PADDLE INDIANA

PADDLE INDIANA

An Access Guide to Canoeing & Kayaking Indiana Lakes & Streams

Alan McPherson

Readers are welcome to write the author or publisher if you discover changes have occurred on the watercourses described herein. Paddling on a lake or stream is a risk activity and your safety and enjoyment depends on responsible personal judgment, knowledge and skill. The author and publisher are not held responsible for any accidents or injuries that may incur while using this guide. All suggestions and comments are welcome. Address all correspondence to: J. L. Waters & Company, 109 N. College Avenue, Bloomington, Indiana 47404
email: roger@jlwaters.com web page: www.jlwaters.com

Published by J. L. Waters & Company
ISBN 0-9672922-0-4
Printed in the USA

Additional Indiana Nature Books by Author

Indiana Best Hikes
Nature Walks in Northern Indiana
Nature Walks in Southern Indiana
Wild Food Plants of Indiana

Cover Photo: Upper Tippecanoe River near Potawatomi Wildlife Park
Back Cover Photos: Author on Sugar Creek; Wyland Lake, Tri-County FWA
Cover and photos by author
Frontispiece, Kayak 2- Winter, Lower Cataract Falls by Rod Bradfield
Text design, page composition and maps, unless otherwise indicated by The Perennial Conspiracy

"Floating up the streams in their canoes
Our fathers were rich, they were in the light....."

Walum Olum
Delaware epic poem-song legend

Table of Contents

Foreword

When Paul, the former store manager of J. L. Waters & Company, asked if I would be interested in compiling a Indiana canoe and kayak guidebook that they would publish, I was surprised, pleased and eager. After outfitting the expedition with a Dagger brand canoe and other related gear, I set out to discover where are the best paddling lakes and streams in Hoosierland. After two seasons of exploring the state, I finally arrived at 70 select lakes, both natural and manmade, and 35 choice creeks and rivers to write up. Although it would take several years more to paddle every mile, I paddled every lake and sampled a section of every river herein.

These publicly accessible waterbodies allow those who love the natural outdoors an alternative to hiking by permitting waterborne travelers to go places they can not reach on foot. Overall Indiana's lakes and streams are rich with wildlife and beauty despite the ravages of two centuries of settlement. Indiana waters accommodate those who prefer casual and placid northern lakes where tamarack and birch thrive on marshy shores or southern lakes where bald cypress provide bald eagles nesting sites. Streams may be as lazy as a prairie river or as fast as a rocky hill country creek. Indiana is somewhere between Canada's north country and the Upper and Deep South bayou country; where deciduous forest has been domesticated but there are remnants of wildness especially around lakes and along streams. Hoosiers and visitors alike are discovering paddling as a popular relaxing outdoor recreation. Canoe and kayak liveries or rentals are available along major scenic streams to accommodate paddlers.

The aim of this book is to inform and guide intrepid paddlers, novice and experienced, where to put in and take out and what to generally expect. Various park agencies and private organizations have established access sites however the lion's share has been established by the DNR's Division of Fish & Wildlife. Another bright spot is that the lakes and streams are less polluted now than in recent years however much needs to be done to bring water closer to pure. Good paddling etiquette means that paddlers keep the waters and adjacent lands free of litter, prevent erosion and respect property rights.

Acknowledgements

The author appreciates the helpful, good natured support of Paul, Roger and Chris at J. L. Waters for the project. Thanks to Dagger Canoe & Kayak Company for supplying the canoe that explored the many lakes and streams. A special thank you to Paula B. for her enthusiastic expertise with the maps and overall book design plus her ability to decipher my scrawlings and correct the awkward run-on sentences. My sincere appreciation goes out to several people I met along this fluvial Hoosier odyssey. A special thank you to my family for their continual support.

Alan McPherson

Paddle Indiana: An Overview

"Low and clear, and pure and deep, ripples of the river
sing—
Water-lilies, half asleep, drowsed with listening:"

With the Current, poem
James Whitcomb Riley, 1883

Paddling has become increasingly popular in the United States and fortunately, the state of Indiana, has an abundance of scenic and semi-wild lakes and streams that are accessible to the paddler. Within its boundaries, Indiana has approximately 90,000 miles of streams and 500 natural lakes and manmade reservoirs, 50 acres and larger. The state boundaries are for the most part defined via the water bodies of Lake Michigan, the Wabash River and Ohio River. About 90% of stream drainage in Indiana flows into the Mississippi River basin. Nearly two thirds of the drainage is by the Wabash River and its tributaries. Roughly 10% of Indiana drains into the Great Lakes and St. Lawrence River basin. Indiana's lakes and streams are rated Class 1 or easy during normal flow by the American Whitewater Association; inviting to nearly everyone looking for stimulating outdoor recreation.

Geologic Past

Indiana's lakes and rivers owe their existence to the last Pleistocene Ice Age that occurred between one million years to about 20,000 years ago. Two glaciers of the Great Ice Age, the Wisconsinian and the Illinoisian, played a major role in shaping the surface of present-day Indiana by leveling the land and forever altering the drainage system. The more recent Wisconsin glaciation covered the northern two thirds of Indiana, grinding down and rounding hills and filling in deep valleys with glacial till rock. Numerous moraines and ice block lakes were left behind with the warming and cooling of the climate. The Fawn, Pigeon and Tippecanoe rivers originate from and drain many glacially-carved lakes. Wisconsin glacier meltwaters carried large quantities of sediments in the major sluiceways such as the Wabash, Eel and Whitewater rivers. The Kankakee, Yellow and Iroquois rivers received the sand and gravel outwash from glacial streams and high winds.

The vast flat land between the Wabash and the hill country to the south received a wide and deep band of Wisconsin glacial till. A few streams in the deeply entrenched area of west central Indiana have carved their way their way through to the deep bedrock: Sugar Creek, Wildcat, Big Walnut and Big Pine; some of the state's most beautiful streams. Both forks of the White River and other streams

INDIANA'S LAKES & STREAMS

SOURCE: INDIANA ADMINISTRATIVE SERVICES

begin "high up" in the plateau country of east central Indiana. What natural lakes that formerly existed in the central till plain are now extinct by drainage, replaced by artificial reservoirs created from streams such as the Wabash, Salamonie and Mississinewa rivers.

While the south central uplands area of Indiana was unglaciated, the southeastern and southwestern areas were glaciated but not by the Wisconsin glacier. The twice-as-old Illinoisian glacier extended further south, forming a lobe around the south central uplands. Illinoisian-carved lakes were nearly non-existent and the ones that did exist were filled in over eons of time. Oxbow lakes, created from meandering rivers such as Hovey Lake, are the only natural lakes in southern Indiana. Today southern Indiana has the largest manmade lakes such as Monroe, Patoka and Brookville. The streams in southern Indiana are older and have had a longer time to cut down to the bedrock and form canyons. Blue River, Little Blue River, Lost River, Muscatatuck Vernon Fork River, White River East Fork and Sand Creek have their share of half and full canyons.

River Rights

In Indiana, a paddler's legal right to travel a stream is based on the concept of navigability and public access. Lake access is determined by whether it has been legally declared a public or private body of water. After accessing a stream or a lake, paddlers will discover most of the bordering land is private property and not public.

The right to paddle a stream in Indiana depends on the stream having been declared navigable as interpreted by law or has public access. A roster of navigable rivers is available from the DNR. If you want to float a stream in Indiana which has not been declared legally navigable, you must have permission of the owners of the river bed to use the river. Indiana law recognizes the "riparian rights doctrine" regarding natural watercourse rights. However a second interpretation of Indiana law gives paddlers the right to use all natural streams and natural lakes which still flow in their natural way (1955 Water Resources Act). A recreational navigability standard generally implies that if a stream can be navigated by recreational paddlers for a significant part of the year, despite hazards and portages, then it is legally navigable and open to public use (prescriptive easement). The right to public use applies only to the water. Legally speaking, if a paddler steps out of the watercraft onto the undeclared nonnavigable stream bottom without permission, the paddler is trespassing. The public may claim a right to use Indiana's rivers for recreation however if a conflict arises and the stream has neither been declared navigable nor designated a recreational stream, the conflict will need to be resolved by the Natural Resources Commission.

Paddlers should always respect the water and land and leave no impact. Conservation officers can help to clarify river rights questions. In Indiana, human powered watercraft such as canoes and kayaks need not be registered or titled. For further information regarding lake and stream rights contact: Indiana DNR, Division of Law Enforcement, 402 W Washington, Rm 255 D, Indianapolis, IN 46204 (317) 232-4010.

Access

Overall access to Indiana lakes and streams is good but more public access sites are needed to meet public demand and safety. Indiana's Public Access Program is a long-term commitment developed by the Division of Fish and Wildlife (since 1953) to provide free access to Indiana waters for all outdoor persons (274 sites). In northern Indiana, most sites are located on natural lakes. In southern Indiana, access sites are half streams and half reservoir lakes. The public access program attempts to develop at least eight new sites each year. Marinas, liveries, fishing camps and other private commercial outlets offer fee access sites to many lakes and streams, some, where no public access or parking is available. Parking is always a major concern for paddlers and most public and private access sites offer adequate security. Be sure your vehicle that brought you to the stream or lake is off the road and not blocking the access ramp. Watch for glass or other sharp objects when parking in hidden grassy road shoulders. Never rush putting on or taking off a canoe or kayak from your vehicle. Don't give vandals the opportunity to trash and rob you vehicle. Park where other vehicles can see yours. Leave no valuables. Check you car insurance policy for coverage. Always take extra caution when transporting a canoe or kayak.

Be careful not to trespass onto private property especially if it is signed or fenced. If confronted by a angry landowner be careful not to upset the situation any further. Be nice and continue on your way. Always be friendly and approachable when on the water.

Water & Boating Safety

There are numerous safety tips to write about or list but the one tip that sums it up is "*use common sense*". Respect the water. Be prepared but expect the unexpected by planning for emergencies. Learn to "read" the water. It is important to know how to swim if capsized. The most important safety item, a personal flotation device or life jacket, is required by Indiana boating law. The best basic protection is the off-shore type or the inflatable life vest with reflective tape. Since your life may depend on your safety vest, keep in mind you get what you pay for. Drowning is the number one cause of death and its usually attributed to the victim not wearing a life jacket (PFD).

Although it is great to be spontaneous, it is best to plan a canoe or kayak trip. Check the weather a week in advance and choose a good day. Check <http://h2o.usgs.gov/public/realtime.html> for current water level readings of select Indiana streams.Check the vessel's condition. Check a day use canoe outing gear list and check the condition of your gear. Check your transport vehicle to make sure it is road worthy. Think of your personal needs, water temperature and warm clothing and comforts during the fluvial venture. Hypothermia is a major cause of drowning and is likely to occur in late winter and early spring but may occur any time of the year. Fatigue from exposure from the elements sets in after four hours of paddling and you are more vulnerable to upset and accident. Know your limits. Have a vacation mind-set and slow down. Leave your paddling plans with a family member or friend.

Paddling solo will offer great experiences but for safety's sake it is best to paddle in numbers. If possible, learn CPR and First Aid. Learn self-rescue. Do not paddle at night or on flooded streams. Do not litter. Always expect to get wet and dress and pack accordingly. Know how to handle an upset. Stay with your boat if capsized. Never give up your paddle. If separated from your watercraft on a stream, float on your back with feet pointed downstream. Know the dam sites and be prepared to portage. Avoid strainers. Don't stand or wade in swift water over knee deep. Wear rubber soled canvas or tennis shoes. Many paddling injuries occur from bare feet. Don't paddle in a lightning storm. Protect yourself from the sun and the possibility of heat exhaustion or heat stroke.

For first-timers, a shorter trip of three to five hours is recommended to provide time to experience the enjoyment of paddling and a chance to learn and practice some of the basic skills without over doing it. A container or two of drinking water should be on board since paddling can be a thirsty recreational experience. There are four waterway markers or navigational aids (traffic signs) worth knowing: red diamond shaped cross on a white background or red diamond for danger, red circle for speed zone, red rectangle for information. Powerboats are expected to give canoes and kayaks the right-of-way however expect to yield to wake and look for danger. A distress signal can be made by waving the arms slowly up and down.

The DNR has conservation officers (COs) trained and fully equipped as a Fast Water Emergency Response Team. COs are taught how to perform a self-rescue, read characteristics of the river, operate boats using the ferrying technique and construct a rope system used to rescue stranded victims. Low dams are common in Indiana streams and are especially dangerous at high water levels. The boil at the base of a dam can be "keepers" of backwash victims who go overboard.

Paddling with Children

Children especially ages 6-12, "The Golden Years" of youth, usually enjoy the outdoors and are keenly observant. They should know how to swim to avoid the fear of water. Children as well as adults are required by law to have Personal Floatation Devices (PFDs, life jackets) at all times while on the water. There are capsizing safety techniques they should know before they go out in a canoe as well as other safety measures.

Take precautionary measures when packing for the trip. Sunscreen, bug repellent, first aid kit, clean water and soapy cloths in a ziplock bag, plus dry clothes and jackets for wind protection. Know the signs of heat prostration and be prepared to land and rest when it is hot, windy or inclement. Don't allow toys that can be ruined by water. Emphasize sitting still and balance to reduce the risk of tipping.

To introduce them to water, begin with a lake or a short river trip and stop often to avoid heat exhaustion, windburn or break the monotony. Stay close to the shore so that they can see land and have a sense of security. Make children comfortable in the center of the canoe. Bring along cushions and get a dip net and bucket for gathering along the shore during exploration breaks. Keep them comfortable and have nourishing food that they will enjoy during the outing. Point out your observations of the natural surroundings and let them have time to notice things on their own.

Strokes & Paddling Tips

After purchasing a canoe or kayak, paddles and life jacket (PFD) plus a roof rack and/or specialized carrier, the paddler is ready to try out the equipment. Cartop your watercraft properly with rope or tiedowns and drive to the nearest water body (lake recommended) of choice to practice and become familiar with paddling procedures. Practice at home with a broom instead of a paddle.

Carry down to the access site from the parking area. Two people in a tandem canoe is safe. The heaviest of the two should sit at the stern or rear seat of the watercraft. If solo, sit near the center where most of the stability and carry capacity is found in a canoe. Keep weight low centered and avoid sudden movements where balance may be lost. Enter and exit a kayak working your way into the cockpit seat. Become familiar and comfortable with your kayak's stability and point of capsizing.

When you are paddling a canoe, your offside hand should be positioned on top of the paddle grip to control the various strokes. The outside hand should be a comfortable distance down the grip, inches above the paddle blade. In a canoe, the more experienced or heavier paddler generally will paddle in the stern and be the main paddling force. The bow paddler pulls straight back. Always paddle unison on opposite sides of the canoe.

The solo kayak paddler has a unique double paddle with blades at both ends. Placing your hands in the correct position along the paddle shaft is important. Hold the double paddle horizontal and slide your hands apart which should be an equal distance from the blades. If right-handed, the right hand is the control or fixed hand and the left hand is the unfixed, loosely gripped hand (opposite for left-handers). After a forward paddle stroke, the fixed hand is dropped so that the paddle is rotated 90 degrees through the unfixed hand. Sweep the forward stroke in a straight line along the gunwale. Match the stroke in intensity on both sides. Keeping the kayak or canoe straight in the water may become frustrating. It will take some practice to establish good paddling rhythm.

The most common directional or steering stroke is the "hook" stroke, which has a slight outward side-pressure at stroke's completion. Until the hook stroke is mastered, a beginning stern paddler can use a rudder-like action every few strokes to keep the canoe on course. A more elaborate hook stroke is the "J" stroke, the basic stern stroke that keeps the canoe on course but loses momentum with the stroke's side motion (figure "J" in the water). The modified "J" or Parallel Turn Stroke is a straight stroke with the paddle culminating in a slight turn outward and the blade turned even with the flow. The main bow stroke is the Power Bow Stroke, a well forward reach and straight back pull stroke. The Bow Rudder and Cross Bow Rudder are considered canoe strokes.

Both the bow paddler and the stern paddler share the same strokes as the Simple Reverse Backwater Stroke, the Draw Stroke, Pry or Pushover Stroke, Sculling Stroke, Reverse Sculling Stroke and the Sweep Stroke. There are several variations and stroke combinations to propel, turn and brace.

A Guide to the Guide

The author attempted to address in the write-ups and capsule data the most common concerns for a safe and stimulating paddling trip. For further enhancement and understanding how this guidebook works read on:

Lake & Stream Name & Corresponding Number-Identifies water body by name and accompanying number corresponds to regional or statewide map. The arranging order of lakes and streams is geographic based, north to south and east to west. The 70 lakes were selected for their naturalness, special features, limited boat traffic, ease of access, quietude, available camping and other amenities. The selection of the 35 streams was primarily based on available water, access, and scenery.

Headliner or Essence Statement- Sums up the fluvial experience in few words. Highlights to catch your attention.

Write-Up-Expands on the headline or essence statement. Succinct what-to-expect summary on a particular paddling outing. Looks at the best and the worst and suggests tips to enjoy the outing. Natural and social history facts included.

Capsule Data:

U.S.G.S. Maps- United State Geological Survey maps 1:24,000 or one inch equals 2,000 feet were consulted. These topographical or "topo", quadrangle or "quad' maps are available at outdoor outfitter stores, the DNR Maps Sales Section, 402 W Washington, W-160, Indianapolis, IN 46204-2742 or the Indiana Geological Survey Publications & Maps Sales, 611 N Walnut Grove & 10th Street, Bloomington, IN 47404 (812) 855-7636 (over the counter or mail order). Public libraries or soil conservation agents often have local map collections. Best map for looking up close at the Indiana landscape. Identifies such natural features as water bodies, islands, marsh, woods, caves, hills, and depressions plus human made features such as buildings, roads, bridges and access sites. Birds eye view! DeLorme's Indiana Atlas & Gazetteer is next best thing. A wall map of Indiana's Lakes & Streams is available from the DNR Map Sales.

Vicinity- Lists the county or counties the water body occupies or runs through and the closest community or communities where supplies may be obtained. Refer to DeLorme Indiana Atlas or the Indiana DOT Highway Map.

Lake Acreage/Depth- Identifies the size of lakes by acres and the deepest point by feet.

Paddling Time (Lakes only)- length of time needed for an unhurried leisurely trip.

Stream Distance/Trips-Stream distance is measured in miles and tenths. Measurements are based on government agency figures (IDEM, DNR, USGS) and a map measuring wheel, rolling over more than 200 maps 1:24,000. Stream mileage is close but not completely accurate. Accurate GSI satellite mileage readings is being compiled and will be available in the future. A trip is considered from access to access. A day's paddling distance varies with individuals. The average paddling speed is two m.p.h., therefore an unhurried 12 mile trip may take about six hours.

Level of Difficulty- All of Indiana's streams and lakes are rated Class I, based on the International River Rating Scale of difficulty by the American Whitewater Affiliation (life threatening, Class VI is the highest). The water characteristics of Class I are easy bends, moving water with some riffles or small rapids and low waves. Obstructions are few but include some downed trees that can turn into strainers and log jams sometimes at bridge pilings. Stream speed is usually less than two person paddling speed. In addition, a stream is considered one class more difficult than normal if the water temperature is below 50 degrees. The level of difficulty rises when extended with overnight camping. It is important to realize that ratings change as water levels rise or fall. A stream that ranks Class I in May could be a Class II or III or higher during April run-off. Some sections of Class I streams are considered Class II or easy unobstructed rapids with waves up to three feet and low ledges in a wide clear channel. For information about daily stream levels check this internet address <http://h2o.usgs.gov/public/realtime.html>

Hazards & Portages- The main hazards on Indiana streams are low head dams, log jams, and strainers. Unseen obstacles such as submerged boulders and logs are potentially dangerous. Portages are required for dams. Always expect the unexpected like capsizing in fast water. Once overboard, the possibility of striking your head on an object is real. Wind in open water can be an obstacle to overcome. Be alert! Power boats, jet skiers and other motorized water traffic can be threatening to the paddler by creating unwanted wake. Low bridges in high water could be deadly. Maps do not show all low bridges or dams.

Info Sources- For information regarding the access, fishing action, water level or other questions about a particular water body contact the listed sources.

Area Outfitters/Liveries- Listing of nearby canoe and kayak rentals. Also great information sources.

Gamefish Species- Listing identifies edible gamefish of a particular water body. To fish in Indiana public lakes, streams or its boundary waters, you must have a valid fishing license and carry it when fishing. There are fines and penalties for fishing without a license. Most licenses are available from independent agents, county clerks and DNR properties. All licenses issued by the DNR are non-transferable and non-refundable. The possession limit on all sport or gamefish is two day's daily bag limit. For further information regarding fishing regulations see current annual issue of DNR fishing guide. Also see fish consumption advisory, Appendix E.

Camping- Lists addresses and phone numbers of places to camp, most are year around state properties. Private seasonal campgrounds are not included. Campgrounds are rated Class A, AA (electric, showers), Class B (showers) and Class C (primitive). Riverside primitive camping is permitted on Hoosier National Forest (Lost River & Little Blue River). More canoe camps on public lands are needed to meet demand.

Medical Assistance- Includes nearby hospitals with ambulance service. In an emergency always dial 911 first. Above all, know some First Aid and CPR (cardiopulmonary resuscitation). Hypothermia is a major concern for paddlers during a cool to cold spring and fall. Drowning is the paddler's nightmare. Head and bodily injury may occur from strainers or submerged objects. Watch for the poisonous massasauga rattlesnake in northern Indiana lake country. The poisonous cottonmouth is not known from Indiana except at a few isolated wetlands in southwest Indiana. Copperheads may occur anywhere in southern Indiana but are usually upland vipers along with the timber rattlesnake.

Access- Directionally describes how to arrive from the main highway to the access site. Access sites usually range in size up to four acres and includes a boat ramp and parking area. In addition to the included highway, vicinity and site maps herein, DeLorme Indiana Atlas and Gazetteer is recommended. The highest use of access sites occurs from April through June. Do your appreciative part by helping to keep access sites clean from litter. The majority of access sites are developed by the DNR's Division of Fish and Wildlife, Public Access Program (since 1953). Providing free access to public waters is the goal of the Public Access Program. Efforts are made to develop eight new access sites a year (the average cost per site is $20,000). Larger than access sites (up to 500 acres), the 20 public fishing areas often provide more than boat ramps and parking. Look for the rectangular brown access directional road signs that are placed at regular intervals.

Abbreviations A-Z

A

a.-acre or acres
alt.-alternative
approx,, apprx.- approximate, approximately
Ave.-Avenue
avg.-average

B

C

CCC-Civilian Conservation Corps

CFS-Cubic Feet per Second (river flow measurement, a cubic foot is eight gallons)

Co., Cos.-County, Counties

CO-Conservation Officer

CR-County Road

D

Div.-Division

DNR-Department of Natural Resources

Dr.-Drive

d.s.-downstream

E

E-East

Elev.-Elevation

Est.-established

F

FR-Forest Road

Ft.-Foot

FWA-Fish & Wildlife Area

G

GPS-Global Positioning System, satellite measures stream miles

H

Hrs.-Hours

Hwy-Highway

I

I-Interstate

Ill, IL-Illinois

Info-Information

Ind., IN-Indiana

IDNR-Indiana Department of Natural Resources

ILDNR-Illinois Department of Natural Resources

IO- Inboard and outboard motors

J

K

Ky-Kentucky

L

Ltd.-Limited

M
MI, Mich.-Michigan
mi.-miles
MDNR-Michigan Department of Natural Resources
MPH-m.p.h., mph, Miles Per Hour

N
N-North
NL-National Lakeshore
NP-Nature Preserve
NWR-National Wildlife Refuge

O
OH-Ohio
ODNR-Ohio Department of Natural Resources

P
PFD-Personal Flotation Device, life jacket
PFA-Public fishing area

Q

R
RA-Recreation Area
Rd-Road
RR-railroad or rural route
Rt-route

S
S-South
SF-State Forest
SPK-State Park
St-Street, Sts.-streets

T

U
US-United States
USGS-United States Geological Survey

V

W
W-West
WCA-Wetland Conservation Area, DNR Fish & Wildlife

X, Y, Z

THE HIAWATHA SYNDROME:

Challenge of Tandem Paddling

by Roger & Carol Kugler

The Illusion
You've seen the commercials, two people happily paddling a tandem (two-person canoe) across a beautiful lake at sunset, sharing the special moment, reveling in the quiet serenity the canoe has allowed them to find. Rubbish.

The Reality
He gets in the back (stern) tells you to get in the front (bow), he shoves off before you're ready an 20 feet from shore starts to tell you everything you are doing wrong. One half hour later you're swearing to never get into another boat with him that is smaller than the Queen Mary.

The Problem
The reason for his behavior is the Hiawatha Syndrome. The Hiawatha Syndrome is a theory in canoesportology that purposes that all males born in North America are implanted with the canoeing gene at birth. It's an instinct, much like the instinct that makes men watch basketball or throw their dirty socks on the floor. Men just know how to canoe regardless if they have never seen a canoe before. This theory can be observed first hand on any Saturday at the local canoe livery. A group of high spirited guys show up ready to "conquer the wilderness". In tow are a few calm women who really just want to enjoy the afternoon and maybe get a suntan. The men immediately grab the canoe paddles and shove off. The women listen to the livery tape and learn a little about how to maneuver the canoe. This illustrates the Hiawatha Syndrome as most people experience it.
Another peculiar behavior you may have observed in your male canoeing partner is the Horizontal Paddle Reflex. Scientists have discovered that deep in the brain near the hypothalamus is tiny gland that secretes a hormone that makes men go ballistic with rage, anger, and fury when a woman paddler, in the bow, places her paddle in the horizontal position across the gunnels of a canoe. So don't get too mad at your male canoeing partner when this happens—it's just natural. (Women place their paddles in this position in response to the Hiawatha Syndrome).
Despite all of this it is possible to paddle your canoe across the lake with bow and stern paddlers enjoying the view, the boat and each other.
Five years later, after much trial and error and with two kids aboard they paddle tandem again. But by now they both know the other one can handle their end of the canoe and Hiawatha no longer paddles with them. They now talk about the scenery and smile alot. Paddling tandem is fun!

Three Elements of Tandem Canoeing

Teamwork, Communication and Skill are required to paddle a tandem well.

Teamwork—Each of the paddlers has a job. Although many people don't know it, the bow paddler is very important if you want to enjoy your day in the canoe. First of all, the bow and stern paddlers should paddle on opposite sides of the boat. If they don't the common saying is: paddle on the same side, swim on the same side. Second, the bow paddler, not the stern person is the one who will set the cadence or the number of strokes per minute. Of course, the stern paddler can give input on whether the cadence is too fast or too slow. This is the beginning of communication.

Communication-Paddlers who have achieved good paddling communication, usually talk in calm, quiet voices about how beautiful the sky is or when they think they'll have to leave. To reach this level you must realize that the bow person is responsible for the front half of the boat. The stern person gets the rest. That means that if there's a rock in front of the boat it's the bow person that must maneuver the boat to avoid it. (And if the bow person takes on this task it is less likely the stern person will tell you which stroke to use). When the maneuver begins, the stern person realizes something must be ahead. "She just did a hard draw to the right. I might want to do a hard pry." And the boat side slips to the right.
Another observation about communicating in a tandem canoe; it's hard to talk normally most of the time. The bow person is facing the same direction as the stern person. There is no eye contact and if there is a little head wind anything short of yelling can't be heard. If this is a problem for you, get solo canoes and paddle side by side. You can talk (and even kiss) with a lot less effort and frustration. Now, a little about skill.

Skill—There isn't enough room and this isn't the right place to give advice on specific strokes. However, it's important to realize the responsibilities of each paddler. Contrary to popular myth, the person in the back does not "steer" the canoe. Each person is responsible for his or her own end of the boat.

To properly maneuver the boat where you want it to go means that you will have to learn how to do draw, a pry and a few other strokes. The bow and stern positions each have their own special strokes that help keep that end of the boat where it should be. To learn more about all of this, take some classes, read some books, watch a few videos and then go practice.
The most important thing to remember is that canoeing is supposed to be fun. So, if you aren't ready for the Olympics next week, don't get frustrated. Take a breath, look at the scenery around you and realize that it takes years of paddling fun to perfect this sport.

Indiana Lakes: An Overview

"A lake is the landscape's most beautiful and expressive feature."
Henry David Thoreau (1817-1862)

The boundaries of present day Indiana, roughly speaking, harbor several hundred natural lakes situated north of the Wabash River and several artificial reservoirs or "lakes" south of the Wabash to the Ohio River. Former gravel pits, limestone quarries and coal mine pits dot the plains and hills statewide and now some serve as recreational water bodies. Oxbow lakes, cut offs from a meandering main stream, are found along the bigger rivers such as the Wabash and White rivers especially along the lower reaches. With all of this vast lake acreage, it is not surprising that development followed along now settled private shores. Fortunately public access was not forgotten. Over half of the 70 lakes mentioned are located in the rural northern third of Indiana, north of the Wabash. Many are concentrated on or behind the Mississinewa and Packerton morainic systems from Steuben County, southwest 75 miles. Outlying morainic systems in northern Indiana include the Valparaiso moraine of Lake, Porter and LaPorte counties and the Maxinkuckee moraine of Marshall, Starke, Fulton and Pulaski counties.

The main criterion for inclusion in this guidebook was rural lakes with undisturbed landscapes that retain a sense of original wildness and urban exceptions that have worthwhile amenities. An undeveloped chain of lakes (connected by channel) offers the ultimate lake experience in northern Indiana. Unlike streams, lakes are always at a dependable water level that is rarely too high or low. Once you communicate with other paddlers, there is a general consensus that northern Indiana, particularly northeast Indiana offers the best lake paddling experiences in Hoosierland.

The Wisconsin glaciation of thousands of years ago accounts for the hundreds of natural northern Indiana lakes. Retreating mile high glaciers left behind ice blocks that settled and melted into kettle and pit glacial water bodies. Lakes, like living beings, once born are destined to die. Since the last ice age, hundreds of lakes have disappeared, some by natural organic sediment and others by speedy land drainage. The last 200 years of settlement has greatly altered the lake landscape. While natural lakes have disappeared, artificial lakes have been created by damming and digging. To the prehistoric and historic native cultures and the early European explorers and American pioneers, the lakes yielded a survivalist way of life. To modern Indiana residents and visitors, the lakes are a source of drinking water and a place to swim, fish, study nature, canoe and kayak.

Lake paddling does not require a shuttle therefore you may go solo

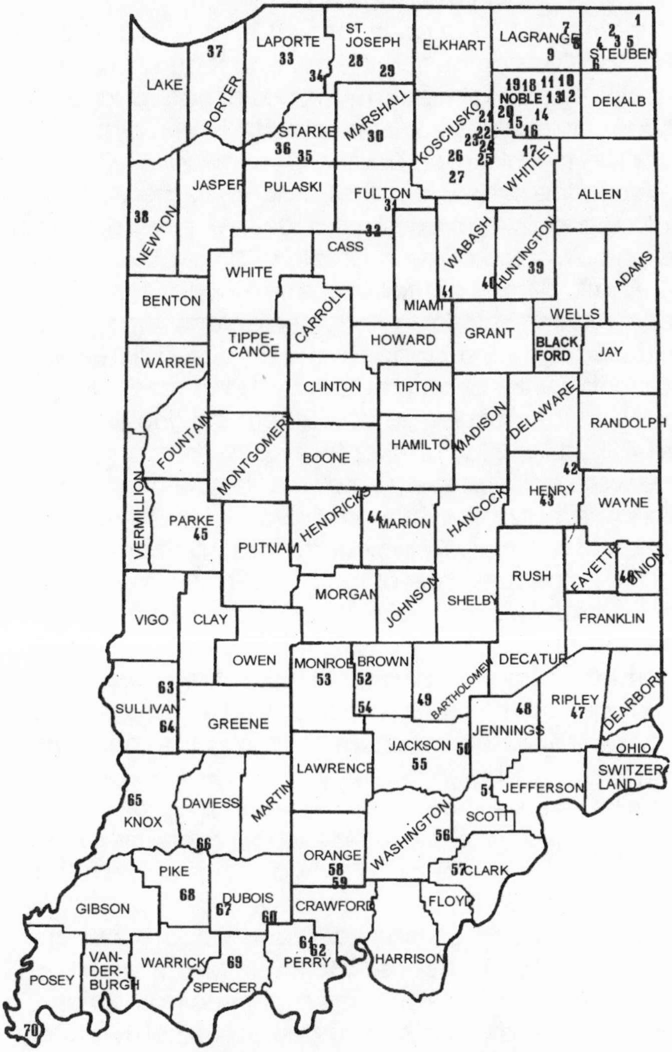

Indiana Lakes

however it is best to share the trip. Peaceful lakes, a good starting point for beginners, seem friendlier than turbulent streams for youngsters and adults who may have a fear of water. Paddlers will discover as they move across the motionless water with their own muscle that each lake has its' own ambiance.

The three northernmost tiers of counties feature about 500 lakes that are greater than five acres each. Nearly one thousand lakes dot the plains and prairie morainic ridges. Two types of natural lakes are the glacial outwash pit lake such as Bass Lake and the more common ice block kettle lake such as Little Gentian Lake. A third type of natural lake is the oxbow lake that reaches its greatest development along the lower Wabash and White river valleys. Hovey Lake along the Ohio River is a prime example of an oxbow lake, a cut off bend. The natural lakes contain more than 240,000 million gallons of water of which rainfall is the primary replenishing source.

Where glaciation advanced, stopped and retreated determined why southern Indiana is without natural lakes. The Wisconsinian glaciation stopped at the north edge of southern Indiana hill country. The older Illinoisian glacial lakes that covered much of southern Indiana were obliterated by time and the elements. But where nature fails to supply lakes, humans have.

The construction of artificial lakes in central and southern Indiana has accelerated over the latter half of the 20th century. These manmade impoundments or reservoirs are considered multiple-use in purpose with flood control, drinking water, wildlife habitat and recreation opportunities. Huntington's Roush Lake, Salamonie Lake and Mississsinewa Lake are prime examples of multiple-use reservoirs. Some of the largest artificial Indiana lakes were constructed over 150 years ago during the canal building days. Sylvan Lake (1837) is an example of a feeder lake still in existence however most no longer exist such as Splunge Creek Reservoir (Clay-Vigo county line) which fed the Wabash & Erie Canal. The need for water has created lakes but the search for coal and other minerals creates lakes as a byproduct. Publicly owned lands that were former coal mines are plentiful in Clay, Vigo, Sullivan, Greene, Knox, Pike and Warrick counties. Current mining reclamation is leaving the lake pits more natural (especially noticeable at the West Dugger Unit of Greene-Sullivan State Forest). If beaver were given greater freedom, they would create their own artificial lakes.

Overall, Indiana lakes are in decline due to the effects of civilization and time. Noble efforts are being made to save our lakes from eutrophic pollution and erosion from agribusiness, industry and domestic housing. The first legal effort to protect Indiana lakes was in the early 1900s when agricultural drainage was dramatically lowering some of the most sought out lakes. For example, Bear Lake was lowered six feet and adjoining High Lake eight feet in 1899. Nearly a century after that first legislative lake protection law in

Indiana, the state seeks to protect the lakes as one of the state's most prime resources. The Indiana Lakes Management Society and numerous local lake associations are dedicated to saving Indiana's lakes. Their mission is to promote and encourage the understanding and comprehensive management of lakes and reservoirs and their watershed ecosystem. They have an enormous task at hand. Trying to stop the spread of exotic water milfoil, purple loosestrife and zebra mussel from one lake to another is only one major battle to save the lakes. If left to their own natural ways, lakes can manage themselves; people require management. It is unfortunate that laws were not in place when Indiana was first settled to prohibit shoreline development and keep the shoreline in public domain (100-yard setbacks). Indiana's Lake Enhancement Program is a statewide strategy for dealing with soil erosion and sedimentation control. IDNR's Division of Soil Conservation is providing technical and financial assistance for lake enhancement needs. For information about lakes with public access sites contact the IDNR's Division of Fish & Wildlife, 402 West Washington Street, Room W 273, Indianapolis, Indiana 46204 (317) 232-4080.

Reflection on Beaverdam Lake, Pigeon River FWA

1. FISH LAKE

- Canoe sparkling waters of one of 101 Steuben County lakes

This mid-sized glacial lake is one of several in northern Indiana place named Fish. The water body lies about a mile south of the Great Lake State of Michigan. Most of the shoreline is level marsh and forest except the northeast shore is upland, open rolling pastureland. Development is limited to Schaeffer's Court; about eight houses set in woodland.

The somewhat hourglass shaped lake has open water with limited shoreline spatterdock and water lily arising from the muck and gravel bottom. There are four deep holes with depths ranging from 27 to 34 feet. Adjacent to the boat ramp south is the outlet for one of several Michianas Fawn Rivers (however this is not the canoeable Fawn, which is located at Orland to the west). Naturewise, Fish Lake's general quiet wildness is semi-secluded, easily accessed and offers leisurely canoeing and fishing.

USGS MAP(S): Angola East, California, Mich.-Ind. 1:24,000
VICINITY: Fremont, Steuben County
LAKE ACREAGE /DEPTH: 59 a. /34'
PADDLING TIME: 1 hour
LEVEL OF DIFFICULTY: Class I
HAZARDS/PORTAGES: IO allowed, 10 mph ltd.
INFO SOURCES: Fawn River Fish Hatchery (219) 829-6241
AREA OUTFITTERS/LIVERIES: Pigeon River Canoe-n-Camp
3490 S 325 W
Pleasant Lake, IN 46779
(219) 351-3537 or 475-5512
GAMEFISH SPECIES: bluegill, largemouth bass, northern pike, redear, sunfish, bowfin
CAMPING: Pokagon State Park, 450 Lane 100 Lake James, Angola, IN 46703 (219) 833-2012, Class A, B, & C
MEDICAL ASSISTANCE: Cameron Memorial Hospital, 410 E. Maumee St., Angola, IN 46703
(219) 665-2141

ACCESS: Exit 144 from the Indiana Toll Road I-80-90 or exit 154 from I-69 at Pokagon State Park and drive east to Fremont on SR 120 or SR 827. From Fremont, take Wayne St./CR 325 E one-mile north to marked access road and turn right/east and continue to the IDNR boat ramp.

FISH LAKE

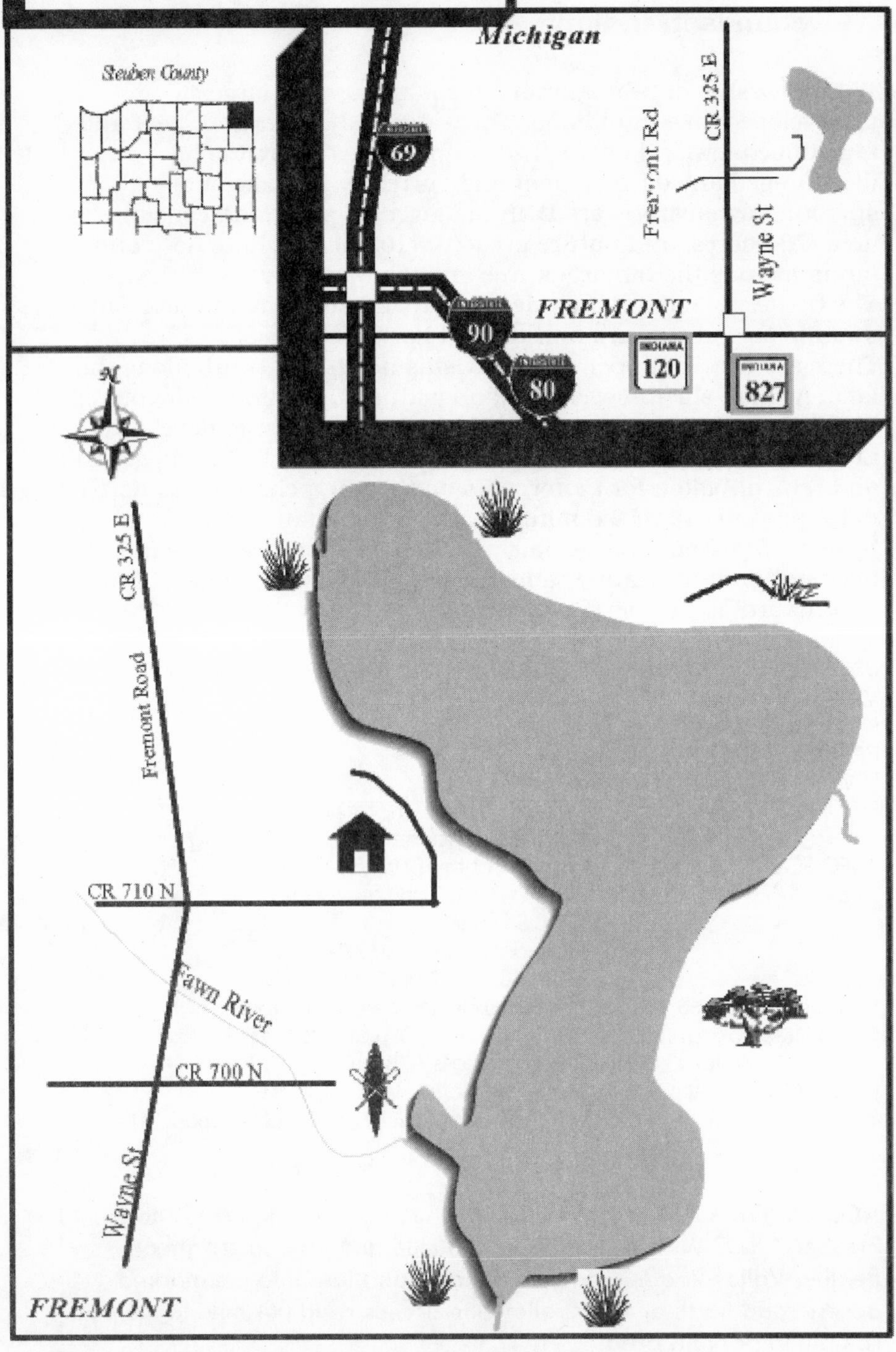
Michigan
Steuben County
69
90
80
FREMONT
Fremont Rd
CR 325 E
Wayne St
120
827
N
CR 325 E
Fremont Road
CR 710 N
Fawn River
CR 700 N
Wayne St
FREMONT

2. MARSH LAKE

- **Experience northern exposure on one of the finest wetlands in Indiana**

Within earshot of I-69, Marsh Lake is the second largest undeveloped lake in Indiana. The water body is an oval, peat and muck filled lowland basin. The swamp forest shoreline has discouraged any development and currently the lake and surrounding environs are DNR managed as a wetland conservation area (734 acres) and nature preserve (103 acres). Rare flora and fauna include the tamarack tree and the Massasauga rattlesnake. The bordering habitat includes cattail and sedge marsh, fen, shrub swamp (poison sumac), and upland hardwood forest.

There are excellent open upland vistas north and south along the lake. A small shrub-covered island with a duck blind adds interest. The Follette Creek outlet channel which flows west to developed Little Otter Lake makes fine canoeing to Oak Hill E-Z Campground and return. Watch for motorboats on the blind channel bends. The noise presence of I-69 diminishes the wild aquatic experience however the scenic vistas, fairly undisturbed naturalness, unique northern flora and fauna, and quality recreational water all lead up to a rewarding northern lake outing.

USGS MAP(S): Angola East 1:24,000
VICINITY: Angola, Steuben County
LAKE ACREAGE /DEPTH: 56 a./38'
PADDLING TIME: 1 1/2 hours
LEVEL OF DIFFICULTY: Class I
HAZARDS/PORTAGES: IO allowed, 10 mph. motorboat traffic in Follette Creek channel, seasonal hunting
INFO SOURCES: Fawn River Fish Hatchery (219) 829-6241
AREA OUTFITTERS/LIVERIES: Pigeon River Canoe-n-Camp
3490 S 325 W
Pleasant Lake, IN 46779
(219) 351-3537 or 475-5512
GAMEFISH SPECIES: bluegill, bass, bullhead, perch, crappie
CAMPING: Pokagon State Park, 450 Lane 100 Lake James, Angola IN 46703 (219) 833-2012, Class A, B & C
MEDICAL ASSISTANCE: Cameron Memorial Hospital, 410 E. Maumee St., Angola, IN 46703 (219) 665-2141

ACCESS: From I-69 exit 154 and continue north along SR 127 to Steuben CR 50 W. Proceed about 0.5 mile and turn east/right on Feather Valley Road. Continue 0.5 mile and turn into the marked access road north or left. Follow the access road 0.4-mile to the boat ramp and parking area.

MARSH LAKE

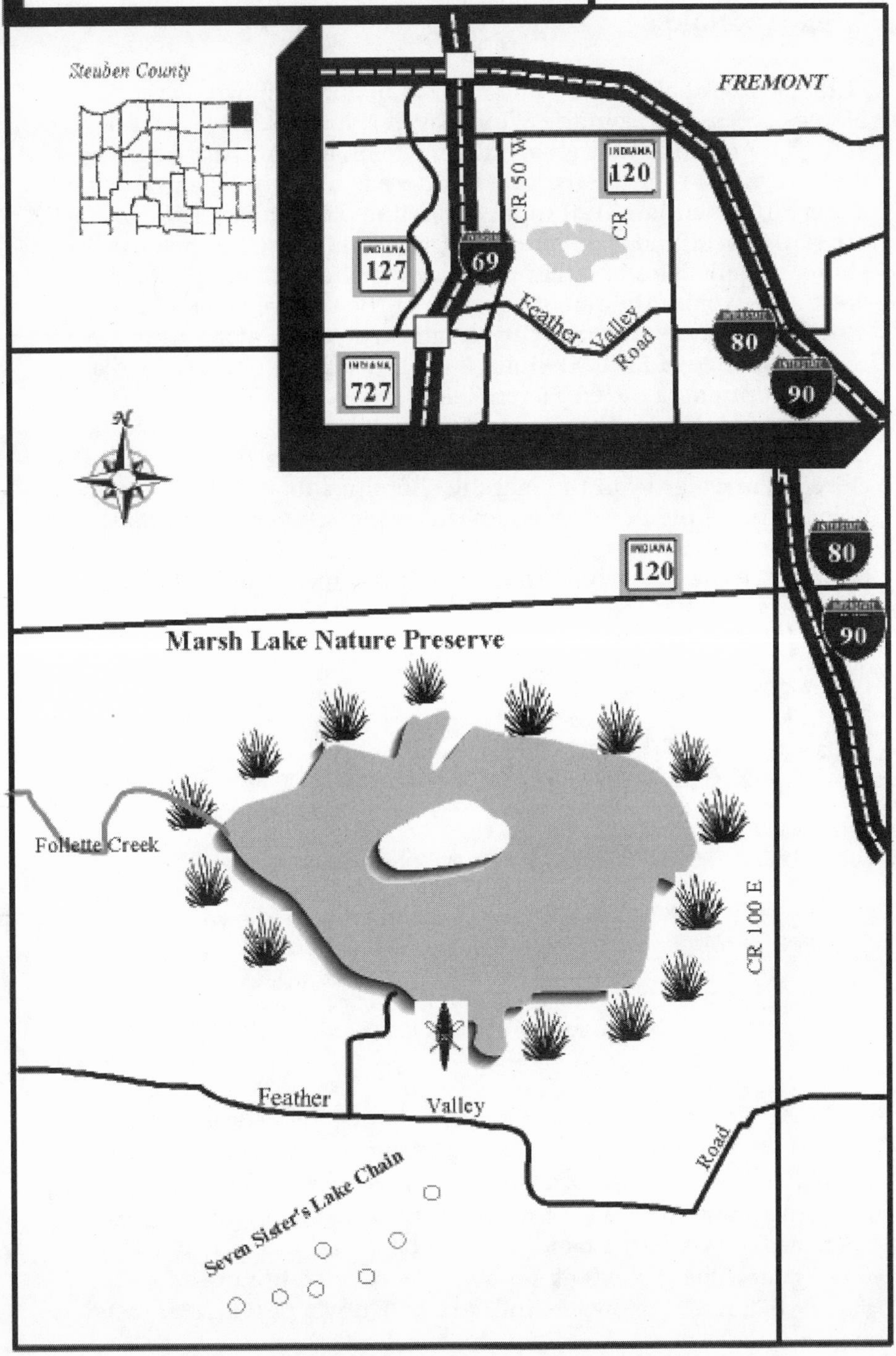
Steuben County
FREMONT
CR 50 W
INDIANA 120
CR
INDIANA 127
69
Feather Valley Road
80
90
INDIANA 727
N
80
90
INDIANA 120
Marsh Lake Nature Preserve
Follette Creek
CR 100 E
Feather
Valley
Road
Seven Sister's Lake Chain

3. LITTLE GENTIAN LAKE

- Kayak the spring-fed pristine waters of glacially carved lakes

Little Gentian Lake is in a chain of small lakes known as the Seven Sisters accessible from the Wing Haven Nature Reserve, a 160-acre sanctuary owned and managed by ACRES, a land trust based in Fort Wayne. From the parking lot there is a 200-yard carry down along Little Gentian Trail to the shoreline pier. Failing Lake and I-69 are to the west and a private campground is along the northwest shore. Helen's Landing pier at the north shore allows paddlers to dock and explore the remote portion of the nature reserve. Look for a narrow channel through the aquatic vegetation along the northeast edge of Little Gentian Lake that allows passage into a smaller unnamed Seven Sisters lake.

The second lake features a stand of yellow birch, tamarack and oak-hickory forest along the west shore. Smaller fringed gentian and closed gentian grow in the marshy shoreline about the lakes. No homes are visible however a handful of piers line the southeast shore. Consider hiking the foot trails while at Wing Haven. Experience the kettle and kame hill landscape of NE Indiana.

USGS MAP(S): Angola East 1:24,000
VICINITY: Angola, Steuben County
LAKE ACREAGE /DEPTH: 22 a./40'
PADDLING TIME: 1 1/2 hours
LEVEL OF DIFFICULTY: Class I
HAZARDS/PORTAGES: carry down can be strenuous on the uphill return, locating the overgrown channel may be difficult
INFO SOURCES: ACRES (219) 422-1004
AREA OUTFITTERS/LIVERIES: Pigeon River Canoe-n-Camp (219) 351-3537
GAMEFISH SPECIES: fishing is not allowed in the nature reserve.
CAMPING: Pokagon State Park, 450 Lane 100 Lake James, Angola, IN 40703 (219) 833-2012, Class A, B & C
MEDICAL ASSISTANCE: Cameron Memorial Hospital, 410 E. Maumee St. Angola, IN 46703 (219) 665-2141

ACCESS: Access to Little Gentian Lake is via Wing Haven Nature Reserve during daylight hours. Wing Haven is located five miles north of Angola near Pokagon State Park. From I-69 exit 154 onto SR 127 and drive south to Steuben CR 400 N. Turn east on CR 400 N and continue 0.4 mile to the main entrance on the left/north side of the road. Follow the gravel entry road to the parking area near the Steward's house. Follow the trailhead path down past the log cabin to the pier.

LITTLE GENTIAN LAKE

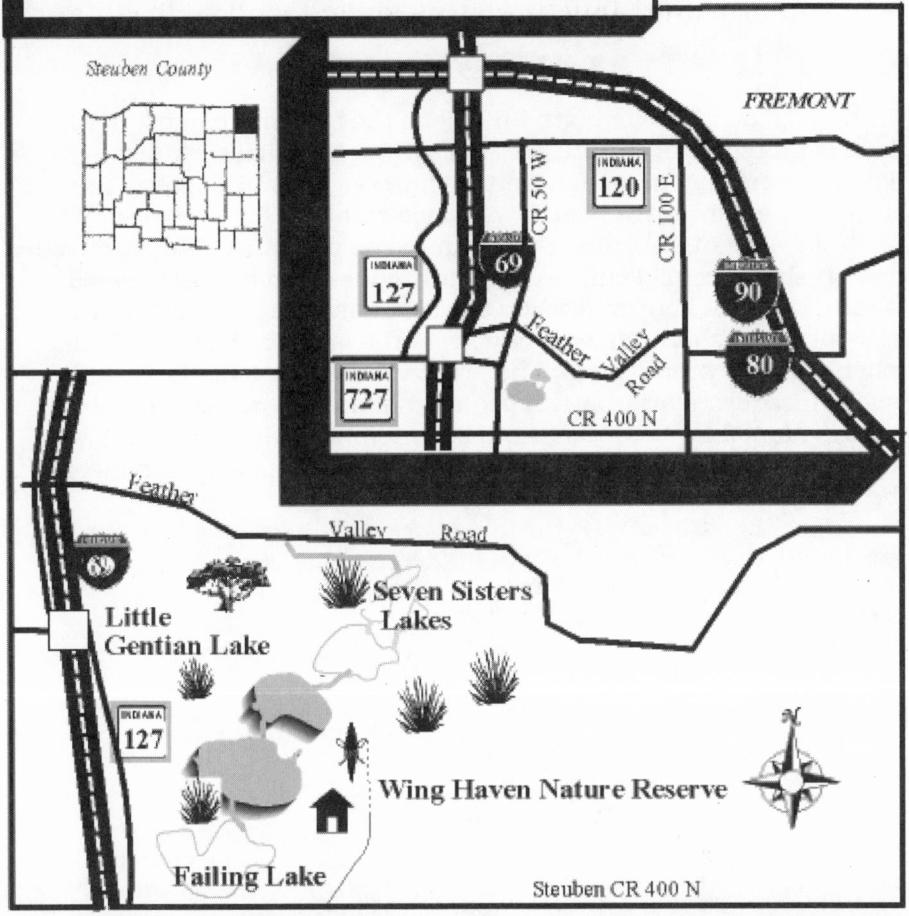

Tuberous Magnolia Water Lily on Little Gentian Lake

4. LOON LAKE

- Skim inviting shallow waters spiked with bulrush and cattail

Although Loon Lake borders I-69 along the east shore, most of the lake is protected by nature preserves (DNR Loon Lake Nature Preserve and the Anspaugh Nature Preserve total 179 acres). The abundance of bulrush, which was once gathered for weaving material, imparts a strong Native American ambiance. The extensive marsh shoreline prevents any landing along the nature-preserved south and west shores however a fine landing may be made at the north central shore where overlooks of the lake can be made from a big bluestem covered knoll. The preserves feature tamarack bog, sedge meadow, marl prairie, open marsh and upland forest. The lake is named for the goose-sized common loon whose piercing wail is heard here on occasion. A sunny Sunday summer morning would be an ideal time to be on the water.

USGS MAP(S): Angola West 1:24,000
VICINITY: Angola, Steuben County
LAKE ACREAGE/DEPTH: 138 a. /14-18′ mostly 4′
PADDLING TIME: 1 1/2 hours
LEVEL OF DIFFICULTY: Class I
HAZARDS/PORTAGES: IO allowed, shallow water restricts access to parts of the lake
INFO SOURCES: Fawn River Fish Hatchery (219) 829-6241
AREA OUTFITTERS/LIVERIES: Pigeon River Canoe-n-Camp
3490 S 325 W
Pleasant Lake, IN 46779
(219) 351-3537 or 475-5512
GAMEFISH SPECIES: bluegill, sunfish, redear, yellow bullhead, yellow perch
CAMPING: Pokagon State Park, 450 Lane 100 Lake James, Angola, IN 40703 (219) 833-2012, Class A, B & C
MEDICAL ASSISTANCE: Cameron Memorial Hospital, 410 E. Maumee St., Angola, IN 46703 (219) 665-2141

ACCESS: DNR public access is located at the northeast shore of Loon Lake, four miles northwest of Angola. From I-69 exit 150 east onto US 20 at Angola and drive about a mile to CR 200 W and turn left or north. Proceed 1.5 mile north on CR 200 W to CR 100 N and turn left. Drive one mile west on CR 100 N driving under I-69 overpass to the access site on the south side of the road.

LOON LAKE

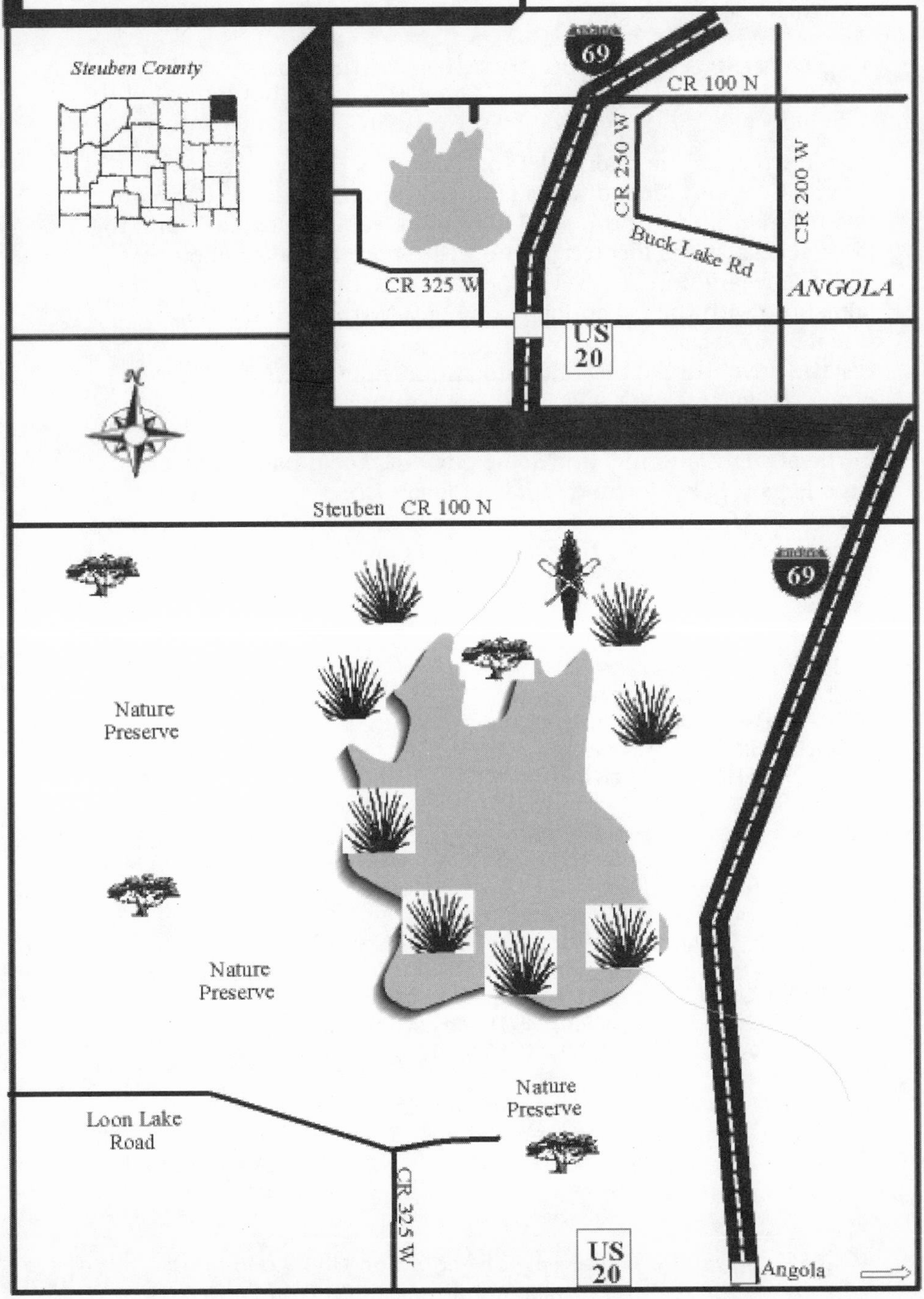

Steuben County
69
CR 100 N
CR 250 W
CR 200 W
Buck Lake Rd
CR 325 W
ANGOLA
US 20
N
Steuben CR 100 N
69
Nature Preserve
Nature Preserve
Nature Preserve
Loon Lake Road
CR 325 W
US 20
Angola

5. PIGEON LAKE

- Traverse a creek-fed standing water body

Pigeon Creek is the main inlet that supplies Pigeon Lake while Ewing, Cole and Metz ditches add their share of water. There are two basins that form the sand bottomed, east to west lake and the DNR access site is located on the west shore of the smaller west basin. Lowland forest cover, especially red maple, surrounds the lakeshore with the exception of one house trailer and an open private campground.

For the adventuresome canoeists and kayakers, the southeast outlet of Pigeon Creek flows 800 feet south from the lake to a smaller unnamed round lake (10 acre, 5 feet deep). Expect log jams in the straight channel and some current. Local paddlers travel from Pigeon Lake downstream via Pigeon Creek to the Golden Lake access and further on to Pigeon River Fish & Wildlife Area access. Expect solitude during the week on this lovely natural lake located east of Angola.

USGS MAP(S): Angola East 1:24,000
VICINITY: Angola, Steuben County
LAKE ACREAGE /DEPTH: 61a./ 38'
PADDLING TIME: 1 1/2 hours
LEVEL OF DIFFICULTY: Class I
HAZARDS/PORTAGES: IO allowed, 10 mph ltd., strainers in Pigeon Creek outlet
INFO SOURCES: Fawn River Fish Hatchery (219) 829-6241
AREA OUTFITTERS/LIVERIES: Pigeon River Canoe-n-Camp
3490 S 325 W
Pleasant Lake, IN 46779
(219) 351-3537 or 475-5512
GAMEFISH SPECIES: bluegill, largemouth bass, crappie
CAMPING: Pokagon State Park, 450 Lane 100 Lake James
Angola, IN 46703 (219) 833-2012
Class A, B, & C
MEDICAL ASSISTANCE: Cameron Memorial Hospital, 410 E. Maumee St., Angola, IN 46703
(219) 665-2141

ACCESS: Drive three miles east of Angola on US 20 and turn north on Steuben CR 200 E. Go 0.75 mile north on CR 200 E and turn right or east on the access road to the DNR boat ramp.

PIGEON LAKE

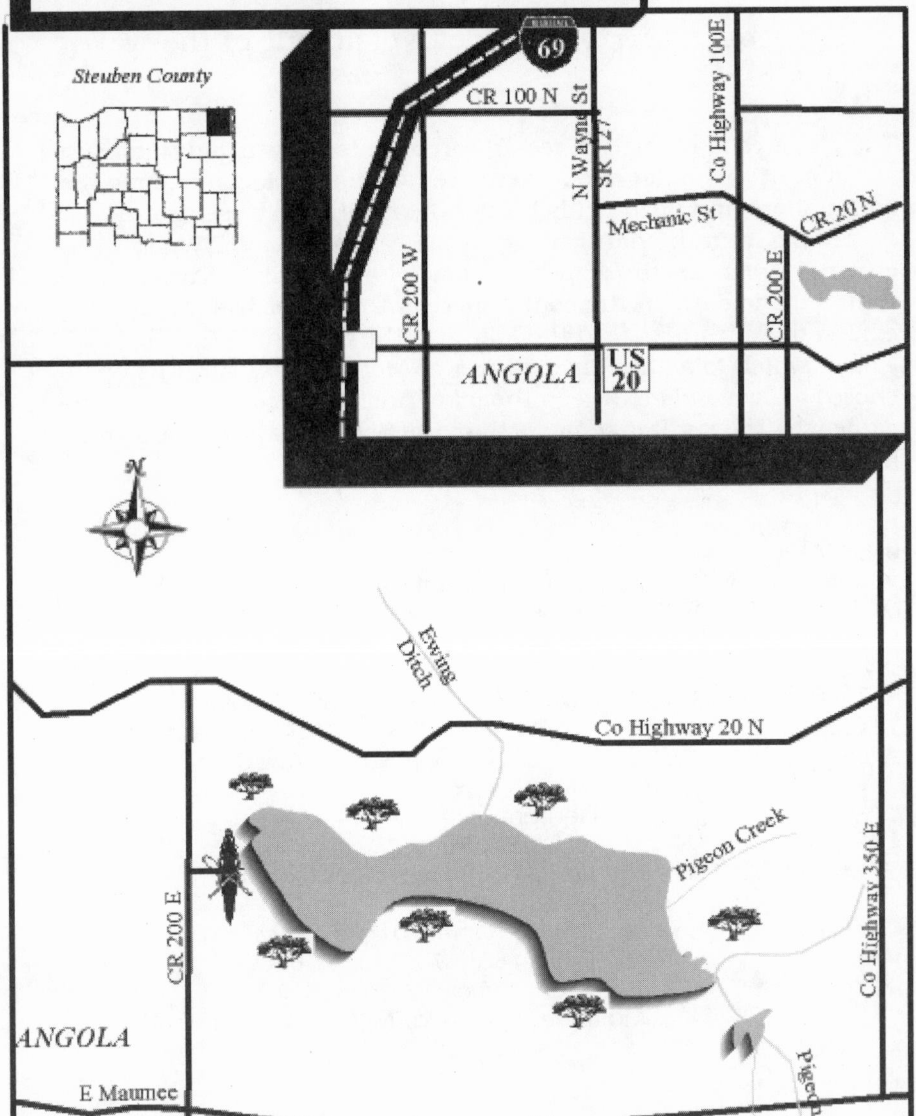

69
Steuben County
CR 100 N
N Wayne St
SR 127
Co Highway 100E
Mechanic St
CR 20 N
CR 200 W
CR 200 E
ANGOLA
US 20
N
Ewing Ditch
Co Highway 20 N
Pigeon Creek
Co Highway 350 E
CR 200 E
ANGOLA
E Maumee
US 20
Pigeon Creek

6. LITTLE TURKEY LAKE

- Enjoy quietude & open views of an out-of-the-way lake

There is a good chance of seeing cormorants, egrets and herons in summer at this quiet lake. There are two houses located along the south shore and farm fields border the north and west shores, detracting from the naturalness of the east shore. A lily pad channel separates the upper and lower basin of Little Turkey Lake. A man made cove on the south shore of the upper basin may be explored. Four inlets feed the lake and the main outlet is Turkey Creek, which joins the Pigeon River at Mongo Reservoir. The open shores allow winds to sweep the lake. Anglers may want to troll for gamefish. The rural lake is north of the Steuben and Dekalb county line, west of Hudson.

USGS MAP(S): Ashley 1:24,000
VICINITY: Ashley & Hudson, Steuben County
LAKE ACREAGE /DEPTH: 58 a./ 30'
PADDLING TIME: 1 hour
LEVEL OF DIFFICULTY: Class I
HAZARDS/PORTAGES: IO allowed, 10 mph ltd. windy at times
INFO SOURCES: Fawn River Fish Hatchery (219) 829-6241
AREA OUTFITTERS/LIVERIES: Pigeon River Canoe-n-Camp
3490 S 325 W
Pleasant Lake, IN 46779
(219) 351-3537 or 475-5512
GAMEFISH SPECIES: bluegill, largemouth bass, black crappie, yellow perch, bullhead
CAMPING: Pokagon State Park, 450 Lane 100 Lake James, Angola, IN 46703 (219) 833-2012, Class A, B & C
MEDICAL ASSISTANCE: Cameron Memorial Hospital, 410 E. Maumee St., Angola, IN 46703 (219) 665-2141

ACCESS: From I-69 exit 140 west onto SR 4. Drive 1.5 miles west on SR 4 past Hudson along the Steuben-DeKalb co line. Turn right or north onto CR 725 W and continue one mile to CR 700 S and turn right or east. Proceed 0.75 mile to the access road and turn right or south. Continue along the wooded lane to the DNR landing on the northeast shore.

LITTTLE TURKEY LAKE

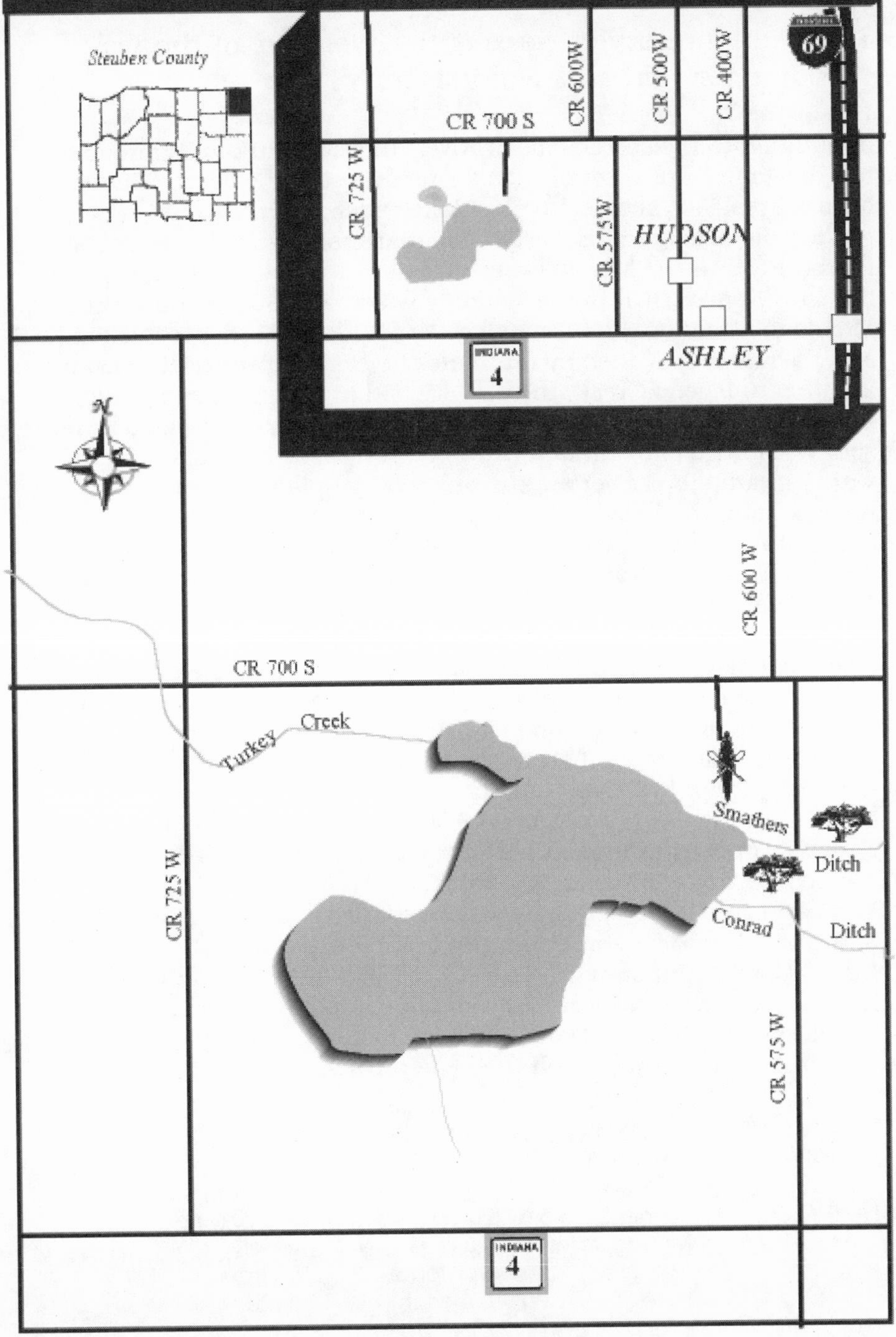

7. PIGEON RIVER FISH & WILDLIFE AREA

- **Experience seven lakes & reservoirs in an area long noted for wild and scenic beauty**

In addition to the scenic Pigeon River, there are 20 ponds and lakes but only a few are accessible to floaters most of the year. Seasonal hunting restricts access to select lakes such as Beaverdam Lake (for closure dates contact property headquarters). Pigeon Creek becomes Pigeon River at the Mongo Dam tailwater. It flows 17 miles through the 11,500-acre DNR property on its way to the St. Joseph River in Michigan (see Indiana Streams section). This DNR property is long and narrow and divided by map into the east and west sections. In addition to Pigeon Creek, the east section includes Stayner Lake, Beaverdam Lake and Mongo Reservoir. Stayner Lake, located at the southeast edge of the area, is a lovely, round, isolated glacial lake with a swamp forest border surrounded by upland forest and prairie. Man, not beaver, has impounded the waters of Beaverdam Lake. The long and narrow scenic lake attracts migratory waterfowl. Mongo reservoir is formed by a dam impoundment on Pigeon Creek. The slow moving current of Pigeon Creek cuts through the extensive lily pad and cattail marsh communities of Mongo Mill Pond, allowing floaters to paddle upstream or down. Downstream from the dam, at the confluence of Pigeon Creek and Turkey Creek and the village of Mongo, the stream is Pigeon River.

The west section of the fish and wildlife area, west of Mongo village, includes Pigeon River and impoundments of Nasby Reservoir and Ontario Mill Pond, Troxel Lake and Aldrich Lake. The "V" shaped Nasby Dam is as unique as is the dry prairie on the north shore. Further downstream near the village of Ontario is the Ontario Mill Pond and river access. The slow current allows paddling upstream and downstream for some distance (dam to Lagrange CR 475 near Curtis Creek trout station). Troxel Lake was impounded in 1967 however the shallow vegetated wetland can prove challenging to paddlers. Near Ontario Dam is Aldrich Lake, a small but undisturbed natural lake off the beaten track.

USGS MAP(S): Orland, Mongo, Lagrange 1:24,000
VICINITY: Orland, Steuben County
Mongo, Ontario & Howe, Lagrange County
LAKE ACREAGE: Stayner Lake 6 a. /20', Beaverdam Lake 20 a./26', Mongo Reservoir 125 a. /15', Nasby Reservoir 31a. /15', Ontario Mill Pond 108 a./15', Troxel Lake 55 a. /avg. 4', Aldrich Lake 10 a./20'
PADDLING TIME: ranges from 1/2 to two hours

LEVEL OF DIFFICULTY: Class I
HAZARDS/PORTAGES: electric only, no IO, select lakes closed during waterfowl season, insects
INFO SOURCES: Pigeon River FWA, Box 71, 8310 E 300 N, Mongo, IN 46771 (219) 367-2164
AREA OUTFITTERS/LIVERIES: Pigeon River Canoe–n-Camp
3490 S 325 W
Pleasant Lake, IN 46779
(219) 475-5512 or 351-3537
Trading Post, Box 132, CR 300 N
Mongo, IN 46771 (219) 367-2493
(April 1-Oct 31)
GAMEFISH SPECIES: redear, bluegill, bullhead, pumpkinseed, sunfish, largemouth bass, warmouth, perch, trout fishing in river & lakes
CAMPING: Pigeon River Fish & Wildlife Area, Mongo campground adjacent to property headquarters (219) 367-2164, Class C
Pokagon State Park near Angola (219) 833-2012, Class A, B, & C
MEDICAL ASSISTANCE; Vencor Hospital, 207 N. Townline Road, Lagrange, IN 46761 (219) 463-2143

ACCESS: East Property: Stayner Lake, from US 20 junction with SR 327, go north one mile on SR 327 and turn left or west on the access road to Stayner Lake. Beaverdam Lake, three miles southwest of Orland on SR 327, west on CR 350 N, turning north on CR 375 N to access road. Pigeon Creek accesses: SR 327, Steuben CR 175 N, Lagrange CR 1200 E, Mongo Reservoir at Mongo campground south edge, Pigeon River Headquarters CR 300 N east of Mongo.
West Property: Pigeon River: Mongo Dam tailwater, Mongo, Lagrange CR 300 N access just west of SR 3, Ontario Bridge, CR 225 E, SE corner of bridge just north of village; Nasby Dam Mill Pond, CR 300 N, E-3 parking lot; B-4 parking lot, CR 300 N & CR 390 E, Troxel-Skips Bridge, west of Curtis Creek Fish Hatchery; Ontario Dam, B-1 parking, CR 450 N; Troxel Lake, A-6 parking, CR 500 N; Aldrich Lake, A-2 parking, CR 450 N, north of Ontario Dam.

Canadian Geese in the Morning Mist of Stayner Lake

PIGEON RIVER FISH & WILDLIFE AREA WEST

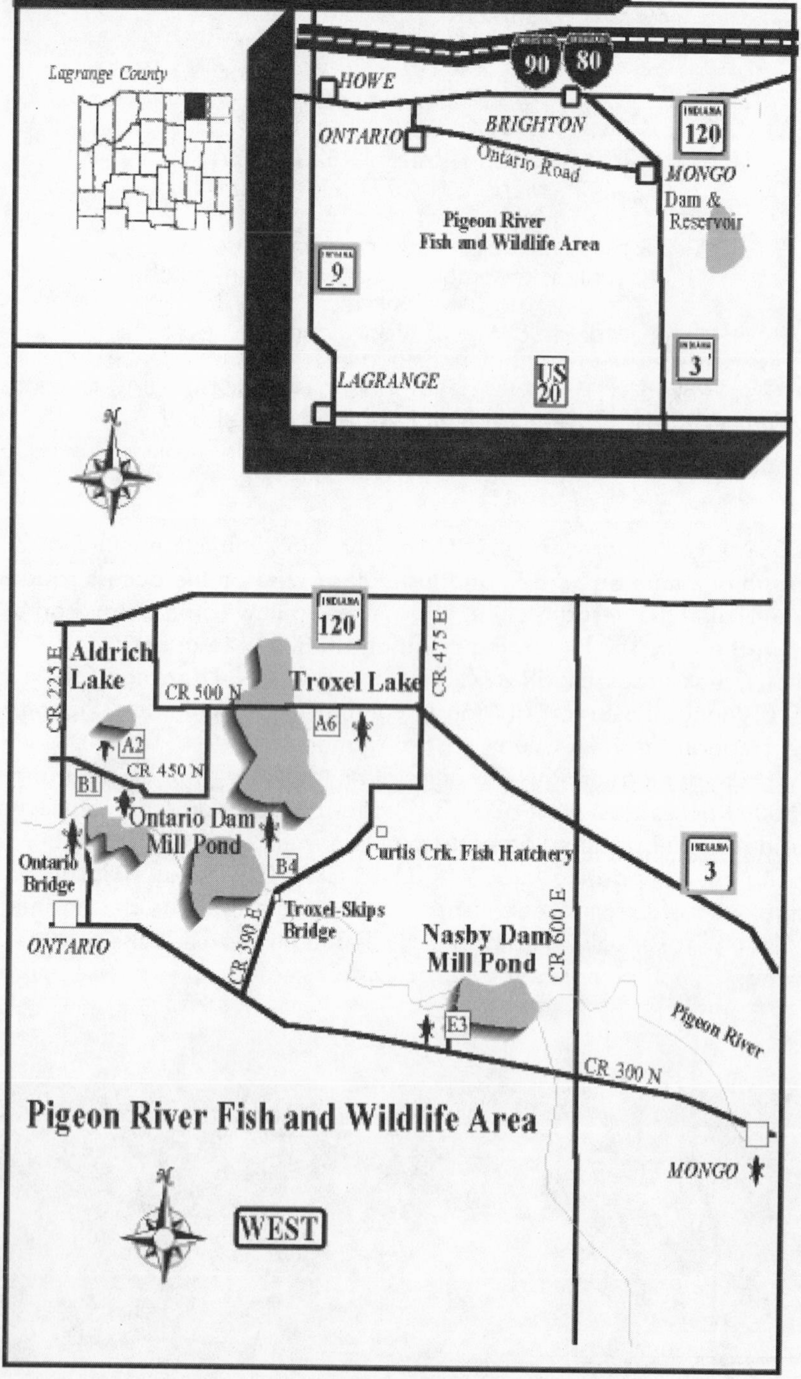
Lagrange County
HOWE
90
80
ONTARIO
BRIGHTON
120
Ontario Road
MONGO
Dam & Reservoir
Pigeon River Fish and Wildlife Area
9
3
LAGRANGE
US 20
N
120
CR 475 E
Aldrich Lake
CR 225 E
CR 500 N
Troxel Lake
A6
A2
CR 450 N
B1
Ontario Dam Mill Pond
Ontario Bridge
B4
Curtis Crk. Fish Hatchery
3
ONTARIO
CR 390 E
Troxel-Skips Bridge
Nasby Dam Mill Pond
CR 600 E
Pigeon River
E3
CR 300 N
Pigeon River Fish and Wildlife Area
MONGO
N
WEST

PIGEON RIVER FISH & WILDLIFE AREA EAST

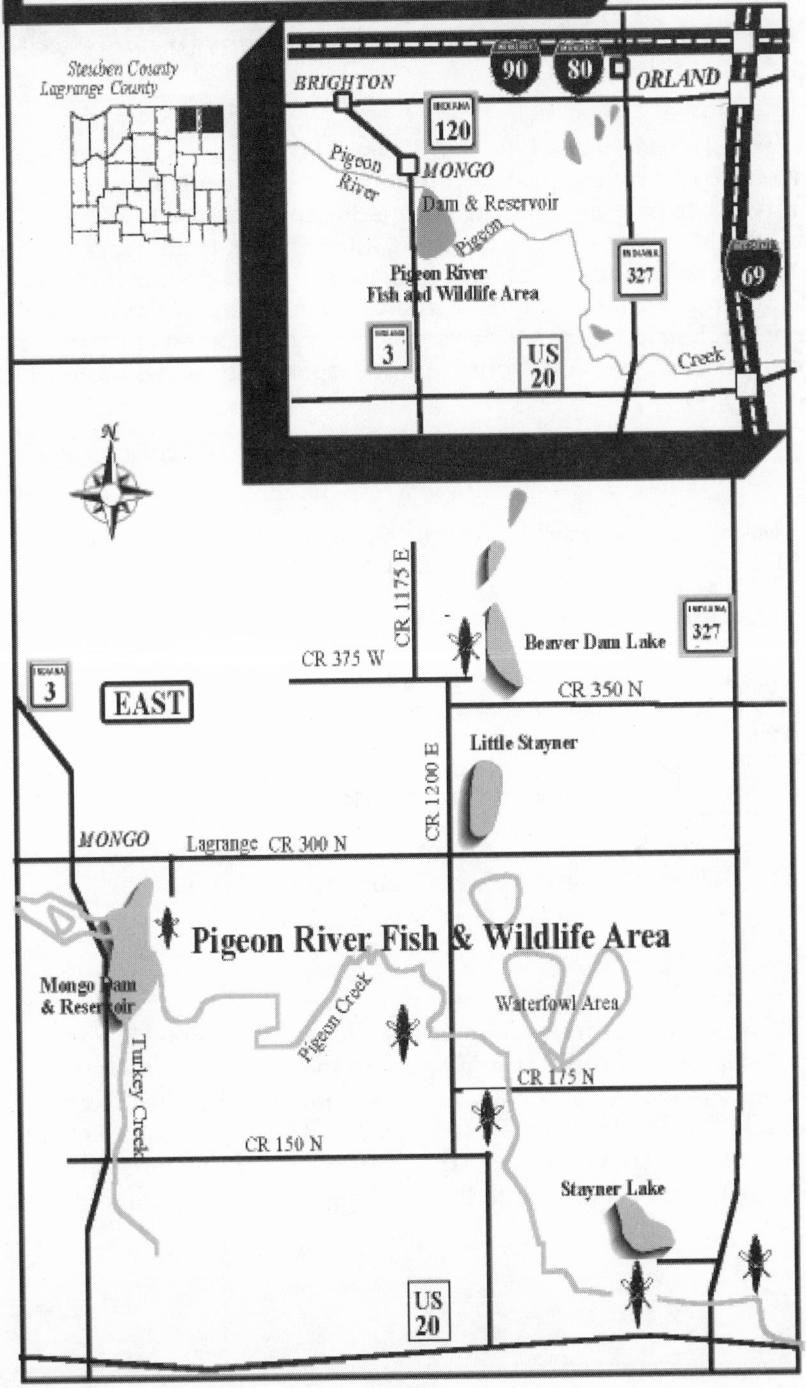

Steuben County
Lagrange County
BRIGHTON
90
80
ORLAND
120
MONGO
Pigeon River
Dam & Reservoir
Pigeon
Pigeon River
Fish and Wildlife Area
327
69
3
US 20
Creek
N
CR 1175 E
CR 375 W
Beaver Dam Lake
327
CR 350 N
3
EAST
Little Stayner
CR 1200 E
MONGO
Lagrange CR 300 N
Pigeon River Fish & Wildlife Area
Mongo Dam & Reservoir
Pigeon Creek
Waterfowl Area
Turkey Creek
CR 175 N
CR 150 N
Stayner Lake
US 20

8. APPLEMAN LAKE

- Take in rolling, rural countryside from the lake water

The oval-shaped glacial lake is positioned in a marshy depression surrounded by rolling pastured uplands of east central Lagrange County. There are no inlets or outlets for this basin lake. The marshy edge along the east shore is filled with cattail, water lily and spatterdock. The appealing and spacious farmscape has limited development with few homes. From the boat ramp at the northeast end of Appleman Lake, paddlers can cover the lake in less than an hour. There are few coves but the wide-open waters invite the wind. A scenic spot.

USGS MAP(S): Stroh, Orland 1:24,000
VICINITY: Brushy Prairie & Stroh, Lagrange County
LAKE ACREAGE /DEPTH: 52 a./ 26′
PADDLING TIME: 1 hour
LEVEL OF DIFFICULTY: Class I
HAZARDS/PORTAGES: IO allowed, 10 mph ltd. windy at times
INFO SOURCES: Fawn River Fish Hatchery (219) 829-6241
AREA OUTFITTERS/LIVERIES: none
GAMEFISH SPECIES: bluegill, sunfish, redear, warmouth, largemouth bass, bullhead
CAMPING: Pigeon River Fish & Wildlife Area, Box 71, 8310 E 300N, Mongo, IN 46771 (219) 367-2164, Class C
MEDICAL ASSISTANCE: Vencor Hospital, 207 N. Townline Rd. Lagrange, IN 47761 (219) 463-2143 or 911

ACCESS: From Lagrange, drive about 10.5 miles east on US 20 through Plato and Brushy Prairie to Lagrange CR 1150 E (near the Lagrange-Steuben County line) and turn right or south. Proceed one-mile south on CR 1150 E to CR 100 S and turn right or west. Continue 0.5 mile on CR 100 S to the access road/CR 1100 E and turn left or south. Follow the short road to the DNR access site on the north shore.

APPLEMAN LAKE

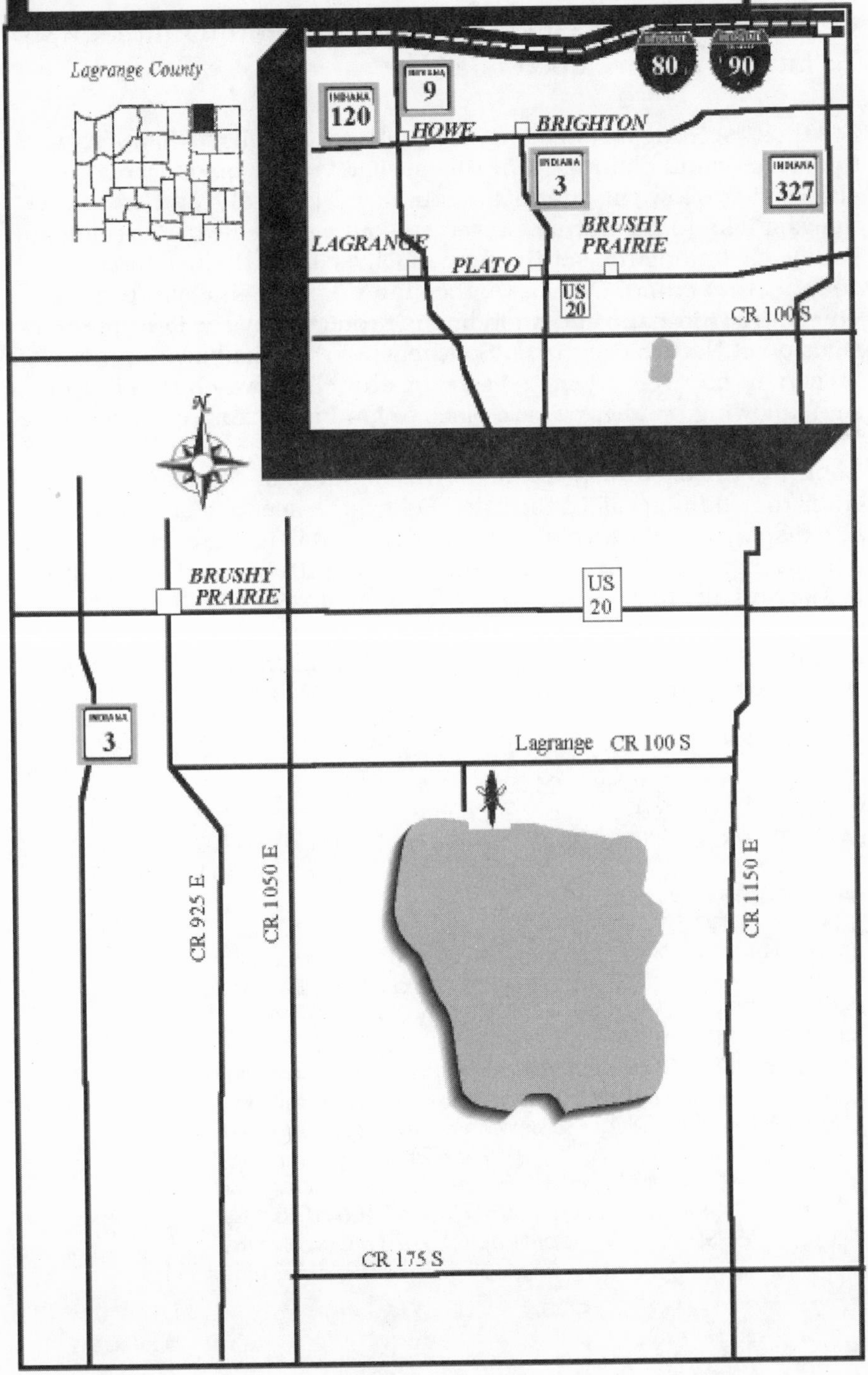

Lagrange County
80
90
INDIANA
120
9
HOWE
BRIGHTON
INDIANA
3
INDIANA
327
BRUSHY
PRAIRIE
LAGRANGE
PLATO
US
20
CR 100 S
BRUSHY
PRAIRIE
US
20
INDIANA
3
Lagrange CR 100 S
CR 925 E
CR 1050 E
CR 1150 E
CR 175 S

9. OLIVER-OLIN-MARTIN-SMITH HOLE LAKES

- Put in & explore a chain-o-lakes including Indiana's largest undeveloped lake

For those seeking a rewarding day's outing, paddlers will appreciate the scenery and distance that this special voyage holds. From the access site follow the channel south into Oliver Lake and cross over the vast lake to the nature preserved south shore near Bass Hole. Paddle east along the south shore of Oliver Lake to the short channel that enters Olin Lake, the states' largest undeveloped lake. The entire Olin Lake and shoreline is protected by the DNR's Division of Nature Preserves. Southeast of the small island, the preserve's nature trail emerges at the shoreline (watch for #5 trail sign) allowing paddlers a rare place to land and explore the preserve (mosquitoes can be prolific).

Continue the excursion to the northeast shore of Olin Lake and enter the channel to Martin Lake. Follow the scenic channel with its fine display of aquatic plants to emerge at Martin Lake where houses line the north shore. Proceed along the wooded south shore of Martin Lake to arrive at a short channel to Smith Hole, the smallest of the four glacial-gouged lakes. To return, reverse the fluvial journey. Most paddlers agree that this chain of lakes is one of the best in northern Indiana.

USGS MAP(S): Oliver Lake 1:24,000
VICINITY: Wolcottville, Lagrange County
LAKE ACREAGE /DEPTH: Oliver Lake 394 a./ 91', Olin Lake 103 a./82', Martin Lake 26 a./56', Smith Hole 2 a./18'
PADDLING TIME: 4 hours
LEVEL OF DIFFICULTY: Class I
HAZARDS/PORTAGES: IO allowed, 10 mph ltd. windy at times, long distance could be challenging
INFO SOURCES: Fawn River Fish Hatchery (219) 829-6241
AREA OUTFITTERS/LIVERIES: none
GAMEFISH SPECIES: bluegill, yellow perch, carp, smallmouth bass, rock bass, largemouth bass, rainbow trout
CAMPING: Pigeon River Fish & Wildlife Area, Box 71, 8310 E 300 N, Mongo, IN 46771 (219) 367-2164 or Bixler Lake Park, Kendallville Parks & Recreation, 211 Iddings Street, Kendallville, IN 467551 (219) 347-1064, Class C
MEDICAL ASSISTANCE: Vencor Hospital, 207 N. Townline Rd., Lagrange, IN 47761 (219) 463-2143 or 911

ACCESS: From Lagrange, drive south on SR 9 to Lagrange CR 450 S and turn right or west. Continue two miles west on CR 450 S to the DNR access site on the northwest shore of Oliver Lake. The access site is about five miles northwest of Wolcottville.

OLIVER, OLIN, MARTIN & SMITH HOLE LAKES

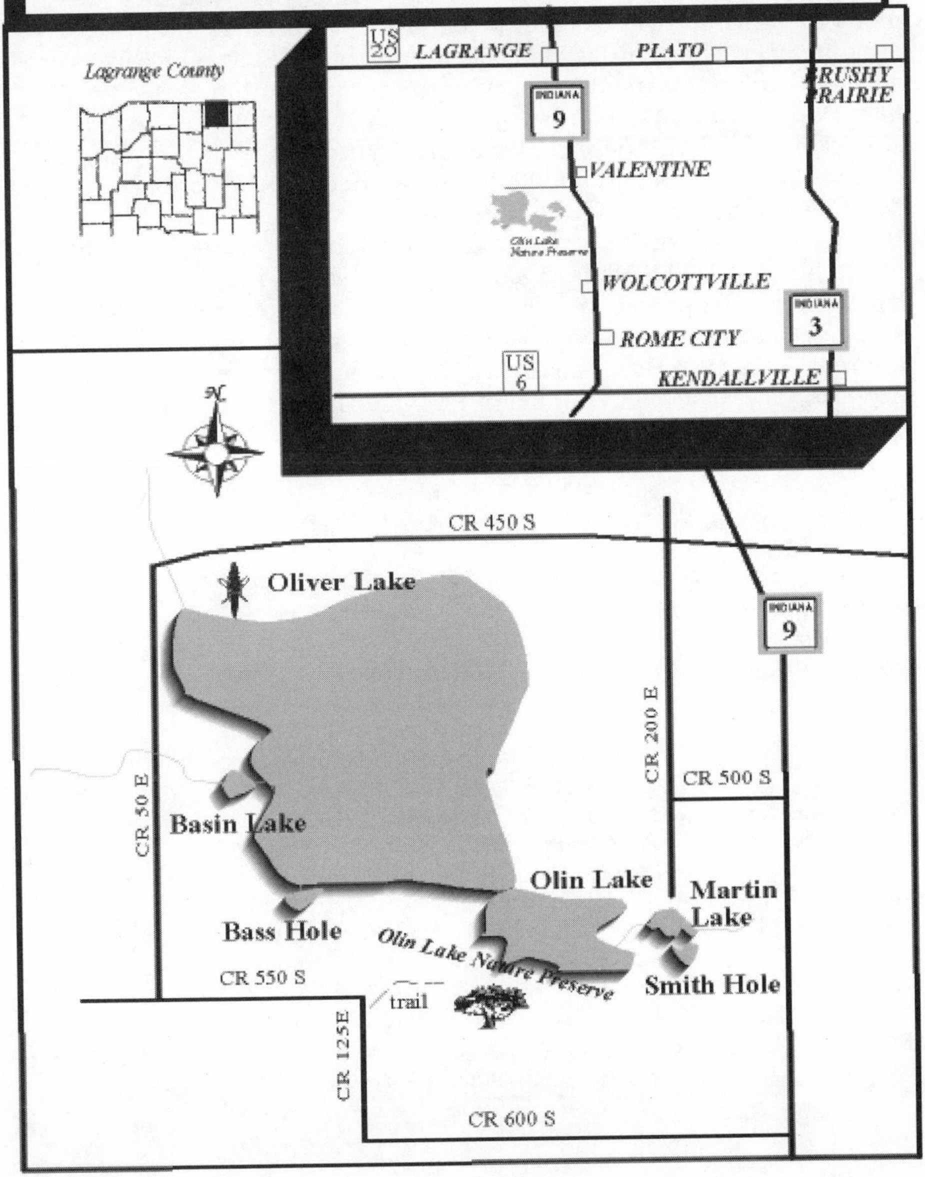

10. SYLVAN LAKE

- Ply the lake author Gene Stratton Porter (1863-1924) explored

Sylvan Lake is a manmade lake created during the 19th century heyday of the canal era to serve as a "feeder". Today the attractive lake is highly developed and motor boats, pontoons and jet skis are heavy especially on summer weekends. Paddlers will find their moments during early morning weekdays. From the Brady's Landing access (fee) at Pit Lake Basin, northeast Sylvan Lake, the shortest and safest paddling path to the Gene Stratton Porter historic site would be to cross over the basin and follow the south shore west around the tip of Boy Scout Island. Once on the south side of Boy Scout Island paddle to the wooded south shore of Cain Lake Basin southeast Sylvan Lake. There are piers in place for landing at the lakefront of the 20-acre state historic site that is open to the public. The DNR managed site includes the home (tours), gardens, woods, picnic shelter and gift shop plus special events such as Chautauqua Days in August. The grounds are open dawn to dusk. Return to Brady's Landing via the same route. Consider exploring the east inlet channel of Pit Lake Basin where few motorboats venture. Pay for boat access at Brady's Landing at the adjacent Granny's Restaurant.

USGS MAP(S): Kendallville, Albion, Wolcottville1:24,000
VICINITY: Rome City, Noble County
LAKE ACREAGE /DEPTH: 669 a. /36'
PADDLING TIME: 3 hours
LEVEL OF DIFFICULTY: Class I
HAZARDS/PORTAGES: IO allowed, watch for motorboat traffic especially weekends, fee for boat access at Brady's Landing. pay at Granny's Restaurant nearby, due to excess amount of motorboats, most of the lake is not recommended
INFO SOURCES: Brady's Landing (219) 854-9498 or Gene Stratton Porter Stratton Historic Site, (219) 854-3790, Tri-Lakes Fisheries Station (219) 691-3181
AREA OUTFITTERS/LIVERIES: none
GAMEFISH SPECIES: bluegill, largemouth bass, channel catfish, perch, walleye, crappie
CAMPING: Chain O'Lakes State Park, 2355 E 75 S, Albion, IN 46701 (219) 636-2654, Class A, B & C
MEDICAL ASSISTANCE: McCray Memorial Hospital, 951 Hospital Drive, Kendallville, IN 46755 (800) 824-5860 (219) 347-1100

ACCESS: Brady's Landing, a private fee charged access site ($1.00 canoes) is located on the northeast shore of Pit Lake Basin of Sylvan Lake. To reach the access site from Rome City, drive north on North Kelly Street/SR 9 to Northport Road and turn right or east. Follow Northport Road about two miles to Noble CR 400 E and turn right or east. Continue on CR 400 E 0.5 mile to Northshore Drive and turn right or east. Proceed on Northshore Drive to the cul de sac parking and Granny's Restaurant at Brady's Landing at 1850 Northshore Drive. There is a DNR public access site at Front Street, Lakeside Park in Rome City just south of the dam however boat traffic is usually heavy in summer.

SYLVAN LAKE

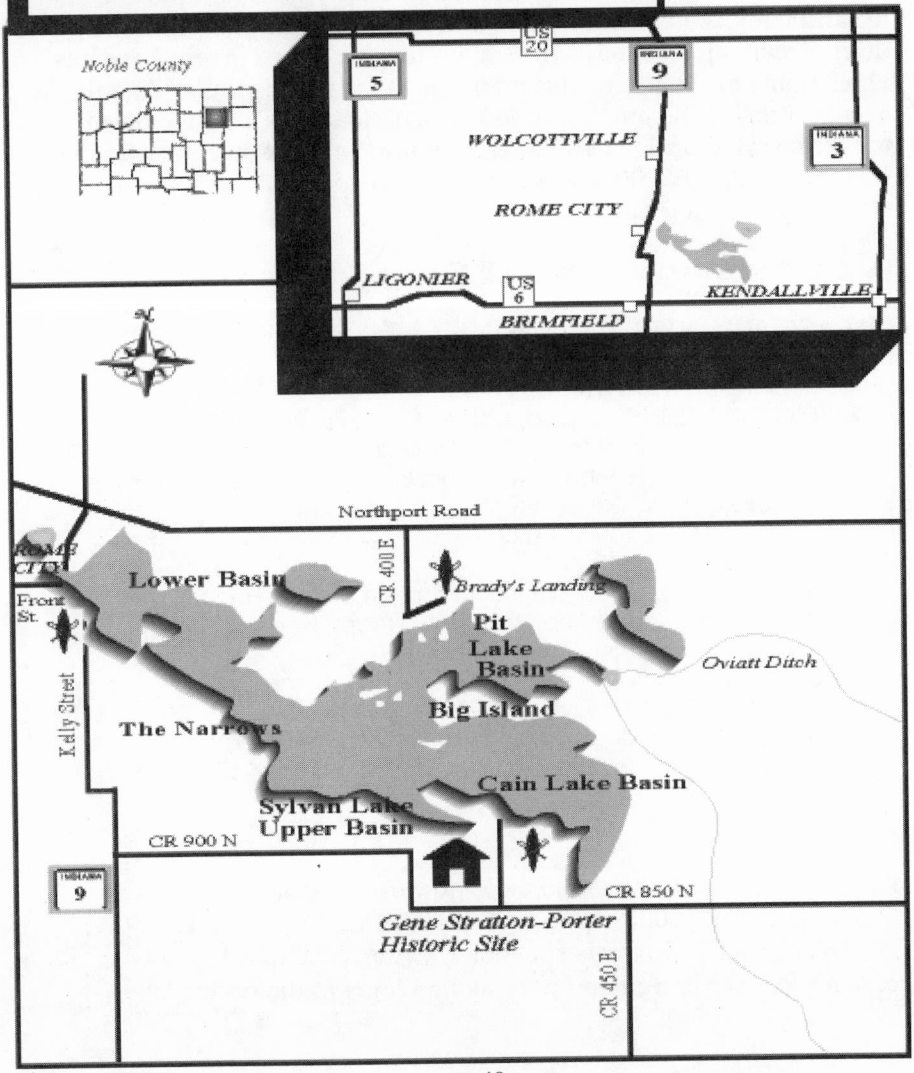

11. WALDRON LAKE

- Go through wetlands upstream to the mouth of a lake

Paddle upstream along the North Branch of the Elkhart River headwaters (normally weak current) through the Hammer Wetlands Nature Preserve (owned by ACRES land trust) to the confluence of Waldron Lake for a unique fluvial journey. Explore the developed chain of lakes known as West Lakes (Waldron, Jones, Steinbarger and Tamarack lakes). The best portion is the quality wetlands between the access site and Waldron Lake. Enroute you may see waterfowl such as the wood duck, coots, blue herons, green herons and mallards and wildflowers such as cardinal flower, marsh marigold, blue flag, iris and marsh mallows. Watch for motorboats up and back. A challenging optional trip would be to float downstream along the North Branch to where the current becomes challenging and back upstream to the Dukes Bridge, Wm T. Malle access site. If the current is too strong, float about a mile down to the Cosperville bridge CR 900 N , the next bridge south (a 1.5 mile car shuttle by CR's 900 N east and 125 W north). Watch for strainers or sweepers.

USGS MAP(S): Oliver Lake, Albion 1:24,000
VICINITY: Rome City, Noble County
LAKE ACREAGE /DEPTH: 216 a. /45'
PADDLING TIME: 2 hours
LEVEL OF DIFFICULTY: Class I
HAZARDS/PORTAGES: IO allowed, watch for motorboat traffic, logjams on the Elkhart River North Branch downstream from access site
INFO SOURCES: Tri-Lakes Fisheries Station (219) 691-3181
ACRES Land Trust (219) 422-1004
AREA OUTFITTERS/LIVERIES: none
GAMEFISH SPECIES: bluegill, largemouth bass, smallmouth bass, channel catfish, perch, crappie, redear, northern pike, warmouth
CAMPING: Chain O'Lakes State Park, 2355 E 75 S, Albion, IN 46701 (219) 636-2654, Class A, B, & C
MEDICAL ASSISTANCE: McCray Memorial Hospital, 951 E Hospital Drive. Kendallville, IN 6755 (800) 824-5860 (219) 347-1100

ACCESS: From Rome City and SR 9, go west 2.5 miles on Front Street/Noble CR 1000 N. Jog right onto CR 1050 N to CR 125 W & turn left or south. Continue south on CR 125 W 0.5 mile to the NW corner of Dukes Bridge and park at the Wm T. Malle access site.

WALDRON LAKE

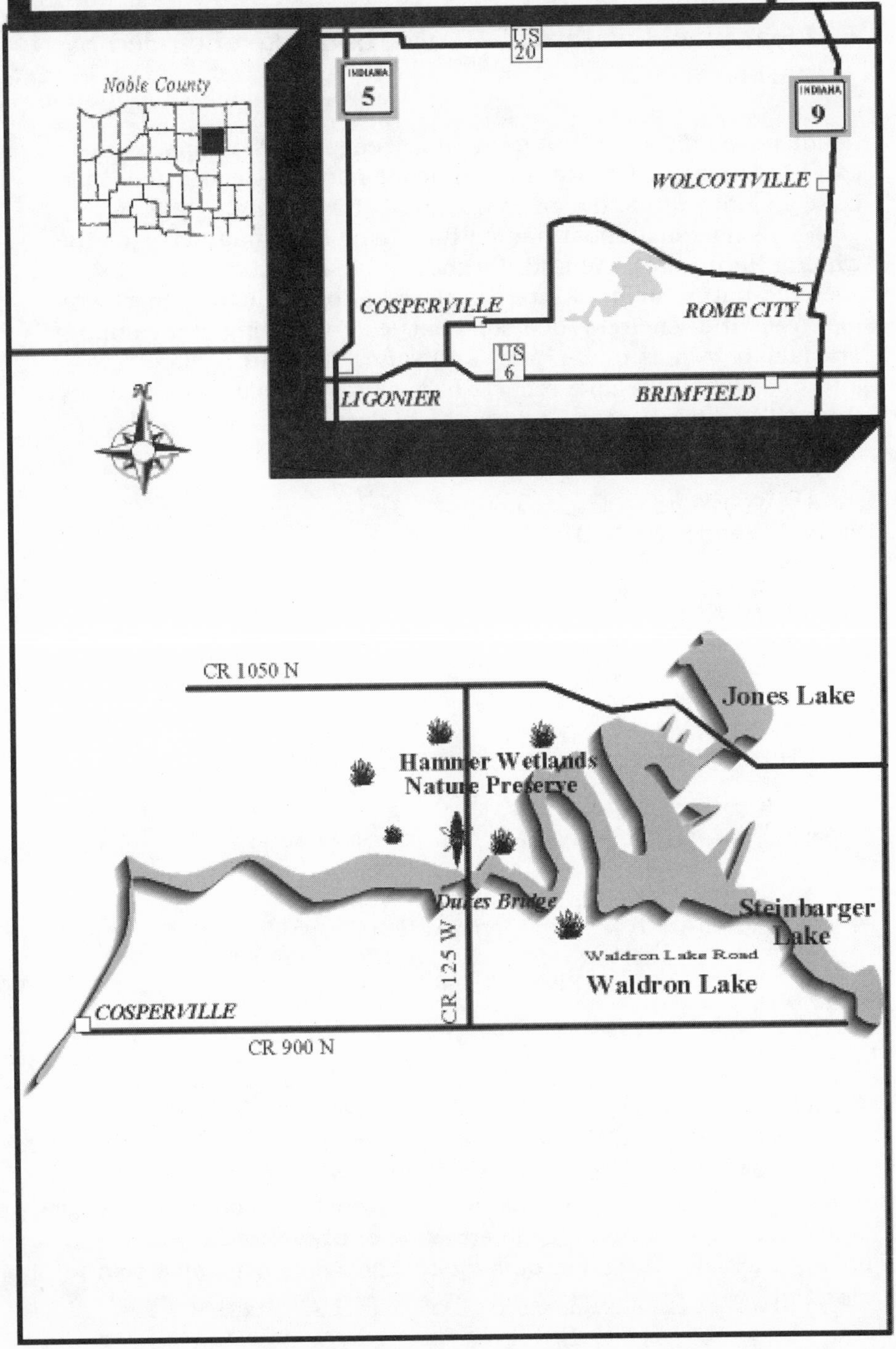

Noble County
US 20
INDIANA 5
INDIANA 9
WOLCOTTVILLE
COSPERVILLE
ROME CITY
US 6
LIGONIER
BRIMFIELD
CR 1050 N
Jones Lake
Hammer Wetlands
Nature Preserve
Dukes Bridge
Steinbarger Lake
CR 125 W
Waldron Lake Road
Waldron Lake
COSPERVILLE
CR 900 N

12. BIXLER LAKE

- Float placid waters of a suburban lake encircled by parkland

Paddlers will discover that even on the edge of urban spaces there can be wildness. The city of Kendallville has long recognized Bixler Lake as a recreational asset since the 1850s. During 1866 and 1867, a small steamboat named the Flying Dutchman cruised the waters. Naturalists will find the south marshy natural shoreline (wetland nature area) of interest. In addition to floating there are foot trails that encircle the lake, beaches, picnicking and camping. The lake bottom is muck, marl and sand. A sun-drenched afternoon when the lake reflects blue sky is a choice time to enjoy this civilized excursion. Great with children.

USGS MAP(S): Kendallville, Corunna 1:24,000
VICINITY: Kendallville, Noble County
LAKE ACREAGE /DEPTH: 120 a. /43'
PADDLING TIME: 1 hour
LEVEL OF DIFFICULTY: Class I
HAZARDS/PORTAGES: IO allowed, motorboat traffic, mosquitoes
INFO SOURCES: Kendallville Park and Recreation Dept.
(219) 347-1064
AREA OUTFITTERS/LIVERIES: none
GAMEFISH SPECIES: bluegill, largemouth bass, smallmouth bass, channel catfish, perch, crappie, redear, northern pike
CAMPING: east shore of Bixler Lake (219) 347-1064 & Chain O' Lakes State Park, 2355 E 75 S, Albion, IN 46701 (219) 636-2654, Class A, B, & C
MEDICAL ASSISTANCE: McCray Memorial Hospital, 951 E Hospital Drive, Kendallville, IN 46755 (800) 824-5860 or (219) 347-1100

ACCESS: From US 6 in east Kendallville, drive south on Fair Street to the "T" intersection at Wayne Street and turn left or east. Drive a short distance and turn right or south onto Park Avenue. Proceed on Park Avenue to Lake Park Drive and turn left or east. Continue on Lake Park Drive to the boat ramp at the intersection of Lake Park Drive and Sherman Street, NW corner of the lake adjacent to McCray Memorial Hospital.

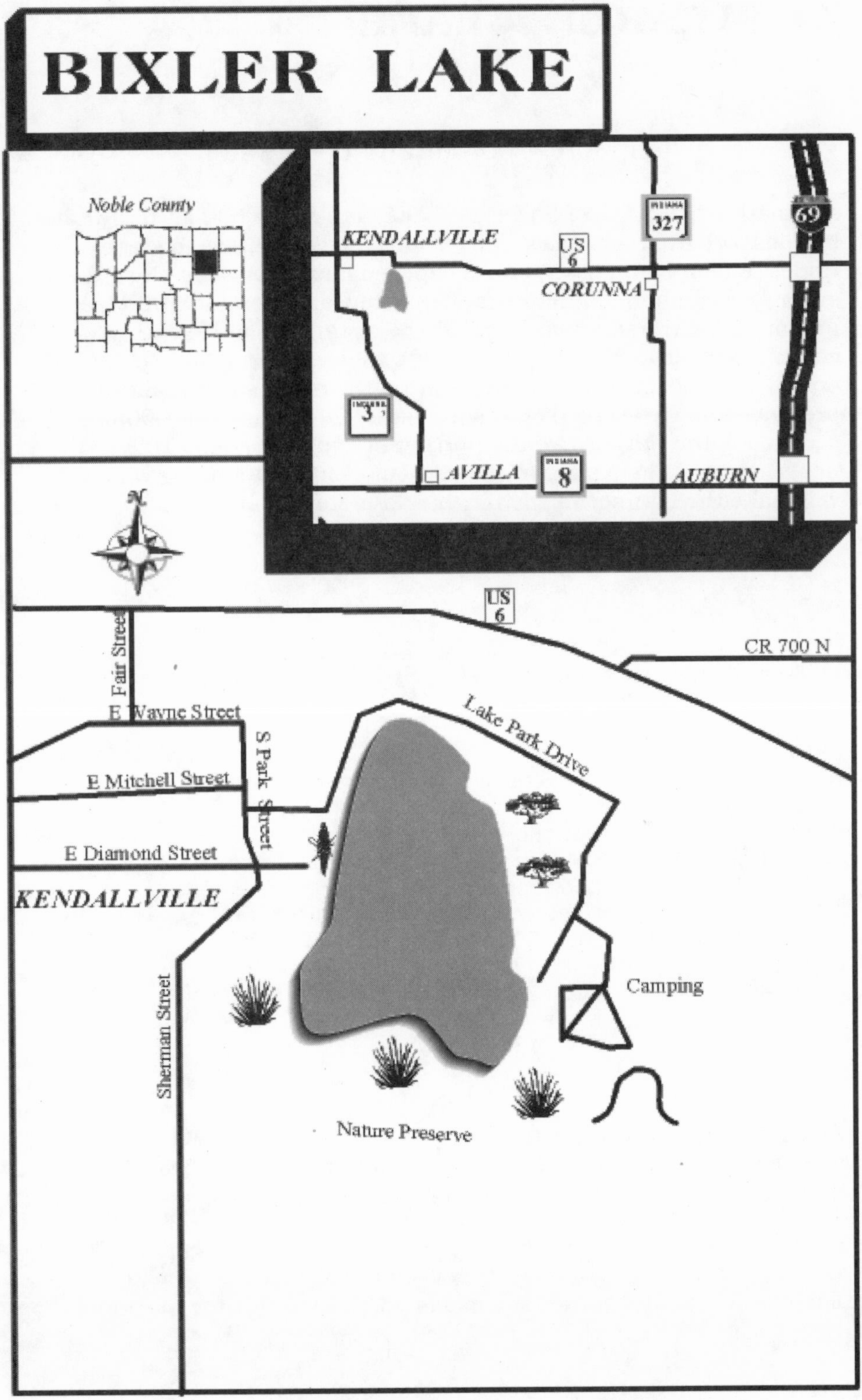

BIXLER LAKE
Noble County
KENDALLVILLE
US 6
327
69
CORUNNA
3
AVILLA
8
AUBURN
US 6
CR 700 N
Fair Street
E Wayne Street
S Park Street
Lake Park Drive
E Mitchell Street
E Diamond Street
KENDALLVILLE
Sherman Street
Camping
Nature Preserve

13. SACARIDER LAKE

- Savor swamp forest border and open waters

A remarkable feature of Sacarider Lake is the deep 60-foot hole that lies offshore from the access site. Toppled trees, unable to stand under punishing high wind have exposed large root wads along the swampy east shore. Agricultural fields appear beyond the thin tree margin along the southwest shore. The open, tree-lined south and east shores allow paddlers to gaze into the swamp forest near the outlet. The sole property homeowner on the north shore makes his presence known with a picturesque barn. Glimpses of CR 600 N are seen along the ridge above the northwest end of the lake. This is a fine water body to explore in the early morning autumn fog which will make the lake seemingly larger and more of a mysterious natural wonder.

USGS MAP(S): Kendallville, 1:24,000
VICINITY: Kendallville, Noble County
LAKE ACREAGE /DEPTH: 33 a. /60'
PADDLING TIME: 1 hour
LEVEL OF DIFFICULTY: Class I
HAZARDS/PORTAGES: IO allowed, watch for motorboat traffic
INFO SOURCES: Tri-Lakes Fisheries Station (219) 691-3181
AREA OUTFITTERS/LIVERIES: none
GAMEFISH SPECIES: bluegill, largemouth bass, bullhead catfish, perch, crappie, redear, sunfish, pumpkinseed
CAMPING: east shore of Bixler Lake, Kendallville City Parks (219) 347-1064 & Chain O' Lakes State Park, 2355 E 75 S, Albion, IN 46701 (219) 636-2654, Class A, B & C
MEDICAL ASSISTANCE: McCray Memorial Hospital, 951 E Hospital Dr., Kendallville, IN 46755 (800) 824-5860 or (219) 347-1100

ACCESS: From SR 3 at Kendallville, go west on Noble CR 600 N about three miles to the access road and turn left or south and proceed to the DNR boat ramp on the northeast side of Sacarider Lake.

SACARIDER LAKE

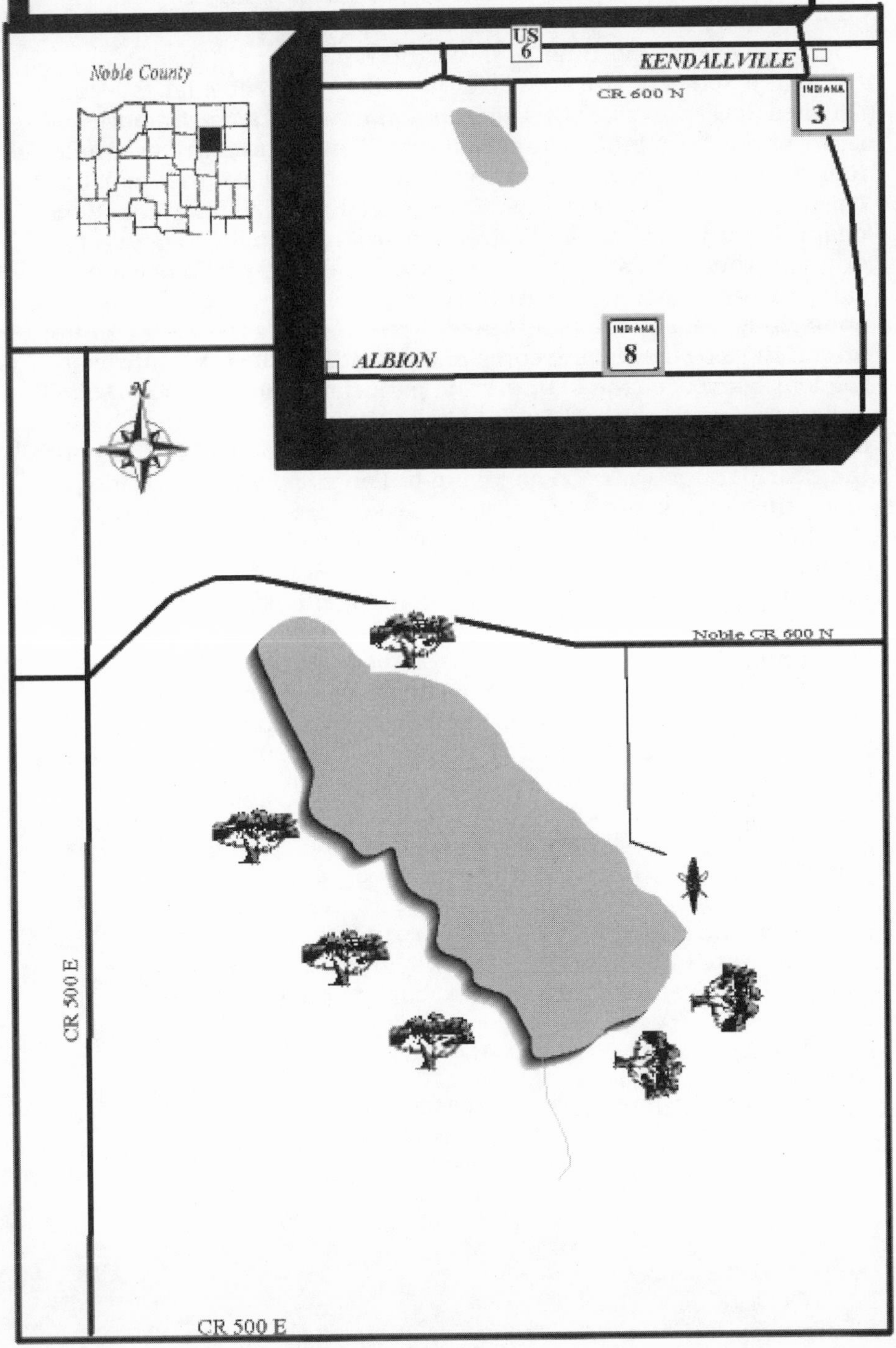

14. CHAIN O'LAKES STATE PARK

- Paddle across a liquid string of glacial lakes

There are a few opportunities in northern Indiana to journey through a series of interconnecting publicly accessible lakes. Chain O'Lakes aptly describes this special aquatic experience from the heart of northern Indiana lake country. Eight lakes form a six-mile long east to west chain from Long Lake to Miller Lake that may be traversed in half a day or less. Experienced paddlers may canoe the chain and turn around and retrace their strokes back to point of origin, rather than shuttle, in one leisurely day or perhaps canoe camp at Rivir Lake, northeast shore.

Long Lake, the second largest lake in the chain, is the ideal point of origin. Explore the private coves and go with the flow west through the long narrow channel, under the park road bridge to Dock Lake. Follow the north shore of Dock Lake to the short connecting channel to Bowen Lake. Float under the Trail 1 footbridge and enter the nearly round water body. Miami Indian villagers once resided along the north shore bluff of Bowen Lake. Locate the channel to Sand Lake along the south shore. The channel leads through the undulating, maturing woodland where maples thrive. It crosses under the park road bridge, then enters Sand Lake; the most developed and largest lake of the Chain O'Lakes. (Canoe rentals and swimming beach on east shore.) Troll for trout as you continue your fluvial excursion along the northwest shore and enter the channel to the most undeveloped and remote section of the trip. Follow the winding channel to river-like Weber Lake, which is much longer than it is wide, where the latter stages of glacial evolution are in evidence. Continue in the clear, center flow of the channel to Mud Lake. A canoe camp is located on the northeast side of the shore as you go under the Trail 4 footbridge to Rivir Lake. Proceed west through the open water to Miller Lake and the north shore access, the last in the chain west. Consider portaging to Norman Lake (less than 100 yards north) and if time and energy allow, reverse the course and retrace the watery route back to point of origin.

USGS MAP(S): Merriam, Ege 1:24,000
VICINITY: Albion, Noble County
LAKE ACREAGE /DEPTH: (east to west flow) Long Lake 40 a. /32', Dock Lake 16 a. /22', Bowen Lake 30 a. / 65', Sand Lake 47 a. /51', Weber Lake 7 a. /20', Mud Lake 8 a. /25', Rivir Lake 24 a. /32', Miller Lake 11 a. /27', Norman Lake 14 a. /46'
PADDLING TIME: 4 hours (one-way)
LEVEL OF DIFFICULTY: Class I
HAZARDS/PORTAGES: electric trolling only, 10 mph ltd., seasonal

low water in the connecting channels, one portage, Miller Lake to Norman Lake, seasonal entrance fee & boat launch fee

INFO SOURCES: Chain O'Lakes State Park, 2355 East 75 S, Albion, IN 46701 (219) 636-2654

AREA OUTFITTERS/LIVERIES: seasonal canoe rentals at Sand Lake

GAMEFISH SPECIES: bluegill, largemouth bass, northern pike, redear, sunfish, warmouth, bullhead, crappie, rainbow trout

CAMPING: Chain O'Lakes State Park canoe camp, Class A, B & C rally, youth, tent, family cabins (219) 636-2654

MEDICAL ASSISTANCE: McCray Memorial Hospital, 951 East Hospital Drive, Kendallville, IN 46755 (219) 347-1100 or (800) 824-5860

ACCESS: From Albion drive south on SR 9 three miles to CR 75 S and turn left at the marked entrance. Drive east to the main gate. All lake chain has access sites except Mud Lake & Weber Lake. Put in at Long Lake to go with the flow.

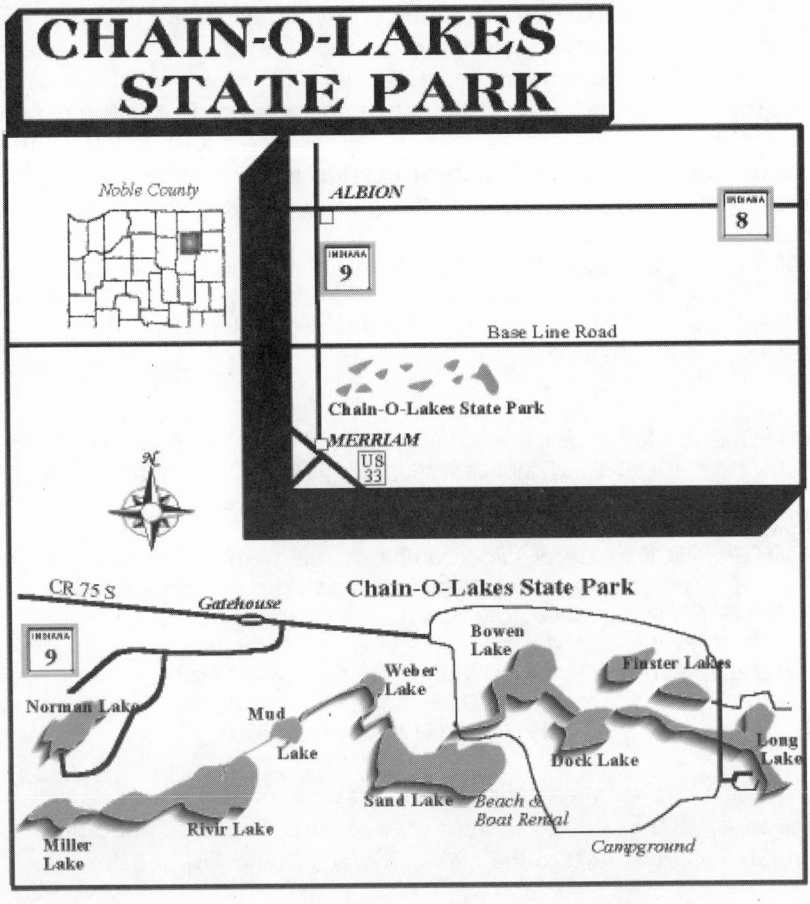

15. BEAR LAKE & HIGH LAKE

- Probe the backwater of two linked northern lakes

A long and narrow ditch connects Bear Lake with High Lake. A short 60-yard portage is necessary in the 0.25-mile long channel at a bridge near the confluence of High Lake. Most of the natural shoreline is owned by Merry Lea Environmental Learning Center of Goshen College. Canoeists are permitted to land along the shore of Merry Lea property to rest and explore the immediate area.

From the DNR boat access at Bear Lake's east shore, just north of the Helen Thomas Memorial Park and Beach, paddle to the south open shore which is owned by Merry Lea. Near mid-point is an open landing one may use to view the beach sand prairie, a former lake bottom. Continue west along the south shore of the deep glacial-formed lake to the channel entrance to High Lake. The "Goose Neck" a secluded cove surrounded by marsh, is located to the west of the channel mouth.

Enter the channel and canoe against the slight current. Shrub and swamp forests thrive on both sides of the channel, home to the least bittern and marsh wren. Deer flies in the channel can prove pesky. The channel narrows near the road bridge that leads to the Merry Lea group camp and a short portage is necessary. Carry the canoe under the bridge, upstream 180' to deeper water and go left on the channel onto High Lake. The best portion is the north end of High Lake. Retrace the route back to the access site at Bear Lake.

USGS MAP(S): Ormas 1:24,000
VICINITY: Wolf Lake, Noble County
LAKE ACREAGE /DEPTH: Bear Lake 136 a. /59' High Lake 123 a. /27'
PADDLING TIME: 3 to 4 hours
LEVEL OF DIFFICULTY: Class I
HAZARDS/PORTAGES: portage into High Lake, distance & insects
INFO SOURCES: Merry Lea, Box 263, Wolf Lake, IN 46796 (219) 799-5869 also Tri-Lakes Fisheries Station, 5570 North Fish Hatchery Road, Columbia City, IN, 46725 (219) 691-3181
AREA OUTFITTERS/LIVERIES: none
GAMEFISH SPECIES: bluegill, largemouth bass, northern pike, redear, sunfish, carp, wamouth, bullhead, crappie, rainbow trout
CAMPING: Chain O' Lakes State Park, E 75 S, Albion, IN 46701 (219) 636-2654, Class A, B & C
MEDICAL ASSISTANCE: McCray Memorial Hospital, 951 East Hospital Drive, Kendallville, IN 46755 (219) 636-2654 or (800) 824-5860

ACCESS: Go one mile south of Wolf Lake on SR 109, then one mile west on CR 200 S. Access at the northeast side of Bear Lake along Lake Shore Drive, next to the Helen Thomas Memorial beach park.

BEAR LAKE & HIGH LAKE

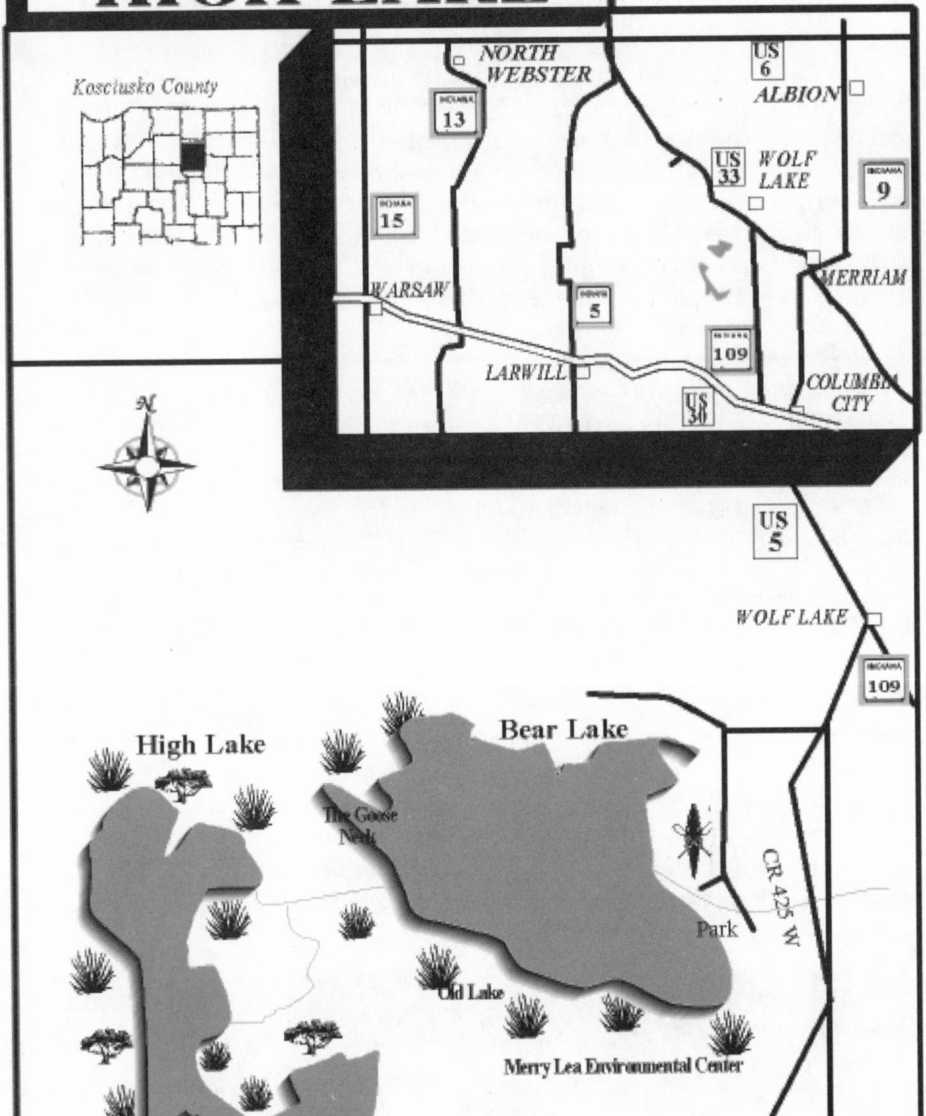

16. CRANE LAKE

- Enjoy the overlooked quietude & easy access

Crane Lake is tucked out of the way. It curves north to south and most of the shore is wooded and has only one homesite. The lake access is at the north shore, south of the junction of CR 500 S and CR 300 W. The narrow long lake allows down and back blissful canoeing, especially along the east and west shore. The outlet at the south end drains the muck-bottomed lake to nearby Big Lake and the Tippecanoe River. Great blue heron and bluegill are common at Crane Lake. People are scarce in this sliver of aquatic wildness.

USGS MAP(S): Merriam 1:24,000
VICINITY: Wolf Lake, Noble County
LAKE ACREAGE /DEPTH: 28 a. /35'
PADDLING TIME: 1 hour
LEVEL OF DIFFICULTY: Class I
HAZARDS/PORTAGES: IO mph allowed
INFO SOURCES: Tri-Lakes Fisheries Station, 5570 North Fish Hatchery Road, Columbia City, IN 46725 (219) 691-3181, Class A, B & C
AREA OUTFITTERS/LIVERIES: none
GAMEFISH SPECIES: bluegill, largemouth bass, perch, redear, warmouth, bullhead, crappie
CAMPING: Chain O'Lakes State Park, 2355 East 75 S, Albion, IN 46701 (219) 636-2654
MEDICAL ASSISTANCE: Whitley County Memorial Hospital, 353 North Oak, Columbia City, IN 46725 (219) 244-6191

ACCESS: From Wolf Lake drive 4.2 miles south on SR 109 to Noble CR 500 S and turn east. Continue 0.7 miles to the junction with CR 300 W and the DNR access site on the south side of CR 500 S. By road, just a few miles north of Crooked Lake.

Canadian Geese Flock in Flight

CRANE LAKE

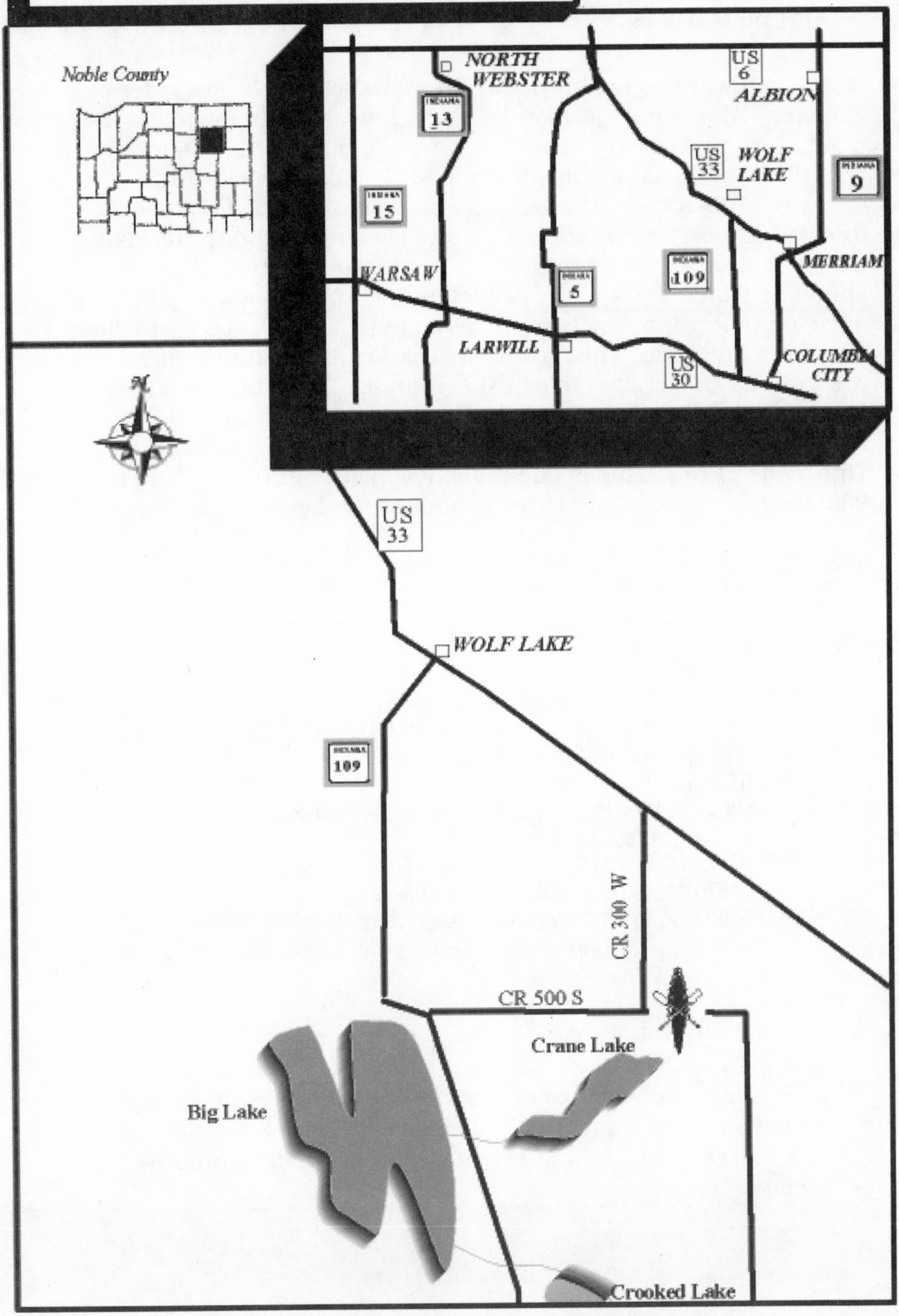

Noble County
NORTH WEBSTER
US 6
ALBION
13
US 33
WOLF LAKE
9
15
MERRIAM
109
WARSAW
5
LARWILL
COLUMBIA CITY
US 30
US 33
WOLF LAKE
109
CR 300 W
CR 500 S
Crane Lake
Big Lake
Crooked Lake

17. CROOKED LAKE

- Travel by water over one of Indiana's cleanest & deepest lakes

Paddlers always comment about the visual clarity of the water at Crooked Lake. The 106-foot deep pristine lake is home to cisco and trout. From the access site along SR 109, paddle the shallow north shoreline southeast alongside the DNR Crooked Lake Nature Preserve (100 acres). The preserve occupies over half a mile of forested slopes, marsh and seeps and even an island in the lake. A few open, level breaks occur along the preserve's knee-deep shoreline which allow canoeists a landing (there is a sharp drop-off a few more feet into the lake). There are two trail loops that follow the shore and bluff. The nature preserve runs the north shore from the Indiana University biological station south to the north shore of 20 acre adjoining Little Crooked Lake. The channel to Little Crooked Lake is exceptionally scenic and is considered the headwaters of the Tippecanoe River. This is one of the few places in northern Indiana lake country to gaze into clear water and see beneath the surface.

USGS MAP(S): Merriam 1:24,000
VICINITY: Merriam, Noble County
LAKE ACREAGE /DEPTH: 206 a. /108'
PADDLING TIME: 2 hour
LEVEL OF DIFFICULTY: Class I
HAZARDS/PORTAGES: IO allowed, wind susceptible
INFO SOURCES: Tri-Lakes Fisheries Station, 5570 North Fish Hatchery Road, Columbia City, IN 46725 (219) 691-3181
AREA OUTFITTERS/LIVERIES: none
GAMEFISH SPECIES: bluegill, largemouth bass, trout, redear, crappie, cisco, perch
CAMPING: Chain O'Lakes State Park, 2355 East 75 S, Albion, IN 46701 (219) 66-2654, Class A, B & C
MEDICAL ASSISTANCE: Whitley County Memorial Hospital, 353 North Oak, Columbia City, IN 46725 (219) 244-6191

ACCESS: The Crooked Lake access site is located five miles south of Wolf Lake on SR 109, east side of the highway near the outlet to Big Lake and three miles south of Merriam, straddling the Noble-Whitley county line.

CROOKED LAKE

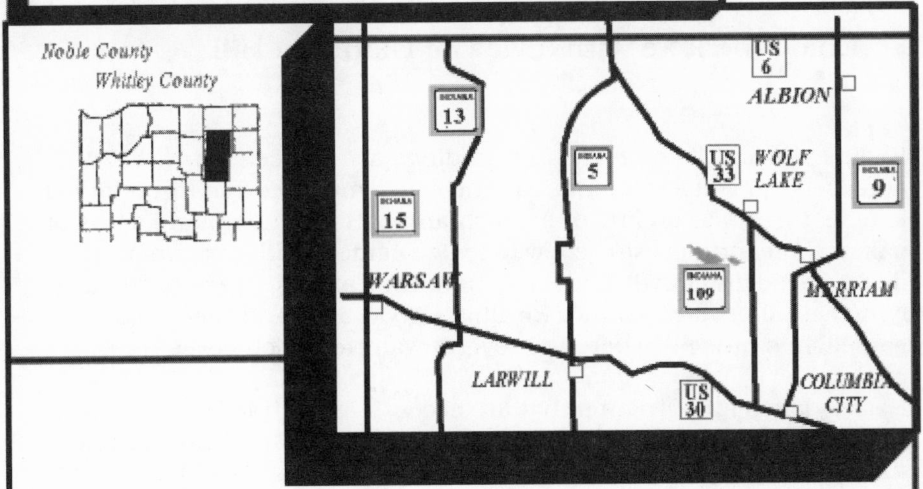

18. EAGLE LAKE

- Enjoy the lake with a view of Diamond Hill

Eagle Lake and its marshy surroundings are protected as a 137-acre wetland conservation area. The sand, muck and marl bottomed lake features a shoreline of bulrush and cattail. The upland areas of oak and hickory forest are few. Scenic Diamond Hill appears in the distance looking north and east above the cattails. There is one low lying cattail-covered island. Birding is good here and the noted gamefish is bluegill. There are several waterfowl rich coves to explore.

Nearby lakes and streams that are accessible include Diamond Lake (south shore), Engle Lake (east shore) and the Mallard Roost Area #2 access along the Elkhart River's South Branch, east of Diamond Lake.

USGS MAP(S): Ligonier 1:24,000
VICINITY: Ligonier, Noble County
LAKE ACREAGE /DEPTH: 81a. /49'
PADDLING TIME: 1-2 hours
LEVEL OF DIFFICULTY: Class I
HAZARDS/PORTAGES: IO allowed, 10 mph ltd., seasonal hunting
INFO SOURCES: Tri-Lakes Fisheries Station, 5570 North Fish Hatchery Road, Columbia City, IN 46725 (219) 691-3181, Tri-County Fish & Wildlife Area, RR #2, Box 522, 8432 N 850 E, Syracuse, IN 46567 (219) 834-4461
AREA OUTFITTERS/LIVERIES: none
GAMEFISH SPECIES: bluegill, largemouth bass, perch, crappie, bullhead, redear, sunfish, bowfin
CAMPING: Chain O'Lakes State Park, 2355 East 75 S, Albion, IN 46701 (219) 636-2654, Class A, B & C
MEDICAL ASSISTANCE: McCray Memorial Hospital, 951 East Hospital Drive, Kendallville, IN 46755 (800) 824-5860 or (219) 347-110

ACCESS: From Ligonier, drive south on SR 33 two miles to Noble CR 500 N and go east or left. Continue on CR 500 N two miles to the lake access at the west shore of Eagle Lake.

EAGLE LAKE

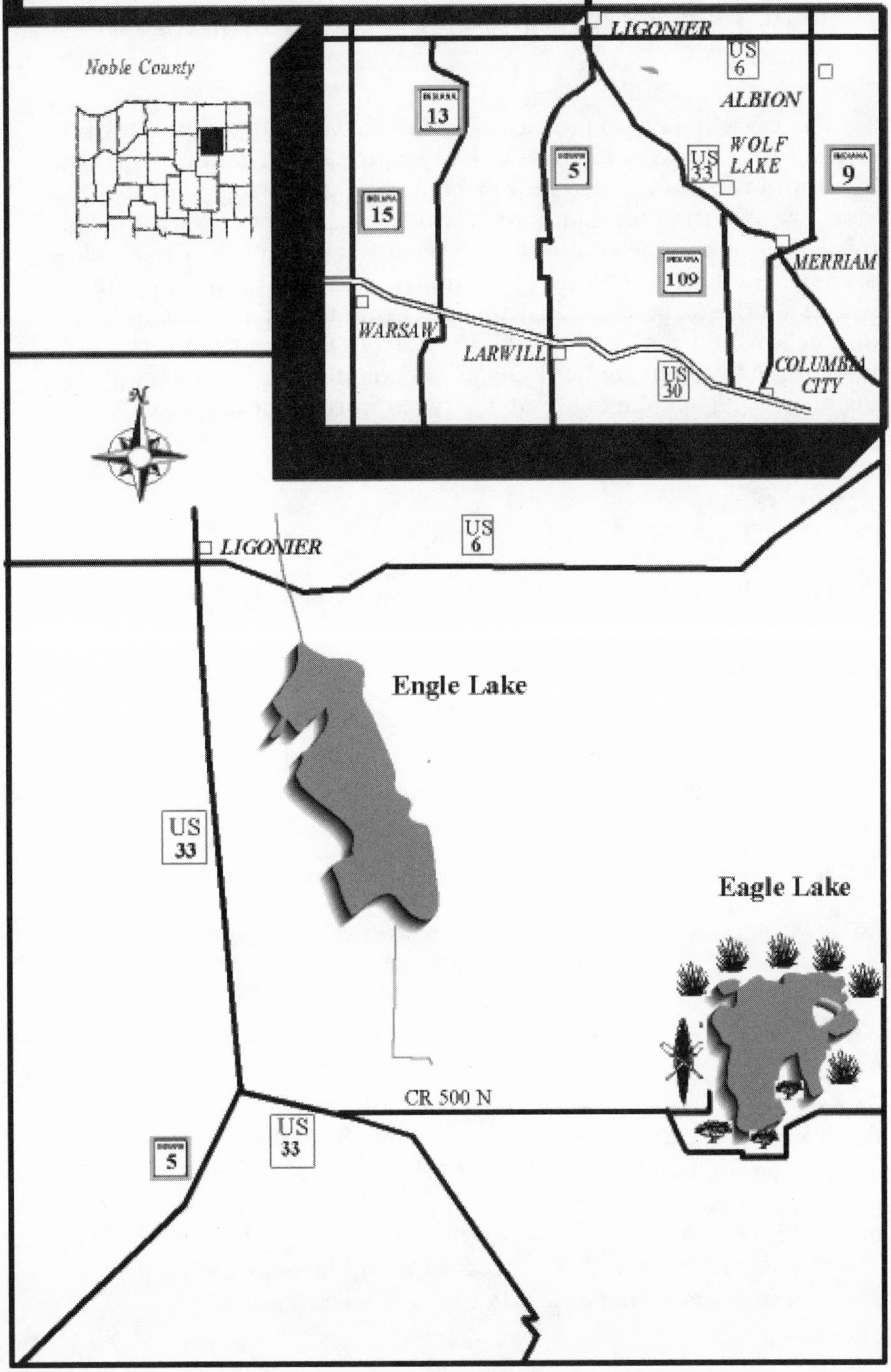
Noble County
LIGONIER
US 6
ALBION
13
WOLF LAKE
US 33
5
9
15
MERRIAM
109
WARSAW
LARWILL
US 30
COLUMBIA CITY
N
LIGONIER
US 6
Engle Lake
US 33
Eagle Lake
CR 500 N
US 33
5

19. ENGLE LAKE

- **Watch for Great White Egrets along shallow marshy coves**

The access site access road CR 750 W is a tree-lined lane that leads down a wooded west facing slope to Engle Lake. The narrow, north to south lake lies cradled in a glacial trough showing relief in the view. Nearly the entire shore is natural and forest cover conceals most set back homes. Otters have been released here. The shallow areas of the lake are filling with aquatic vegetation. In late summer watch for the large three foot tall, all-white heron with black legs and yellow bill; the Great White Egret from the South. Overall the lake imparts a removed or isolated feeling despite its closeness to Ligionier. Engle Lake is about 1.5 miles northwest of Eagle Lake.

USGS MAP(S): Ligonier 1:24,000
VICINITY: Ligonier, Noble County
LAKE ACREAGE /DEPTH: 48 a. /29'
PADDLING TIME: 1 hour
LEVEL OF DIFFICULTY: Class I
HAZARDS/PORTAGES: IO allowed, 10 mph ltd., low, shallow places
INFO SOURCES: Tri-Lakes Fisheries Station, 5570 N. Fish Hatchery Rd., Columbia City, IN 46725 (219) 691-3181
AREA OUTFITTERS/LIVERIES: none
GAMEFISH SPECIES: bluegill, largemouth bass, northern pike, redear, sunfish, crappie, perch, bullhead, warmouth
CAMPING: Chain O'Lakes State Park, 2355 E 75 S, Albion, IN 46701 (219) 636-2654, Class A, B & C
MEDICAL ASSISTANCE: McCray Memorial Hospital, 951 East Hospital Drive, Kendallville, IN 46755 (800) 824-5860 or (219) 347-1100

ACCESS: From Ligonier drive 0.5 mile south from the US 6 and SR 5 junction on SR 5 and turn east or left on Noble CR 650 N. Continue another half mile on CR 650 N to CR 750 W and turn south. Proceed another half mile on CR 700 W to the access gravel road marked CR 750 W. Turn right or west and proceed along the wooded lane to the shore access site on the east side of Engle Lake.

ENGLE LAKE

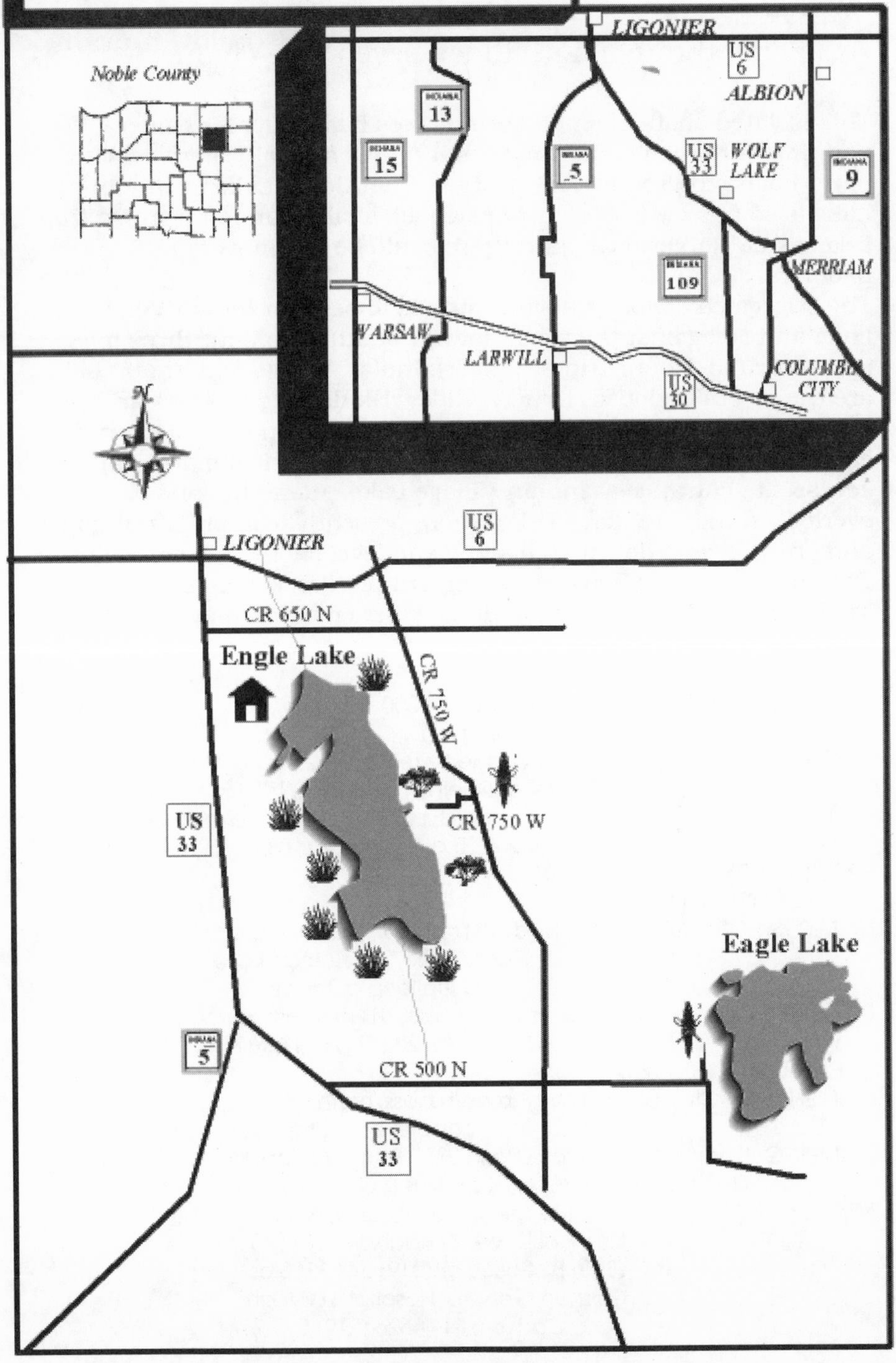
Noble County
LIGONIER
US 6
ALBION
13
15
5
US 33
WOLF LAKE
9
109
MERRIAM
WARSAW
LARWILL
COLUMBIA CITY
US 30
N
LIGONIER
US 6
CR 650 N
Engle Lake
CR 750 W
CR 750 W
US 33
Eagle Lake
5
CR 500 N
US 33

20. INDIAN VILLAGE LAKE-KNAPP LAKE CHAIN

- Paddle through a secluded seven lake chain

This isolated chain of small scenic lakes has plenty for camera pointing. Although canoes must share this special waterway with motorboats, the connecting channel from Gordy Lake to Hindman Lake is so narrow (room for one canoe), shallow and overgrown that it keeps out larger boats and there could be log liftovers for paddlers.

The suggested canoe or kayak route is to begin at Indian Village Lake and go against the weak flowage southeast about three miles and return (3-5 hour trip or longer). Indian Village and Knapp Lake are the most developed. Druely, Rider, Hindman and Moss are the most pristine and picturesque. A Boy Scout camp is located on the east shore of Gordy Lake. According to the historical marker at the access site entrance at Indian Village Lake, Miami Indians once overlooked Indian Village Lake where presently, camping trailers and grazing cows dot the hill slope and level shore. The combined waters flow to Lake Wawasee along Turkey Creek from Indian Village Lake. This one is a paddling experience you may want to repeat. The lake chain deserves nature preserve protection.

USGS MAP(S): North Webster, Ormas 1:24,000
VICINITY: Indian Village, Noble County
LAKE ACREAGE /DEPTH: Indian Village Lake 12 a./22', Druely Lake (also Durley or Dueley Lake) 21a./19', Rider Lake 5 a./16', Gordy Lake 31a./35', Hindman Lake 13 a./20', Moss Lake 10 a./19', Knapp 88 a. /59'
PADDLING TIME: 3-4 hours (one-way)
LEVEL OF DIFFICULTY: Class I
HAZARDS/PORTAGES: IO allowed, 10 mph ltd., possible choked channel Gordy Lake to Hindman Lake, consider round trip long distance
INFO SOURCES: Tri-Lakes Fisheries Station, 5570 North Fish Hatchery Rd. Columbia City, IN 46725 (219) 691-3181
AREA OUTFITTERS/LIVERIES: none
GAMEFISH SPECIES: bluegill, largemouth bass, northern pike, redear, sunfish, crappie, bullhead, warmouth
CAMPING: Chain O'Lakes State Park, 2355 E 75 S, Albion, IN 46701 (219) 636-2654, Class A, B & C
MEDICAL ASSISTANCE: McCray Memorial Hospital, 951 East Hospital Drive, Kendallville, IN 46755 (800) 824-5860 or (219) 347-1100 or Goshen General Hospital, 200 High Park, Goshen, IN 46526 (219) 533-2141

ACCESS: The Indian Village Lake access site is located at the south edge of Indian Village on the east side of SR 5 in southwest Noble County. To reach the Knapp Lake access site from SR 9 at Indian Village go east on CR 100 N about two miles to CR 1000 W and turn south or right. Follow the road curves south and turn south on Knapp Lake Road. Continue to the east shore of Knapp Lake and access site.

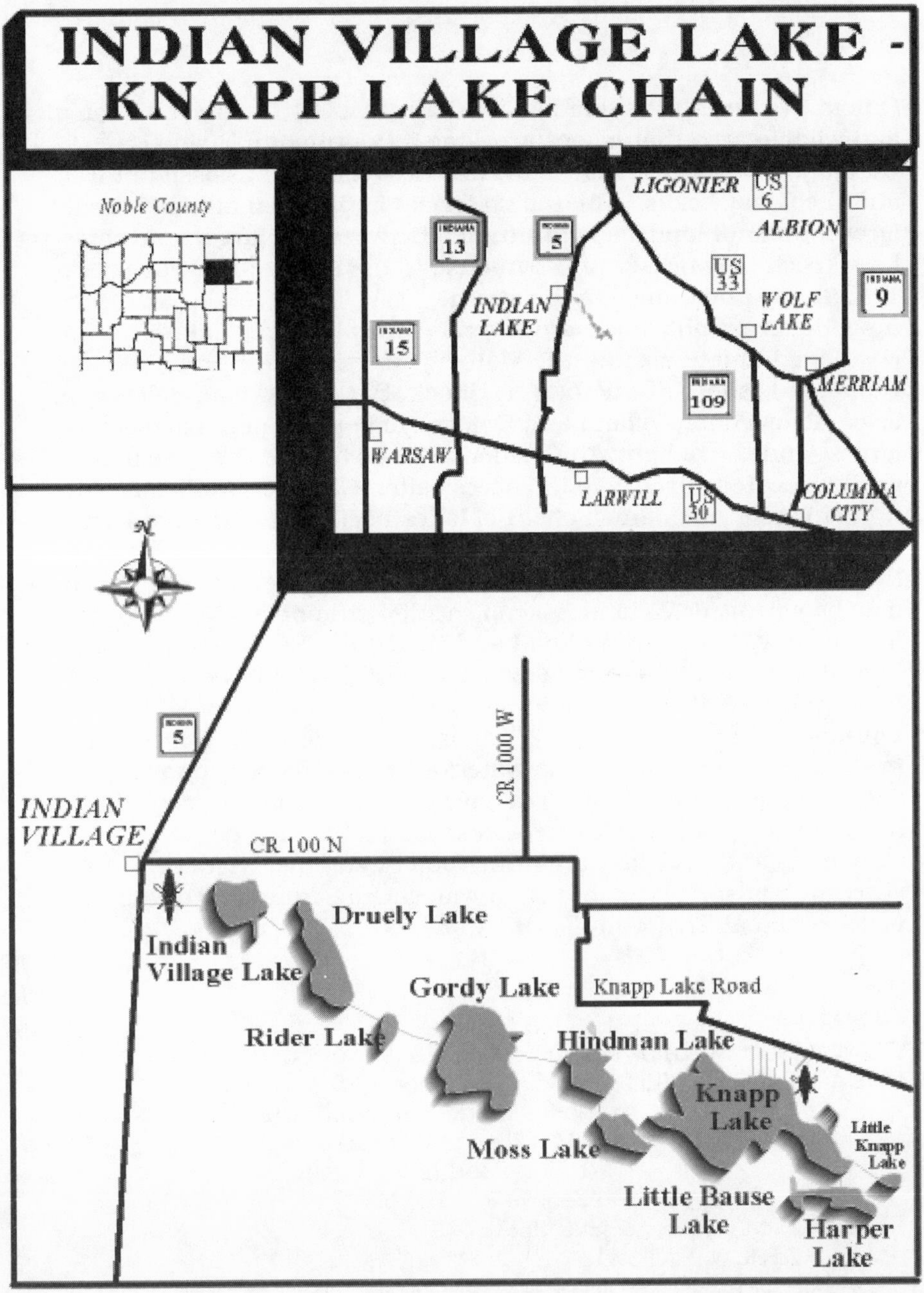

21. TRI-COUNTY FISH & WILDLIFE AREA

- Delve into lake and pond-pocked landscape of glacial-carved "Hoss Hills"

One in five acres is wetland at Tri-County, a 3,487 acre state fish and wildlife area that is located along a Continental Divide watershed where drainage is divided between the Mississippi River and the Great Lakes. The rolling glacial kettle (wetland) and kame (gravel upland) landscape is situated between the larger lakes of Papakeechie, Wawasee and Syracuse to the north and Webster, Tippecanoe and James to the south.

A paddler's delight, there are several canoeable small lakes positioned in and around the Flatbelly Marsh area: Spear, Hammond, Allen, Rothenberger, Shock, Barrel and One Half, Long, Price, Bass Pond, Wyland and Goldeneye Pond. Spear Lake is the largest and the old growth Greider's Woods Nature Preserve (loop trail) is located enroute to the access site. Hammond, Allen and Rothenberger are a small chain of lakes northeast of the property headquarters that could be portaged. Barrel and One Half Lake is the closest lake from property headquarters. Long and Price Lakes may be portaged. Wyland Lake, a scenic kettle hole lake has trout fishing only. Shock, Bass Pond and Goldeneye Pond are some of the largest water bodies. Most lakes have access sites however Loon Pond would require a carry-in portage.

With exception of Wyland Lake, all lakes are closed to fishing early in October and Spear Lake, a waterfowl refuge, is closed to fishing/canoeing the first three days of teal season. Check with headquarters for lake closure and seasonal hunting dates. Mosquitos and deer flies are numerous in summer. Aquatic vegetation is spreading into open water. Unfortunately no camping is permitted at Tri-County at this time.

USGS MAP(S): North Webster 1:24,000
VICINITY: North Webster, Kosciusko, Noble & Whitley counties
LAKE ACREAGE /DEPTH: Spear 45 a., Hammond 7.5 a., Allen 5.5 a., Rothenberger 6 a., Barrel and One Half 14 a., Long 6 a., Price 6 a., Shock 14 a., Bass Pond 18 a., Wyland 6 a., Goldeneye Pond 26 a.
PADDLING TIME: 2 days of lake trips
LEVEL OF DIFFICULTY: Class I
HAZARDS/PORTAGES: electric trolling only, no swimming, all lakes

except Wyland are closed from October to freeze, check with headquarters, insects

INFO SOURCES: Tri-County Fish & Wildlife Area , RR#2, Box 522, 8432 N 850 E, Syracuse, IN 46567 (219) 834-4461

AREA OUTFITTERS/LIVERIES: none

GAMEFISH SPECIES: bluegill, largemouth bass, northern pike, redear, sunfish, channel cat, crappie, rainbow trout.

CAMPING: Chain O'Lakes State Park, 2355 E 75 S, Albion, IN 46701 (219) 636-2654, Class A, B & C

MEDICAL ASSISTANCE: Kosciusko Community Hospital, 2101 East Dubois Drive, Warsaw, IN 46580 (219) 267-3200

ACCESS: Tri-County Fish and Wildlife Area lies south of Syracuse & north of North Webster, east of SR 13 & west of SR 5 & Indian Village. Property headquarters is located east of Hoss Hills Road. Access ramps at all lakes except Loon Pond.

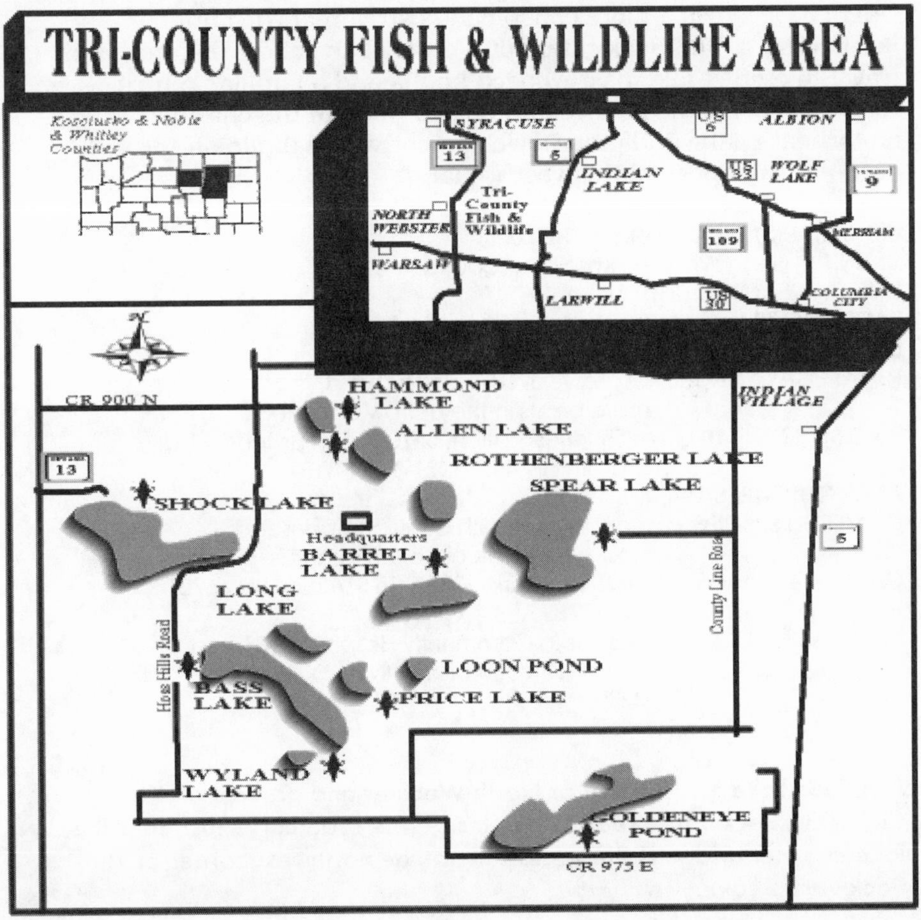

22. THE BACKWATERS & KISER LAKE

- Propel through isolated backwaters of Tippecanoe River to a secluded lake

The Backwaters resulted when a dam was constructed to create adjoining Webster Lake. From the access site follow the obvious channel southeast through the spatterdock and water lily thick, stagnant backwaters (motorboats and main current keep the channel from growing over). Curve past the only inhabited shore in The Backwaters near the south end. Continue upstream along the narrow channel past upland studded knolls of oak and hickory enroute to Kiser Lake; a small isolated natural lake. The Tippecanoe River flows into and through The Backwaters and on through Webster Lake, James Lake, Tippecanoe Lake and Oswego Lake where it becomes a more conspicuous stream at the outlet.
For paddlers, The Backwaters of Webster Lake offers distance and travel to a quiet lake past wooded knolls and a familiar return route. Expect some motorboats but no wake in the channel. More motorboat traffic and other development would diminish the outdoor experience of this vast wetland.

USGS MAP(S): North Webster 1:24,000
VICINITY: North Webster, Kosciusko County
LAKE ACREAGE /DEPTH: 140 a. /6'
PADDLING TIME: 2 hours
LEVEL OF DIFFICULTY: Class I
HAZARDS/PORTAGES: IO allowed, 10 mph ltd., wind, motorboats in the narrow channel
INFO SOURCES: Tri-Lakes Fisheries Station, 5570 N. Fish Hatchery Rd., Columbia City, IN 46725 (219) 691-3181
AREA OUTFITTERS/LIVERIES: none
GAMEFISH SPECIES: bluegill, largemouth bass, pumpkinseed, redear, yellow perch, black crappie
CAMPING: Chain O'Lakes State Park, 2355 E 75 S, Albion, IN 46701 (219) 636-2654, Class A, B & C
MEDICAL ASSISTANCE: Kosciusko Community Hospital, 2101 East Dubois Drive, Warsaw, IN 46580 (219) 267-3200

ACCESS: Take SR 13 south of North Webster and go east on Kosciusko CR 550 N/Backwater Road two miles. At the road curve just after the lake channel bridge is the access site at the northwest corner of The Backwaters Lake.

THE BACKWATERS & KISER LAKE

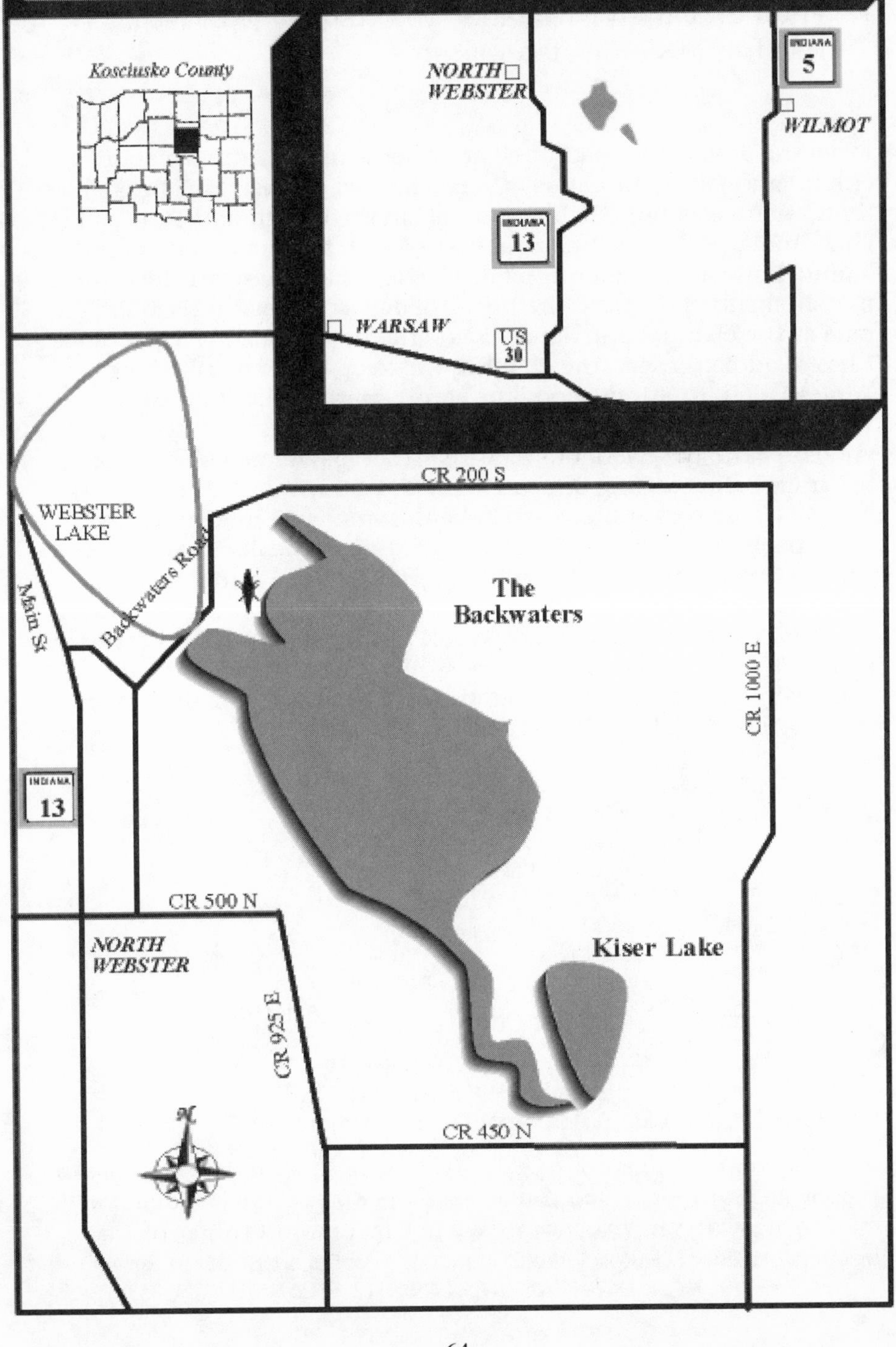

23. TIPPECANOE LAKE & JAMES LAKE

- Paddle extensive wetlands where black oak islands rise from wildlife-rich marsh

From the access site, paddle right or north under Armstrong Road culvert and follow the Grassy Creek channel downstream through the wetland expanse. Go about a mile to the mouth and Tippecanoe Lake, Indiana's deepest natural lake. Watch for motorboaters in the channel. At the lake mouth paddle right or east between the cattail marsh-shrub border and the buoys of deeper water for about half a mile to the channel into James Lake, the upper basin of Tippecanoe Lake. Paddle through the channel and keep to the south shore of James Lake. Continue along the south shore to the Ball' Wetlands/Camp Crosley YMCA pier. (Permission is required to land and enter the Ball Wetlands Nature Preserve (249 acres) and hike the trail. Before setting out call (219) 834-2331 summer and (317) 288-4448 the rest of the year.) Take the same two-mile or so water route back to the Grassy Creek access. Expect weak current on Grassy Creek return. Motorboaters, jetskiers and waterskiers are active on Tippecanoe and James lakes from late morning to dark in summer. Best time to canoe or kayak is during the week in the early morning and the best seasons are spring, late summer and fall. Upstream on Grassy Creek from the access site is a small dam and the developed Barbee Chain O'Lakes.

USGS MAP(S): Leesburg, North Webster 1:24,000
VICINITY: North Webster, Kosciusko County
LAKE ACREAGE /DEPTH: Tippecanoe Lake 768 a. /123'
James Lake 282 a. /63'
PADDLING TIME: 3 hours
LEVEL OF DIFFICULTY: Class I
HAZARDS/PORTAGES: IO allowed, unlimited horsepower, waves from motorboats, wind, long distance
INFO SOURCES: YMCA Camp Crosley, RR#2, Box 151A, North Webster, IN 46555 (219) 834-2331 and Tri-Lakes Fisheries Station, 5570 N. Fish Hatchery Road, Columbia City, IN 46725 (219) 691-3181
GAMEFISH SPECIES: bluegill, largemouth bass, northern pike, redear, black crappie, warmouth, channel cat, rock bass.
CAMPING: Chain O'Lakes State Park, 2355 E 75 S, Albion, IN 46701 (219) 636-2654, Class A, B & C
MEDICAL ASSISTANCE: Kosciusko Community Hospital, 2101 E. Dubois Drive, Warsaw, IN 46580 (219) 267-3200

ACCESS: The DNR Grassy Creek access site may be reached from US 30 by driving north on SR 13 at Pierceton east of Warsaw. Go north on SR 13, 7.5 miles to CR 500 N/Armstrong Road. Drive two miles west on Armstrong Road to the shaded Grassy Creek access on the south side of the road, three miles east of Oswego.

TIPPECANOE LAKE & JAMES LAKE

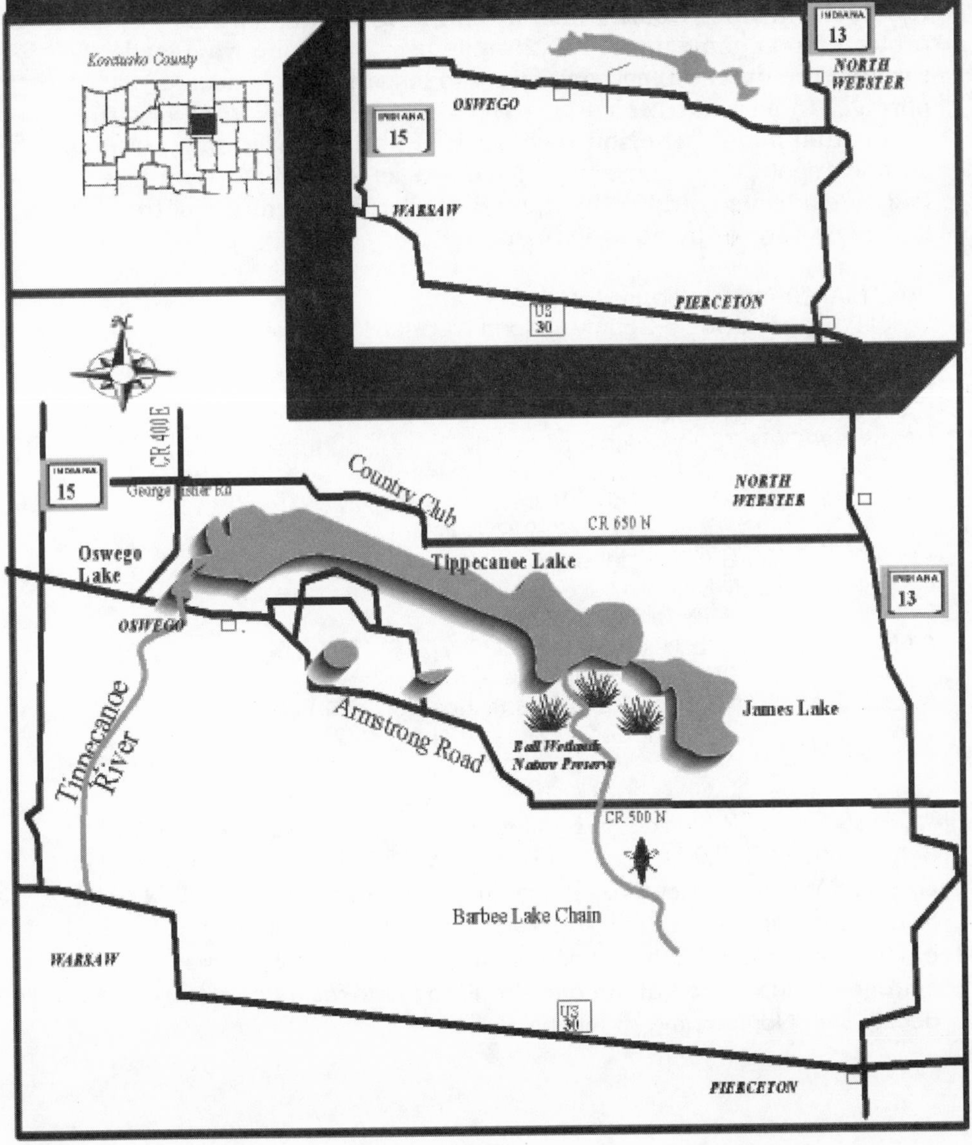

24. DURHAM LAKE & PISGAH LAKE

- Sample Canadian ambiance of two far away lakes

These two small lakes and surrounding marshlands have northern flavor. Durham Lake and its environs comprise a 178-acre wetland conservation area. There is a 60-yard carry down from the parking lot to Durham Lake with its small but all-natural shore.
Further east 0.2 mile from Durham Lake, across the Pisgah Marsh Non Game Area is the mini-parking site for Pisgah Lake on the north side of Kosciusko CR 350 N/Whitely CR 850 N near the Kosciusko-Whitley County line. (No hunting allowed in this protected non-game area). A 0.25-mile user path (one-way) leads through the upland black oak forest to Pisgah Lake, a scenic portage. Tamarack trees run the rim between the oak knoll and the vast cattail marsh. The southwest corner at the beaver dam outlet is an open spot to put in. Nearly the same size as level Durham Lake, Pisgah Lake sits craddled by upland oak forest and much of the lake is overgrown by aquatic plants.

USGS MAP(S): North Webster 1:24,000
VICINITY: Wilmot, Noble County & North Webster, Kosciusko County
LAKE ACREAGE: Durham Lake 18 a., Pisgah Lake 17 a.
PADDLING TIME: 3-4 hours
LEVEL OF DIFFICULTY: Class I
HAZARDS/PORTAGES: electric motors only, 5 mph., portage to Pisgah Lake a half mile total
INFO SOURCES: Tri-County Fish & Wildlife Area, 8432 N 850 E Syracuse IN 46567 (219) 834-4461
AREA OUTFITTERS/LIVERIES: none
GAMEFISH SPECIES: Durham Lake-bluegill, largemouth bass
Pisgah Lake-bluegill
CAMPING: Chain O'Lakes State Park, 2355 E 75 S, Albion, IN 46701 (219) 636-2654, Class A, B & C
MEDICAL ASSISTANCE: Kosciusko County Hospital, 2101 East Dubois Dubois Dr., Warsaw IN 46580 (219) 267-3200

ACCESS: From SR 5 about two miles south of Wilmot turn west or right onto Whitley CR 850 N. Proceed west on CR 850 N about a mile and cross the Whitley-Kosciusko county line, now Kosciusko CR 350 N. The Pisgah Lake and Marsh mini-parking area is on the right or north side of the gravel road. Durham Lake is further west 0.2 mile to the entrance road. Go left at the entry road to the lakeside and carry down access site. No camping at this time.

DURHAM LAKE & PISGAH LAKE

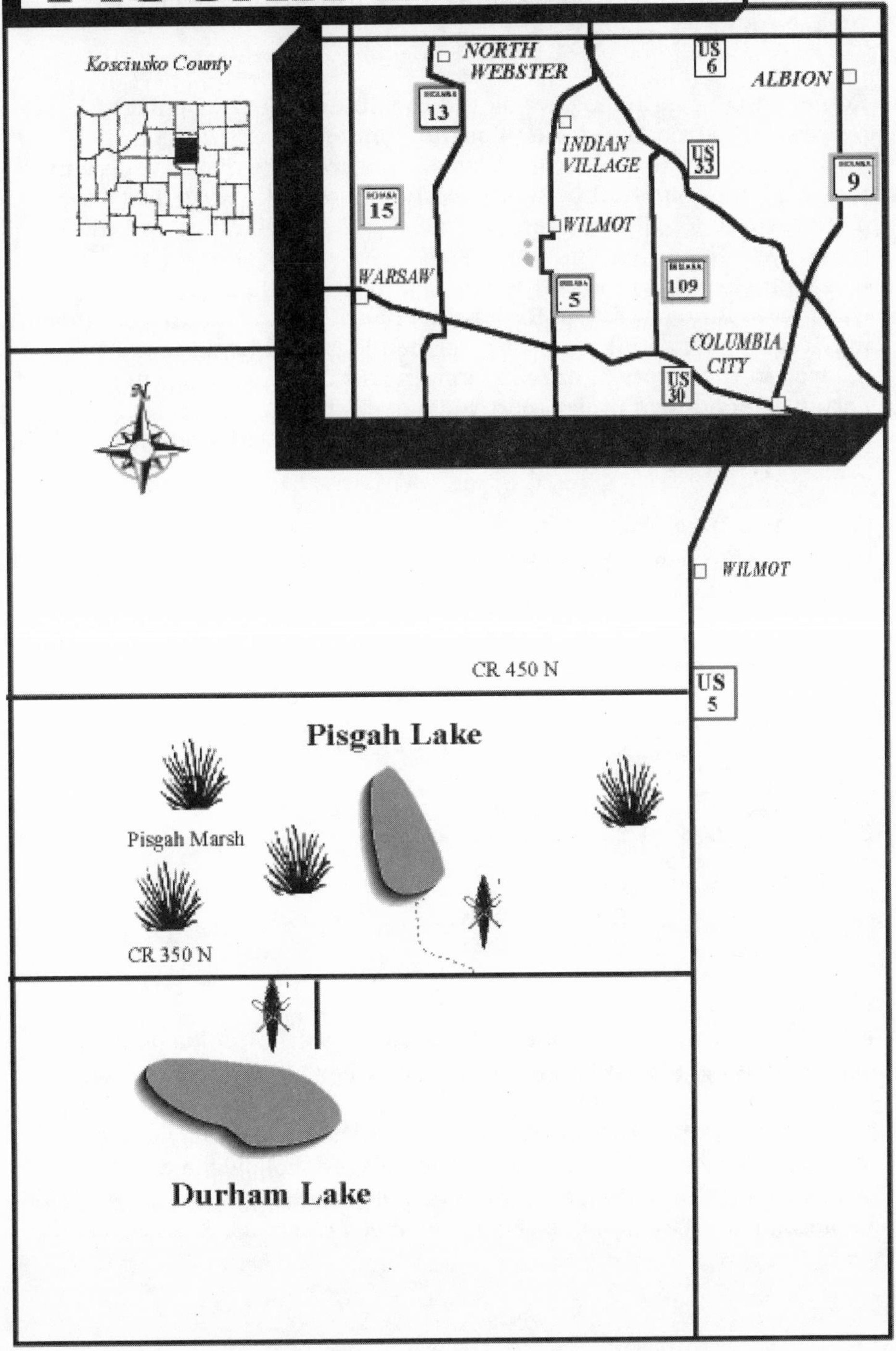

25. ROBINSON LAKE & RINE LAKE

- **Picturesque northern lake and forest preserve; a paddler's environs plus camping**

Robinson Lake is the focus point of the 300-acre DNR Deniston Natural Resource Area located at the Whitley-Koscuisko County line. In addition to paddling on the all-natural lake there is carry in tent camping. Situated between Old Robinson Lake Road and US 30 a substantial forest has been preserved between the lake and the roadways. The outlet and pond at the west end of the lake is interesting to explore and there is a canoeable 0.25 mile inlet channel to Rine Lake. The Rine Lake channel at the southeast shore may require canoe liftovers over downed logs. Fall hunting is allowed in the resource area. Swimming and open fires are not permitted. Paddlers prefer more ideal areas like Robinson Lake with its scenery, wildlife, camping, adventure and preservation.

USGS MAP(S): Pierceton 1:24,000
VICINITY: Pierceton, Kosciusko & Larwill, Whitley County
LAKE ACREAGE /DEPTH: 59 a./51', 15 a./15'
PADDLING TIME: 2 hours
LEVEL OF DIFFICULTY: Class I
HAZARDS/PORTAGES: IO allowed, 10 mph ltd., channel to Rine Lake may be clogged, seasonal hunting
INFO SOURCES: Tri-County Fish & Wildlife Area, 8432 850 E Syracuse, IN 46567-8378 (219) 834-4461
AREA OUTFITTERS/LIVERIES: none
GAMEFISH SPECIES: bluegill, largemouth bass, crappie
CAMPING: Robinson Lake, Deniston Resource Area, ltd. walk-in tent sites (219) 834-4461, Class C
MEDICAL ASSISTANCE: Kosciusko County Hospital, 2101 E. Dubois Drive, Warsaw, IN 46580 (219) 267-3200

ACCESS: Robinson Lake is located eight miles west of Columbia City and ten miles east of Warsaw on West Lincolnway/Old US 30 at the Whitley-Kosciusko county line. From US 30 at Larwill go north on SR 5 to W. Lincolnway Hwy/Old US 30. Turn left and drive one mile to the marked entrance at the Deniston Resource Area. Follow the access road about 0.25 mile to the access site at the northeast shore of Robinson Lake. Use uphill parking area away from lake & access site.

ROBINSON LAKE & RINE LAKE

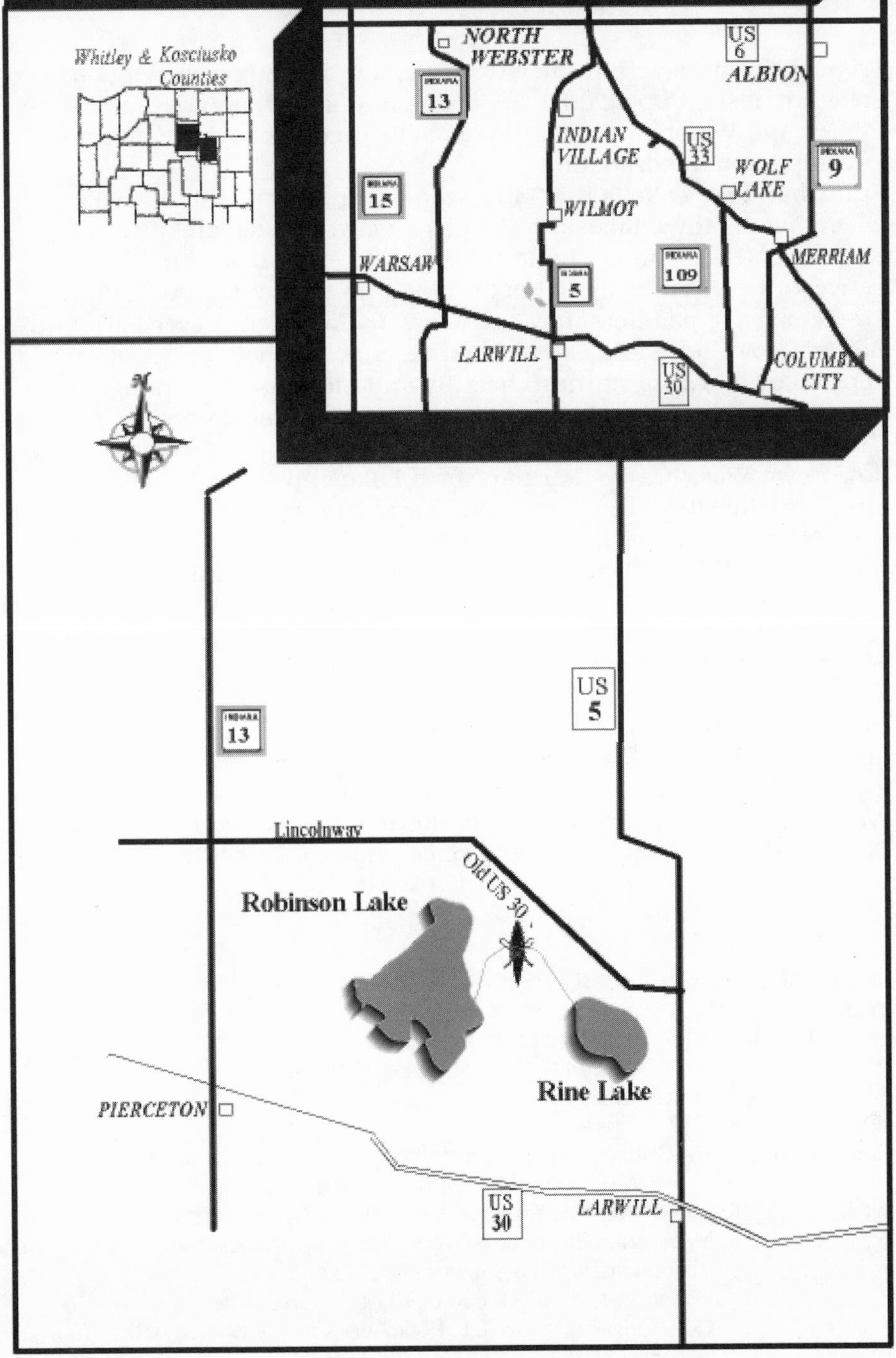
Whitley & Kosciusko Counties
NORTH WEBSTER
US 6
ALBION
13
INDIAN VILLAGE
US 33
WOLF LAKE
9
15
WILMOT
WARSAW
109
5
MERRIAM
LARWILL
COLUMBIA CITY
US 30
N
US 5
13
Lincolnway
Old US 30
Robinson Lake
Rine Lake
PIERCETON
US 30
LARWILL

26. PIKE LAKE

• Go afloat & ashore within the "City of Lakes"

Tree-laden parks within the city of Warsaw and adjacent Winona Lake are nestled up against the urban and suburban lakes of Pike, Center and Winona. All three lakes have access sites for canoeing, kayaking and motorboating.

Suburban Pike Lake is the "closest to nature" of the three "civilized" lakes, having three lakeside (city of Warsaw) parks along its level to rolling southwest shore. In addition to Pike Lake boat ramp located between the beach (fishing boat rental) and the campground (April 15-October 1), paddlers may carry down at adjacent Beyer Park and Baker's Boy Club Park/Camp Lucerne Park. The city parks have kept Pike Lake semi-natural, healthy and picturesque making it a fine place to live for residents of its north and west shores.

Center Lake is the most urban of the three lakes; the "showpiece" of downtown Warsaw. Nye Park at North Lake and North Buffalo streets is the site of the access ramp and city park office. Additional parks located around the south end of the lake include Funk Park, the Warsaw Biblical Gardens and Bixler Park that feature a beach, concessions, picnicking, playgrounds, ball courts and fields. Water-skiing and speedboats are not permitted on Center Lake.

Winona Lake, the largest of the three, is a handsome suburban lake. Access is located at Kiwanis Park on east Smith Street via Hackleman Road in the city of Winona Lake at the northwest lakeshore. Winona City Park on the east shore near Grace College is a carry down site and canoe rentals are available during summer. Waterskiing and speedboats are permitted. The Winona Mineral Springs along the east shore was once known for its lithia spring bottled water.

USGS MAP(S): Warsaw, Leesburg 1:24,000
VICINITY: Warsaw & Winona Lake, Kosciusko County
LAKE ACREAGE /DEPTH: Pike Lake 230a. /35', Center Lake 140 a. /42', Winona Lake 562 a. /79'
PADDLING TIME: 1 hour each
LEVEL OF DIFFICULTY: Class I
HAZARDS/PORTAGES: IO allowed, 10 mph ltd. on Pike Lake, powerboats on Winona Lake, urban noise, potenial wind
INFO SOURCES: City of Warsaw Parks & Recreation Department, Nye Park, Center Lake, N. Buffalo Street, Warsaw IN 46580 (219) 372-9554 or Kosciusko County Visitors Bureau (800) 800-6090 or Winona Lake City Parks Dept., 1590 N Park Avenue, Winona Lake, IN 46590 (219) 267-2310 (summer only)

AREA OUTFITTERS/LIVERIES: summer park rentals at Pike Lake & Winona Lake
GAMEFISH SPECIES: bluegill, largemouth bass, northern pike, redear, sunfish, walleye, yellow perch, black crappie
CAMPING: Pike Lake Park, Warsaw City Parks, N. Arthur Street (April 15-Oct.1) Warsaw, IN 46580 (219) 372-9554
MEDICAL ASSISTANCE: Kosciusko Community Hospital, 2101 East Dubois Dr., Warsaw, IN 46580 (219) 267-3200

ACCESS: Pike Lake Park and access is located two blocks from SR 15 N/ Detroit Street and Center Lake in north Warsaw. Follow Arthur Street to the lake and the park from SR 15 N/ Detroit Street. Access to Center Lake is from SR 15 N/ Detroit Street, Canal, Buffalo and North Lake streets north three blocks of downtown. Two miles southeast of Warsaw is Winona Lake and city. Best carry down access is at Winona Lake City Park along Park Avenue, east shore. There is a public boat ramp along Hackleman Road & Smith Street along the northeast shore of Winona Lake.

Beyer Park Access at Pike lake

PIKE LAKE

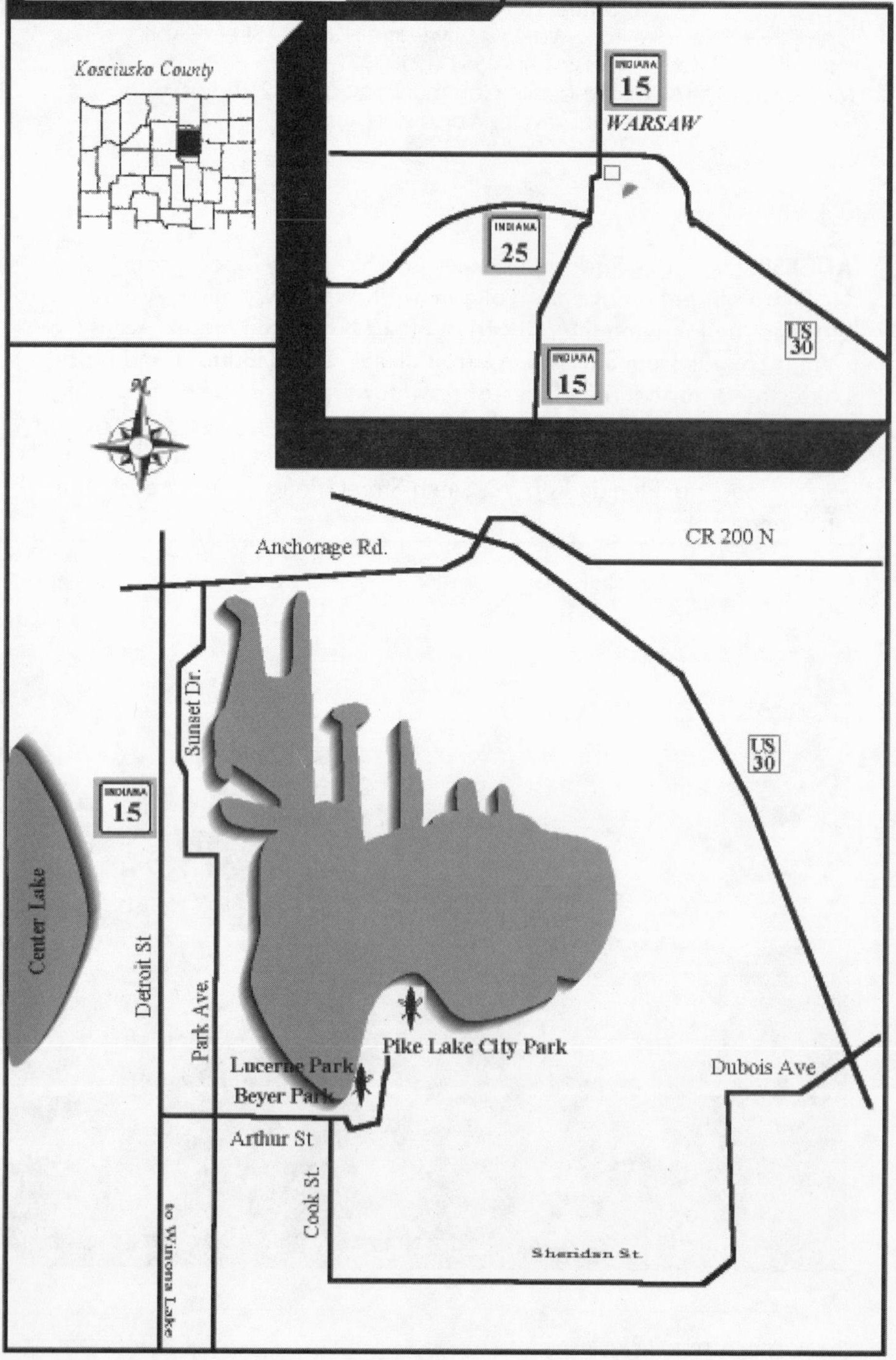
Kosciusko County
INDIANA 15
WARSAW
INDIANA 25
US 30
INDIANA 15
Anchorage Rd.
CR 200 N
Sunset Dr.
US 30
INDIANA 15
Center Lake
Detroit St
Park Ave.
Pike Lake City Park
Lucerne Park
Beyer Park
Dubois Ave
Arthur St
Cook St.
to Winona Lake
Sheridan St.

Carr Lake Fisherman

Woody Shoreline at the Menominee Lake Access

27. CARR LAKE

- Go adrift & let summer zephyrs carry you across the water

There is a strong rural character to Carr Lake. Only in recent years have new homes been erected on its natural north shore. Brown's Landing, a fishing camp on the south shore, is not too intrusive for its size since it has woodland cover. Much of the shore is vegetated however there are expansive countryside vistas to the southeast of the access site. The mix of sand, gravel, muck and marl bottom provides aquatic plants a fertile root bed. The DNR access site is at the northwest corner of the lake east of the inlet from Reed Lake. Carr Lake sheds its water to Walnut Creek and the Tippecanoe River.

USGS MAP(S): Warsaw 1:24,000
VICINITY: Warsaw, Kosciusko County
LAKE ACREAGE /DEPTH: 79 a. /35'
PADDLING TIME: 1 hour
LEVEL OF DIFFICULTY: Class I
HAZARDS/PORTAGES: IO allowed, 10 mph ltd., wind potential
INFO SOURCES: Tri-Lakes Fisheries Station, 5570 North Fish Hatchery Road, Columbia City, IN 46725 (219) 691-3181
AREA OUTFITTERS/LIVERIES: none
GAMEFISH SPECIES: bluegill, largemouth bass, black crappie, yellow perch, catfish
CAMPING: Chain O'Lakes State Park, 2355 E 75 S, Albion, IN 46701 (219) 636-2654, Class A, B & C
MEDICAL ASSISTANCE: Kosciusko Community Hospital, 2101 East Dubois Drive, Warsaw, IN 46580 (219) 267-3200

ACCESS: From SR 15 south of Warsaw and north of Silver Lake near Claypool, drive east on Kosciusko CR 550 S. Go 0.5 mile to CR 200 W or Kinsey Road and turn north or left. Continue one mile to the access lane on the east side of CR 200 W. Turn and drive down the wooded lane to the marked access site on the northwest side of Carr l ake.

CARR LAKE

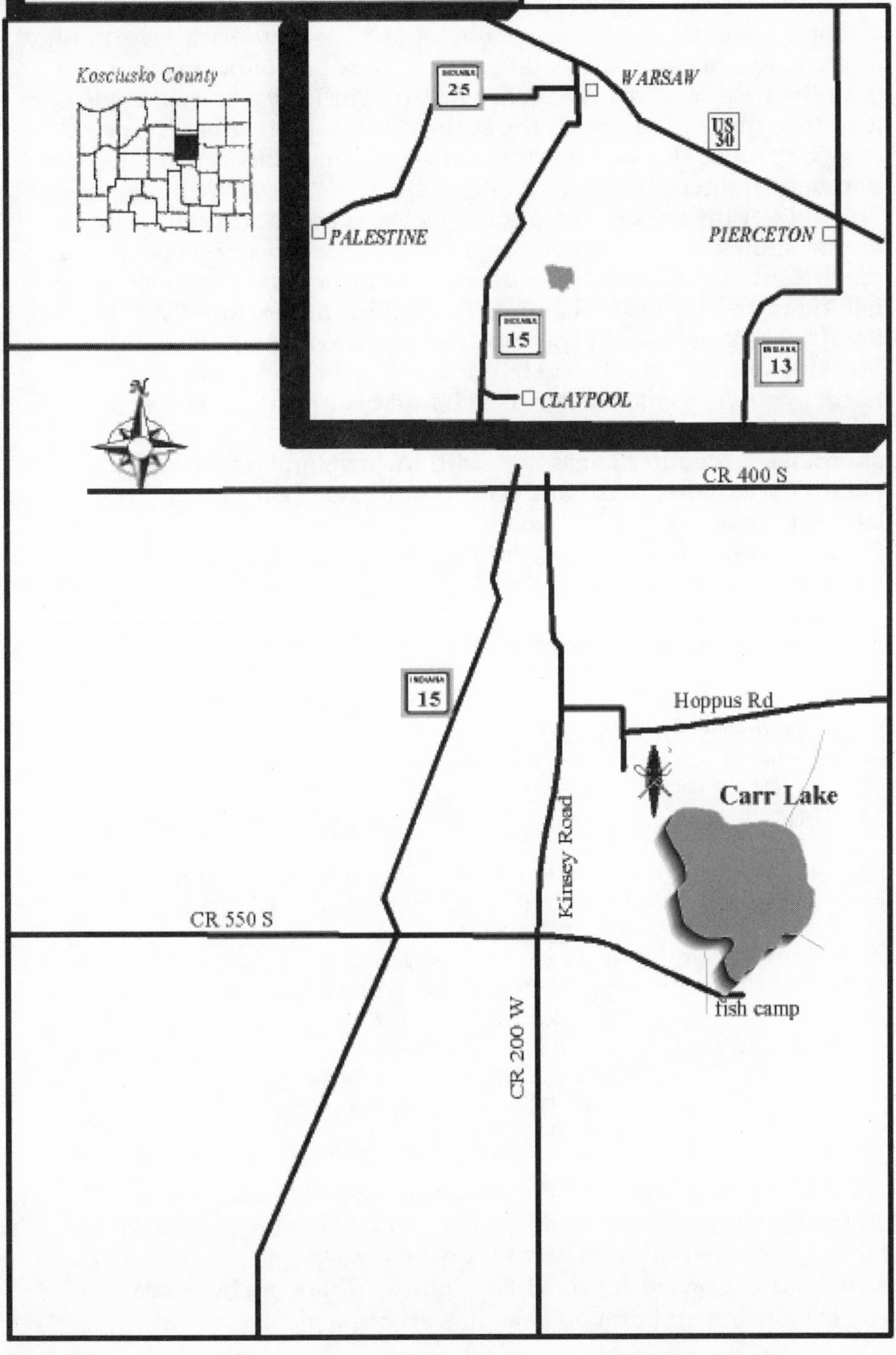

Kosciusko County
WARSAW
25
US 30
PALESTINE
PIERCETON
15
13
CLAYPOOL
CR 400 S
15
Hoppus Rd
Carr Lake
Kinsey Road
CR 550 S
fish camp
CR 200 W

28. WORSTER LAKE

- Enjoy a short or long watery state park outing

Worster Lake, the centerpiece of Potato Creek State Park (est. 1977), is the result of damming Potato Creek. The state park was founded with the help of Darcy Worster, a self-taught local naturalist who lead the efforts to establish the lake and recreation area. Expect company since the state park is one of the most highly attended parks in northern Indiana.

The bulk of the park's recreational facilities are located along its scenic shores. A narrow neck separates the 327-acre reservoir into an east and west basin; both basins having access launch sites and fishing piers. The east basin has the wildest nature and features Potato Creek inlet along the south shore. The Swamp Rose Nature Preserve drains from the east. The northeast shore harbors the nature center, picnic shelter, beach and boat rentals. The west basin has the linear dam site on the north shore while the south shore has a "country character" with its barn and picnic area. Potato Creek flows north and south to the Kankakee River. This lake experience is a great one for families.

Canoe rentals, naturalist programs, fishing, biking, swimming, picnicking, hiking and camping are some of the activities offered at this north central Indiana state park. A seasonal launch fee permit is necessary to paddle the lake.

USGS MAP(S): Lakeville 1:24,000
VICINITY: North Liberty, St. Joseph County
LAKE ACREAGE /DEPTH: 327 a. /25'
PADDLING TIME: 3 hours
LEVEL OF DIFFICULTY: Class I
HAZARDS/PORTAGES: electric motors only, watch for snags, wind potential
INFO SOURCES: Potato Creek State Park, 25601 SR 4, North Liberty, IN 46554 (219) 656-8186
AREA OUTFITTERS/LIVERIES: summer concession rental at beach
GAMEFISH SPECIES: bluegill, largemouth bass, black crappie, channel cat, rainbow trout
CAMPING: Potato Creek State Park, Class A sites (219) 656-8186
MEDICAL ASSISTANCE: Madison Center S Hospital, 403 East Madison St., South Bend, IN 46617 (219) 234-0061

ACCESS: Worster Lake and Potato Creek State Park are located about 12 mi. SW of South Bend and four mi. E of North Liberty. Take US 31 S to SR 4 near Lakeville and turn W. Continue seven mi. W on SR 4 to park entrance on the N side of the highway. There are two access ramps: one in east basin and one in west basin of Worster Lake.

WORSTER LAKE

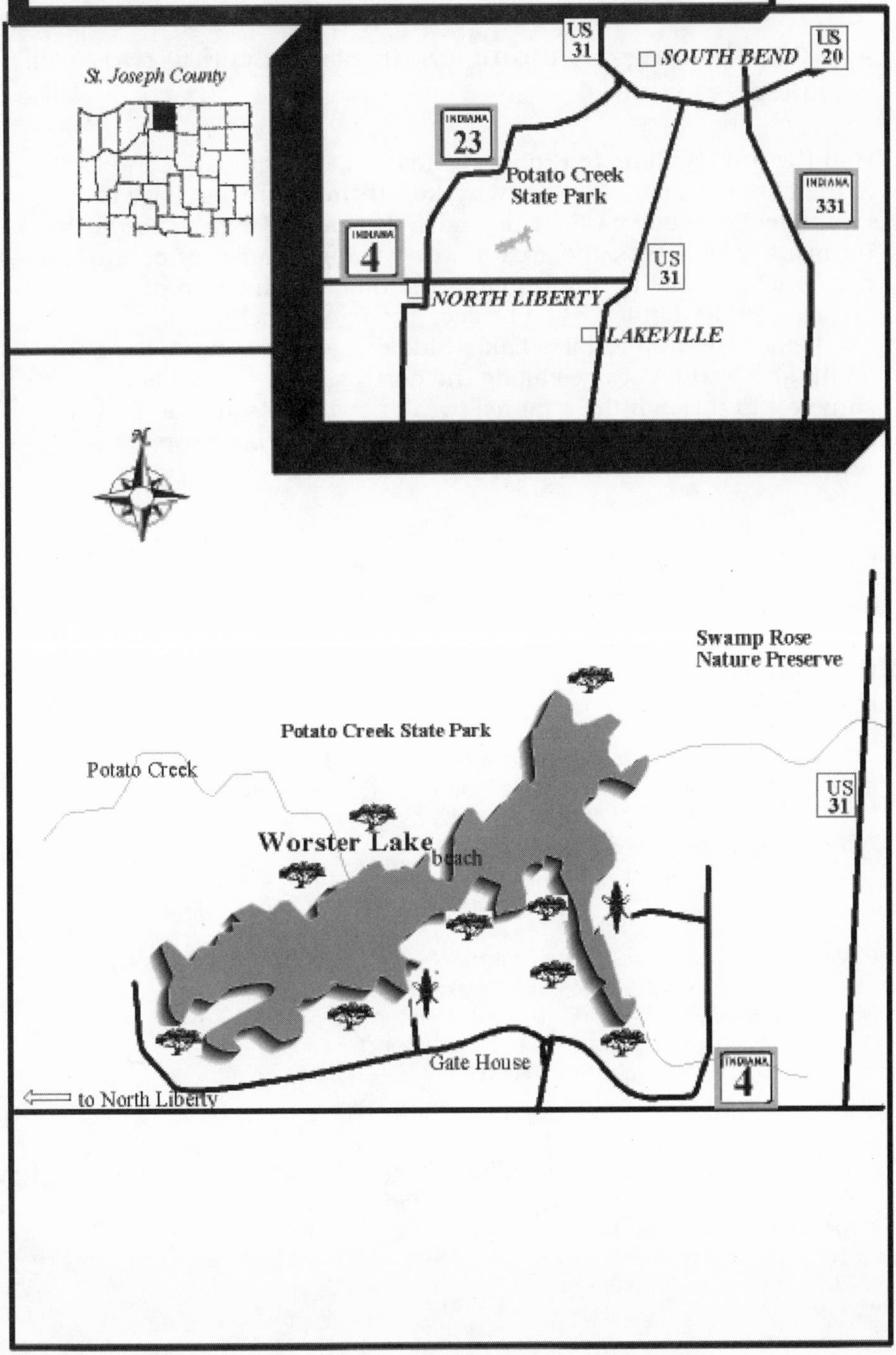
St. Joseph County
US 31
SOUTH BEND
US 20
INDIANA 23
Potato Creek
State Park
INDIANA 331
INDIANA 4
US 31
NORTH LIBERTY
LAKEVILLE
N
Swamp Rose
Nature Preserve
Potato Creek State Park
Potato Creek
US 31
Worster Lake
beach
Gate House
INDIANA 4
to North Liberty

29. PLEASANT LAKE & RIDDLES LAKE

- Take the long & winding channel connecting two lakes

Half the fun paddling to Riddles Lake from Pleasant Lake and back is the channel that joins the two lakes at the southeast edge of Lakeville. Busy noisy US 31 degrades the natural experience at the Pleasant Lake access site area however things change once entering the outlet channel to Riddles Lake. Paddle with the current, crossing under Linden Road bridge, as the channel becomes ditch-like before entering Riddles Lake. Riddles Lake is natural along the south shore with cottages along the north shore. Return is the same route through the channel (weak flow). The sense of distance and the large degree of natural vegetation make these two lakes a pleasant half-day sojourn.

USGS MAP(S): Lakeville, LaPaz 1:24,000
VICINITY: Lakeville, St. Joseph County
LAKE ACREAGE /DEPTH: Pleasant Lake 29 a./39'
Riddles Lake 77a./20'
PADDLING TIME: 3 hours
LEVEL OF DIFFICULTY: Class I
HAZARDS/PORTAGES: IO allowed, 10 mph ltd.,
traffic noise & possible wind
INFO SOURCES: Bass Lake Fisheries Station, 6718 E Winona Ave,
Knox, IN 46534 (219) 772-2353
AREA OUTFITTERS/LIVERIES: none
GAMEFISH SPECIES: bluegill, largemouth bass, crappie,
warmouth, bullhead, pumpkinseed, sunfish,
perch
CAMPING: Potato Creek State Park, 25601 SR 4, POB 908, North Liberty, IN
46554 (219) 656-8186 Class A sites
MEDICAL ASSISTANCE: Madison Center S Hospital, 403 East
Madison St., South Bend, IN 46617
(219) 234-0061

ACCESS: The access site is located at the south edge of Lakeville adjacent to US 31 on the south side of the highway. Look for the marked access signs. No public access site at Riddles Lake.

PLEASANT LAKE & RIDDLES LAKE

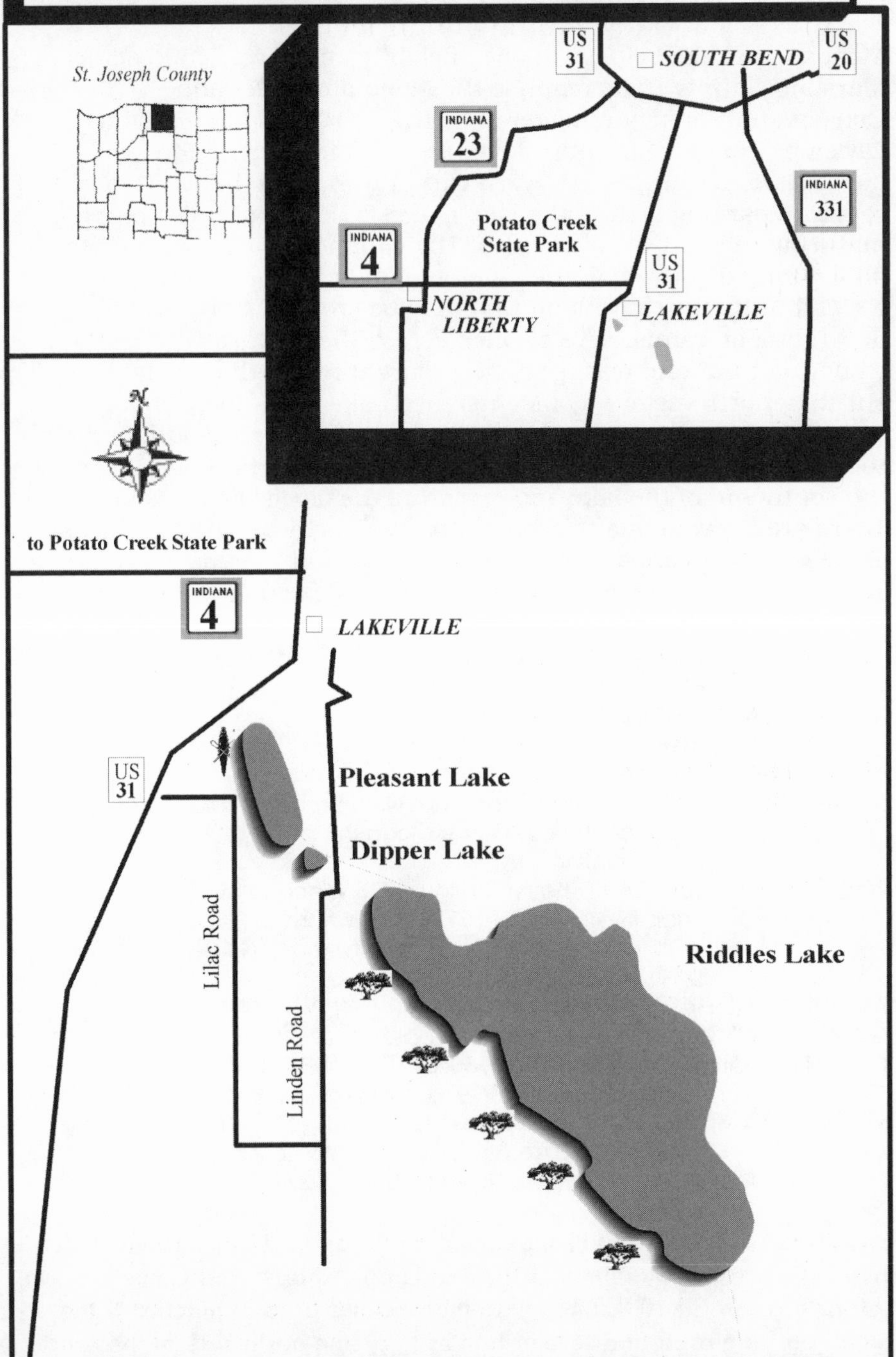

30. MENOMINEE LAKE

• Portage a pine-covered slope to a wetland conservation area

Menominee Lake belongs to one of eight tracts (over 1,800 acres) in Marshall County that comprise the Menominee Wetland Conservation Area administered by the DNR's Fish and Wildlife Division. (No name for the lake appears on maps therefore Menominee Lake). The 100-yard carry down from the blufftop roadside parking area to the lake makes a scenic portal through the maturing red and white pineries. The glimmering lake will be seen on a sunny day through the pine breaks. At the base of the slope is a small buttonbush wetland that may be crossed by boat or foot depending on rainfall levels. Once across the 60 yard-wide wetland, a short get-out and portage is necessary through the pin oaks to a shrubby northwest cove of Menominee Lake. Look for a break in the buttonbush border to launch. A distance vista of the south end of the lake reveals wooded oak-hickory upland. Consider landing at the south end of the lake and exploring the clogged channel on foot. There are a few permanent homes on the northeast and southeast shores. Beavers are active around the lake and there is waterfowl. The same land-water route of arrival is suggested for return.

USGS MAP(S): Donaldson 1:24,000
VICINITY: Plymouth, Marshall County
LAKE ACREAGE /DEPTH: 40 a. /20'
PADDLING TIME: 2-3 hours
LEVEL OF DIFFICULTY: Class I
HAZARDS/PORTAGES: electric motors only, wind problem, take care on the pine slope along the portage, seasonal hunting
INFO SOURCES: Bass Lake Fisheries Station, 6718 Winona Ave., Knox, IN 46534 (219) 772-2353 Winamac Fish & Wildlife Area, RR #4 Box 115, Winamac, IN 46996 (219) 946-4422
AREA OUTFITTERS/LIVERIES: none
GAMEFISH SPECIES: bluegill, largemouth bass
CAMPING: Potato Creek State Park, 35601 SR 4, POB 908 North Liberty, IN 46554 (219) 656-8181 Class A
MEDICAL ASSISTANCE: St. Joseph's Hospital of Marshall County 1915 Lake Ave., Plymouth, IN 46563 (219) 936-3181 or (800) 660-4274

ACCESS: From US 30 at Plymouth exit south on SR 17 and drive about five miles west to Marshall CR 10 B at Union Chapel and Cemetery. Go left or east on CR 10 B, one mi. to the wooded area at hillcrest & the small parking area at a former homesite on the north side of the road.

MENOMINEE LAKE

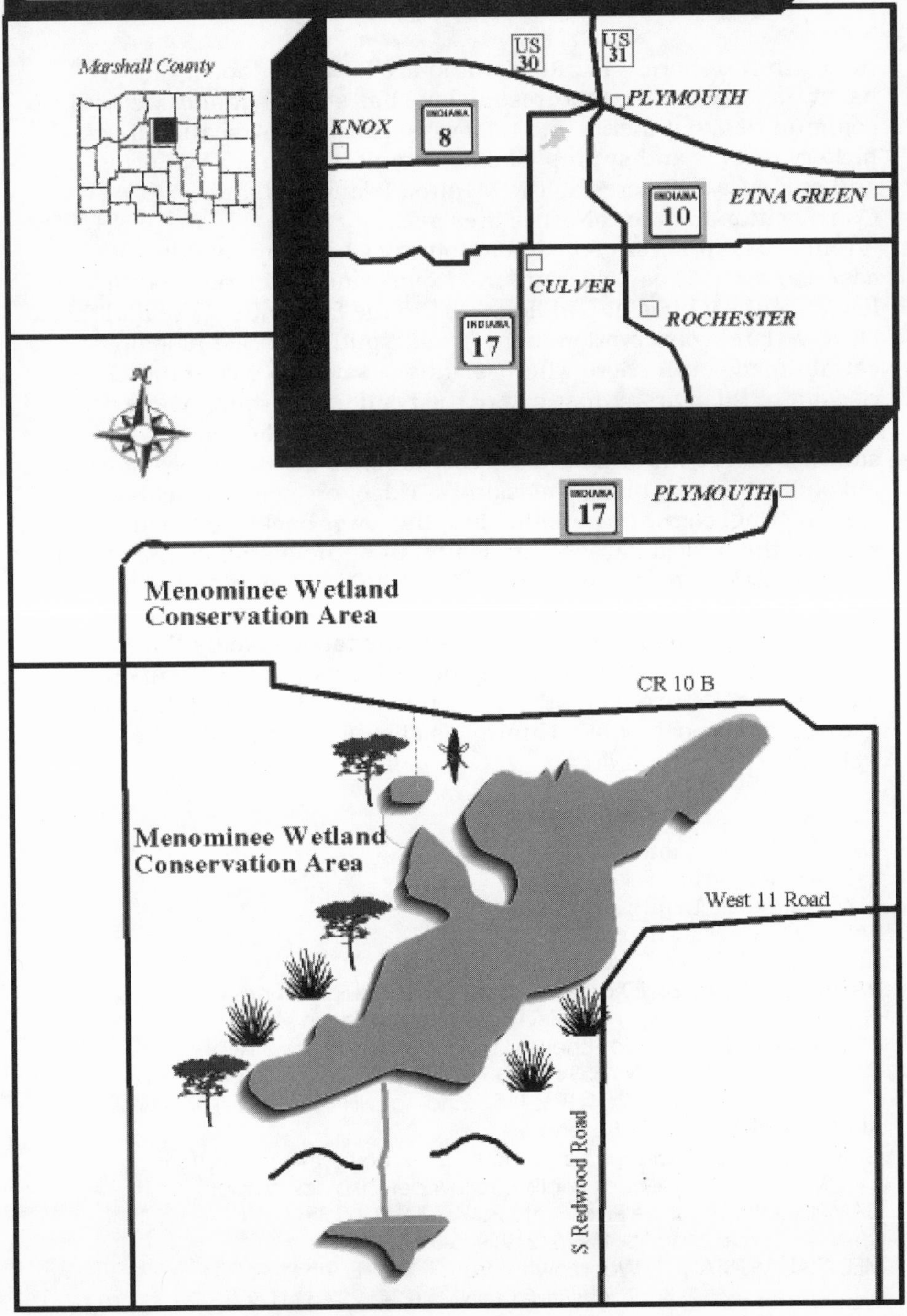

31. LAKE MANITOU

- Land an oak savanna-covered island & follow a deer path

Although the shores of Lake Manitou are 80% developed, the backwater area of the picturesque lake has several quality wetland communities that merge into tall grass, cattail flats, scattered oak-hickory islands and swamp islands of tamarack. The DNR owns and manages 298 acres as the Manitou Island Wetland Conservation Area and Nature Preserve.

From the DNR access site along Country Club Drive paddle the east shore south past year around homes and at the neck of the lower southeast basin, paddle across to the far south shore and the DNR wetland conservation area. Paddle south and east along the cattail-lined south shore where islands of savanna oak and hickory rise out of the marsh. Just before the bend in the shore where the lake narrows, an old pier and boardwalk will appear, leading to a savanna island where deer and other animals have trampled a 0.25 mile hikeable path along the island's "ridge" or "spinal" backbone. After resting, continue paddling into the lower backwaters where some of the best tamarack stands jut out of the marsh as low shrub islands. Lake Manitou was created in 1826 by damming the Mill Creek outlet combining five deep ponds. A devil-like monster or Ma-nit-to was said to inhabit the depths of the taboo lake by the Potawatomi (circa. 1800) and they never ate fish or floated upon its dark waters. Return along the same route but stay within the buoys to avoid motorboat traffic. Hunting is allowed in season in the wetland conservation area.

USGS MAP(S): Rochester 1:24,000
VICINITY: Rochester, Fulton County
LAKE ACREAGE /DEPTH: 713 a. /35'
PADDLING TIME: 3-4 hours
LEVEL OF DIFFICULTY: Class I
HAZARDS/PORTAGES: IO allowed, boat traffic could be heavy at times, wind potential, hunting in season
INFO SOURCES: Bass Lake Fisheries Station, 6718 E. Winona Avenue, Knox, IN 46534 (219) 772-2353, Winamac Fish & Wildlife Area, RR# 4, Box 115, Winamac, IN 46996 (219) 946-4422
AREA OUTFITTERS/LIVERIES: none
GAMEFISH SPECIES: bluegill, largemouth bass, northern pike, catfish redear, sunfish, yellow perch, black crappie
CAMPING: Tippecanoe River State Park, 4200 N. US 35 Winamac, IN 46996 (219) 946-3213 Class A
MEDICAL ASSISTANCE: Woodlawn Hospital, 1400 E. 9th Street Rochester, IN 46975 (219) 223-3141

ACCESS: The Lake Manitou access site is located on the east shore along Country Club Drive. From the junction of SR 25 & SR 14 in east Rochester, drive 1.5 miles east on SR 14 to Bessmore Park Road/East Shore Drive & turn right or south. Go 0.6 mile to Country Club Drive/ Fulton CR 400 E & turn right or west. The access site will be on the right just after the turn at a channel cove.

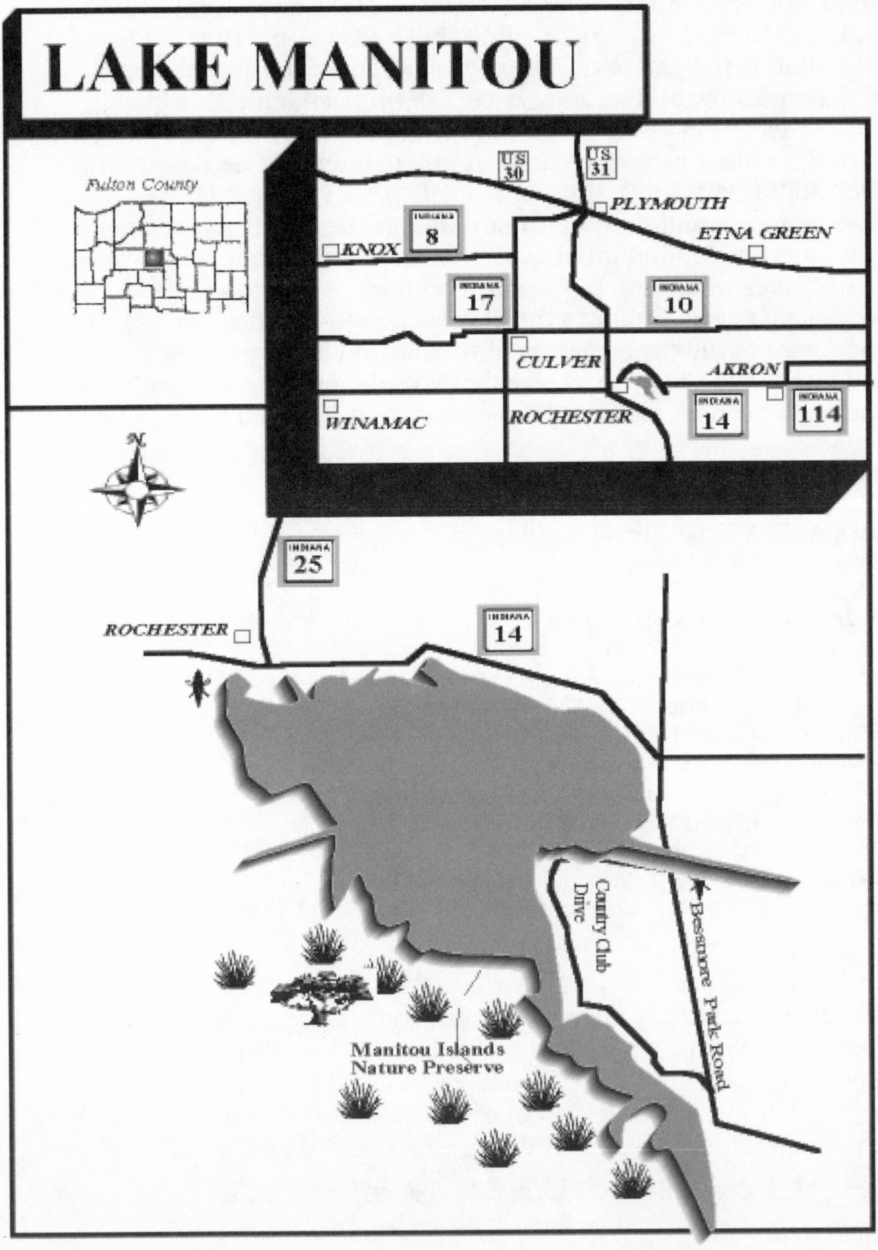

32. FLETCHER LAKE

- Tour a bucolic lake scene where people are scarce

Fletcher Lake borders the Fulton-Cass county line and is one of 20 lakes found in Fulton County. The small, deep glacial lake is accessible from the northeast shore adjacent west from the church and cemetery. The three-acre access site is community park-like with its large white oaks shading the grassy bluff. Much of the shoreline is natural with a mix of swamp and hardwood forest, grassy meadow and aquatic border of bulrush, cattail, willow, spatterdock and water magnolia lily. Aside from the small village, Fletcher Lake has so far survived an onslaught of homes strung around its handsome shores. The village of Fletcher with its few homes and fishing "resort" is situated at the southeast edge of the lake and has limited intrusion. The east to west lake has two deep kettle holes in its muck and sand bottom. The lake waters are shed to Grassy Creek and onto the Tippecanoe River. Fletcher Lake is at the near southwest terminus of the natural lake region of northern Indiana (Lake Cicott, southwest of Logansport is often considered the most outlying natural lake in northern Indiana).

USGS MAP(S): Fulton 1:24,000
VICINITY: Fulton, Rochester, Fulton County
LAKE ACREAGE /DEPTH: 45 a./40'
PADDLING TIME: 1 hour
LEVEL OF DIFFICULTY: Class I
HAZARDS/PORTAGES: IO allowed, 10 mph ltd. westerly winds can be strong
INFO SOURCES: Bass Lake Fisheries Station, 6718 East Winona Ave., Knox, IN 46534 (219) 772-2353
AREA OUTFITTERS/LIVERIES: none
GAMEFISH SPECIES: bluegill, largemouth bass, yellow perch, black crappie, channel catfish
CAMPING: Tippecanoe River State Park, 4200 N. US 35, Winamac, IN 46996 (219) 946-3213 Class A
MEDICAL ASSISTANCE: Woodlawn Hospital, 1400 E. 9th Street, Rochester, IN 46975 (219) 223-3141

ACCESS: From Rochester & US 31 exit south on SR 25 & drive about eight mi. to Fulton & turn west on SR 114. Follow SR 114 west about four mi. to CR 500 W & turn south. Follow CR 500 W south about two mi. to CR 950 S & turn left/ east. Proceed east 0.25 mi. on CR 950 S & turn right/south on CR 475 W & go another 0.25 mi. to the marked access site on the northeast shore of Fletcher Lake.

FLETCHER LAKE

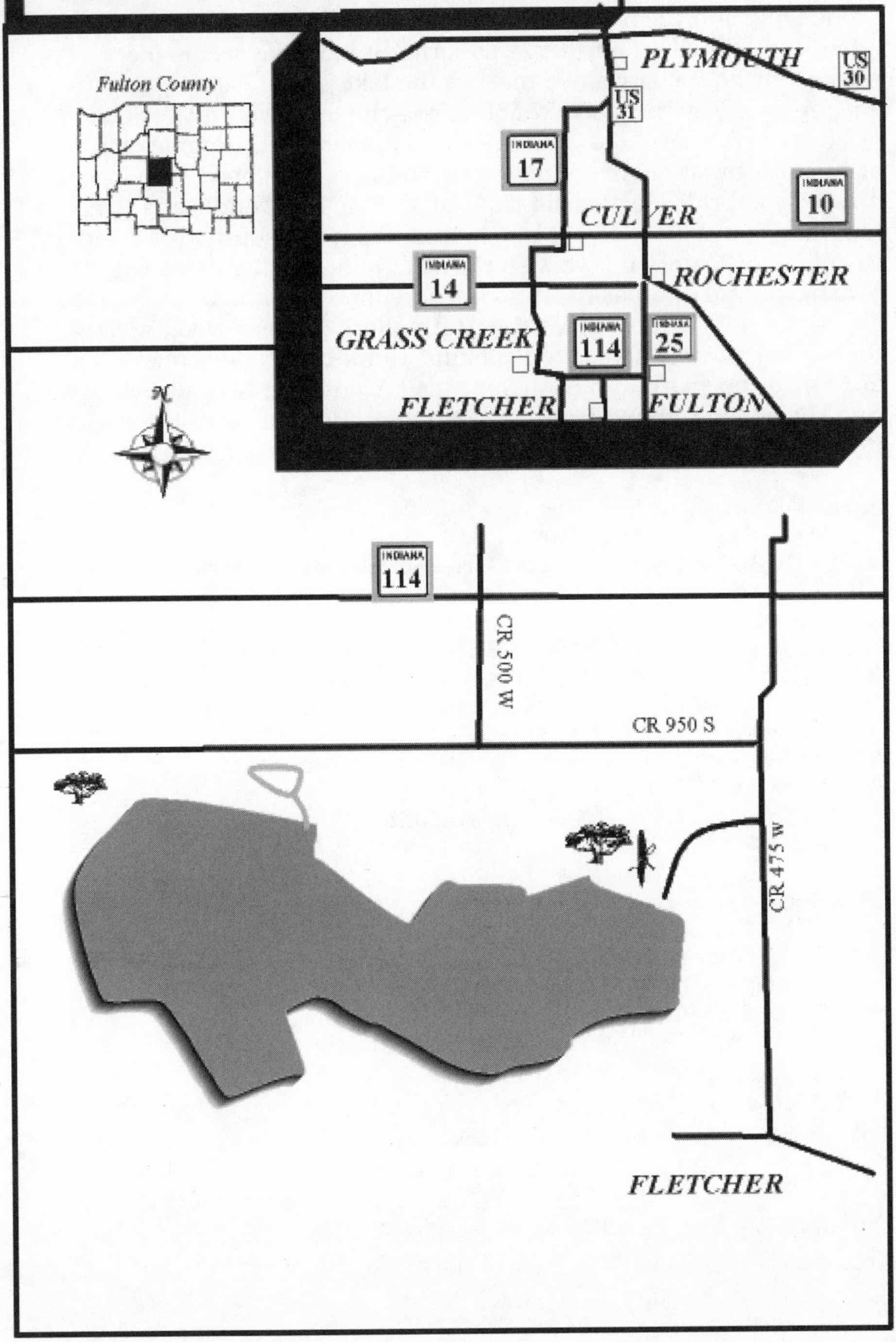

Fulton County
PLYMOUTH
US 30
US 31
INDIANA 17
INDIANA 10
CULVER
INDIANA 14
ROCHESTER
GRASS CREEK
INDIANA 114
INDIANA 25
FLETCHER
FULTON
INDIANA 114
CR 500 W
CR 950 S
CR 475 W
FLETCHER

33. STONE LAKE & CLEAR LAKE

- Come & go on two lakes within the "Lake City"

Stone Lake and Clear Lake lie within a few city blocks of each other's shorelines in northeast LaPorte. Stone Lake seems more removed from the city since most of the lake and the shore are encompassed by the wooded 556-acre Soldiers Memorial Park. A public beach is situated at the northeast shore. A navigable channel at the northwest shore connects the 564 acre developed Pine Lake. A metal footbridge spans the channel to Pine Lake and leads south to hiking trails. The access site is located on the south shore and many motorboaters use this site to access Pine Lake. Clear Lake, nearby, is also in a park setting but it is more urban. The 170-acre Fox Memorial Park occupies the north shore of Clear Lake, where the access site is also located. Distant views of the LaPorte skyline appear to the south and east. Truesdell Avenue and Hoelocker Drive ring the shallow lake. Birding is good here. Both in-town lakes are rich in social and natural history.

USGS MAP(S): LaPorte East, LaPorte West 1:24,000
VICINITY: LaPorte, LaPorte County
LAKE ACREAGE /DEPTH: Stone Lake 25 a. /36' Clear Lake 106 a./12'
PADDLING TIME: 1 hour each
LEVEL OF DIFFICULTY: Class I
HAZARDS/PORTAGES: IO allowed, 10 mph ltd. on both lakes
INFO SOURCES: LaPorte Parks and Recreation Dept., Soldiers Memorial Park, 205 Pine Lake Avenue, LaPorte, IN 46350 (219) 326-9600
AREA OUTFITTERS/LIVERIES: summer boat rental at Soldiers Memorial Park beach (219) 326-9600
GAMEFISH SPECIES: bluegill, largemouth bass, northern pike, walleye redear, warmouth, perch, bullhead, crappie
CAMPING: Indiana Dunes National Lakeshore, 110 N. Mineral Springs, Road, LaPorte, IN 46304 (219) 926-9600 Class A
Indiana Dunes State Park, 1600 N. 25 E, Chesterton, IN (219) 326-1234, Class A & B
MEDICAL ASSISTANCE: LaPorte Hospital, 1007 Lincolnway LaPorte, IN 46350 (219) 326-1234

ACCESS: To reach Stone Lake in NW LaPorte from US 35/SR 39/Pine Lake Ave. W of overpass & downtown, left on Weller Ave. 0.8 mi. to Craven Dr., turn right. Go a short distance to Lakeshore Dr. & left 0.3 mi. to access site. Follow signs. Clear Lake is reached from US 35/SR 39/Pine Lake Ave. near the overpass, turning right or north on Truesdell Avenue and proceed to Fox Park at the N end of lake. Access is near Hoelocker Drive.

STONE LAKE & CLEAR LAKE

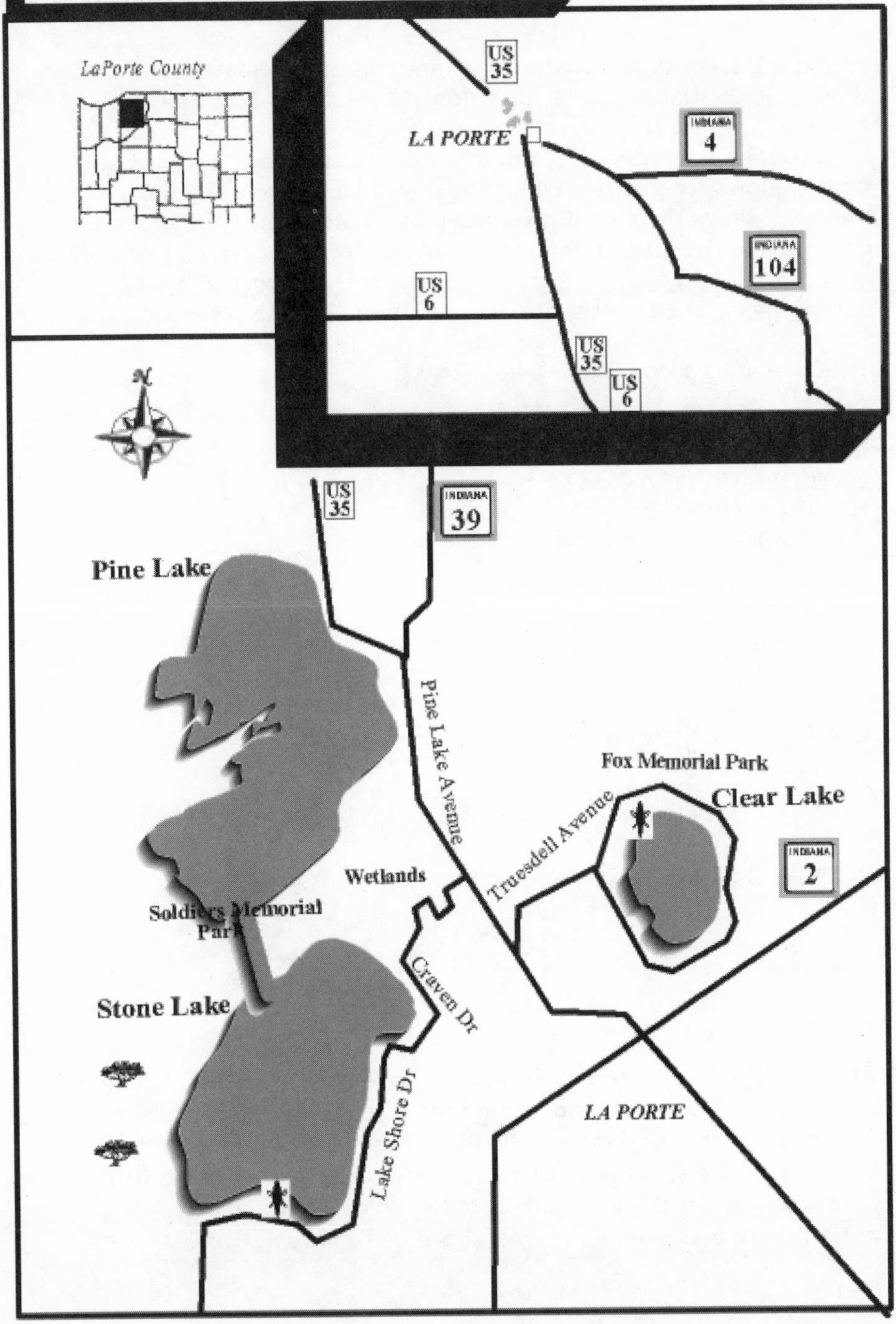

LaPorte County
US 35
LA PORTE
INDIANA 4
INDIANA 104
US 6
US 35
US 6
US 35
INDIANA 39
Pine Lake
Pine Lake Avenue
Fox Memorial Park
Clear Lake
Truesdell Avenue
INDIANA 2
Wetlands
Soldiers Memorial Park
Craven Dr
Stone Lake
Lake Shore Dr
LA PORTE

34. TAMARACK LAKE

- Glide across the surface of a Grand Kankakee marsh lake

Tamarack Lake is situated at the east end of Kingsbury Fish and Wildlife Area just south of the coldwater Mix-saw-bah Fish Hatchery and north of the Kankakee River access site. The shallow, muck bottom lake is bordered by encroaching spatterdock and marsh which allows for prairie vistas. Deep well water from the fish hatchery flows through Tamarack Lake replenishing the marsh. Contrary to the place name, there are no tamarack trees however an introduced bald cypress survives north of the access site and fishing pier. The rich birdlife adds to your floating pleasure.

USGS MAP(S): LaPorte East, Stillwell 1:24,000
VICINITY: LaPorte, LaPorte County
LAKE ACREAGE /DEPTH: 20 a. /9'
PADDLING TIME: 1 hour
LEVEL OF DIFFICULTY: Class I
HAZARDS/PORTAGES: electric motors only, hunter safety zone
INFO SOURCES: Kingsbury Fish & Wildlife Area
5344 S. Hupp Rd.,
LaPorte, IN 46350
(219) 393-3612
AREA OUTFITTERS/LIVERIES: none
GAMEFISH SPECIES: bluegill, largemouth bass, northern pike, catfish
CAMPING: Kingsbury FWA (219) 393-3612
18 Class C sites Potato Creek State Park
25601 SR 4, POB 908
North Liberty, IN 46554 (219) 656-8186
Class C
MEDICAL ASSISTANCE: LaPorte Hospital
1007 Lincolnway
LaPorte, IN 46350
(800) 235-6204 or (219) 326-1234

ACCESS: The best access to Tamarack Lake is from SR 104, 8.5 miles northwest of Walkerton and about four miles southeast of Stillwell. Turn south at the road marked Mix-saw-bah Fish Hatchery/LaPorte CR 700 E. Drive south & enter the fish and wildlife area at the fish hatchery gate & continue south about 1.5 mile & turn left to the parking & access site on the west shore of Tamarack Lake.

TAMARACK LAKE

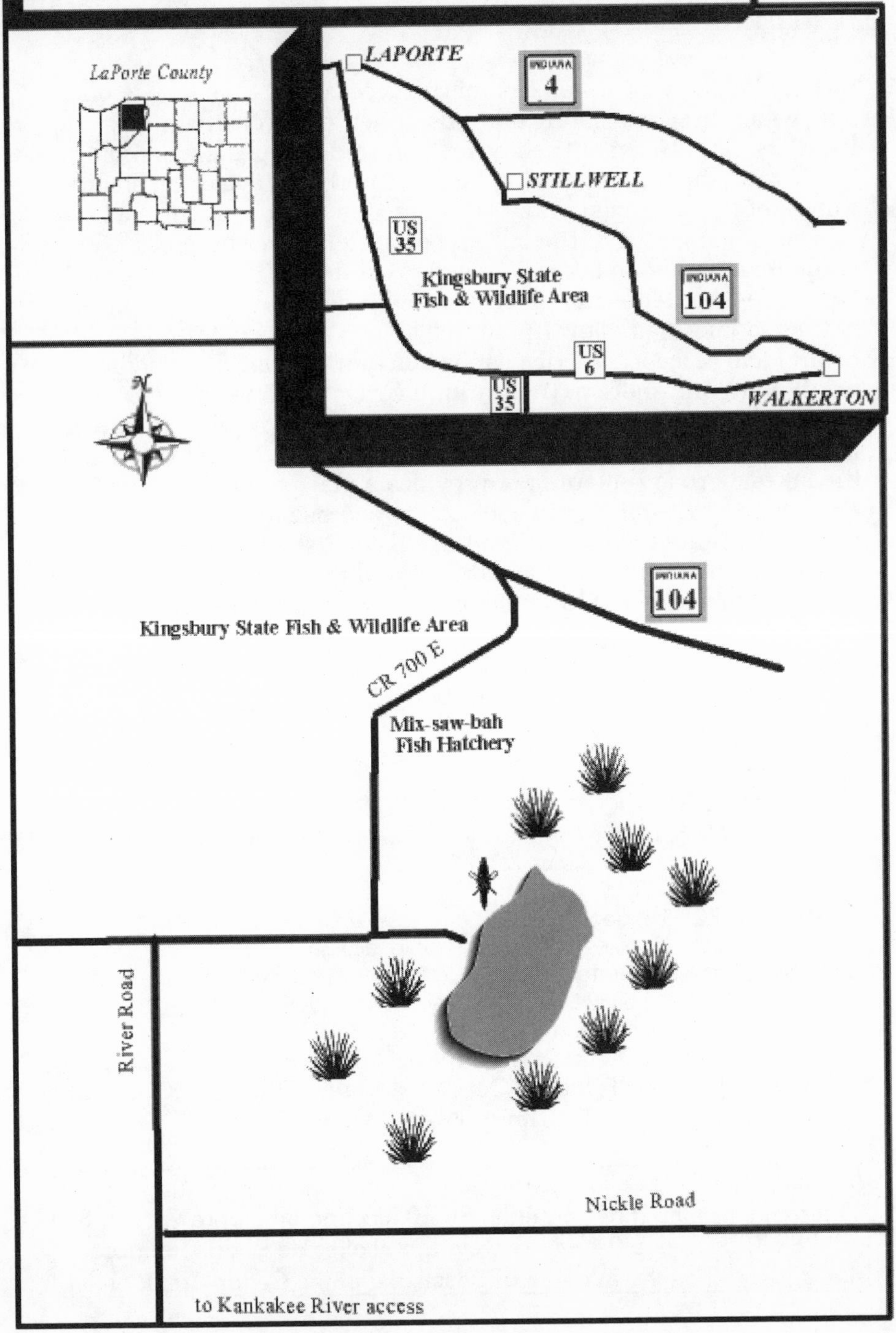

LaPorte County
LAPORTE
INDIANA 4
STILLWELL
US 35
Kingsbury State Fish & Wildlife Area
INDIANA 104
US 6
US 35
WALKERTON
INDIANA 104
Kingsbury State Fish & Wildlife Area
CR 700 E
Mix-saw-bah Fish Hatchery
River Road
Nickle Road
to Kankakee River access

35. BASS LAKE

- Canoe a quiet cove on Indiana's fourth largest natural lake

Bass Lake has vast vistas east of the access site. This lake is one mile wide, three miles long and has eleven miles of shoreline. Paddlers can discover "The Pocket", an undeveloped portion of Bass Lake, west shore in the south basin. Motorboats avoid the shallow waters of the west basin however pontoons do not. From the DNR access site adjacent to the outlet, paddle left or north about 100 yards (past ten or so lakeside residences) to the thick wet wooded shoreline where fine stands of river birch dominate. The sandy bottomed lake is shallow (three to five feet) at this point and could be an ideal place to practice canoe safety with children. Paddle north along the shore to the tranquil cove, "The Pocket", where water magnolia lily finds shelter from the open water in the muck. Paddle on north along the shore to about where the trees end and the lakeside road pullout spot provides a place to land and rest. Retrace the half-mile route back to the access site.
Bass Lake State Beach and the Bass Lake Fisheries Station are located in the north basin, southeast and northeast shores. Springs and flowing wells are found along the east and northeast shores.

USGS MAP(S): Bass Lake 1:24,000
VICINITY: Bass Lake & Knox, Starke County
LAKE ACREAGE /DEPTH: 1,345 a./30'
PADDLING TIME: 1-2 hours
LEVEL OF DIFFICULTY: Class I
HAZARDS/PORTAGES: IO allowed, 10 mph ltd., wind & wave action
INFO SOURCES: Bass Lake Fisheries Station, 6718 E. Winona Ave., Knox, IN 46534 (219) 772-2353
AREA OUTFITTERS/LIVERIES: none
GAMEFISH SPECIES: bluegill, largemouth bass, white bass, northern pike, walleyes, crappie, catfish
CAMPING: Bass Lake State Beach, 5838 S SR 10, Knox, IN 46534 (219) 772-3382 Memorial Day to Labor day, also Tippecanoe River State Park, 4200 N. US 35, Winamac, IN 46996 (219) 946-3213, Class A
MEDICAL ASSISTANCE: Starke County Memorial Hospital, 102 E. Culver Rd., Knox, IN 46534 (219) 772-6231

ACCESS: The Bass Lake access site is located six mi. S of Knox on US 35 turning E at the (flashing light) SR 10 junction on Starke CR 600 S (Old SR 10). Drive E 0.4 mi., curving S on Lakeside Road. The access site is located on the SW side of Bass Lake at the Cedar Creek outlet.

BASS LAKE

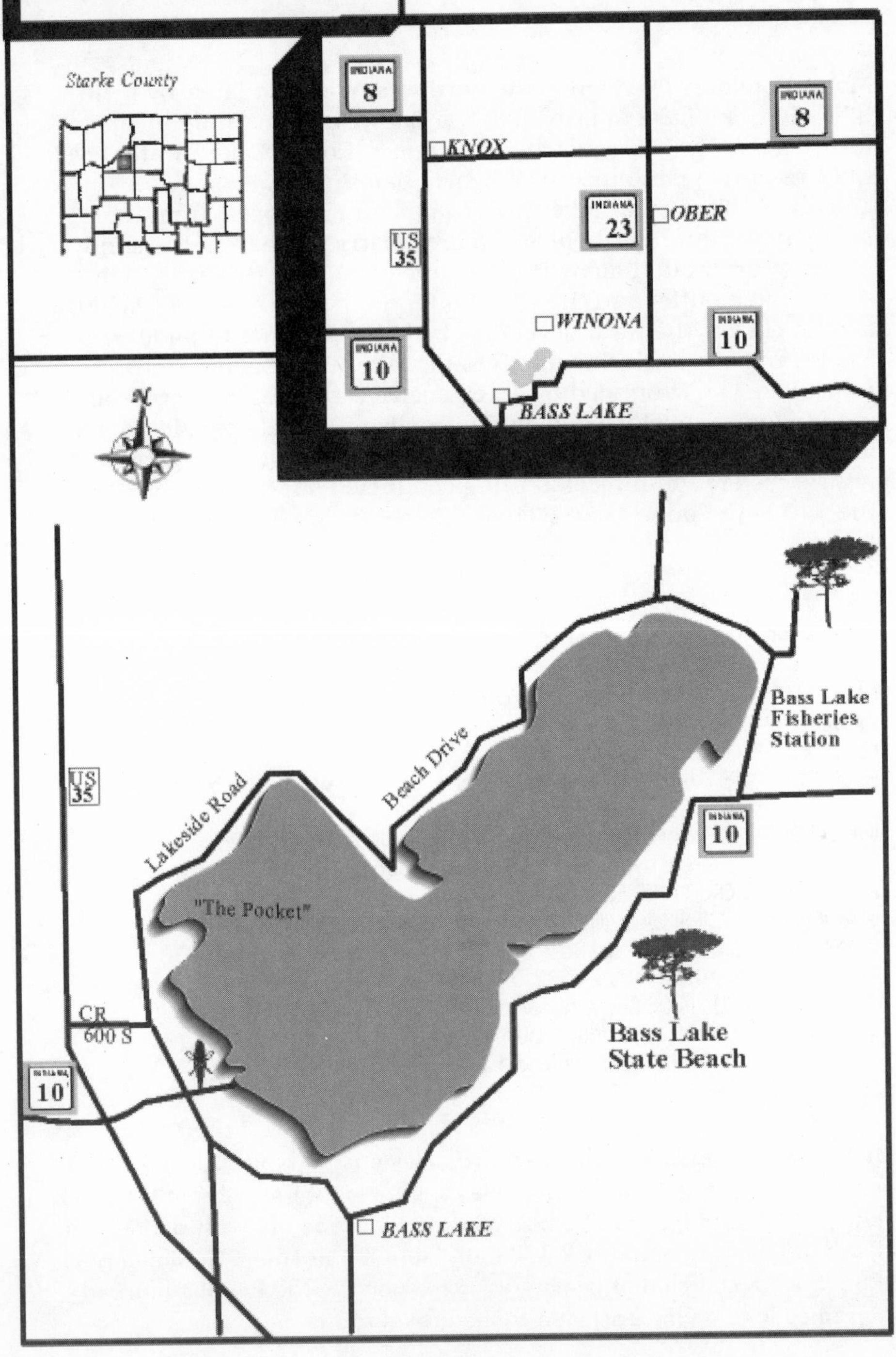
Starke County
INDIANA 8
INDIANA 8
KNOX
INDIANA 23
OBER
US 35
WINONA
INDIANA 10
INDIANA 10
BASS LAKE
N
US 35
Lakeside Road
Beach Drive
Bass Lake Fisheries Station
INDIANA 10
"The Pocket"
CR 600 S
INDIANA 10
Bass Lake State Beach
BASS LAKE

36. ROUND LAKE

- Be waterborne in the home of ancient Mound Builders

Mound builders lived along the northwest shore and nearby sand hills of Round Lake approximately 1,200 years ago. In the near future a dam will be constructed to regain Round Lake's water level, until recently maintained by a beaver dam.

To access the circular lake (DNR owned and managed) from the sandy parking former homestead area, carry down from the sandy parking turnaround along the dry muck lane east 60 yards to the Smith Ditch outlet and the site of a former beaver dam that held the lake in check. The water level may be to low at times to paddle up the channel through the marsh to the lake. The shallow, natural muck lake is surrounded by an extensive cattail marsh border and swamp forest which wildlife find attractive. Several rare plants are found in the wetlands and hardwood trees thrive in the uplands. A prairie restoration project is being conducted on the south edge of the 140-acre Round Lake Wetland Conservation Area and Nature Preserve.

USGS MAP(S): Denham 1:24,000
VICINITY: Knox, Starke County
LAKE ACREAGE /DEPTH: 29 a. /9' (dammed to 100 a.)
PADDLING TIME: 1 hour
LEVEL OF DIFFICULTY: Class I
HAZARDS/PORTAGES: electric trolling only, shallow water, seasonal hunting
INFO SOURCES: Kankakee Fish & Wildlife Area, 4320 W Toto Rd., POB 77, North Judson, IN 46336 (219) 896-3522
AREA OUTFITTERS/LIVERIES: none
GAMEFISH SPECIES: bluegill, largemouth bass, crappie, bowfin
CAMPING: Bass Lake State Beach (Memorial Day-Labor Day) 5838 S SR 10 (219) 772-3382 & Tippecanoe River State Park 4200 N US 35. Winamac, IN 46996 (219) 946-3213, Class A
MEDICAL ASSISTANCE: Starke County Memorial Hospital, 102 E. Culver Road. Knox, IN 46534 (219) 772-6231

ACCESS: Round Lake is located five miles east of North Judson, three miles southeast of Toto and six miles southwest of Knox. From the south edge of Knox at the US 35 and Toto Road junction, go west on the Toto Road 2.5 miles to Starke CR 150 E and turn left or south. Continue past Round Lake church and cemetery 1.6 mile on CR 150 E to the marked entrance lane on the east side of the gravel road.

ROUND LAKE

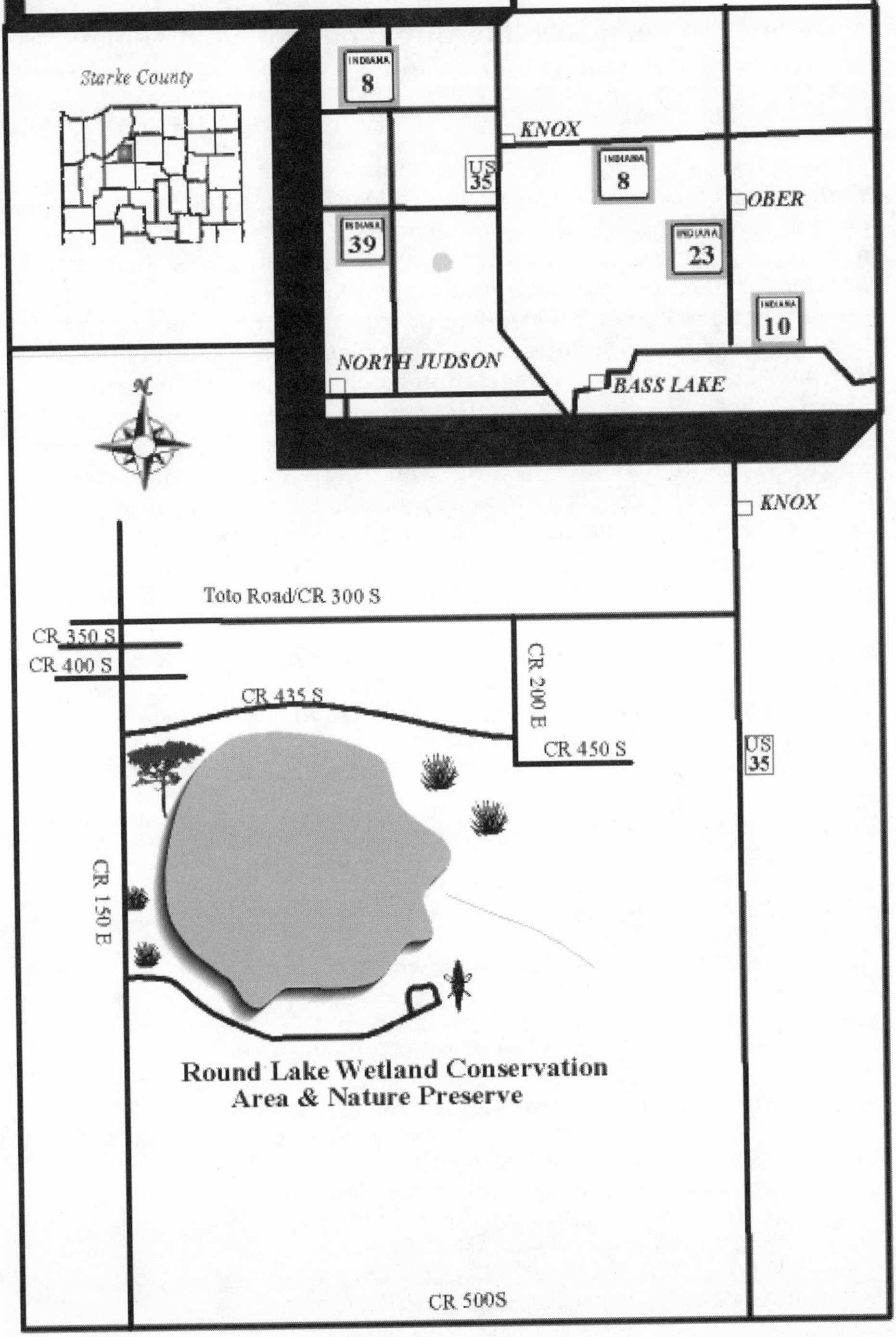
Starke County
INDIANA 8
KNOX
US 35
INDIANA 8
OBER
INDIANA 39
INDIANA 23
INDIANA 10
NORTH JUDSON
BASS LAKE
N
KNOX
Toto Road/CR 300 S
CR 350 S
CR 400 S
CR 435 S
CR 200 E
CR 450 S
US 35
CR 150 E
Round Lake Wetland Conservation
Area & Nature Preserve
CR 500S

37. LONG LAKE

- **Scout out a shallow interdunal pond amidst golden sands of a national lakeshore**

Thousands of years ago, this tranquil interdunal pond was a long, shallow lagoon of fast-receding Lake Chicago, stretching from present-day Long Lake eastward to Dunes State Park. Today visitors may access the lake via a 60-yard carry down from a West Beach parking lot to an observation overlook at lakeside. Once on the vegetating lake, fine dunal vistas appear to the north where Long Lake and West Beach hiking trails crisscross. To the south of the narrow lake a filter strip of vegetation blocks the view of the South Shore railroad. Spatterdock is attempting to close the remaining open waters. The east-to-west lake is a resting spot for migratory waterfowl. Rarities include tundra swan, brant and Eurasian wigeon but paddlers are more likely to see grebes, herons, wood ducks, hooded mergansers, pintails, coots, bitterns and marsh wrens. Long Lake provides a rare paddling opportunity within the Dunes natural region.

Kayakers may find the buoyed safety zone of Lake Michigan conducive for sea kayaking. All Indiana Dunes national lakeshore beaches require carrydown: Central Beach, Lakeview, Kemil Beach, West Beach and Miller Beach/Lake Street City Park; also Dunes State Park beach.

USGS MAP(S): Porter 1:24,000
VICINITY: Portage, Porter County
LAKE ACREAGE /DEPTH: 25 a. /8'
PADDLING TIME: 1 hour
LEVEL OF DIFFICULTY: Class I
HAZARDS/PORTAGES: carry down 60 yards from parking lot, wind potenial, plenty of spatterdock
INFO SOURCES: Indiana Dunes National Lakeshore, 1100 N. Mineral Springs Road, Porter, IN 46304 (219) 926-7561, Visitor Center at Kemil Road & US 12
AREA OUTFITTERS/LIVERIES: Jordan's Wilderness Shop & Outfitters, 7940 Hawthorne Place, Dyer, IN 46311 (800) 644-9955
GAMEFISH SPECIES: bluegill, largemouth bass
CAMPING: Indiana Dunes National Lakeshore, Class A (219) 926-7561 & Indiana Dunes State Park, 1600 N 25th E, Chesterton, IN 46304 (219) 942-0552 (219) 926-1952, Class A & B
MEDICAL ASSISTANCE: Methodist Hospitals, 600 Grant St. Gary, IN 46402, (219) 886-4315

ACCESS: Long Lake is located at West Beach, Dunes National Lakeshore near the Porter-Lake county line & Ogden Dunes. From I-94 exit 16 north on SR 51 & proceed 0.5 miles to US 20. Turn east on US 20 & drive one mi. to County Line Road & turn north. Continue 2 mi. on County Line Road to the marked West Beach National Lakeshore entrance. Summer season entrance fee. Or, from I-94, exit 19 north on SR 249 to US 12 & turn west. Go about four mi. on US 12 to County Line Road, turn north & proceed to the marked entry ramp. From the entrance control station, park at first parking area in West Beach.

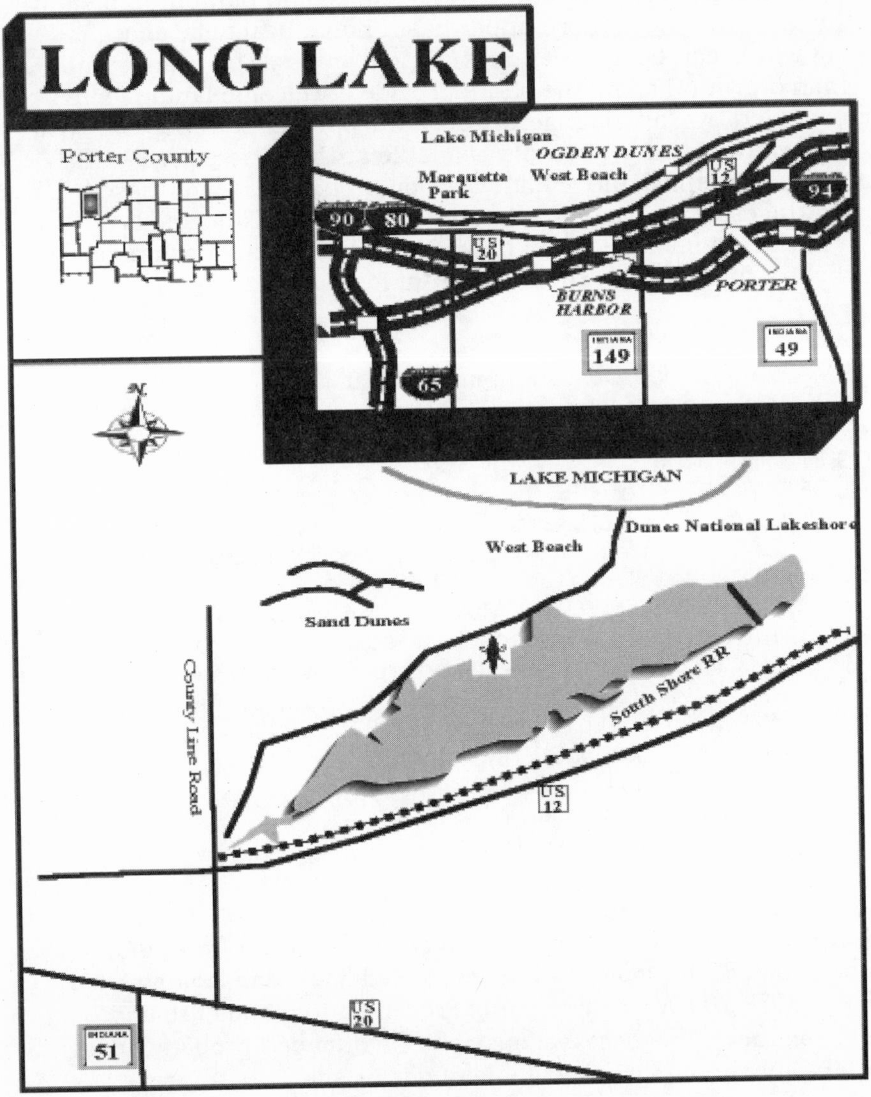

38. J.C. MURPHEY LAKE

- **Float under prairie skies on a vast shallow lake**

J.C. Murphy Lake is an artificial water body, completed in 1951. It is situated in the 9,956 acre Willow Slough Fish and Wildlife area in northwestern Indiana's sand prairies. The huge lake is divided into an upper north basin and lower south basin. Several small wooded islands separate the two basins. Marsh borders the north distant end of the lake and black oak savanna upland and pin oak flats are common habitat along the shore. A lakeside sand blowout and sand prairie along the west shore upper basin has a beachlike effect. Strong winds can be a threat on the open waters. The islands and the higher ground along the shore provide a welcome landing site if not occupied by Canadian geese. J.C. Murphey Lake is popular with fishermen in johnboats (rentals available at the concession building). Waterfowl and wildlife are common. The lake is closed during the early teal and main waterfowl season. Canoeing is allowed during fishing season only. Check with headquarters on the southwest shore next to the boat rental for closed dates.

USGS MAP(S): Morocco, Donovan, Ill-Ind 1:24,000
VICINITY: Morocco, Newton County
LAKE ACREAGE /DEPTH: 1,300 a. /8′ average 2′-4′
PADDLING TIME: 4 hrs
LEVEL OF DIFFICULTY: Class I
HAZARDS/PORTAGES: wind, insects, hunting allowed in season,
electric only, access only during fishing season
INFO SOURCES: Willow Slough Fish and Wildlife Area
2042 S 500 W RR#2, Morocco, IN 47963 (219) 285-2704
AREA OUTFITTERS/LIVERIES: Willow Slough concessionaire, johnboats
GAMEFISH SPECIES: bluegill, largemouth bass, channel catfish,
northern pike, redear, sunfish, crappie, carp
CAMPING: Willow Slough Fish & Wildlife Area, 75 Class B sites
MEDICAL ASSISTANCE: Jasper County Hospital
104 East Grace Street
Rensselaer, IN 47978
(219) 866-5141

ACCESS: From US 41 in west central Newton County, go west at Morocco on SR 114 and drive 2 miles to the Illinois and Indiana State Line Road/CR 700 W and turn north. Proceed north to the fish and wildlife entrance. The access site is near the dam and property headquarters. Johnboat rentals available at access site.

J.C. MURPHEY LAKE

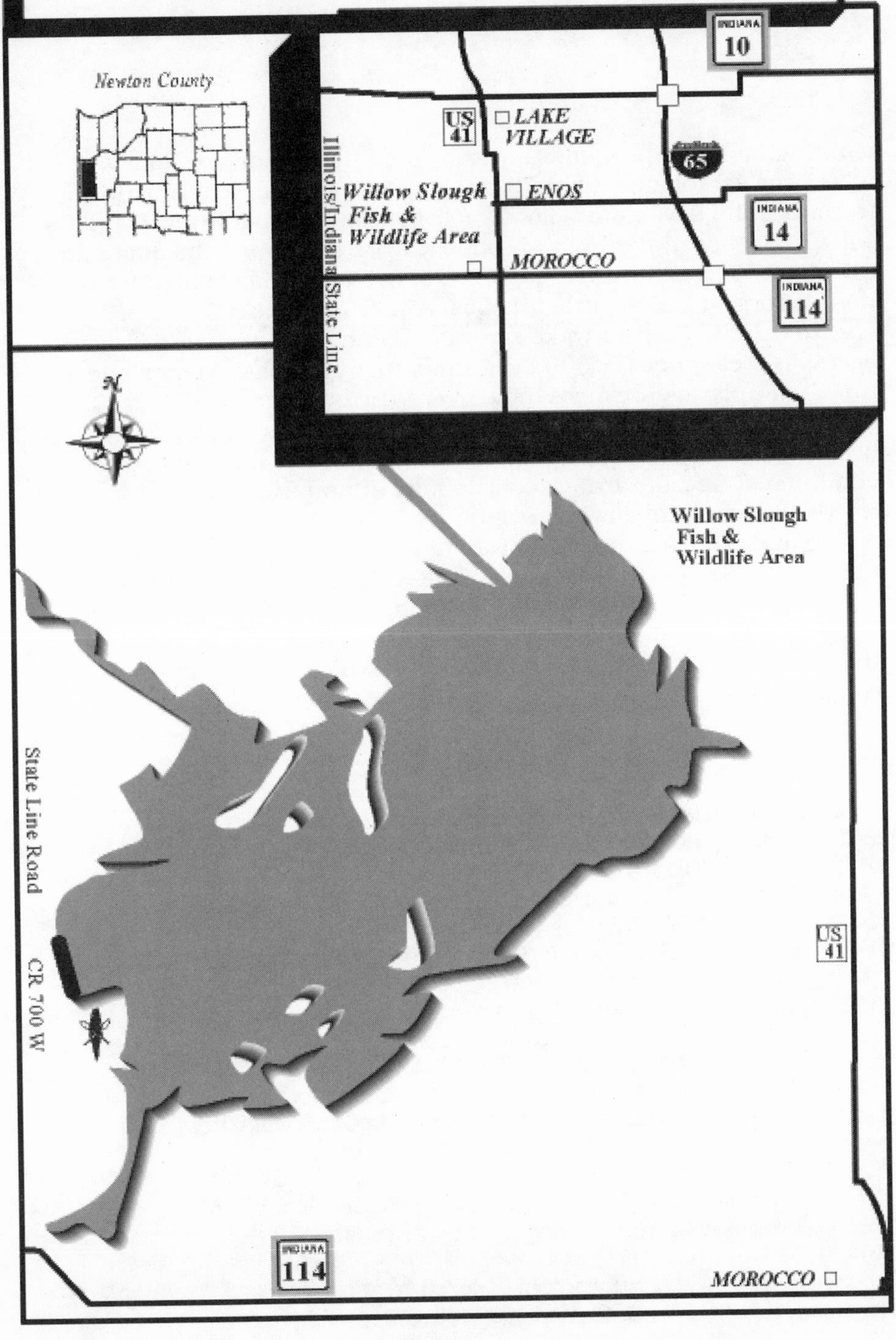
Newton County
INDIANA 10
US 41
LAKE VILLAGE
65
Illinois/Indiana State Line
Willow Slough Fish & Wildlife Area
ENOS
INDIANA 14
MOROCCO
INDIANA 114
Willow Slough Fish & Wildlife Area
State Line Road
CR 700 W
US 41
INDIANA 114
MOROCCO

39. HUNTINGTON/ROUSH LAKE

- Paddle quiet backwaters of the only Wabash River reservoir

Huntington Lake, now officially known as the J. Edward Roush Lake, was established in 1970 by the US Army Corps of Engineers to control the devastating floodwaters of the Wabash River. Paddlers will want to avoid the busy speedboat waters between the dam and SR 5 east to the Huntington CR 200 E bridge. The best area for the non-motorized and shuttle free boater is from the CR 200 E bridge east to CR 375 E, a no-wake-no-wash fishing idle zone. A mid-point access is located at CR 300 E. Canoe upstream past islands and timbered uplands to where the current turns your vessel downstream. Going east, the reservoir widens near the CR 200 E bridge. Numerous standing and submerged water drowned snags add interest and hazard. Canoeists may attempt to explore the wooded coves of the lower reservoir near the dam during off-season spring and fall. Hunting is allowed in season.
Consider a 300 pace carry-in to Wahk-shin-gah Lake (25 acres/20' deep) south of the causeway bridge along CR 200 E. In addition to canoeing or kayaking, the property offers a swimming beach, hiking trails, picnicking and playground sites, naturalist programs, camping and more.

USGS MAP(S): Majenica, Markle 1:24,000
VICINITY: Huntington, Markle, Huntington County
LAKE ACREAGE /DEPTH: 870 a. /40'
PADDLING TIME: 1 hour to a full day
LEVEL OF DIFFICULTY: Class I
HAZARDS/PORTAGES: submerged snags, speedboats, hunting in season, wind on open water
INFO SOURCES: Huntington Lake (J. Edward Roush Lake)
517 North Warren Road
Huntington, IN 46750 (219) 468-2165 or 2166
AREA OUTFITTERS/LIVERIES: none listed, check local marinas
GAMEFISH SPECIES: bluegill, largemouth, smallmouth & white bass, white crappie, channel cat, carp
CAMPING: Two Class C campgrounds, Kil-so-quah SRA and Little Turtle SRA at Huntington Lake (219) 468-2165 or 2166
MEDICAL ASSISTANCE: Huntington Memorial Hospital
1215 Etna Avenue
Huntington, IN 46750
(219) 356-3000

ACCESS: From I-69 exit 86 at Markle onto US 224 and go west toward Huntington.Wahk-shin-gah Lake is reached from US 224 by turning at Huntington CR 200 E and driving south across the causeway about a mile to a roadside parking lot on the left and carry in. To reach the backwater of Huntington Lake continue south on CR 200 E to CR 100 S and turn east. Proceed east on CR 100 S to CR 300 E and turn north. Go N on CR 300 E about a mi. to the "T" junction. Carry down access is left at the "T" where the road ends in water on East Division Road.

HUNTINGTON LAKE /ROUSH LAKE

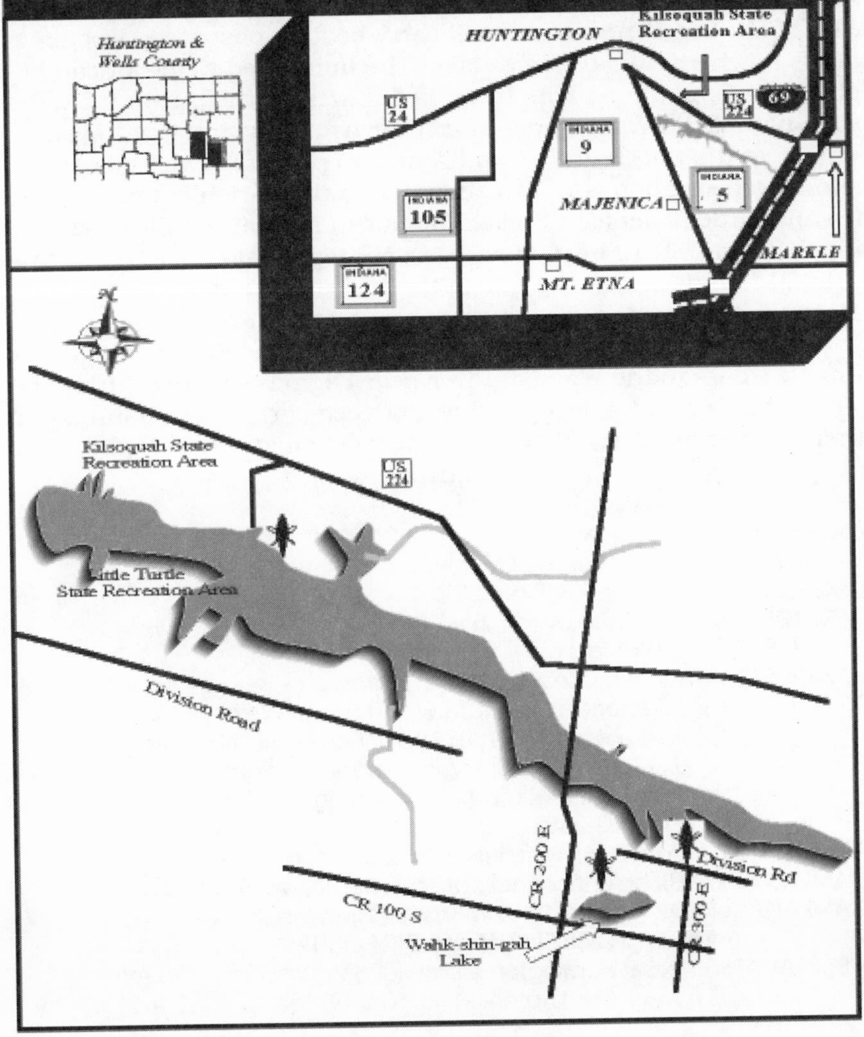

40. SALAMONIE LAKE

- Explore the upper reaches where river meets reservoir

Salamonie Lake is the middle upper Wabash reservoir, located between Huntington or Roush Lake and Mississinewa Lake. The Army Corps of Engineers built all three and Salamonie has been operational since 1966. The backwaters merit exploration by paddlers. The no–wash-no-wake fishing zone has calm muddy waters, many snags and forested bluffs. Paddle east, from Mt. Etna's main street access, through the backwaters, upstream to the incoming Salamonie River. Also, consider paddling a scenic horseshoe bend of the river without a necessary car shuttle. The put-in site (unsigned) is north of SR 124 along Huntington CR 400 W just east of Mt. Etna.The current will carry boaters past steep wooded bluffs to where river becomes lake. The unmarked take–out can be difficult to find after a trip, but it is due west of the put-in 0.5 miles via a potholed drivable lane. After your trip return on foot to your vehicle at the put-in access and return to pick-up at the take-out site. Another option is to investigate the wildlife-rich coves of Majenica and Little Majenica Creeks. The put-in is north of Mt. Etna and the SR 9 and SR 124 junction. From SR 9 go east on CR 400 E to CR 600 N and turn north and go to the dead end boat ramp. Mosquitoes can be prolific during the warm months in the backwaters. In addition, the short segment of the Salamonie River from the dam to the Wabash River near Lagro is inviting during the winter drawdown (mid-September to December). To be assured that there is enough released dam water, groups may write or phone the Corps office to plan their fluvial trips.

USGS MAP(S): Mt. Etna, Andrews, Largo 1:24,000
VICINITY: Mt. Etna, Huntington County
LAKE ACREAGE /DEPTH: 2,855 a./65'
PADDLING TIME: 1 hour to overnights
LEVEL OF DIFFICULTY: Class I
HAZARDS/PORTAGES: log snags, insects, motorboats, seasonal hunting
INFO SOURCES: Salamonie Lake, 9214 W Lost Bridge West, SR 105, Andrews, IN (219) 468-2124 or (219) 468-2125 also U.S. Army Corp of Engineers, South Salamonie Dam Road, Route #1, Box 40, Lagro, IN 46941 (219) 782-2358
AREA OUTFITTERS/LIVERIES: none listed, try local marinas
GAMEFISH SPECIES: bass, channel catfish, walleye, white crappie.
CAMPING: Salamonie Lake, 9214 W, Lost Bridge West, SR 105, Andrews, IN 46072 (219) 468-2124 or 2125, Class A & C
MEDICAL ASSISTANCE: Huntington Memorial Hospital, 1215 Etna Ave Huntington, IN 46750 (219) 356-3000

ACCESS: Four access sites at or near Mt. Etna. Salamonie backwaters- From SR 124 at Mt. Etna go north to the lake on Main Street or Huntington CR 600 W. Salamonie River horseshoe bend & backwaters- East of Mt. Etna on SR 124, drive north on Huntington CR 400 W to the put in site on the east side of the access road down a lane to the river. The take out is west 0.5 mile on the drivable farm lane just north of the launch site to the river. A solo non-shuttle trip. CR 550 S backwater dead end- From the junction of SR 124 & SR 9 at Mt. Etna, drive north on SR 9 and turn right or east on Huntington CR 500 S, the first road across the bridge. Follow CR 500 S to CR 600 W and turn south. Go a short distance and turn east on CR 550 S. Continue on CR 550 S, curving right at the junction of CR 500 W. Proceed down the narrowing wooded lane to the reservoir and dead end. Majenica Creek access- north of the junction of SR 124 and SR 9 at Mt. Etna. From SR 9 go east on Huntington CR 400 S to CR 600 W. Drive north on CR 600 W to the dead end and access site across the causeway bridge.

Salamonie Lake Backwaters, Sunset

SALAMONIE LAKE

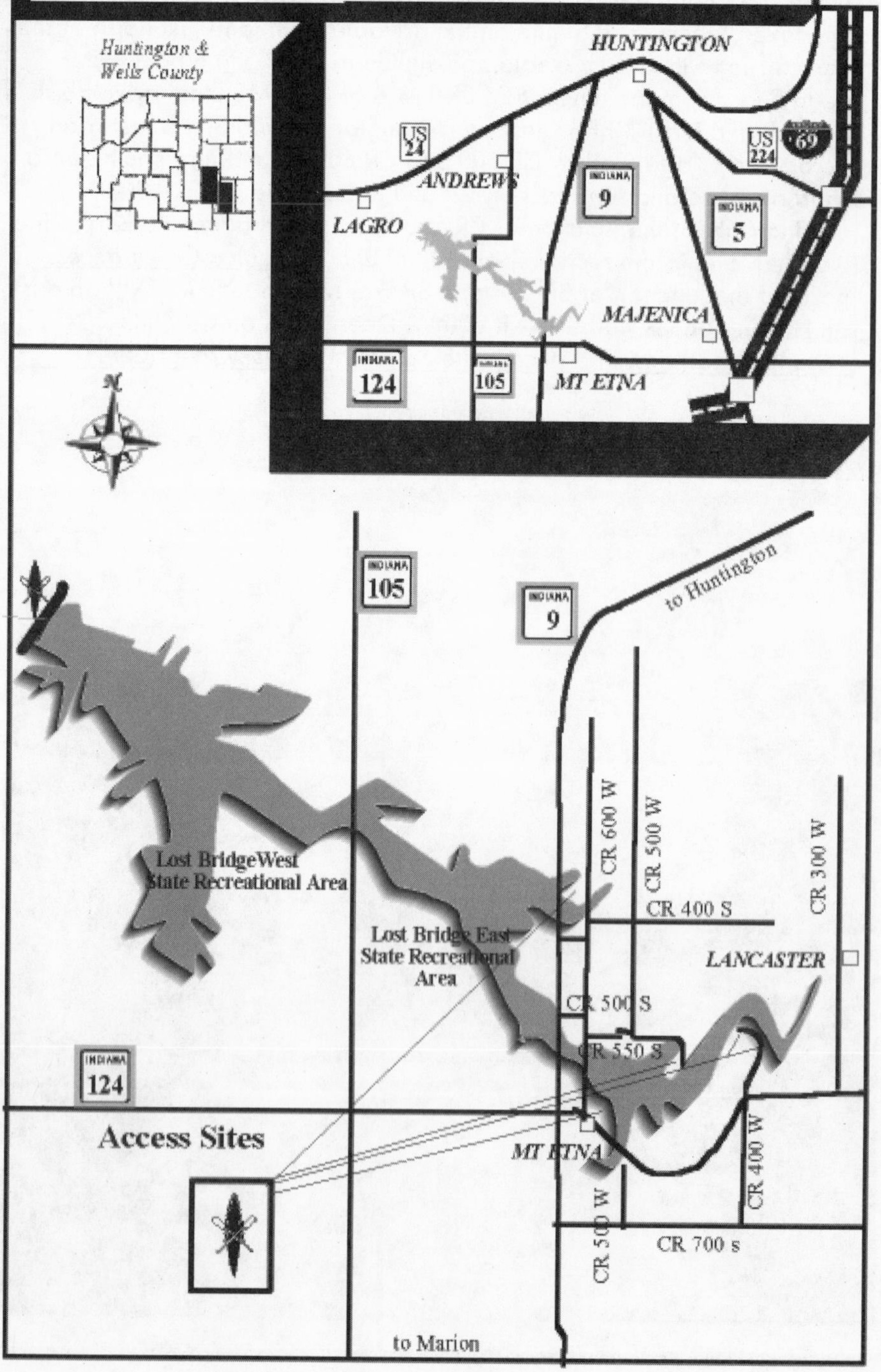

MISSISSINEWA LAKE

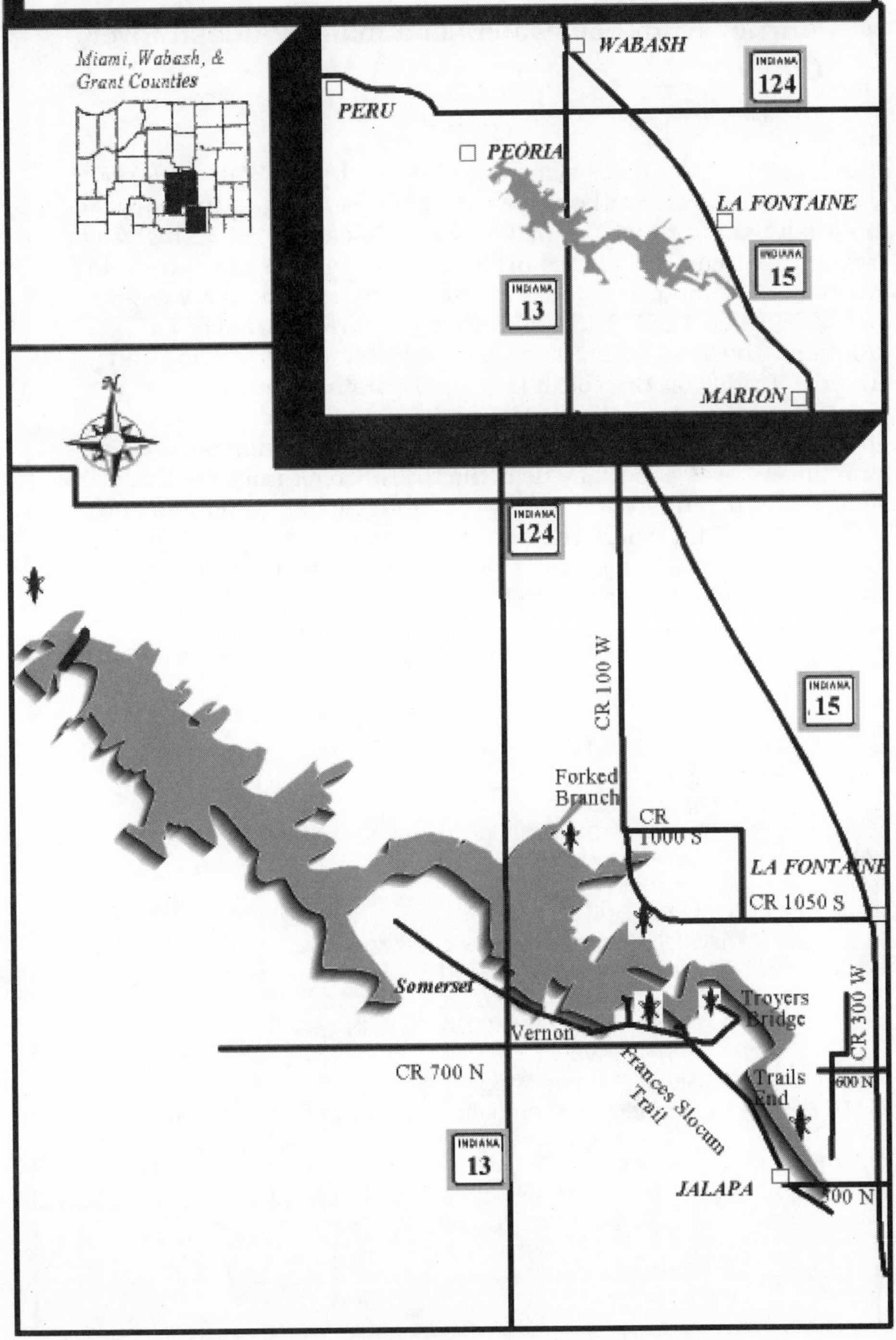

Miami, Wabash, & Grant Counties
WABASH
INDIANA 124
PERU
PEORIA
LA FONTAINE
INDIANA 15
INDIANA 13
MARION
INDIANA 124
CR 100 W
INDIANA 15
Forked Branch
CR 1000 S
LA FONTAINE
CR 1050 S
CR 300 W
Somerset
Troyers Bridge
Vernon
CR 700 N
Frances Slocum Trail
Trails End
600 N
INDIANA 13
JALAPA
500 N

41. MISSISSINEWA LAKE

- Journey calm backwaters of a major Wabash River tributary

The largest of the "three sister lakes" of the upper Wabash River country, Mississinewa Lake offers remote paddling in the no-wake-no-wash fishing zone. The paddling area is east of SR 13 highway bridge, upstream to Troyers Bridge and up against the current to about Trail's End access near Jalapa. There are five carry down access sites east of SR 13 and Somerset: Forked Branch, La Fontaine and Trail's End lie on the north bank and Vernon and Troyer's Bridge on the south bank. LaFontaine access site is considered the best with central positioning and ease of access; located west of SR 15 and LaFontaine. Wooded peninsulas, islands and finger coves especially near the Grant Creek inlet are admirable features. A trip upstream to Troyer's Bridge (old foundation) and beyond to a point where the current becomes too strong near Trail's End, makes a half a day trip. Consider paddling from the dam and tailwater Peoria fishing site to the Wabash River and Peru during the winter drawdown, (mid-September to December).

USGS MAP(S): Peoria, Somerset, LaFontaine 1:24,000
VICINITY: Peru, Miami County,
Marion, Grant County,
Wabash, Wabash County
LAKE ACREAGE /DEPTH: 3,210 a./65'
PADDLING TIME: 1 hour to full day
LEVEL OF DIFFICULTY: Class I
HAZARDS/PORTAGES: hidden snags, wind, seasonal hunting
INFO SOURCES: Mississinewa Lake DNR, Rt. #1, Box 194, Peru, IN 46970 (765) 473-6528, US Army Corps of Engineers, Rt#1, Box 202A, Peru, IN 46970 (765) 473-9745
AREA OUTFITTERS/LIVERIES: none listed, try local marinas
GAMEFISH SPECIES: bluegill, largemouth, smallmouth & white bass, white crappie, channel catfish, carp
CAMPING: Mississinewa Lake, (765) 473-6528, Class A & C
MEDICAL ASSISTANCE: Duke Memorial Hospital, 275 W. 12th St., Peru, IN 46970, (765) 473-6621

ACCESS: Five access sites (carry down) east of SR 13 and Somerset & west of SR 15 & LaFontaine: Forked Branch access-Wabash CR 1000 S & CR 100 W, west to lake. South of the model airplane flying field. Views of the SR 13 hwy bridge. LaFontaine access-west of LaFontaine and SR 15 via Wabash CR 1050 S. Good midpoint access & wildlife viewing area. Halfway between Troyers Bridge and SR 13 hwy bridge. No-wash no-wake zone. Trails End access-west of SR 15 near Jalapa. Behaves like a river at this point. Good take-out access for Mississinewa River trips. From SR 15 go W on Grant CR 600 N to CR 300 W, south to access, south of LaFontaine. Near historic site 1812 Battle of Mississinewa. Vernon and Hogback access-east of Somerset and north of Frances Slocum Trail Road on Wabash CR 25 E. Near 2 peninsulas along a gravel access road that ends in water. Troyers Bridge access-most remote site. Between Somerset and Jalapa, east of the Frances Slocum Trail. Bridge no longer exists. Carry down a slippery mud bank.

Mississinewa Cove

42. SUMMIT LAKE

- Poke around backwaters of east central Indiana's newest state park

Summit Lake is the major feature of Indiana's 19th state park. Established in 1988, 800-acre Summit Lake was formed by damming Big Blue River and other smaller tributaries such as Brown Run and Seerington Ditch. The eastern backwaters of the lake make the best paddling. Wildlife appears in the dead standing tree snags of the finger coves. Early morning or early evening is the best time to be out on the water. The wetlands east of Henry CR 500 E are off limits to floaters. The backwaters range from 5 to 20 feet deep and the bottom is a mix of clay, gravel, sand and muck. Use the boat launch at the northeast end of the lake for least traffic of the three launches. The reservoir is popular with small boat (idle speed) fishermen. A foggy morning adds to the experience. The surrounding old herbaceous meadows make the skies seem more spacious. Summit Lake also has a lifeguard beach (Memorial Day to Labor Day), seasonal canoe rental, picnicking and camping available. Entrance fee and launch fee during the summer season. Due north ten miles is Prairie Creek Reservoir, which is administered by the city of Muncie Park Department but owned by the Indiana Water Company. This 1,252-acre stream-fed lake has launching and camping facilities on the east shore at Delaware CR 560 E and CR 450 S, north of the beach. Paddling is best mid to late fall on this popular lake.

USGS MAP(S): Mt. Pleasant 1:24,000
VICINITY: Mount Summit, Henry County
LAKE ACREAGE /DEPTH: 835 a./60'
PADDLING TIME: 2 hour to half day
LEVEL OF DIFFICULTY: Class I
HAZARDS/PORTAGES: snags, wind, motor boats (idle speed only)
INFO SOURCES: Summit Lake State Park, Rt# 4, Box 33c,
New Castle, IN, 47362 (765) 766-5873
AREA OUTFITTERS/LIVERIES: Seasonal concessionaire at beach
GAMEFISH SPECIES: bluegill, channel catfish, perch, sunfish
largemouth bass, redear, crappie, carp
CAMPING: Summit Lake State Park, (765) 766-5873, Class A
Prairie Creek Reservoir, (765) 747- 4776, Class A & C
MEDICAL ASSISTANCE: Henry County Memorial Hospital, 1000
North 16th Street, New Castle, IN 47362
(765) 521-0890

ACCESS: Summit Lake State Park is located four miles north and east of New Castle. Take SR 3 north to Mount Summit and turn east onto U S 36 near Mooreland. Go east about two miles to Henry CR 600 N and turn north. The entrance is at CR 600 N and Messick Road. The three launch sites are located in the campground (for campers only), the Harvey Shelter picnic area access, and the recommended launch north of the beach area. County roads 75 N and 500 E access the north and west portions of the park (no boat access).

SUMMIT LAKE

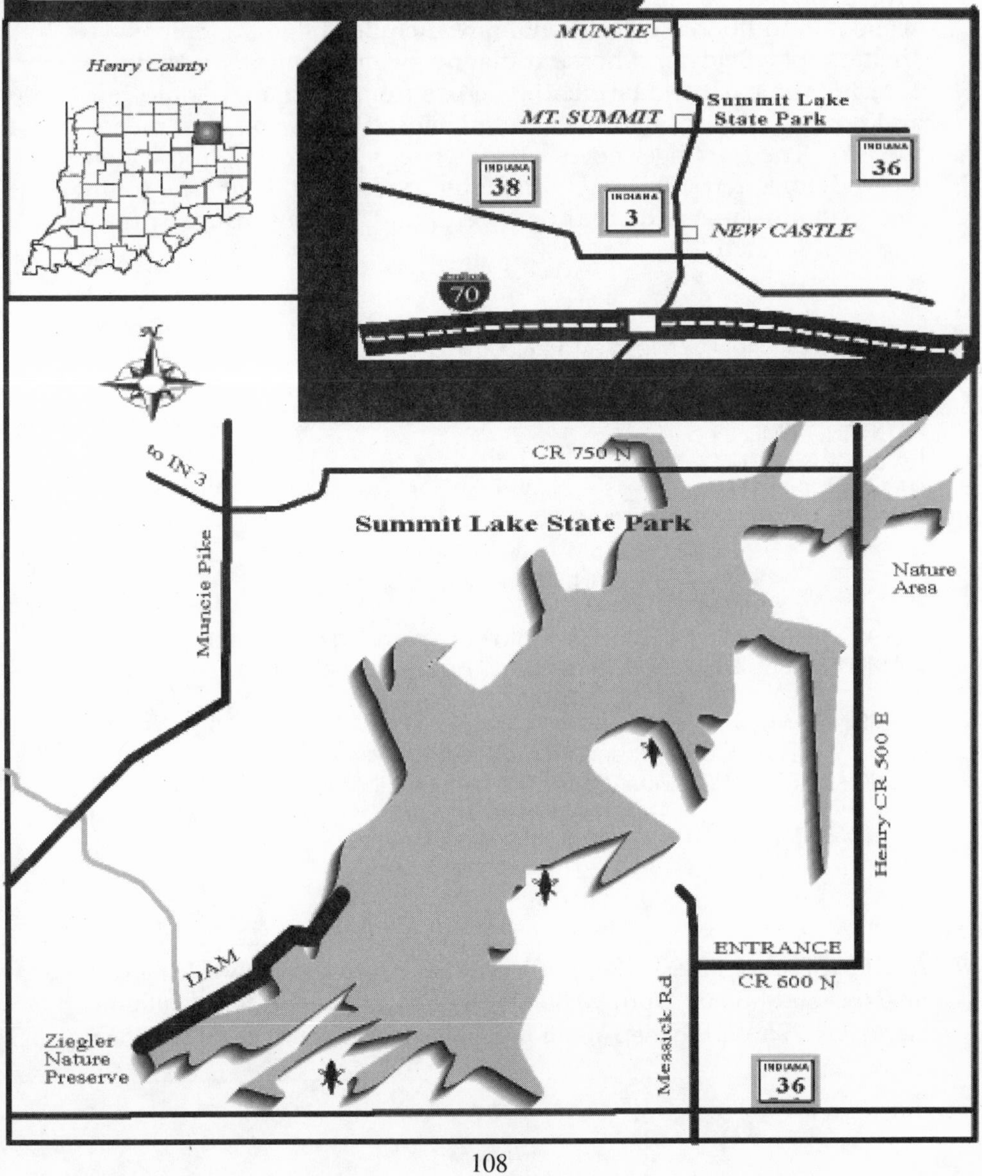

43. WESTWOOD LAKE

- Acquaint yourself with "Raintree County"

Westwood Lake and Park has been owned and operated by the Big Blue River Conservancy District since its beginning in 1974. The 630-acre park's main attraction is the 180 lake, formed by an earthen dam across Westwood Run, a small tributary to Big Blue River. The park is open all year for canoeing but camping is seasonal. Additional recreational fare includes hiking, picnic shelters, playfields and horse trails (no swimming beach). Upon entering the park and launching across from the dam, paddle east and north to the scenic upper waters where Westwood Run meets the lake. The few finger coves provide cozy spots to rest and watch for wildlife. Electric trolling is the limit (no motor boats). The rolling wooded landscape adds to the peaceful and scenic setting. Entrance and boat launch fees.

USGS MAP(S): New Castle West 1:24,000
VICINITY: New Castle, Henry County
LAKE ACREAGE /DEPTH: 180 a./40'
PADDLING TIME: 2 hours
LEVEL OF DIFFICULTY: Class I
HAZARDS/PORTAGES: none
INFO SOURCES: Westwood Park
1900 S CR 275 W
New Castle, IN, 47362
(765) 521-0890
AREA OUTFITTERS/LIVERIES: none, rentals are planned at Westwood
GAMEFISH SPECIES: bluegill, largemouth bass, channel catfish, redear, crappie.
CAMPING: Westwood Park (May 1-October 31) at Point Campground (765) 766-5873 Class A
MEDICAL ASSISTANCE: Henry County Memorial Hospital
1000 N 16th Street
New Castle, IN 47362
(765) 521-0890

ACCESS: From I-70 exit 123, north on SR 3 & drive to New Castle & the intersection of SR 38. Turn W on SR 38 and go 2.5 mi & turn south on Henry CR 275 W. Proceed south two miles to the entrance at the road curve.

WESTWOOD LAKE

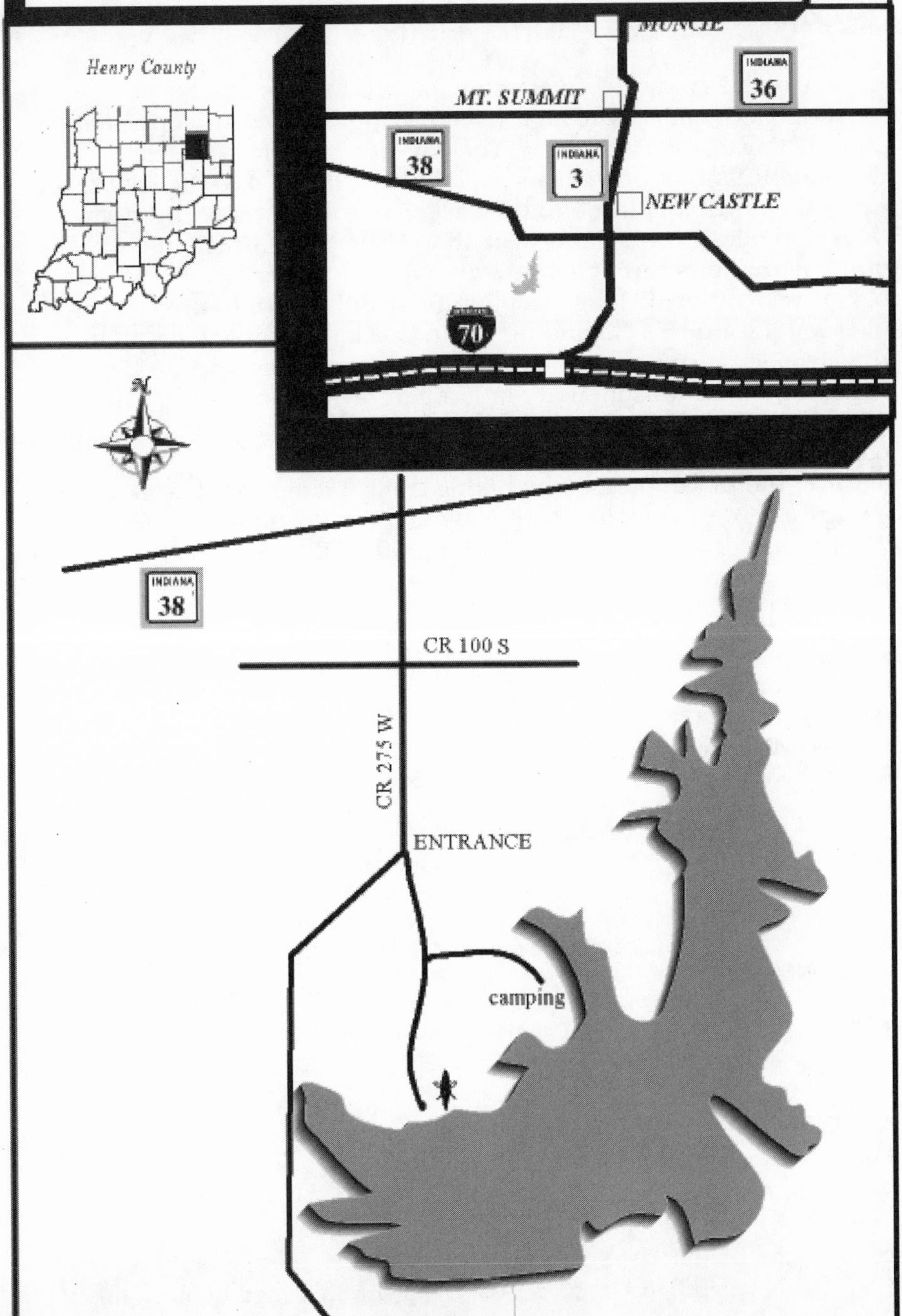

44. EAGLE CREEK RESERVOIR

- Drift on liquid wildness at the edge of Indiana's Capitol City

Eagle Creek Park, the former estate of J.K. Lilly, is nearly surrounded by interstate highways. It is now owned and operated by Indy Parks and Recreation. The day-use park had densely wooded bluffs that provide a scenic buffer from I-74 to the south, I-65 to the north and I-465 to the east. There are several finger coves to explore along the upland west shore. The Shoal Creek inlet, west of the dam, flows through a 297-acre nature preserve of deciduous old growth situated along steep bluffs. Paddle north to the backwaters, under I-65 and up Eagle Creek or Fishback Creek to the stronger current or shallows. Boating is off limits within the 125-acre waterfowl sanctuary (a former gravel pit) near the 71st Street, North Gate. Paddleboats only on the five acre Lilly Lake. The park closes at dusk. Although the 1,350-acre reservoir is the main feature, the urban park offers hiking trails, picnicking, playgrounds, a nature center and small fishing ponds. Entry and launch fees. Electric motors only. No boats within 500' of the dam

USGS MAP(S): Zionsville, Clermont, 1:24,000
VICINITY: Indianapolis, Marion County
LAKE ACREAGE /DEPTH: 1,350 a./40'
PADDLING TIME: 2 hours
LEVEL OF DIFFICULTY: Class I
HAZARDS/PORTAGES: wind, traffic
INFO SOURCES: Eagle Creek Park, 7840 W. 56th Street, Indianapolis, IN 46254 (317) 327-7110
Nature Center (317) 327-7148
AREA OUTFITTERS/LIVERIES: Seasonal boat rental at marina along Dandy Trail (317) 327-7130
GAMEFISH SPECIES: bluegill, largemouth bass, channel catfish, striped bass, redear, white crappie, carp
CAMPING: Shades State Park, Rt#1, Box 72, Waveland, IN 47989 (765) 435-2810, Class B
MEDICAL ASSISTANCE: St. Vincent Hospitals & Health, 3400 Lafayette Rd., Indianapolis, IN 46222 (317) 290-3626

ACCESS: Eagle Creek Reservoir & Park are located on the northwest side of Indianapolis, west of I-465 between I-65 to the north and I-74 to the south. Access is from 38th Street (exit 17, I-465), 56th street (exit 19, northbound only I-465) and 71st Street (exit 124, I-65). Canoes and kayaks may be launched near the Ranger Station (best site) or at the 42nd Street ramp. Trailered boats can only be launched at the 42nd Street access.

EAGLE CREEK RESERVOIR

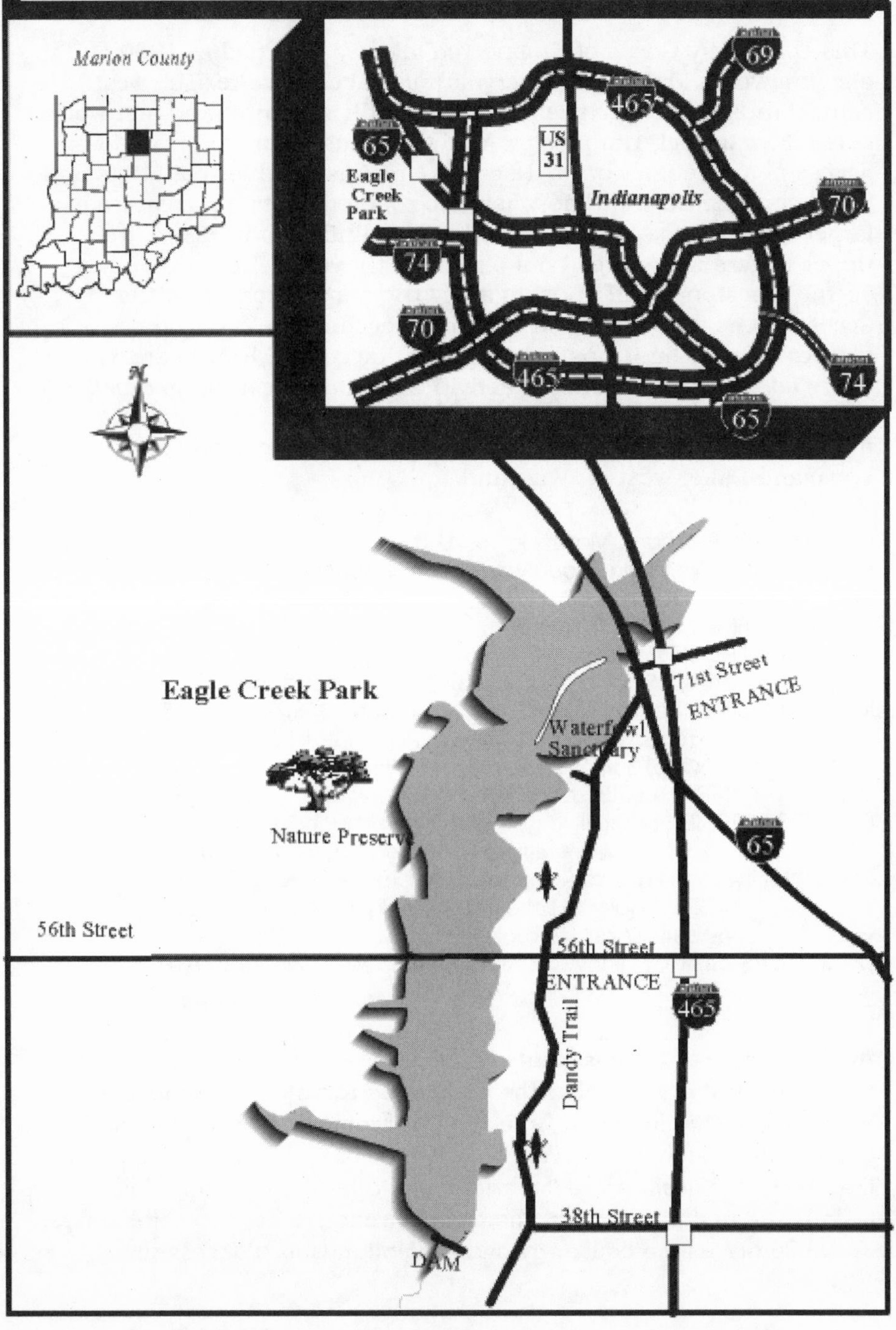

Marion County
69
465
US 31
65
Eagle Creek Park
Indianapolis
70
74
70
465
65
74
Eagle Creek Park
Waterfowl Sanctuary
71st Street
ENTRANCE
Nature Preserve
65
56th Street
56th Street
ENTRANCE
465
Dandy Trail
38th Street
DAM

45. CECIL M. HARDEN LAKE

- Withdraw to the upper reservoir reaches & Big Raccoon Creek

This U.S. Army Corps of Engineered lake was opened in 1960 and is also known as Mansfield Reservoir and Raccoon Lake. The west central Indiana property is about evenly divided into land and water acres. Five launch ramps surround the lake but only Portland Mills access near the inlet of Big Raccoon Creek is ideal for canoeists and kayakers. The no-wake-no-wash idle zone provides a retreat from larger motorized vessels. Depending on rainfall and season, the upper waters may spread out and flood the adjacent woodland. A scenic limestone bluff appears along the north shore from the access to the first upstream bend of Raccoon Creek. Logjams further up may limit upstream access. Raccoon S.R.A. near the dam offers additional recreational activities including camping. Smaller nearby lake reservoirs that are seasonally open to paddling and motorboats include Rockville Lake northeast of Rockville and Waveland Lake, west of Waveland.

USGS MAP(S): Bellmore, Mansfield 1:24,000
VICINITY: Rockville, Parke County & Putnam County
LAKE ACREAGE /DEPTH: 2,060 a./60'
PADDLING TIME: 2 hours to half day
LEVEL OF DIFFICULTY: Class I
HAZARDS/PORTAGES: wind, motorboats, ltd. hunting in season
INFO SOURCES: Cecil M. Harden Lake, Raccoon SRA, RR 1, Box 48, 160 S. Raccoon Parkway, Rockville, IN 47872 (765) 334-1412 & (765) 344-1884
AREA OUTFITTERS/LIVERIES: none listed, try marinas
GAMEFISH SPECIES: bluegill, largemouth bass, channel catfish, carp, walleye, striped bass, redear, white crappie
CAMPING: Harden Lake at Raccoon SRA, Class A, B, & C (765) 344-1412 or Rockville Lake, RR#1, Rockville, IN 47872 (765) 569-6541 (April 1-October 21)
MEDICAL ASSISTANCE: Clay County Hospital, 1206 E. National Ave Brazil, IN., 47834, (812) 448-2675

ACCESS: Harden Lake is located 50 miles west of Indianapolis and nine miles east of Rockville. The best canoe ramp is the Portland Mills access where Big Raccoon Creek enters. From US 36 near the Parke and Putnam county line, go north on Putnam CR 1170 about 2.5 miles to the access site, just before the bridge and after the Portland Mills historic site and picnic area. The main entrance to Raccoon SRA is west on US 36 across the causeway and the Hollandsburg access site.

CECIL M. HARDEN LAKE

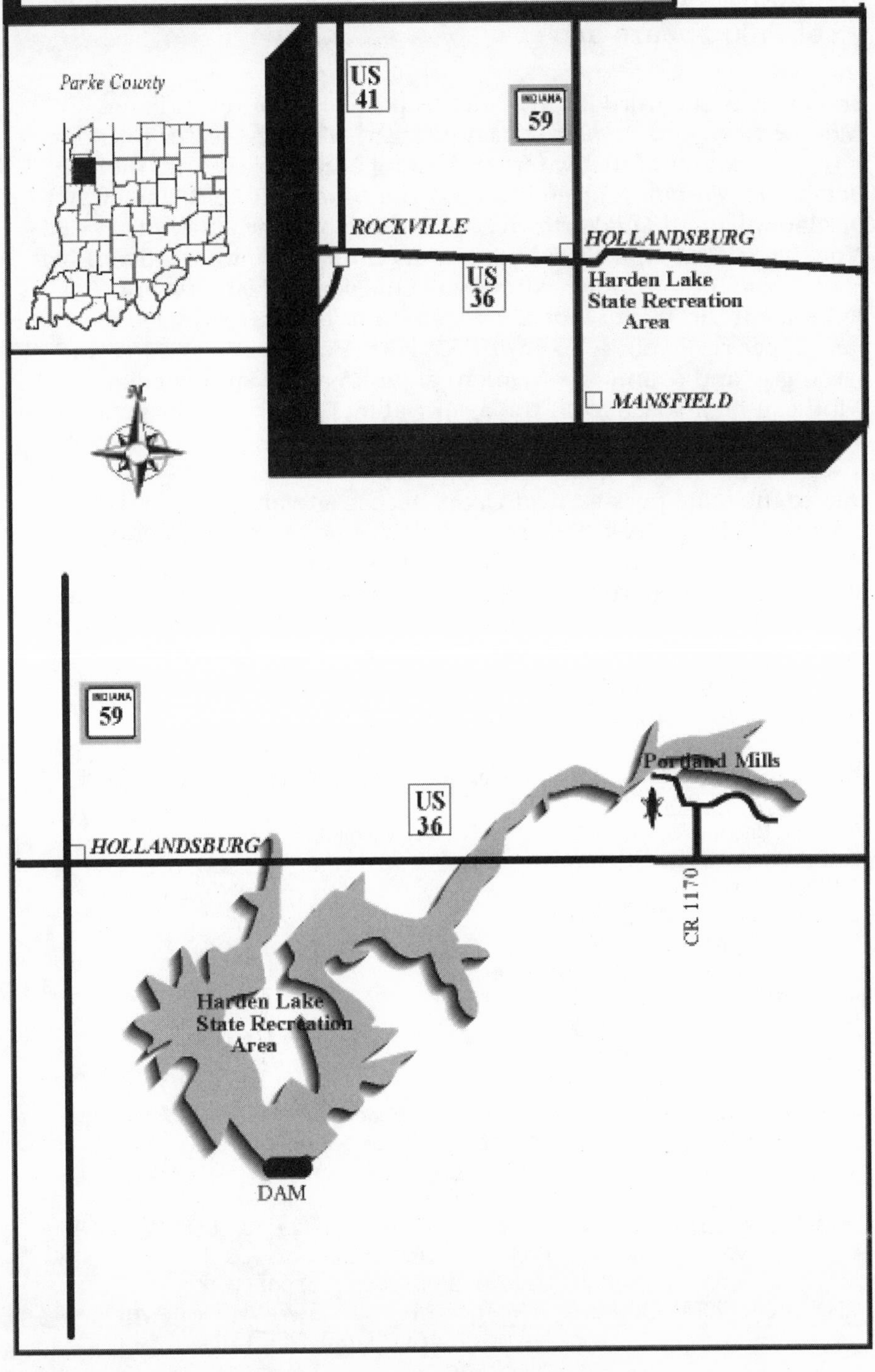

46. BROOKVILLE LAKE

- Paddle former haunts of prehistoric Mound Builders of 7,000 years ago

Brookville is the third largest and deepest reservoir in Indiana. (Monroe Lake and Patoka Lake are larger). The best water to explore is the backwater of the waterfowl resting area (closed from mid-October to March). It stretches from the Union CR 75 S causeway to Dunlapsville and Quakertown SRA north along the shore of Whitewater State Park, and upstream on the Whitewater River East Fork to the SR 44 bridge. Numerous snags, small islands and coves lie between the Treaty Line access south to the open waters of this vast upper reservoir; a lake within a lake. Birdlife such as heron, egret, gull and osprey are frequent sight on a late summer day. Wind can be a struggle on the open water. The lake teems with power boaters on weekends.
A suggested route begins at Treaty Line access and floats south and east to the state park's Silver Creek access site and beyond to the mouth of Silver Creek. Return is along the same route. In addition to paddling, Brookville Lake offers waterskiing, swimming beach, playgrounds, sheltered picnicking, seasonal naturalist, and hiking at Mounds SRA and Quakertown SRA (access SR 101, then west at CR 75 S). Fully developed Whitewater State Park offers a canoeable 199-acre Whitewater Lake with access to Brookville Lake and boats may be rented. Fine family adventure.

USGS MAP(S): Everton, New Fairfield, Brookville, Whitcomb,
Liberty1:24,000
VICINITY: Brookville, Franklin County & Liberty, Union County
LAKE ACREAGE /DEPTH: 5,260 a./116′
PADDLING TIME: 3 hours
LEVEL OF DIFFICULTY: Class I
HAZARDS/PORTAGES: snags, shallow water, wind, motorboats,
hunting in season
INFO SOURCES: Brookville Lake DNR
P.O. Box 100
Brookville, IN 47012
(765) 647-2657 & 2658
AREA OUTFITTERS/LIVERIES: none listed, try marinas
GAMEFISH SPECIES: bluegill, largemouth bass, channel catfish,
striped bass, walleye, crappie, carp,
muskellunge, trout at tailwater
CAMPING: Quakertown SRA, Mounds SRA (765) 647-2657& 2658, Class AA&A
Whitewater State Park, (765) 458-5565, Class A & B
Franklin Co. Park, US 52 at Brookville (765) 647-4422
MEDICAL ASSISTANCE: Fayette Memorial Hospital, 1941 Virginia Ave.
Connersville, IN 47331 (765) 825-5131

ACCESS: There are ten access sites around Brookville Lake however the best for small watercraft is at the Treaty Line access in the backwaters where river meets reservoir. To reach Treaty Line access, drive west from Liberty on SR 44 about 5 miles and cross the highway bridge over the Whitewater River East Fork entrance at SR 101 and turn left at the first road. Go south & turn east near the dead end & proceed to the Treaty Line access site. Mounds SRA access SR 101.

BROOKVILLE LAKE

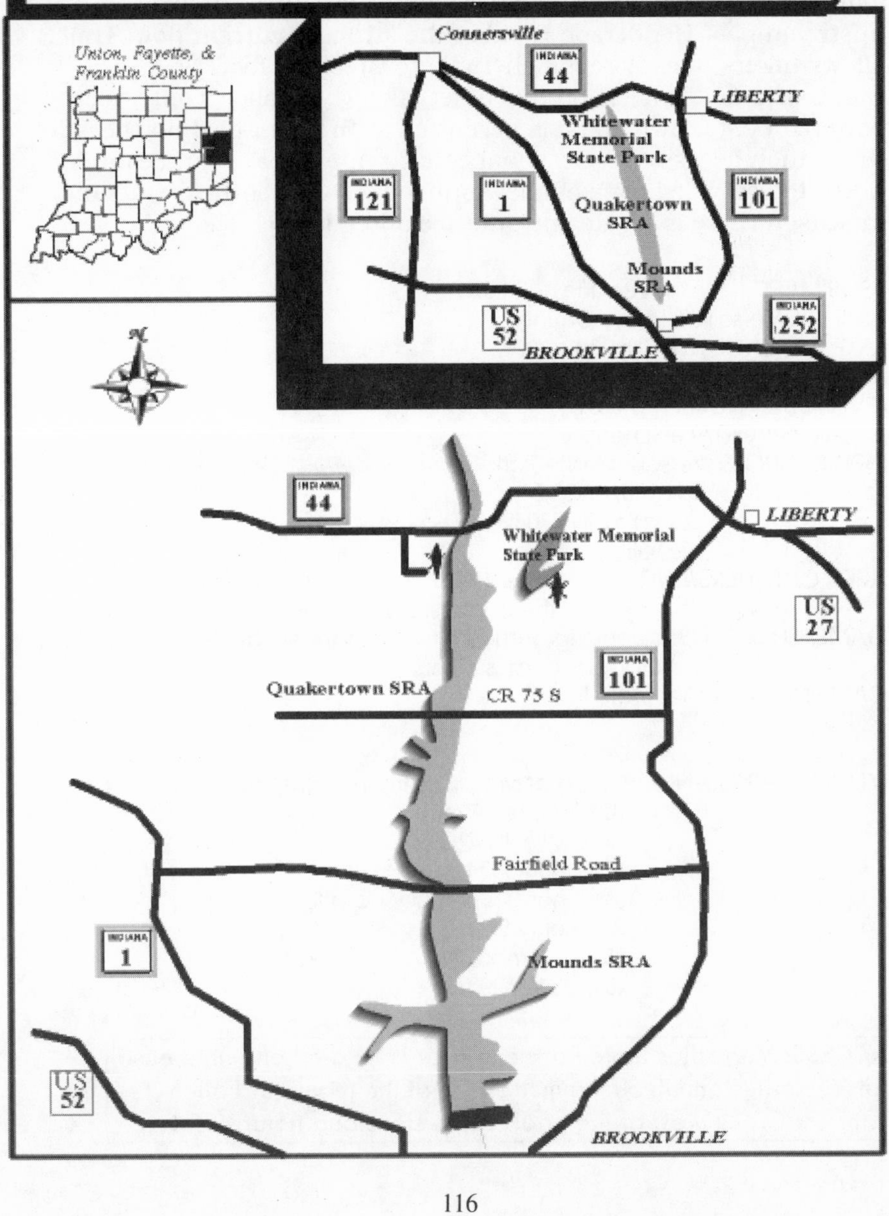

47. VERSAILLES LAKE

• Jaunt from lake to creek & back

Laughrey Creek, Cedar Creek, and Fallen Timbers Creek are the main contributors to Versailles Lake, the heart of Versailles State Park. There are open water and scenic bluffs looking south towards the dam. Cedar Creek and Fallen Timbers Creek are too shallow for inspection far beyond its' mouth. However, Laugherey Creek, the main inlet stream, allows paddlers to venture about a mile upstream past Henderson Bend to the stronger current flow. Trail 3 allows hikers to explore Fallen Timbers Creek on foot. No fear of wakes and motor noise on this quiet lake which allows only electric powered boats. Swimming is permitted at the park pool northeast of the launch access site. Seasonal canoe rental. Year round camping. Never too crowded. One of a few public lakes in southeast Indiana. In season there is a gate entrance fee and a launch fee.

USGS MAP(S): Milan, Versailles 1:24,000
VICINITY: Versailles, Ripley County
LAKE ACREAGE /DEPTH: 230 a./30'
PADDLING TIME: 2 hours
LEVEL OF DIFFICULTY: Class I
HAZARDS/PORTAGES: none
INFO SOURCES: Versailles State Park
Box 205, US 50 E
Versailles, IN 47042
(812) 689-6424
AREA OUTFITTERS/LIVERIES: boat rentals at the launch ramp, west of the camp store
GAMEFISH SPECIES: bluegill, largemouth bass, channel catfish, crappie, carp, suckers
CAMPING: Versailles State Park
Class A
(812) 689-6424
MEDICAL ASSISTANCE: Margaret Mary Community Hospital
321 Mitchell Ave.
Batesville, IN 47006
(765) 934-6624
Jennings Community Hospital
301 Henry St.
North Vernon, IN 47265
(812) 346-6200

ACCESS: Versailles State Park entrance is located one mile east of Versailles on US 50. Launch site is at the mouth of Fallen Timbers Creek west of the pool, camp store and nature center.

VERSAILLES LAKE

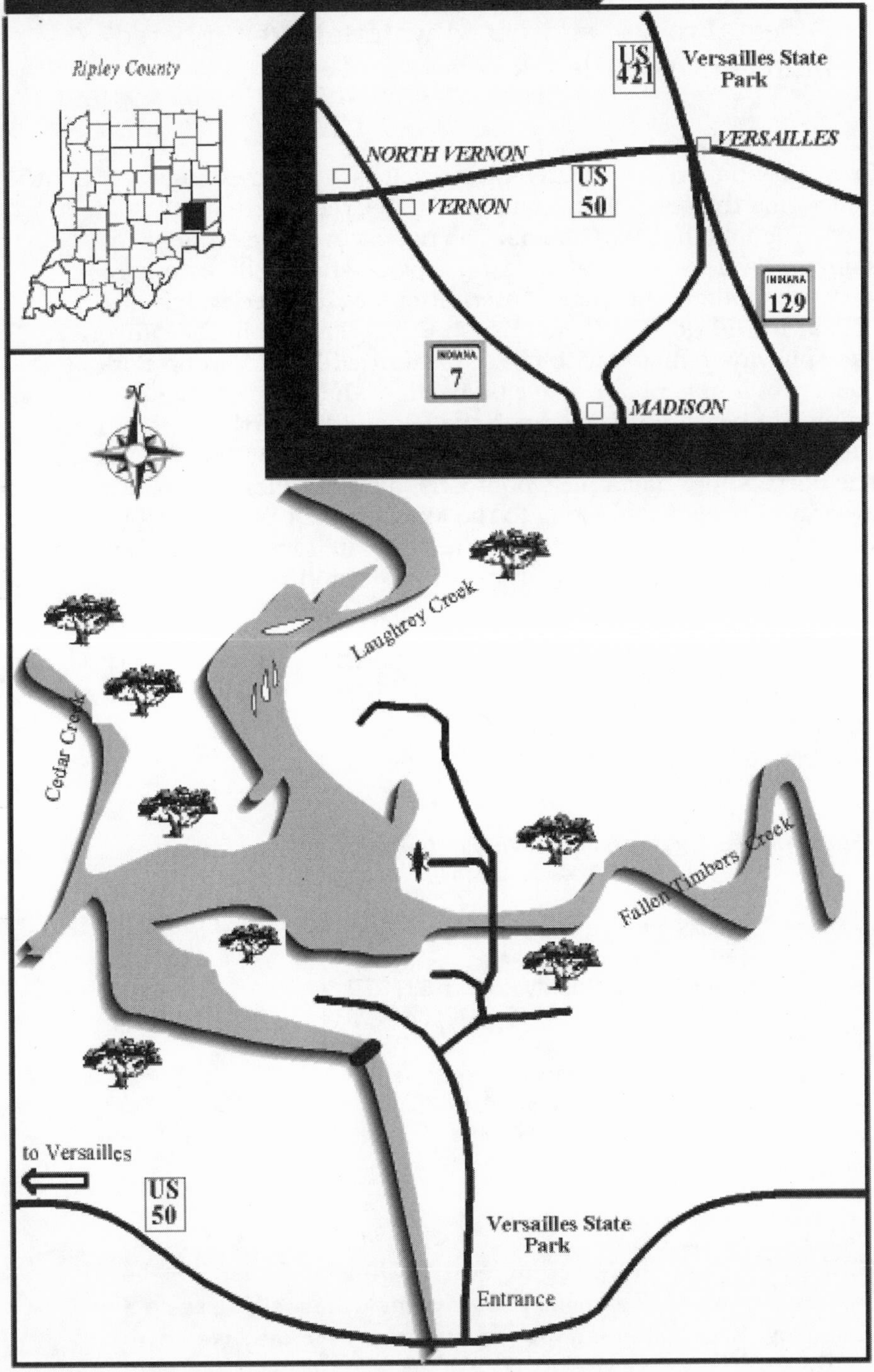
Ripley County
US 421
Versailles State Park
VERSAILLES
NORTH VERNON
VERNON
US 50
INDIANA 129
INDIANA 7
MADISON
N
Laughrey Creek
Cedar Creek
Fallen Timbers Creek
to Versailles
US 50
Versailles State Park
Entrance

48. BRUSH CREEK RESERVOIR

- **Pedestal rocks, staircased waterfalls & timbered bluffs envelop the lake**

Crescent-shaped Brush Creek Reservoir is a picturesque water body that forms the south boundary of Brush Creek Fish and Wildlife Area. The lake has two basins. The narrow west basin near the spillway dam has several pedestal or vase-shaped limestone rock formations along the shore. Intermittent, staircased waterfalls appear in the wooded coves. Brush Creek flows from the canyon-like spillway to merge with the Muscatatuck River Vernon Fork, a quarter of a mile north. The east basin of the reservoir has open water. Timbered bluffs overlook the lake to the north. Brush Creek enters at the east inlet. Cormorants may be seen in late summer. The north shore has a pier, pontoons, a picnic shelter, observation tower and trails that belong to the Muscatatuck State School located nearby. The level access site is located in a protected north to south finger cove, south shore, at lake's mid-point.

USGS MAP(S): Butlerville 1:24,000
VICINITY: Butlerville, Jennings County
LAKE ACREAGE /DEPTH: 267 a. /32'
PADDLING TIME: 2-3 hours
LEVEL OF DIFFICULTY: Class I
HAZARDS/PORTAGES: snags
INFO SOURCES: Crosley Fish and Wildlife Area, 2010 S SR 3,
North Vernon, IN 47265 (812) 346-5596
AREA OUTFITTERS/LIVERIES: none
GAMEFISH SPECIES: bluegill, redear, largemouth bass, catfish,
crappie, suckers
CAMPING: Muscatatuck County Park, 325 N SR 7 & 3
North Vernon, IN 47265 (812) 346-2953
MEDICAL ASSISTANCE: Jennings Community Hospital
301 Henry Street
North Vernon, IN 47265
(812) 346-6200

ACCESS: From North Vernon go east on US 50 to Butlerville, then drive north one mile on CR Jennings 550 E to the access site. Use caution on the narrow, steep, winding, paved access road to the lake cove.

BRUSH CREEK RESERVOIR

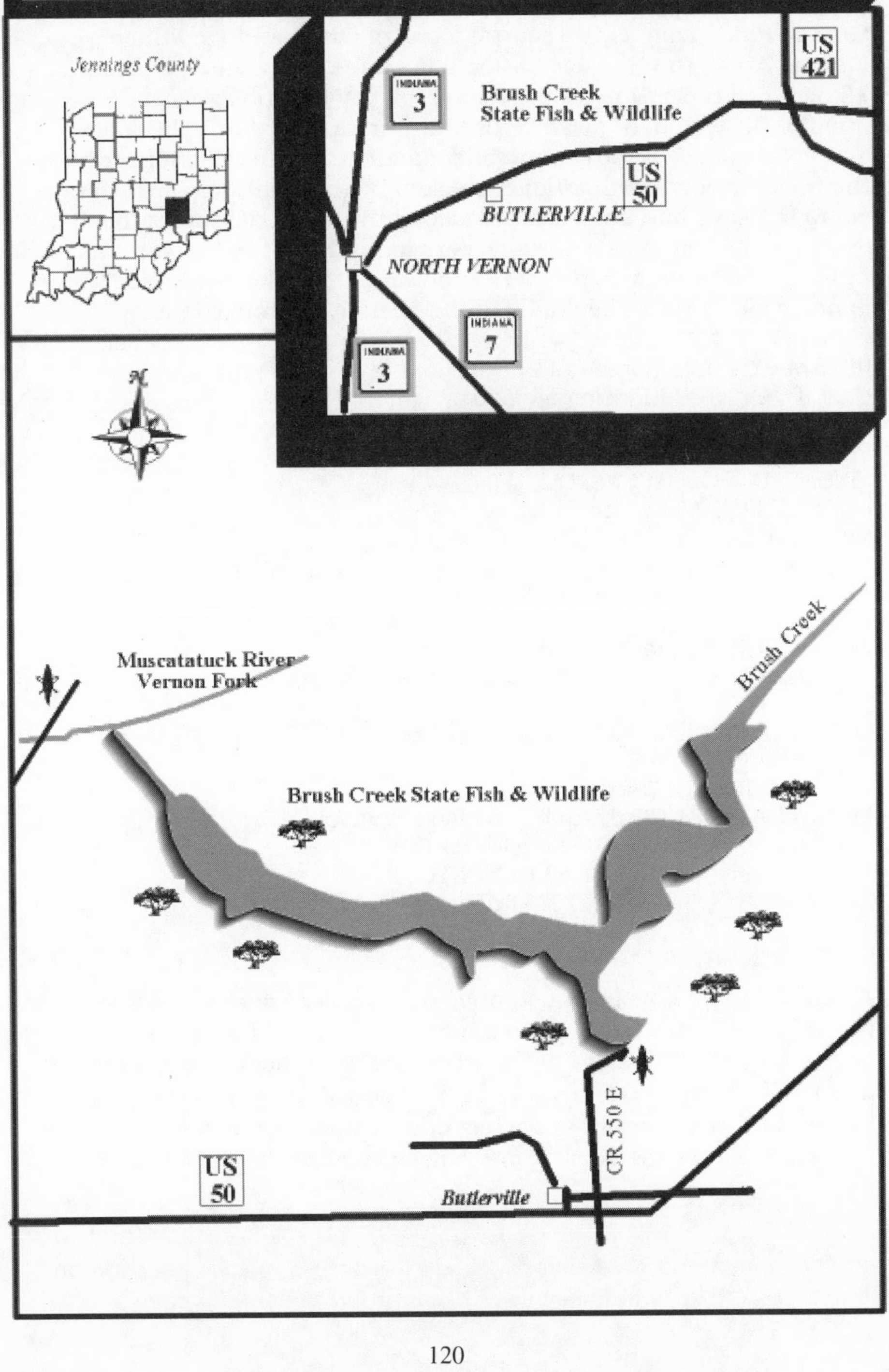
Jennings County
Indiana 3
Brush Creek
State Fish & Wildlife
US 421
US 50
BUTLERVILLE
NORTH VERNON
Indiana 7
Indiana 3
N
Muscatatuck River
Vernon Fork
Brush Creek
Brush Creek State Fish & Wildlife
CR 550 E
US 50
Butlerville

49. GROUSE RIDGE LAKE

• Canoe & camp in southern Indiana hill country

Grouse Ridge Lake is the central focus of Grouse Ridge Public Fishing Area. The Hoosier National Forest is a few miles west of the 26 acre reservoir. It is off the main highway and has a sleepy quality. Buttonbush, swamp rose, buttercup, silver maple, willow and cottonwood hug the shoreline. Paddle the curving shore edge of the finger coves. Fish the lake, stocked by the DNR, for dinner and camp in peace and semi-solitude along the shaded north ridge that overlooks the lake. The outlet waters join White Creek about half a mile east of the dam. The average depth of the lake is 15 feet. There is no drinking water available in the primitive campground.

USGS MAP(S): Waymansville 1:24,000
VICINITY: Ogilville, Bartholomew County
LAKE ACREAGE /DEPTH: 26 a./31′
PADDLING TIME: 45 minutes
LEVEL OF DIFFICULTY: Class I
HAZARDS/PORTAGES: none, electric motors only
INFO SOURCES: Crosley Fish and Wildlife Area
2010 South St., SR 3
North Vernon, IN 47265
(812) 346-5596
AREA OUTFITTERS/LIVERIES: none
GAMEFISH SPECIES: bluegill, largemouth bass, channel catfish, redear, crappie
CAMPING: Grouse Ridge Public Fishing Area
(812) 346-5596
10 Class C sites
MEDICAL ASSISTANCE: Columbus Regional Hospital
2075 Lincoln Park Dr.
Columbus, IN 47201
(812) 376-8292

ACCESS: From I-65 exit 64 and drive west and south on SR 58 through North Ogilville and Ogilville to Bartholomew CR 525 S and turn west. Follow CR 525 S 0.5 miles to CR 700 W and turn south. Continue south on CR 700 W about 0.5 miles to the marked entrance on the west side of the road. There are two concrete boat ramps: one on the north shore and one on the south shore. Fifteen miles southwest of Columbus.

GROUSE RIDGE LAKE

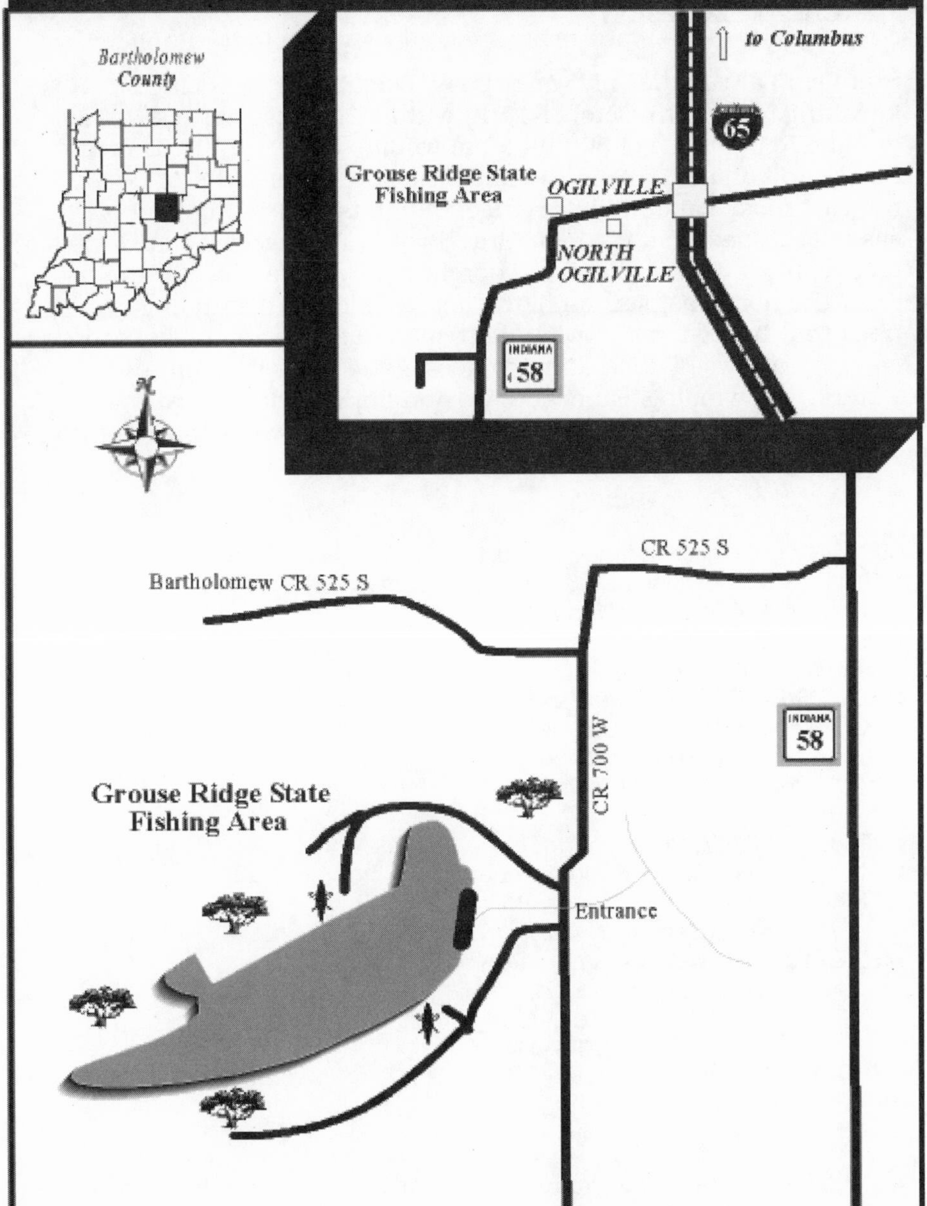
Bartholomew
County
to Columbus
65
Grouse Ridge State
Fishing Area
OGILVILLE
NORTH
OGILVILLE
INDIANA
58
CR 525 S
Bartholomew CR 525 S
CR 700 W
INDIANA
58
Grouse Ridge State
Fishing Area
Entrance

50. STANFIELD LAKE

- **Bring binoculars on this aquatic national wildlife refuge excursion**

Stanfield Lake is the only water body available for canoeing or kayaking (May 15th-October 15th) within the Muscatatuck National Wildlife Refuge, one of 500 national wildlife refuges in the United States and one of three in Indiana. The lake is located just east of the vast Moss Lake (wildlife refuge, off limits for boating) and is easily accessed from the main gravel road. The level vegetated landscape of the surrounding shoreline provides a place to stop and rest. The northeast section of the lake is filled with standing dead trees that harbor waterfowl and other wildlife. Diving ducks, osprey, cormorants, wood duck, Canada geese, and coots frequent the waters. The winding, canoeable Vernon Fork of the Muscatatuck River forms the south boundary of the refuge however there are no river access sites on the property.

USGS MAP(S): Chestnut Ridge 1:24,000
VICINITY: Seymour, Jackson & Jennings County
LAKE ACREAGE /DEPTH: 125 a./15'
PADDLING TIME: 1 hour
LEVEL OF DIFFICULTY: Class I
HAZARDS/PORTAGES: hidden snags, wind
INFO SOURCES: Muscatatuck National Wildlife Refuge
12985 East US 50
Seymour, IN 47274
(812) 522-4352
AREA OUTFITTERS/LIVERIES: none
GAMEFISH SPECIES: bluegill, largemouth bass, crappie
CAMPING: Muscatatuck County Park, 325 N SR 7,
North Vernon, IN 47265 (812) 346-2953
MEDICAL ASSISTANCE: Columbus Regional Hospital
2400 E 17th
St., Columbus, IN 47201
(812) 379-4441

ACCESS: From I-65 at Seymour exit 49 onto US 50. Drive three miles to the national wildlife refuge entrance on the south side of the highway. Travel 0.5 mile south, past the electronic gate (closes automatically at dusk) to the visitor center and bookstore. Continue south on the refuge gravel road to Stanfield Lake marked access site.

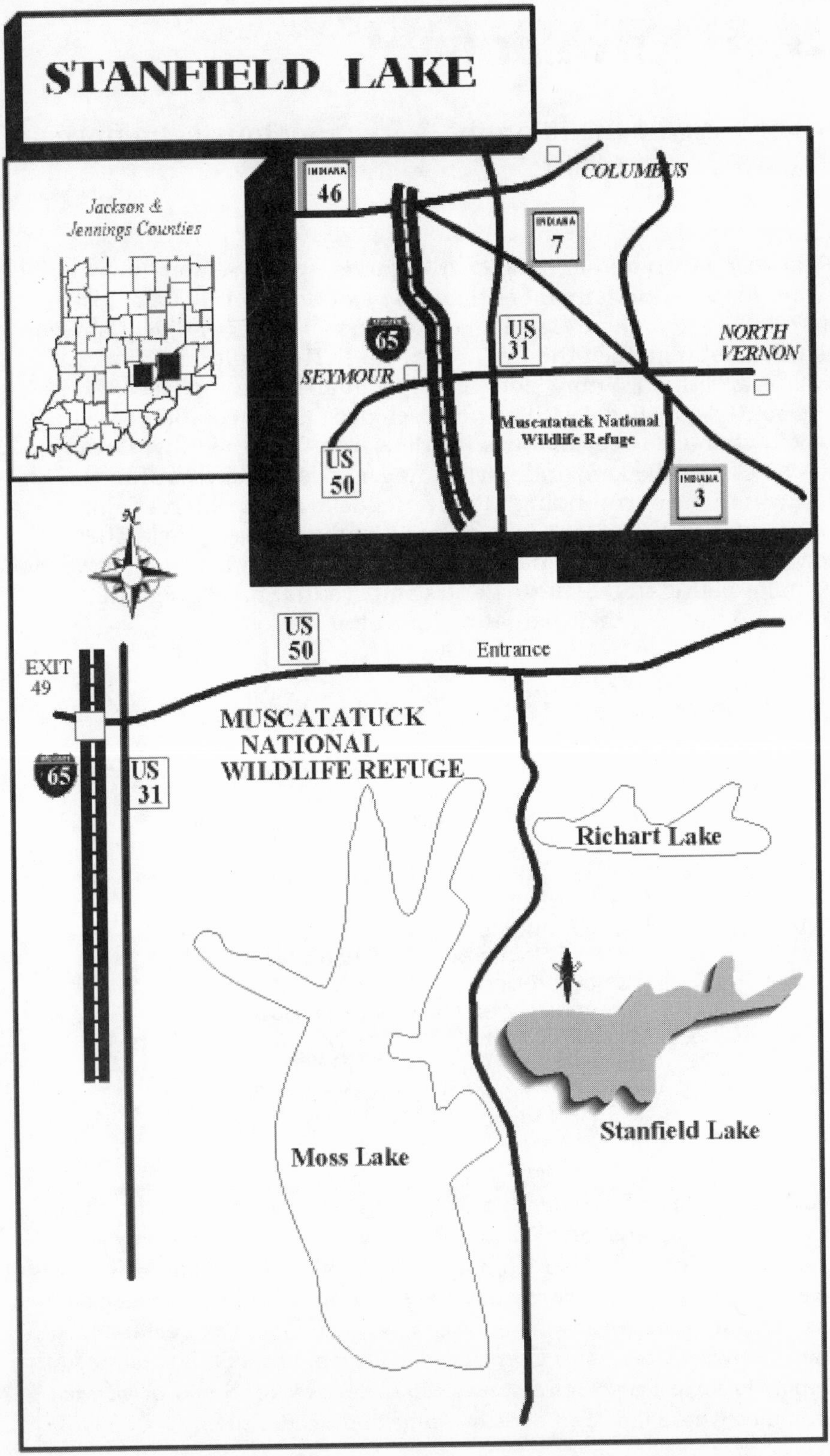
STANFIELD LAKE
Jackson &
Jennings Counties
INDIANA
46
COLUMBUS
INDIANA
7
65
US
31
NORTH
VERNON
SEYMOUR
Muscatatuck National
Wildlife Refuge
US
50
INDIANA
3
N
US
50
Entrance
EXIT
49
65
US
31
MUSCATATUCK
NATIONAL
WILDLIFE REFUGE
Richart Lake
Stanfield Lake
Moss Lake

51. HARDY LAKE

- Investigate the idle zone & its numerous calm finger coves

Quick Creek and other smaller tributaries, which seldom allow the water level to fluctuate more than one foot, feed Hardy Lake (est. 1973). The east shore Carmel boat ramp is best for paddlers since it is the most remote of the five access sites. The additional four ramps are Alpha, Sunnyside, Shore Bluff and Wooster located on the southwest shore, within the developed DNR recreation area, which charges a seasonal fee. Paddle south from the Carmel ramp and seek out the long and narrow finger coves or bays within the idle zone. The surrounding area shoreline is a mix of forest and open meadows. The lake is usually quiet during weekdays. The lower reservoir near the dam includes the swimming beach, rowboat rentals, hiking trails, marina and campground. Fishermen are expected to clean their fish at the cleaning station.

USGS MAP(S): Deputy 1:24,000
VICINITY: Austin & Deputy, Scott & Jefferson counties
LAKE ACREAGE /DEPTH: 741a./38′
PADDLING TIME: 1 hour to half day
LEVEL OF DIFFICULTY: Class I
HAZARDS/PORTAGES: wind, powerboats, waterskiing, seasonal hunting
INFO SOURCES: Hardy Lake, RR#4, Box 174, Scottsburg, IN 47170 (812) 794-3800
AREA OUTFITTERS/LIVERIES: boat rentals at Alpha launch marina & Carmel village launch area
GAMEFISH SPECIES: bluegill, redear, northern pike, bullhead, crappie, tiger muskellunge, walleye
CAMPING: Hardy Lake SRA, Class A & C (812) 265-3800
Clifty Falls State Park, Class A & C (812) 265-1331
MEDICAL ASSISTANCE: King's Daughter's Hospital, King's Daughter's Dr., Madison, IN 47250 (812) 265-5211

ACCESS: From I-65 exit 33 onto SR 256 and go east through the city of Austin. Continue east on SR 256 about five miles to the four way stop and the junction of SR 203. Turn north on Scott SR 400 E and drive about two miles to the Hardy Lake SRA entrance. There are five access sites and four are within the seasonal fee zone. The best fee-free canoe/kayak access is at Carmel launch ramp. From SR 3 south of Deputy turn west onto Jefferson CR 300 N/Blake Road and drive west two miles where the road ends in water and access site.

HARDY LAKE

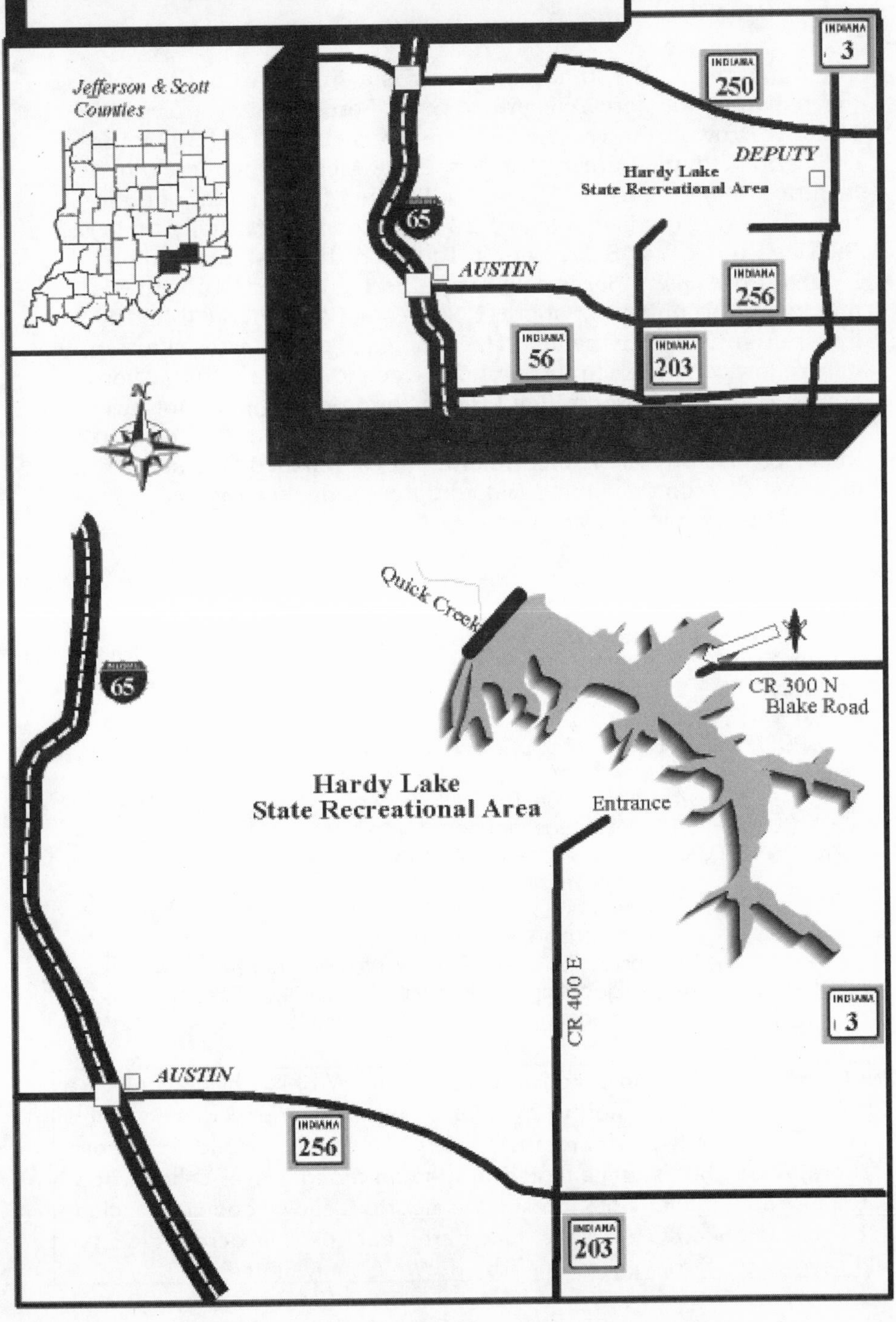

Jefferson & Scott Counties
INDIANA 3
INDIANA 250
DEPUTY
Hardy Lake State Recreational Area
65
AUSTIN
INDIANA 256
INDIANA 56
INDIANA 203
Quick Creek
CR 300 N Blake Road
65
Hardy Lake State Recreational Area
Entrance
CR 400 E
INDIANA 3
AUSTIN
INDIANA 256
INDIANA 203

52. YELLOWWOOD LAKE

- Float among water lotus amidst wooded Brown County hills

The north to south 130-acre reservoir is a small part of the extensive 23,365 acre Yellowwood State Forest that occupies western Brown County. The lake was constructed is 1939 by the CCC and WPA men during the New Deal. Most of the recreational facilities along the east shore are still intact from that era and in use. The ridge-cradled lake is 1.25 miles long with heavily timbered Bill Jack Ridge and Scarce-O-Fat Ridge on the west and Dubois Ridge on the east. A large colony of American water lotus crowds the mucky marsh northeast shore. Colonies of bats emerge from the forest at sunset over the lake. Jackson Creek, the main tributary, fills Yellowwood Lake and then flows beyond the dam to the North Fork of Salt Creek; John Floyd Hollow and Sol Pogue Hollow are significant tributaries. This is some of the most beautiful country in the Hoosier state. Nashville Indiana, an established tourist town, is just east of Yellowwood and Bloomington, a diverse Big Ten university town is due west.

USGS MAP(S): Belmont 1:24,000
VICINITY: Nashville, Brown County
LAKE ACREAGE /DEPTH: 133 a. /32'
PADDLING TIME: 2 hours
LEVEL OF DIFFICULTY: Class I
HAZARDS/PORTAGES: seasonal public hunting, electric motors only
INFO SOURCES: Yellowwood State Forest, 772 Yellowwood Lake Road, Nashville, IN 47448 (812) 988-7945
AREA OUTFITTERS/LIVERIES: seasonal boat rentals
GAMEFISH SPECIES: bluegill, largemouth bass, catfish, sunfish, redear, white crappie, rainbow trout, (Jackson Creek at dam outlet), warmouth
CAMPING: Yellowwood State Forest, Class C, sites adjacent to lake
MEDICAL ASSISTANCE: Bloomington Hospital, 601 West 2nd Street, Bloomington, IN 47403 (812) 336-6821

ACCESS: Yellowwood Lake is located six mi. W of Nashville via SR 6 to Knight's Corner, then north two miles on the curving paved road to the lake. There are two boat ramps. One is at the spillway and dam (east shore) & another is at the marshy north end along gravel Yellowwood Lake Road. Smaller state forest lakes nearby Yellowwood Lake include 13 acre Crooked Creek Lake, nine acre Bear Lake; 17 acre Ogle Lake & seven acre Strahl Lake in nearby Brown County State Park.

YELLOWWOOD LAKE

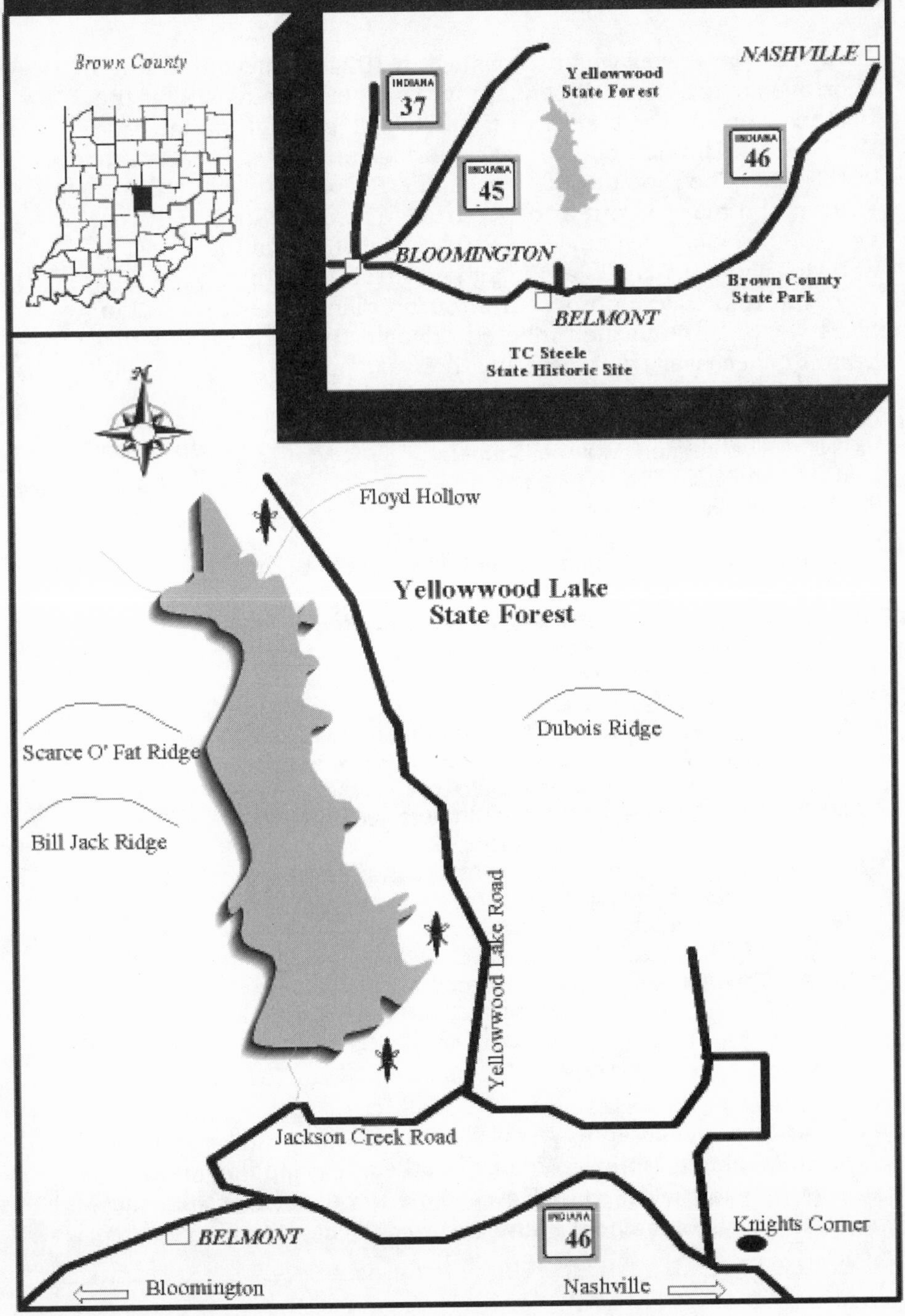
Brown County
INDIANA
37
INDIANA
45
INDIANA
46
Yellowwood
State Forest
NASHVILLE
BLOOMINGTON
BELMONT
Brown County
State Park
TC Steele
State Historic Site
N
Floyd Hollow
Yellowwood Lake
State Forest
Dubois Ridge
Scarce O' Fat Ridge
Bill Jack Ridge
Yellowwood Lake Road
Jackson Creek Road
INDIANA
46
BELMONT
Knights Corner
Bloomington
Nashville

53. GRIFFY LAKE

- **Paddle where scenery, recreation & relaxation combine at city edge**

Griffy Lake reservoir was established in 1924 to alleviate a water shortage for the city of Bloomington. From the access site at the northeast end of the lake near the Griffy Creek inlet, paddle under the Headley-Hinkle Road causeway bridge and enter the main body of the lake. The Bloomington Parks and Recreation Department has written and mapped out a "canoe trail". The fluvial trip features wetlands, geology, sycamore, yellow poplar, fish habitat, erosion and riparian life. This is a fine aquatic "trail" for children. A 240-acre nature preserve borders the south upland lakeshore. Hiking trails weave through the timbered ridge north shore. A daily boat permit is necessary when the boathouse is open.

USGS MAP(S): Bloomington 1:24,000
VICINITY: Bloomington, Monroe County
LAKE ACREAGE /DEPTH: 130 a. /36'
PADDLING TIME: 1 to 2 hours
LEVEL OF DIFFICULTY: Class I
HAZARDS/PORTAGES: electric motors, ltd. number of boats (only 22) on the lake at any time
INFO SOURCES: Bloomington Parks and Recreation,
401 North Morton
Bloomington, IN 47402
(812) 349-3700
AREA OUTFITTERS/LIVERIES: Griffy boathouse, April (weekends) 9 a.m. to 6 p.m. daily, May to September 7a.m. to 7p.m.
GAMEFISH SPECIES: bluegill, largemouth bass, sunfish, redear, channel cat, crappie
CAMPING: Morgan-Monroe State Forest
Class C (765) 342-4026
Riddle Point Park at Lake Lemon
(812) 332-5220 (canoe rental also)
MEDICAL ASSISTANCE: Bloomington Hospital
601 West 2nd St.
Bloomington, IN 47403
(812) 336-6821

ACCESS: From the SR 46/45 bypass, northeast Bloomington, turn north at the stop light and follow Matlock Road east to Headley Road curving north to Hinkle Road. Descend the slope and cross the causeway & turn right at the boat house and ramp access parking area.

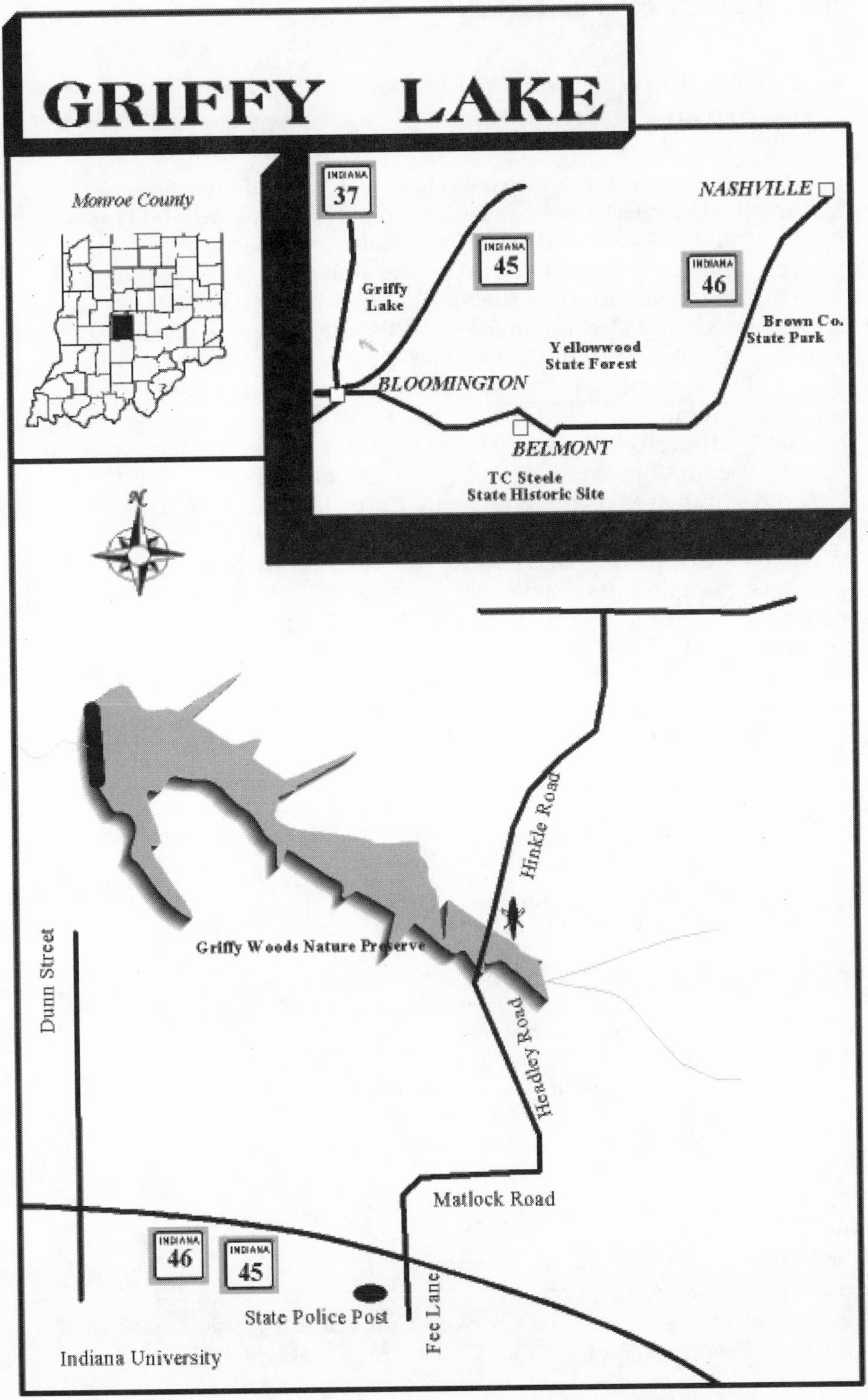
GRIFFY LAKE
Monroe County
INDIANA 37
INDIANA 45
INDIANA 46
NASHVILLE
Griffy Lake
Yellowwood State Forest
Brown Co. State Park
BLOOMINGTON
BELMONT
TC Steele State Historic Site
Hinkle Road
Griffy Woods Nature Preserve
Dunn Street
Headley Road
Matlock Road
INDIANA 46
INDIANA 45
State Police Post
Fee Lane
Indiana University

54. MONROE LAKE

- Retreat to backwater wilderness on Indiana's largest inland lake

Established in 1966, Monroe Lake has 119 miles of shoreline, making it the largest reservoir in Indiana. The vast water body is divided into two basins at the SR 446 Salt Creek causeway. The preferred paddling water lies east of the causeway (a 5-mph idle zone for motorized boats). Crooked Creek provides the best access for paddlers due to its' remoteness and shallow waters. Even in the upper reaches of the Salt Creek Middle Fork area of the lake it is vast and wide open vistas of the scenic forest and round hills are in every direction.

Paddle south from the Crooked Creek access across the lake to the Charles Deam Wilderness shore. Overnight camping is permitted in the wilderness area or the U.S. Army Corps land to the northeast of the Middle Fork inlet. To the east is the Middle Fork Salt Creek Waterfowl Area (closed Oct. 1-April 15). The Pinegrove access allows paddlers to explore the backwater North Fork Salt Creek waterfowl resting area (closed Oct. 1-April 15). Topographical maps recommended.

USGS MAP(S): Allen's Creek, Elkinsville 1:24,000
VICINITY: Bloomington, Monroe County
LAKE ACREAGE /DEPTH: 10,750 a. /54'
PADDLING TIME: half day to overnites
LEVEL OF DIFFICULTY: Class 1
HAZARDS/PORTAGES: wind, seasonal hunting, powerboats
INFO SOURCES: Monroe Lake, 4850 S. SR 446, Bloomington, IN 47401 (812) 837-9546
AREA OUTFITTERS/LIVERIES: none, four marinas: Paynetown, Fairfax, Cutright, & Moore's Creek SRA's
GAMEFISH SPECIES: bluegill, channel catfish, walleye, crappie, largemouth, smallmouth, yellow & striped bass, warmouth, sunfish, northern pike
CAMPING: Class A, B & C: Monroe Lake (812) 837-9546
HNF Hardin Ridge, Deam Wilderness (812) 275-5987
US Army Corps of Engineers (812) 824-9136
MEDICAL ASSISTANCE: Bloomington Hospital, 601 West 2nd Street Bloomington, IN 47403 (812) 336-6821

ACCESS: Monroe Lake is 10 mi. SE of Bloomington. SR 446 crosses mid-reservoir. Of nine ramps Pinegrove & Crooked Creek access sites are the best access for paddlers. Pinegrove SRA is E of SR 446 at Pinegrove Rd. dead end. The Crooked Creek SRA is located south of SR 46 (2nd road south of Knight's Corner) on Crooked Creek Road.

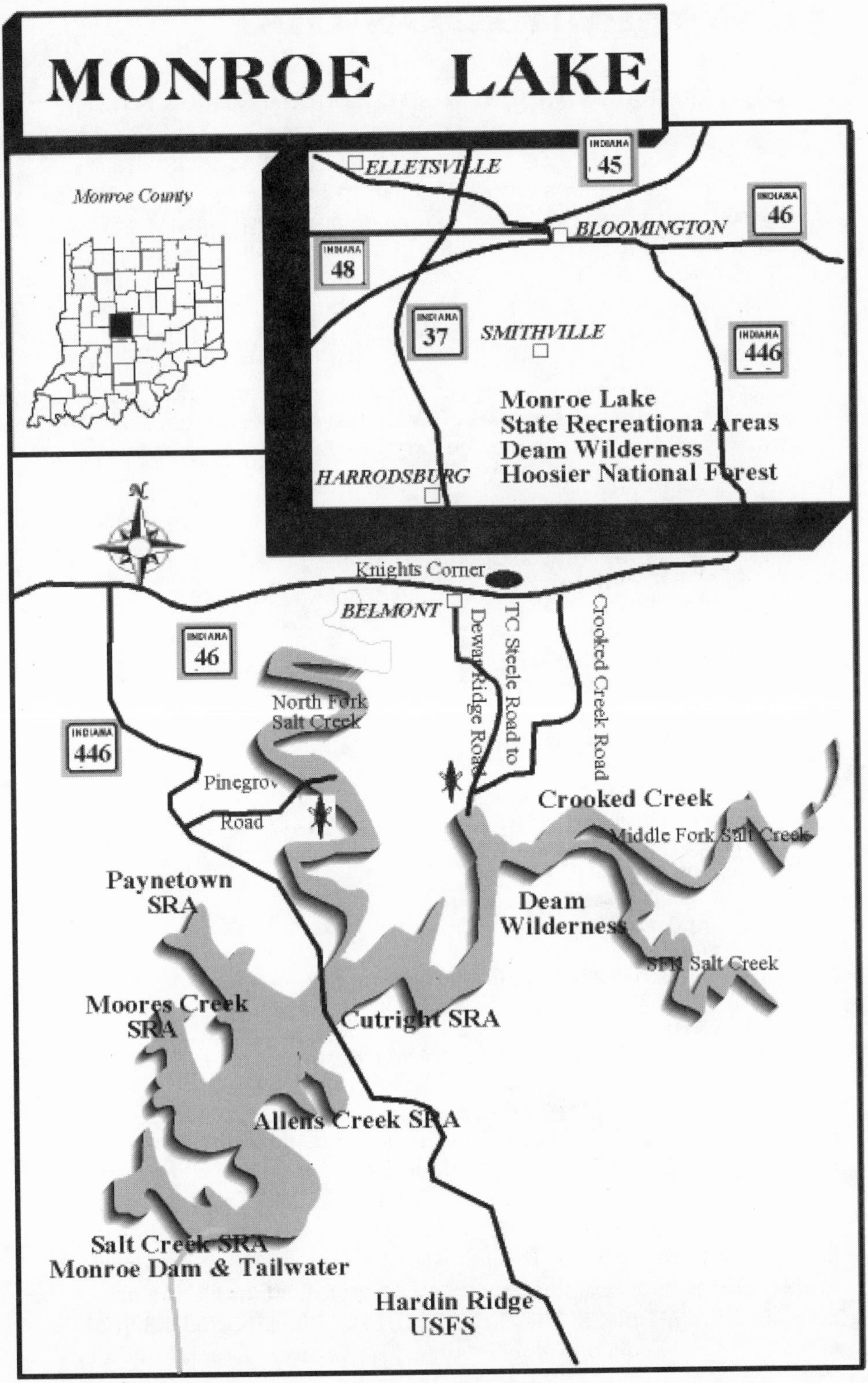
MONROE LAKE
Monroe County
ELLETSVILLE
INDIANA 45
INDIANA 46
BLOOMINGTON
INDIANA 48
INDIANA 37
SMITHVILLE
INDIANA 446
Monroe Lake
State Recreationa Areas
Deam Wilderness
Hoosier National Forest
HARRODSBURG
Knights Corner
BELMONT
TC Steele Road to
Dewar Ridge Road
Crooked Creek Road
INDIANA 46
North Fork
Salt Creek
INDIANA 446
Pinegrov
Road
Crooked Creek
Middle Fork Salt Creek
Paynetown
SRA
Deam
Wilderness
SFK Salt Creek
Moores Creek
SRA
Cutright SRA
Allens Creek SRA
Salt Creek SRA
Monroe Dam & Tailwater
Hardin Ridge
USFS

55. STARVE HOLLOW LAKE

- Dip into serene waters where Knobs overlook Lake

What makes Starve Hollow Lake special (established 1938) are the reflective, ethereal knobs along the east and southeast shore. These nearly round timbered hills (850' elev.) offer a sharp contrast to the watery plain of the lake and adjoining marsh. Aquatic vegetation is choking much of the 145 acre Starve Hollow Lake. Planted bald cypress along the north shore adds a southern charm. Driftwood Fish Hatchery is situated at the base of the dam west of the spillway outlet. Mill Creek flows south to the Muscatatuck River. Seasonal daily permit or annual pass fee required to access the lake. Wooded lakeside tent camping is available along the northeast shore. During the warm season, the lake can be very busy.

USGS MAP(S): Vallonia 1:24,000
VICINITY: Brownstown, Jackson County
LAKE ACREAGE /DEPTH: 145 a. /20'
PADDLING TIME: 2 hours
LEVEL OF DIFFICULTY: Class I
HAZARDS/PORTAGES: electric motors only, choked vegetation
INFO SOURCES: Starve Hollow SRA
4345S CR 275 W
Vallonia, IN 47281
(812) 358-3464
AREA OUTFITTERS/LIVERIES: seasonal boat rental at beach
GAMEFISH SPECIES: bluegill, largemouth bass, catfish, bowfin, crappie, warmouth.
CAMPING: Starve Hollow SRA
Class A & B
(812) 358-3464
Knob Lake
Jackson-Washington State Forest
(812) 358-2160
Class C
MEDICAL ASSISTANCE: Memorial Hospital, 411 West Tipton St., Seymour, IN 47274 (812) 522-2349

ACCESS: From I-65 exit 49 and go east on US 50 through Seymour to Brownstown and SR 135. Drive south on SR 135 to Vallonia and turn east on Lake Road. Continue about 2.5 miles on Lake Road to the entrance. The boat access is 0.25 miles south of the park entrance near the dam and fish hatchery. This is a seasonal fee access in season. There are also ramps at the beach and campground areas.

STARVE HOLLOW LAKE

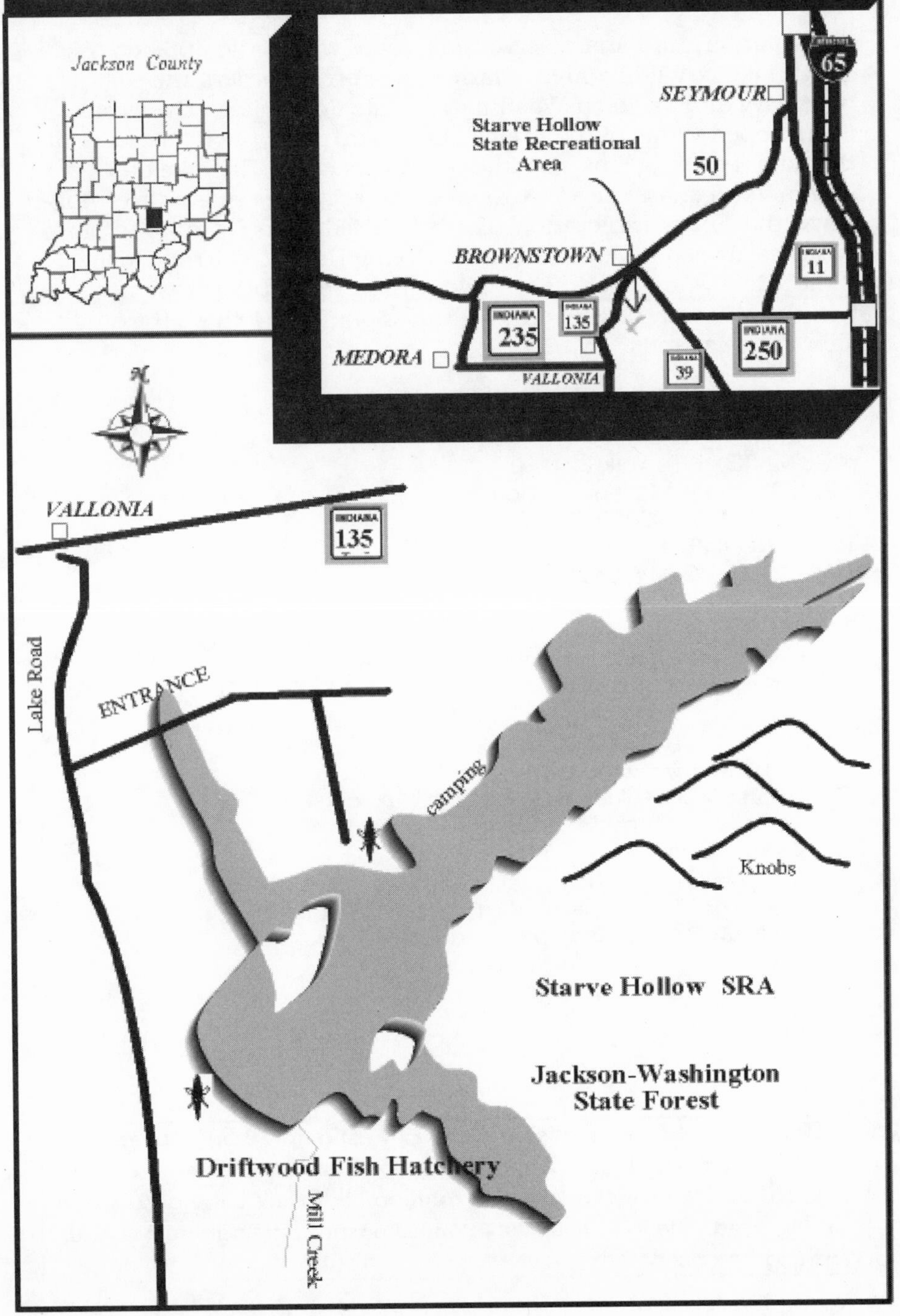
Jackson County
SEYMOUR
65
Starve Hollow
State Recreational
Area
50
BROWNSTOWN
11
235
135
MEDORA
VALLONIA
39
250
VALLONIA
135
Lake Road
ENTRANCE
camping
Knobs
Starve Hollow SRA
Jackson-Washington
State Forest
Driftwood Fish Hatchery
Mill Creek

56. ELK CREEK LAKE

- Buoy up where the Knobstone Trail passes through

This southern Indiana reservoir is located within the 666 acre Elk Creek Fish & Wildlife Area. Clark State Forest borders the east boundary and Jackson-Washington State Forest is on the west. Scenic open vistas of the Knobs nearly surround the lake except at the dam (power pylons straddle the Knobs east). The lake has several level shoreline spots to land and relax. There are three finger coves that invite exploration. The lake is fed by forest runoff from steep hardwood covered hills into Nowing Hollow, Garrett Hollow, Smith Hollow and McKnight Hollow. Elk Creek outlet flows north to join the Muscatatuck River. The Knobstone Trail follows the south shore and uplands.

USGS MAP(S): Little York 1:24,000
VICINITY: Salem, Washington County
LAKE ACREAGE /DEPTH: 47a. /23'
PADDLING TIME: 1 hour
LEVEL OF DIFFICULTY: Class I
HAZARDS/PORTAGES: electric motors only, seasonal public hunting
INFO SOURCES: Crosley Fish and Wildlife Area
2010 S SR3
North Vernon, IN 47265
(812) 346-5596
AREA OUTFITTERS/LIVERIES: none
GAMEFISH SPECIES: bluegill, largemouth bass, channel catfish, redear.
CAMPING: Delaney County Park
(812) 883-5101
10 miles northeast of Salem, east of SR 135 N
MEDICAL ASSISTANCE: Scott Memorial Hospital
1451 N. Gardner
St., Scottsburg, IN 47170
(812) 752-3456

ACCESS: From I-65 at Scottsburg exit 29 west onto SR 56. Proceed west on SR 56 about 7.5 miles and turn south on Elk Creek Lake Road or Ratts Road. Continue two miles south to Elk Creek Lake access and parking area. The lake is about 10 miles east of Salem in east central Washington county.

ELK CREEK LAKE

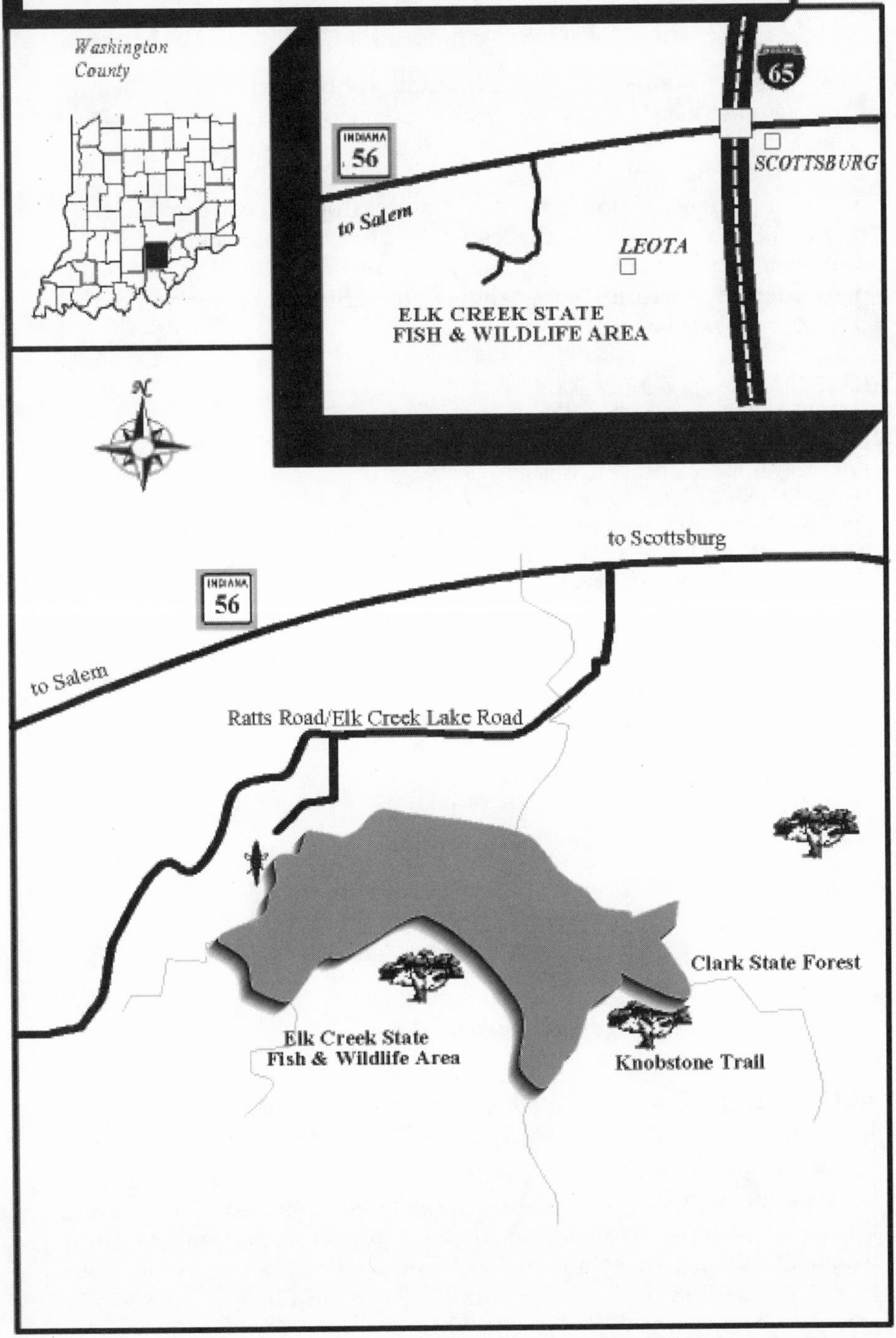

Washington
County
INDIANA
56
65
SCOTTSBURG
to Salem
LEOTA
ELK CREEK STATE
FISH & WILDLIFE AREA
N
to Scottsburg
INDIANA
56
to Salem
Ratts Road/Elk Creek Lake Road
Clark State Forest
Elk Creek State
Fish & Wildlife Area
Knobstone Trail

57. DEAM LAKE

- **Canoe at the base of Waggoner Knobs in Indiana's oldest state forest**

The 194-acre lake (est. 1956) is named in honor of Charles Deam, Indiana's first state forester and foremost botanist. The 1,300 Deam Lake State Recreation Area, one of four SRAs managed by the Division of Forestry, is part of Clark State Forest, Indiana's "Cradle of Forestry" (est. 1903). There are several finger coves in which to paddle. The west shore includes the boat ramp, picnicking with shelters, beach, playground, nature center and boat rental. This area offers opportunities for families for renting a canoe, to fish, and discover aquatic nature.

USGS MAP(S): Speed 1:24,000
VICINITY: Sellersburg, Clark County
LAKE ACREAGE /DEPTH: 194 a. /33'
PADDLING TIME: 2 hours to half-day
LEVEL OF DIFFICULTY: Class I
HAZARDS/PORTAGES: wind, seasonal hunting, electric motors only
INFO SOURCES: Deam Lake, RR#2, Box 568, Borden, IN 47106,
(812) 246-5421
AREA OUTFITTERS/LIVERIES: seasonal boat rental
GAMEFISH SPECIES: bluegill, bass, catfish.
CAMPING: Deam Lake
Class A & B
(812) 294-4306
Clark State Forest
Class C
(812) 294-4306
MEDICAL ASSISTANCE: Clark Memorial Hospital
1220 Missouri Avenue
Jeffersonville, IN 47130
(812) 282-6631
Washington County Memorial
911 N. Shelby St.
Salem , IN 47167
(812) 883-5881

ACCESS: Deam Lake is located nine miles northwest of Sellersburg and five miles southeast of New Providence. From I-65 exit 7 northwest onto SR 60. Go northwest on scenic SR 60 to Carr Road and turn north. Proceed through Carwood and curve north on Waggoner Knob Rd to the park entrance. Seasonal fees. There are also seven small lakes within Clark State Forest (all north of Deam Lake). Exit 19 from I-65 at Henryville and go one mile north on US 31 to the Clark SF entrance.

DEAM LAKE

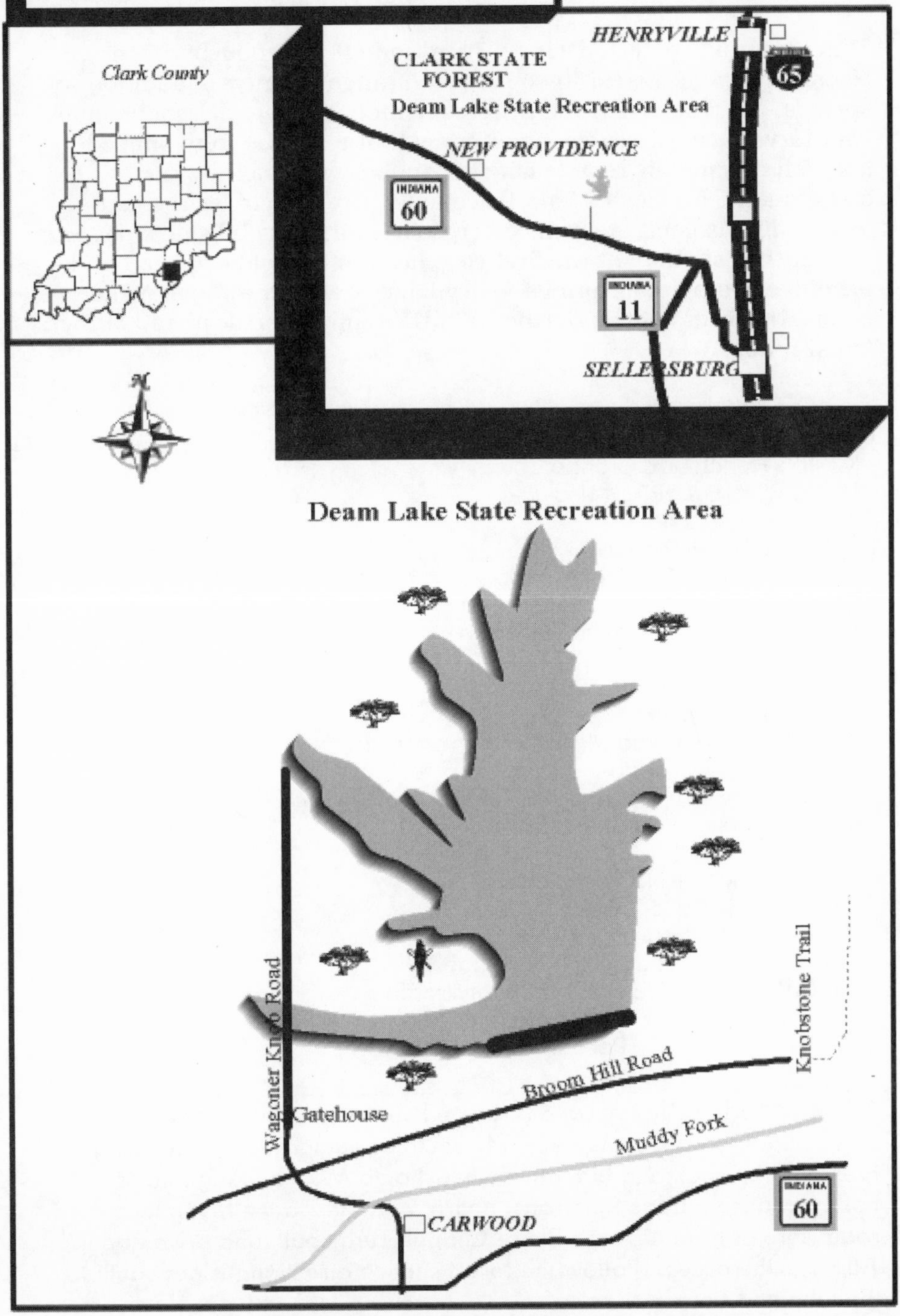
Clark County
CLARK STATE
FOREST
Deam Lake State Recreation Area
HENRYVILLE
65
NEW PROVIDENCE
INDIANA
60
INDIANA
11
SELLERSBURG
Deam Lake State Recreation Area
Wagoner Knob Road
Knobstone Trail
Broom Hill Road
Gatehouse
Muddy Fork
INDIANA
60
CARWOOD

58. SPRINGS VALLEY LAKE

- Sweep across a spring fed national forest lake

This tranquil lake (est. 1965) is surrounded by a thousand acres of Hoosier National Forest in southwest Orange County. In addition to springs, the reservoir is fed by forest runoff. French Lick is the main tributary. There are three major coves that form the "bird shaped" lake. The seemingly remote lake is popular with anglers. The abandoned 5.5 miles Buffalo Trace hiking trail encircles the lake and birding is good. A spring emerges from a rocky hillside along the southwest shore at the first cove north of the old trailhead and primitive camp area. Springs Valley Lake is also known as Tucker Lake. The access site is northeast of the dam at the dead end of the forest road.

USGS MAP(S): Greenbrier 1:24,000
VICINITY: French Lick, Orange County
LAKE ACREAGE /DEPTH: 141 a. /39'
PADDLING TIME: 2 hours
LEVEL OF DIFFICULTY: Class I
HAZARDS/PORTAGES: electric motors only, seasonal hunting area
INFO SOURCES: Hoosier National Forest
811 Constitution Ave.
Bedford, IN 47421
(812) 275-5987
AREA OUTFITTERS/LIVERIES: none
GAMEFISH SPECIES: bluegill, largemouth bass, crappie,
redear, sunfish, carp, warmouth, longear,
green sunfish, channel catfish
CAMPING: Springs Valley RA
Class C
Hoosier National Forest
(812) 275-5987
upper campground is closed
limited camping at lakeside
MEDICAL ASSISTANCE: Orange County Hospital
642 W. Hospital Rd.,
Paoli, IN 47454, (812) 723-2811

ACCESS: Springs Valley Lake is located six miles southeast of French Lick. From French Lick, take SR 145 south about three miles crossing French Lick Creek and turning southeast onto Moore's Ridge Road. Follow Moore's Ridge Road east nearly 2.7 miles to the first paved road right beyond Moore's Ridge Chapel. Turn south and drive about 1.5 mi to the access. Follow the forest service directional signs south to the lake and access.

SPRINGS VALLEY LAKE /TUCKER LAKE

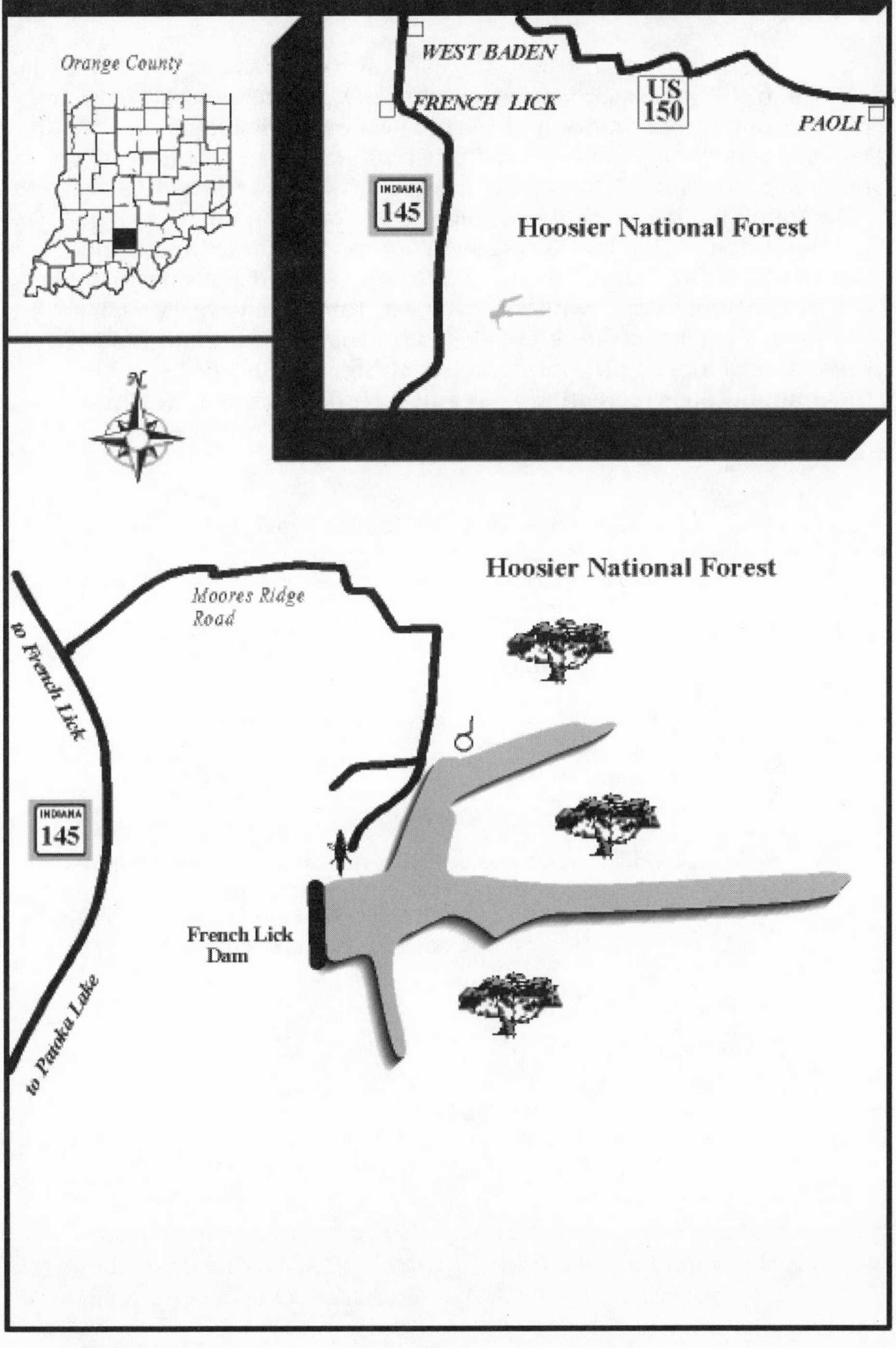

59. PATOKA LAKE

- Wander backwater coves of one of southern Indiana's largest lakes

Patoka Lake, Indiana's second largest reservoir, has few places for canoes in the vast open water (sea kayaks will fare better). There are nine launch ramps but only three (no–wake-no-wash) are recommended for paddlers: Painter Creek Ramp (easiest access, go upstream on Painter Creek and Jordan Branch cove); the Wall's Lake Ramp (south of Painter Creek, bigger water, many snags, go upstream to the Patoka River inlet, Youngs Creek inlet and Cane Branch inlet.) and the Little Patoka Ramp; (three deep waterfowl coves, Sycamore Cove & Allen Cove best, ramp busy weekends). Portions of the backwaters are closed during the waterfowl resting season in October until Spring. Newton-Stewart SRA (fee area) is the main outdoor recreation area and includes camping. Rolling hills and scenic rock outcroppings surround Patoka Lake.

USGS MAP(S): Cuzco, Greenbrier, Birdseye, Taswell 1:24,000
VICINITY: French Lick, Orange County
English, Crawford County
Jasper, Dubois County
LAKE ACREAGE /DEPTH: 9,032 a. /53'
PADDLING TIME: half day to overnites
LEVEL OF DIFFICULTY: Class I
HAZARDS/PORTAGES: wind, powerboats, seasonal hunting
INFO SOURCES: Patoka Lake
RR#1, Box 290
Birdseye, IN 47513
(812) 695-2464
AREA OUTFITTERS/LIVERIES: none, motorboat rental at reservoir marinas.
GAMEFISH SPECIES: bluegill, largemouth bass, northern pike, redear, sunfish, catfish, crappie, walleye, warmouth, white bass, rock & smallmouth bass
CAMPING: Patoka Lake
Newton-Stewart SRA
Class A & C
(812) 685-2464
MEDICAL ASSISTANCE: Orange County Hospital
642 W. Hospital Rd.,
Paoli, IN 47454
(812) 723-2811

ACCESS: Patoka Lake is situated in Dubois, Crawford and Orange counties, about 12 miles northeast of Jasper. From I-65 exit 72 onto SR 145 and drive north to Birdseye and turn east on SR 64. Turn north again on SR 145 to Wickliffe and the lake at Newton-Stewart SRA. Three ramps are of interest to paddlers:
Painter's Creek Ramp: access adjacent to SR 145 highway bridge, northeast corner, north of the SR 164 and SR 145 junction. Paddle east and north on Painter Creek & west & north on Jordan Branch cove.
Wall's Lake Ramp: From SR 145, south of the Painter Creek Ramp, turn east onto Newton-Stewart Road (Orange CR 875 S) and drive two miles to CR 625W and turn south. Proceed 2.6 miles on CR 625W to the access site. Area closed during the waterfowl season.
Little Patoka Ramp: From Taswell and SR 64 go north along paved country roads (Jerico Road and Red Hill Road) curving west to the water and cross Sycamore Creek bridge. This is the most remote of the three accesses. There are three coves nearby. Sycamore Marsh is a long, shallow, wildlife rich wetland and mud flat. Allen's Creek Cove and Little Patoka River Cove are closed during autumn waterfowl season.

Painted Turtle

PATOKA LAKE

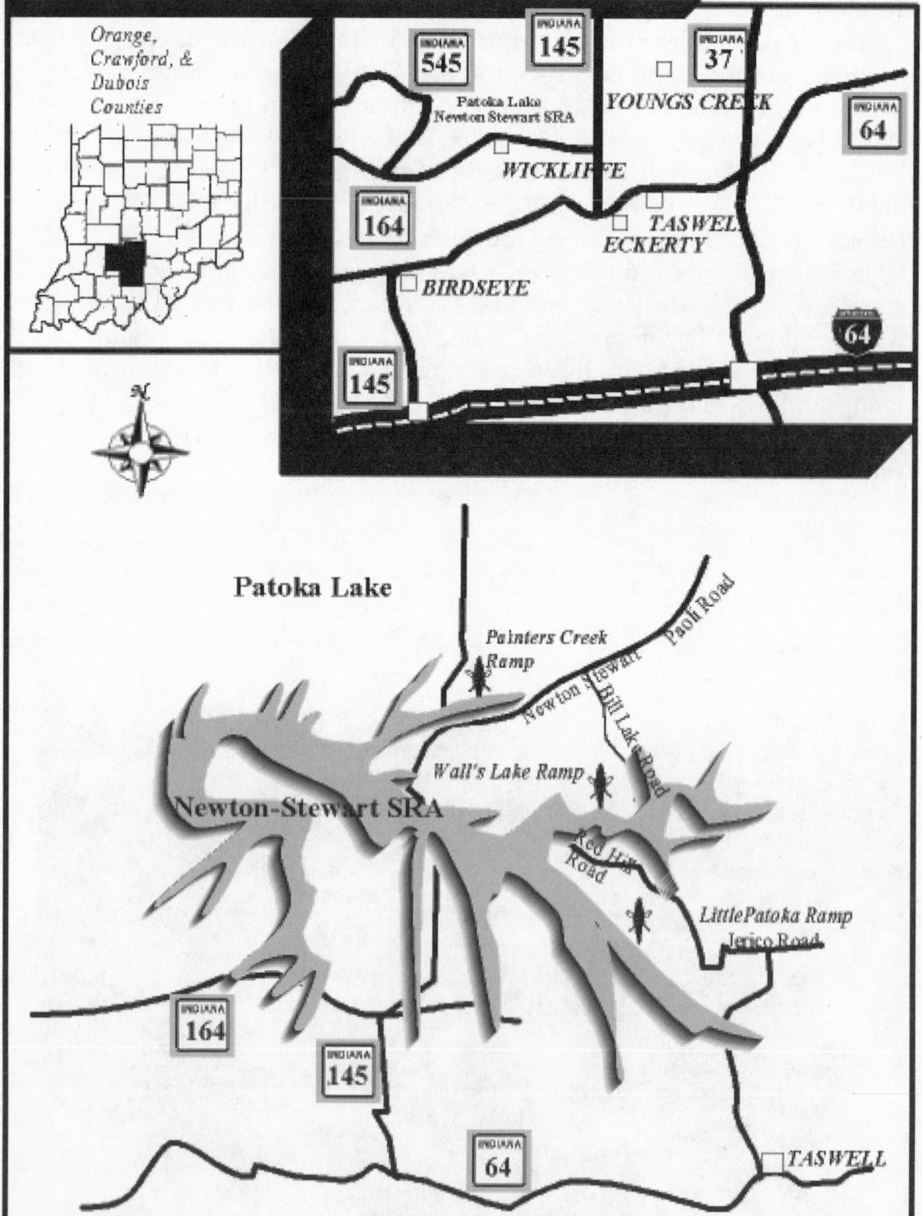

Orange,
Crawford, &
Dubois
Counties
INDIANA 545
INDIANA 145
INDIANA 37
Patoka Lake
Newton Stewart SRA
YOUNGS CREEK
INDIANA 64
WICKLIFFE
INDIANA 164
TASWELL
ECKERTY
BIRDSEYE
64
INDIANA 145
N
Patoka Lake
Painters Creek
Ramp
Paoli Road
Newton Stewart
Bill Lake Road
Wall's Lake Ramp
Newton-Stewart SRA
Red Hill
Road
LittlePatoka Ramp
Jerico Road
INDIANA 164
INDIANA 145
INDIANA 64
TASWELL

Lifejacket at Work

Coots on a Log

60. FERDINAND LAKE

- Drift on tree reflected waters

Ferdinand Lake lies within the 7,657 acre Ferdinand State Forest in a scenic hollow. The long and narrow reservoir is bordered by steep upland forest along the south shore, a level incoming creek valley to the west, the dam and campground to the east and the developed north tree-studded shore with its shaded picnic tables, sandy beach and boat rental. The lake drains southeast to Hurricane Creek. The beautiful forest lake was established in 1934 as a Civilian Conservation Corps (CCC) camp. Large specimens of white, short leaf and red pine shade the leisure-centered north shore. Great spot for families. Camp and hike for a complete visit to southern Indiana outdoors.

USGS MAP(S): St. Anthony 1:24,000
VICINITY: Ferdinand, Dubois County
LAKE ACREAGE /DEPTH: 42 a./22'
PADDLING TIME: 1 hour
LEVEL OF DIFFICULTY: Class I
HAZARDS/PORTAGES: electric motors only, seasonal hunting
INFO SOURCES: Ferdinand State Forest
6583 E SR 264
Ferdinand, IN 47532
(812) 367-1524
AREA OUTFITTERS/LIVERIES: summer boat rental
GAMEFISH SPECIES: bluegill, largemouth bass, sunfish, crappie, channel catfish, perch, warmouth
CAMPING: Ferdinand State Forest
(812) 367-1524
Class C sites
MEDICAL ASSISTANCE: St. Joseph's Hospital
1900 Medical Arts Dr.
Huntingburg, IN 47542
(812) 683-2121

ACCESS: The state forest is located five miles northeast of Ferdinand on SR 264. From I-64 at Ferdinand exit 63 and go north on SR 162 through the community to the SR 264 junction and turn east. Go east & north on SR 264 to the state forest entrance and lake. Seasonal entrance fee. Paddlers must have a seasonal permit. A concrete ramp and boat rental is on the northeast shore and carry down from the picnic area.

FERDINAND LAKE

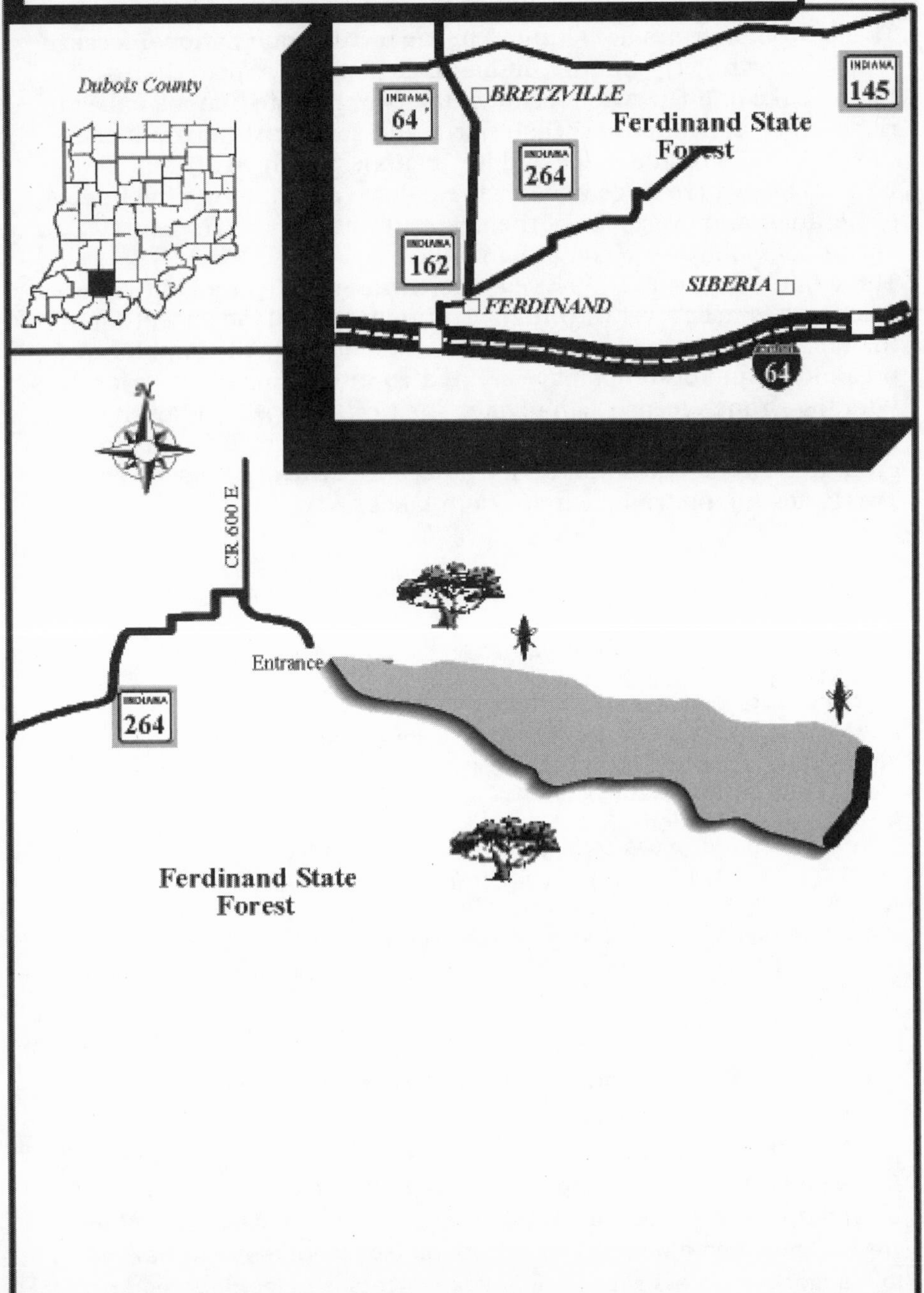

Dubois County
INDIANA 64
BRETZVILLE
INDIANA 145
Ferdinand State Forest
INDIANA 264
INDIANA 162
SIBERIA
FERDINAND
64
CR 600 E
Entrance
INDIANA 264
Ferdinand State Forest

61. INDIAN LAKE & CELINA LAKE

- Escape from the ordinary into the wild

These two reservoirs are situated in the picturesque national forest lands of north Perry County. Indian Lake is more remote than Celina Lake and the most scenic of the two. Forested knobs and ridges appear on the northeast, north and southeast horizons of Indian Lake. A marsh is located in the upper northeast basin of Indian Lake where large boulder breakdown and outcropping invites exploration and overlooks of the peaceful water body. The Middle Fork Anderson River feeds Indian Lake.

Three miles east via FR 501 near the entrance is Celina Lake. The lakeshore is near level with the surrounding woodland except for the north and southeast shore near the dam where the boulder breakdown and outcrops have created an interesting place to land. Winding Branch feeds Celina Lake. The North Slope and South Slope campground loops are located at Celina Lake and a picnic ground is situated at Indian Lake adjacent to the access site. The Two Lakes hiking trail encircles both lakes.

USGS MAP(S): (Celina Lake) Bristow (Indian Lake) Branchville 1:24,000
VICINITY: St. Croix, Perry County
LAKE ACREAGE /DEPTH: 164 a. /41' Celina, 154 a./34' Indian
PADDLING TIME: 2 hour each
LEVEL OF DIFFICULTY: Class I
HAZARDS/PORTAGES: electric motors only, snags, seasonal hunting
INFO SOURCES: Hoosier National Forest
811 Constitution Ave.
Bedford, IN 47421
(812) 275-5987
Tell City Ranger Office (812) 547-7051
AREA OUTFITTERS/LIVERIES: none
GAMEFISH SPECIES: bluegill, largemouth bass, warmouth, redear, sunfish, channel cat, crappie
CAMPING: Celina Lake, Hoosier National Forest, Class A & C two campground loops
MEDICAL ASSISTANCE: Perry County Memorial Hospital, 1 Hospital Road, Tell City, IN 47586 (812) 547-7011

ACCESS: From I-64 at St. Croix, northern Perry County, exit 79 onto SR 37 and drive three miles to Forest Road 501 marked entrance and turn west. Continue to the entry control station (seasonal fee) and beyond to the marked access sites. Celina Lake access is at the dead end at the first left beyond the entry station. Indian Lake access is a dead end (road ends in water), located three miles west of the control station.

INDIAN LAKE & CELINA LAKE

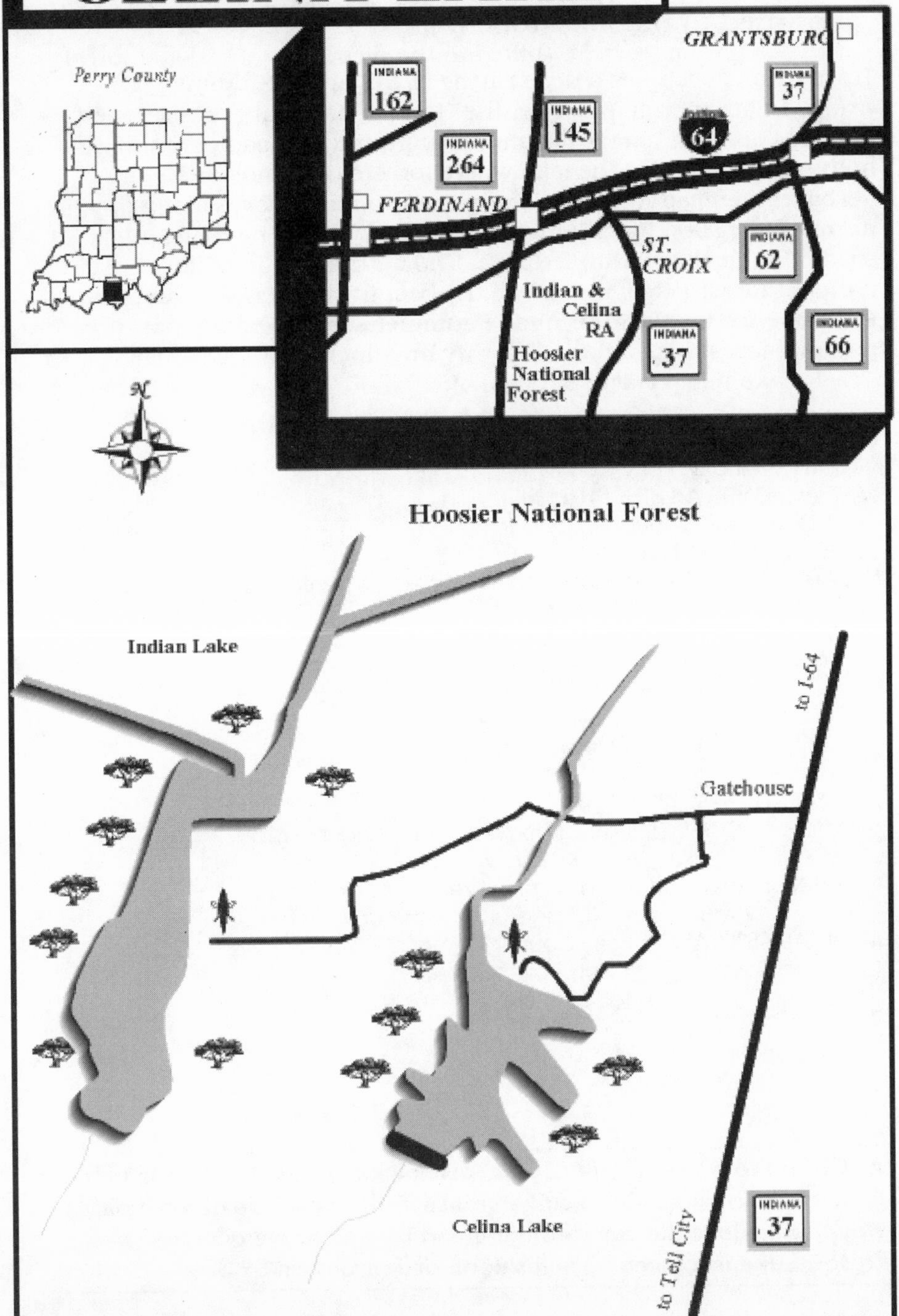
Perry County
GRANTSBURG
INDIANA 162
INDIANA 145
INDIANA 264
INDIANA 37
64
FERDINAND
ST. CROIX
INDIANA 62
Indian & Celina RA
INDIANA 37
INDIANA 66
Hoosier National Forest
N
Hoosier National Forest
Indian Lake
to I-64
Gatehouse
Celina Lake
INDIANA 37
to Tell City

62. TIPSAW LAKE

- Relax and enjoy a southern Indiana lake that is nestled in the limestone hills

Tipsaw Lake occupies a deep ravine of the upper Sulphur Fork Creek. In addition to the lake, the Hoosier National Forest property includes a beach, picnic ground, playground and campground. A hiking trail encircles the lake where forested uplands and herbaceous meadow thrive. There are two major coves along the narrow long lake. Families would especially enjoy paddling and swimming in the stream-fed lake. The natural setting, like all national forest lakes, is some of the best in southern Indiana. Entrance fee in effect during the summer season. Additional national forest lakes in the Tell City area include 39-acre Deer Creek Lake and 41-acre Saddle Lake.

USGS MAP(S): Bristow 1:24,000
VICINITY: Tell City, Perry County
LAKE ACREAGE /DEPTH: 141a./34'
PADDLING TIME: 1 hour
LEVEL OF DIFFICULTY: Class I
HAZARDS/PORTAGES: aquatic growth , seasonal hunting, electric motors only
INFO SOURCES: Hoosier National Forest
811 Constitution Ave.
Bedford, IN 47421
(812) 275-5987
Tell City Office
(812) 547-7051
AREA OUTFITTERS/LIVERIES: none
GAMEFISH SPECIES: bluegill, largemouth bass, channel cat, redear, sunfish, warmouth
CAMPING: Tipsaw Lake, family, primitive, & electric loops, group camp. (Closed Oct. 19 through winter)
MEDICAL ASSISTANCE: Perry County Memorial Hospital
1 Hospital Road
Tell City, IN 47586
(812) 547-7011

ACCESS: From I-64 exit 79 at St. Croix south onto SR 37 and continue three miles to Forest Road 503 entrance at the west side of the highway. Continue to the control station and beyond to the access site. Tipsaw Lake is located 13 miles north of Tell City on SR 37.

TIPSAW LAKE

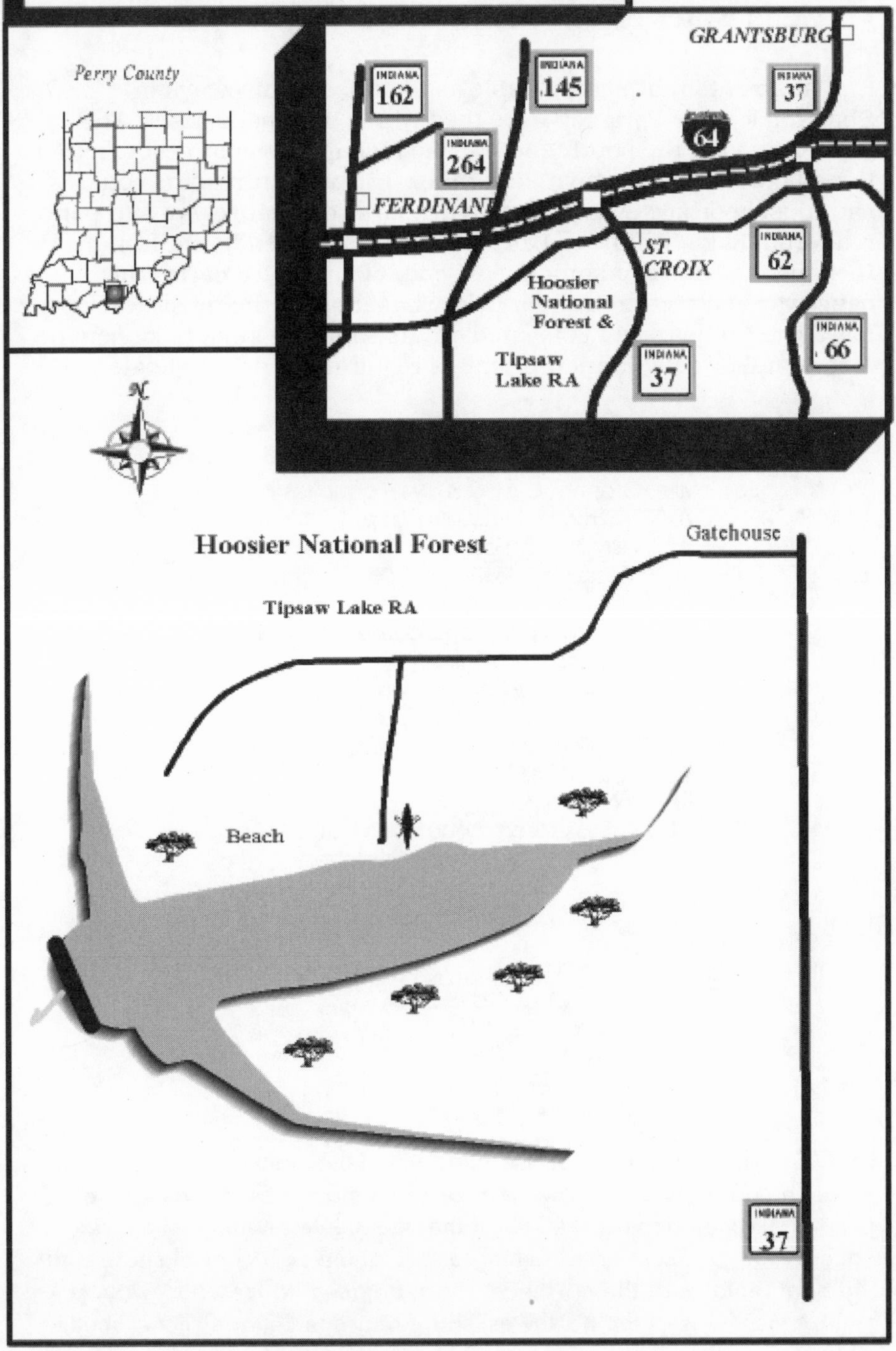
Perry County
INDIANA 162
INDIANA 145
GRANTSBURG
INDIANA 37
64
INDIANA 264
FERDINAN
ST. CROIX
INDIANA 62
Hoosier National Forest &
Tipsaw Lake RA
INDIANA 66
INDIANA 37
N
Hoosier National Forest
Tipsaw Lake RA
Gatehouse
Beach
INDIANA 37

63. LAKES SHAKAMAK, KICKAPOO & LENAPE

- Tread water of three adjoining lakes

Embankments that serve double as motorized causeways in Shakamak State Park separate these three manmade lakes. The main dam is at the south end of Lake Kickapoo, the largest lake. All three lakes have their own boat ramp. The adventuresome could cautiously portage over the low-lying park road causeway and park road from Lake Lenape to Lake Kickapoo (south end) and from Lake Kickapoo to Lake Shakamak (east end, 60-100 yard carry, the causeway is closed to traffic). Lake Shakamak is the most developed lake. The campground is located on the south shore of Lake Lenape. A seasonal or daily launch permit is required for private boats.

USGS MAP(S): Jasonville, Hymera 1:24,000
VICINITY: Jasonville, Greene, Clay & Sullivan counties
LAKE ACREAGE /DEPTH: 156 total a./ avg. depth
PADDLING TIME: half day to a full day
LEVEL OF DIFFICULTY: Class I
HAZARDS/PORTAGES: electric motors only, 10 mph, portage the two park road causeways that seperate the lakes
INFO SOURCES: Shakamak State Park
Rt #2, Box 120
6265 W SR 48
Jasonville, IN 47438
(812) 665-2158
AREA OUTFITTERS/LIVERIES: seasonal boat rental at Lake Kickapoo, NW shore
GAMEFISH SPECIES: bluegill, largemouth bass, perch, redear, sunfish, crappie
CAMPING: Shakamak State Park, Class A (812) 665-2158
MEDICAL ASSISTANCE: Greene County General Hospital
Lone Tree Rd. & SR 54 E
Linton, IN 47441
(812) 847-2281

ACCESS: There are three boat ramps within the state park, one at each lake. The park entrance is located one mile northwest of Jasonville. Lake Shakamak access is south of the aquacenter, southeast shore. Lake Kickapoo access and fishing pier is at the east central shore and the boat rental is at the northeast shore adjacent to the causeway. Lake Lenape access is at the northwest shore near the Lenape picnic shelter.

LAKES SHAKAMAK, KICKAPOO & LENAPE

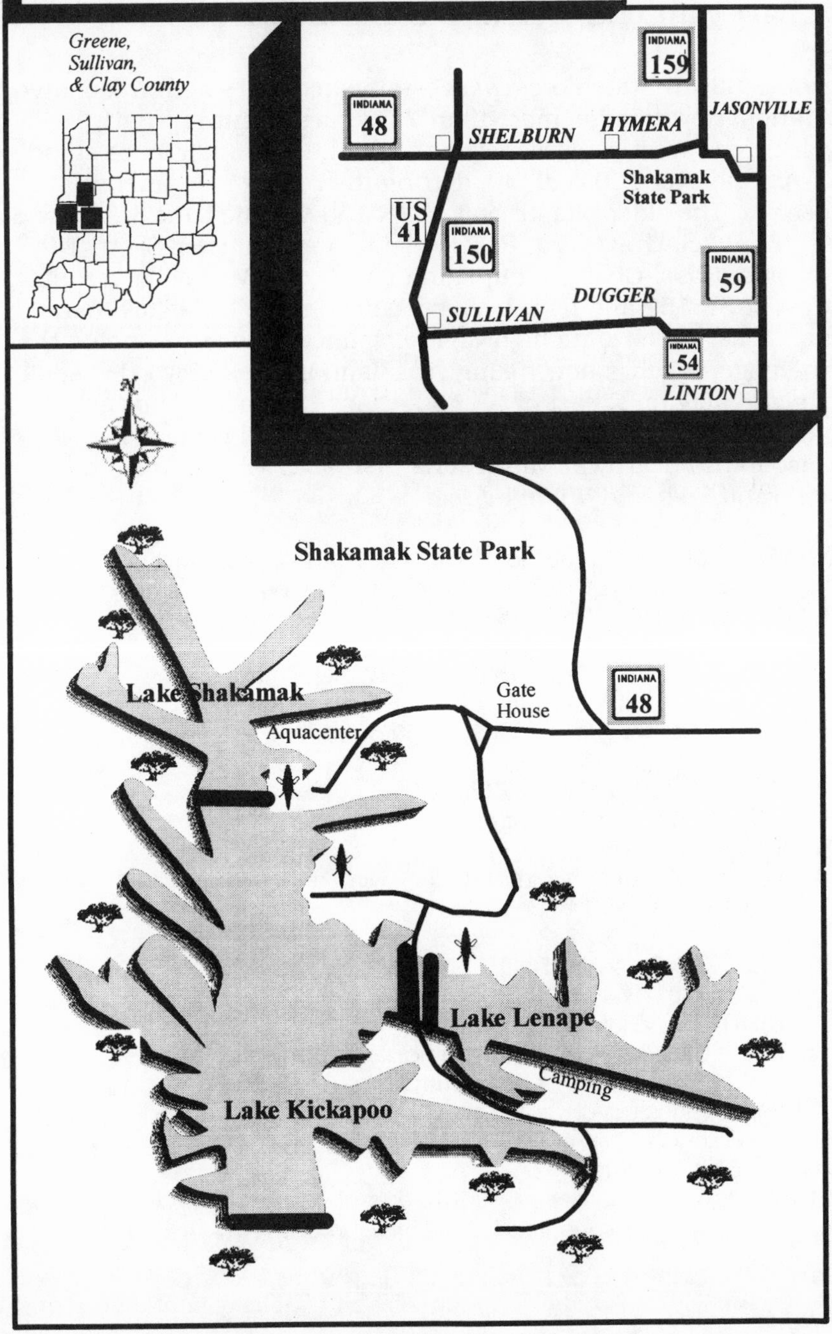

64. GREENE-SULLIVAN STATE FOREST

- Chart your craft across reclaimed coal pit lakes

Greene-Sullivan State Forest was established in 1936 from donated coal lands, now totaling more than 7,000 acres since recently acquiring the West Dugger reclamation unit. Seven pit lakes stand out from the over 100 coal pits dotting the rolling man-altered landscape. The older pits lie east of SR 159: Airline Lake (rainbow trout), Benefiel, Graveyard, Reservoir 26, and Wampler-Scott. The newer pits, Bass, Goose, Pump and Long of the West Dugger unit, lie west of SR 159 and have been reclaimed more like lakes than "canals" east of the state highway. Reclaimed land surrounding the West Dugger lakes is now rolling grassland instead of wooded spoil banks and slag hills, east of SR 159. Class C campgrounds are situated at Wampler Lake and Reservoir #26. Paddleable lake pits are also found nearby at Minnehaha Fish and Wildlife Area and Hillenbrand Fish and Wildlife Area.

USGS MAP(S): Dugger, Linton, Sandborn, Bucktown, Scott 1:24,000
VICINITY: Linton, Greene County, Sullivan, Sullivan County
LAKE ACREAGE /DEPTH: Airline 25 a./67'
Benefiel 60 a./40'
Graveyard 48 a./50'
Reservoir #280 a./38'
Wampler-Scott 80 a./38'
Bass 220 a./50'
Goose 72 a./50'
PADDLING TIME: 1 hour to overnites
LEVEL OF DIFFICULTY: Class I
HAZARDS/PORTAGES: electric motors only, wind on the larger lakes
INFO SOURCES: Greene-Sullivan State Forest
Rt #1, Box 382
Dugger, IN 47848
(812) 648-2810
AREA OUTFITTERS/LIVERIES: none
GAME FISHSPECIES: bluegill, largemouth bass, rainbow trout, redear, sunfish, buffalo, crappie, carp
CAMPING: Greene-Sullivan State Forest
Class C
(812) 648-2810
MEDICAL ASSISTANCE: Greene County General Hospital,
Lone Tree Rd., SR 54 E, Linton, IN 47441
(812) 847-2281
Mary Sherman Hospital
320 N. Section St.
Sullivan, IN 47882 (812) 268-4311

ACCESS: Greene-Sullivan State Forest is located 1.5 miles south of Dugger, six miles east of Linton and eight miles west of Sullivan via SR 159 and SR 54. All lake pits are accessible from SR 159 & SR 54:
Airline: From SR 159 (one mile south of headquarters) go east on Sullivan CR 350 S to County Line Road/1600 W/900 E and turn south. Continue to Truck Road and turn east to access.
Reservoir #26: From SR 159 north of Bucktown, go east on Sullivan CR 500 S to the access road on the north side of the road.
Wampler Lake: From SR 159 go east on Sullivan CR 500 S to Sassafras Rd & Greene CR 1500 W.
Graveyard Lake: From SR 159 south of Bucktown, access road north of Sullivan CR 700S, east side of highway.
Benefiel Lake: Northwest edge of Pleasantville. From SR 159 go north on Sullivan CR 850 E to access.
West Dugger Unit: South of SR 54, east of Sullivan CR 200 E & west of SR 159. Includes Bass Lake, Goose Lake, Pump Lake & Long Lake.
Bass Lake: SR 54 south on Sullivan CR 450 E.
Goose Lake: SR 54 south on Sullivan CR 450 E.

Reclaimed Coal Mine Pit

GREENE-SULLIVAN STATE FOREST

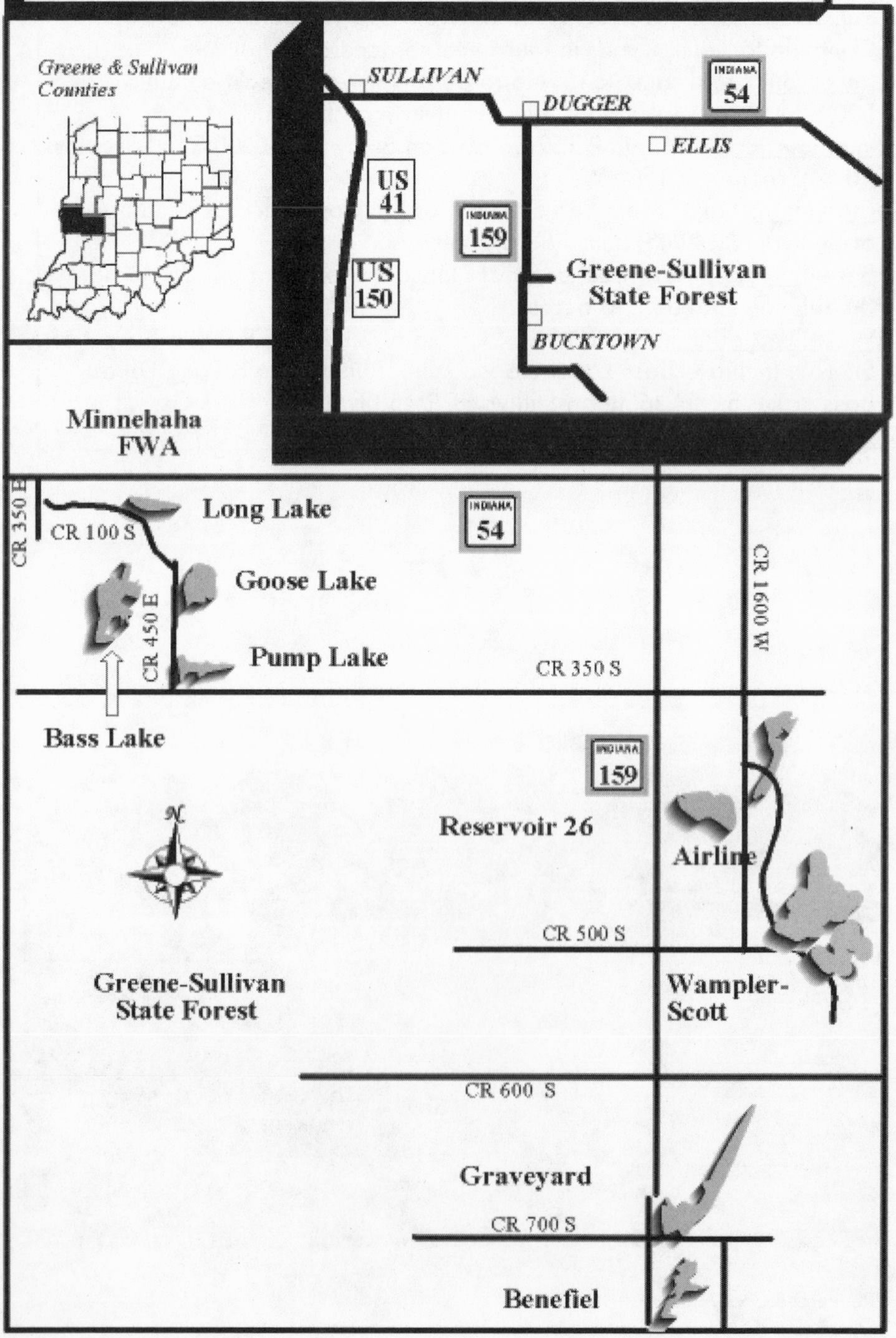

Greene & Sullivan Counties
SULLIVAN
DUGGER
INDIANA 54
ELLIS
US 41
INDIANA 159
US 150
Greene-Sullivan State Forest
BUCKTOWN
Minnehaha FWA
CR 350 E
CR 100 S
Long Lake
INDIANA 54
Goose Lake
CR 450 E
Pump Lake
CR 350 S
CR 1600 W
Bass Lake
INDIANA 159
N
Reservoir 26
Airline
CR 500 S
Greene-Sullivan State Forest
Wampler-Scott
CR 600 S
Graveyard
CR 700 S
Benefiel

Coil of a Banded Water Snake

American Lotus on Dogwood Lake

65. BIG & LITTLE WHITE OAK LAKES

- Lay back, camp, fish and canoe

This public fishing area is a welcome respite in the broad agricultural open landscape of northern Knox County. The combination of water and adjacent woods is an oasis for paddlers looking for a near natural outing. Primitive camping is available for overnight tent visitors. Fishermen and other user paths follow the shore and through the connecting old growth woods of numerous white oaks. The South Fork of Smalls Creek flows from the lakes. Paddlers enroute to the other aquatic destinations such as Hovey Lake will discover White Oak as an ideal rest spot.

USGS MAP(S): Fritchton 1:24,000
VICINITY: Bruceville, Knox County
LAKE ACREAGE /DEPTH: 31 a./20', 7 a./10'
PADDLING TIME: 2 hours
LEVEL OF DIFFICULTY: Class I
HAZARDS/PORTAGES: none
INFO SOURCES: Public Access Sites South
RR#2, Box 300
Montgomery, IN 47358
(812) 644-7731
AREA OUTFITTERS/LIVERIES: none
GAMEFISH SPECIES: largemouth bass, crappie
CAMPING: White Oak Public Fishing Area
Class C sites
(812) 644-7731
MEDICAL ASSISTANCE: Good Samaritan Hospital
520 S. 7th St.
Vincennes, IN 47591
(812) 882-5220

ACCESS: From the junction of SR 550 and SR 67 in Bruceville go southwest 0.5 mile on SR 67 to Knox CR 300 E (unmarked) and turn south. Continue one mile on paved CR 300 E to the public fishing area entrance. Turn left. Each lake has a separate access.

BIG & LITTLE WHITE OAK LAKES

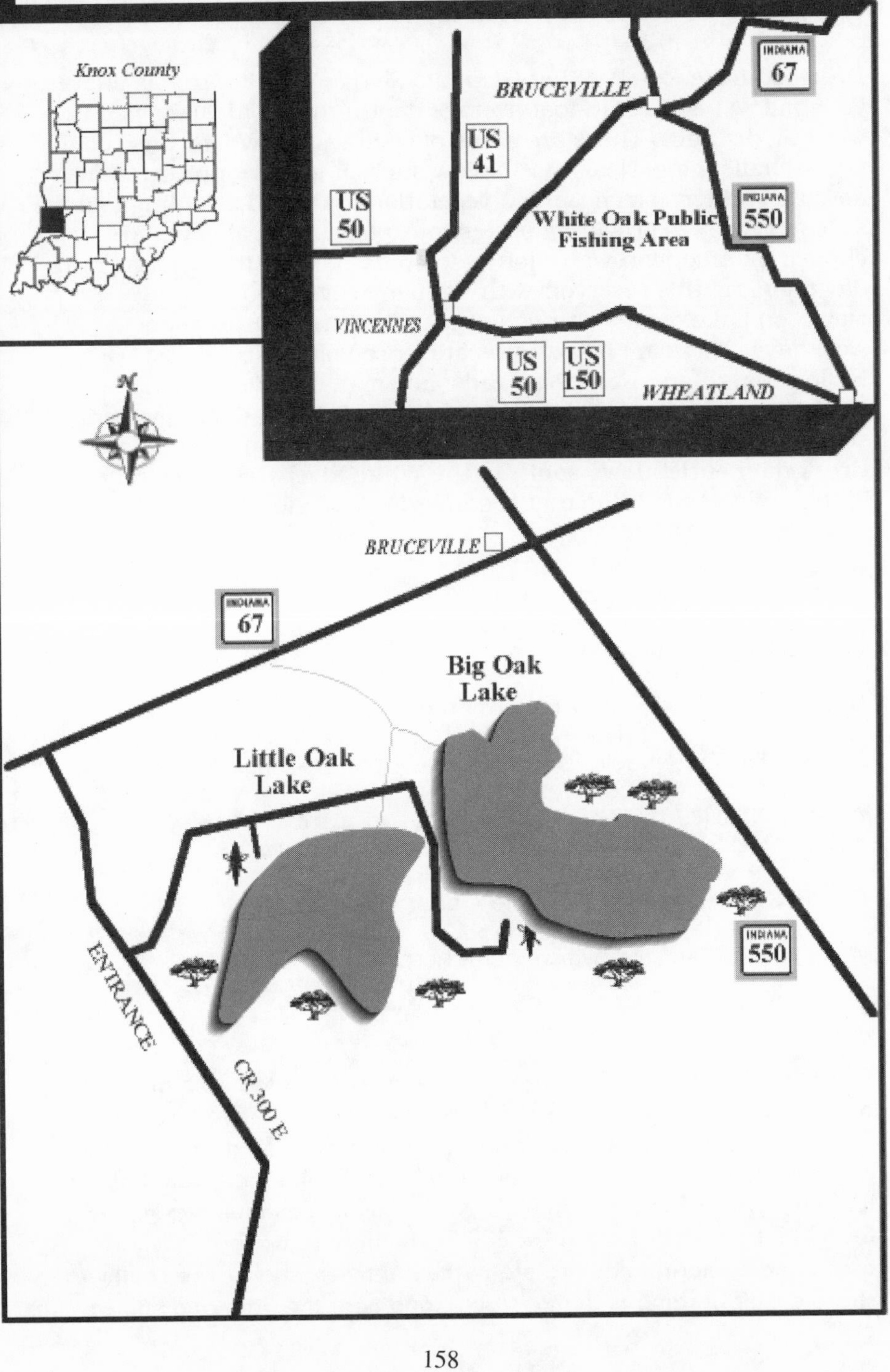

66. DOGWOOD LAKE

- **Steer a course through standing & submerged snags & coves of water lotus**

Dogwood Lake (est.1965) at Glendale Fish & Wildlife Area is a large, yet shallow reservoir (8 foot average depth) that is ideal for paddlers wanting distance. There are areas of open waters where wind could prove challenging. Near the shallow shore it is more protected by aquatic and terrestrial upland vegetation and dead standing and submerged trees providing places to explore. Several coves are choked by American water lotus. It would be easy to pass an entire day paddling this reservoir with its many coves.
Dogwood Lake teems with fishermen. Go during sunrise on weekdays. There are also ramps at Goose Pond, Wren Pond, Dove Hollow Marsh and Redwing Ponds; all small impoundments, all less than ten acres. Dogwood Lake is closed to boating during waterfowl season. The East Fork Fish Hatchery is open to tours. The Mud Creek dam outlet flows south to the White River East Fork. The Flatrock access is located at the East Fork White River.

USGS MAP(S): Glendale 1:24,000
VICINITY: Washington, Daviess County
LAKE ACREAGE /DEPTH: 1,400 a./42'
PADDLING TIME: half to full day
LEVEL OF DIFFICULTY: Class I
HAZARDS/PORTAGES: wind, no swimming, seasonal hunting, (closed Oct 23-Nov 1)
INFO SOURCES: Glendale Fish and Wildlife Area, RR #2, Box 300, Montgomery, IN 47558
AREA OUTFITTERS/LIVERIES: seasonal rentals adjacent to office
GAMEFISH SPECIES: bluegill, largemouth bass, perch, crappie redear, sunfish, catfish
CAMPING: Glendale Fish & Wildlife Area (812) 644-7711 Class A & C
MEDICAL ASSISTANCE: Daviess County Hospital, 1314 Grand Ave., Washington, IN 47501, (812) 254-2760

ACCESS: The southeast Daviess County lake is located 10.5 miles SE of Washington & 1.5 miles SE of Glendale. There are two boat ramps located on the SW & NW opposite shore. From US 50 at Montgomery go south eight miles on Sportsmen Rd/CR 650 E 4.5 mi. to CR 400 S & turn west. Go 0.5 mi. to CR 600 E. & turn south. Continue two mi. on CR 600 E to the entrance at CR 600 S. The boat ramp, boat rental, office and campgrounds are along the northwest shore. The southwest shore auxiliary ramp is along Waco Road near the dam and spillway.

DOGWOOD LAKE

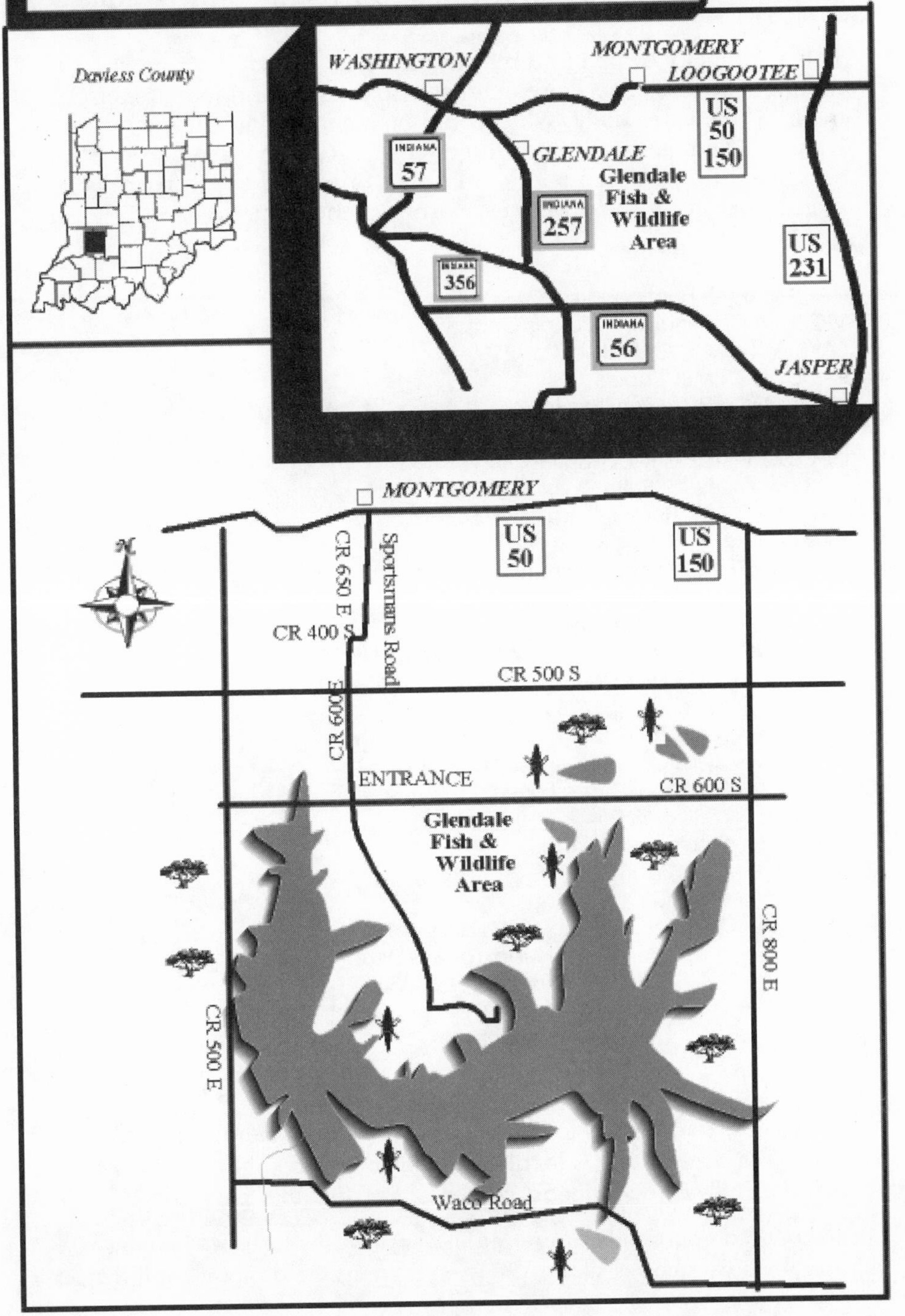

67. HUNTINGBURG LAKE

Enjoy a city lake beyond the suburbs at country edge

This idyllic city owned and maintained lake is ideal for non-motorized boats. There are open country vistas and forest encircles most of the water body. Wind could be a concern in the open waters. There are two major finger coves. A golf course borders the southeast finger cove making an upland pastoral scene.There is a picnic shelter on the northwest corner of the dam.

USGS MAP(S): Huntingburg 1:24,000
VICINITY: Huntingburg, Dubois County
LAKE ACREAGE /DEPTH: 147 a./21'
PADDLING TIME: 2 hours
LEVEL OF DIFFICULTY: Class I
HAZARDS/PORTAGES: wind
INFO SOURCES: City of Huntingburg
508 4th St
Huntingburg, IN 47542
(812) 683-2211
AREA OUTFITTERS/LIVERIES: none
GAMEFISH SPECIES: crappie, largemouth bass, carp, sauger
CAMPING: Sugar Ridge Fish & Wildlife Area
2310 E. SR 364
Winslow, IN 47958
(812) 789-2724
Class C
Ferdinand State Forest
6583 E. SR 264
Ferdinand, IN 47532
(812) 367-1524
Class C
MEDICAL ASSISTANCE: St. Joseph's Hospital
1900 Medical Arts Dr.
Huntingburg, IN 47542
(812) 683-2121
Ambulance 911

ACCESS: Lake access is located two miles west of Huntingburg on SR 64. The access lane is located on the south side of the highway, near the spillway & northeast corner of the dam in a pine grove.

HUNTINGBURG LAKE

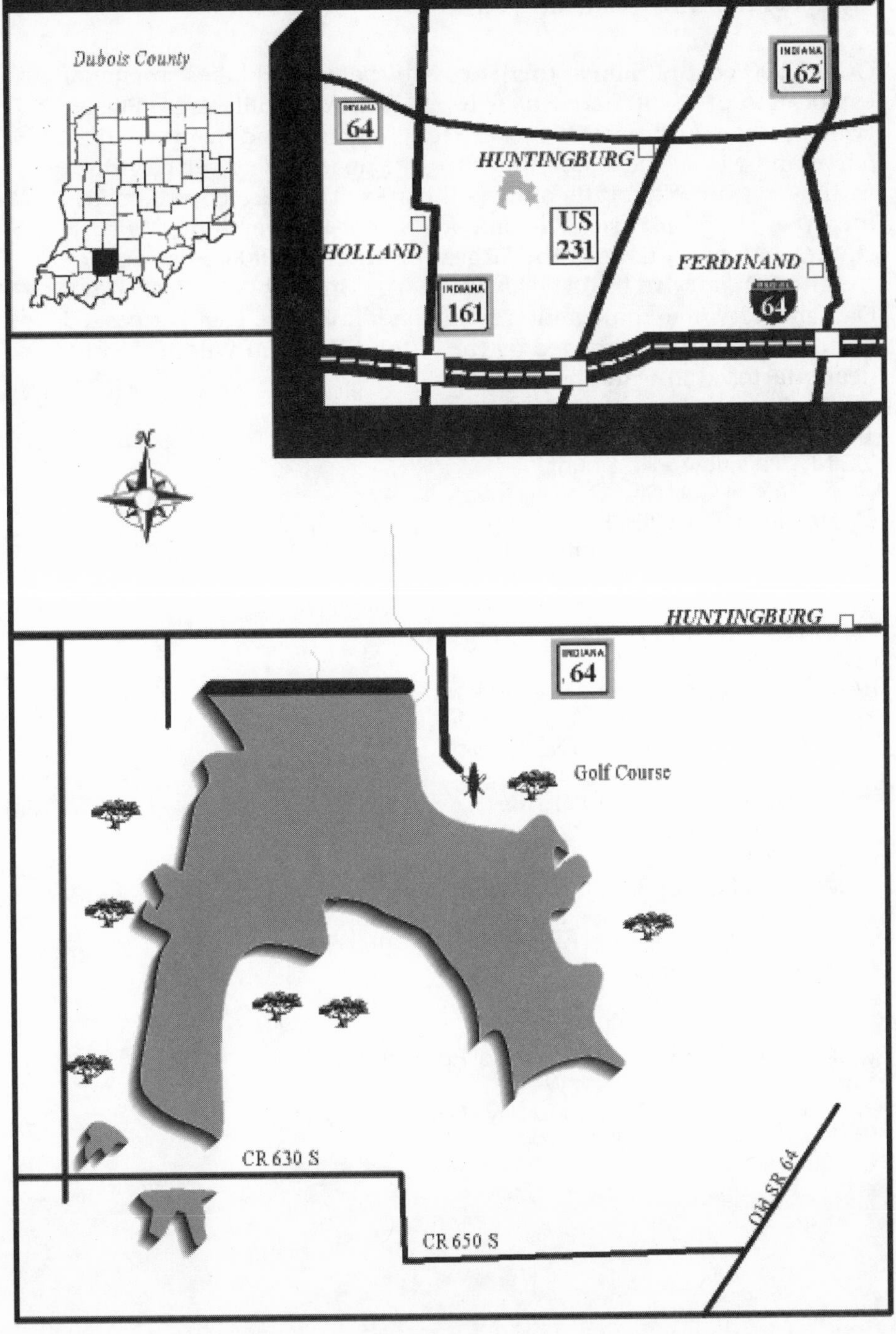

68. SUGAR RIDGE FISH & WILDLIFE AREA

- Explore man-carved "canals"

Out of 100 coal pit lakes, there are five coal mined lakes worthy of exploration at 7,300 acre Sugar Ridge Fish & Wildlife Area. Pigeon, Beaver, Bass, and Barrett Pits are long, narrow and deep pits that curve and wind. These channels are like deadwater river corridors with exposed rocky bluffs and spoil banks. They are covered with evergreens reminiscent of a compact bonzai-like version of North Ontario. Augusta Lake is the largest however the lake is so acidic that no fish survive in its clear water. The Snakey Point Marsh near Oakland City also makes interesting paddling. The easily accessed natural wetland is managed by the Patoka National Wildlife Refuge, headquartered in Oakland City.

USGS MAP(S): Augusta, Oakland City, Winslow, Folsomville 1:24,000
VICINITY: Winslow, Pike County
Oakland City, Gibson County
LAKE ACREAGE /DEPTH: Pigeon 22 a., Augusta Lake 33 a.,
Barrett Pit 10.8 a., Beaver Pit 17 a.,
Bass Pit 22 a., Snakey Point-Oakland City
Patoka NWR 280 a. swamp
PADDLING TIME: 1 to 2 hours per pit
LEVEL OF DIFFICULTY: Class I
HAZARDS/PORTAGES: electric motors only, downed trees, aquatic growth, low water, seasonal hunting
INFO SOURCES: Sugar Ridge Fish & Wildlife Area
2310 E SR 364
Winslow, IN 47598
(812) 789-2724
AREA OUTFITTERS/LIVERIES: none
GAMEFISH SPECIES: bluegill, largemouth bass, warmouth, redear, catfish, trout (Bethel Pit only), no fish at Augusta Lake (too acid)
CAMPING: Sugar Ridge FWA
Class C sites
(812) 789-2724
MEDICAL ASSISTANCE: Wirth Regional Hospital
SR 64 W
Oakland City, IN 47660
(812) 749-6111

ACCESS: Sugar Ridge FWA is located in Winslow-Stendahl area of east central Pike County. There are six areas but only Areas II, IV & VI are recommended:

Area II- Pigeon Lake- Curving linear lake. Forest bluff outcrops and a slag hill near access site. From Indiana SR 61, south of Winslow & SR 364, go west on Royalty Road. Follow the short road to Pike CR 475 S and turn west. Proceed on CR 475 S to the marked access road near CR 125 E.

Area IV-Augusta Lake, Largest pit lake on the property. Plenty of snags. Two major finger coves. Access is carry down at 4A parking area. From the property headquarters junction of SR 61 & SR 364, go east on SR 364 three miles to Pike CR 450 E and turn south. Proceed 0.6 miles to the access road left & 4A parking site at the dam, NW corner spillway.

Area VI-Beaver Pit, Bass Pit and Barrett Pit: Along Haul Road. All 3 pits are long, narrow canal-like waterways. From SR 64 (east of SR 64 and SR 61 junction) go south two miles on Scottsburg Road to Pike CR 900 S and turn east. Continue 2.2 miles east just past Bethel Church to the Area VI entrance and Haul Road. Proceed south to Beaver Pit and Bass Pit. Go east on CR 1000 S and proceed to Barrett Pit, west of SR 257 at Stendal on CR 1000 S.

Snakey Point, Patoka NWR-Marsh along the swampy bottoms of the Patoka River South Fork. Access is carry down. From SR 64, 1.3 miles east of Oakland City and the Patoka NWR office, turn north onto CR 1275 E and follow the curve north and east 1.3 miles to Snakey Point Marsh (812) 749-3199.

Wind Dancer

SUGAR RIDGE FWA

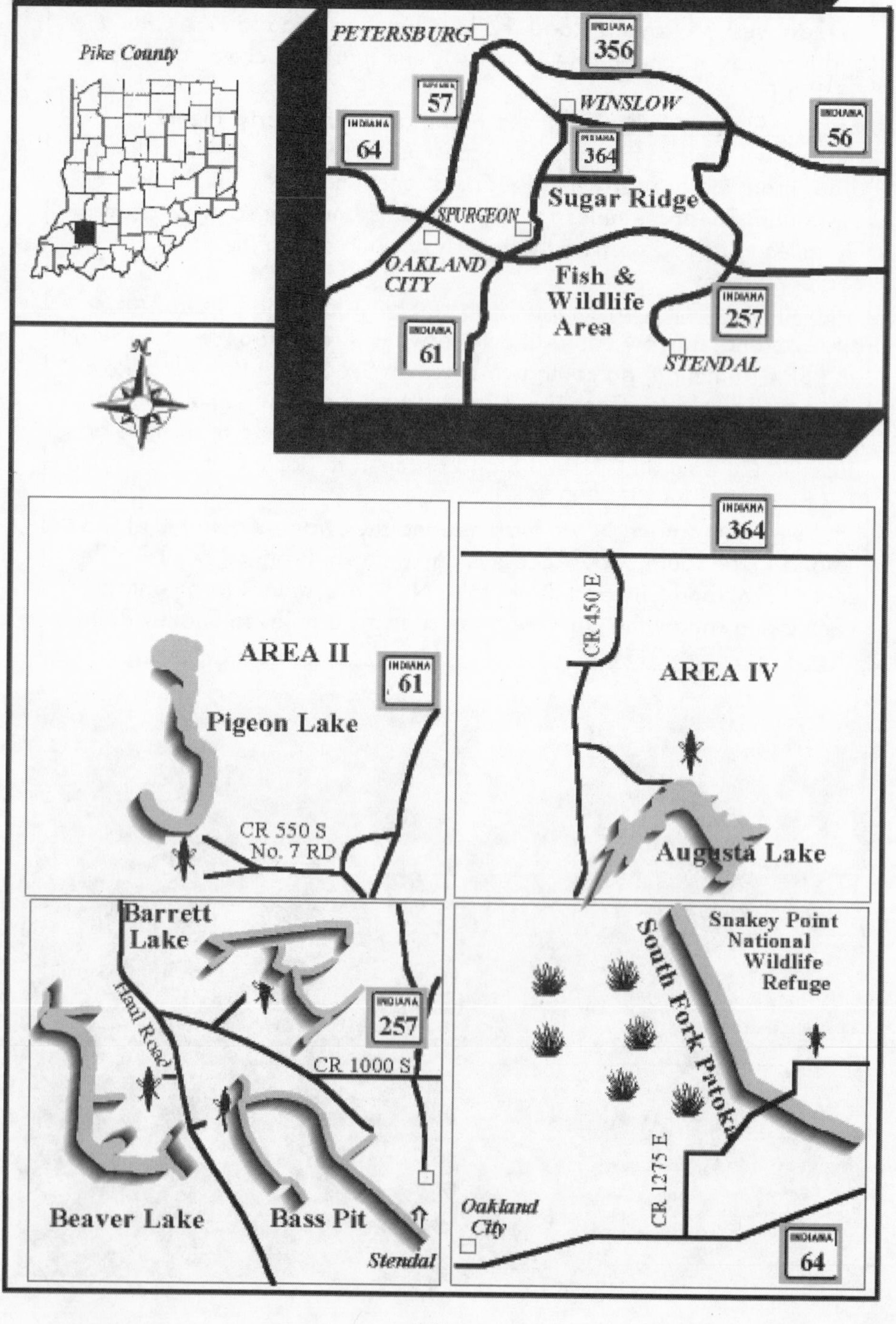

Fall Sunrise on Lincoln Lake

Bald Cypress at Hovey Lake

69. LINCOLN LAKE

- Paddle near Abraham Lincoln's boyhood home

Peaceful Lake Lincoln lies within Lincoln State Park, just south of Abraham Lincoln's boyhood home, which is now a national monument. This is an ideal lake for families. Canoes may be rented by the hour or day. Additional watercraft on the reservoir may include rowboats and paddleboats with trolling electric motors. Concessions may be purchased at lakeside in the upper level of the beach bathhouse from Memorial Day to Labor Day. The lakeside picnic shelter near the boat ramp, beach, boathouse and boat rental overlooks the lake. There are two fishing piers. Camping and family cabins allow visitors to stay overnight. A state fishing license may be purchased at the park office. A former fish hatchery operated at the base of the dam. Hiking Trail 1 encircles the lake. A seasonal permit is required to launch private boats.

USGS MAP(S): Santa Claus 1:24,000
VICINITY: Dale, Spencer County
LAKE ACREAGE /DEPTH: 77 a./24'
PADDLING TIME: 2 hours
LEVEL OF DIFFICULTY: Class I
HAZARDS/PORTAGES: wind, electric motors only
INFO SOURCES: Lincoln State Park
Box 216
Lincoln City, IN 47552
(812) 937-4710
AREA OUTFITTERS/LIVERIES: seasonal boat rental near beach
GAMEFISH SPECIES: bluegill, largemouth bass, crappie,
redear, sunfish, catfish
CAMPING: Lincoln State Park, Class A & C (812) 937-4710
MEDICAL ASSISTANCE: St. Elizabeth Ann Seton Hospital
1116 Millis Ave.
Boonville, IN 47601
(812) 897-4800

ACCESS: From I-64 exit 57 south onto US 231/SR62 and travel through Dale to SR 162 at Gentryville. Go east on SR 162 to Lincoln State Park and Lake Lincoln just south of Lincoln Boyhood National Memorial and Lincoln City. The boat ramp is a few yards west of the beach.

LINCOLN LAKE

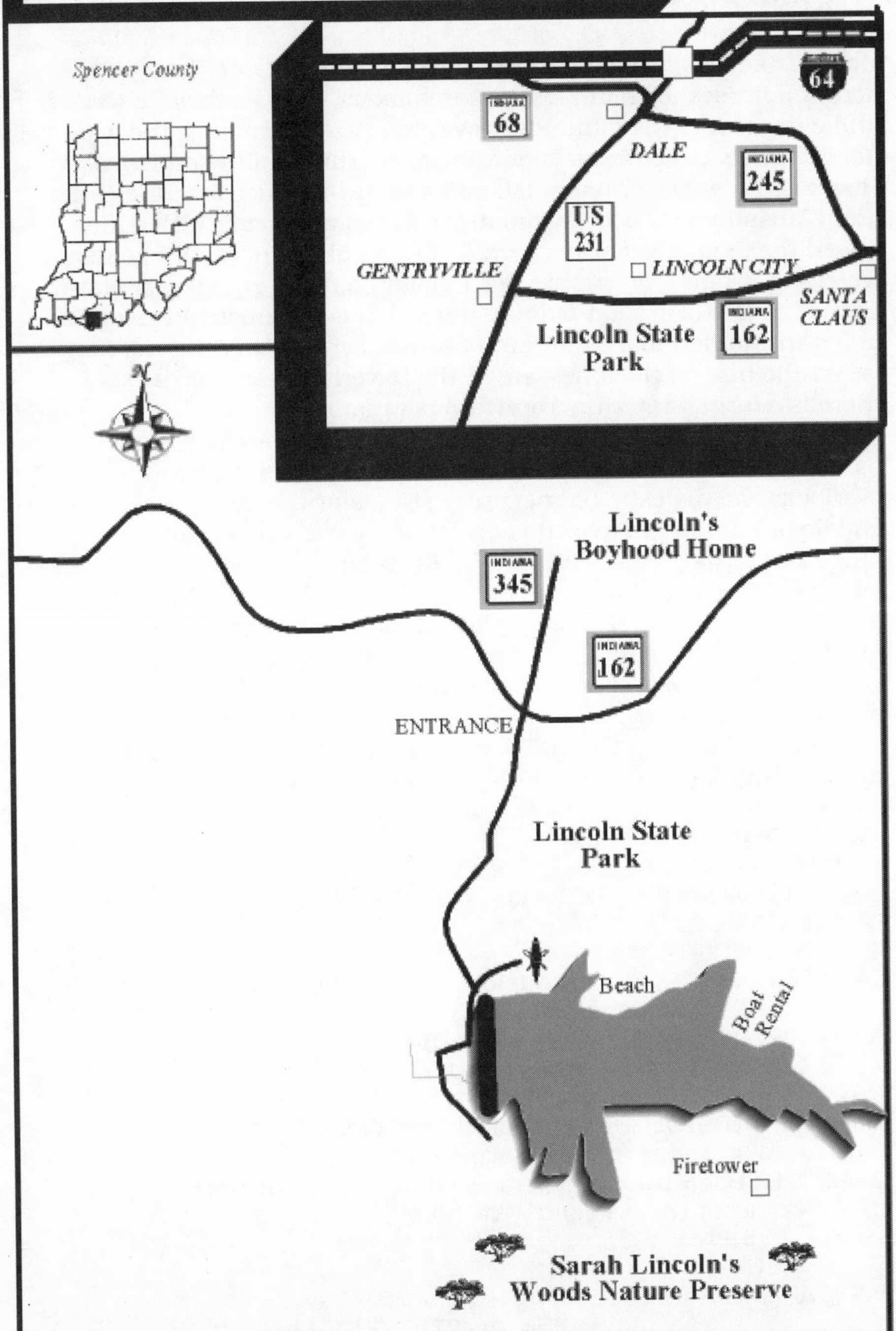
Spencer County
64
INDIANA 68
DALE
INDIANA 245
US 231
GENTRYVILLE
LINCOLN CITY
SANTA CLAUS
INDIANA 162
Lincoln State Park
N
Lincoln's Boyhood Home
INDIANA 345
INDIANA 162
ENTRANCE
Lincoln State Park
Beach
Boat Rental
Firetower
Sarah Lincoln's Woods Nature Preserve

70. HOVEY LAKE

- **Weave between bald cypress on Indiana's southernmost lake**

Hovey Lake was formed 500 years ago when the Ohio River cut across a horseshoe bend leaving an oxbow lake. During late winter and early spring the Ohio River overflows and inundates the wide floodplain that separates lake from river. Three miles southwest of Hovey Lake, above Wabash Island near the confluence of the Ohio and Wabash rivers is the Uniontown Locks and Dam, which have raised the Ohio River water level 7-11 feet above normal. The dam waters that have spilled over have resulted in an even larger Hovey Lake. The DNR Division of Fish and Wildlife administers Hovey Lake and surrounding marsh lowlands (4,400 acres). After many years lapse, the bald eagle is nesting in the towering bald cypress and there is a large wintering waterfowl population.

From the access site adjacent east of property headquarters office, paddle the shoreline south and east where an observation tower overlooks the majestic bald cypress stands at the lake's center. Paddle out and maneuver through the trees, which are alive with migratory birds during spring. Wind can be a problem on the open lake. Mississippian Indian villages (prior to 1,500 B.C.) once occupied the higher ground of the shoreline. The lake is named for Alvin P. Hovey, Indiana governor (1888-1892) who once was landlord of the lake. If adventuresome, consider a carry down and paddle west of Hovey Lake on the Big Cypress Oxbow Slough where there is access along CR 400W west of Hovey Lake. Several miles north is Half Moon Pond, another canoeable DNR unit.

USGS MAP(S): Uniontown 1:24,000
VICINITY: Mount Vernon, Posey County
LAKE ACREAGE /DEPTH: 1,400 a./50'
PADDLING TIME: half to full day
LEVEL OF DIFFICULTY: Class I
HAZARDS/PORTAGES: IO allowed, 10 mph ltd., wind,
seasonal hunting
INFO SOURCES: Hovey Lake Fish and Wildlife Area
1298 W. Graddey Road, RR#5, Mt. Vernon, IN
47620 (812) 838-2927
AREA OUTFITTERS/LIVERIES: johnboat rental at property office &
access site
GAMEFISH SPECIES: bluegill, largemouth bass, crappie, catfish
CAMPING: Hovey Lake Fish and Wildlife Area
(812) 838-2927
Class C
MEDICAL ASSISTANCE: Deaconess Hospital, 600 Mary St.
Evansville, IN 47710, (812) 426-3000

ACCESS: Hovey Lake is located nine miles southwest of Mount Vernon on SR 69. The boat ramp is adjacent to the headquarters, rentals & campground on the west side of the lake. Big Cypress Slough is two miles west of Hovey Lake on Posey CR 1500 S, then north on CR 425 W. Half Moon Pond is north on CR 300 W, from 1500 S to CR 1100 S west towards the Wabash River.

HOVEY LAKE

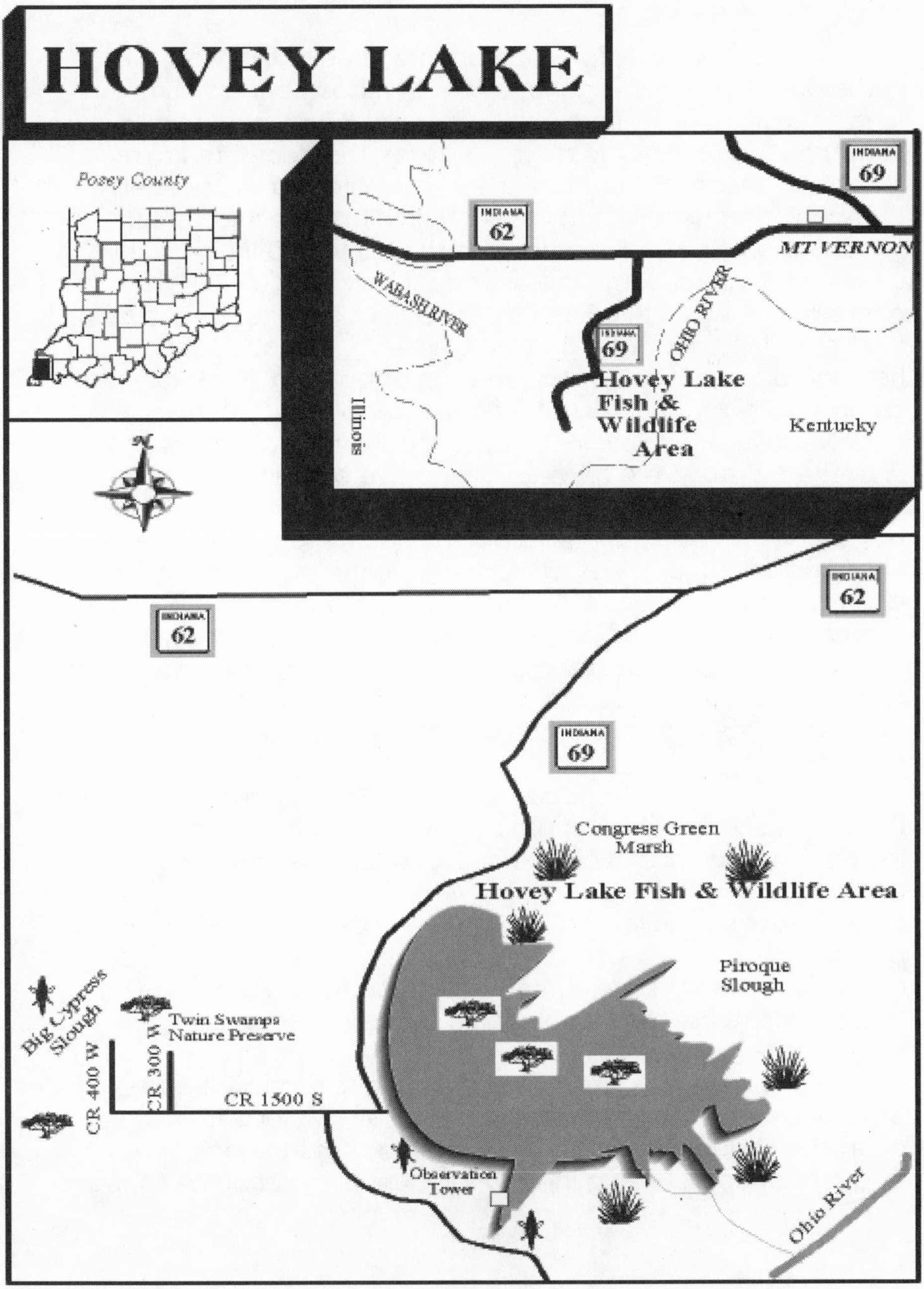

Indiana Streams: An Overview

*" where th' ripples on th' river,
kinda chuckle as they flow,"*

from *Ain't God Good to Indiana*
by William Herschell, 1940

Indiana's streams, its forks or branches, creeks and rivers, are numerous. A stream is a generic term that describes a volume of running water moving from point A to point B that may greatly vary in volume from a brook to a river. The largest surface streams are known as rivers and streams of a lesser size are known as rivulets, branches, prongs, forks and creeks. Rainfall is the primary source of all surface water in Indiana and one third of total annual rainfall is carried away by streams. The abundant precipitation (38"-42" annually) is shed by three major drainage basins: the Great Lakes, the Upper Mississippi River and the Ohio River. This aquatic natural heritage offers canoe and kayakers an opportunity to explore places along easy going streams not readily available on foot.

Unlike lakes which are static water bodies that stay calm and unexcited, streams are always on the move even in deep winter, returning volumes of water downstream to their oceanic sources. Unlike lakes, exploring will require a shuttle on streams since few would paddle and pole back upstream to the starting point. Too low and too high water levels may not permit paddling. The 35 select streams normally have adequate flowage, some seasonally, legal access availability and scenery however expect some despoliation in urban areas as well as rural areas. The majority of streams are declared legally navigable and paddling recreational usage is permitted.

The majority of public access sites are owned and maintained by the Indiana DNR, Division of Fish and Wildlife yet there are several regional, municipal and private access sites. These mini-parks that allow aquatic passage are usually well marked by brown highway signs. Always park in the designated site or as far off the highways as possible for safety sake. Never block access. Do your part to keep access sites clean. Drive carefully from access to access and home and back. Use care when unloading or loading boats along roadsides. Arrive alive.

Indiana streams vary in flowage season to season. Streams statewide are at their highest flow during late winter and early spring, oftentime flooded. Fast water in spring may not take long to reach the takeout point. Finding the right amount of water at the right time

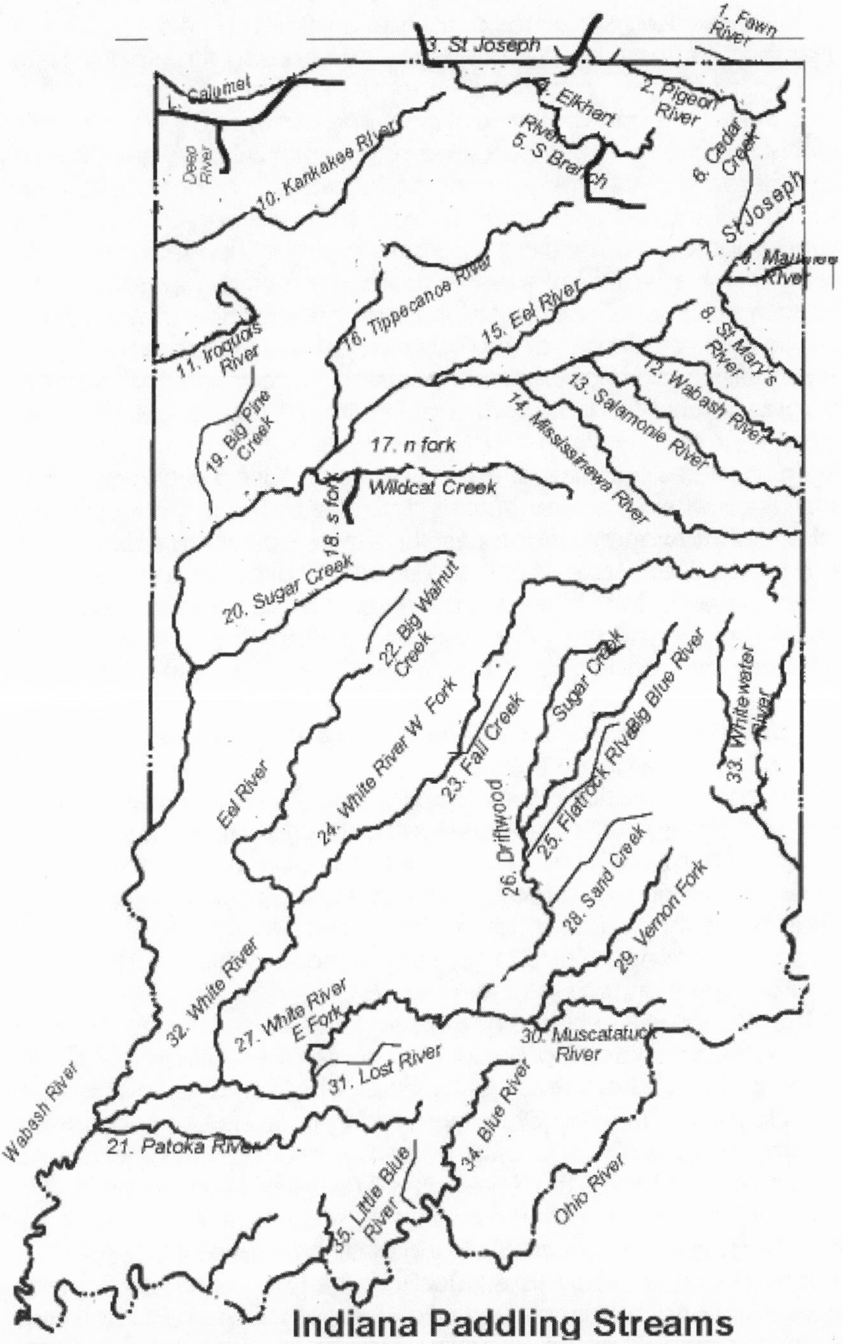

1. Fawn River
3. St Joseph
Calumet
2. Pigeon River
4. Elkhart River
5. S Branch
Deep River
10. Kankakee River
6. Cedar Creek
7. St Joseph
River
8. St Mary's River
16. Tippecanoe River
15. Eel River
11. Iroquois River
12. Wabash River
13. Salamonie River
14. Mississinewa River
19. Big Pine Creek
17. n fork
Wildcat Creek
18. s fork
20. Sugar Creek
22. Big Walnut Creek
Sugar Creek
Big Blue River
33. Whitewater River
23. Fall Creek
24. White River W Fork
Eel River
25. Flatrock River
26. Driftwood
28. Sand Creek
29. Vernon Fork
32. White River
27. White River E Fork
30. Muscatatuck River
31. Lost River
Wabash River
21. Patoka River
34. Blue River
Ohio River
35. Little Blue River

Indiana Paddling Streams

is the first challenge of paddling a stream. The northern Indiana, lake-fed streams such as the Fawn River and Tippecanoe River insure steady dependable flow. South of the lake country, streams are more dependent on rainfall or springs, unless dammed. The central plain and southern hill streams nearly go dry as summer passes into fall except during a summer downpour or reservoir drawdown. It can be a frustrating and unpleasant paddling experience in low water with numerous carrys. The 35 streams are rated Class 1 and are considered easy however during periods of above normal flow sections of some streams can approach Class 2 and Class 3 with dangerous rapids. Paddling is possible anytime the weather permits and when the water level is adequate. The most dangerous paddling moments occur at high flow when strainers may trap the canoe and kayak and/or you or when running low dams. Hypothermia may happen in any season. Topographical maps are always useful to the outdoorsman. A six to ten mile long distance is far enough for a day trip

Indiana shares paddling streams with neighboring Michigan, Ohio and Illinois within the Great Lakes drainage basin. The St. Joseph of Lake Michigan and its tributaries: the Fawn, Pigeon and Elkhart rivers empty into Great Lake Michigan (Northern Lakes Natural Region). Deep River and the Little Calumet River East Branch also stream to Lake Michigan (Northwestern Morainal Natural Region). The Maumee River and its tributaries: Cedar Creek, St. Joseph River and St. Marys River flow to Lake Erie (Black Swamp Natural Region and Bluffton Till Plain Section). The Great Lake basin has well sustained stream flow throughout the year.

The Upper Mississippi River basin includes the Kankakee River and its largest tributary, the Iroquois River; both originate in northwestern Indiana within the Grand Prairie Natural Region. Both of these prairie streams have been altered by drainage in Indiana however in neighboring Illinois they retain their greatest naturalness. Establishment of a national wildlife refuge along the Kankakee River will restore some of its former glory.

The Wabash River drains nearly two thirds of Indiana, forming Indiana's largest drainage of 24,206 square miles (mostly central till plain). Indiana's State River rises in adjacent Ohio and flows west and south to merge with the Ohio River, taking in numerous floatable streams along its 500 mile journey: the Salamonie, Mississinewa, Eel, Tippecanoe, Wildcat, Big Pine, Sugar Creek, Patoka and White rivers.

The White River is a short 50 mile long stream but its east and west forks are several hundred miles long and have several tributary streams that offer accessible paddling. The East Fork is considered more rustic and rural and even wild whereas the West Fork is thought of as considerably urban in the upper half while the lower segment becomes rural and remote. The East Fork paddlable tributaries include Sand Creek, Muscatatuck River (Bluegrass Natural Region)

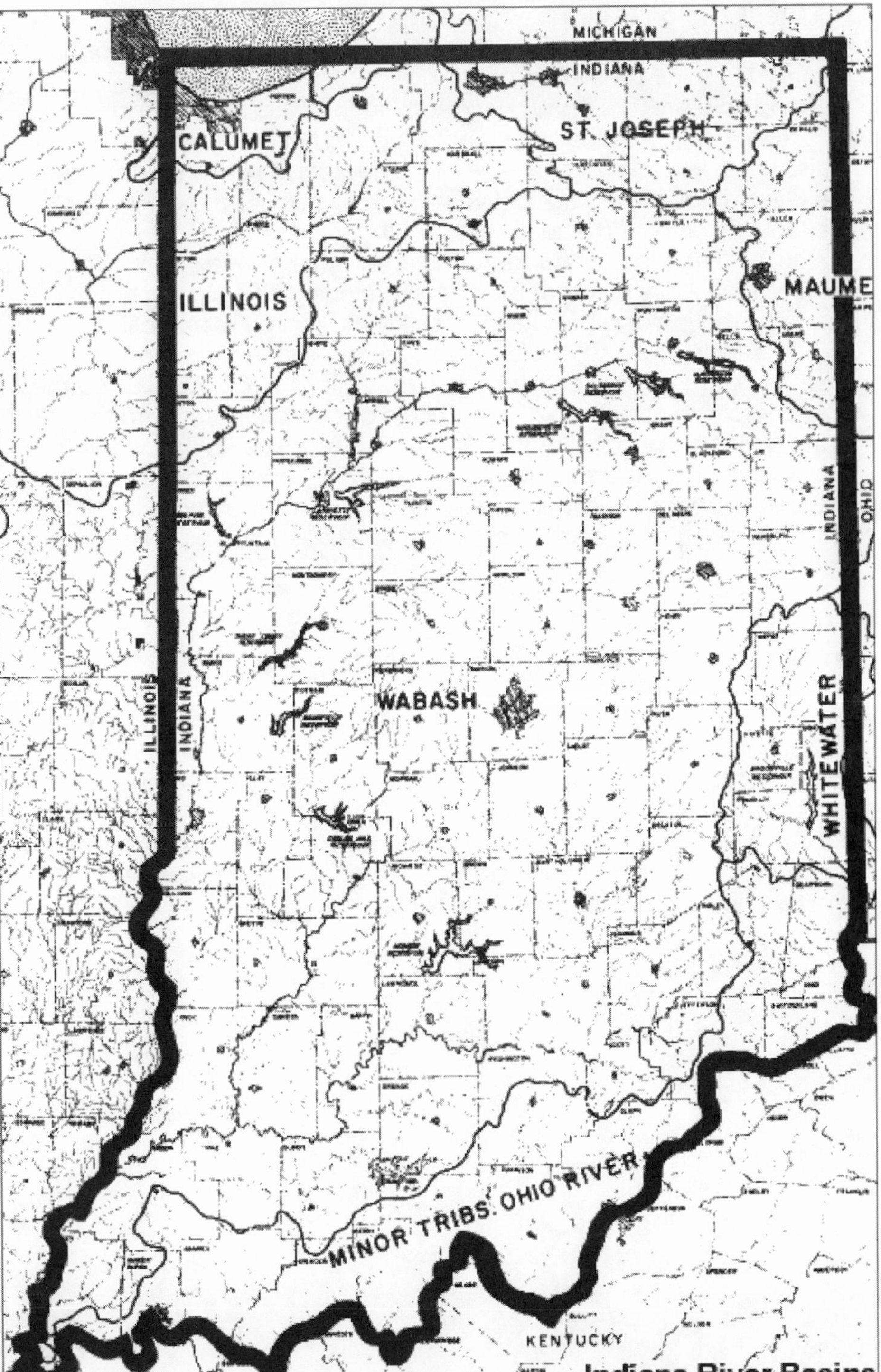

Source: IDNR Division of Water

and Lost River (Shawnee Hills Natural Region). The West Fork features Fall Creek (Tipton Till Plain Section), the southern Eel River (Shawnee Hills Natural Region) and Big Walnut Creek (entrenched valley of Central Till Plain Natural Region).

Paddable streams that flow directly to the Ohio River includes the Blue River and Little Blue River (Shawnee Hills Natural Region). The Whitewater River flows into the Ohio (Bluegrass Natural Region) via the Great Miami River, about five miles upstream from the mouth of the Ohio River, extreme southwest Ohio.

In 1973, the Indiana General Assembly passed the Indiana Rivers Preservation Act to protect Indiana's remaining free flowing natural streams. The Indiana DNR Resources Rivers Program is primarily focused on ten river segments which are considered the most representative natural and scenic river sections in the state. Since the passage of the act, three streams have been designated into the Natural, Scenic and Recreational River System: Blue River, Cedar Creek and Wildcat Creek, The following three streams may be eligible for designation: Sand Creek, Big Walnut Creek and Tippecanoe River. The following rivers have been studied for inclusion in the River Program: Big Pine Creek, Elkhart River South Branch, Sugar Creek and the Whitewater River.

Additional programs exist in the DNR to further the protection and enhancement of Indiana's rivers. In 1991, the Operation Clean Stream program was initiated by the Division of Law Enforcement to reduce pollution, litter and alcohol and drug abuse on Indiana rivers.

During 1992, the DNR organized the first Rivers Advisory Group to help assist the DNR in the development of a new river cleanup program to be administered by the DNR. What evolved through this effort was the Hoosier Riverkeepers and Riverwatch programs. The mission of the program is to heighten water quality awareness and improve riparian stewardship.

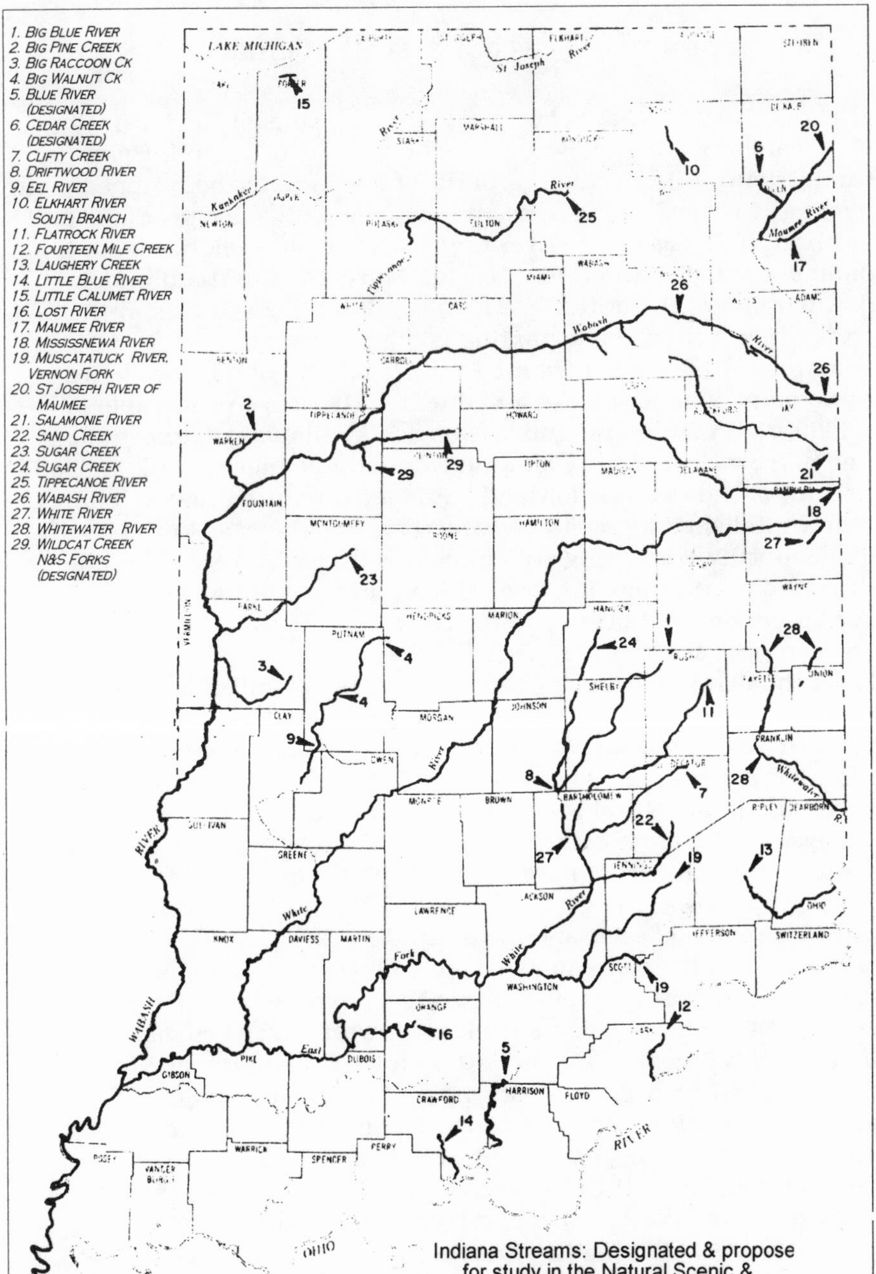

Indiana Streams: Designated & propose for study in the Natural Scenic & Recreational Stream System

Source: IDNR, Outdoor Recreation Division

1. FAWN RIVER

- Be swept away by a cool & swift Michiana stream

This relatively unknown northern stream begins at the Fawn River Fish Hatchery dam spillway at the north edge of Orland. Upstream from Orland, this circuitous course of a wild water body appears on maps as Crooked Creek; a scenic segment with some deadfalls and low bridge portages. The river that rises from a creek begins at the Jimmerson Lake outlet near Nevada Mills. The first road bridge downstream of the outlet (Steuben CR 600 W) has access at the SE corner however roadside parking is not permitted.

More than 40 lakes contribute to the delightful and beloved stream as do many smaller creeks and ditches. There is considerable wildlife-rich marshland and streamside swamp shrub forest along this narrow clear river. Oak-studded morainic hills and till knolls rise out of the swampy lowlands. Protected nature preserves have been established along its' vegetated banks. The east-to-west and finally northwest flowing stream passes under I-80-90 toll road three times and there are several road bridge crossings and portages along its' journey to the St. Joseph River of Lake Michigan. The compact size of the river is ideal for paddlers.

From the fish hatchery at Orland to Greenfield Mills, (Rinkel Mill still grinding), the river gradually widens. From the Greenfield mill pond there is a portage or shuttle around the mill race to Lagrange CR 1050 E bridge, 150 yards north. The river veers north, crossing under the Indiana Toll Road I-80-90, and enters neighboring Michigan. In Branch county, (P.L.) at the Gunthrope Rd. and the Danber Rd. culverts. Entering St. Joseph County, MI, the Fawn flows through the village of Fawn River. Fawn River Road bridge provides roadside access; (P.L.) around the bridge and old breached dam adjacent downstream (sharp bend). Downstream a short distance, paddlers may enter Fawn River via Lee Lake access channel. The stream curves back southwest from Michigan and then southwest of the Indiana 80-90 toll road and under SR 9 bridge. The river begins to back up and flows past and over Star Mill and two dams (P.R.) at the lane road before the first dam and carry 100 yards beyond bypassing the second dam). Flowing to and northwest of Scott, the river turns abruptly north to re-enter Michigan near Aldrich Lake and Pickerel Lake. Meandering northwest, near the US 12 crossing, the stream is within a mile's reach of the Pigeon River which is also on its' way to the St. Joseph River; separated by moraine. Northwest of Klinger Lake, the Fawn River curves west toward Hay Bridge Rd. (roadside access). Downstream, the Sevision Rd. bridge, SE corner, provides level access. The Fawn River begins to back up at Lutz Rd. from the Simplex Dam, downstream at Constantine (P.R.). Downstream from the Simplex Dam, the river picks up speed in it's final 30 minute segment to the St. Joseph. Novices may want to take out at the Simplex Dam (P.R.). Just beyond the Norfolk & Southern Railroad bridge is the old Tumble Dam ruins and a sharp bend in the river (P.L.). There are strainers about the Featherstone Rd. bridge wooded flood plain. Enter the St. Joseph River, downstream 300 feet from the Constantine Dam and paddle another 1,000 feet to the access before the US 131 bridge on the left or south bank in Constantine, MI. The next access downstream on the St. Joseph River is at Mottville (6 mi).

USGS MAP(S): Indiana & Michigan topos:
Angola West, Orland, Bronson South, Burr Oak, Sturgis, Lagrange, Shipshewana. Klinger Lake, Constantine 1:24,000
VICINITY: Nevada Mills, Orland, Steuben County,
Greenfield Mills, Star Mill, Howe, Scott, Lagrange County, IN
Fawn River, Sturgis, Constantine, St. Joseph County, MI
STREAM DISTANCE/TRIPS: approx. 60 miles, 6 or more trips
LEVEL OF DIFFICULTY: Class I
HAZARDS/PORTAGES: portages at low dams, culverts, weirs & low bridges esp. during high water, swift current, deadfall snags, deepwater, sharp bends, strainers, lack of water July to fall, fast water at Constantine
INFO SOURCES: Pigeon River Canoe-n-Camp
(219) 475-5512 or 351-3537
Fawn River Fish Hatchery
6889 N SR 327
Orland, IN 46776
(219) 829-6241
Three Rivers Canoe Rental
(888) 314-7444
St. Joseph County, MI Parks and Recreation
POB 4327
Centreville, MI 49032
(616) 467-6361
Michigan DNR
Fisheries Div. 12
621 N. 10th St.
Plainwell, MI 49080
(616) 685-6851 (800) ASK-FISH
AREA OUTFITTERS/LIVERIES: Pigeon River Canoe-n-Camp
3490 S 325 W
Pleasant Lake, IN 46779
(219) 475-5512 or 351-3537
Three Rivers Canoe Rental
1509 S. Main
Conservation Park
Three Rivers, MI 49093
(888) 314-7444 (616) 279-9326

St. Joseph Parks and Recreation
POB 4327
Centreville, MI 49032
(616) 467-6361

GAMEFISH SPECIES: largemouth & smallmouth bass, pike, catfish

CAMPING: Pigeon River Fish and Wildlife Area
Box 71, 8310 E 300 N
Mongo, IN 46771
(219) 367-2164
Class C
Nottawa Park at Sand Lake
St. Joseph County Parks & Recreation
60778 Railroad St.
Nottowa, MI 49075
(616) 467-5519 (seasonal)
Class A, B & C

MEDICAL ASSISTANCE: Cameron Memorial Hospital
410 E. Maumee St.
Angola, IN 46703
(219) 665-2141
Vencor Hospital
207 N. Townline Dr.
Lagrange, IN 46761
(219) 463-2143
Sturgis Hospital
916 Myrtle Ave.
Sturgis, MI 49091
(616) 651-7824
Three Rivers Area Hospital
1111 W. Broadway
Three Rivers, MI 49093
(616) 278-1145

ACCESS SITES	SECTION	RIVER MILES
A. NW of Nevada Mills, Steuben CR 600 W, SE roadside, (no parking)	A-B	4.5 miles
B. Fawn River Fish Hatchery, Orland, SR 327 N, (P.L.) dam, (1st best access)	B-C	5.5 miles
C. Greenfield Mills, mill pond, CR 750 N, next to Rinkel Mill, roadside pullout NW bank (low bridge at last county rd (CR 1100 E) before mill pond, (P.R.)	C-D	150 yard carry/shuttle
D. Greenfield Mills, Lagrange CR 1050 bridge, portage or shuttle to pullout & carry		

down, (150 yds north of Rinkel Mill) Note* Two SE to SW portages (P.L.) around culverts in Branch County, MI	D-E	14 miles
E. Fawn River, MI, Fawn River Rd. bridge, MI, (P.L.) at SE corner before bridge & old breached dam, put-in at SW corner	E-F	2 miles
F. Lee Lake MDNR access via channel, Fawn River Rd. pullout, west of Fawn River Village, MI.	F-G	7 miles
G. Star Mill & Dams, Lagrange CR 700 N, 0.5 mi W of SR 9, north roadside pullout or take lane road north to Star Mill site & dams. Portage dams by landing at lane road (P.R.) & carry 100 yards beyond 2nd dam (alt. access upstream at Lagrange CR 100 E, SE corner, E of SR 9 or downstream at CR 250 W/ Balk Rd., MI,	G-H	11 miles
H. Lagrange CR 600 W bridge, SW corner, NW parking, roadside north of Scott	H-I	11.5 miles
I. Hay Bridge Road bridge access, St. Joseph Co., MI, 100 yards west of SW corner, roadside pull out & access. (alt. access at Roberts Bridge, Dickinson Rd. upstream or Sevison Rd., SE corner, downstream)	I-J	5.5 miles
J. Simplex Dam, (P.R.) Old Centreville-Constantine Rd. west from Kalamazoo Rd.		
K. Constantine public access, Water St., east of US 131	J-K	1.5 miles

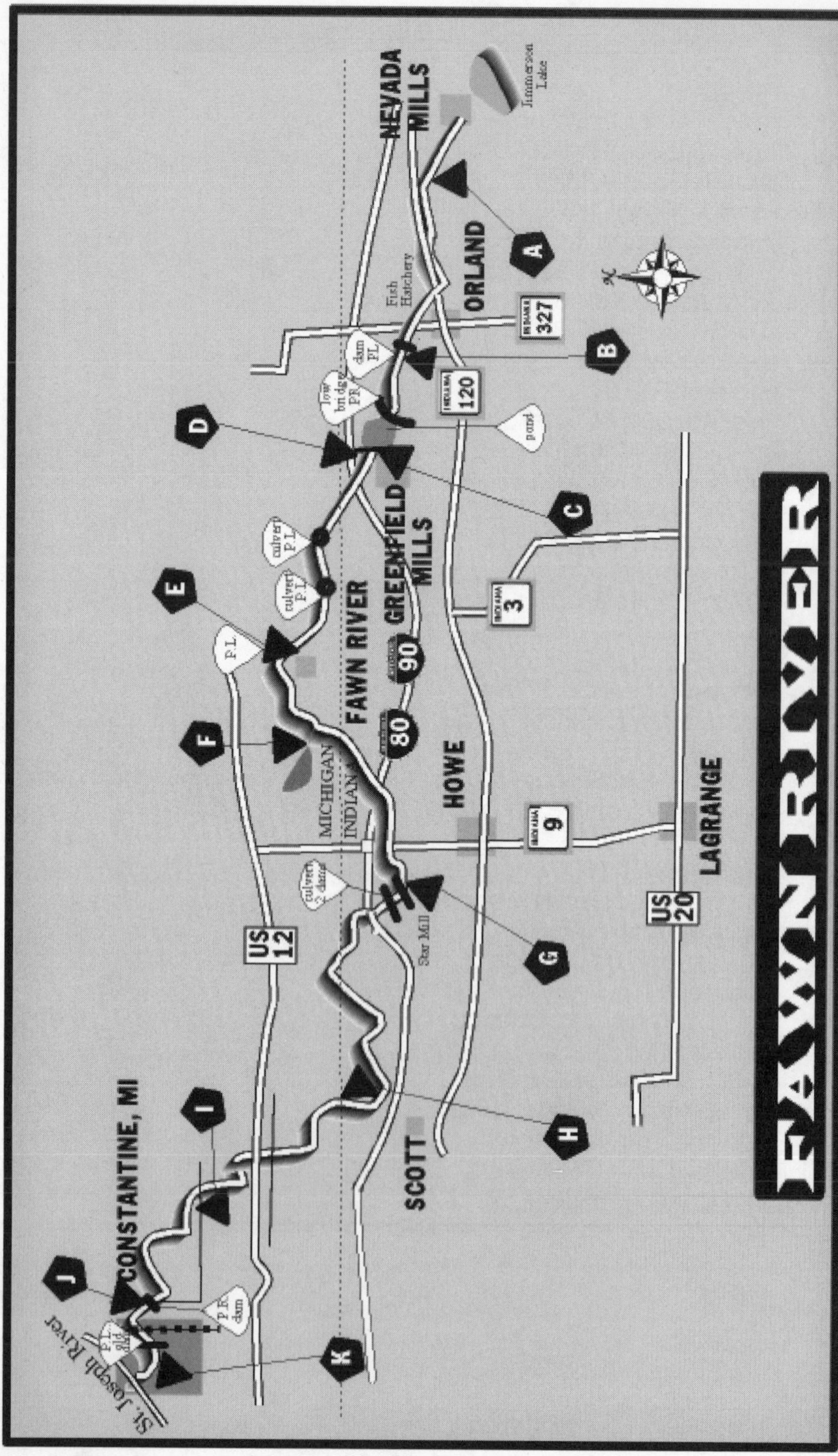
FAWN RIVER
NEVADA MILLS
Jimmerson Lake
ORLAND
Fish Hatchery
327
120
dam P.L.
low bridge P.L.
pond
GREENFIELD MILLS
culvert P.L.
culvert P.L.
P.L.
FAWN RIVER
90
80
MICHIGAN
INDIANA
HOWE
3
9
LAGRANGE
US 20
US 12
culvert 2 dams
Star Mill
SCOTT
CONSTANTINE, MI
P.R. dam
P.L. old
St. Joseph River
A
B
C
D
E
F
G
H
I
J
K

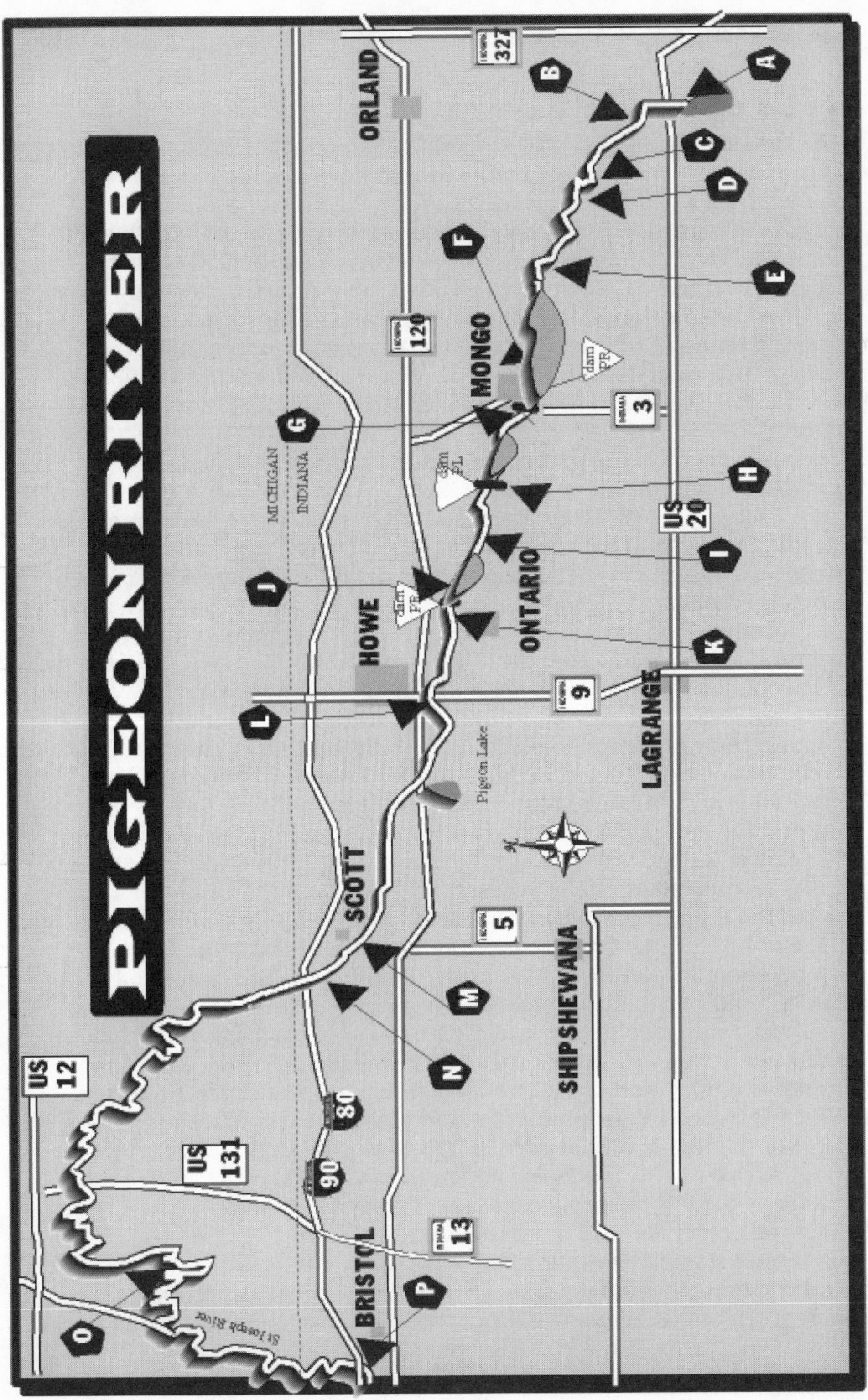
PIGEON RIVER
ORLAND
MONGO
HOWE
ONTARIO
LAGRANGE
SCOTT
SHIPSHEWANA
BRISTOL
MICHIGAN
INDIANA
Pigeon Lake
St Joseph River
dam PR
dam PL
US 12
US 131
90
80
13
5
9
3
120
327
US 20
A
B
C
D
E
F
G
H
I
J
K
L
M
N
O
P

2. PIGEON RIVER

- Let northern wildness reveal itself

If the Pigeon River were human it would have a name like the Potawatomi Chief Wahbememe or White Pigeon for whom the stream is named. Geographically young, the narrow and shallow 70 mile long river drains more than 50 lakes within its' 350 square miles of watershed. The tannic-stained, light brown waters flow over a sand and gravel bottom. The fall is greatest near its' source at Cedar Swamp (1,000' elev. northeast Steuben County) and its' mouth at the St. Joseph River (752' elev. Indiana-Michigan line north of Bristol, south of Mottville) and more gradual in its' central course.

Access is good overall and spaced at appropriate distances. Local paddlers have started at Pigeon Lake, west of Angola and followed a lake chain to Pigeon River Fish & Wildlife Area. There are numerous deadfall snags and strainers in the river downstream from the Ontario access to the St. Joseph River (29 miles). There are nine uncleared miles in Michigan. Canoeing is best during the days of late summer and early fall when insects and humidity are low and autumn colors are happening.

The cool, lake-fed stream begins in northeast Steuben County at the outlet of Cedar Swamp (a drained lake and a DNR wetland conservation area) and is place-named Pigeon Creek. The young creek flows south to and through Pigeon Lake west of Angola and gradually west to Long Lake. From here, Pigeon Creek follows an accessable and paddlable chain o' lakes course through Little and Big Bower Lakes, Golden Lake, Hogback Lake, and Otter Lake (the first recommended public access).

From the Otter Lake put-in, the swift creek flows northwest to the SR 327 access, NE bridge corner and the east boundary of the 11,500 acre Pigeon River Fish and Wildlife Area. The river is off limits to all but waterfowl hunters from mid-October to January (contact property office for exact dates). For the next fourteen miles, the river carves its' way through the fish and wildlife area, broken by three dams: Mongo (P.R.), Nasby (P.L.) and Ontario (P.R.) former NIPSCO hydroelectric plants. Paddlers enroute through the Cliff's Hole of the fish & wildlife area will discover the Goose Neck, High Banks, Dry Fly Run, a tamarack swamp, the Horseshoe and Rainbow Run. From the junction of Turkey Creek and Pigeon Creek at Mongo reservoir and dam, the creek becomes a river. Pigeon River continues its northwest flow, backing up at the Nasby Dam and Ontario Dam into small lakes. West of Howe, the Pigeon River meanders to Pigeon Lake and out, heading north, crossing SR 120, flowing on the north side of the Lagrange Moraine. The river curves northwest to Scott Mill County Park and DNR Public Fishing Area

access. The 120 acre Lagrange County Park at Scott features a covered walking bridge to an island adjacent to the access and limited primitive camping on the north bank.
Downstream, Lagrange CR 750 N is the last Indiana access before flowing under the I-80-90 toll road and entering Michigan where the stream is officially known as White Pigeon River. Separated by a narrow morainal ridge, the White Pigeon River is less than a mile away from the Fawn River, east of Marl Lake. There are seven road crossings including two state highways enroute to the St. Joseph River within St. Joseph County, Michigan but the only designated access is at Vistula Road bridge just south of Silver Creek Road, NE corner, southeast of Mottville. The 58 acre White Pigeon River Nature Sanctuary is located upstream from the Vistula access, downstream from the Blue School Road bridge (alt. access). From the confluence with the larger St. Joseph River it is a short journey (7mi.) downstream to Bristol, Indiana and the Apollo Street, Hermance Park access, South Bend.

USGS MAP(S): Indiana & Michigan topos:
Orland, Mongo, Lagrange, Shipshewana,
Klinger Lake, Constantine, Mottville1:24,000
VICINITY: Mongo, Ontario, Howe, Scott, Lagrange County, IN
White Pigeon, Mottville, St. Joseph County, MI
Bristol, Elkhart County, IN
STREAM DISTANCE/TRIPS: approx 50 miles
five trips or more
LEVEL OF DIFFICULTY: Class I
HAZARDS/PORTAGES: log jams, dams, sharp bends, meanders,
strainers, low bridges
INFO SOURCES: Pigeon River Fish & Wildlife Area
Box 71, 8310 E 300 N
Mongo, IN 46771
(219) 367-2164
Three Rivers Canoe Rental
(888) 314-7444
Trading Post Canoe Rental
(219) 367-2493
Michigan DNR
Fisheries Div. 12
621 N. 10th St.
Plainwell, MI 49080
(616) 685-6851 (800) ASK-FISH
AREA OUTFITTERS/LIVERIES: Pigeon River Canoe-n-Camp
3490 South CR 325 W
Pleasant Lake, IN 46779
(219) 351-3537 (219) 475-5512
Three Rivers Canoe Rental
1509 S. Main
Conservation Park

Three Rivers, MI 49093
(616) 279-9326
Trading Post Canoe Rental
Box 132, CR 300 N
Mongo, IN 46771
(219) 367-2493 (April 1-Oct 31)

GAMEFISH SPECIES: largemouth & smallmouth bass, rock bass catfish, northern pike, trout, bluegill, sunfish, bullhead, carp, sucker

CAMPING: Pigeon River Fish and Wildlife Area,
Box 71, 8310 E 300 N
Mongo, IN 46771
(219) 367-2164
Class C
Nottowa Park at Sand Lake
St. Joseph County Park, MI
60778 Railroad St.
Nottowa, MI 49075
(616) 467-5519
Class A, B & C
Trading Post Canoe Rental
Box 132, CR 300 N
Mongo, IN 46771
(219) 367-2493 (April 1-Oct 31)
Class A & B

MEDICAL ASSISTANCE: Vencor Hospital
207 Townline Dr.
Lagrange, IN 46761
(219) 463-2143
Sturgis Hospital
916 Myrtle Ave.
Sturgis, MI 49091
(616) 651-7824
Three Rivers Area Hospital
1111 W Broadway
Three Rivers, MI 49093
(616) 278-6108

ACCESS SITES	SECTION	RIVER MILES
A. Otter Lake, 7 miles west of Angola on US 20	A-B	0.7 miles
B. SR 327 bridge, NE corner, L-6 parking lot, Pigeon River FWA	B-C	1.5 miles
C. Steuben CR 175 N, SW corner, I-3 parking, PRFWA	C-D	0.5 miles

D. Steuben CR 1100 W, SW corner, I-4 parking, PRFWA	D-E	4.5 miles
E. Lagrange CR 900 E, NW corner, G-3 parking, PRFWA	E-F	1.7 miles
F. Mongo Campground, Lagrange CR 300 N, Mongo Reservoir, G-1 parking, PRFWA		
G. Mongo Dam (PR), Mongo village, CR 300 N & SR 3, park at dam, (P.R.),PRFWA	G-H	2.6 miles
H. Nasby Dam (P.L.), Lagrange CR 300 N, E-3 parking, PRFWA	H-I	1.5 miles
I. Lagrange CR 375 E/475 E, C-3 parking, PRFWA, SW of Curtis Creek FH	I-J	1 mile
J. Ontario Dam, B-1 parking, Lagrange CR 450 N, (P.R.), PRFWA	J-K	0.5 miles
K. Ontario access, Lagrange CR 225 E bridge, SE corner, north of Ontario	K-L	3 miles
L. SR 9 bridge, NW corner. south of Howe	L-M	8.5 miles
M. Scott Mill Park & DNR PFA, 2 mi. N of SR 120 on Lagrange CR 675 W, SE corner	M-N	1.5 miles
N. Lagrange CR 750 N bridge SW corner	N-O	14 miles
O. Vistula Park bridge, NE corner, one mi. S of US 12 on Vistula Rd., MI	O-P	7 miles
P. St. Joseph River, Hermance Park access, Apollo St. in Bristol, IN		

3. ST. JOSEPH RIVER OF LAKE MICHIGAN

- Canoe one of the best trout & salmon rivers in the continental United States

French explorers, including LaSalle, and Roman Catholic missionaries named the St. Joseph River after the patron saint of New France. The native Potawatomi called this stream Sahg-wah-se-be, Sagwasepe, or Kawk-wawk-sil-buck, meaning "mystery river" or "the mystery" in reference to its' sudden water level rise after a rain. The St. Joseph is primarily a Michigan stream (168 mi.) making its' way from Hillsdale, Michigan to Lake Michigan at Benton Harbor and St. Joseph, Michigan. The Indiana section (42 miles), the "south bend" of the river, flows through the predominately metro corridor of Elkhart, Osceola, Mishawaka, and South Bend where numerous municipal parks line its' banks. More than 40 access sites are scattered at intervals from Sturgeon Lake at Colon, Michigan to Lake Michigan. Along its' paddling course eleven hydroelectric dams span the river from near Mendon, Michigan to Berrien Springs, Michigan. There are four dams in Indiana. The construction of five interstate fish ladders provide safe passage for salmon and steelhead trout around the dams from the Lake Michigan river mouth upstream through Mishawaka to Twin Branch Dam, making for fine fishing (special regulations apply). The dams are also obstacles for paddlers although portages are permitted around most dams. Boating buoy barriers prevent drifting to close to the hydros. The South Bend East Race, the first artificial whitewater course in North America, is open to public canoeing, kayaking, and rafting in summer (city park, fee).
The most undeveloped section of the St. Joseph River in Michigan begins east of I-69 and Tekonsha near Claredon, south of M160 at the Twenty-Mile Road bridge. The river flows southwest through Tekonsha, Burlington, Union City, Union Lake and on to Colon at Sturgeon Lake (20 mi.). Only Union Lake and county road bridges provide access.
The best canoeing along the St. Joseph River may be in St. Joseph County, Michigan (which has more navigable streams than any other Michigan county) downstream to Bristol, Indiana: Sturgeon Lake to Mendon, Three Rivers to Constantine Dam, Constantine to Mottville dam and Mottville to Bristol. Great Michigan "side trips " include the White Pigeon River (expect log jams) from the Vistula Bridge access down to the St. Joseph River and Bristol (7 mi.) or the Long Lake and Trout Creek access to the St. Joseph River and Bristol (5 mi.). Additional tributaries that may be combined with the St. Joseph River within St. Joseph County, Michigan include the

Fawn, Prairie, Rocky and Portage Rivers and Nottawa Creek. The river passes by several city parks along the Indiana section. Dams are located at Elkhart (P.R.), Twin Branch (P.L.) and Central Park in Mishawaka (P.R.), and Century Center in South Bend (P.R.). Once beyond South Bend and starting from St. Patrick's County Park access, the river is not quite so developed as it makes it way towards the Niles, Michigan dam. The Niles Dam to Buchanan Dam, Michigan segment is also popular canoeing. The river becomes Lake Chapin from Buchanan to Berrien Springs. Motorized boat traffic becomes plentiful near Lake Michigan.

USGS MAP(S): Michigan Origins, St. Joseph County, MI:
Lyon Lake, Colon, Nottawa, Mendon,
Three Rivers East, Three Rivers West, Constantine, Mich.-Ind., Mottville, Mich.-Ind. 1:24,000
Indiana Central, "south bend of the river":
Bristol Elkhart, Osceola, South Bend East
South Bend West 1:24,000
Michigan Finale, Berrien County,
MI: Niles West,Mich.-Ind., Berrien Springs
Baroda South, Benton Harbor 1:24,000

VICINITY: Michigan Origins: Colon, Mendon, Three Rivers, Constantine, Mottville, St. Joseph County, MI
Indiana Central: Bristol, Elkhart, Elkhart County
Osceola, Mishawaka, South Bend, St. Joseph County
Michigan Finale: Bertrand, Niles, Buchanan, Berrien Springs, Benton Harbor & St. Joseph, Berrien County, MI

STREAM DISTANCE/TRIPS: 100 miles total
15 or more trips

LEVEL OF DIFFICULTY: Class I

HAZARDS/PORTAGES: numerous dams, wind, power boats, snags, dead water, seasonal hunting

INFO SOURCES: Friends of the St. Joseph Association
POB 354
Athens, MI, 49011
(616) 729-5174
St. Joseph County, MI
Parks and Recreation
Department
(616) 467-6361
Three Rivers Canoe Rental
(800) 314-7444
Bristol Canoe & Kayak
(219) 848-4465
Niles Canoe Rental
(616) 683-5110
St. Joseph River Fishing Info
(219) 257-8477
Michigan DNR
Fisheries Div. 12
621 N. 10th St.

Plainwell, MI 49080
(616) 685-6851 (800) ASK-FISH

AREA OUTFITTERS/LIVERIES: Mendon Country Inn
440 W. Main
Mendon, MI 49072
(800)-304-3366 (616) 496-8132
Three Rivers Canoe Rental
1509 S Main, Conservation Park
Three Rivers, MI 49093 (800) 314-7444
St. Joseph County, MI Parks
& Recreation
POB 427
Centreville, MI 49032
(616) 467-5519 or 6361
Bristol Canoe & Kayak
402 SR 15 N
Bristol, IN 46507
(219) 848-4465
Ferretie-Baugo Creek
St. Joseph, IN, County Parks
(north of US 33)
Osceola, IN 46561
(219) 674-9765
St. Patricks County Park
St. Joseph County, IN, Parks
50651 Laurel Rd.
(west of US 33 at state line)
South Bend, IN 46637
(219) 277-4828
Niles Canoe Rental
1430 N Business US 31
Niles, MI 49120
(616) 683-5110

GAMEFISH SPECIES: bluegill, largemouth & smallmouth bass, rock bass, crappie, redear, muskie, northern pike, walleye, carp, suckers, catfish, steelhead trout & chinook salmon from Lake Michigan upstream to the Twin Branch Dam Mishawaka (63 mi.)

CAMPING: Nottawa Park at Sand Lake
St, Joseph County Park, MI
60778 Railroad Street
Nottawa, MI 49075
(June to August)
(616) 467-5519, or 6316, or 7848
Potato Creek State Park
25601 SR 4, POB 908
North Liberty, IN, 46554
(219) 656-8186
Class A
Warren Dunes State Park
Route 1, Red Arrow Highway

Sawyer, MI 49125
(616) 426-4013
Class A (seasonal)

MEDICAL ASSISTANCE: Three Rivers Area Hospital
1111 West Broadway
Three Rivers, MI 49091
(616) 278-1145
Sturgis Hospital
916 Myrtle Ave
Sturgis, MI 49091
(616) 651-7824
Elkhart General Hospital
600 E Boulevard
Elkhart, IN 46514
(219) 294-2621
St. Joseph Community Hospital
215 W 4th Street
Mishawaka, IN 46544
(219) 259-2431
St. Joseph Medical Center
801 E LaSalle Ave.
South Bend, IN 46617
(219) 237-7111
Memorial Hospital of South Bend
615 N Michigan St.
South Bend, IN 46601
(219) 234-9041
Lakeland Medical Center
31 N St. Joseph Ave
Niles, MI 49120
(616) 683-5510
Lee Memorial Hospital
420 W High St.
Dowagiac, MI 49047
(616) 782-8681
Lakeland Medical Center
6418 Dean's Hill Road
Berrien Center, MI 49102
(616) 473-3074
Lakeland Medical Center
1234 Napier Ave.
St. Joseph, MI 49085
(616) 927-5469

ACCESS SITES	SECTION	RIVER MILES
A. Sturgeon Lake, SE shore, MDNR access, Blackstone Ave. N from MI 86/Colon Rd at Colon, MI	A-B	11 miles
B. Mendon, Reed Riverside Park, south of Main & Nottawa Sts intersection in Mendon, S of MI 60	B-C	0.7 miles
C. Mendon, MDNR access, S of Main St./MI 60 on S Railroad St., lake-like to Sturgis Dam	C-D	6 miles
D. Sturgis Dam, (P.L.), Covered Bridge Park, three mi. north of Centreville on Switzer Rd.	D-E	10 miles
E. Noah Lake, S River Rd., east of Three Rivers, MI	E-F	4 miles
F. Jefferson access, city of Three Rivers, (P.R.) before dam	F-G	0.5 miles
G. Three Rivers, Conservation Park & Skidmore Park, downtown Three Rivers, MI 86 & MI 60 (canoe rental)	G-H	5 miles
H. Florence Withers Bridge, Withers Rd., E of SR 131, ltd parking at the SE & NE bridge corner (lake-like to Constantine Dam)	H-I	3 miles
I. Constantine Canoe Park, (P.L.) Constantine Dam. (No vehicular access) (P.R.) to take out at hydro access	I-J	0.25 miles
J. Constantine public access US 131 to Water St. across from police station	J-K	6 miles
K. Mottville Canoe Park, Riverside Dr., (P.L.) at dam north of US 12	K-M	7.5 miles
L. L1.Long Lake access to Trout Creek to St. Joseph River	L1-M	5 miles

ACCESS	SECTION	RIVER MILES
L2.Fawn River, NE Dickinson Bridge to St. Joseph River	L2-M	15 miles
L3. Pigeon River, NE Vistula Bridge access to St. Joseph River	L3-M	7 miles
M. Bristol, IN, Hermance Park, S bank, one block N of SR 120 on Apollo St.	M-N	4.8 miles
N. Six Span Bridge, from SR 120 go 0.25 miles N of CR 17 N, SE corner (expect deadwater from here to Elkhart Dam) (P.R.), 200 yd portage Elkhart dam, crossing Johnson St. bridge (not recommended)	N-O	4 miles
O. Island Park, Bicentennial Park & Beardsley Park, mouth of the Elkhart River, downtown Elkhart, Main St. & Beardsley Ave.	O-P	0.7 miles
P. Sherman St. Bridge, city of Elkhart, W of Main on Jackson Blvd., Clyde St., Jefferson & Riverside Dr.	P-Q	1.5 miles
Q. McNaughton Park, city of Elkhart, N bank, US 20 S, on West Blvd.	Q-R	2 miles
R. Treasure Island County Park, 0.8 mi. W of SR 19, N of Indiana Ave./CR 16	R-S	4.5 miles
S. Baugo Bay, Ferrettie-Baugo Creek County Park, St. US 33 & SR 219 in Osceola, (canoe rental)	S-T	3.8 miles
T. Twin Branch Dam (P.L.) US 33, N on Power Rd. in east Mishawaka	T-U	0.3 miles
U. Frank Zappia public access, corner of Lincolnway Hwy E/US 33 & Capitol Ave.	U-V	1 mile
V. Eberhart-Petro Municpal Golf Course, Mishawaka,		

ACCESS SITE	SECTION	RIVER MILES
US 33, N on Merrifield Ave., in Mishawaka	V-W	0.6 miles
W. Merrifield Park, US 33/ Lincolnway Ave E of Logan St.	W-X	0.6 miles
X. Central Park, Mishawaka, (P.R.) dam & first ladder	X-Y	0.75 miles
Y. Lincoln Park, Mishawaka, Lincolnway Ave./US 33, east of Logan St.	Y-Z	1.5 miles
Z. Veteran's Memorial park, South Bend, Northside Blvd., N bank, W of Ironwood Dr. & Indiana University Campus	Z-AA	2 miles
AA. Downtown South Bend, East Race & Century Center Dam (P.R.) at East Race pier boardwalk, 100 yds to launch below dam	AA-BB	4 miles
BB. Keller Park, South Bend, Riverside Dr., N of Angola Blvd. (downstream Woodlawn Park, carry down, Riverside & Woodlawn Blvd.)	BB-CC	1.8 miles
CC. Riverside Park, Riverside Dr., South Bend, S of Darden Rd., N of the I-80-90 toll Rd.	CC-DD	1.8 miles
DD. St. Patrick's County Park, St. Joseph County, IN Parks, W of US 31/33/N Michigan St. at Laurel & Auten Rds, then N on Laurel, E bank	DD-EE	5 miles
EE. St. Joseph Park & Public access, Bond Rd.& Fort St. in Niles, MI, French Paper Dam site, (P.R.) public access below dam 0.25 mi	EE-FF	1.5 miles
FF. Public access site, N Niles, Front St./US 31 to Marmont St., W to the river	FF-GG	8 miles

ACCESS	SECTION	RIVER MILES
GG. Upper Buchanan dam access, (P.R.) bridge at Walton & Mead Rds, NE corner (further access downstream, 32 mi. to Lake Michigan, expect bigger water & boats	From GG 100 yard carry	
HH. Public access site, below Buchanan Dam, N Redbud Trail in Buchanan		

St. Joseph River, East Race View of Century Center, Downtown South Bend

ST JOSEPH RIVER indiana central & michigan finale

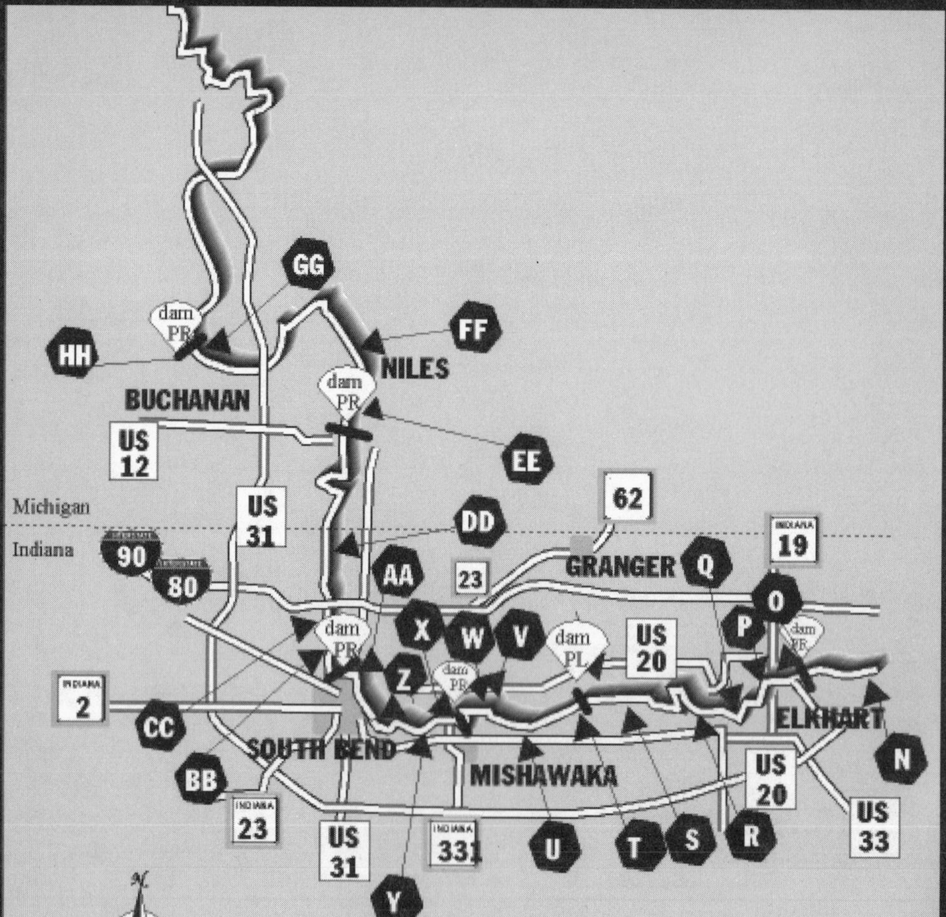

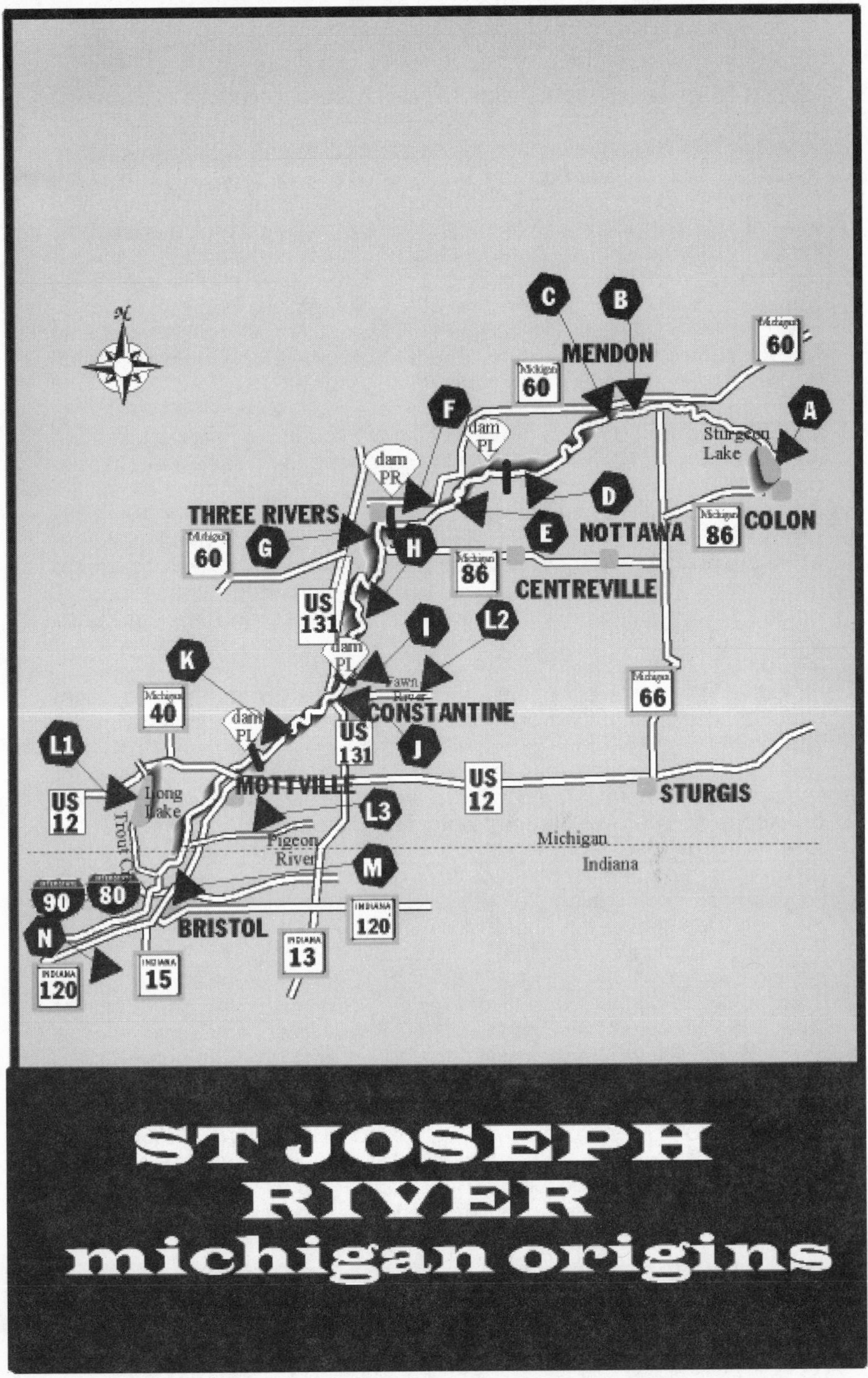

ST JOSEPH RIVER
michigan origins

FURTHER NOTES:

Lake Michigan Tributaries, Northwest Indiana Streams

The Little Calumet River East Fork is not recommended for paddling at this time primarily due to logjams and poor access. The steep, stinging-nettle covered, spoil banks, as well as stinging insects, make portaging around the jams difficult. The last mile can develop potentially threatening whitewater conditions. From this point on, the Little Calumet is channelized to its confluence with the West Fall of the Little Calumet River and Burns Ditch to empty at Lake Michigan.The 60 mile East Fork or Arm of the Little Calumet River originates in LaPorte County and is channelized via the Kemper Ditch to near Chesterton, then meanders through Chesterton and Porter and enters the Indiana Dunes National Lakeshore at US 20 and Mineral Springs Road. For the next 5.7 miles the stream flows through the national lakeshore and exits 0.5 miles downstream from the confluence with Salt Creek (10 miles canoeable).

The best section for the paddler is from Howe Road near the Bailly Homestead to Indiana SR 149. There are no designated river access sites within the national lakeshore however plans are to develop five access and parking sites: Howe Road bridge access, Bailly Homestead canoe landing, Indiana 149 bridge access, Boos Road bridge access and the Burns Ditch River access. Current access is at road right-of-ways and other unimproved sites. (USGS MAP(S): Chesterton & Portage 1:24,000).

For further information about the Little Calumet River contact: Indiana Dunes National Lakeshore, 1100 North Mineral Springs Rd., Porter, IN 46304, (219) 926-7561.

Deep River is excluded from the main list of paddlable Indiana streams because of numerous logjams, low water, limited access and rurban development. However the most natural section of this short stream is the seven mile segment from the Deep River County Park canoe ramp just downstream from the John Woods 1876 grist mill to Lake George and Jerry Pavese Park, north shore take-out in Hobart. If continuing on the next ten miles, portage right at the Hobart dam and flow northeast through a rurban residential-industrial corridor to US 6 (Riverview & Bicentennial Parks access), curving west, and portaging left at a small dam downstream from the Liverpool Road bridge. Deep River joins the West Fork of the Little Calumet River. The take-out site is along the Little Calumet River and Central Avenue near I-65 and I-80-94 intersection in Lake Station (a total of 17.5 paddle miles, seasonal rentals available).

For further information about Deep River contact; Lake County Parks & Recreation, 2293 N. Main, Crown Point, Indiana 46307 (219) 755-3685; Deep River County Park, 9410 Old US 30/Lincolnway Hwy., Hobart, IN 46342 (219) 947-1958, (seasonal canoe rental); Hobart City Parks & Recreation (219) 942-2987; or Bass Lake Fisheries Station, 6718 E. Winona Ave., Knox, IN 46534 (219) 772-2353. (USGS MAP(S): Palmer, Crown Point, Gary, Portage 1:24,000).

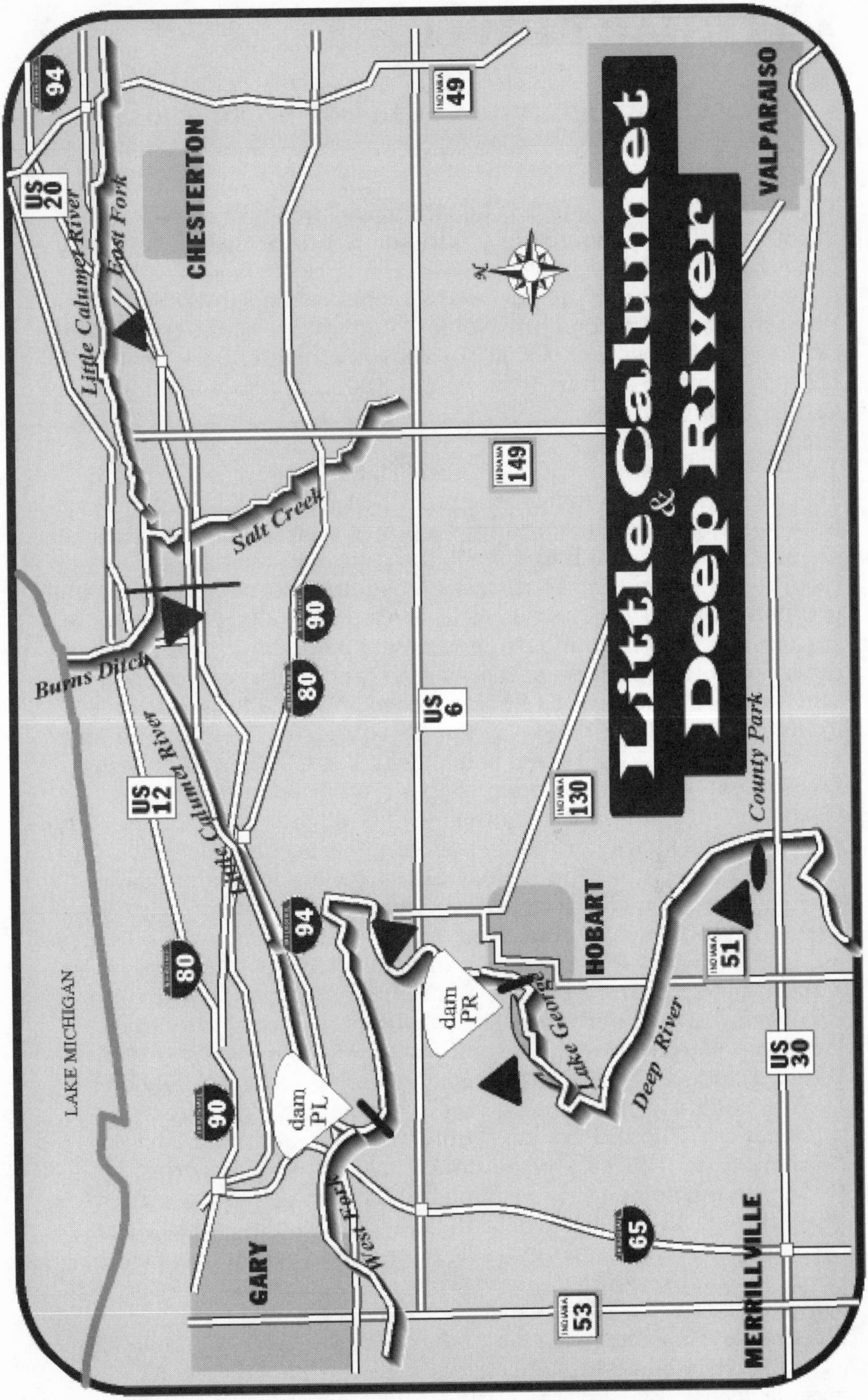
Little Calumet & Deep River
LAKE MICHIGAN
CHESTERTON
GARY
HOBART
VALPARAISO
MERRILLVILLE
Burns Ditch
Little Calumet River
East Fork
Salt Creek
Little Calumet River
West Fork
Lake George
Deep River
County Park
dam PL
dam PR
US 20
US 12
US 6
US 30
94
94
80
80
90
90
65
INDIANA 49
INDIANA 149
INDIANA 130
INDIANA 51
INDIANA 53

4. ELKHART RIVER

• Navigate through rural wetlands & urban wilds

The Elkhart River drains 573 square miles and is 38 miles long, heading at the junction of its' North and South Branches between Ligonier and Wawaka, just north of US 6 in Noble County. The shallow and slow moving, lake-fed stream flows northwestward through Ligonier and on into Noble County to its' confluence at the St. Joseph River within the city of Elkhart at Island Park. Major tributaries of the Elkhart River within Elkhart County include Stony Creek, Solomon Creek, Turkey Creek, Rock Run Creek and Yellow Creek.

The first access site is the SR 13 bridge, SW corner, just south of Millersburg where Stony Creek enters east of the bridge (33 mi. from mouth). Roadside parking is a problem on the narrow sloping shoulder, however Elkhart CR 37, the next road west, has plenty of room to park along the southeast and southwest road shoulder and less of a carry down. There is little development along the banks to Benton (28.5 mi. from mouth, houses are being built) and much of the land on the south bank is leased to hunting (private property). The Nature Conservancy's 21 acre Leacock Woods (unmarked) is located at a roadside bend, 1.2 mi. (by road) from Benton. The River Preserve County Park (1,055 acres) begins at the Benton Landing access west of the US 33 bridge and stretches on and off to the Goshen Pond Dam on the south side of Goshen. The wetlands and floodplain forest are fairly intact making this section the best paddling of the river. The Benton, Bainertown and Goshen dams (former NIPSCO hydroelectric dams). have created much of the wetlands (750 acres) within River Preserve. Adjacent to each dam is a canoeable canal that offers a manmade alternative to the river for a short distance. The Benton Dam, Spillway Park and Hydro, Baintertown Dam, Park, and Hydro offer places within the River Preserve to stop and rest. Once beyond SR 15 the Elkhart River becomes wide and quiet like a lake, backing up from the Goshen Dam (19.55 mi. from mouth, access). Within the city of Goshen the stream skirts Shoup-Parsons Nature Preserve, Shanklin (access), New and Rogers parks and continues its' northwest flow through the city to the suburbs. Development has encroached upon the river along the US 33 corridor where the cities of Goshen and Elkhart are becoming one. A few float miles later, the river borders Ox Bow County Park, providing a quiet respite and access site (no canoe camp). The river becomes wider as it makes it way past new housing development, passing underneath the US 20 bypass. The city of Elkhart has established several parks along its' banks that provide access: Elkhart Environmental Center, Baker Park,

Studebaker Park, F.O.P. Park, American Park, Riverwalk, Burton Upon Trent, Riverwalk, Bicentennial Park and Island Park. (watch for a low dam (P.L.) at American Park, about 0.5 mile upstream from the mouth). Taking out at Riverwalk Park, Island Park, Bicentennial Park, or Beardsley Park works well.
Most area historians believe the place name Elkhart is derived from the elk heart-shaped Island Park of which the Potawatomi called Me-sheh-weh-ou-deh-ik or Mi-siwa-o-daik-se-be, "elk heart river" but other legends refer to Shawnee chief of that name or a band of Potawatomi that resided in the area, or possibly for the former abundance of elk or wapiti (Cervus elaphus) in the Elkhart Prairie area.

USGS MAP(S): Millersburg, Goshen, Milford, Foraker, Elkhart 1:24,000
VICINITY: Millersburg, Benton, Goshen, Elkhart, Elkhart County
STREAM DISTANCE/TRIPS: apprx. 28 miles, 2-3 or more trips
LEVEL OF DIFFICULTY: Class 1
HAZARDS/PORTAGES: dams, log jams, strainers, sharp bends, low water, low bridges, seasonal hunting
INFO SOURCES: Fawn River State Fish Hatchery
(219) 829-6241
Goshen Parks & Recreation
(219) 534-2901
Elkhart Parks & Recreation
(219) 295-7275 or 7529
Elkhart County Parks & Recreation
(219) 535-6458
AREA OUTFITTERS: Goshen Parks & Recreation
607 W. Plymouth
Goshen, IN 46526
(219) 534-2901
Elkhart Parks & Recreation
131 Tyler St.
Elkhart, IN 46516
(219) 295-7275 or 7529
GAMEFISH SPECIES: smallmouth bass, catfish, northern pike, rock bass
CAMPING: Chain O' Lakes State Park
2355 E. 75 S
Albion, IN 46701
(219) 636-2654
Class A, B, & C
MEDICAL ASSISTANCE: Goshen General Hospital
200 W. High Park Ave.
Goshen, IN 46526
(219) 533-2141
Elkhart General Hospital
600 E. Blvd.
Elkhart, IN 46514
(219) 294-2621

ACCESS SITE	SECTION	RIVER MILES
A. SR 13 bridge, SW corner, one mile south of Millersburg, parking for 2 cars roadside carry down, (see B alternative site)	A-B	1.1 miles
B. Elkhart CR 37 bridge, SE & SW corner, carry down, one mile west of SR 13	B-C	3.4 miles
C. Benton Landing, US 33 bridge, NW corner, ramp & parking, River Preserve County Park	C-D	0.8 miles
D. Benton dam, canal, spillway site, CR 31, River Preserve County Park (upstream of CR 31 bridge is the Benton Dam (P.R.) if continuing on the river, stay right on canal, downstream to spillway (P.L.) to reconnect to river or if continuing on canal to hydro & dam (P.R.) go right. Downstream (P.L.) at Baintertown dam or follow 2nd canal left to Baintertown Park & hydro, dam (P.L.) watch for low bridges	D-E	3 miles
E. Baintertown Park, carry down, to canal, CR 29 & CR 142, 0.5 mile east of SR 15	E-F	0.25 miles
F. Baintertown Hydro, carry down to dam (P.L.), junction of canal & river, CR 29, 0.4 mile east of SR 15	F-G	3 miles
G. Goshen Dam Pond acCess (P.R.), west of SR 15 at Goshen College on Westwood Drive to dam & hydraulic canal, (portage or carry down to either canal or river, canal reconnects river near Lincoln Ave near Rogers Park)	G-H	4.5 miles

ACCESS SITE	SECTION	RIVER MILES
H. Shanklin Park, Goshen City Park, east bank public access site, (canal or river access) Plymouth St./SR 119 entrance	H-I	1.8 miles
I. Rogers Park, Goshen City Park, access south of US 33 on Chicago Ave	I-J	0.7 miles
J. Ox Bow County Park, US 33 to Dunlap, turn north on CR 15 & left on CR 45/ Hammond St. to park entrance (fee)	J-K	5.5 miles
K. Elkhart Environmental Center, east of US 33 & Sterling Ave. at 1717 W. Lusher Ave.	K-L	1.2 miles
L. Baker, Studebaker, & FOP park complex, Elkhart City Parks, US 33/S. Main east of Fetters St. to McDonald St. between Middlebury St. & Indiana Ave. & Goshen Rd.	L-M	1.5 miles
M. American Park, Elkhart City Park, S. Main east on Division St., then north at bridge, (P.L.) at low dam downstream between Johnson & Franklin)	M-N	1.2 miles
N. Elkhart City Parks: Riverwalk Park & Burton Upon Trent Park, upstream from Jacobs Blvd. bridge; Bicentennial Park, Island Park & Beardsley Park, mouth of Elkhart River at St. Joseph River. Parking between Beardsley Ave., Main St., Jackson Blvd. & Johnson St.		

5. ELKHART RIVER SOUTH BRANCH

- Cut through "The Spread"

The South Branch of the Elkhart River is a 20 mile long, slow-flowing stream that heads up at the outlet of Hawk Lake. The headwater flows northeastward through the largest unbroken wetlands in northern Indiana to join the North Branch of the Elkhart River near Ligonier, forming the Elkhart River. The lower 12 canoeable miles of the lake-fed branch has been studied for inclusion in the DNR's Natural and Scenic River Systems (between Noble CR 100 N and the US 6 bridge). The unique stream meanders through the low marshly mucklands interspersed with morainic ridges and till hills that are rich with wildlife; locally known as "The Spread". The low-level banks allow the slightest rise in water level to "spread" over the wide floodplain of cattail flats dotted with willow, ash, maple, and cottonwood. Being lake-fed, it usually has adequate water for paddling even during dry spells but the muddy muck banks discourage landing and the cattail glades discourage exploring on foot. The entire branch flows through west central Noble County. Paddlers may put-in southwest of Albion at River Road bridge/CR 250 N, SW corner and park along the roadside pullout (room for two cars). The access site is located 0.5 mile north of the ACRES Lloyd W. Bender Memorial Forest Preserve (parking area). The stream forms part of the north and west boundary of the 116 acre land trust and there are several logjams and strainers in this segment. The narrow branch and weak current widens from swampy woodlands into glade-like wetlands on its' way northwest to the next access, Mallard Roost #3 access (7.25 mi.) flowing under four country road bridges and one railroad bridge. (Paddlers could put in or take out at Long Lake Rd., NE corner of bridge, CR 330 N bridge SW corner and the CR 350 N bridge, SW corner enroute). At the CR 550 W bridge access, Mallard Roost #3, the stream enters the 760 acre DNR's Mallard Roost Wetland Conservation Area; one of the most outstanding publicly-owned wetlands in northern Indiana (seasonal hunting allowed). Rising above the cattail marsh to the northwest is the 1,000-foot high Diamond Hill, adding to the wide open scenery. Just over a mile north is the second WCA access, Mallard Roost #2 at CR 600 N. The final segment flows on through the "everglade-like" marsh to the US 6 access, Mallard Roost # 1, just before joining the North Branch to form the Elkhart River. The adventuresome may consider floating the nearby North Branch Elkhart River from Waldron Lake, Wm. T. Malle access downstream about three miles distance to the CR 900 N bridge (the first bridge downstream) at Cosperville. Be prepared for strainers.

USGS MAP(S): Albion, Ligonier 1:24,000
VICINITY: Albion, Wawaka, Ligonier, Noble County
STREAM DISTANCE/TRIPS: 12 miles approx
one or two trips
LEVEL OF DIFFICULTY: Class 1
HAZARDS/PORTAGES: logjams, strainers, mucky banks, seasonal hunting
INFO SOURCES: Tri-Lakes Fisheries Station
5570 N. Fish Hatchery Road
Columbia City, IN 46725
(219) 691-3181
DNR Div. of Outdoor Recreation
Streams & Trails
402 W. Washington Rm. 271 W
Indianapolis, IN 46204
(317) 232-4070
AREA OUTFITTERS: none
GAMEFISH SPECIES: catfish, carp
CAMPING: Chain O' Lakes State Park
2355 E 75 S
Albion, IN 46701
(219) 636-2654
Class A, B & C
MEDICAL ASSISTANCE: McCray Memorial Hospital
951 E Hospital Drive
Kendallville, IN 46755
(219) 347-1100

ACCESS SITES	SECTION	RIVER MILES
A. River Road/Noble CR 250 N bridge, SW corner, two miles SW of Albion. (parking for two cars at pullout)	A-B	7.25 miles
B. Noble CR 550 N, Mallard Roost #3, SW bridge corner, two miles SE of Diamond Lake	B-C	1.5 miles
C. Noble CR 600 N, Mallard Roost # 2, NW bridge corner, about a mile from Diamond Lake (parking for four cars)	C-D	3 miles
D. US 6, Mallard Roost #1 access, NE bridge corner, three miles west of Wawaka & about 4.5 miles east of Ligonier		

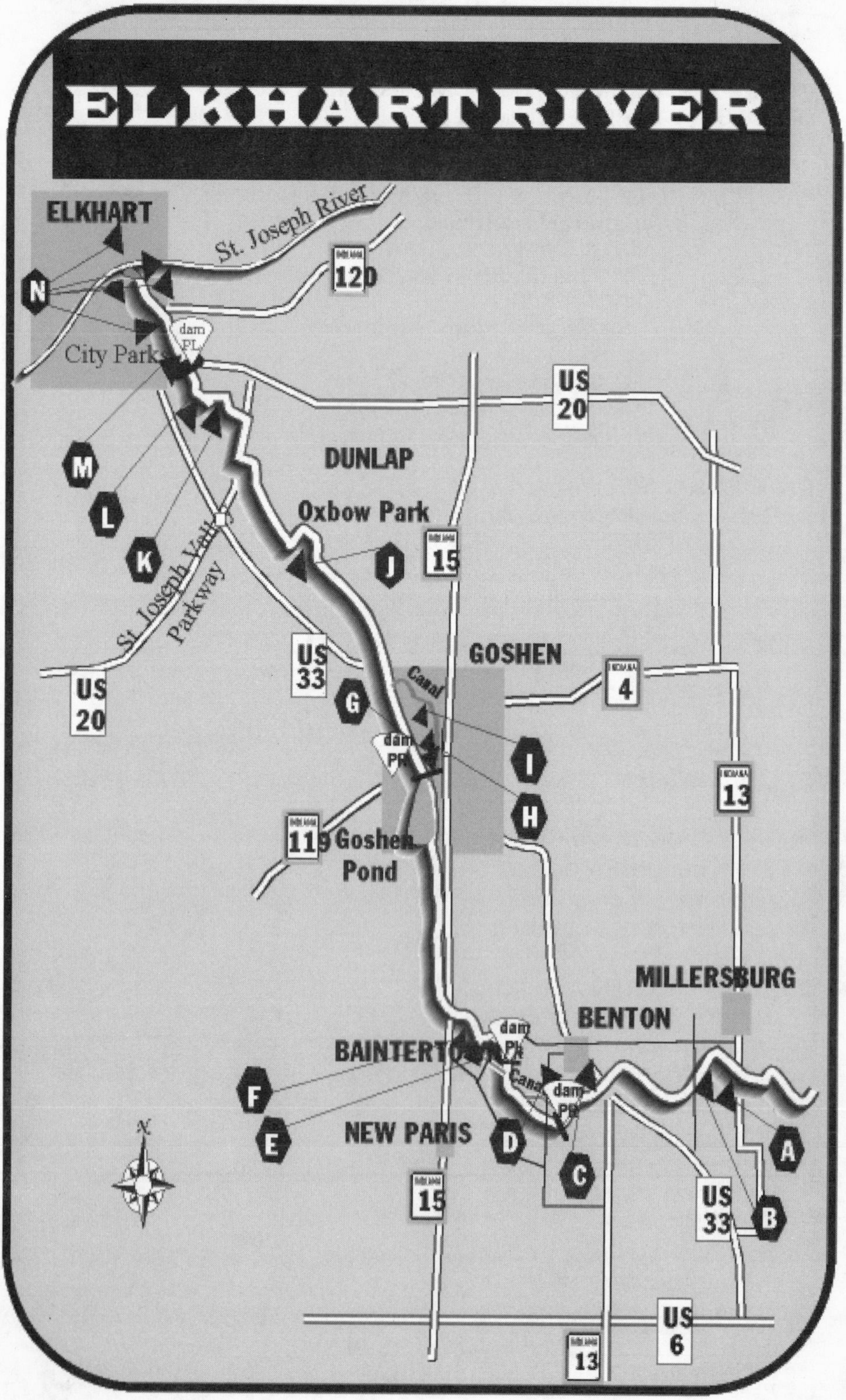

ELKHART RIVER
ELKHART
St. Joseph River
120
N
dam FL
City Parks
US 20
DUNLAP
M
L
K
Oxbow Park
J
15
St. Joseph Valley Parkway
US 33
GOSHEN
US 20
G
Canal
4
I
dam PR
H
13
119
Goshen Pond
MILLERSBURG
BENTON
dam PR
BAINTERTOWN
Canal
dam PR
F
E
NEW PARIS
D
A
C
15
US 33
B
US 6
13
N.

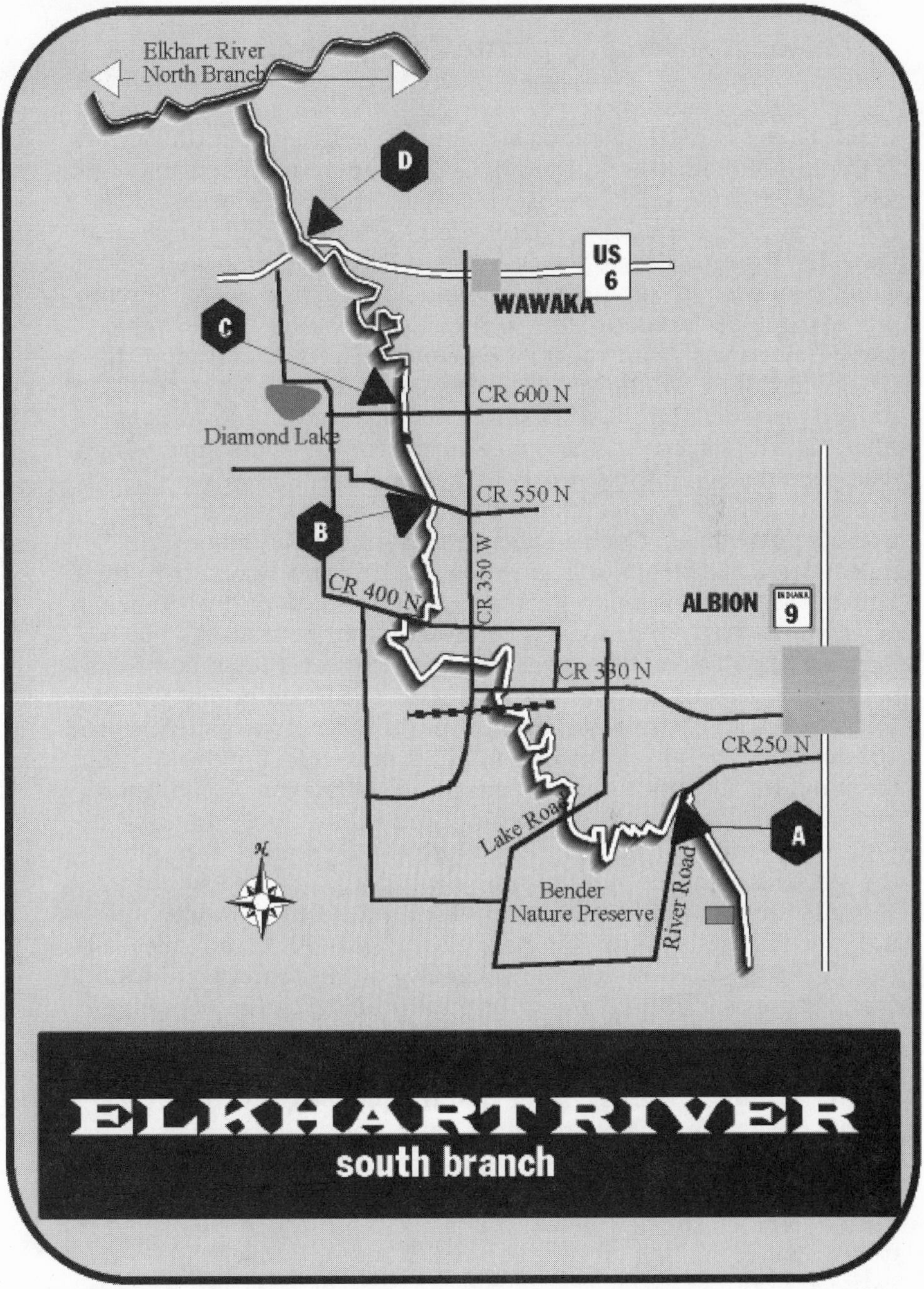
Elkhart River
North Branch
D
US
6
WAWAKA
C
CR 600 N
Diamond Lake
CR 550 N
B
CR 350 W
CR 400 N
ALBION
9
CR 330 N
CR250 N
Lake Road
A
River Road
Bender
Nature Preserve
ELKHART RIVER
south branch

6. CEDAR CREEK

• Meander through a picturesque canyon

Cedar Creek is a 40 mile long stream that originates at the outflow of Cedar Lake, northwest DeKalb County and curves south merging with the St. Joseph River of the Maumee, the river's largest tributary, near Cedarville, Allen County. From DeKalb CR 68 near the Allen County Line to the St. Joseph River (13.7 miles), Cedar Creek has been designated an Indiana Natural and Scenic Stream, one of three declared streams in the Hoosier state. The deeply carved, narrow stream valley or canyon features steeply sloped, timbered ridges, wildflower-filled ravines and floodplain forest. Five nature preserves have been established along its banks plus two Allen County parks. The compact but intense creek is surprisingly wild considering how close it is to metropolitan Fort Wayne. Paddlers will not be disappointed by the beauty however in the upper reaches from Cook's Landing to Tonkel Road (about five miles) there are plenty of frustrating logjams and strainers in high flow but if you don't mind getting in and out or the time it takes, it is worth the trip. From Cook's Landing, a four acre Allen County Park on Shoaff Road, the creek crosses Coldwater Road and flows southeast, picking up Willow Creek from the Bicentennial Woods Nature Preserve. There are few houses or other development as the stream skirts half canyons and full canyons, crossing the Wabash Moraine. Rodenbeck Nature Preserve and Vandolah Nature Preserve provide scenic passage underneath Cedar Canyons Road and I-69. Within two intimate miles is Tonkel Road, the second access and the starting point for most paddlers especially during low water. There is ample parking along the wide level shoulder where a carry down or out is necessary (no ramp). Within another two miles is the Hursh Bridge (access) and the beginning of Metea County Park. Prairie flora is scattered along the south-facing bluffs overlooking Cedar Creek within the Meno-aki ("blessed earth", Potawatomi) Nature Preserve of Metea County Park. The Brittany Overlook is about the only human evidence that the paddler is within the county park, a fine place to rest or if need be, a 300 yard carry to the parking lot. Watch for the old low dam near the SR 1 bridge and stay left to pass through. The last access site before the St. Joseph River will be on the southeast side of the SR 1 bridge. To extend the trip, consider floating on down on the St. Joseph River to Shoaff Park Golf Course and access site at Fort Wayne (about four hours) or continue on down to Johnny Appleseed Park and dam (P.R.). The place name, Cedar Creek, was derived from the Potawatomi village of Musk-waw-se-peo-tan (1795-1828), "village on the old red wood creek", near the confluence on the north bank near present-day Cedarville. Although few are seen, "the old red wood" refers to the eastern red cedar (Juniperus virginiana) which in the virgin forest was restricted to the high bluffs and banks of streams where it could compete with other forest trees. Prehistoric mounds and earthworks were once numerous along the upper valley of Cedar Creek in DeKalb County.

USGS MAP(S): Garrett, Huntertown, Cedarville 1:24,000
VICINITY: Huntertown, Cedarville, Ft. Wayne, Allen County
STREAM DISTANCE/TRIPS: apprx. 17 miles
three trips
LEVEL OF DIFFICULTY: Class 1
HAZARDS/PORTAGES: strainers, logjams, low water, swift current
INFO SOURCES: Allen County Parks & Recreation
c/o Fox Island County Park
7324 Yohne Rd.
Ft. Wayne, IN 46809
(219) 747-7846
Div. of Outdoor Recreation
Streams and Trails
402 W. Washington Rm. 271 W
Indianapolis, IN 46204
(317) 232-4070
ACRES Land Trust
(219) 422-1004
Root's (Canoe Rental)
(219) 484-2604 (800) 669-ROOT
AREA OUTFITTERS: Root's
6844 N. Clinton St.
Ft. Wayne, IN 46825
(219) 484-2604
GAMEFISH SPECIES: smallmouth bass, bluegill, catfish, sunfish
CAMPING: Appleseed Municipal Park
Coliseum Blvd. E
(April-Oct)
(219) 427-6720
c/o Ft. Wayne Park & Recreation
705 E. State Blvd.
Ft. Wayne, IN 46805
(219) 483-0057
MEDICAL ASSISTANCE: Parview Memorial Hospital
1234 E. Dupont Rd.
Ft. Wayne, IN 46825
(219) 489-6660
Parkview Memorial Hospital
2200 Randallia Dr.
Ft. Wayne, IN 46805
(219) 480-6636

ACCESS SITES	SECTION	RIVER MILES
A. Cook's Landing, 4 acre Allen County Park, NE of Huntertown near the junction of SR 327/ Coldwater Rd. & Shoaff Rd. & Chapman Rd., one mile south of the DeKalb-Allen County Line.*Note water can be low and logjammed to Tonkel Rd.	A-B	4 miles
B. Tonkel Road, NW bridge corner, roadside parking, carry down access	B-C	4.3 miles
C. Cedarville DNR public access, SE bridge corner, SR 1, west Cedarville	C-D	8.5 miles
D. St. Joseph River, Shoaff Park, St. Joe Rd., east bank, between Evard Rd. & St. Joe Center Rd., NE Ft. Wayne *Note this access is on the St. Joseph River, for those who want to combine stream trips and continue		(less than 1 mi to St. Joseph River)

Cedar Creek , Upstream from Brittany Overlook, Metea County Park

CEDAR CREEK

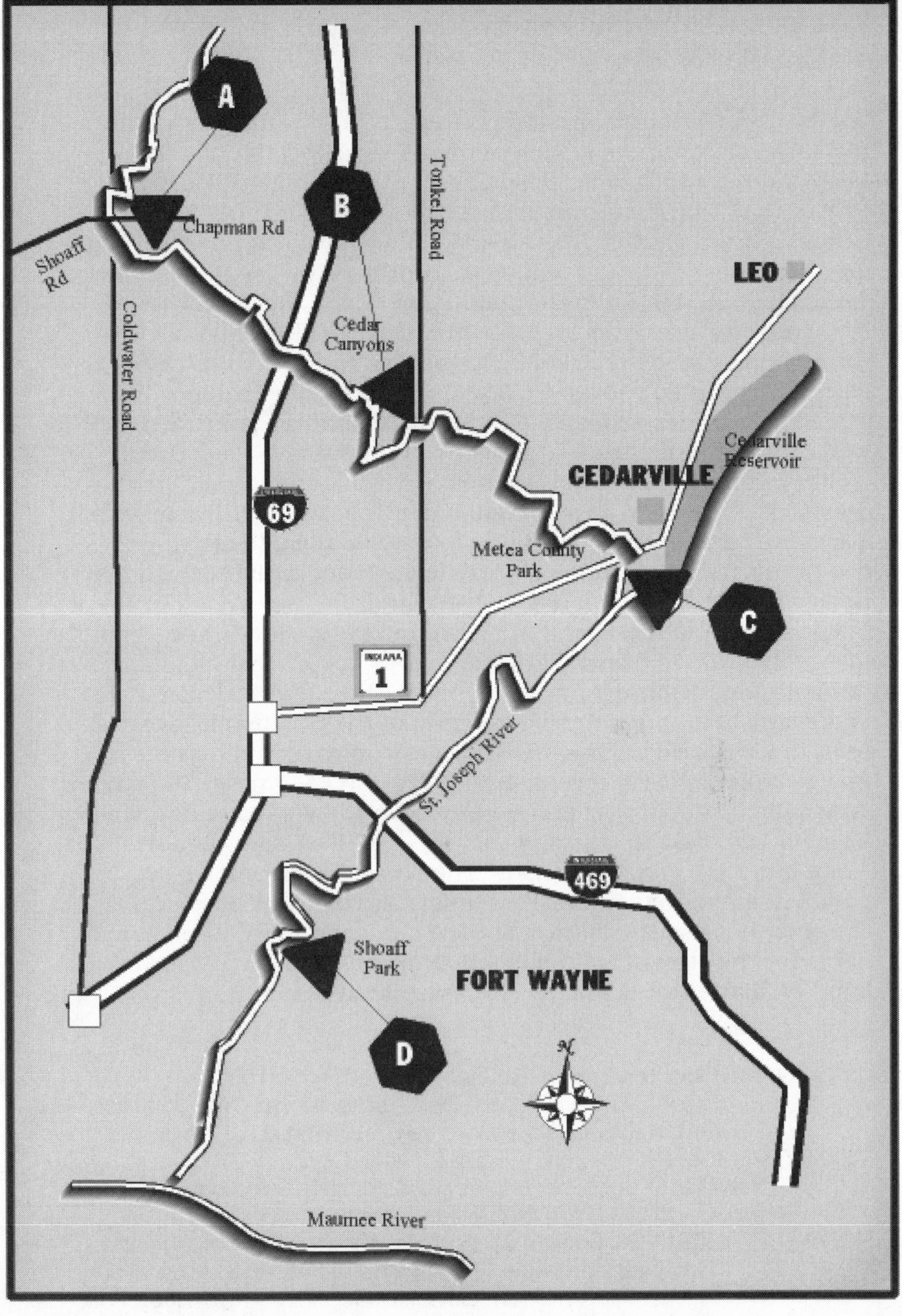
A
B
Chapman Rd
Shoaff Rd
Tonkel Road
Coldwater Road
LEO
Cedar Canyons
Cedarville Reservoir
CEDARVILLE
69
Metea County Park
C
INDIANA 1
St. Joseph River
469
Shoaff Park
FORT WAYNE
D
N
Maumee River

7. ST. JOSEPH RIVER OF THE MAUMEE

- **Course through timbered banks with meadow, woodlot & farmland beyond**

The headwaters of the St. Joseph River of the Maumee begin about two miles south of the origins of the St. Joseph River of Lake Michigan near Hillsdale, Hillsdale County, Michigan. The East Branch and the West Branch of the St. Joseph River of the Maumee heads up from glacially-carved lakes, flowing southwards, crossing into northwest Ohio and joining to form the river, south of Pioneer, Ohio near U.S. 20. From the confluence of the east and west branches, the lazy river of gentle flow travels 75 miles southwest through man-made prairie-like farmscape to unite with the St. Mary's River in downtown Ft. Wayne, creating the Maumee River. The river becomes wider as it carves its meandering way across the well-drained agricultural lake plains of the former Black Swamp country of northwest Ohio and northeast Indiana. As the stream draws closer to Ft. Wayne, development follows. Paddlers may find the river too slow and boat traffic too much along the eight-mile deadwater back up (460-acre lake) from Spencerville to Cedarville. Be aware of the low dam (P.L.) upstream from the covered bridge at Spencerville and the dam (P.R.) at Johnny Appleseed Park. From the Cedarville Dam to Shoaff Park the river is surprisingly wild however downstream to Johnny Appleseed Park, the city reveals itself. Paddlers will discover the best portion of the St. Joseph River is from the Montpelier, Ohio ODNR access downstream to the Spencerville, Indiana covered bridge (approx. 44 miles). The stream is usually floatable year around but expect low water riffles, some logjams and even strainers in the upper Ohio reaches and wind along lower more open portions. The recessed streambed gives paddlers a removed and more intimate fluvial experience. Cedar Creek is the largest tributary of the St. Joseph River. The Miami name for the stream is Ko-chis-oh-se-pe or "bean river". The Wea band of Miami called the river Weasepe or Weasepon.

USGS MAP(S): Ohio: Montpelier, Blakeslee, Edgerton, 1:24,000
Indiana: Butler East, Ind.-Ohio, Hicksville, Ind-Ohio, Saint Joe, Grabill, Cedarville, Ft. Wayne East 1:24,000

VICINITY: Montpelier, Edgerion, Williams County, Ohio
Newville, St. Joe, Spencerville, DeKalb County, Indiana
Leo, Cedarville, Ft. Wayne, Allen County

STREAM DISTANCE/TRIPS: approx. 27 mi. from Montpelier to Ohio-Indiana state line;17 mi. from state line to Spencerville; 12 mi. from Cedarville to Johnny Appleseed Park

3-4 trips or more possible

LEVEL OF DIFFICULTY: Class 1

HAZARDS/PORTAGES: dams, wind, snags, boulders, deadwater, motorized boats

INFO SOURCES: Lake La Su An Wildlife Area
Route 1, Box 88
Montpelier, OH 43543
(414) 459-4676
Ohio DNR
Div. of Watercraft 6
1630 Sycamore Line
Sandusky, OH 44870
(419) 621-1402
Ft. Wayne Parks & Recreation
705 E. State Blvd.
Ft. Wayne, IN 46805
(219) 483-0057
Roots Livery
6844 N. Clinton St.
Ft. Wayne, IN 46825
(219) 484-2604

AREA OUTFITTERS: Roots (219) 484-2604

GAMEFISH SPECIES: smallmouth bass, crappie, carp, channel catfish, suckers

CAMPING: Johnny Appleseed Park
Coliseum Blvd. E.
Ft. Wayne Parks & Recreation (seasonal)
(219) 427-6720 or 483-0057

MEDICAL ASSISTANCE: Community Hospitals-Williams Co.
433 West High Street
Bryan, Ohio
(419) 636-1131
DeKalb Memorial Hospital
1316 E. 17th St.
Auburn, IN 46706
(800) 925-4600
Parview Memorial Hospital
1234 E. Dupont Rd.
Ft. Wayne, IN 46825
(219) 489-6660
Parkview Memorial Hospital
2200 Randallia Dr.
Ft. Wayne, IN 46805
(219) 480-7156 or 6636

ACCESS SITES	SECTION	RIVER MILES
A. ODNR access, Montpelier, OH, Williams County Fairgrounds, from Ohio SR 107 (alt site, SR 34 bridge)	A-B	15 miles
B. Williams, OH, CR J/39, NE of Edgerton	B-C	8 miles
C. Williams-Defiance, OH, County Line Road Clarksville bridge	C-D	4 miles
D. DeKalb CR 40/OH SR 249, Ohio-Indiana state line, SE corner of bridge	D-E	12 miles
E. St. Joe IDNR public access, 0.5 mi. east of St. Joe on SR 1, then south on DeKalb CR 63rd Rd., across railroad track to access	E-F	5 miles
F. Spencerville Covered Bridge, south of SR 1 on Mill St./CR 68, SW corner *Note (P.L.) at low dam 100 yards before covered bridge. Deadwater from Spencerville to Cedarville Lake Dam.	Bypass Cedarville Resevoir. If paddling thru access available at Leo, Cedarville, (P.R.) at Cedarville dam	
G. Cedar Creek access, Cedarville, SR 1 bridge, SE corner , put-in only	G-H	8.5 miles
H. Shoaff Park & Golf Course, east bank access, St. Joe Road north of St. Joe Center Road	H-I	3.4 miles
I. Johnny Appleseed Park, west bank access, *Note (P.R.) before Municipal Dam, just south of Coliseum Blvd./US 33/30/24, east of Clinton St. & bordered by Parnell Ave., California Dr., & Harry Baals Dr. (seasonal camping. Ft. Wayne Parks and Recreation)		

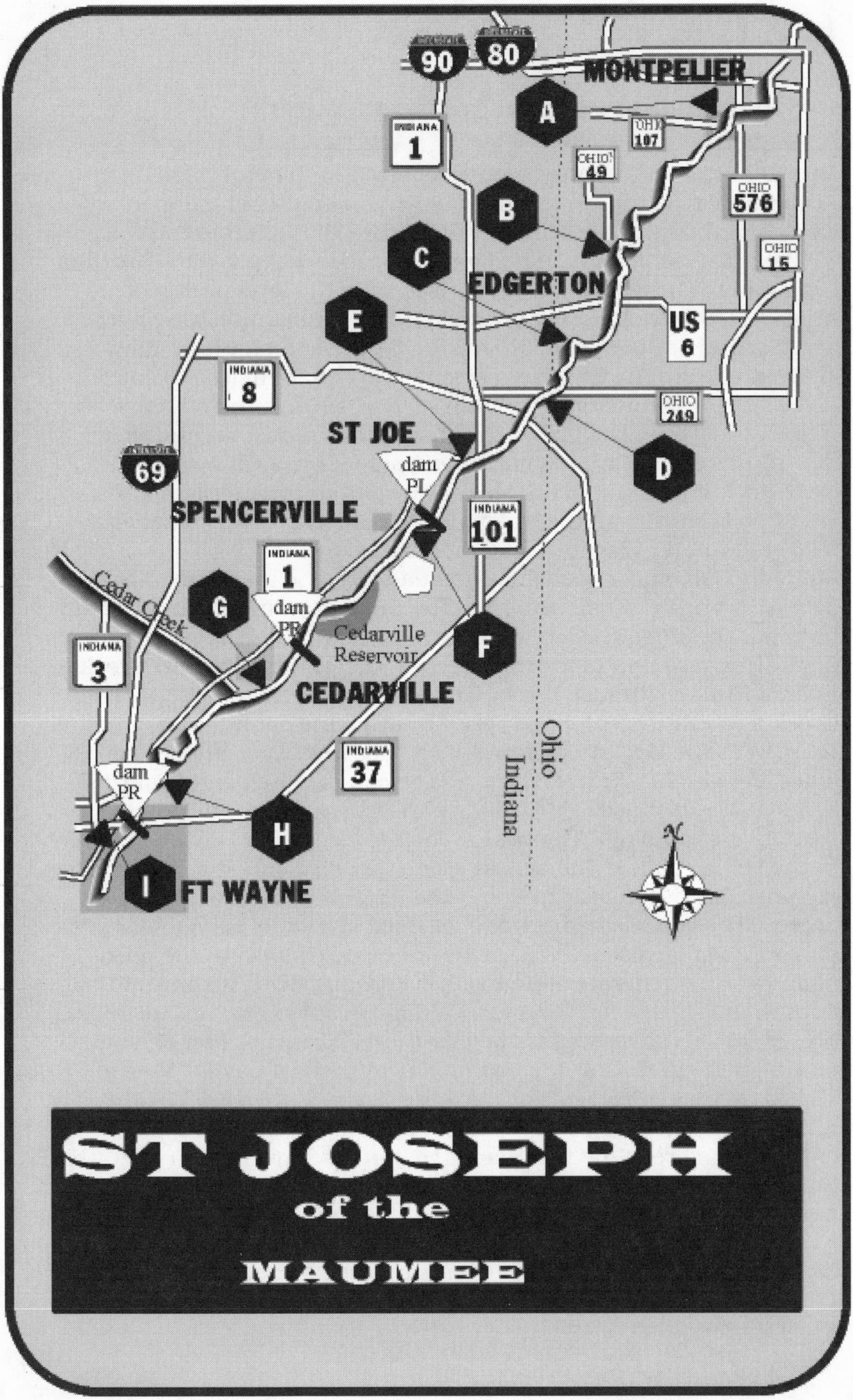

ST JOSEPH
of the
MAUMEE

8. ST. MARY'S RIVER

- Go a languid pace on quiescent waters

Over 200 years ago, army scouts reported to General "Mad" Anthony Wayne that the St. Mary's River would only "support canoes and those only at high water". The US military report of 1794 applies today. If you go light, the canoe will ply with less than high water. The St. Mary's River rises from the level prairie of Auglaize County, Ohio not far west of New Bremen, flowing north and northwest 90 miles to marry the St. Joseph and form the Maumee River. The St. Marys drains 450 square miles of Ohio before entering Indiana. The Ohio section of the stream has frequent logjams, sluggish current and poor public access; therefore the upper reaches are recommended only for the adventuresome. Near Rockford, Ohio, the St. Mary's begins to run nearly parallel to US 33, continuing all the way to Ft. Wayne and the confluence; following the Ft. Wayne glacial morainal ridge.

Willshire, Ohio near the Ohio-Indiana state line marks the first access to put-in (40 mi. from St. Joseph to Maumee). Crossing into Indiana, the sluggish, muddy stream picks up Blue Creek. Further downstream the St. Mary's will receive the waters of Yellow Creek, Borum Run, Holthouse Ditch, Gerke Ditch, Nickelsen Creek, Trier Creek and Little St. Mary's River. Decatur, the county seat of Adams County, is the largest community on the river between the Ohio state line and Ft. Wayne. Decatur's streamside Kekionga Park (55 acres) is the most sizeable public park between the canoeable section (no camping). The best section to paddle runs from Willshire to the village of Poe. The access points are situated at a comfortable distance apart. Decatur to Poe is the longest section without good access. The recessed, limestone-exposed stream is carved below the surrounding farmscape and more protected from wind the open plain country generates. Timing is everything when it comes to finding the right water level for paddling (not too low, not too high).

The St. Mary's River was named by the 17th century French who occupied Ft. Miamis at the confluence in present day Ft. Wayne. The St. Mary's is known as Ca-ko-the-ke or "kettle river" by the Shawnee, Ke-ke-ong-se-pe by the Huron and Mah-ma-i-quah-se-pe or "sturgeon creek" by the Miami. Historians have written about the St. Mary's as a voyageur portage route between tributary waters of western Lake Erie and the Ohio River.

USGS MAP(S): Willshire, Ohio-Ind., Wren, Decatur, Hoagland, Poe, Ft. Wayne West 1:24,000

VICINITY: Willshire, Van Wert County, Ohio
Pleasant Mills, Decatur, Adams County,
Poe, Ft. Wayne, Allen County

STREAM DISTANCE/TRIPS: approx. 40 miles
five or more trips possible
LEVEL OF DIFFICULTY: Class 1
HAZARDS/PORTAGES: low water, snags, deadwater, wind, steep banks
INFO SOURCES: Ohio DNR
Div. of Watercraft 2
1976 Buck Creek Lane
Springfield, OH 45502
(937) 323-1582
Decatur & Adams County Parks & Recreation
231 East Monroe
Decatur, IN 46733
(219) 724-2520
Ft. Wayne Parks & Recreation
705 E. State Blvd.
Ft. Wayne, IN 46805
(219) 483-0057
Tri-Lakes Fisheries Station
5570 N. Fish Hatchery Rd.
Columbia City, IN 46725
(219) 691-3181
AREA OUTFITTERS: none
GAMEFISH SPECIES: smallmouth bass
CAMPING: Ouabache State Park
4903 E SR 201
Bluffton, IN 46714
(219) 824-0926
Johnny Appleseed Park
Coliseum Blvd. E
c/o Ft. Wayne Parks & Recreation
(219) 483-0057 or 427-6720
MEDICAL ASSISTANCE: Adams County Memorial
805 High St.
Decatur, IN 46733
(219) 724-2145
Lutheran Hospital of Indiana
7950 W. Jefferson Blvd.
Ft. Wayne, IN 46804
(219) 435-7001

ACCESS SITES	SECTION	RIVER MILES
A. Willshire, OH, SR 49/81 bridge, NW corner, adjacent to OH SR 49, pullout or streetside parking	A-B	4 miles
B. Pleasant Mills, Adams CR 225 N, pullout & carry down, NE of SR 101 bridge or streetside parking	B-C	6 miles
C. Decatur, Kekionga Park, US 224/Monroe St. south to Mercer Ave., then east to Parkview Dr.	C-D	18 miles
D. Poe, Taylor St., village park, adjacent SE to Hoagland Bridge, steep banks, user path, carry down from playground	D-E	3.2 miles
E. Bostick Rd. bridge, NE corner, ltd. roadside parking	E-F	4 miles
F. Ft. Wayne Parks:		
F1. Tillman Park, Tillman & Hanna St.	F1-F2	2 miles
F2. Foster Park/Indian Village Park, Bluffton Rd. & Hartman Road	F2-F3	2 miles
F3. West Swinney Park/East Park/Camp Allen Park, Jefferson Blvd. & Washington Blvd.	F3-F4	0.8 miles
F4. Guldlin Park/Bloomingdale Park, Superior St.	F4-F5	0.8 miles
F5. Historic Old Ft. Wayne, Spy Run Ave.		

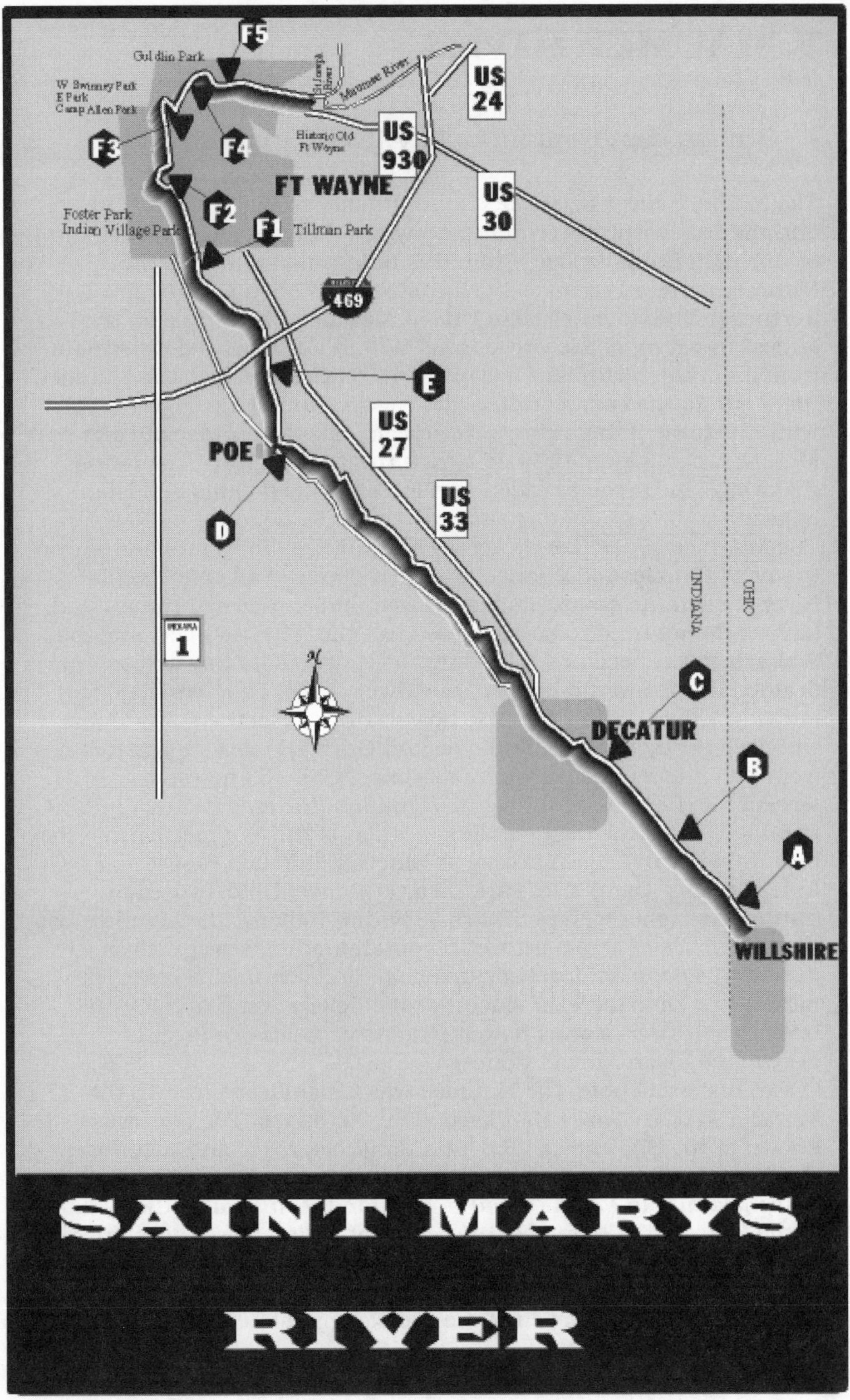

SAINT MARYS RIVER

9. MAUMEE RIVER

- Stream east from inner city to outer countryside

The Maumee River begins at the confluence of the St. Mary's River and the St. Joseph River in downtown Ft. Wayne, just downstream of the Main Street bridge. From this fluid union of rivers, the Maumee travels 175 miles northeast, across Allen County and northeast Ohio to enter Lake Erie at Maumee Bay in Toledo, the largest tributary of the Great Lake. Within a few miles downstream from its urban birthplace (beyond I-469/US 24 bridge), the Maumee River enters the open countryside, carving its way through the western shore of the ancient Pleistocene lake bed of glacial Lake Maumee, now a rich, drained agricultural plain. The meandering rocky stream begins to widen and forested steep bluffs and islands appear.

The Maumee glides quietly across the Indiana-Ohio state line where the next 43 miles to Defiance has been declared an Ohio Scenic River section (no dams, limited access). Indiana-owned canoes and kayaks do not need to be registered in Ohio. The Maumee, like the Wabash River, becomes "big water" as it makes its way across the drained Black Swamp lands of northwest Ohio. Paddlers may paddle all the way to Lake Erie however hydroelectric power dams will need portage east of Defiance and Grand Rapids. Downstream from the Independence Dam to Maumee, Ohio (53 miles), the stream has Recreational River designation (the river nearly doubles in size). Overall the best paddling section of the Maumee is from the Bull Rapids carry down access at Bluecast, Indiana east to Independence Dam State Park, near Defiance, Ohio, especially during the higher waters of spring. Within Indiana, the Maumee has seen its share of abuse with PCB contamination, sewage, river widening, floodplain forest destruction, and streamside gravel pit mining but Ohio (at least since 1974) officially respects the water body to a greater degree; however the lower Maumee River is designated as an Area of Concern,

On an historical note, the Maumee was a significant river to the Miami and other tribes that lived along its banks. The river was known to the Shawnee as the "standing rock river" and Ottawasepe. The French who built forts near the confluence altered the tribal name Miami into Maumee and referred to the stream as the " Miami of the Lakes". The Maumee, the center of Indian power, was broken by the American General "Mad" Anthony Wayne, "the General who never sleeps", during the Battle of Fallen Timbers 1794 near Maumee, Ohio which opened the Old Northwest Territory to American settlement.

USGS MAP(S): Ft. Wayne West, Ft. Wayne East, Maples, Grabill, Woodburn N, Ind.-Ohio, Antwerp, Paulding, Sherwood, Defiance West, Defiance East 1:24,000
VICINITY: Ft. Wayne & New Haven, Allen County, Indiana
Antwerp & Cecil, Paulding County, Ohio
Defiance, Defiance County, Ohio
STREAM DISTANCE/TRIPS: nearly 70 miles from Ft. Wayne to Independence Dam State Park
8 or more trips
LEVEL OF DIFFICULTY: Class 1
HAZARDS/PORATGES: wind, shallow water, boulders, dams
INFO SOURCES: Ft. Wayne Parks & Recreation
705 E. State Blvd.
Ft. Wayne, IN 46805
(219) 483-0057
Tri-Lakes Fisheries Station
5570 N. Fish Hatchery Rd.
Columbia City, IN 46725
(219) 691-3181
Ohio DNR Div. Of Natural Areas & Preserves
Scenic Rivers Program
Fountain Square, Bldg. F
Columbus, Ohio 43224
(614) 265-6458
AREA OUTFITTERS: none
GAMEFISH SPECIES: smallmouth bass, walleye
CAMPING: Johnny Appleseed Park
Coliseum Blvd. East
Ft. Wayne Parks & Recreation
(seasonal)
(219) 427-6720 or 483-0057
Independence Dam State Park
27722 SR 424, Rt. 4
Defiance, OH 43512
(419) 784-3263
MEDICAL ASSISTANCE: Parkview Memorial Hospital
2200 Randallia Drive
Ft. Wayne, IN 46805
(219) 484-6636
Defiance City Hospital
1206 E 2nd St.
Defiance, Ohio 43512
(419) 783-6955

ACCESS SITES	SECTION	RIVER MILES
A. Guldlin Park, Ft. Wayne, Sherman Blvd. & Michaels Ave. on St. Mary's River, float down to the confluence of St. Joseph River & Maumee River. (2.6 mi) downstream, (P.L.) at Hosey Dam just upstream from Anthony Blvd. bridge	A-B	6.7 miles
B. Maumee Park, Ft. Wayne, east of US 30 on Lake Ave./North River Rd., south side of road, north bank (best access to begin river trip)	B-C	14 miles
C. Bull Rapids Road & Doehrman Road Bridge, NW corner at the dead end adjacent to Zion Lutheran Church & graveyard, park & carry down, north of US 24 near Bluecast	C-D	2 miles
D. SR 101 Robert B. Shirley Memorial Bridge, NW corner, roadside parking & carry down	D-E	14.3 miles
E. Antwerp, Ohio city roadside park, US 24 east, south bank, carry down along service road in NE corner of city park	E-F	14.5 miles
F. Roadside rest area, junction of US 24 & US 127, east of Cecil, OH, south bank, carry down	F-G	8 miles
G. ODNR access off Bend Rd./Defiance CR 134, 0.5 mile north of US 24, south of The Bend, Ohio, south bank	G-H1	
H1. Pontiac Park, Defiance, 0.25 mile east of Ohio		

ACCESS SITE	SECTION	RIVER MILES
SR 66 bridge on Ohio SR 18/424, north bank	H1-H2	11.3 miles
H2. Kingsbury Park, Defiance, north of E. 2nd St. off Front St., along Auglaize St. south bank, east across from Ft. Defiance historic park, mouth of Auglaize River (camping)	H2-I	3.7 miles
I. Independence Dam State Park, Ohio SR 424, east of Defiance, north bank, (P.L.) at dam		

Scenic Maumee River, Ohio SR 49, north of Antwerp

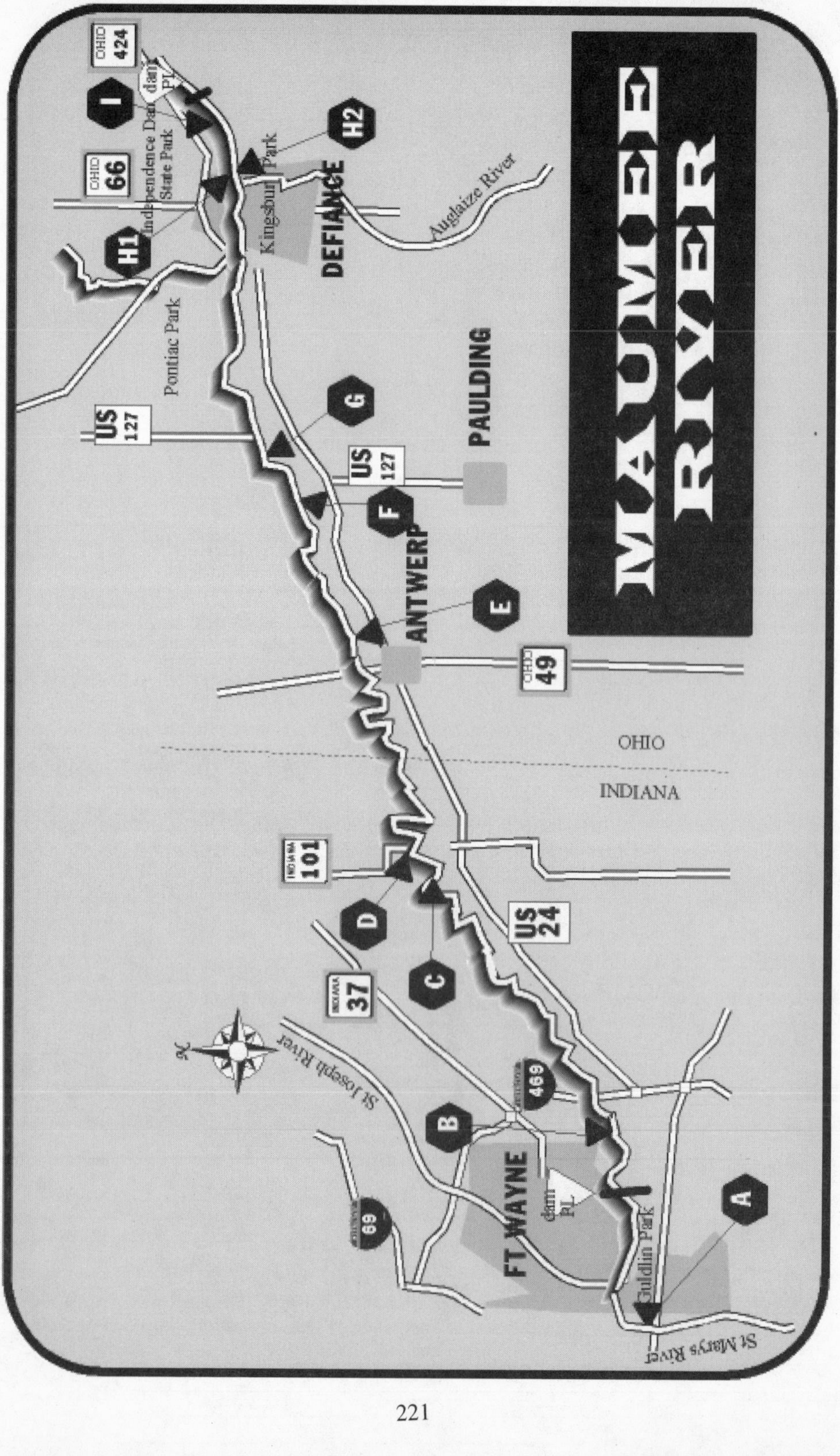
MAUMEE RIVER
DEFIANCE
PAULDING
ANTWERP
FT WAYNE
OHIO
INDIANA
Pontiac Park
Independence Dam State Park
Kingsbury Park
Auglaize River
St Joseph River
St Marys River
Guldin Park
dam PL
OHIO 424
OHIO 66
US 127
OHIO 49
INDIANA 101
US 24
INDIANA 37
469
69
A
B
C
D
E
F
G
H1
H2
I

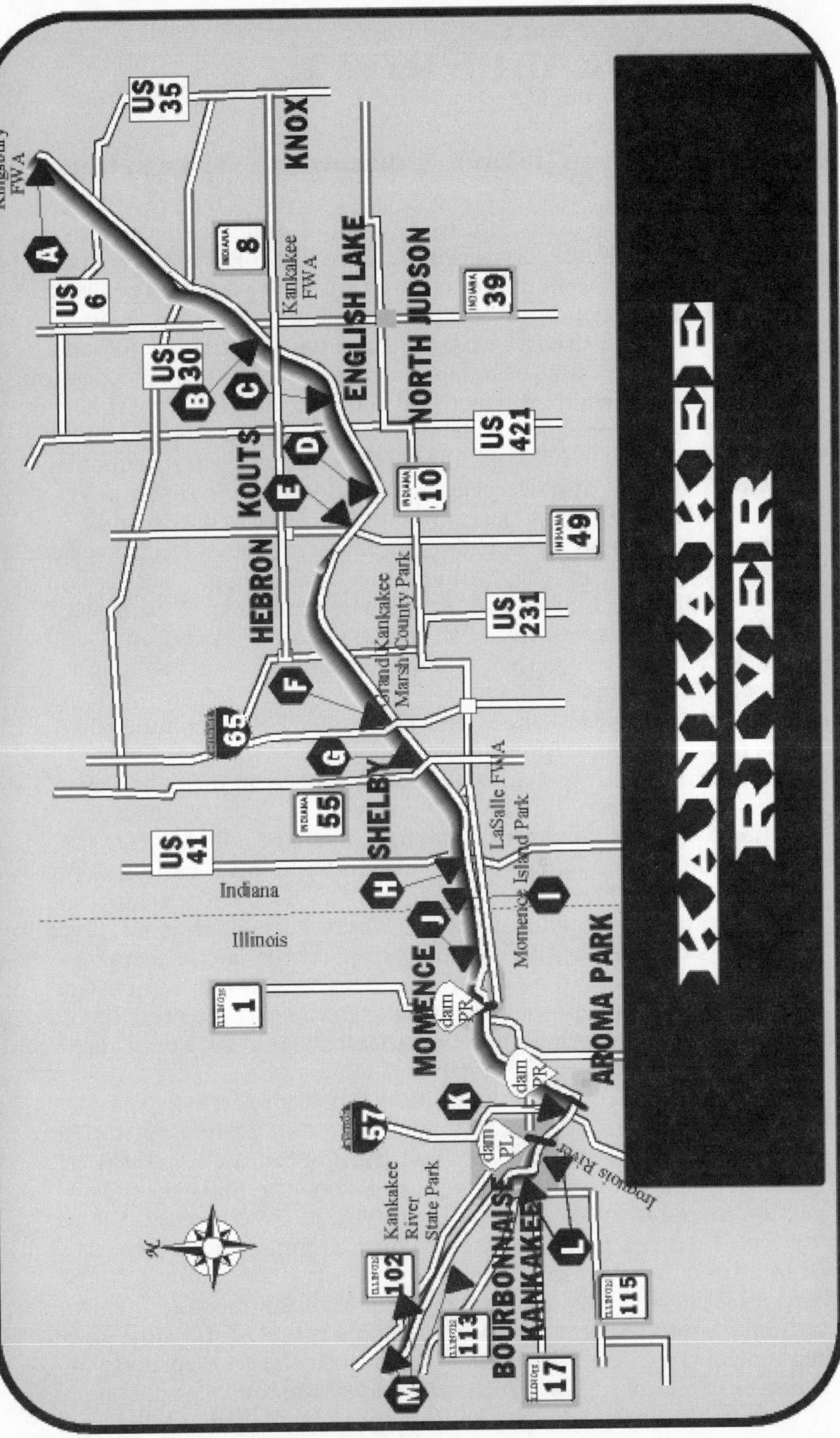
KANKAKEE RIVER
Kingsbury FWA
Kankakee FWA
Grand Kankakee Marsh County Park
LaSalle FWA
Momence Island Park
Kankakee River State Park
Iroquois River
Indiana
Illinois
KNOX
ENGLISH LAKE
NORTH JUDSON
KOUTS
HEBRON
SHELBY
MOMENCE
AROMA PARK
BOURBONNAISE
KANKAKEE
US 35
US 6
US 30
US 421
US 231
US 41
8
39
10
49
65
55
1
57
102
113
17
115
dam PR
dam PR
dam PL
A
B
C
D
E
F
G
H
I
J
K
L
M

10. KANKAKEE RIVER

- Do the ditch in Indiana & discover the river in Illinois

Before channelizing (early 1900s), the wild Kankakee River and adjoining 500,000 acre Grand Marsh were like a Florida everglade; a vast wildlife-rich wetland punctuated with savanna and prairie in northwest Indiana and northeast Illinois. Today, the manmade stream is a shorter dredged channel in Indiana but at the Illinois state line, the Kankakee becomes a natural river; one of the cleanest in the midwest. Despite the fact that the river and much of the marsh has been converted to serve agriculture, the stream still has travel appeal especially for paddlers who are looking for remoteness, fairly swift current and exercise; by making time and distance via paddling. The Indiana section is not about a leisurely trip amid scenic beauty but about experiencing a vastly altered river. Access sites are spaced about the right distance and campgrounds are not far out of the way. Insects can be overwhelming from June to frost. Efforts are underway to establish the Grand Kankakee Marsh National Wildlife Refuge that would eventually encompass and restore 30,000 acres.
The 159 mile long Kankakee River (250 miles before channelizing) heads in St. Joseph County in mucklands, southwest of South Bend, flowing southwest and into Illinois, merging with the Des Plaines River to form the Illinois River, west of Joliet, A sizeable volume of water is shed within the 3,000 square mile basin of the "East Branch of the Illinois River". The Indiana ditch section of the river is 75 to 1880 feet wide, four to five feet deep with one foot fall per mile and three to four mph flow. Much of the ditch is cut down and depressed allowing no sweeping views of the open Kankakee sand prairie beyond. The cut off meanders have few gravel bars or islands to land. Mosquitoes can be horrendous. There are a few logjams. Although seemingly remote, Chicago and its' sprawl are positioned to the not-so-far north and west.
The Yellow River (canoeable from Knox's Wythougan city park access down a linear ditch to Kankakee FWA near the English Lake confluence and access) is the largest tributary of the Kankakee in Indiana. Some of the interesting places along the Kankakee River include Kingsbury FWA (camping), Kankakee FWA (access, Yellow River confluence), Lomax historic village, Dunn's Bridge (access), Grand Kankakee Marsh (Lake) County Park (access), Badal Trust Area, and LaSalle FWA (access) in Indiana. Kankakee State Park (camping), northwest of Kankakee, Illinois is one of the most scenic sections of the river. The Iroquois River is the largest tributary of the river in Illinois. Dams at the Momence, Kankakee and Wilmington, Illinois raise the water level to to accommodate large

motorized boats however the trip from the Indiana state line to Momence and down to Aroma Park confluence and from Bird Park in Kankakee to Kankakee River State Park offer some of the best paddling in Illinois (limestone bluffs, islands, backwaters, inlets). In Indiana, Kankakee FWA to English Lake or Dunn's Bridge and on downstream to Grand Kankakee Marsh County Park and LaSalle FWA is okay canoeing.
Historically, the Potawatomi called the river and its broad, marsh-like floodplain Teh-yak-ki-ki or "swampy country", the source of the name Kankakee. The French explorer LaSalle entered the "Land of Lincoln" via the Kankakee. Since the mid 1800's, the Kankakee valley has known environmental change and economic conquest but the river has survived man's onslaught and will be making a comeback from Indiana's most endangered river in the 21st century with the proposed national wildlife refuge.

USGS MAP(S): Stillwell, Hamlet, Kingsford Heights, Knox West, English Lake, LaCrosse, San Pierre, Wheatfield, Kouts, Hebron, Demotte, Shelby, Schneider, Illiana Heights, Ill.-Ind., Momence, St. Anne, Kankakee, West Kankakee, Bourbonnais, Bonfield, 1:24,000

VICINITY: LaPorte & LaCrosse, LaPorte County
Knox, English Lake, North Judson, Starke County
Kouts & Hebron, Lake County
Wheatfield & Demotte, Jasper County
Shelby & Schneider, Lake County
Momence, Aroma Park, Kankakee, Bourbonnais, Kankakee County, Illinois

STREAM DISTANCE/TRIPS: 100 miles & more
ten or more trips

LEVEL OF DIFFICULTY: Class 1

HAZARDS/PORATGES: insects, dangerous low bridges in high water (especially US 41), steep banks, deep water, drop off, hunting in season, undertow, strong current, no glass bottles on rivers in Illinois

INFO SOURCES: Kingsbury FWA
5344 S. Hupp Rd.
LaPorte, IN 46350
(219) 393-3612
Kankakee FWA
4320 W. Toto Rd.
POB 77
North Judson, IN 46366
(219) 896-3522
Lake County Parks & Recreation
2293 N. Main St.
Crown Point, IN 46307
(219) 769-PARK
LaSalle FWA
4752 W. 1050 N
Lake Village, IN 46349

(219) 992-3019
Kankakee River State Park
POB 37
Bourbonnais, IL 60914
(815) 932-0488
Illinois Div. of Fisheries
(217) 782-6424

AREA OUTFITTERS: Daily Canoe Trips
313 E. 2nd
Aroma Park, IL 60910
(815) 939-2486
Reed's Canoe Trips
907 N. Indiana Ave.
Rt. 50
Kankakee, IL 60901
(815) WE-CANOE 939-3117
Kankakee River State Park Canoe Trips
RR#1
Bourbonnais, IL 60914
(815) 932-0488

GAMEFISH SPECIES: smallmouth, largemouth, & rock bass, walleye, bluegill, channel catfish, crappie, northern pike

CAMPING: Kingsbury FWA
(219) 393-3612
18 Class C sites
Jasper-Pulaski FWA
5822 N. Fish & Wildlife Lane
Medaryville, IN 47957
(219) 843-4841
51 Class C sites
Willow Slough FWA
2042 S 500 W
Morroco, IN 47963
(219) 285-2704
Class B
Kankakee River State Park, IL
(815) 933-1383
Class A, B, C & D

MEDICAL ASSISTANCE: LaPorte Hospital
1007 Lincolnway
LaPorte, IN 46350
(800) 235-6204
Starke Memorial Hospital
102 E. Culver Rd.
Knox, IN 46534
(219) 772-6231
Jasper County Hospital
1104 E. Grace
Rensselaer, IN 47978
(219) 866-5141
St. Anthony Medical Center
201 S. Main

Crown Point, IN 46307
(219) 738-2100 757-6310
St. Mary's Hospital
500 W. Court St.
Kankakee, IL 60901
(815) 937-2490

ACCESS SITE	SECTION	RIVER MILES
A. Kingsbury FWA, 10 mi SE of LaPorte, south of River Rd. from SR 104 or US 35	A-B	16 miles
B. Kankakee FWA, 0.5 mi west of junction of SR 8 & SR 39 on SR 8, north side of hwy, west bank	B-C	5.3 miles
C. English Lake access, Yellow River, north on Starke CR 650 W	C-D	8.3 miles
D. Dunns Bridge access, Porter County Park, NE corner, CR 500 E	D-E	4 miles
E. SR 49 bridge, NE corner, pullout parking & carry down	E-F	14.4 miles
F. Grand Kankakee Marsh County Park, Lake County Park, Range Line Rd	F-G	15 miles
G. Shelby access site SR 55 bridge, NE corner north of Thayer, south of Shelby	G-H	7 miles
H. LaSalle FWA, LaSalle/White Oak Bayou access, US 41, east end of property (at mid-point, Black Oak access, 3A parking, LaSalle FWA)	H-I	3.8 miles
I. LaSalle FWA, State Line access, NE side of bridge on State Line Rd., one mile north of SR 10	I-J	9 miles
J. Momence, IL, Momence Island Park & Momence Ramp (dam downstream from Dixie Hwy bridge (P.R.) or take channel left past Island Park to avoid dam)	J-K	11 miles

ACCESS SITE	SECTION	RIVER MILES
K. Aroma Park, boat launch, Front St. N bank, river mouth, Potawatomi Park (dams at Aroma Park (P.R.) & Kankakee, (P.L.), deadwater from Aroma Park to Kankakee)	K-L	5 miles
L. Jeffers Park, boat launch, 0.8 mi.down-stream from Kankakee Dam, SW of SR 115 Water St., Kankakee, IL, or downstream at Bird Park, Court St. & Wall St	L-M	9 miles
M. Kankakee River State Park, SR 102, NW of Kankakee, three access sites: Shell Pipeline Rd., Island Nature Preserve, Warner Bridge Rd		

Kankakee River, Historic Marker Acknowledging French Explorer LaSalle

Kankakee River, Dangerous Low Bridge in High Water, US 41

Kankakee River, Kankakee River State Park, Illinois

11. IROQUOIS RIVER

- Make your watery way across the Grand Prairie into the Land of Lincoln

The 94 mile long Iroquois River heads up in Jasper County, north of Rensselaer, the county seat, and slowly meanders southwest into Newton County and on into Illinois, bending northwest at Watseka to join the Kankakee River at Aroma Park. The sluggish and turbid river drains 2,175 square miles of rural prairie countryside within Indiana (50 miles) and northeast Illinois (44 miles). The drop in stream gradient is measured in inches most of the level course except at the "Rensselaer Rapids" and the last six miles (Sugar Island bridge to confluence) where the drop is 2.3 feet per mile. The stream still shows evidence of being dredged in Indiana (early 1900's) however the Iroquois has not been channelized in Illinois where it retains more of its native beauty.

Paddlers can expect logjams from Indiana to Watseka where the river widens after being joined by Sugar Creek. Floods of 1993 and 1995 persisted during late spring and resulted in the death of numerous bankside trees that are piling up in the river. Bring a paddling friend to help portage around the logjams (no woodland stinging nettle noticed). Expect to paddle all the way in the seemingly still current. Wind can be a concern on the open wide river north of Watseka. Incoming streams include Sugar Creek, Prairie Creek, Pike Creek, Langan Creek, Spring Creek, and Beaver Creek. Motorboats can navigate a short distance up the Iroquois from the pool formed on the Kankakee River behind the dam in Kankakee. The Iroquois is not a sought out canoeing stream except by locals. Access is adequate but in short supply. The best paddling section of the river is between the Newton County Fairgrounds, Pumpkinvine Road bridge and Watseka.

From marshland, the Iroquois grows from waters of large ditches and after 20 miles of gathering strength it reaches Rensselaer and the first public access. The "Rapids of the Iroquois" may be examined up close from the Rensselaer access to Bicentennial Park, two miles downstream. Devonian limestone streambed is exposed along the Iroquois at Rensselaer. From Rensselaer to Brook the river is ditch-like, showing past dredging and therefore is not recommended for paddling. From Brook (two separate access sites) to the Indiana-Illinois state line there are several logjams and strainers (flooding has created tree bank dieback). The last best take-out or put-in, in Indiana, is at the Newton County Fairgrounds (the State Line Road & bridge/Newton CR 700 W, 55 mi. from mouth is closed). The 50' foot wide lackadaisical stream enters Illinois and brushes the south edge of the village of Iroquois, crossing a former Potawatomi foot trail to Chicago. Continuing its natural course towards Watseka through some of the best farmland in the world there is little development. Access at Texas Bridge is mid point between the Indiana state line and Watseka. In Watseka near the confluence of Sugar Creek (the largest tributary of the Iroquois) is an Illinois DNR ramp at the end of West Main. The river changes its southwest flowing course and heads north, widening substantially. The woody growth on the bottoms thrives with southern cottonwood, American elm, hackberry, silver maple, willow, swamp white oak and sycamore. The last major meanders are near the Plato Bridge (fee access) and development in the form of river cottages lines the banks. The next few miles are nearly straight north however at Sugar Island Bridge, six miles above the Kankakee mouth, rocky rapids appear. The prairie stream meets and merges with the Kankakee River at Aroma Park where access is provided at Potowatomi Park, north bank. The Iroquois River derives its name from an Iroquois war party that was subdued by the Potawatomi.

USGS (MAPS): Rensselaer, Mount Ayr, Goodland, Kentland, Sheldon, Ill.-Ind.
Watseka, Crescent City, L'Erable, Kankakee 1:24,000
VICINITY: Indiana: Rensselaer, Jasper County,
Brook, Kentland, Newton County
Illinois: Iroquois, Watseka, Iroquois County
Kankakee, Aroma Park, Kankakee County
STREAM DISTANCE/TRIPS: 70 mi possible
eight or more trips
LEVEL OF DIFFICULTY: Class 1
HAZARDS/PORTAGES: logjams, portages, wind, slow current
INFO SOURCES: Bass Lake Fish Hatcheries Station
6718 E. Winona Ave.
Knox, IN 46534
(219) 772-2353
Daily Canoe Trips
(815) 939-2486
Ilinois DNR
(800) ASK-FISH
Illinois DNR Div. of Fisheries
(217) 782-6424
AREA OUTFITTERS: Daily Canoe Trips (rental only, no shuttle)
313 E. 2nd
Aroma Park, IL
(815) 939-2486
GAMEFISH SPECIES: smallmouth, largemouth, & rock bass, walleye, northern pike, crappie, bluegill, channel catfish, carp
CAMPING: Willow Slough FWA
2042 S. 500 W
Morocco, IN 47963
(219) 285-2704
Class C
Kankakee River State Park
SR 102, POB 37

Bourbonnais, IL 60914
(815) 933-1383
Class A, B, C & D

MEDICAL ASSISTANCE: Jasper County Hospital
1104 E. Grace St.
Rensselaer, IN 47978
(219) 866-5141
Iroquois Memorial Hospital
200 E. Fairman
Watseka, IL 60970
(815) 432-5841
Provena St. Mary's Hospital
500 W. Court St.
Kankakee, IL 60901
(815) 933-1671 or 935-7494

ACCESS SITES	SECTION	RIVER MILES
A. Rensselaer, DNR access, SR 114 E bridge NE corner	A-B	1.9 miles
B. Rensselaer, Bicentennial City Park, Washington St., south bank	section B-C not recommended	
C. SR 16 E bridge, two mi. E of Brook, NE bank, steep slope, use caution (located NW of George Ade, Hazleton home, humorist prose writer (1866-1944)	C-D	2.2 miles
D. S Highway St./Rd. bridge, S 0.5 mi. of Brook, SE corner, pullout & carry down, (alt. site to C)	D-E	11 miles
E. Newton CR 450 N/Pumpkinvine Rd. bridge, NW corner, adjacent to Newton County Fairgrounds & access road	E-F	14 miles
*Note: No State Line Rd./Newton CR 700 W bridge to access. Bridge out & road closed. Possible take-out at Iroquois, IL, US 52 bridge, SE corner, Twp 407/2120 N Rd. no parking, park at		

	town park, follow the survey marker and gaging station edge		
F.	Texas Rd. Bridge/Iroquois CR 2500 E, NE corner, N of US 24, N of CR 1900 N junction, midway between state line & Watseka	F-G	4.8 miles
G.	West Main St., NW Watseka, W two blocks from SR 1, IL DNR & Friends of Old Town Park access	G-H	14 miles
H.	Plato Bridge/Iroquois CR 2400 N (fee)	H-I	12.5 miles
I.	Sugar Island Rd. Bridge/ Kankakee CR S 776 E, NW corner, (respect private property) , also Sainman Ford access 4 mi SW of Aroma Park on E side of river	I-J	6.4 miles
J.	Kankakee River, Potawatomi Park access, Aroma Park, IL, Front St., north bank at confluence, near Shannon Island		

Clear Tributary Joins Muddy River

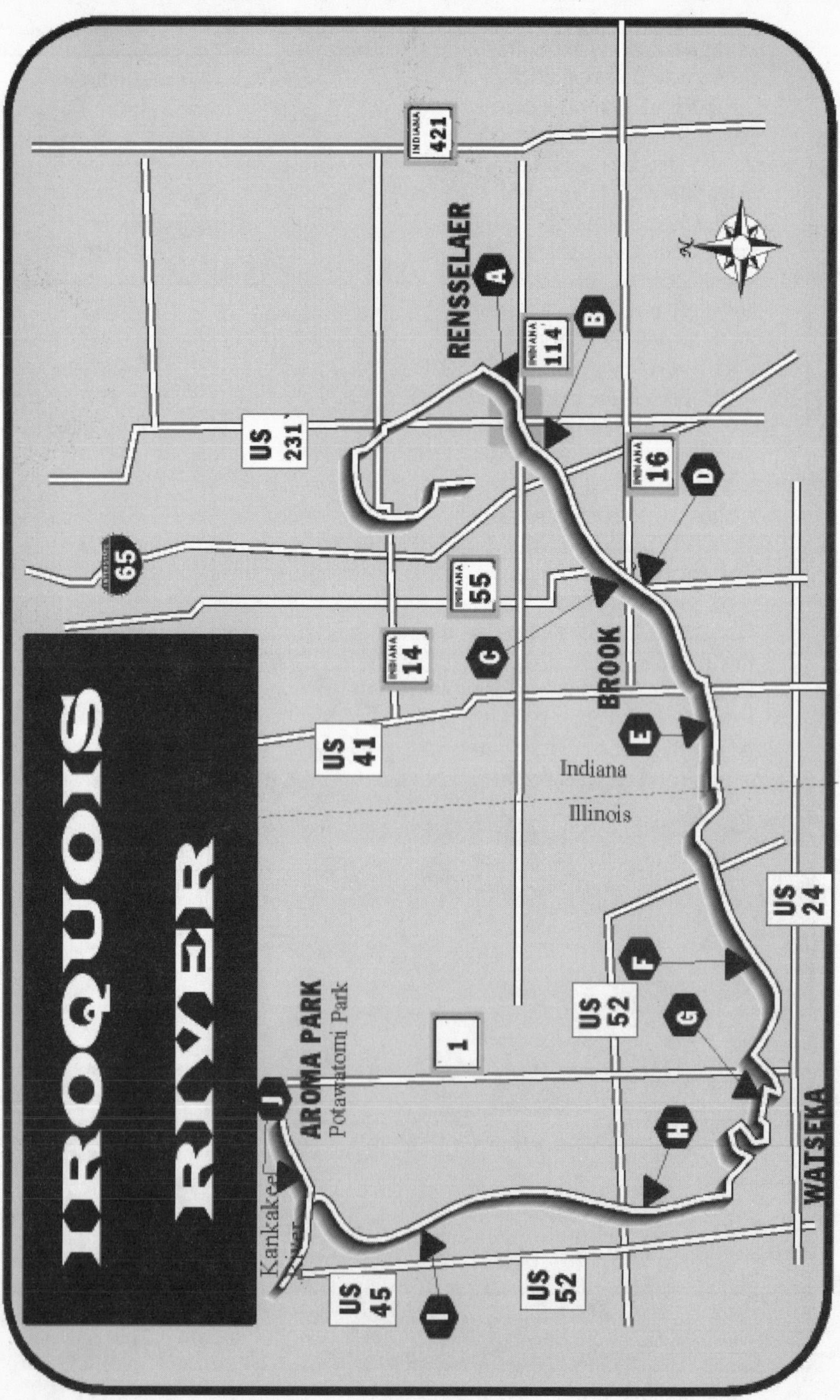
IROQUOIS RIVER
RENSSELAER
BROOK
Indiana
Illinois
AROMA PARK
Potawatomi Park
WATSEKA
Kankakee River
INDIANA 421
US 231
INDIANA 114
INDIANA 16
65
INDIANA 55
INDIANA 14
US 41
US 24
US 52
1
US 52
US 45
A
B
C
D
E
F
G
H
I
J
N

Wabash River, Kienly Island, Logansport

Wabash River, Mouth of Sugar Creek

12. WABASH RIVER

- Be far away on Indiana's State River

Rich in cultural and natural heritage, the Wabash is "The River of Indiana" through which our state history flows. The nearly 500 mile long river begins south of Fort Recovery, Ohio and flows north and northwest into Indiana, then west and south to merge with the Ohio River. Over 33,000 square miles (over 70 Indiana counties) drain into the Wabash River, which runs through 17 Indiana counties. Since 1991, the Wabash River Heritage Corridor Commission has been working "to promote the conservation and development of the natural, cultural and recreational resources of the corridor" much to the benefit of most.

Paddling-wise, the first best access (normal flow and above) is located at the Adams County Park of Linn Grove, (52 river miles from its Ohio drainage ditch source), Paralleling SR 116 from Linn Grove northwest to the east edge of Huntington/Roush Lake at Markle (28 miles), the Wabash cuts through rural countryside with the exception of Bluffton. Natural areas and parks enroute include Ouabache State Park (camping), the Bluffton River Greenway and the ACRES Along the Wabash Nature Preserve near Murray. This section of the Wabash is considered some of the best due to its relatively small navigable size and lack of development.

Bypassing the 8.5-mile long Huntington/Roush Lake (see Lake Section) the Wabash becomes a stream again at the dam tailwater along SR 5 south of the city of Huntington. Approximately 2.5 miles downstream of the Huntington Lake dam near the Etna Avenue bridge is a low dam (P.R.) adjacent to the city of Huntington water works (north bank) and the ACRES Tel-Hy Nature Preserve (south bank).Two and a half miles further downstream from the low dam is the Forks of the Wabash where the Little (Wabash) River joins the mainstream (access via SR 9 bridge, SE corner or carry down from the Historic Forks grounds, NW corner).

Downstream from the Forks, 147 miles to Covington, Fountain County is considered the best paddling on the entire Wabash River. The river retains a compact and private experience despite the fact that the water body becomes wider and cities crowd upon its banks. Communities that formerly turned away from the Wabash are now embracing the river with new parks and walkways along their waterfronts. Islands and timbered bluffs are more commonplace. Highlights along this section include Hanging Rock Nature Preserve, Little Turtle Waterway, France Park, French Post Park, Trailhead Park, Prophetstown State Park, Davis Ferry Park, Wabash Heritage Trail, Heron Island Nature Preserve, Fort Ouiatenon, Ross Hills County Park, Goose Island Nature Preserve, Zachariah Cicott County Park, Portland Arch Nature Preserve and numerous city

parks that line the banks. The big water, while rocky and boulder infested, affords easy paddling especially during normal or above normal flow. During Pleistocene times the river acted as a glacial sluiceway, known as the Teays River.
The Middle Wabash from Covington south 84 miles to Darwin, Illinois is the least appealing section for paddlers. The river is wide, often straight and with few natural areas, features or even trees to line its banks. However the middle section is more remote than the upper Wabash and there are several large islands. The largest number of eagles in Indiana are found near the power plants that are situated along the river, Only a few communities are located enroute: Perrysville, Montezuma, Clinton, and Terre Haute; all connected by SR 63.
The Lower Wabash River from Darwin, Illinois to the Ohio River confluence is by far the most remote and wild section. There are few highway bridges or other landmarks along the 166 miles of river. The riverbanks turn into wide sandy beach strands. Large islands inhabit the deep watery expanse of meandering stream. Bends are longer in distance. The floodplain forest features plants that thrive further south. The word bayou appears on the map. Cut offs in the shifting river channel has left behind isolated oxbow lagoons and lakes or bayous, cutoff from mainstream: Pearl Island, Bull Island, Ribeyre Island, Hermann Island and Greathouse Island. Choice areas along the Lower Wabash include Merom Bluff, Ouabache Trails Park, George Rogers Clark Memorial, Beall Woods State Park (Illinois), New Harmony and Harmonie State Park. The big river needs respect from canoeists who will have to deal with the wind in the wide openess. Staying close to shore will provide overhanging shade and a safer position from the path of larger boats that ply the river. Always be on the alert for submerged objects.
Those who prefer to travel to the Ohio River confluence at Wabash Island and continue downstream ten miles to the Shawneetown, Illinois take-out, are advised to hug the Ohio's north bank and be prepared for tug-boats and barges that threaten to capsize smaller crafts with their large wake (avoid the Ohio River if at all possible, in a kayak or canoe).
The place name Wabash is derived from the Miami, Wah-bah-shik-ki or "white shining path" in reference to the white Niagara limestone bed in the upper course of the river.

UPPER WABASH: Linn Grove, IN to Covington, IN

USGS MAP(S): Linn Grove, Bluffton, Uniondale, Markle, Majenica, Andrews, Lagro, Wabash, Rich Valley, Peru. Bunker Hill, Onward, Twelve Mile, Logansport, Anoka, Clymers, Lucerne, Burrows, Yeoman, Delphi, Brookston, Lafayette East, Lafayette West, Otterbein, West Point, Attica, Williamsport, Stonebluff, Covington 1:24,000

VICINITY: Linn Grove, Adams County; Bluffton, Wells County; Markle, Huntington, Andrews, Huntington County; Lagro, Wabash, Rich

Valley, Wabash County; Peru, Miami County; Lewisburg, Logansport, Georgetown, Cass County; Lockport, Delphi, Carroll County; Americus, Lafayette, W. Lafayette, Tippecanoe County; Independence, Williamsport, Warren County; Covington, Fountain County

STREAM DISTANCE/TRIPS: 189 miles canoeable
20 trips or more

LEVEL OF DIFFICULTY: Class 1

HAZARDS/PORTAGES: low water, high water, rocky shallows, rock ledges, submerged objects, logjams, bridge & bend pile ups, two dams at Huntington, wind

INFO SOURCES: Wabash Heritage Corridor
DNR Div. Of Outdoor Recreation
402 W. Washington St. Rm. W 271
Indianapolis, IN 46204
(317) 232-4070
US Army Corps of Engineers
Huntington/Roush Lake
735 N Warren Rd.
Huntington, IN 46750
(219) 356-8648
Tri-Lakes Fisheries Station
5570 N. Fish Hatchery Rd.
Columbia City, IN 46725
(219) 691-3181
Bass Lake Fisheries Station
6718 E. Winona Ave.
Knox, IN 46534
(219) 772-2353

AREA OUTFITTERS: River Junction Canoe Rental
6614 SR 25 N.
Lafayette, IN 47904
(765) 589-3875
(serves Lafayette area)

GAMEFISH SPECIES: bass, catfish, carp, crappie, walleye, sauger, bluegill

CAMPING: Ouabache State Park
4930 E. SR 201
Bluffton, IN 46714
(219) 824-0926
Class A & B
Huntington/Roush Lake
517 N. Warren Rd.
Huntington, IN 46750
(219) 468-2165
Class C
Salamonie Lake
9214 W. Lost Bridge West
Andrews, IN 46702
(219) 468-2124
Class A & C
Mississinewa Lake
RR#1, Box 194

Peru, IN 46970
(765) 473-6528
Class AA, A, B & C
France Park
US 24 W
Logansport, IN 46947
(219) 753-3938
Class A
River Junction Canoe Rental
6614 SR 25 N
Lafayette, IN 47905
(765) 589-3875
(camp & access, Tippecanoe River confluence at Americus)
Prophetstown State Park
(opens year 2000)
Battle Ground, IN 47920

MEDICAL ASSISTANCE: Wells Community Hospital
1100 S. Main St.
Bluffton, IN 46714
(219) 824-3210
Huntington Memorial Hospital
1215 Etna Ave.
Huntington, IN 46750
(219) 356-3000
Dukes Memorial Hospital
275 W. 12th St.
Peru, IN 46970
(765) 473-6621
Logansport Memorial Hospital
1101 Michigan Ave.
Logansport, IN 46947
(219) 753-7541
St. Elizabeth Medical Center
1501 Hartford St.
Lafayette, IN 47904
(765) 423-6011
St. Vincent Williamsport Hospital
412 N. Monroe St.
Williamsport, IN 47993
(765) 762-2496

MIDDLE WABASH RIVER: Covington to Darwin, Illinois

USGS MAP(S): Covington, Newport, Kingman, Montezuma, Dana, Clinton, New Goshen, Terre Haute, Denniston, Hutton 1:24,000
VICINITY: Covington, Fountain County
Perrysville, Cayuga, Newport, Clinton, Vermillion County
Montezuma, Parke County
Terre Haute, Vigo County
Darwin, Clark County, Illinois
STREAM DISTANCE/TRIPS: 84 miles total
5 or more trips
LEVEL OF DIFFICULTY: Class 1
HAZARDS/PORTAGES: wind, submerged objects, motorized river traffic
INFO SOURCES: Wabash Heritage Corridor
DNR Div. Of Outdoor Recreation
402 W. Washington St. Rm. W 271
Indianapolis, IN 46204
(317) 232-4070
Cikana Fish Hatchery
2650 SR 44
Martinsville, IN 46151
(765) 342-5527
Avoca Fish Hatchery
POB 16
Avoca, IN 47420
(812) 279-1215
AREA OUTFITTERS: none
GAMEFISH SPECIES: catfish, carp, sturgeon, crappie, sauger, walleye, largemouth bass
CAMPING: Turkey Run State Park
RR #1, Box 164
Marshall, IN 47859
(765) 597-2635
Class A & B
Lieber SRA
Cagles Mill Lake
1317 W. Lieber Rd. Suite 1
Cloverdale, IN 46120
(765) 795-4576
Class A, B, & C
Prairie Creek Park
Vigo County Parks & Recreation
c/o Courthouse Rm. 13
Terre Haute, IN 47801
(812) 462-3391
Class A
MEDICAL ASSISTANCE: United Samaritan Medical Center
600 Sager St.
Danville, IL 61832
(217) 443-5000
Culver-Union Hospital
US 231 N. 1710 Lafayette Rd.

Crawfordsville, IN 47933
(765) 362-2800
Terre Haute Regional Hospital
3901 S. 7th St.
Terre Haute, IN 47802
(812) 232-0021

LOWER WABASH RIVER, Darwin Illinois to Shawneetown, Illinois

USGS MAP(S): Hutton, Fairbanks, West Union, Hutsonville, Merom, Heathsville, Russelllville, Oaktown, Tippecanoe, Decker, St. Francisville, East Mt. Carmel, Mt. Carmel, Keensburg, Grayville, New Harmony, Solitude, Maunie, Emma, Wabash Island 1:24,000
(several of these topos are shared with Illinois)
VICINITY: Darwin, Clark County, IL; Hutsonville, Crawford County, IL; Merom, Sulllivan County; Russellville, Lawrence County, IL; Vincennes, Knox County, St. Francisville, Lawrence County, IL; Mt. Carmel, Wabash County, IL; East Mt. Carmel, Gibson County; Grayville, Edwards & White County, IL; New Harmony, Posey County; Maunie, White County, IL; Old Shawneetown, Gallatin County, IL
STREAM DISTANCE/TRIPS: 166 miles
12 or more trips
LEVEL OF DIFFIFCULTY: Class 1
HAZARDS/PORTAGES: wind, unseen objects, motorized river traffic
INFO SOURCES: Wabash Heritage Corridor
DNR Div. Of Outdoor Recreation
402 W. Washington St. Rm. W 271
Indianapolis, IN 46204
(317) 232-4070
Avoca Fish Hatchery
POB 16
Avoca, IN 47420
(812) 279-1215
Sugar Ridge Fish & Wildlife Area
2310 E. SR 364
Winslow, IN 47598
(812) 789-2724
AREA OUTFITTERS: none
GAMEFISH SPECIES: largemouth bass, catfish, carp, sauger
CAMPING: Shakamak State Park
6265 W. SR 48
Jasonville, IN 47438
(812) 665-2158
Class A & C
Greene-Sullivan State Forest
2551 S. SR 159
Dugger, IN 47848
(812) 648-2810
Class C
Ouabache Trails Park
Knox County Parks & Recreation
Ft. Knox Rd.

Vincennes, IN 47591
(812) 882-4316
Class A
Harmonie State Park
RR #1, Box 5A
New Harmony, IN 47631
(812) 682-4821
Class A
Hovey Lake Fish & Wildlife Area
1298 W. Graddy Rd.
Mt. Vernon, IN 47620
(812) 838-2927
Class C

MEDICAL ASSISTANCE: Mary Sherman Hospital
320 N. Section St.
Sullivan, IN 47882
(812) 268-4311
Crawford Memorial Hospital
1000 N. Allen St.
Robinson, IL 62454
(618) 544-3131
Good Samaritan Hospital
520 S. 7th St.
Tippecanoe, IN 47591
(812) 882-5220
Wabash General Hospital
1418 College Dr.
Mt. Carmel, IL 62863
(618) 262-8621
Gibson General Hospital
1808 Sherman Drive
Princeton, IN 47670
(812) 385-3401
White County Hospital
400 Plum St.
Carmi, IL 62821
(618) 382-4171
Deaconess Hospital
600 Mary St.
Evansville, IN 47715
(812) 477-6436

ACCESS	SECTION	RIVER MILES
	Upper Wabash	
A. Linn Grove, Adams County Park, east bank, 52 mi. d.s.from Ohio headwaters, (Ouabache State Park, long carrydown)	A-B	12 miles
B. Bluffton, White Bridge, east Bluffton Green-way, end of River Rd. (alt. site, Kehoe Park, SR 1 & SR 124, Bluffton)	B-C	15.5 miles
C. Markle, one mile east on SR 116 to Wells CR 500 W, south to ramp, east end Huntington/ Roush Lake	C-D	Huntington/Roush Reservoir not recommended
D. Huntington Dam (no portage) & Tailwater, Arrowhead N area, SR 5 (downstream (P.R.) at the spillway dam, Huntington Water Works)	D-E	6 miles
E. Forks of the Wabash, SR 9 bridge, SE or NW corner	E-F	13 miles
F. Lagro, SR 524 bridge, NE corner, park streetside at historic toll station & carry down, user access	F-G	8 miles
G. Wabash, DNR access site west of SR 13/15 bridge, west of Miami St. on Smith St.	G-H	6 miles
H. Omar Cole, DNR access, Old US 24, Wabash-Miami county line	H-I	9.5 miles
I. Peru, Wayne St. bridge, NE corner, power plant parking, (alt. site, d.s. SR 19 bridge, NW corner Cole Porter Depot Park)	I-J	20 miles
J. Logansport, no developed access, best access is down-stream at France Park, how-ever paddlers may consider: J1 the old Cass CR 600 E bridge		

ACCESS SITES	SECTION	RIVER MILES
Upper Wabash		
just south of Old US 24, an abandoned bridge upstream from Rock Island, J2 the 18th St. bridge, first bridge at Logansport city limits, ltd. pullout parking, SE corner, also called Morgan Hill Rd J3 SR 25 bridge, NW corner, downstream from the confluence of the Eel River. Little Turtle Gateway & Overlook has carry down town access	J-K	7 miles
K. France Park, DNR access, 3.2 miles west of Logansport on US 24, south 1.6 mi. on W Georgetown Rd.	K-L	9 miles
L. Lockport, French Post Park, S bank (camping) 3.7 mi. W of Burrows & SR 25 on Carroll CR 900 N to CR 275 W, then north one mi.	L-M	12 miles
M. Pittsburg, downstream 0.25 mi. of US 421/SR 18 & 39 bridge	M-N	10 miles
N. Americus, Tippecanoe River mouth, River junction Canoe Rental, west of Americus on SR 25, ($ minimal fee for access)	N-O	6.5 miles
O. Davis Ferry, Tippecanoe County Park, two mi. N of Lafayette, on Ferry St., south bank	O-P1	3 miles
P. Lafayette & West Lafayette access sites:		
P1. Mascouten Park, rest park, W bank, SR 443, near Happy Hollow Park	P1-P2	1 mile
P2. Digby Park, E bank	P2-P3	1 mile
P3. Tapawingo Park, W bank	P3-P4	0.5 miles
P4. Shamrock Park, E bank	P4-Q	4.5 miles
Q. Fort Ouiatenon historic park,		

	S. River Rd., West Lafayette	Q-R	5 miles
R.	Granville Bridge, NW corner, eight mi. W of West Lafayette on S. River Rd. & Division Rd. & Tippecanoe CR 700 W bridge	R-S	16 miles
S.	Attica, Potawatomi Park, downstream from the US 41/ Paul Dresser Bridge, SW bank, Market St. to Jackson St.	S-T	17.5 miles
	Middle Wabash		
T.	Covington, Five Crossings city park, three blocks W of the N side of the Fountain County courthouse	T-U	16.5 miles
U.	SR 234 bridge, SW corner E of Cayuga, W of Lodi, developed site, new access planned for Big Vermillion	U-V	15.5 miles
V.	Montezuma, Reeder Park, E bank, downstream from SR 36 bridge on First St.	V-W	10 miles
W.	Clinton, city park, NW SR 163 bridge, NW corner	W-X	8.5 miles
X.	Tecumseh, Kearns DNR access, from SR 63 N of Terre Haute, go E on Tecumseh Rd. To Pottsville Rd., then S 0.5 mile	X-Y	9 miles
Y.	Terre Haute, Fairbanks Park, S of US 40 and W of US 41	Y-Z	24 miles
Z.	Darwin Ferry site, Darwin, IL, access both sides of Wabash River, E of IL SR 1	Z-AA	19 miles
	Lower Wabash		
AA.	Hutsonville, IL, access ramp at SW bridge corner of SR 154, W bank	AA-BB	6.5 miles
BB.	Merom, access site on Bluff Rd., SR 58 & SR 63	BB-CC	24 miles
CC.	Russellville, IL, launch ramp	CC-DD	12 miles
DD.	Vincennes, Kimmell Park (camping), access		

ACCESS SITE	SECTION	RIVER MILES
also George Rogers Clark bridge, NW corner, IL side of river	DD-EE	11.5 miles
EE. St. Francisville, IL, d.s. of toll bridge Knox CR, 950 S	EE-FF	16.5 miles
FF. East Mt. Carmel, Patoka Island access site, River Rd. S (alt. site, Mt. Carmel, IL, mouth of White River confluence)	FF-GG	8 miles
GG. Crawleyville, Gibson CR 475, & CR 1400 W, launch ramp	GG-HH	17.5 miles
HH. Grayville, IL I-64 to SR 1 follow cut-off to town waterfront	HH-II	9.5 miles
II. New Harmony, SE corner of toll bridge, IN SR 66/IL 2	II-JJ	4 miles
JJ Harmonie State Park, SR 69, S of New Harmony, access SE Indiana shore from Mink Island (d.s. access at Maummee, IL)	JJ-KK	10.5 miles
KK. Dogtown Ferry, access is 3.3 miles west of Mt. Vernon on SR 62, then 3 mi. N on Raben Rd. and 2 mi. W on Posey CR 450 S, last access before mouth of the Wabash River	KK-LL	37.5 miles
LL. Ohio River, Old Shawneetown, IL, IL 13 & KY 56 toll bridge, IL side, NE corner by levee, 10 mi. d.s. of Wabash River mouth		

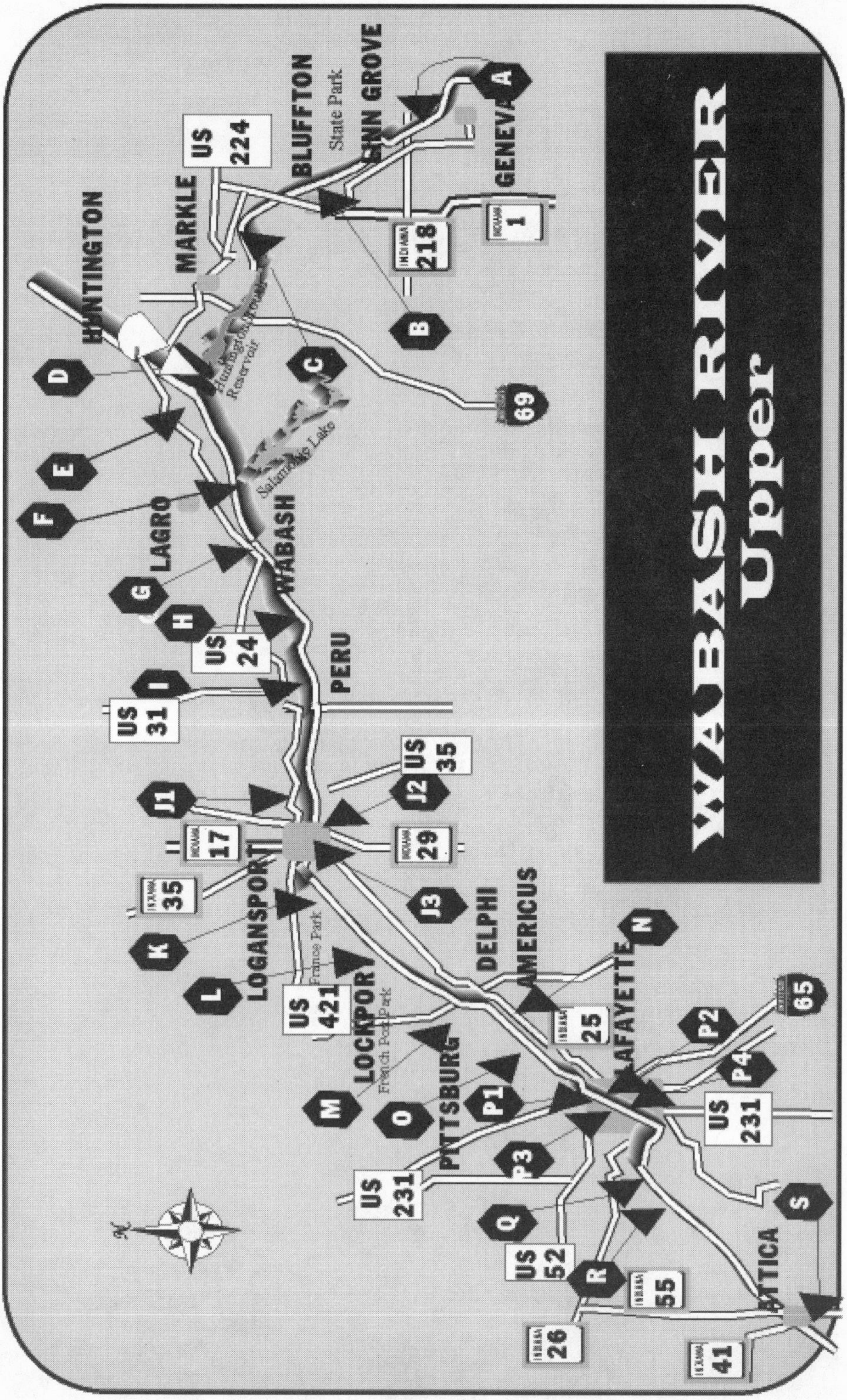
WABASH RIVER
Upper
HUNTINGTON
MARKLE
BLUFFTON
LINN GROVE
State Park
GENEVA
Huntington Lake
Reservoir
Salamonie Lake
LAGRO
WABASH
PERU
LOGANSPORT
France Park
LOCKPORT
French Post Park
DELPHI
AMERICUS
PITTSBURG
LAFAYETTE
ATTICA
US 224
US 24
US 31
US 35
US 421
US 231
US 52
218
1
17
35
29
25
55
26
41
69
65
A
B
C
D
E
F
G
H
I
J1
J2
J3
K
L
M
N
O
P1
P2
P3
P4
Q
R
S

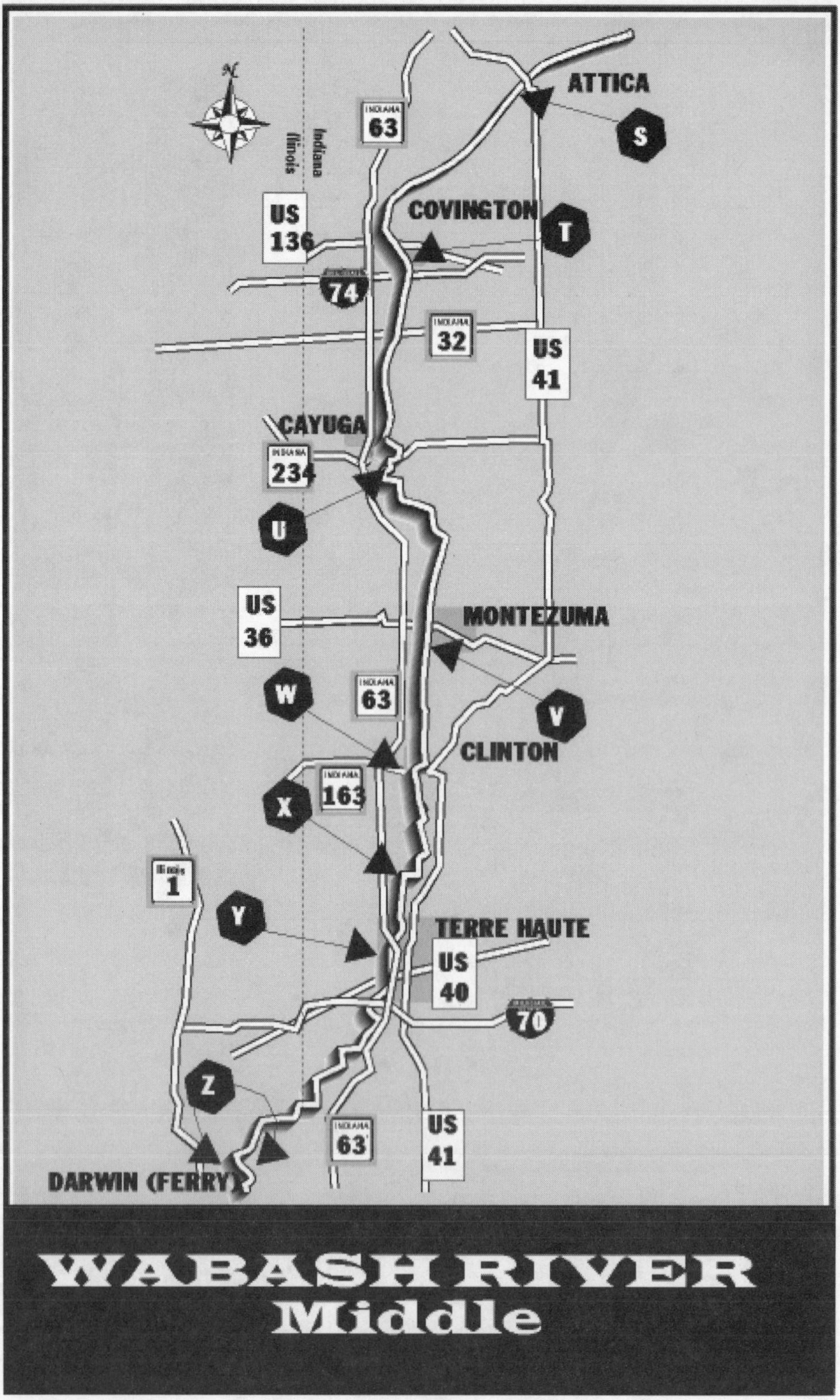

WABASH RIVER Middle

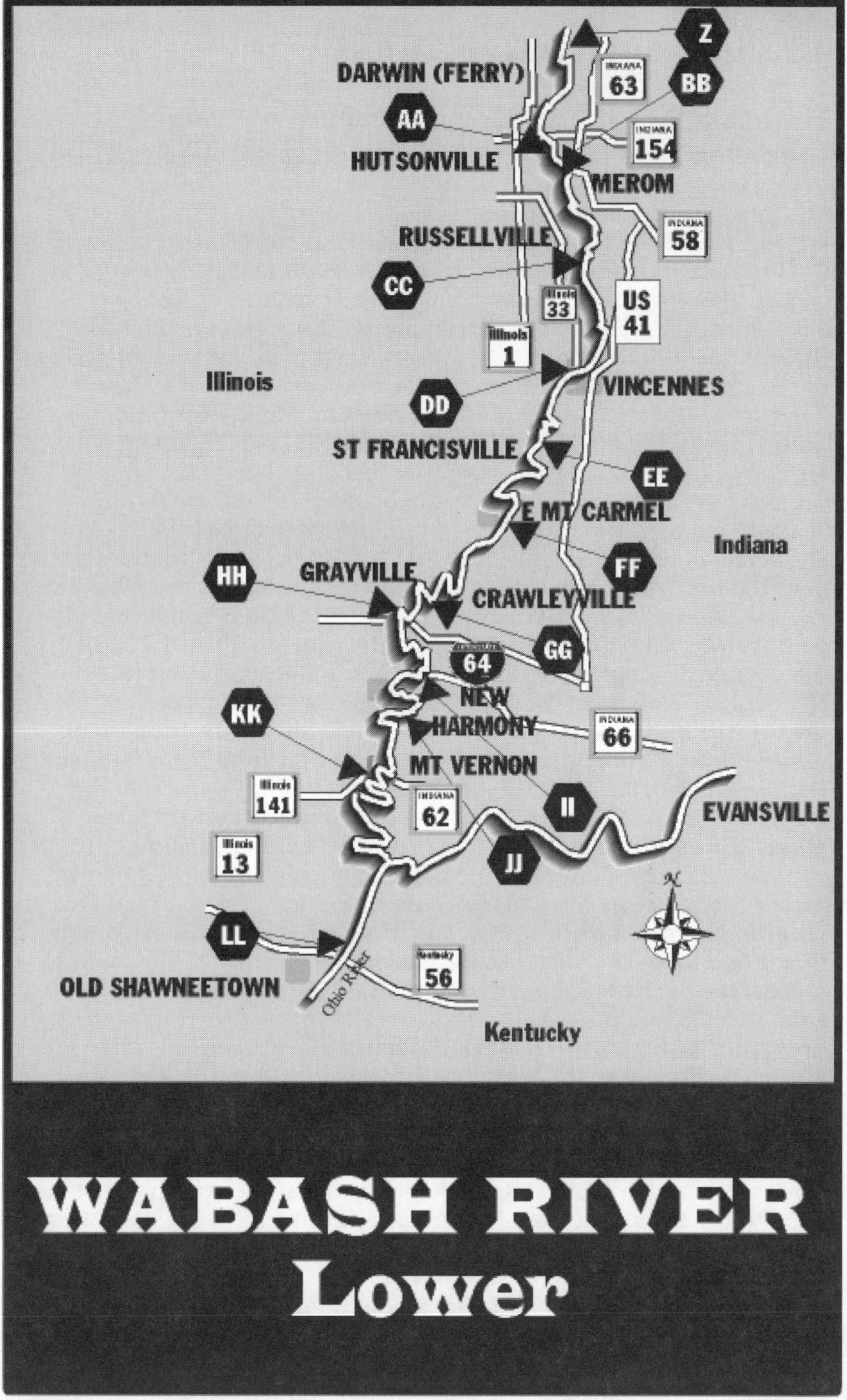

WABASH RIVER Lower

13. SALAMONIE RIVER

- Take a fluvial trip along an obscure & entrenched stream

The tame and docile Salamonie is seldom thought of as a floatable stream. The relatively small drainage basin is sandwiched between the Wabash and Mississinewa rivers and seasonal flow is best in the spring. The 88-mile long Salamonie River originates in southwest Jay County near the village of Salamonia. The stream is ditched through most of Jay County as it flows northwest, held in check by the Salamonie Moraine. Entering Blackford County, the stream flows along the north edge of Matamoras and Montpelier (first access, upstream 50 mi. from the Wabash) where it begins to appear more like a river (accessible).

Crossing over into Wells County, the boulder-ridden stream gathers strength from Prairie Creek near the village of Jeff. Downstream a few bends is the SR 3 bridge, the first best carry down access. Put-in at the northwest corner where bridgeside parking is available for two cars along adjacent Willow Road. From the SR 3 highway bridge down to Warren, Huntington County, the river parallels SR 218 on the near east, crossing under the SR 218 bridge at Warren (access NW corner). Watch for two low dams close together, upstream from the SR 218 bridge. Continue the fluvial venture northwest passing under the I-69 bridges and enter the deadwater from the Belleville Dam (P.L.) at Belleville Road and Huntington CR 700 S. From the Belleville Dam to Salamonie Lake, (considered the best section above Salamonie Lake) the entrenched river follows winding bends with scenic timbered bluffs. The boulder-lined stream loops its way across SR 124 near Mt. Etna and enters Heiney's Bend. There are six access sites between the SR 124 crossing and the Mt. Etna Main Street take-out. The current weakens and dissipates upstream from D-4 access as the stream enters from the 17-mile long Salamonie Lake. (see Salamonie Lake).

Continue the aquatic trek at the Salamonie Dam and Tailwater access, north bank. The short but sweet segment to the Wabash River normally has enough released water to paddle especially in fall during the annual drawdown. Downstream from the dam, the Salamonie passes through the picturesque Salamonie State Forest. Once entering the Wabash, paddle upstream, if the current is weak, about 0.5 miles to Hanging Rock on the south side of the river. Rest and explore the silurian reef and continue downstream to Lagro and the SR 524 bridge, NE corner take-out near the historic canal/interurban toll station. The Miami name for the Salamonie River is O-sah-mo-nee or On-sah-la-mo-nee, "yellow paint", the color that is obtained from the spring flowering bloodroot (Sanguinaria canadensis) which grows along the riverbanks.

USGS MAP(S): Montpelier, Liberty Center, Warren, Mt. Etna, Andrews, Lagro
1:24,000
VICINITY: Montpelier, Blackford County
Warren, Mt. Etna, Huntington County
Lagro, Wabash County
STREAM DISTANCE/TRIPS: approx. 40-45 miles
3 or more trips possible
LEVEL OF DIFFICULTY: Class 1
HAZARDS/PORTAGES: low dams at (P.L.)Warren & Belleville,
hidden boulders, snags, low water
INFO SOURCES: DNR Salamonie Lake
9214 W. Lost Bridge West
Andrews, IN 46702
(219) 468-2124
US Army Corps of Engineers
Rt. 1, Box 40
Lagro, IN 46941
(219) 782-2358
Tri-Lakes Fisheries Station
5570 N. Fish Hatchery Road
Columbia City, IN 46725
(219) 691-3181
AREA OUTFITTERS: none
GAMEFISH SPECIES: bass, walleye, catfish, crappie, carp
CAMPING: Salamonie Lake
9214 W. Lost Bridge West
Andrews, IN 46702
(219) 468-2124
Class A & C
MEDICAL ASSISTANCE: Blackford County Hospital
503 E. Van Cleve
Hartford City, IN 47348
(765) 348-0300
Huntington Memorial Hospital
1215 Etna Ave.
Huntington, IN 46750
(219) 356-3000
Wabash County Hospital
710 N. East St.
Wabash, IN 46992
(219) 563-3131

ACCESS	SECTION	RIVER MILES
A. Montpelier, Blackford CR 500 E & Cummins Rd., NE corner (high flow only) or Fireman River Park just upstream	A-B	9.5 miles
B. SR 3 bridge, NW corner, bridgeside parking (above normal flow only)	B-C	6.5 miles
C. Warren, SR 218 bridge, NW corner (two dams (P.L.) just upstream) (watch for Belleville Dam (P.L.) downstream of I-69 bridges)	C-D1	9 miles
D. Salamonie Lake backwaters, between SR 124 & Mt. Etna take-out:		
D1. South of Lancaster, 0.2 mi. N of SR 124, Huntington CR 300 W, E bank	D1-D2	1 miles
D2. W of Lancaster, Huntington CR 543 S, 0.8 mi., W bank	D2-D3	1.5 miles
D3. N of SR 124 between the Salamonie River bridge & the inlet cove bridge, E of Mt. Etna, W bank	D3-D4	3.5 miles
D4. W of D3 along a farm lane, E bank	D4-D5	0.75 miles
D5. SR 9, N of Mt. Etna to Huntington CR 400 S, E to CR 550 S	D5-D6	1.5 miles
D6. Mt. Etna, Main St. N to Salamonie Lake	D1-D6	8.25 miles
E. Salamonie Dam & Tailwater, N bank, Wabash CR 600 E	E-F	3.25 miles
F. Lagro bridge, SR 524, NE corner		

SALAMONIE RIVER

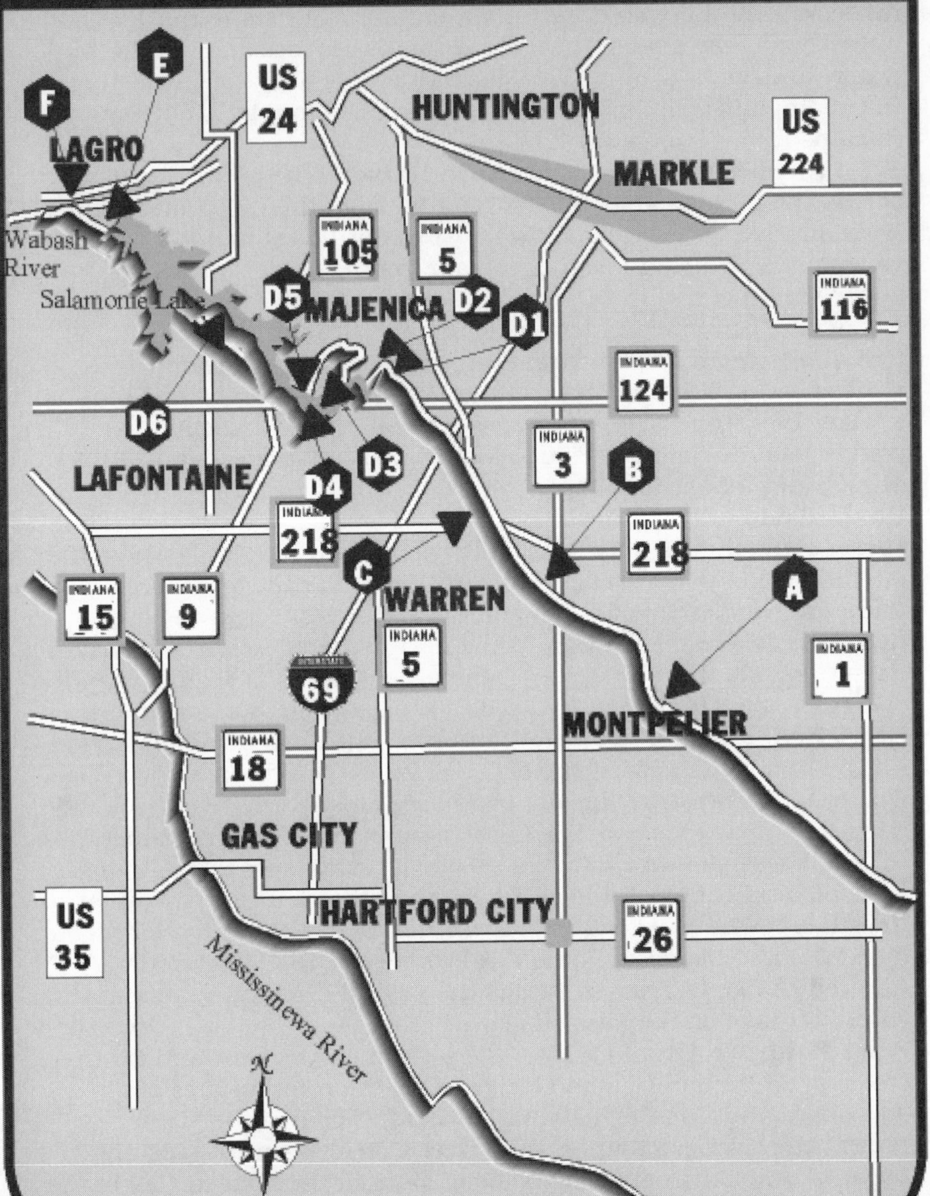

E
F
LAGRO
US 24
HUNTINGTON
US 224
MARKLE
Wabash River
Salamonie Lake
INDIANA 105
INDIANA 5
D5
MAJENICA
D2
D1
INDIANA 116
INDIANA 124
D6
D3
D4
INDIANA 3
B
LAFONTAINE
INDIANA 218
INDIANA 218
C
WARREN
A
INDIANA 15
INDIANA 9
INDIANA 5
INDIANA 1
69
MONTPELIER
INDIANA 18
GAS CITY
HARTFORD CITY
INDIANA 26
US 35
Mississinewa River
N

14. MISSISSINEWA RIVER

- Paddle the "river that slants", one of the swiftest streams in Indiana

Dropping an average of 3.3 feet per mile, the Mississinewa River is one of the fastest flowing streams in the Hoosier State. The Miami name Mis-chi-sin-wah or Nah-mah-chi-sin-wi refers to the numerous rocky shallow riffles and rapids as "much fall in the water" and/or "it slants". The Mississinewa is a beloved stream of the Miami and remnants granted to Chief Godfroy by U.S. treaty remains under Miami ownership.

The 110 miles long river heads up in Darke County, Ohio, just across the Indiana state line and not far from the headwaters of the Wabash River. The stream flows west to northwest in a low wide valley to the Wabash River, upstream from Peru. For nearly the entire length of the 15,000-year-old river, it follows the south edge of glacial Mississinewa Moraine. Outstanding silurian rock formations occur downstream from the Mississinewa Dam particularly the Seven Pillars of the Mississinewa, an eroded bluff of shallow limestone caves or alcoves. Overall the best sections to paddle include the Ridgeville to Matthews section and from SR 15 to Mississinewa Lake at Jalapa.

Dredged and ditched, the Mississinewa River flows nearly horizontal across Randolph County from Ohio until about Ridgeville where the stream begins to naturally meander. Within the Ridgeville area there are two developed Randolph County access sites: CR 100 W near Deerfield and CR 750 N at the north edge of McVey Memorial Forest. Paddle this section only when the water is at high flow and watch for the 3/4 dam at Ridgeville. The gathering stream enters Delaware County and borders the south edge of Albany where there is a carry down access at the old steel trestle bridge on Strong Road. Curving southwest for the last time from Albany, the river hooks northwest near the Campbell Creek confluence. Crossing under SR 67, the Mississinewa continues its northwest course through the agricultural Bluffton Till Plain where the river brushes up against the small towns and villages of Granville, Eaton, Wheeling (floodgate dam P.L.) and Matthews (dam P.R.) where the 1877 Cumberland Covered Bridge (access) still fords the stream; the only remaining covered bridge on the Mississinewa.

From Matthews, Grant County, the stream curves west and north, crossing SR 26 and I-65 and on, dividing the communities of Jonesboro and Gas City (city park access). North of the "Twin Cities", the river gains water from Deer Creek, Walnut Creek and Lugar Creek, skirting the east side of Marion, the "Queen City of the Valley". Crossing SR 18, the river becomes the Marion Mississinewa Riverway, a linear city park from 18th Street downstream to Matter

Park (access) where portage (P.R.) is necessary at the low dam. North of Marion the river crosses SR 9 and SR 15 (access) and enters the Mississinewa Lake boundary. Jalapa and the Trail's End access is the last site before the flatwater of Mississinewa Lake (see Mississinewa Lake).

The Mississinewa River continues beyond the dam at the tailwater Peoria Fishing Site and Frances Slocum State Forest (north bank access and parking). The steady release of the dam waters assures enough water for paddling however during fall drawdown time the stream is at higher than normal flow (higher flow may be arranged by calling the US Army Corps Office). The trip downstream to Peru via the Wabash River is a scenic stretch and includes the Seven Pillars of the Mississinewa natural feature. Beyond the SR 124-highway bridge (access) there is a series of fast moving riffles before the river joins the Wabash River. Continue down the Wabash to Peru and exit at the Wayne Street bridge (first bridge) adjacent to the power plant or the next bridge downstream (SR 19 bridge) at the Old Depot Park (also called the Cole Porter Park). Steep take-out at both Peru north bank access sites.

USGS MAP(S): Deerfield, Ridgeville, Redkey, Eaton, Wheeling, Hartford City West, Gas City, Fairmont, Marion, Van Buren, LaFontaine, Somerset, Peoria, Bunker Hill, Peru 1:24,000

VICINITY: Ridgeville, Randolph County
Albany & Eaton, Delaware County
Matthews, Jonesboro, Gas City, Marion, Jalapa, Grant County
Peru, Miami County

STREAM DISTANCE/TRIPS: approx. 70 miles
ten or more trips possible

LEVEL OF DIFFICULTY: Class 1

HAZARDS/PORTAGES: low dams, low water, hidden snags & boulders, rock ledges

INFO SOURCES: Mississinewa Lake DNR
RR #1, Box 194
Peru, IN 46970
(765) 473-6528
US Army Corps of Engineers
Route #1, Box 202a
Peru, IN 46970
(765) 473-5946
Tri-Lakes Fisheries Station
5570 N. Fish Hatchery Rd.
Columbia City, IN 46725
(219) 691-3181

AREA OUTFITTERS: none

GAMEFISH SPECIES: sunfish, bass, crappie, walleye, catfish

CAMPING: Mississinewa Lake
RR #1, Box 194
Peru, IN 46970

(765) 473-6528
Class AA, A, B, C sites

MEDICAL ASSISTANCE: Blackford County Hospital
503 E. Van Cleve
Hartford City, IN 47348
(765) 348-0300
Marion General Hospital
441 N. Wabash Ave.
Marion, IN 46952
(765) 662-4694 or 1441
Dukes Memorial Hospital
275 W. 12th St.
Peru, IN 46970
(765) 473-6621

ACCESS SITES	SECTION	RIVER MILES
A. Randolph CR 100 W, just N of SR 28, W of Deerfield (high flow only, 3/4 dam at Ridgeville)	A-B	10 miles
B. McVey Memorial Forest, Randolph CR 750 S, S of SR 28 & W of SR 1, 60 yd. carry down from parking lot adjacent to old farm (high flow only)	B-C	6.5 miles
C. Albany, Delaware CR N 800 E/Strong Rd. Bridge, NW corner, pullout parking, turn S from SR 28, S on Water St. or Mississinewa Ave.	C-D	6.5 miles
D. Delaware CR E 700 N, NW corner, pullout parking, carry down (SR 67 not recommended due to heavy traffic)	D-E	2 miles
E. Granville, E on Gregory Rd./Delaware CR 879 N/E CR 850 N to roadside pullout parking, S bank, E of flowing spring	E-F	11 miles
F. Wheeling, E of and N of W. Eaton-Wheeling Pike on Delaware CR 364 W bridge, SW corner, pullout		

parking & carry down	F-G	3.25 miles
G. Matthews, Third St., Cumberland Covered Bridge, Hurst-Lions Memorial Park, SW corner	G-H	5.25 miles
H. Grant CR 700 S, NW & NE pullout & carry down	H-I	6.5 miles
I. Gas City Park, from US 35/SR 22/Main St. go S on Broadway to South H St. & Rogers St.	I-J1	6 miles
J. Marion City Parks:		
J1. Riverside Park, corner of	J1-J2	0.5 miles
Spencer Ave. & River Dr.	J2-J3	0.5 miles
J2. Charles Mill Park, (P.R.)		
and dam	J3-K	2.5 miles
Charles St.& Washington St.		
J3. Matter Park, Matter Park Rd.		
K. Four Mile Bridge access, SR 15 bridge, NW corner	K-L	3.5 miles
L. Trails End access, Grant CR 300 W, near Jalapa via CR 600 N from SR 15 (last access before deadwater from Mississinewa Lake, (see Mississinewa Lake)		
M. Mississinewa Lake & Dam Tailwater, Peoria Fishing Site, Frances Slocum State Forest, NE bank, carry down from parking lot	M-N	5 miles
N. SR 124 bridge, NW corner (last access before Wabash River confluence)	N-O	4.25 miles
O. Peru, Wayne St. bridge, NE corner, power plant overflow parking or Old Depot Park, SR 19 bridge, NW corner, steep slope		

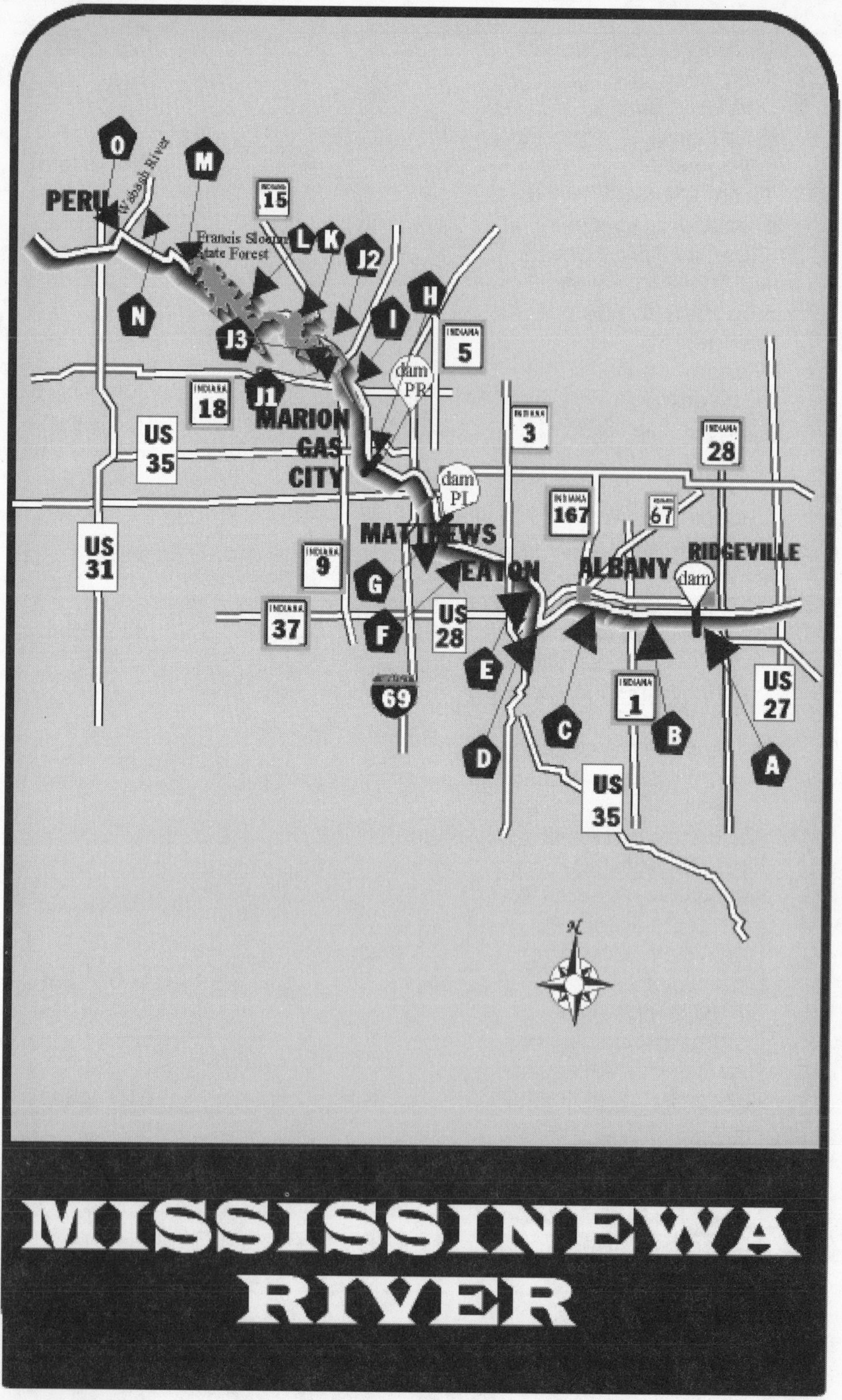

MISSISSINEWA RIVER

Mississinewa River, Trails End Access Near Jalapa

Mississinewa River, Overlook, Seven Pillars Nature Preserve

15. EEL RIVER OF THE WABASH

- Curl around cool & shady bends in the former haunts of Little Turtle, Porcupine & The Soldier

The Eel River heads up southwest of Hunterstown in northwestern Allen County and journeys 110 miles southwest through bucolic farmscape and small towns, arriving at Logansport and the Wabash River confluence. Geologically, the Eel River valley train cuts through the Salamonie Moraine and the Mississinewa Moraine in Whitley County and skirts the Packerton Moraine along its north valley to its mouth at the Wabash River. The numerous tributaries that contribute to the Eel River include Blue River and various creeks: Spring, Sugar, Hurricane, Plunge, Swank, Simonton, Pony, Clear, Otter, Silver, Beargrass, Squirrel, Paw Paw, Flowers, Weasau, Twelve Mile, Tick and Horney. The Eel was and is a river of special significance to the Miami's Eel River band who call the stream, and their former main village, Ken-na-pe-kwo-ma-kwa or "snake fish" in reference to (Anguilla rostrata) which they relished as food.

Even though the villages of the Eel River Miami band no longer line its banks and the serpentine eel no longer run its waters, the paddler will discover the stream offers scenery, good regular current and plenty of motion-filled, boulder-lined riffles (average fall is 2.7 feet a mile). However there are pockets of deadwater due to several unmarked low dams (some that can be breached with the right amount of flow). Small islands line the stream and there are springs that emerge from the sometimes steep wooded banks. Development is limited but there are several houses located between Denver and Mexico in north Miami County. The best sections of the Eel for paddling are from the Collamer Dam to North Manchester, Laketon to Denver and downstream from US 31 bridge to the Adamsboro access. During autumn the shallow water is clear and offers fine stream bottom wildlife viewing.

The first recommended access begins at the South Whitley Community Park or just downstream beyond the SR 5 bridge at Hagan Memorial Park (66 mi. from the mouth). The Eel flows quickly at first, widening as it goes but the water becomes quiet from the Collamer Dam at Collamer (portage left and carry about 60 yards). The stream flows southwest, twisting and turning, from Whitley County into Kosciusko County and on into Wabash County. Positioned near the Wabash-Kosciusko county line is the Taylor Wildlife Sanctuary (east bank) which is owned and managed by the local chapter of the Audubon Society. Watch for the low dam at Liberty Mills (P.R.) not far upstream from the public access site. The river skirts Manchester College and North Manchester east and south, flowing under SR 114, a covered bridge and over a small dam (P.R.) between a railroad bridge and a highway bridge). Near

Laketon is the Laketon Bog Nature Preserve situated along the northwest bank. The gathering stream continues through more quiet countryside on its southwest journey flowing through Laketon (public access site), across SR 15 (Beargrass public access site) to Roann (covered bridge access) and on through deadwater to the dam at Stockdale (P.L. at public access site). Just upstream from the SR 19 bridge at Chili there is a low dam (P.R.) or if the water is at the right level, paddle through the right corner. Continue on to Denver and access the Meridian Road bridge at the northwest corner (little road shoulder for parking, however parking available at the town park north less than 0.5 mile). Housing development is noticeable between Denver and the US 31 bridge. The dam at Mexico is collapsed left of center and can be breached at above normal flow or portage left. West of US 31, the river takes on a wild character again, downstream to the Adamsboro bridge access. Between the village of Hoover and Adamsboro was the historic three-mile long Miami riverside community of Ken-na-pe-kwo-ma-kwa, "snake fish" or "Olde Towne". From the Adamsboro access to Spencer Park access, Logansport suburbs are in view along the east bank. The adventuresome may continue on to the Wabash River however a dam portage (P.R.) will be necessary just downstream from Riverside Park, another possible take-out via carry. A new access will be located on the east bank before the SR 17 bridge. Beyond the Riverside dam and the SR 17 bridge are the "Rapids of the Eel" along the Front Street Park, downstream from the Third Street bridge/SR 17 to the Wabash River confluence. The next public access is on the Wabash River at France Park, north bank (alt. access at SR 25 bridge, NW corner).

USGS MAP(S): South Whitley East, South Whitley West, North Manchester North, North Manchester South, Laketon, Roann, Rich Valley, Peru, Twelve Mile, Logansport 1:24,000

VICINITY: South Whitley, Whitley County
Liberty Mills, North Manchester, Laketon, Roann, Wabash County
Chili, Denver, Mexico, Miami County
Logansport, Cass County

STREAM DISTANCE/TRIPS: 70 canoeable miles
4-5 or more possible trips

LEVEL OF DIFFICULTY: Class 1

HAZARDS/PORTAGES: rocks, wind, snags, low water, deadwater, low dams, summer insects, some logjams require portage

INFO SOURCES: Tri-Lakes Fisheries Station
5570 N. Fish Hatchery Road
Columbia City, IN 46725
(219) 691-3181
Salamonie Lake
9214 W. Lost Bridge West
Andrews, IN 46702 (219) 468-2124
Mississinewa Lake
RR#1, Box 194

Peru, IN 46970
(765) 473-6528
France Park
Cass County Park
4505 US 24 W
Logansport, IN 46947
(219) 468-2124 or 753-2928

AREA OUTFITTERS: none
GAMEFISH SPECIES: bass, walleye, catfish, crappie, carp
CAMPING: Salamonie Lake
9214 W. Lost Bridge West
Andrews, IN 46702
(219) 468-2124
Class A & C
MEDICAL ASSISTANCE: Whitley Memorial Hospital
353 N. Oak St.
Columbia City, IN 46725
(219) 244-6191
Wabash County Hospital
710 N. East St.
Wabash, IN 46992
(219) 563-3131
Dukes Memorial Hospital
275 W. 12th St.
Peru, IN 46970
(765) 473-6621
Logansport Memorial Hospital
1101 Michigan Ave.
Logansport, IN 46947
(219) 753-7541
(800) 243-4512

ACCESS	SECTION	RIVER MILES
A. South Whitley Community Park, one block E of Main St./SR 5 then S behind City Hall, N bank	A-B	2.6 miles
B. Collamer Dam, (P.L.) at dam,100 yd. carry, access, SW corner of downstream bridge, 0.25 mi. S of SR 14 at Collamer	B-C	6.2 miles
C. Liberty mills, DNR public access, (P.R). at dam upstream, go E of SR 13 on Martin Rd. to Liberty Mills and turn S from Main St. on Second St., 0.5 mi.		

to access on right, E bank, Wabash CR 325 E	C-D	10.3 miles
D. Laketon DNR public access, at the SE edge of Laketon, SW corner of bridge, Wabash CR 200 W (P.R.) dam at N. Manchester	D-E	4 miles
E. Beargrass Creek, DNR public access, SR 15 near Wabash CR 300 N	E-F	4.5 miles
F. Roann Covered Bridge, Wabash CR 700 W, N of SR 16 at Roann, NW corner, carry down	F-G	1 mile
G. Stockdale, DNR public access, (P.L.) at dam, access above dam, S bank, SR 16, one mi. W of Roann (P.L. at Chili Dam, upstream from SR 19 bridge, an alt. access)	G-H	13.4 miles
H. Denver, Meridian Rd. bridge, NW corner, 0.5 mi. S of SR 16 at Denver	H-I	19.1 miles
I. Adamsboro, DNR public access, US 24 E of Logansport, to Cass CR 600 E, N 0.5 mi. to CR 150 N & turn W to NE bridge corner	I-J	4 miles
J. Spencer Park, Logansport, S bank, High St. & Plaza Dr. (alt. site at Riverside Park, Riverside Dr., W of High St. (P.R.) downstream dam) New river access north of SR 17 bridge, south bank, High St., also Front St. Park	J-K	7 miles
K. France Park, Wabash River, N bank, US 24 W from Logansport to Towpath Rd./Georgetown Rd., left & follow the river to the S boundary of the park & access site at Paw Paw Creek confluence		

EEL RIVER of the Wabash

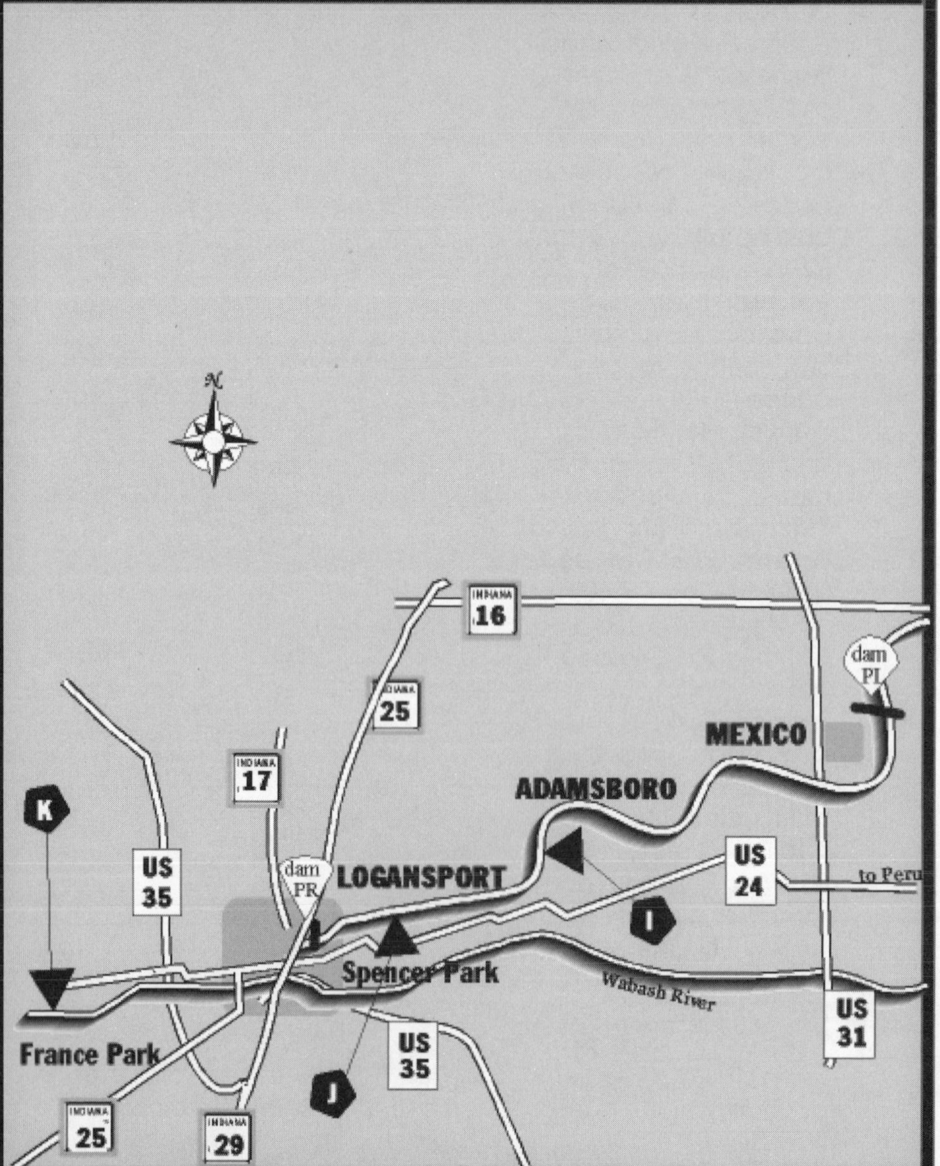

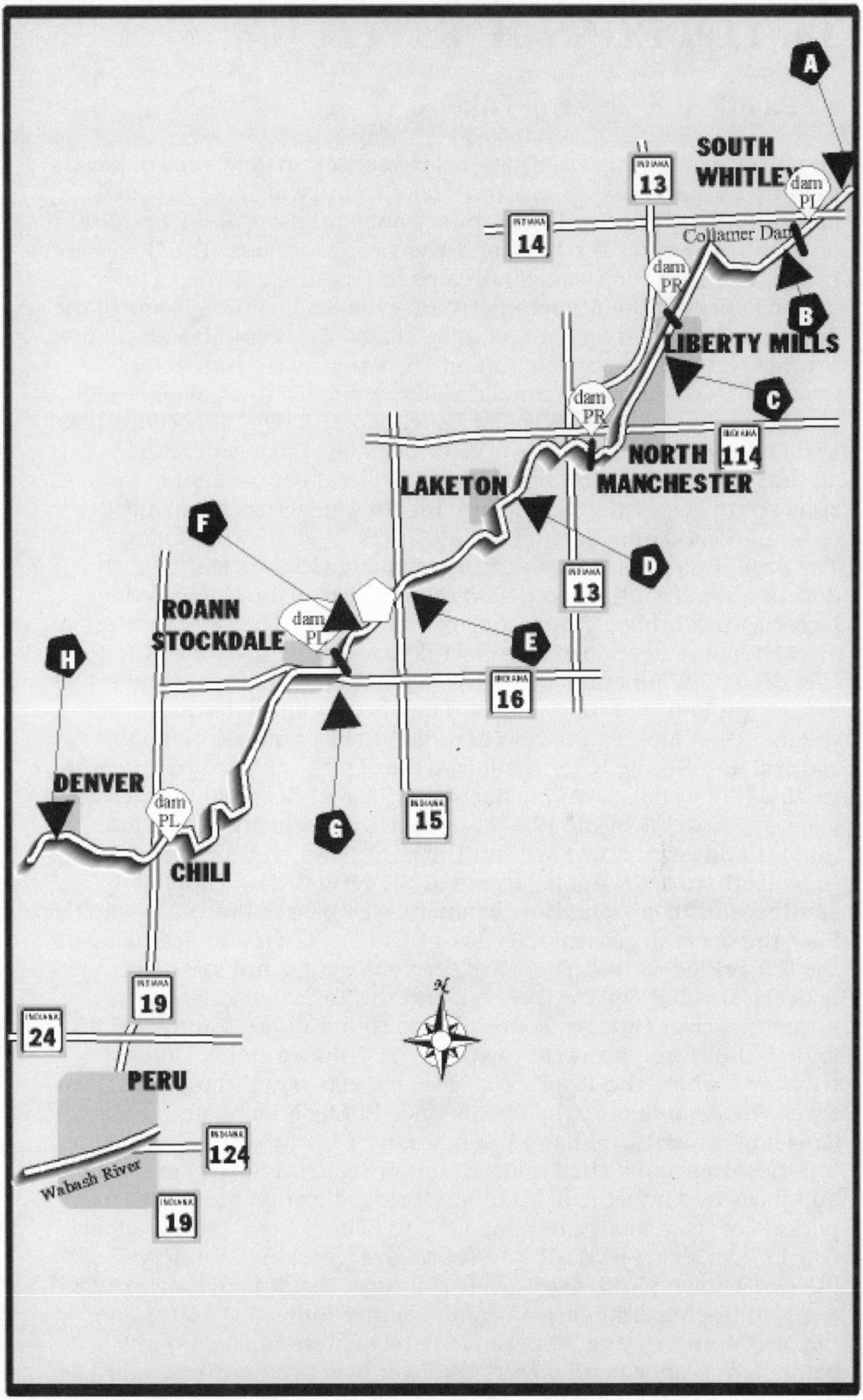
A
SOUTH
WHITLEY
dam
PL
INDIANA
13
INDIANA
14
Collamer Dam
dam
PR
B
LIBERTY MILLS
dam
PR
C
INDIANA
114
NORTH
MANCHESTER
LAKETON
F
D
INDIANA
13
ROANN
STOCKDALE
dam
PL
E
H
INDIANA
16
DENVER
dam
PL
CHILI
G
INDIANA
15
INDIANA
19
INDIANA
24
N
PERU
INDIANA
124
Wabash River
INDIANA
19

16. TIPPECANOE RIVER

- Paddle the "River of Lakes"

The Tippecanoe River or "Tippy" as it is affectionately known, begins high up in northeastern Indiana's lake country at Little Crooked Lake along the Whitley-Noble county line and flows southwest 200 or so miles to enter the Wabash River near Americus. The "River of Lakes" is one of the cleanest streams in Hoosierdom due to the settling effect of the numerous tributary lakes including some of the largest and deepest in Indiana. Like beads on a liquid necklace, the young steam gathers strength and flows northwest connecting Crooked Lake, Big Lake, Smalley Lake, Baugher Lake, Wilmot Mill Pond, The Backwaters, Webster Lake, James Lake, Tippecanoe Lake and Oswego Lake. From the outlet at Oswego Lake (where the stream actually becomes a river) the physical course changes and runs southwest, twisting and curving its way across farmland, crossing US 30 and skirting the northwest Warsaw city limits. The first access point (park & carry down) is located just downstream from the Old US 30 river bridge at the Chenworth historic steel bridge, Tippecanoe roadside park. The river continues along housing developed shores and farmscape. Kosciusko CR 100 N & CR 700 W junction at the NW bridge corner is the next possible access (pullout and carry down). The next 16 miles downstream to the mouth of Moores Ditch in Marshall County qualify as a DNR Natural and Scenic River section. West of Crystal Lake, the river has retained its wetlands and dense swamp forest floodplain (watch for logjams). Kosciusko CR 125 N bridge, SE corner, provides a fine pullout and carry down access. The river flows on through wildness to Mollenhour DNR public access at SR 19 & SR 10. Dipping southwest, the growing river winds its way past Potawatomi Wildlife Park (no access), crossing SR 331 at Old Tip Town and accessing at the NW bridge corner. There are several logjams and strainers between the Old Tip Town access and the Talma access and numerous river cottages south of SR 110 in Fulton County. SR 25 follows the river southwest to about the Chippewanuck Creek tributary, where the Tippecanoe goes its wild way through the Dead River Woods area onto the Menomonee Public Fishing access. Crossing under the old and the new US 31 bridges, the river brushes up against the Fulton County Historical Society grounds and flows northwest near Germany Bridge through farmscape and pockets of river cottage development to Leiters Ford (access along Old 17 N), Delong (Old SR 17 RR bridge access) and Monterey (Kleckner town park). Over geological time, the stream has breached a gap in the Maxinkuckee Moraine to enter Pulaski County. Beyond Monterey, the Tippecanoe barely enters Starke County before a hoseshoe bend directs the river abruptly southwestward from its northwesterly course. Southwest of Ora, the river enters Tippecanoe River State Park where there is an access and adjacent canoe camp. A floodplain nature preserve has been set aside north of the riverside picnic shelter where a sandy landing allows access downstream from the canoe camp access. After seven miles of state park, the Tippy flows on to the developed banks of Winamac where there is an access at the town park along a horseshoe bend. More islands appear as the river widens south of Winamac where another access is located south of US 35. The village of Pulaski has a DNR access along the west bank. The current slows to near deadwater nearing Buffalo (back-up from Shafer Lake). The SR 39 bridge, NE corner, where a gaging station is located, is the best take-out before entering Lake Shafer and the Norway Dam, Monticello, Lake Freeman and the Oakdale Dam (there are access sites between the dams; Norway Dam, Blue Water Beach City Park and Lake Freeman access Dodge Camp Road). These man made lakes are highly recreationally active during the warm months and are not recommended for paddlers. The final section, which concludes at the Wabash River, begins at the SR 18 bridge, NW corner, east of Brookston. Usually there is ample water for paddling due to the steady water release from Oakdale Dam. A possible take-out is at River Junction canoe livery located directly across from the mouth of the Tippecanoe River on the south side of the Wabash River. Consider going on the Wabash and taking out at Davis Ferry County Park, Tippecanoe County located between Lafayette and Battle Ground. Overall there is a 2.1 fall per mile along its eight county course, draining over 1,900 square miles of northern Indiana. The best sections to canoe are Kosciusko CR 100 N to Old Tiptown access, SR 331, Marshall County and from Monterey's Kleckner Park to Haschel Bridge access, Pulaski CR 215 E. There are several canoe liveries. The place name Tippecanoe is a corruption of the Miami Ke-tap-kwon or Potawatomi Ki-tap-i-kon or "buffalo fish".

USGS MAP(S): Leesburg, Atwood, Burket, Bourbon, Mentone, Argos,
Rochester, Pershing, Kewanna, Culver, Bass Lake, Winamac,
Buffalo, Monticello North, Monticello South, Yeoman, Delphi,
Brookston 1:24,000

VICINITY: Warsaw, Etna Green, Kosciusko County
Old Tip Town, Tippecanoe, Marshall County
Talma, Rochester, Leiters Ford, Delong, Fulton County
Monterey, Winamac, Pulaski, Pulaski County
Buffalo, Monticello, White County
Americus, Lafayette, Tippecanoe County

STREAM DISTANCE/TRIPS: nearly 100 miles of canoeable stream
eight or more trips

LEVEL OF DIFFICULTY: Class 1

HAZARDS/PORTAGES: logjams, strainers, snags, low water, insects,
two dams at Monticello

INFO SOURCES: Tri-Lakes Fisheries Station
5570 N. Fish Hatchery Rd.
Columbia City, IN
(219) 691-3181
Bass Lake Fisheries Station
6718 E. Winona Ave.
Knox, IN 46534
(219) 772-2353

AREA OUTFITTERS: Tippe-Canoe Float Trips
4903 N. 750 W
Leiters Ford, IN 46945
(219) 542-2777
Zellers Canoe Rental
RR# 1, Box 15
Winamac, IN 46996
(219) 946-3781
Hodges Canoe Trips
2761 N. 1275 W
Delphi, IN 46923
(765) 564-6806
Tippecanoe Rental
RR# 3, Box 115
Monticello, IN 47960
(219) 278-7841
River Junction
6614 SR 25 W
Lafayette, IN 47905
(765) 589-3875

GAMEFISH SPECIES: smallmouth bass, largemouth bass, rock bass, white bass, spotted bass, striped bass, northern pike, walleye, yellow perch, catfish

CAMPING: Tippecanoe River State Park
4200 N. US 35
Winamac, IN 46996
(219) 946-3213
canoe camp, Class A
rent-a-tent, group camp

MEDICAL ASSISTANCE: Kosciusko Community Hospital
2101 E. Dubois Dr.
Warsaw, IN 46580
(219) 267-3200
Woodlawn Hospital
1400 E. 9th St.
Rochester, IN 46975
(219) 223-3141
Pulaski Memorial Hospital
616 E. 13th St.
Winamac, IN 46996
(219) 946-6131
White County Memorial Hospital
1101 O'Conner Blvd.
Monticello, IN 47960

(219) 583-7111

ACCESS SITES	SECTION	RIVER MILES
A. Tippecanoe Roadside rest park, Old US 30/Lincoln Hwy, W of Warsaw, log-jammed section, scenic W of Crystal Lake (alt. pullout carry down access at Kosciusko CR 700 W & S CR 100 N, NW bridge corner & CR 125 N, SE bridge corner)	A-B	10 miles
B. Mollenhour DNR access, 2 mi. S of Etna Green on SR 19, just S of junction SR 10 & SR 19, NE bridge corner	B-C	6 miles
C. Old Tip Town DNR access, between Old Tip Town & Tippecanoe on SR 331, NW bridge corner	C-D	7 miles
D. Talma DNR access, Fulton CR 675 N at road curve, 0.5 mi. W of Talma, W bank	D-E	7 miles
E. Menominee PFA, DNR access, 3 mi. N of Rochester on Old US 31 to Fulton CR 350 N, E to site S bank	E-F1	16 miles
F. F1. Leiters Ford N of the cemetery on Old SR 17	F1-F	6 miles
F.Monterey, Kleckner Park, N bank, access near old band shell	F-G	15 miles
G. Tippecanoe River State Park, canoe campsite & access, N of Winamac via US 35	G-H	5 miles
H. Haschell Bridge, 2.5 mi. N of Winamac on US 35, then 3 mi. E on Pulaski CR 250 N, upstream from the bridge 0.5 mi. on CR 215 E	H-I	5 miles
I. Winamac Town Park, Washington St. entrance, W		

ACCESS SITES	SECTION	RIVER MILES
bank in E side of park, 0.3 mi. E from US 35	I-J	5 miles
J. Winamac DNR access, 1.5 mi. S of Winamac on US 35, then E on Pulaski CR 150 S to CR 50 E & S 0.5 mi. to CR 200 S, 0.5 mi., follow the brown access signs	J-K	7 miles
K. Pulaski DNR access, N. Main St., W bank	K-L	12 miles
L. Buffalo, NE corner of SR 39 bridge at gaging station, stay close to bridge, (do not trespass). Landing and carry out not easy (Tippecanoe River is damned at Norway and Oakdale, forming Lake Shafer & Lake Freeman, N & S of Monticello)	Take out only at Buffalo	
M. SR 18 bridge, NW corner, not a developed access, put in only	Three access sites between dams M-N	9 miles
O. Americus, W SR 25 at River Junction Livery, access fee unless renting canoe	N-O	6 miles
P. Wabash River, Davis Ferry site, Tippecanoe County Park, 2 mi. N of Lafayette on Ferry St., SE bridge corner		

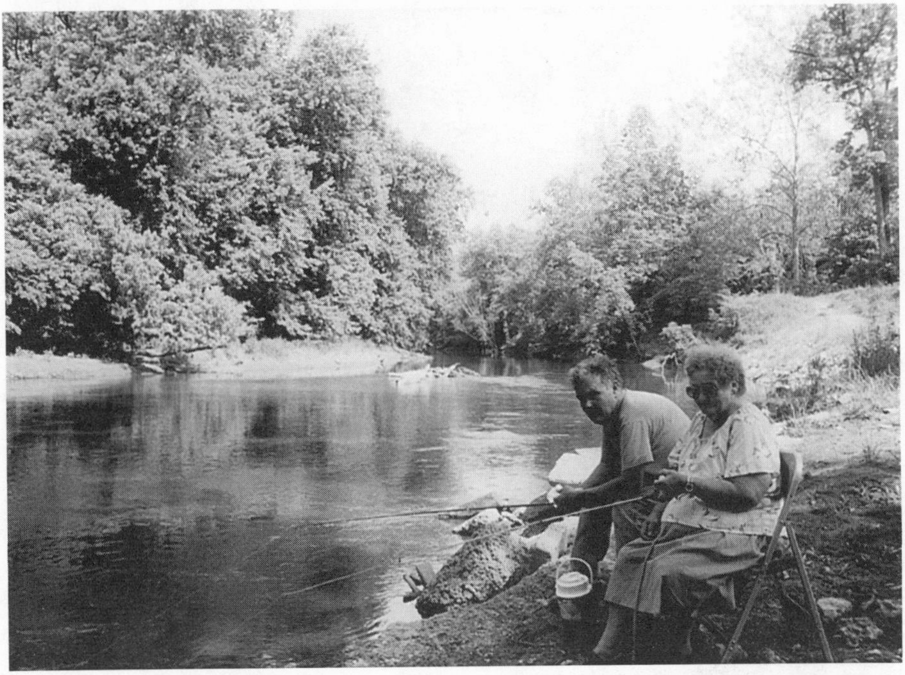

Fishing at Menominee PFA Near Rochester

Tippecanoe River Between the Dams at Monticello

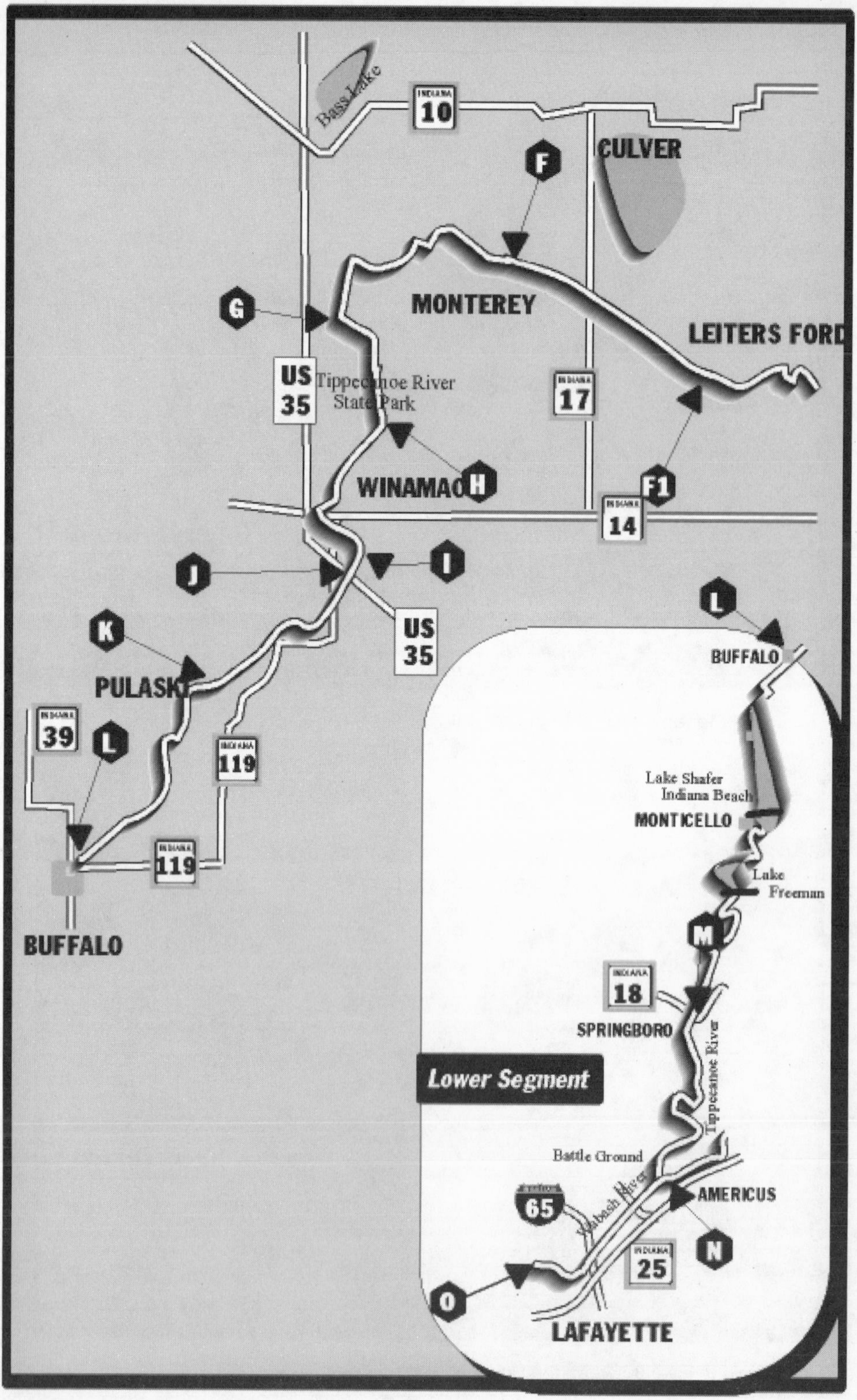
Bass Lake
INDIANA 10
CULVER
F
MONTEREY
G
LEITERS FORD
US 35
Tippecanoe River State Park
INDIANA 17
H
WINAMAC
F1
INDIANA 14
J
I
L
K
US 35
BUFFALO
PULASKI
INDIANA 39
L
INDIANA 119
Lake Shafer
Indiana Beach
MONTICELLO
INDIANA 119
Lake Freeman
BUFFALO
M
INDIANA 18
SPRINGBORO
Tippecanoe River
Lower Segment
Battle Ground
65
Wabash River
AMERICUS
N
INDIANA 25
O
LAFAYETTE

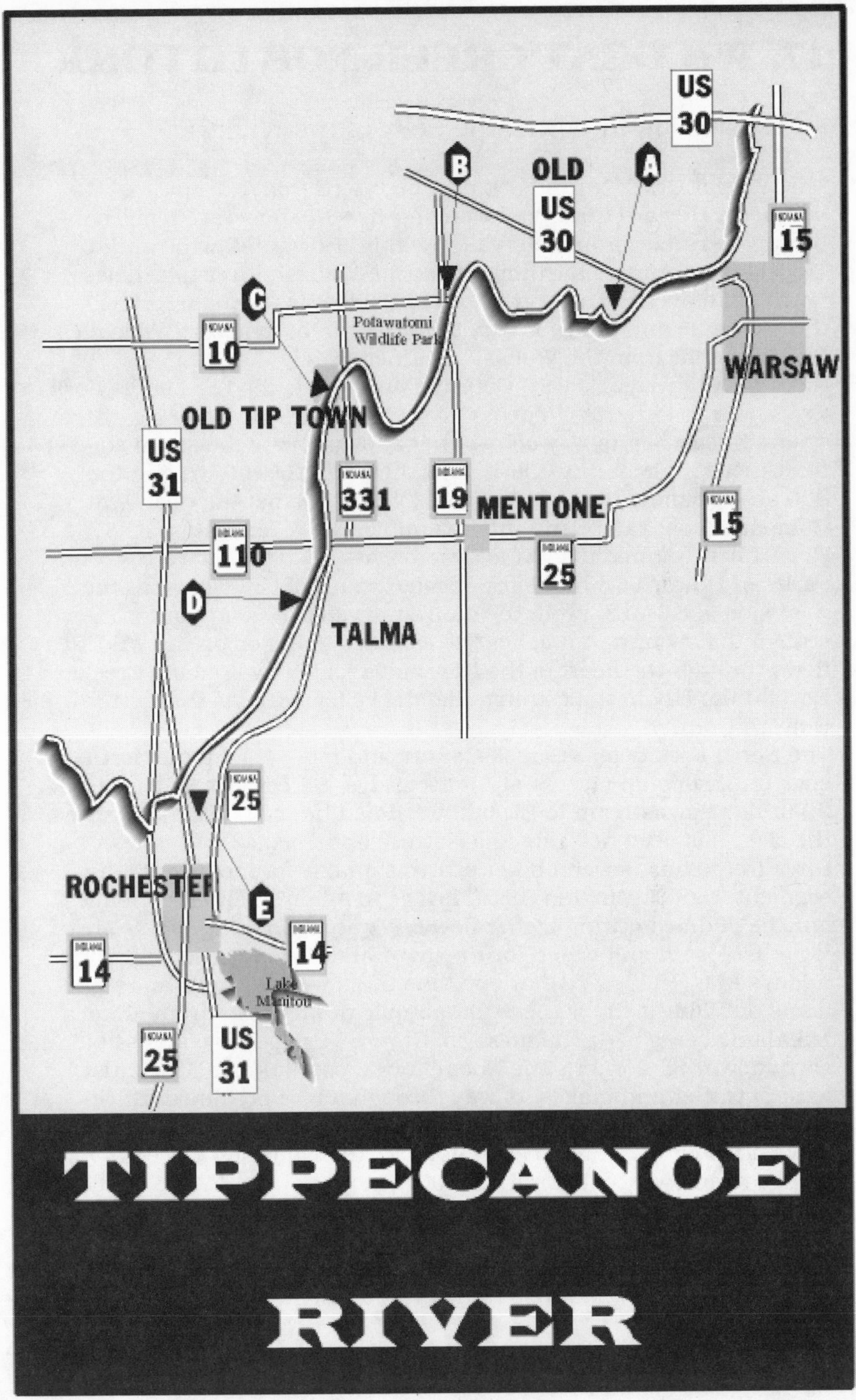

US 30
B
OLD US 30
A
INDIANA 15
C
INDIANA 10
Potawatomi Wildlife Park
WARSAW
OLD TIP TOWN
US 31
INDIANA 331
INDIANA 19
MENTONE
INDIANA 15
INDIANA 110
INDIANA 25
D
TALMA
INDIANA 25
ROCHESTER
E
INDIANA 14
INDIANA 14
Lake Manitou
INDIANA 25
US 31

TIPPECANOE RIVER

17. WILDCAT CREEK NORTH FORK

- Be swallowed down "the belly of the Wild Cat"

The Wildcat Creek North Fork may be traced from extreme southeast Howard County, flowing northwest and west 75 miles through a rather prominent valley within, Howard, Carroll and Tippecanoe counties to culminate at the Wabash River four miles north of Lafayette. The North Fork of Wildcat is the main fork of three (Middle and South Forks) that eventually comprise Wildcat Creek, not far from the Wabash confluence.

Near West Liberty, Howard County, Mud Creek and the Middle Fork Creek join to form the Wildcat Creek North Fork. The creek gathers strength, carving its way across the till plain along the south edge of the Union City Moraine, moving northwest to Greentown and the 800 acre Kokomo Reservoir, owned by the Indiana American Water Company (boat ramp) and the Kokomo Parks & Recreation Department. A nine mile canoe trip begins upstream at Pe-che-wah Park, an Howard County Park, located south of Greentown at the west side of SR 213. From the dam's tailwater, it is not far for the stream to flow until it reaches the confines of Kokomo. The Wildcat flows through the heart of the city and is joined by Kokomo Creek. Beyond the city in the countryside, the valley deepens through Howard County.

The North Fork enters Carroll County and moves along the north edge of Burlington (access at SR 29 bridge, SE corner). From the SR 29 bridge downstream to Eisenhower Road bridge in east Lafayette, the river has been designated a Natural and Scenic River (one of three in Indiana, several other streams qualify for inclusion). The segment from Burlington SR 29 bridge to Adam's Mill PFA should only be paddled during higher flow but watch for sharp bends and logjams. Listen and watch for the low dam (P.L.) at Cutler's historic Adam's Mill (1845-1951). At one time there were 12 mills and 12 dams on Wildcat Creek. Less than a mile downstream from Adam's Mill dam access is the Adam's Mill Covered Bridge (also accessible, carry down, SE corner). The North Fork crosses under SR 75 just west of Cutler and makes its way through a tree-bottomed fringe with islands and bluffs. Prince William Road bridge provides access (NW corner, pull out and carry) however the Lancaster Covered Bridge near Owasco, Carroll CR 500 W does not. US 421/SR 39 at Owasco is the last major highway until I-65 at Lafayette. The Knop Lake PFA does not provide a canoe camp, however it is a fine place to land and explore the bank and upland lake. Be aware of the Pyrmont Dam (P.R.) downstream of Knop Lake access, upstream from Pyrmont.

Cross over into Tippecanoe County at County Line Road bridge however do not expect a developed canoe access at CR 900 E bridge

(Aca-pi-ki- access site, as the map shows) although CR 775 E/CR 725 E bridge, the next bridge downstream has the Mis-so-la access site, SW corner. From the Mis-so-la access it is a short scenic trip on down to the First Wildcat Park at the confluence of the South Fork of the Wildcat. (The Middle Fork merges with the South Fork near Monitor).

Wildcat Creek flows its final few miles through a growing residential Lafayette. The last access site before the Wabash River union is at Peters Mill 100 yds. d.s. of the Eisenhower Bridge, NW corner (first bridge downstream of the First Wildcat Park, private, day use only), just upstream from the blufftop Clegg Botanic Garden, east bank. Cross under I-65, a railroad trestle, SR 25 and then merge with the Wabash River. It is less than a mile on the Wabash River to Davis Ferry Park access, a Tippecanoe County park (a railroad, highway and walking bridge cross the river here). The access site is on the south bank. Consider canoeing through Lafayette to Ft. Ouiatenon Park and access site (there are several city parks enroute along the Wabash in Lafayette and West Lafayette that have access sites).

The Wildcat derives its name from Miami Chief Pin-ji-wa-mo-tai or Pen-che-wah "belly of the Wild Cat"; his Christian name, J.B. Richardville. The Miami chief (from 1814-1841) was granted the "Big Reserve", (present day mostly Howard County), where the Wildcat flowed through the middle of the vast acreage. A Miami war party routed an American military unit near Pyrmont during the War of 1812 that is known as Spur's Defeat, "the second Battle of Tippecanoe".

USGS MAP(S): Burlington, Rossville, Pyrmont, Lafayette East, Lafayette West
1:24,000
VICINITY: Burlington, Cutler, Owasco, Pyrmont, Carroll County
Buck Creek, Lafayette, Tippecanoe County
STREAM DISTANCE/TRIPS: 43 miles
4 or more trips possible
LEVEL OF DIFFICULTY: Class 1
HAZARD/DIFFICULTIES: snags, logjams upper reaches, low water, low dams at
Cutler & Pyrmont
INFO SOURCES: Tippecanoe County Parks & Recreation
4448 SR 43 N
W. Lafayette, IN 47906
(765) 463-2306
Monitor Canoe Trips
(765) 589-3506
Div. of Outdoor Recreation, Streams & Trails
402 W. Washington Rm. 271 W
Indianapolis, IN 46204
(317) 232-4070
Bass Lake Fisheries
6718 E. Winona Ave.
Knox, IN 46534
(219) 772-2353

AREA OUTFITTERS: Monitor Canoe Trips
7736 SR 26 E
Lafayette, IN 47905
(765) 589-3506

GAMEFISH SPECIES: smallmouth, rock & white bass, crappie, catfish, sauger, sunfish

CAMPING: Big Fish-N-Camp
5831 S 900 E
Lafayette, In 47905
(765) 296-2346
Mar Len Park
c/o Tippecanoe County Parks & Recreation
3 miles south of Lafayette on 18th St.
(primitive tent along the north bank of Wea Creek)

MEDICAL ASSISTANCE: Elizabeth Medical Center
1501 Hartford St.
Lafayette, IN 47904
(765) 423-6011

ACCESS SITES	SECTION	RIVER MILES
A. Burlington, SR 29 bridge, SE corner along Mill St	A-B	9 miles
B. Adam's Mill DNR Fishing Area, low dam (P.L.) also carry down access at near-by Adam's Mill Covered Bridge (0.25 mi. via road and 1 mi. via creek), NE of Cutler, Carroll CR 500 S on CR 75 E	B-C	8 miles
C. Prince William Road bridge, Prince William Rd., creek access on the right bank downstream of the bridge (not a recommended access)	C-D	6 miles
D. Knop Lake DNR Fishing Area, S bank, north of Carroll CR 650 S near Pyrmont, up-stream 0.5 mi. from Pyr-mont Dam (P.R.)	D-E	6 miles
E. Mis-so-la access site, S bank, Tippecanoe CR 775 E/725 E bridge, SW corner (no devel-oped Aca-pi- ki access site on Tippecanoe CR 900 E/Heath Rd, SE corner)	E-F	3 miles

F. First Wildcat park, Tippecanoe County Park, confluence of N & S Forks of Wildcat Creek	F-G	2 miles
G. Peter's Mill, Eisenhower Rd. Bridge, NW corner, 100 yds. N, gate open during daylight hours	G-H	7 miles
H. Wabash River, Davis Ferry Park, Tippecanoe County Park, SE corner of Canal St./Ferry bridge, one mi. downstream of Wildcat Creek confluence with Wabash River, (alt. access site at the following parks in downstream Lafayette area: Mascouten Park, Digby Park, Tapawingo Park, Shamrock Park, Ft. Ouiatenon)		

Confluence of North & South Forks, First Wildcat Park Near Lafayette

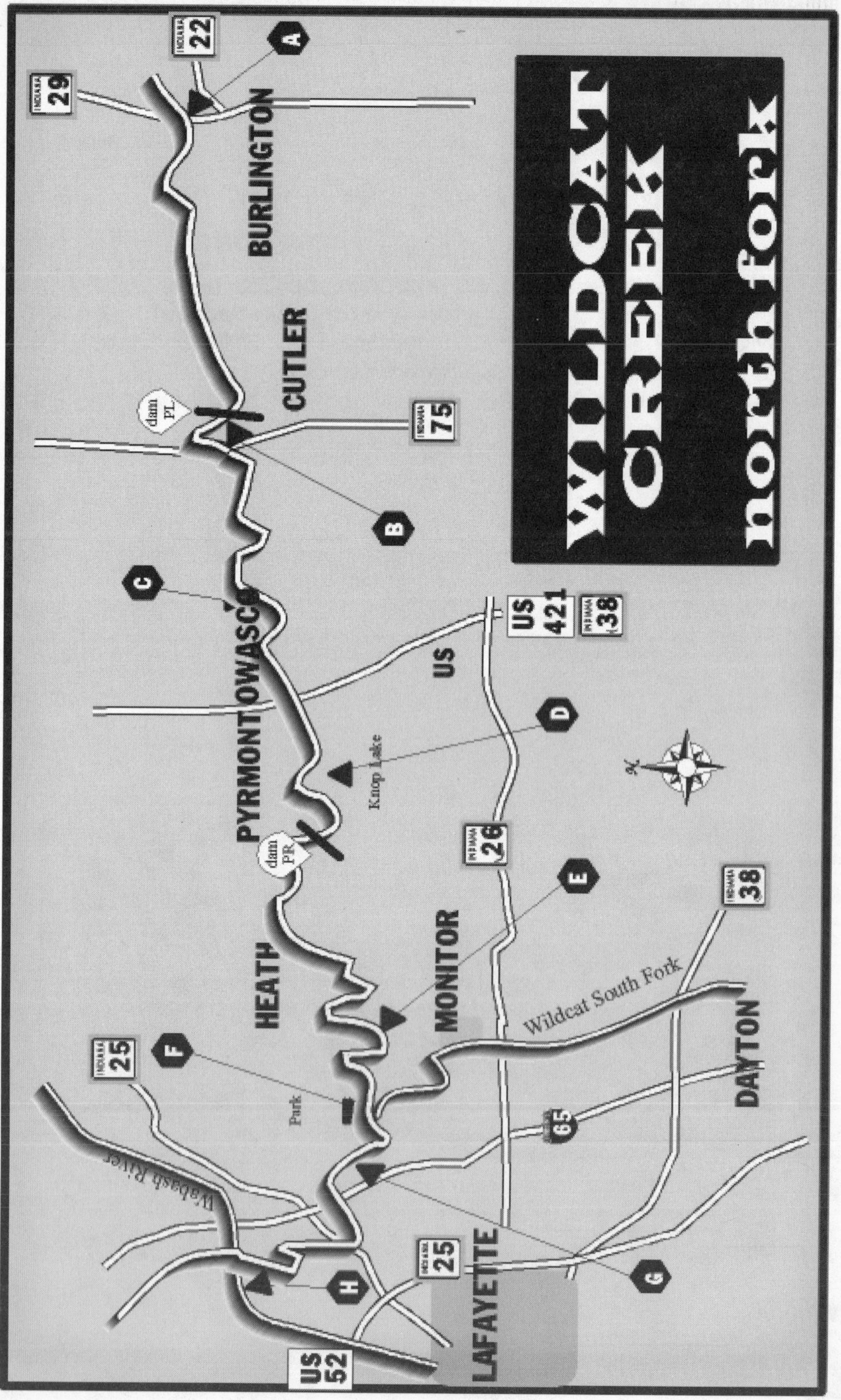
WILDCAT
CREEK
north fork
BURLINGTON
CUTLER
PYRMONT
OWASCO
HEATH
MONITOR
DAYTON
LAFAYETTE
US
Knop Lake
Wildcat South Fork
Wabash River
Park
dam PL.
dam PR.
A
B
C
D
E
F
G
H
INDIANA 22
INDIANA 29
INDIANA 75
US 421
INDIANA 38
INDIANA 26
INDIANA 38
INDIANA 25
65
INDIANA 25
US 52

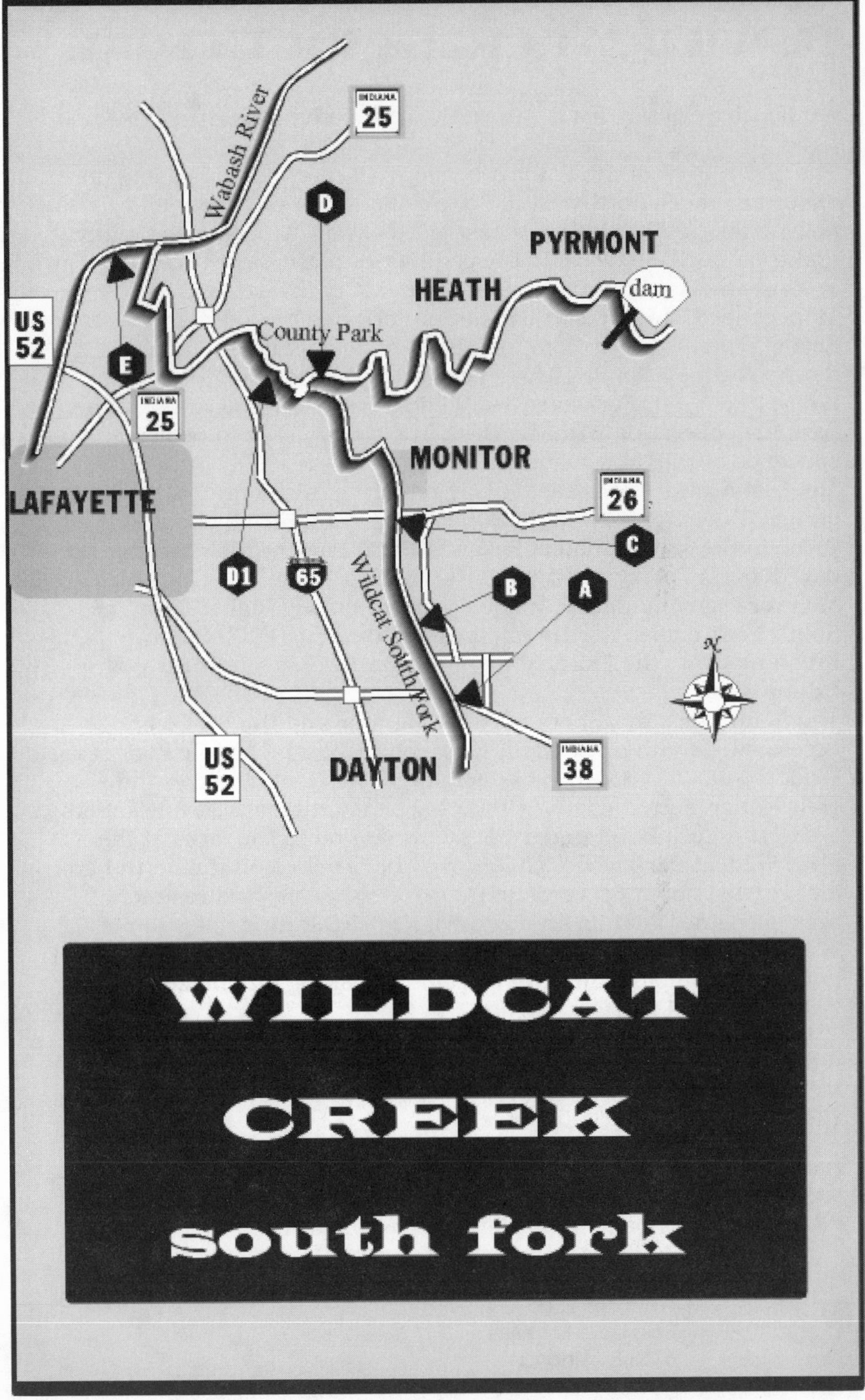

WILDCAT CREEK south fork

18. WILDCAT CREEK SOUTH FORK

- Experience a fork, a creek and a river in one float

The South Fork of the Wildcat is about 45 miles long, heading up about two miles northwest of Scircleville, Clinton County and flowing about 27 miles northeast of Stockwell, Tippecanoe County, and then northeastward to the confluence of the North Fork to form Wildcat Creek, about four miles northeast of Lafayette at a Tippecanoe County park. The South Fork has been declared a state Scenic River segment from the SR 38 bridge at Dayton (access) downstream 10.2 miles (three bridges), to the confluence of the South and North Forks at First Wildcat Park, a Tippecanoe County park in cooperation with the DNR. The stream should be floated in spring or during above normal flow.

The first access site is east of Dayton at the SR 38 bridge, southeast corner. Take Tippecanoe CR 800 E north from SR 38 about 200 yards to the access road of Pathway Park. Park in the spacious paved lot and carry down 60 yards to the stream. The Dayton to Monitor segment should only be paddled during higher flow. The South Fork curves northwest, crossing under CR 200 S and brushing up to the Fairfield Fishing Area (access site & three strip fishing pits).

The South Fork meanders north to Monitor and the SR 26 bridge access site, southeast corner. North of SR 26, the Middle Fork of the Wildcat joins the South Fork, northwest of Monitor village and greatly increases the flow. After a big bend and few short meanders the South Fork flows under CR 100 N and on to the forks at the First Wildcat Park where canoes may be beached on the north bank and carried about 60 yards to the parking, picnic and restroom area. Consider floating on down Wildcat Creek nine miles to the Wabash River confluence and Davis Ferry Park, a few miles north of Lafayette. Sampling all three streams of varying size makes a fulfilling fluvial journey.

USGS MAP(S): Lafayette East, Lafayette West 1:24,000
VICINITY: Dayton, Monitor, Lafayette, Tippecanoe County
STREAM DISTANCE/TRIPS: 10.2 miles
one to two trips
LEVEL OF DIFFICULTY: Class 1
HAZARDS/PORTAGES: low water, snags, logjams upper reaches, high water
INFO SOURCES: Tippecanoe County Parks & Recreation
4448 SR 43 N
W. Lafayette, IN 47905
(765) 463-2306
Bass Lake Fisheries
6718 E. Winona
Knox, IN 46534

(219) 772-2353
DNR Div. of Outdoor Recreation
Streams & Trails
402 W. Washington St. Rm 271 W
Indianapolis, IN 46204
(317) 232-4070

AREA OUTFITTERS: Monitor Canoe Trips
7736 SR 26 E
Lafayette, IN 47905
(765) 589-3506
(5 miles E of Lafayette)

GAMEFISH SPECIES: smallmouth bass, sunfish, catfish

CAMPING: Mar Len Park c/o Tippecanoe County Parks
4448 SR 43 N
W. Lafayette, IN 47906
(765) 463-2306
(S. 18th St., primitive tent camping on Wea Creek)
McAllister Park c/o Lafayette Parks Dept.
1915 Scott St.
Lafayette, IN
(465) 447-9351
(Wabash River, W 9th St. primitive tent camping)

MEDICAL ASSISTANCE: St. Elizabeth Medical Center
1501 Hartford St.
Lafayette, IN 47904
(765) 423-6011

ACCESS SITES	SECTION	RIVER MILES
A. Dayton access site, SR 38 bridge & Tippecanoe CR 800 E, NE corner (Pathway Park, 60 yard carry down from spacious parking area)	A-B	3 miles
B. Fairfield Fishing Area, Tippecanoe County Park, CR 750 E	B-C	3 miles
C. Monitor, SR 26 bridge, SE corner	C-D	4 miles
D. First Wildcat Park, Tippecanoe County Park	D-D1	2 miles
D1. (alt. access), Peter's Mill, Eisenhower Rd. Bridge, NW corner, 100 yds. N	D1-E	7 miles
E. Wabash River, Davis Ferry Park, two miles N of Lafayette on Ferry & Canal Sts.		

19. BIG PINE CREEK

- Kayak a seasonal whitewater stream

Big Pine Creek's headwaters are found in the prairie counties of White and Benton counties, flowing southwest and southeast 51 miles through till plain of Warren County to the Wabash River at Attica. The intense stream has cut through the till end moraine around Rainsville, down to the red-brown Mansfield sandstone, Pennsylvanian bedrock. The steep banks quickly funnel the water through the gravel and bedrock streambed making it some of the best whitewater canoeing in Indiana. Finding the right amount of flowing water is the first challenge of floating Big Pine. Spring rains may prove too much of a paddling challenge for a novice while summer's dryness may prove too little (late June at the latest). A 10.5 mile segment of Big Pine Creek in Warren County, from Rocky Ford, southwest of Rainsville, downstream to CR 131 bridge qualifies for inclusion in the Indiana Natural and Scenic River program. Botanist Charles Deam believed the best Indiana spring wildflowers grow in Big Pine Creek area. Native white pines scattered along the stream's sandstone outcroppings give rise to the place name. Shale is exposed along the stream and snow trillium is found in the cool mini-canyons of adjacent ravines.

There are three access sites along the 15 miles of floatable stream including a 0.4-mile segment of the Wabash River. The upper seven miles from Rainsville Bridge to Twin Bridges include the Rocky Ford ledges that can be dangerous rapids in high water. The somewhat steep gradient in the upper reaches can move paddlers along at a fast clip.The Nature Conservancy 163 acre Fall Creek Gorge preserve is located just south of the Twin Bridges. Consider parking in the nature preserve parking lot. A short ridge trail leads to a five-foot waterfall on Fall Creek and above a series of water-carved potholes or basins. The only developed ramp is at the Ouabache Potawatomi Park along the Wabash River at Attica via Canal Street. The parking is limited at the Rainsville Bridge and it may be more secure at the village square (a store, spring, church and homes) 0.25 mi. south. There is enough parking at Twin Bridges alongside the gravel road pullouts and the nature preserve parking lot. Historically, American General Harrison and his army of "Yellow Jackets" forded and camped on Big Pine Creek, 1.5 miles northeast of Carbondale, enroute to Battle Ground and the Battle of Tippecanoe, early November, 1811. Believe it or not, this beautiful valley was saved from being dammed, to create a reservoir. Fortunately public opinion saved the picturesque Big Pine from an artificial fate that would have destroyed some of the best natural area left in Indiana.

USGS MAP(S): Pine Village, Williamsport 1:24,000
VICINITY: Pine Village & Rainsville, Warren County
Williamsport, Warren County
Attica, Fountain County
STREAM DISTANCE/TRIPS: 14.5 miles of paddling stream
three trips possible
LEVEL OF DIFFICULTY: Class 1 to Class 2
HAZARDS/PORTAGES: high fast water, low water, rock ledges, mandatory portage Rocky Ford Rapids, seasonal stream
INFO SOURCES: Bass Lake Fisheries Station
6718 E. Winona
Knox, IN 46534
(219) 772-2353
DNR Div. Outdoor Recreation, Streams & Trails
402 W. Washington St., Rm. 271 W
Indianapolis, IN 46204
(317) 232-4070
AREA OUTFITTERS: none
GAMEFISH SPECIES: sunfish, smallmouth bass
CAMPING: Shades State Park
Route 1, Box 72
Waveland, IN 47989
(765) 435-2810
Turkey Run State Park
Route 1, Box 164
Marshall, IN 46204
(765) 597-2635
MEDICAL ASSISTANCE: St. Vincent Williamsport Hospital
412 N. Monroe St.
Williamsport, IN 47993
(765) 762-2496

ACCESS SITES	SECTION	RIVER MILES
A. Rainsville bridge, Warren CR 25 E, SW corner, about 0.5 mi. N of Rainsville village, parking is roomier & safer at the Rainsville square (Big Pine Creek runs alongside Rocky Ford Rd. for 3 mi., pullouts and carry down access)	A-B	7 miles
B. Twin Bridges/CR 33 E, NW corner, roadside pullouts between bridges	B-C	8.1 miles
C. Wabash River, Potawatomi Park, city of Attica, S bank, downstream from the Paul Dresser bridge/US 41		

BIG PINE CREEK

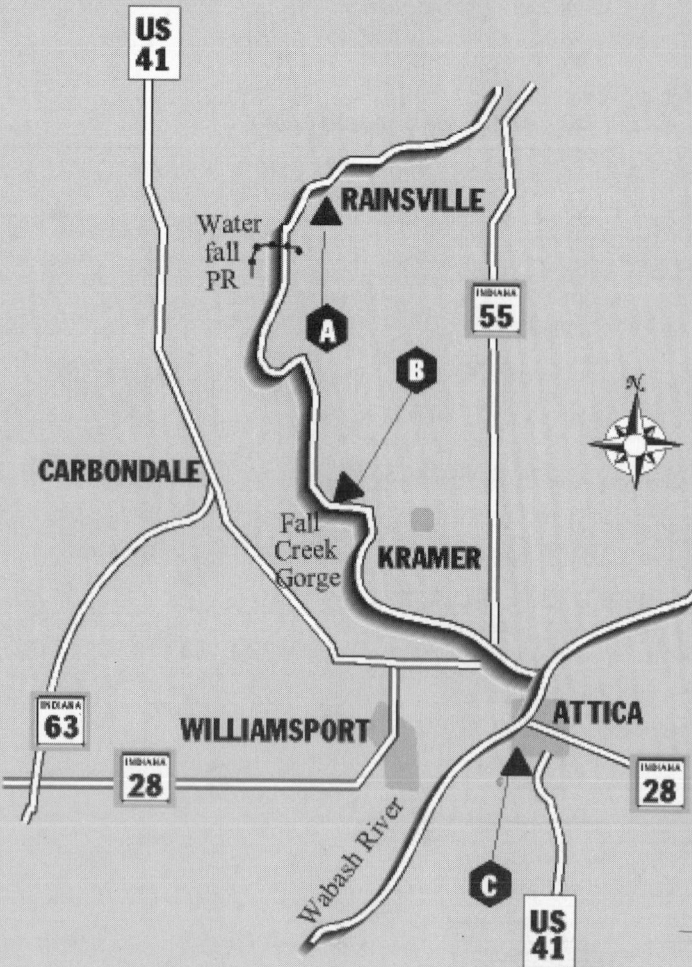

Rocky Ford Ledge

Rocky Ford Falls

SUGAR CREEK

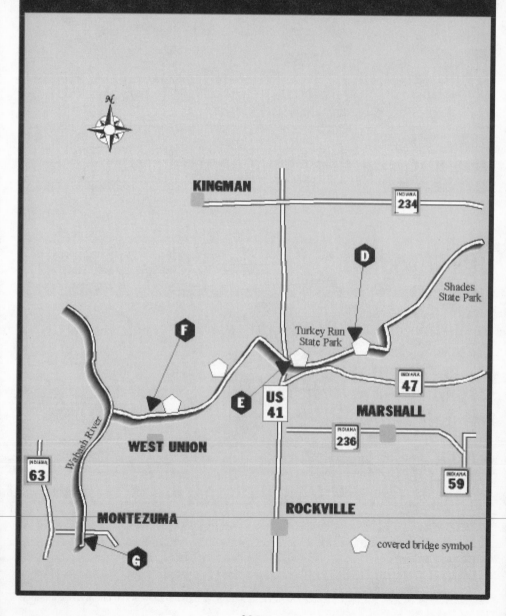

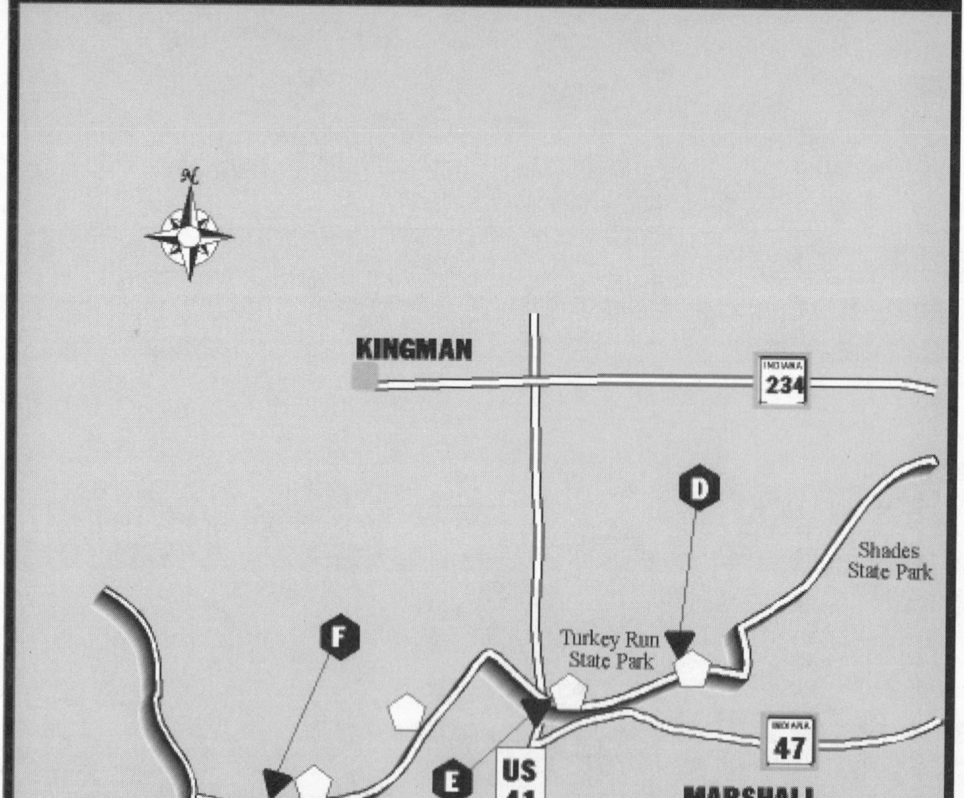
N
KINGMAN
INDIANA 234
D
Shades State Park
F
Turkey Run State Park
INDIANA 47
E
US 41
MARSHALL
INDIANA 236
WEST UNION
Wabash River
INDIANA 63
INDIANA 59
ROCKVILLE
MONTEZUMA
covered bridge symbol
G

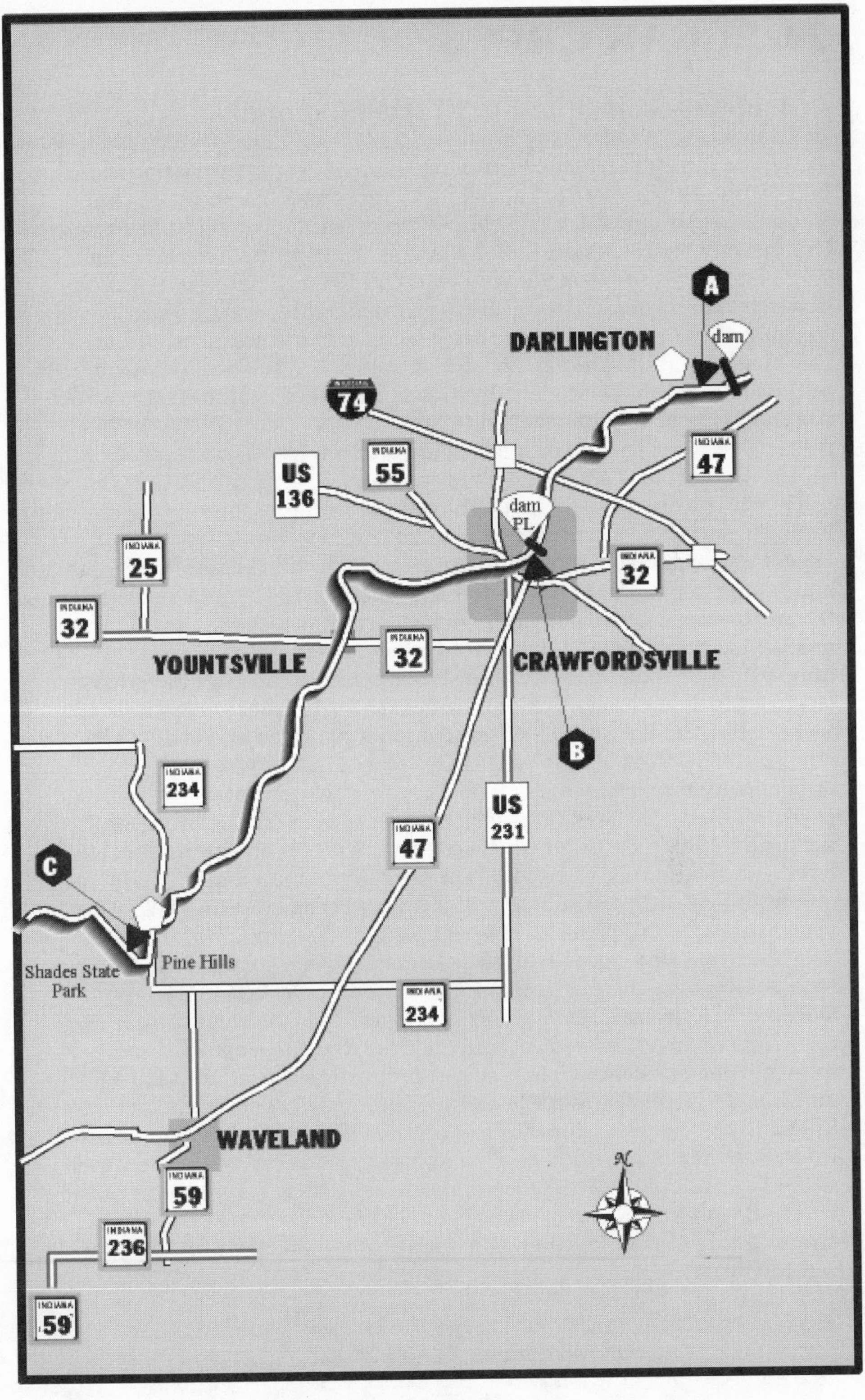
A
DARLINGTON
dam
74
US 136
INDIANA 55
INDIANA 47
dam PL
INDIANA 25
INDIANA 32
INDIANA 32
INDIANA 32
YOUNTSVILLE
CRAWFORDSVILLE
B
INDIANA 234
US 231
INDIANA 47
C
Pine Hills
Shades State Park
INDIANA 234
WAVELAND
INDIANA 59
INDIANA 236
INDIANA 59
N

20. SUGAR CREEK

- Paddle the most beautiful stream in Indiana

There are several streams in Indiana named Sugar Creek but there is only one Sugar Creek that paddlers recognize. The west central Indiana Sugar Creek has 50 canoeable miles, out of 100 miles total, that qualify for inclusion in the Natural and Scenic River program (from Darlington Covered Bridge and Old Dam, Montgomery County downstream to the Wabash River confluence at the Parke and Vermillion county line). There are several natural features and areas that are unmatched along Hoosier streams. Sugar Creek's beauty and unique qualities attract throngs of paddlers (est. 20,000 annually) especially on weekends.
Sugar Creek begins in common fields and ditches of southwest Tipton County and southern Clinton County, flowing nearly 100 miles southwest, cutting through geologic end moraine to join the Indiana State River. The deeply carved and narrow valley turns especially scenic south of Yountsville and SR 32. Bluffs of sandstone are capped with eastern hemlock and Canada yew along the north face and mixed undisturbed deciduous forest, particularly oak and hickory, occupies the south face. Seasonal spring waterfalls appear in the cool, steep ravines. Floodplain forest, that includes virgin walnut, inhabits Turkey Run State Park. Rock formations are plentiful in the deep riffles of the compact canyons and half canyons. The canoe camp at Shades State Park offers an opportunity for overnighters to listen to the water flow. The clean current is usually swift (average fall is five feet per mile) over the sand and rubble bottom but the average 2-4 feet of water may give out in early summer depending on rainfall; so plan a spring trip or one after a plentiful summer or fall rain. Access sites are well spaced and five sites are at covered bridges (Darlington, Deer's Mill, The Narrows, Cox Ford, and West Union). Downstream from Turkey Run State Park, the picturesque valley ends near West Union Covered Bridge and the Wabash floodplain begins. Montezuma, on the Wabash River, is less than five miles from the Sugar Creek mouth, east bank (active Newport Ammunition Plant, west bank) and has an access site in the city riverside park. The Friends of Sugar Creek help to maintain the natural integrity of the stream. A rafting service is provided by Clements Canoe livery when the water is too high to canoe. The place name is near literal translation of the Miami Sa-na-min-dji-si-pi-wi or Ke-an-kek-se-pe, "sugar tree stream" in reference to the sugar maple (Acer saccharum) sap they would gather.

USGS MAP(S): Darlington, Crawfordsville, New Market, Alamo, Wallace, Kingman, Montezuma, Dana 1:24,000
VICINITY: Darlington, Crawfordsville, Waveland, Montgomery County

Marshall, Rockville, West Union, Montezuma, Parke County
STREAM DISTANCE/TRIPS: over 50 miles canoeable
4 or more trips possible
LEVEL OF DIFFICULTY: Class 1
HAZARDS/PORTAGES: hidden boulders, high water, high canoe traffic, two low dams (upper creek)
INFO SOURCES: Shades State Park
Rt. 1, Box 72
Waveland, IN 47989
(765) 435-2810
Turkey Run State Park
Rt. 1, Box 164
Marshall, IN 47859
(765) 597-2635
Cikana Fish Hatchery
2650, SR 44
Martinsville, IN 46151
(765) 342-5527
AREA OUTFITTERS: Clements Canoes
613 Lafayette Ave.
Crawfordsville, IN 47933
(765) 362-2781 or 362-9864
Sugar Valley Canoe Trips
SR 47 Rt. 1, Box 166a
Marshall, IN 47859
(765) 597-2364 or 597-2336
(800) 422-6638
Turkey Run Canoe Trips
311 W. Ohio
Rockville, IN 47872
(765) 597-2456
(765) 569-6705
GAMEFISH SPECIES: smallmouth, largemouth, spotted & rock bass, channel cat
CAMPING: Shades State Park
(765) 435-2810
Class B, Canoe Camp
Turkey Run State Park
(765) 597-2635
Class A & B
Clements Canoes
(April-September)
SR 234, Woods Canyon
(765) 362-2781
MEDICAL ASSISTANCE: Culver-Union Hospital
US 231 N
1710 Lafayette Ra.
Crawfordsville, IN 47933
(765) 362-2800
Terre Haute Regional Hospital
3901 S. 7th St., Terre Haute, IN 47802
(812) 232-0021

ACCESS SITES	SECTION	RIVER MILES
A. Darlington Covered Bridge Park & Dam	A-B	10.2 miles
B. Crawfordsville's Elston Park dam (P.L.),upstream from Old US 231 bridge, south bank	B-C	16.1 miles
C. Deer Mill Covered Bridge access, Shades State Park, SR 234, N bank, large overnite parking area on S bank, canoe camp downstream two mi., S bank, permit required from Shades State Park	C-D	11.1 miles
D. Narrows Covered Bridge access, Turkey Run State Park, old mill site, N bank, Parke CR 280 E	D-E	3 miles
E. Cox Ford Covered Bridge, Turkey Run State Park, Parke CR 30 E/58, ltd. parking	E-F	9.5 miles
F. West Union Covered Bridge, north of West Union village, S bank	F-G	7 miles
G. Wabash River, Montezuma, Reeder Park, S of US 36 bridge		

Shades State Park

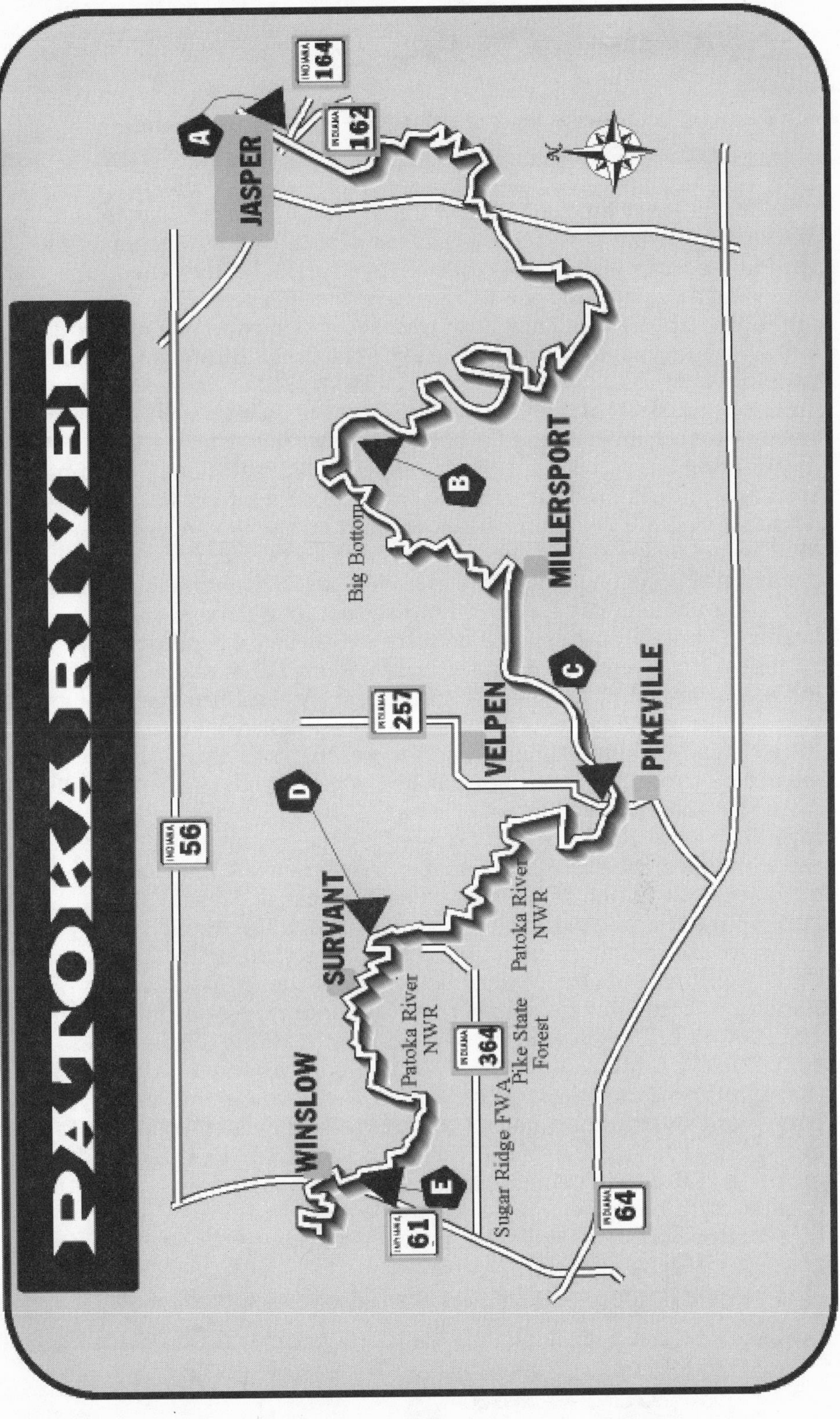
PATOKA RIVER
A
JASPER
164
162
B
Big Bottom
MILLERSPORT
C
PIKEVILLE
257
VELPEN
D
56
SURVANT
Patoka River NWR
Patoka River NWR
Pike State Forest
364
WINSLOW
Patoka River NWR
Sugar Ridge FWA
E
61
64
N

21. PATOKA RIVER

- Pursue a watery way through a national wildlife refuge

The Patoka River has been one of the most environmentally abused of Indiana's rivers however it 'got respect' with the establishment of the Patoka River National Wildlife Refuge in 1994. Since then, accessing and canoeing the Patoka is now easier and more appealing. The Patoka Lake dam releases a steady supply of normal and above normal flow during the dry spell of fall drawdown. From Winslow west to the Wheeling Covered Bridge, the remote river was dredged and straightened in the 1920's; a big change from the early 1800s when pioneers plied flatboats laden with goods on the meandering river (5 day trip from Jasper to Wabash River). The final section is natural and meandering from US 41 south of Patoka (town of) to Hell's Bend and Patoka Island on the Wabash at East Mt. Carmel (access site). The best undisturbed section lies between Jasper and Winslow, a distance of about 40-45 miles.

The 100 mile long Patoka River (860 sq. mi. long narrow basin) heads in Orange County's hill country southeast of Paoli and within 25 miles, the stream drops 300 feet and feeds Patoka Lake (see Patoka Lake). From the dam tailwater, the Patoka River resumes its wild course, curving alongside the Southern Railroad southwest towards Dubois and Jasper. Near Jasper, the river enters and meanders through the ancient flat bed of glacial Lake Patoka totally unlike its hilly national forest origins.

Riverview Park at the SR 162 bridge in Jasper is the first best recommended access. West of Jasper a few miles by road, 20 miles downstream by river, is the second best access at Stewart Road bridge. In a few miles the Patoka flows through the wooded wetlands of Big Bottom enroute to Pike County. Near the Rock Creek confluence is the eastern boundary of the Patoka River National Wildlife Refuge, one of three national refuges in Indiana. The SR 257 bridge provides access north of Pikeville (future access site). The silt bottomed, sluggish stream loops its way northwest through Pike State Forest on its way to Winslow. Several oxbow ponds and swamps lie adjacent to the winding river. The take-out is at the SR 61 bridge, southeast corner in Winslow. The origin and meaning of the Native American place name is uncertain however it is believed to be named after a Kickapoo chief and yet, Patoka may be a Miami word for Comanche, a southern Great Plains tribe.

USGS MAP(S): Jasper, Huntingburg, Velpen, Otwell, Augusta, Winslow
1:24,000

VICINITY: Jasper, Dubois County
Winslow, Pike County
Oakland City, Gibson County

STREAM DISTANCE/TRIPS: approx. 45 miles
four or more trips
LEVEL OF DIFFICULTY: Class 1
HAZARDS/PORTAGES: deadfall, low water, snags, steep, muddy banks, strainers, seasonal hunting
INFO SOURCES: Patoka River National Wildlife Refuge
510 ½ W Morton/SR 64
POB 217
Oakland City, IN 47660
(812) 749-3199
Sugar Ridge Fish & Wildlife Area
(812) 789-2724
AREA OUTFITTERS: none
GAMEFISH SPECIES: bluegill, catfish, carp
CAMPING: Sugar Fish & Wildlife Area
2310 E. SR 364
Winslow, IN 47598
(812) 789-2724, Class C
Pike State Forest
2310 E. SR 364
Winslow, IN 47598
(812) 789-2724, Class C
MEDICAL ASSISTANCE: Jasper Memorial Hospital
800 W. 9th St.
Jasper, IN 47546
(812) 482-2345
St. Joseph's Hospital
1900 Medical Arts Dr.
Huntingburg, IN 46542
(812) 683-2121
Wirth Regional Hospital
SR 64 W
Oakland City, IN 47660
(812) 749-6111

ACCESS SITES	SECTION	RIVER MILES
A. Jasper, Riverview Park, SR 162 at Patoka River, launch & parking	A-B	19 miles
B. Stewart bridge, DNR access, SR 231 south from Jasper to Division Rd. & Dubois CR 600 W, 4 mi.	B-C	10.5 miles
C. SR 257, N of Pikeville, old site of covered bridge (future developed site)	C-D	5 miles
D. Survant Rd. bridge, E of Winslow, N of SR 364	D-E	6 miles
E. Winslow, SR 61, Patoka River bridge in Winslow, SE corner		

22. BIG WALNUT CREEK

- Take a trip down one of Indiana's most scenic streams in covered bridge country

Although the Big Walnut is entirely in Putnam County it originates in southwest Boone and northwest Hendricks counties with the North, Middle and South forks of the Big Walnut converging southwest of the Hendricks-Putnam county line. It is graced with seven covered bridges. Downstream less than a mile is the first access with enough water (March-early June); the Hendricks-Putnam County Line Road/CR 900 E bridge, NW corner with pullout parking at the north end of the green iron bridge. The County Line Road access is also the beginning of the Indiana Natural and Scenic segment (eligible) that flows 10.5 miles to the US 36 bridge east of Bainbridge. The landscape changes south of US 36 to a modern day encroaching agricultural scene as it hurries south to join Mill Creek to form the Eel River of the White River West Fork, south of I-70 and west of Cagles Mill Lake Dam. The U.S. Park Service has declared Big Walnut, like Sugar Creek, a National Natural Landmark.

The best time to paddle is during the spring when rains provide a swift moderate current through riffles, around boulder rock and over gravel and sand. The Big Walnut is deeply carved creating mini-canyons. The best part of the Big Walnut to paddle is north of and just south of US 36 in northeast Putnam County. There are five bridges between County Line Road bridge access and the US 36 bridge access; the first three are modern concrete linear structures (difficult to access) and the last two are 19th century covered bridges (Pine Bluff and Rollingstone have easier access with pullout & path). The 1,200-acre Big Walnut Nature Preserve straddles the stream between the covered bridges. Three north-facing bluffs have a Canadian fringe of eastern hemlock trees and yew shrubs. The south facing slopes are covered with oak and hickory while shade-rich ravines harbor beech and maple. Big Walnut could be place named Big Hemlock since the largest eastern hemlock (Tsuga canadensis) in Indiana thrives in the preserve. Just downstream of the US 36 highway bridge along the west bank is the 94 acre Hall Woods Nature Preserve where it is possible to land and walk the loop trail. This portion of the Big Walnut Nature Preserve features old growth floodplain forest and mixed wood upland; a healthy buffer to Big Walnut. The next bridge downstream from Hall Woods is Bakers Camp Covered Bridge/Old US 30. The section from Bakers Camp Covered Bridge (the first bridge south of US 36) downstream to Dunbar Covered Bridge, northwest of Greencastle has six county bridges, one railroad bridge and one low dam upstream from the US 231 bridge (P.R.) at Greencastle and the surroundings are agricultural. There is good access at Putnam CR 300 N & CR 325 E bridge, SW corner and CR 100 E, NW corner. Although the Dunbar Covered Bridge will suffice as access (NE corner), CR 125 S bridge and the west bank of Grenel Road/CR 200 W downstream is oftentimes used as a take-out. Drive about 100 yards south on gravel CR 200 W to the roadside pullout, part of an old bridge embankment.

To extend the Big Walnut Creek trip, continue downstream from Greencastle passing under the Oakalla Covered bridge (Grenel Rd), Houch Covered bridge (CR 550 S & CR 475 W) and Dick Huffman Covered bridge (CR 1050 S & CR 575 W). Follow the covered bridge road signs just north of I-70. Mill Creek flows west from Cagles Mill Lake tailwater to join Big Walnut Creek which forms Eel River of White River.

USGS MAP(S): North Salem, Roachdale, Greencastle, Clinton Falls, Reelsville
1:24,000
VICINITY: Bainbridge & Greencastle, Putnam County
STREAM DISTANCE/TRIPS: 24.5 miles recommended paddling
two or more trips possible
LEVEL OF DIFFICULTY: Class 1
HAZARDS/PORTAGES: logjams, strainers, sharp bends, low water,
(P.R.) at low dam upstream from US 231 at
Greencastle waterworks
INFO SOURCES: DNR Div. of Outdoor Recreation
Streams & Trails
402 W. Washington, Rm 271
Indianapolis, IN 46204
(317) 232-4070
DNR Div. of Nature Preserves
402 W. Washington, Rm. 267 W
Indianapolis, IN 46204
(317) 232-4052
AREA OUTFITTERS: none
GAMEFISH SPECIES: smallmouth bass, rock bass, sunfish, suckers, carp
CAMPING: Cecil M. Harden Lake
Raccoon SRA
160 S. Raccoon Parkway
Rockville, IN 47872
(765) 344-1412
Class A, B, & C
Cagles Mill Lake
Lieber SRA
1317 W. Lieber Road
Cloverdale, IN 46120
(765) 795-4576
Class A & B
MEDICAL ASSISTANCE: Putnam County Hospital
1542 S. Bloomington St.
Greencastle, IN 46135
(765) 653-5121

ACCESS SITES	SECTION	RIVER MILES
A. Putnam-Hendricks County Line Rd./Putnam CR 900 E, green iron bridge, NW corner, carry down, pullout parking at bridge N end	A-B	10 miles
B. US 36 hwy bridge, 1.5 mi. E of Bainbridge, NW corner, limited roadside parking, busy traffic, carry down (alt. access possible at upstream & downstream covered bridges)	B-C	14 miles
C. Grenel Road access, 2nd street south of courthouse in Greencastle, W 1.25 mi. on west Walnut/CR 125 S & turn left on Grenel Rd./CR 200 W, 0.25 mi. south (alt. take-out at Dunbar Covered Bridge, NE corner, Dunbar Rd., US 231 to CR 25 S, NW Greencastle. (alt. sites, three covered bridges downstream. Dick Huffman last bridge before I-70 crossing. Eel River is considered okay paddling to near Bowling Green)		

Big Walnut Creek at Hall's Woods Nature Preserve

BIG WALNUT CREEK

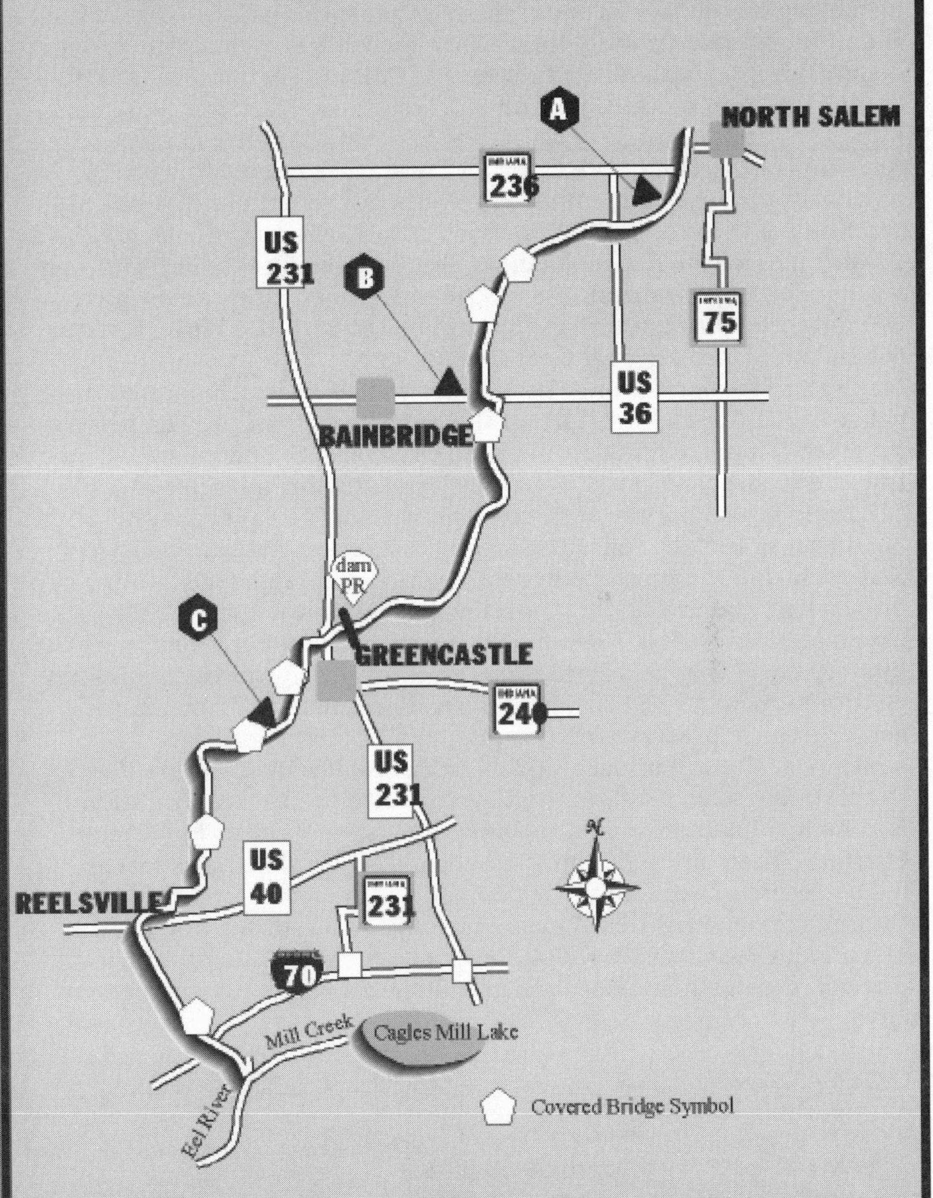
A
NORTH SALEM
236
US 231
B
75
US 36
BAINBRIDGE
dam
PR
C
GREENCASTLE
240
US 231
US 40
231
REELSVILLE
70
Mill Creek
Cagles Mill Lake
Eel River
N
Covered Bridge Symbol

23. FALL CREEK

- Head through wild riparian nature on the Capitol suburban outskirts

Fall Creek is a 75 mile long stream that starts up in Henry County near Sulphur Springs, flowing southwest to join the White River West Fork in downtown Indianapolis. Most of the stream is rarely canoeable due to lack of water (Lick Creek is the largest tributary, Hamilton-Madison county line). The canoeable section of the creek begins 0.5 mi. south of the tailwater of Geist Reservoir dam at 79th St. (17 mi. from mouth), flowing on through Ft. Harrison State Park (3,5 miles), under I-465 near Skilles Test Park and the northeast terminus of the Fall Creek Corridor Park access and on as a greenway through residential neighborhoods to the southwest terminus of the Fall Creek Corridor Park near Keystone Avenue, SR 37 and Allisonville Road. The final section downstream of Fall Creek loses much of its naturalness as the waterway continues its linear concrete way through Indianapolis to merge with the White River at the Indiana University Medical Center.

Meltwater streams flowing through ice-walled channels formed the valley of Fall Creek. The "fall" in the name occurs at the Pendleton waterfall (Miami, Chank-tun-oon-gi, Delaware, Sokpehellak) where the stream drops 25 feet in one mile. The shallow stream has a sand and gravel bottom with some alluvium. The valley is wide northeast of Indianapolis. The steady release of water from Geist Reservoir and the increase in release during September's "winter drawdown" makes paddling possible beyond a wet spring. Fall Creek cuts through 1,700 acre Ft. Harrison State Park (former military base) that represents the largest tract of unbroken forest in central Indiana (no access, long carry down, fishing, trails, nature center, nature preserve, no camping). Fall Creek continues southwest, flowing under I-465, south of Skilles Test Nature Park. Downstream from I-465 to the Keystone Avenue Bridge, the stream and its floodplain becomes an Indianapolis Park called Fall Creek Corridor. There are ten stop sites along the corridor that serve as canoe access. Complete the trip at the south terminus of the Fall Creek Corridor Park near Keystone Avenue and Allisonville Road along Fall Creek Parkway. Fall Creek offers an aquatic excursion through the northeast suburbs of Indianapolis, the Hoosier capitol city.

USGS MAP(S): McCordsville, Fishers, Indianapolis East, Indianapolis West 1:24,000
VICINITY: Lawrence, Castleton, NE Indianapolis, Marion County
STREAM DISTANCE/TRIPS: ten floatable miles
two or more trips

LEVEL OF DIFFICULTY: Class 1
HAZARDS/PORTAGES: low water, urbanization
INFO SOURCES: Indy Parks Greenways
1426 W. 29th St.
Indianapolis, IN 46208
(317) 327-7431
Riverside Restaurant & Marina
3001 N. White River Park, West Dr.
Indianapolis, IN 46222
(317) 327-2628
Cikana Fish Hatchery
Martinsville, IN 46151
(765) 342-5527
AREA OUTFITTERS: Riverside Restaurant & Marina
3001 N. White River Pkwy. West Dr.
Indianapolis, IN 46222
(317) 327-2628
GAMEFISH SPECIES: smallmouth bass, bluegill, channel catfish
CAMPING: Mounds State Park
4306 Mounds Road
Anderson, IN 46017
(765) 642-6627
Class A
Summit Lake State Park
5993 N. Messick Rd.
New Castle, IN 47362
(765) 766-5873 Class A
MEDICAL ASSISTANCE: Community Hospital North
7150 Clearvista Drive
Indianapolis, IN 46256
(317) 849-6262

ACCESS SITES	SECTION	RIVER MILES
A. 79th St. bridge, NE corner, below Geist Reservoir dam, Fall Creek Rd. at 79th St/82nd (long carry down at Ft. Harrison State Park)	A-B	5 miles
B. W of I-465, Fall Creek Corridor Park, NE terminus Fall Creek Parkway	B-C	5 miles
C. Fall Creek Corridor Park, SW terminus, Fall Creek Parkway near Keystone Ave., Allisonville Rd. & SR 37		

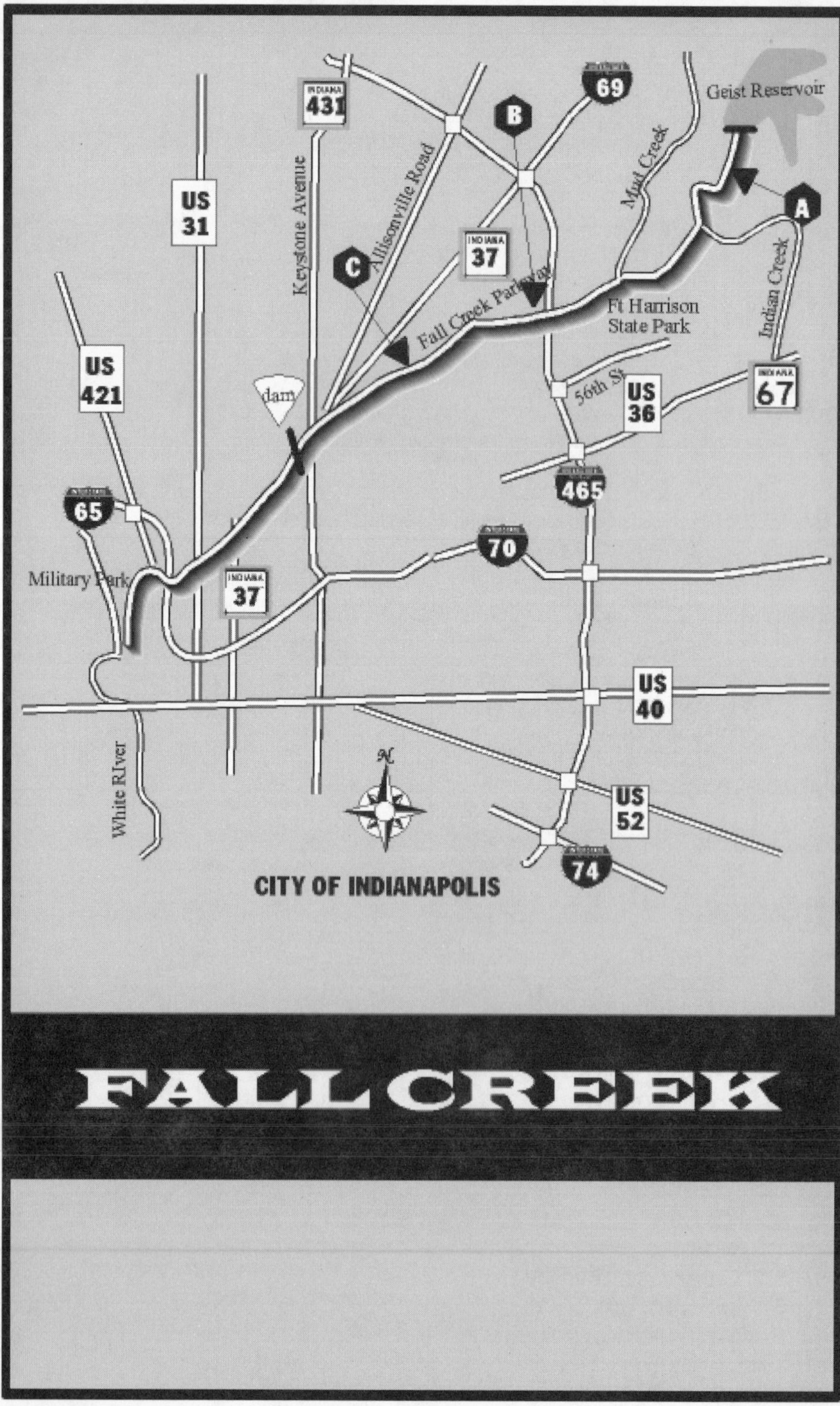
Geist Reservoir
Mud Creek
Indian Creek
Ft Harrison
State Park
Fall Creek Parkway
Allisonville Road
Keystone Avenue
56th St
dam
Military Park
White RIver
A
B
C
US 31
US 421
US 36
US 40
US 52
INDIANA 431
INDIANA 37
INDIANA 67
69
65
465
70
74
N
CITY OF INDIANAPOLIS

FALL CREEK

Fall Leaves on Fall Creek

Heron Rookery, Fort Harrison State Park

24. WHITE RIVER WEST FORK

- Cut through Indiana's heartland river

The West Fork of the White River is one of Indiana's "big rivers", a former Pleistocene glacial sluiceway. The 353-mile long stream basin has a 5,746 square mile watershed. Over 300 miles of the West Fork is paddling water. The average drop per mile is 3.2 feet in the river's upper half to one foot in the lower river. Over 70 streams contribute to the West Fork. No stranger to people, nearly 2,000,000 Hoosiers live within a 15 minute drive of the West Fork. The West Fork has been designated as one of the top 20 most threatened rivers in North America by the American Rivers organization. It is born high up in the east central Indiana plateau country of Randolph County not far from Snow Hill. The young stream flows northeast 10 miles to Harrisville and abruptly turns west in the face of the Union City Moraine. Paralleling SR 32 to the south and the moraine to the north, the stream skims the north edge of Winchester and continues west crossing under SR 1 south of Farmland. The first suggested access at normal and above flow is three bridges downstream west of SR 1 at Randolph CR 1100 W, NW corner. It is shallow going to Muncie and there are five low dams that require portage enroute. Little White River flows in at the Randolph-Delaware county line and Prairie Creek Reservoir gives up its overflow at the southeast edge of Muncie. The city of Muncie occupies the former village sites of the Munsee or Wolf Clan of the Delaware who gave the river the name Wappi-hanne or "white river". West Fork follows the rurban corridor of "Munsonapolis" (Muncie, Anderson, Indianapolis) beginning at Muncie, where development has captured and engulfed much of the true nature of the river. Yorktown, Daleville (access), and Chesterfield are growing, filling in the countryside between Muncie and Anderson. SR 32 continues to run parallel to the West Fork skirting the north edge of and crossing under I-69 and entering Madison County. Mounds State Park is situated on the east bank between Chesterfield and Anderson (camping and access). The park preserves earthworks of the prehistoric Adena and Hopewell cultures.

In Anderson, the White River banks are a linear park along the Indian Trails Riverwalk (Edgewater Park access) downtown for a mile which includes the Killbuck Wetlands Nature Preserve at Broadway and Grant Streets. Flowing west to northwest from Anderson. the West Fork skirts Edgewood and enters the developing countryside. The SR 13 bridge, NE corner at Perkinsville (Madison and Hamilton county line) offers the next best access.

From Perkinsville on down through Strawtown (access) to Riverwood (access) (P.R. d.s. dam jetty) is one of the most undeveloped sections along the upper West Fork. Potters Covered Bridge (restored,

access) spans the West Fork. The West Fork parallels SR 37 through Hamilton County to Fishers and the river turns southwest at Strawtown, just east of SR 37, north of Noblesville. Access to the stream is available at Forest Park in north Noblesville.
The West Fork flows along the west edge of Conner Prairie Pioneer Settlement at Allisonville Road. South of the suburban development in southern Hamilton County, the West Fork enters fast growing suburban Marion County and Indianapolis (P.R. at 4 city dams). The Indy Metro Park Department has established a canoe trail with numerous access sites from 96th St. downstream to Riverside Marina (access and canoe rental at 30th & White River Parkway). The Central Canal runs adjacent to the river (no boating). The West Fork borders and cuts through several parks such as Broad Ripple, Marott, Holliday, Friedmann, Riverside Regional, Municipal Gardens, White River State Park and Southwestway Park (most with access or carry down). Much of the White River south from 16th Street to I-465 has levee, wide channel and concrete and riprap stone banks matching the feral industrial landscape.
Beyond I-465, the West Fork breaks out of the seemingly unending sprawl. The river changes character flowing fast over gravel and rock from pool to riffle. The stream enters Morgan County, the "Gateway to Southern Indiana. The river bumps up against Fox Cliff, Bernard Hill, and Clark Hill along Blue Bluff (826-850' el.) and continues south and west (P.R. at dam) within a safe distance of Martinsville. The section from Martinsville southwest to the East Fork confluence and Petersburg is considered some of the best paddling along the West Fork (remoteness, size of river, natural areas). SR 37 runs contiguous to the West Fork however north of Martinsville the river shifts further southwest and runs alongside SR 67, southwest to Edwardsport, Knox County. The valley plain widens in Greene County at the confluence of the Eel River and continues wide to the East Fork and on down to the White River. The meandering West Fork forms the county line boundary between Knox County and Daviess County (from Elnora to the East Fork). The few communities that reside on or near its banks in southern Indiana (most with access include: Paragon, Gosport, Spencer (McCormicks Creek State Park), Freedom, Farmers (former ferry service), Worthington (Eel River confluence), Bloomfield, Newberry, Elnora, Edwardsport, Washington, and Petersburg (White River access).

USGS MAP(S): Farmland, Muncie East, Muncie West, Gilman, Middletown, Anderson South, Lapel, Frankton, Omega, Riverwood, Noblesville, Fishers, Carmel, Indianapolis West, Maywood, Bargersville, Martinsville, Mooresville East, Mooresville West, Cope, Paragon, Modesto, Gosport, Spencer, Freedom, Arney, Bloomfield, Scotland, Lyons, Epson, Plainville, Bicknell, Washington, Wheatland, Sandy Hook, Monroe City 1:24,000
VICINITY: Farmland, Randolph County

Muncie, Yorktown, Daleville, Delaware County
Chesterfield, Anderson, Perkinsville, Madison County
Strawtown, Noblesville, Fishers, Hamilton County
Indianapolis, Marion County
Waverly, Martinsville, Paragon, Morgan County
Gosport, Spencer, Freedom, Farmers, Owen County
Worthington, Bloomfield, Newberry, Greene County
Elnora, Washington, Daviess County
Edwardsport, Bicknell, Knox County
Petersburg, Pike County

STREAM DISTANCES/TRIPS: 320 miles canoeable
30 or more trips possible

LEVEL OF DIFFICULTY: Class 1

HAZARDS/PORTAGES: snags, submerged objects, low dams

INFO SOURCES: Tri-Lakes Fisheries Station
5570 N. Fish Hatchery Road
Columbia City, IN 46725
(219) 691-3181
Cikana State Fish Hatchery
2650 SR 44
Martinsville, IN 46151
(765) 342-5527
Avoca State Fish Hatchery
POB 16
Avoca, IN 47420
(812) 279-1215
Mounds State Park
(765) 642-6627
Indy Parks & Recreation
1426 W. 29th St.
Indianapolis, IN 46208
(317) 327-0000

AREA OUTFITTERS: Canoe Country
7109 S. River Road
Daleville, IN 47334
(888) 378-7358
River Bend Campground
(317) 773-3333
Riverside Restaurant & Marina
3001 N. White River Pkwy. West Dr.
Indianapolis, IN 46222
(317) 327-2628
Swartz's Bait & Tackle
118 Cicero Rd./SR 19
Noblesville, IN 46060
(317) 776-0129
Ramona Canoe Rental
Box 459 Ramona Rd.
Spencer, IN 47460
(812) 829-0120

GAMEFISH SPECIES: bass, bluegill, sunfish, catfish, crappie, carp, sucker

CAMPING: Prairie Creek Reservoir

c/o Muncie City Parks Dept.
Muncie, IN 47302
(765) 747-4776 or 4872
Class A & C
Mounds State Park
4306 Mounds Rd.
Anderson, IN 46017
(765) 642-6627
Class A
River Bend Campground
21695 SR 37 N
Noblesville, IN 46060
(317) 773-3333
White River Camping
Hamilton Co. Parks & Rec.
1299 E. 234th
Noblesville, IN 46060
(317) 984-2705
McCormicks Creek State Park
Rt. #5 Box 282
Spencer, IN 47460
(812) 829-2235
Class A, B, C
Morgan-Monroe State Forest
6220 Forest Rd.
Martinsville, IN 46151
(765) 342-4026
Class C
Shakamak State Park
6265 W. SR 48
Jasonville, IN 47438
(812) 665-2158
Class A & C
Greene-Sullivan State Forest
2551 S. SR 159
Dugger, IN 47848 (812) 648-2810
Class C
West Boggs Creek Reservoir
US 231 entrance
POB 245
Logootee, IN 47553
(812) 295-3421
Class A, B, C
Glendale FWA
RR#2, Box 300
Montgomery, IN 47558
(812) 644-7711
Class A & B

MEDICAL ASSISTANCE: Randolph County Hospital
325 S. Oak St.
Winchester, IN 47394
(765) 584-9001

Ball Memorial Hospital
2401 University Ave.
Muncie, IN 47303
(765) 747-3111
Anderson Community Hospital
1515 N. Madison Ave.
Anderson, IN 46011
(765) 642- 8011
Riverview Hospital
395 Westfield Rd.
Noblesville, IN 46060
(317) 773-0760
Methodist Hospital
1604 N. Capitol
Indianapolis, IN 46202
(317) 929-8355
Wishard Hospital
1001 W. 10th
Indianapolis, IN 46202
(317) 639-6671
Kendrick Memorial Hospital
1201 Hadley Rd.
Mooresville, IN 46158
(317) 831-1160
Morgan County Memorial Hospital
2209 John R. Wooden Dr.
Martinsville, IN 46151
(765) 342-8441
Bloomington Hospital
601 W. 2nd St.
Bloomington, IN 47403
(812) 336-6821
Greene County General Hospital
Lone Tree Road SR 54
Linton, IN 47441
(812) 847-2281
Daviess County Hospital
1314 Grand Ave.
Washington, IN 47501
(812) 254-2760
Good Samaritan Hospital
520 S. 7th St.
Vincennes, IN 47591
(812) 882-5220

ACCESS SITES	SECTION	RIVER MILES
	Upper Section	
A. Farmland, Randolph CR 1100 W bridge, three mi. SW of Farmland, 1100 W bridge, NW corner, two		

ACCESS SITE	SECTION	RIVER MILES
car parking at roadside, 100 yds N on E side (alt. site next bridge downstream at Randolph CR 1250 W, Windsor bridge, NE corner, (P.R.) at dam upstream from bridge (narrow chute cut through mid-dam. Five dams d.s. in Muncie	A-B	15.5 miles
B. Muncie:		
B1. Riverview Park, Ball Rd. & Carver Dr. (dam P.R.)	B1-B2	.5 miles
B2. McCulloch Park, N. Broadway between White River & Centennial (dams P.L. & P.R.) north terminus of Cardinal Greenway W of SR 32 bridge	B2-B3	1.5 miles
B3. Tuhey Park, White River Blvd. & Wheeling Ave. (P.R. at dam) roadside parking	B3-B4	1.7 miles
B4. Westside Park, between S Nichols & Tillotson along White River Blvd.	B4-B5	1.2 miles
B5. White River Corridor Park, dam breached, canoe thru in higher flow, (P.R.) across from Muncie Wastewater Plant	B5-C	9 miles
C. Daleville Park & access, Delaware CR 900 W/River Rd. N of stoplight in Dale ville	C-D	1.5 miles
D. Wallbridge Acres Park, Chesterfield, east edge of town, SR 32, north to park & access	D-E	3.4 miles
E. Mounds State Park, east bank access in north park, Mounds Rd. between Chesterfield & Anderson	E-F1	3 miles

ACCESS SITE	SECTION	RIVER MILES
F. F1. Anderson, Edgewater Park, 10th & Wilcom Sts. parking & ramp north bank	F1-F2	1 mile
F2. Killbuck Creek access, Indian Trails, Anderson, Grand Ave., east of SR 9/ Broadway	F2-F3	0.5 miles
F3. Derby Downs & Madison Ave. Little League, Anderson, Madison Ave., SE corner	F3-G	13.5 miles
G. Perkinsville, SR 13 bridge, & Madison CR 280 N, NE corner	G-H	4 miles
H. Strawtown, SR 37 bridge, NE corner, roadside parking, carry down along bridge	H-I	3.5 miles
I. Riverbend Campground, 21695 SR 37 N of Noblesville, east bank (fee) (P.R.) at power plant dam downstream, signed portage path at jetty	I-J	4 miles
J. Indiana Transportation Museum, Forest Park, Noblesville, White River public access (alt. site upstream at Potter's Covered Bridge)	J-K1	12.5 miles
	Central Section	
K. K1. 96th St bridge, Indianapolis (P.R.) at 4 dams thru Indianapolis)	K1-K2	2.8 miles
K2. 86th St. bridge, Indianapolis	K2-K3	0.5 miles
K3. Broad Ripple Park, Broad Ripple Ave. 62nd St. (P.R. dam downstream before Westfield Blvd., Marott Park)	K3-K4	1.5 miles
K4. Marott Park, Broad Ripple Cornell Ave.	K4-K5	1.5 miles
K5. Holliday Park, 64th St. at Meridian St.	K5-K6	1.5 miles
K6. Friedman Park at Kessler Blvd.	K6-K7	0.5 miles
K7. Riverside Park (E & S banks) access E bank, S		

ACCESS SITES	SECTION	RIVER MILES
of 38th St., White River parking. (P.R. dam downstream from bridge)	K7-K8	3 miles
K8. White River State Park, W & E banks, across from Zoo, River Promenade Walk (P.R.) d.s. 2 dams between US 36 & I-465	K8-L	20 miles
L. Waverly access, 2.2 mi. W of Waverly on SR 144 to Old SR 144, one mi. to dead-end access	L-M	5 miles
M. S. Henderson Ford Bridge, 4.5 mi. N of Martinsville on SR 37, 0.7 mi. W on Henderson Ford Rd., SW corner, (potentially dangerous dam near Martinsville, 0.75 mi. d.s. of power plant (P.R.)	M-N	10.2 miles
N. SR 39 bridge, Martinsville, SE corner	N-O	20 miles
	Southern Section	
O. Texas Ridge Rd. old iron bridge, upstream from new bridge, park at either side, 100 yd. carry down, 2.2 mi. S of SR 67 & Gosport	O-P	8.3 miles
P. Spencer public access, 1.4 mi. E of Spencer on SR 46, SW 1 mi. on Owen CR 225 E/Old Southport Rd.. (alt. site at Cooper Commons, Spencer city park, downstream, N bank, Main & Cooper)	P-Q	15 miles
Q. Freedom, Owen CR 590 S bridge, SE corner, take out 100 yds. downstream from bridge	Q-R	5 miles
R. Farmers, Greene CR 990 N, former ferry crossing, 1.6 mi. E of US 231/SR 67	R-S	7 miles
S. Worthington, public access 1.1 mi. SE on SR 157, NE 'corner	S-T	9 miles

ACCESS SITE	SECTION	RIVER MILES
T. Bloomfield, upstream NW from US 231/SR 54 bridge, via Greene CR 150 W, 0.2 mi. west bank near mouth of Latta's Creek	T-U	20 miles
U. Elnora public access, 2.6 NW of Elnora & SR 57 Daviess CR 1550 W to CR 400 E	U-V	23 miles
	Lower Section	
V. Carnahan public access, W on SR 358 from Plainville & SR 57, SE bridge corner	V-W	14.5 miles
W. Washington public access, 3.8 mi. west on W. National Hwy. from junction of SR 57 at Washington. From US 50/150 turn north on Daviess CR 300 W at Maysville between new & old US 50/150	W-X	16 miles
X. White River, Petersburg public access, SR 61 bridge, NW corner		

Bank Swallow Nests

WHITE RIVER West Fork

upper section

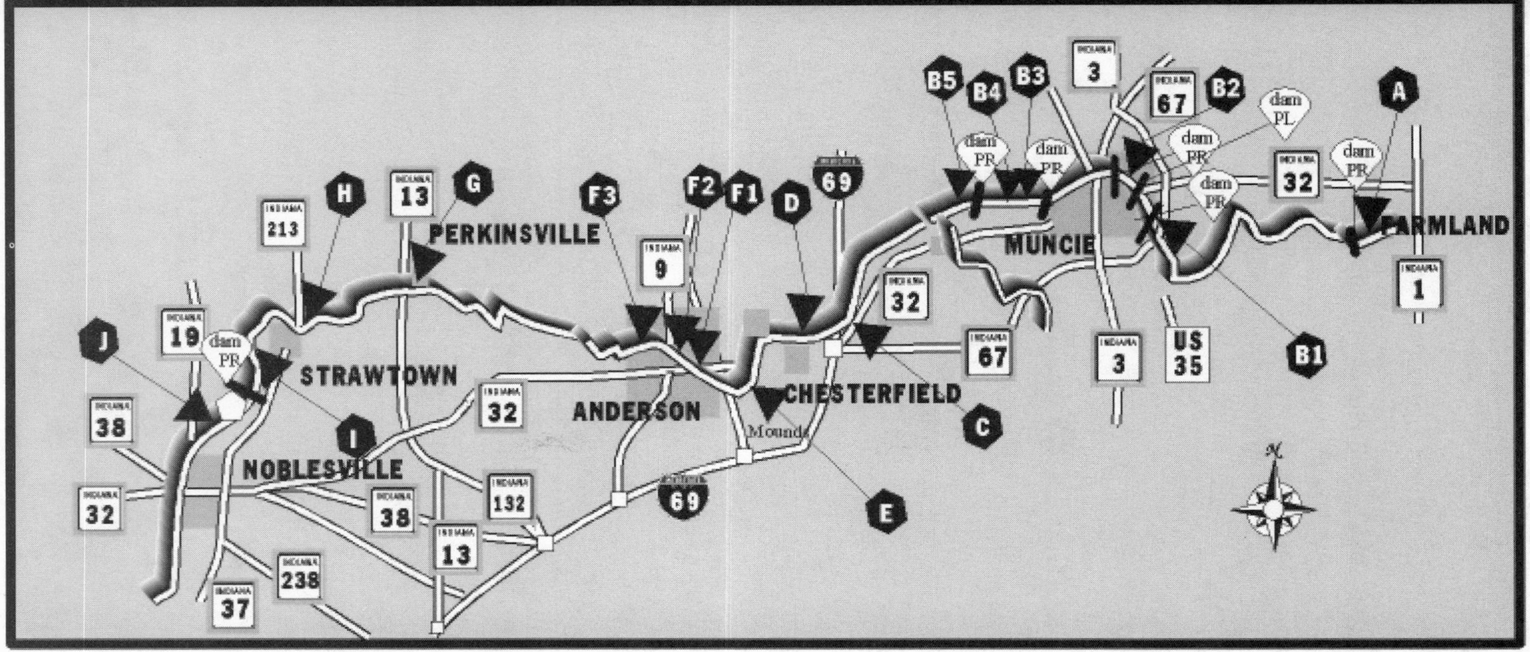

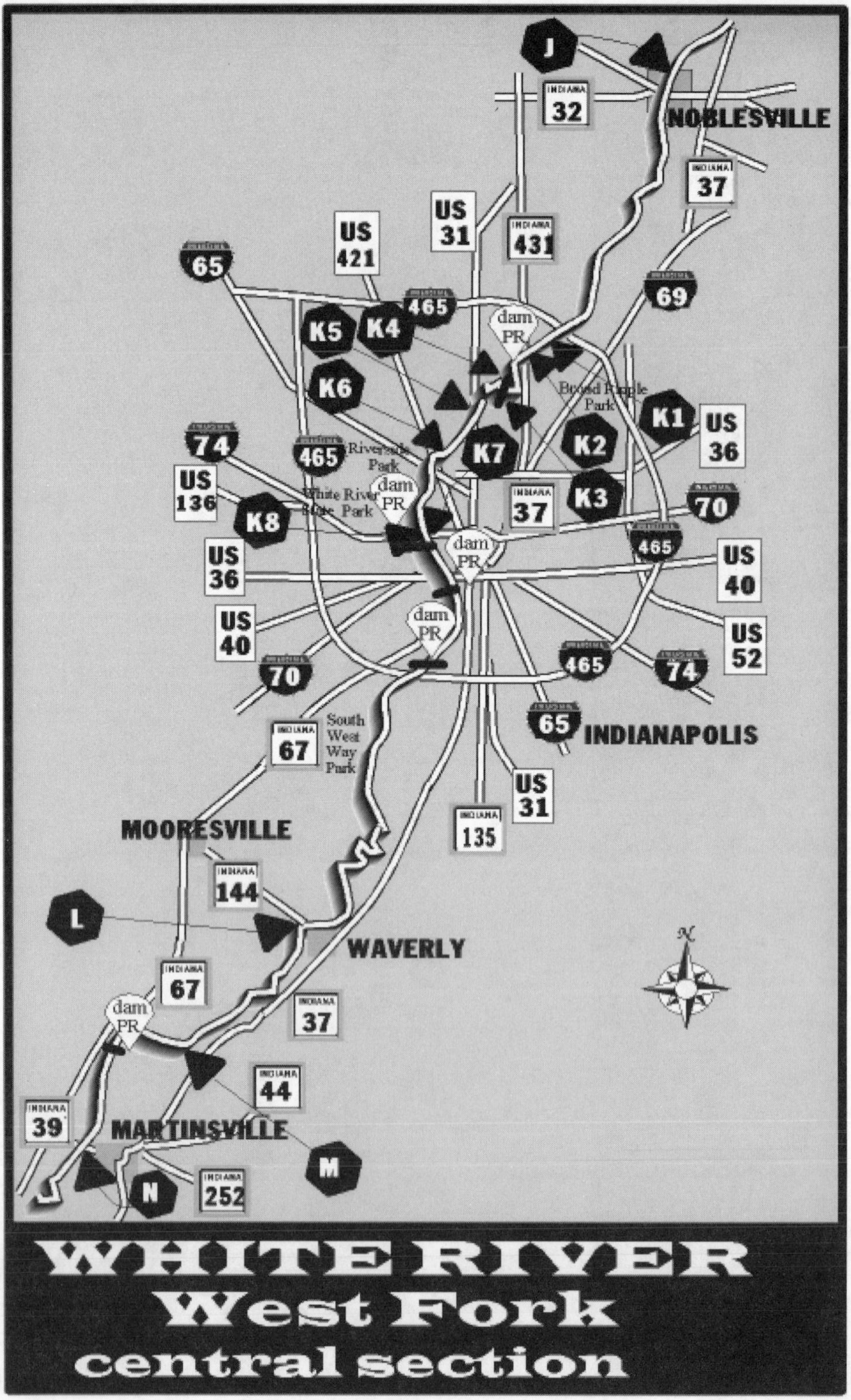

WHITE RIVER
West Fork
central section

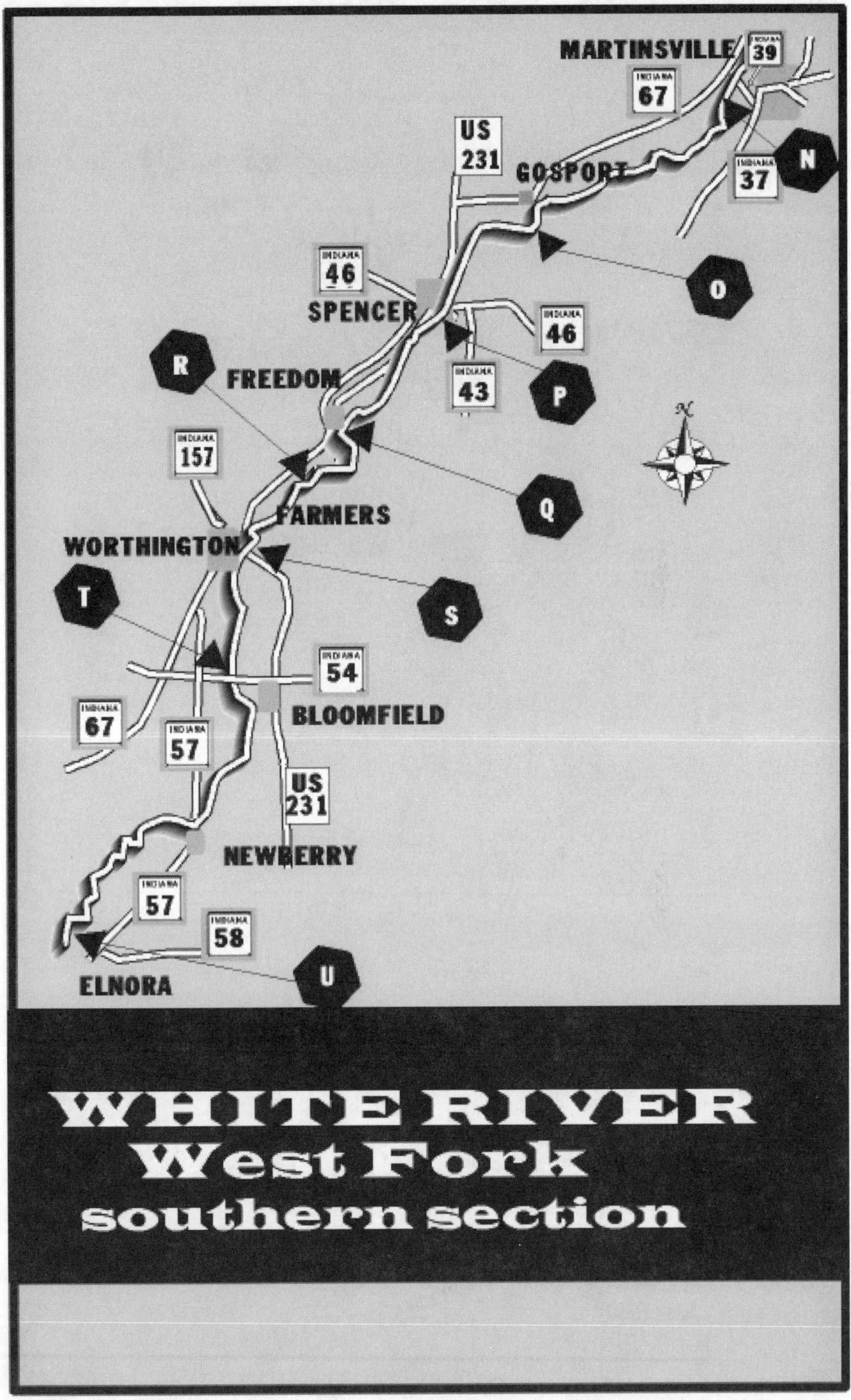

WHITE RIVER
West Fork
southern section

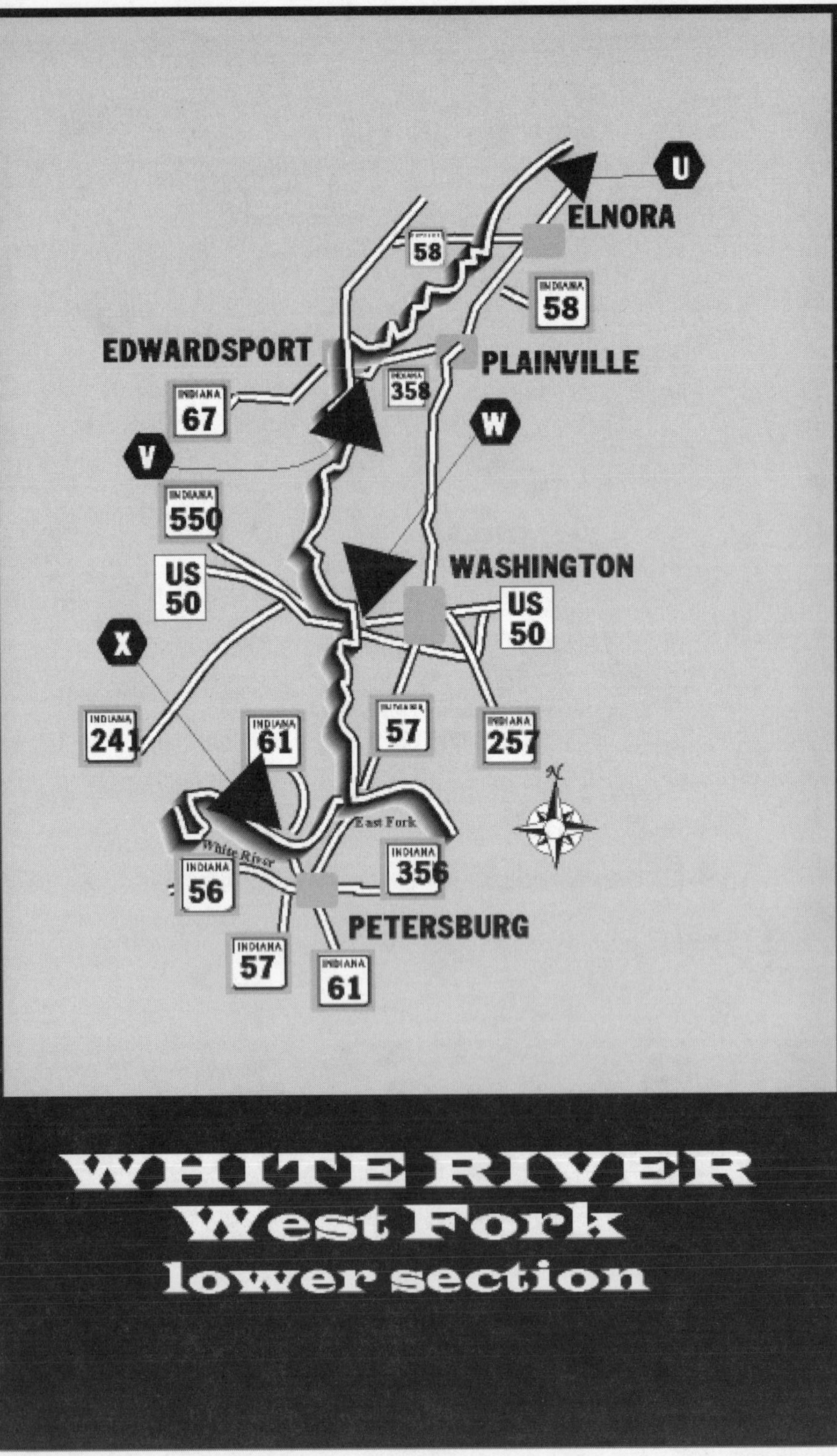

WHITE RIVER
West Fork
lower section

FLATROCK RIVER

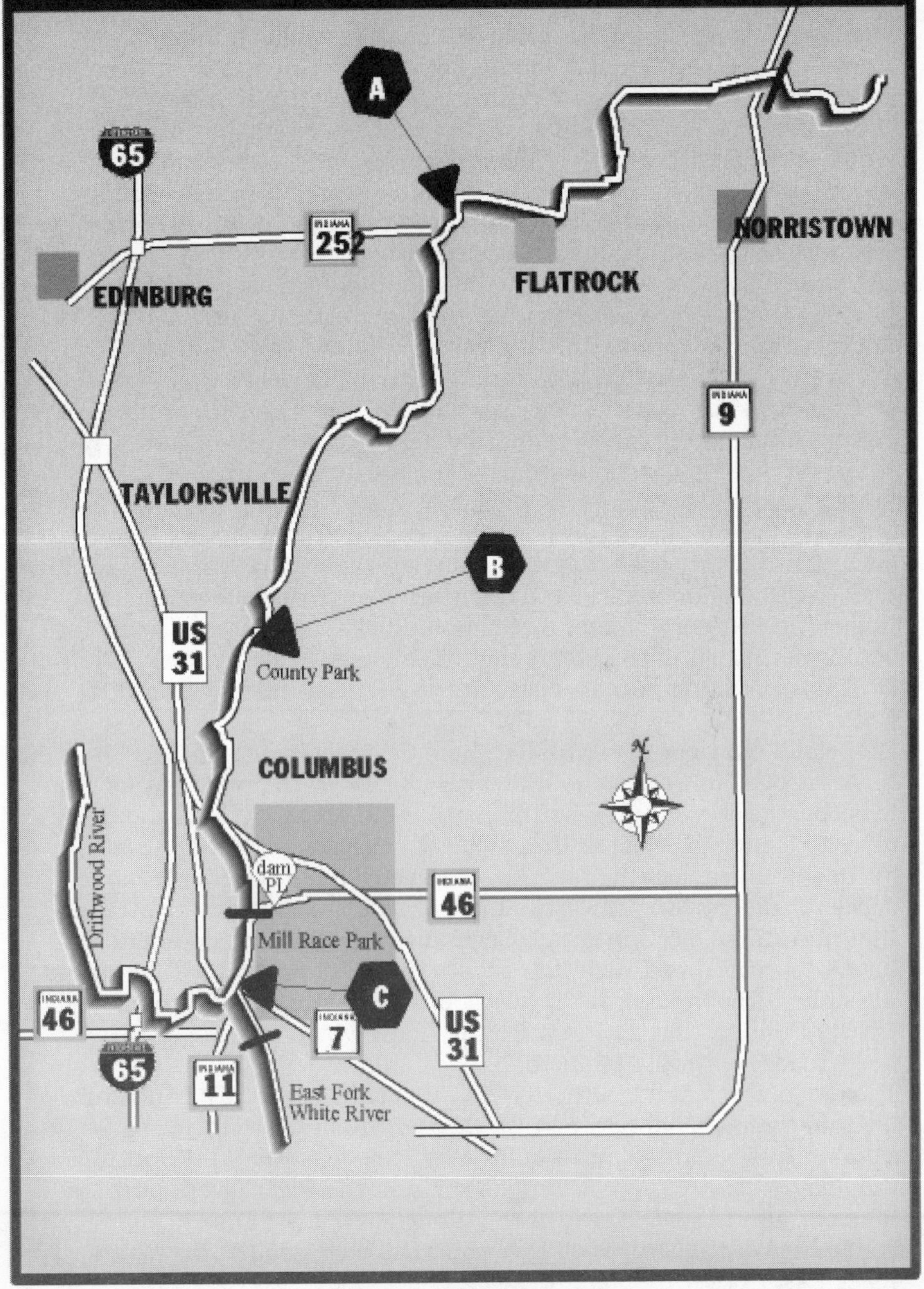

25. FLAT ROCK RIVER

- Wash over sparkling rocky riffles amidst driftwood snags

The Flat Rock River (or Flatrock) headwaters originate near Mooreland, Henry County, Indiana, flowing south and west through a five county course, over 90 miles before merging with the Driftwood River at Columbus where the two streams become the White River East Fork. The 532 square mile basin does not provide enough drainage for canoeing in the upper three counties. Dredged and ditched through Henry County, the rural Flat Rock is allowed to meander in agricultural Rush County where four covered bridges cross (Norris Ford, Smith, Forsythe Mill and Moscow covered bridges). Near I-74, in Decatur County, the Flat Rock and Little Flat Rock join and nearly double the volume of flow. Near St. Paul, it skims over an extensive limestone bed that the Delaware referred to as Pack-op-ka or puck-op-ka, "rock bed of stream". Numerous water powered mills ad dams were built along the river during the early settlements days but the dams are the only visible proof of their former presence.

The river broadens and deepens as it enters Shelby County at St. Paul. There are two low dams at Geneva (about 28 mi from mouth). The Flat Rock, looking more like a river, flows over a low dam and under the SR 9 bridge (not a recommended access) steadily curving southwest, skirting the north edge of the village of Flat Rock. The DNR has provided public access at the SR 252 bridge west of Flat Rock.

Pockets of river cottages cluster along the level banks of the Flat Rock enroute to Columbus, (the only city along the river but for the most part there is little development). Sand and gravel bars are more in evidence. Most of the stream banks are vegetated however in the lower reaches the farm fields have claimed the fragile banks accelerating erosion. There are numerous dead trees in the stream that need to be circumvented. Several of the sharp eroded bends have been riprapped with "flat rock" chunks of concrete. Take-out is possible at Bartholomew CR 800 N but downstream a few miles is Owens Bend, a Bartholomew County Park which provides a much needed access (trails, picnicing).

The city of Columbus, although heard is rarely seen until the dam (P.L. no trespassing) between US 31 and SR 11, not far from a railroad trestle bridge and Noblitt City Park (east bank). Continue the float downstream to Millrace Park and the River Overlook vista take out and the beginning of the White River East Fork at the confluence of the Driftwood River and the beginning of the White River East Fork.

USGS MAP(S): Lewis Creek, Hope, Edinburg, Columbus 1:24,000
VICINITY: Flat Rock, Shelby County
Columbus, Bartholomew County
STREAM DISTANCE/TRIPS: 17 canoeable miles
three or more trips possible
LEVEL OF DIFFICULTY: Class 1
HAZARDS/PORTAGES: logjams, snags, strainers, submerged boulders, logs, low dam (P.L.) at Columbus between US 31 & SR 11
INFO SOURCES: Atterbury Fish & Wildlife Area
7970 S. Rowe St.
Edinburgh, IN 46124
(812) 526-2051
Cikana Fish Hatchery
2650 SR 44
Martinsville, IN 46151
(765) 342-5527
Driftwood Fish Hatchery
4931 S. CR 250 W
Vallonia, IN 47281
(812) 358-4110
AREA OUTFITTERS: none
GAMEFISH SPECIES: smallmouth bass, striped bass, suckers, catfish
CAMPING: Johnson County Park
2949 E. North St.
Edinburgh, IN 46124
(812) 526-6809
Brown County State Park
POB 608
Nashville, IN 47448
(812) 988-6406
MEDICAL ASSISTANCE: Columbus Regional Hospital
2400 E. 17th St.
Columbus, IN 47201
(812) 379-4441
W.S. Major Hospital
150 W. Washington, IN
Shelbyville, IN 46176
(765) 392-3211
(765) 392-4222

ACCESS SITE	SECTION	RIVER MILES
A. Flat Rock River, DNR access, Willow Park, I mi. W of Flat Rock, SR 252 bridge, NW corner	A-B	7.6 miles
B. Owens Bend County Park, Bartholomew CR 550 N & River Rd. SE corner, W of Clifford	B-C	9 miles
C. Millrace Park, Columbus City Park, west end of 5th St., adjacent to SR 46, River Overlook vista, Driftwood River Confluence, White River East Fork begins watch for low dam upstream, (P.L.). Do not trespass		

Gravel Bar Rest Stop, Flat Rock River

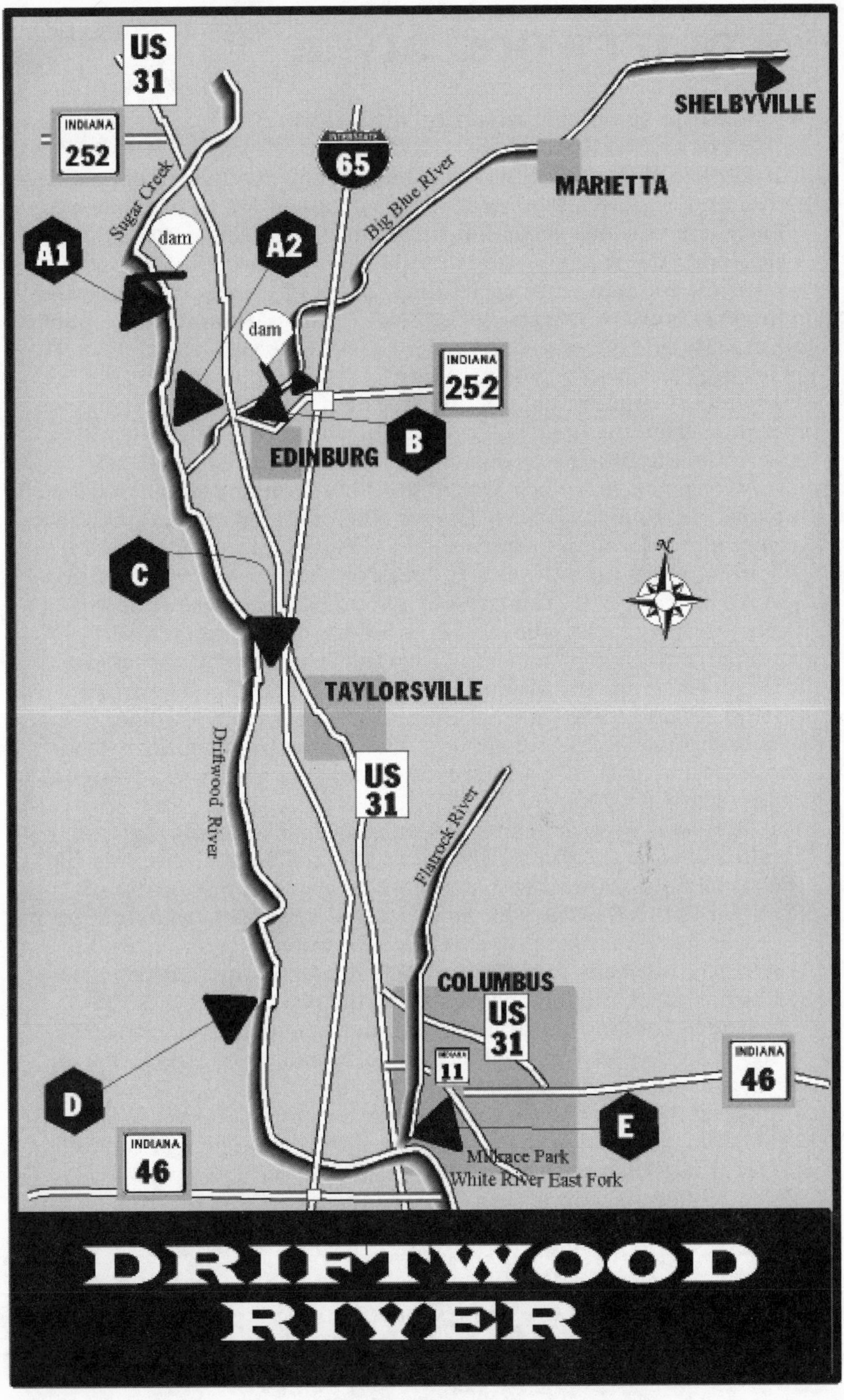
US 31
INDIANA 252
65
SHELBYVILLE
MARIETTA
Sugar Creek
Big Blue RIver
dam
A1
A2
dam
INDIANA 252
B
EDINBURG
C
N
TAYLORSVILLE
Driftwood River
US 31
Flatrock River
COLUMBUS
US 31
INDIANA 11
INDIANA 46
D
E
Millrace Park
White River East Fork
INDIANA 46
DRIFTWOOD
RIVER

26. DRIFTWOOD RIVER

- Sample two streams that make one

The Driftwood River is born river-made at the confluence of Sugar Creek and Big Blue River near the SE Johnson-NE Bartholomew county line in south central Indiana. Sugar Creek is around 80 miles long and begins in west central Henry County, flowing south, southwest through rural agricultural lands of Hancock, Shelby and Johnson counties. Atterbury FWA is the only parkland with a public access site along Sugar Creek. The Big Blue River is about 100 miles long and also begins in Henry County originating at the tailwaters of Summit Lake State Park dam; separated by end moraines from the headwaters of Sugar Creek and the Flatrock River. The Big Blue River has canoe access in the upper Henry County reaches at Wilbur Wright FWA but paddling water may be lacking. Big Blue joins Little Blue at Shelbyville where a DNR public access site is located at Sunset Park (Mechanic St.) north of SR 9 (about 24 miles from the Sugar Creek confluence and the Driftwood River). The river gathers more water from the incoming Brandywine Creek, west of Shelbyville. South of SR 44 to the Sugar Creek confluence is the best canoeing section of Big Blue but access is limited. There are few bridges to access between Sunset Park, at Shelbyville and Irwin Park, at Edinburgh. There is a low dam (P.L.) at Edinburgh, SR 252 bridge upstream a mile from the Driftwood River headwater (USGS MAP(S): Shelbyville, Lewis Creek, Marietta, Edinburgh 1:24,000).

The Driftwood River is a short 16 miles from its origin to the confluence with the Flatrock River at Millrace Park, Columbus, and the birth of the White River East Fork (also called the Driftwood Fork White River). There are ample access sites that begin on Sugar Creek or Big Blue River. There is no headwater access at the confluence adjacent to Driftwood PFA. A watercourse influenced by glaciation, the Driftwood passes along the glacial trough of the Scottsburg Lowland natural region. From the confluence, the Driftwood flows past the public fishing area (former gravel pits) on the east bank accessible from US 31, south of the Blue River bridge and along the east edge of the Camp Atterbury Maneuver Training Center (no trespassing). Downstream of the confluence of Nineveh Creek, the river leaves the military property and flows past Heflin Memorial Park (access). With few meanders, the stream drops nearly straight south to Lowell Bridge & historic site (access), one of the few bridge crossings along its watery route. The river is surprisingly wild sandwiched between I-65 to the east and county roads to the west. As the name suggests, there are plenty of dead trees in the Driftwood that need to be negotiated. Although I-65 and US 31 run parallel to the Driftwood, there is enough greenbuffer to keep the highways out of sight but not always out of earshot. There is one crossing under I-65 (north of Exit 68) as the Driftwood turns east to Columbus and Millrace Park terminus.

The place name Driftwood is a literal interpretation of the Miami On-gwah-sah-kah, "driftwood".

USGS MAP(S): Franklin, Nineveh, Edinburgh, Columbus 1:24,000
VICINITY: Edinburgh, Johnson County
Columbus, Bartholomew County
STREAM DISTANCE/TRIPS: 24 miles total
two or more trips
LEVEL OF DIFFICULTY: Class 1
HAZARDS/PORTAGES: log snags, hidden objects, strainers, seasonal hunting
INFO SOURCES: Atterbury FWA
7970 S. Rowe St.
Edinburgh, IN 46124
(812) 526-2051
Bartholomew County Parks
c/o Bartholomew County Planning
123 Washington, St. #8
Columbus, IN 47201
(812) 376-2550
Cikana Fish Hatchery
2650 SR 44
Martinsville, IN 46151
(765) 342-5527
Driftwood Fish Hatchery
4931 S CR 250 W
Vallonia, IN 47281
(812) 358-4110
AREA OUTFITTERS: Blue's Canoe Livery
CR 700 N
(entrance to Heflin Memorial Park)
Columbus, IN 47201
(812) 526-9851
(812) 376-6293
GAMEFISH SPECIES: bluegill, bass, catfish, carp
CAMPING: Johnson County Park
2949 E. North St. (within Atterbury FWA)
Edinburgh, IN 46124
(812) 526-6809
Heflin Memorial Park
CR 700 N
c/o Bartholomew County Parks
(812) 378-9960
(seasonal)
Brown County State Park
POB 608, Nashville, IN 47448
(812) 988-6406
MEDICAL ASSISTANCE: Columbus Regional Hospital
2400 E. 17th St., Columbus, IN 47201
(812) 379-4441

ACCESS SITE	SECTION	RIVER MILES
A. Sugar Creek access, Atterbury Fish & Wildlife Area A1. Johnson CR 650 S./, Pisgah Rd. E, dam site, parking & carry down A2. Camp Atterbury Rd./ Hospital Rd. bridge, upstream 100 yds on River Rd, E bank, 0.5 mi. W of SR 252 S US 31 junction	A1-A2 A2-C	2 miles 6 miles
B. Edinburgh Bait Shop, Thompson Dam site. Eisenhower /SR 252 S & River Rd. (alt. site Irwin Park upstream from dam)	B-C	6 miles
C. Heflin Memorial Park, from I-65 north of Taylorsville exit 76B & drive north to the first road left & turn south on Heflin Park Rd. Curve west on Heflin Pk Rd/Bartholomew CR 700 N & drive to the park entrance next to canoe rental (park gate may be closed)	C-D	5 miles
D. Lowell Bridge, DNR access site, SW corner, 1.5 mi. N of Columbus, on US 31, then 2.5 mi. W on Lowell Rd.	D-E	5 miles
E. Millrace Park, Columbus City Park, W 5th St., confluence of Driftwood & Flatrock Rivers, River View Overlook , 50 yd carrydown. Also boat ramp downstream 100 yds. on White River before dam		

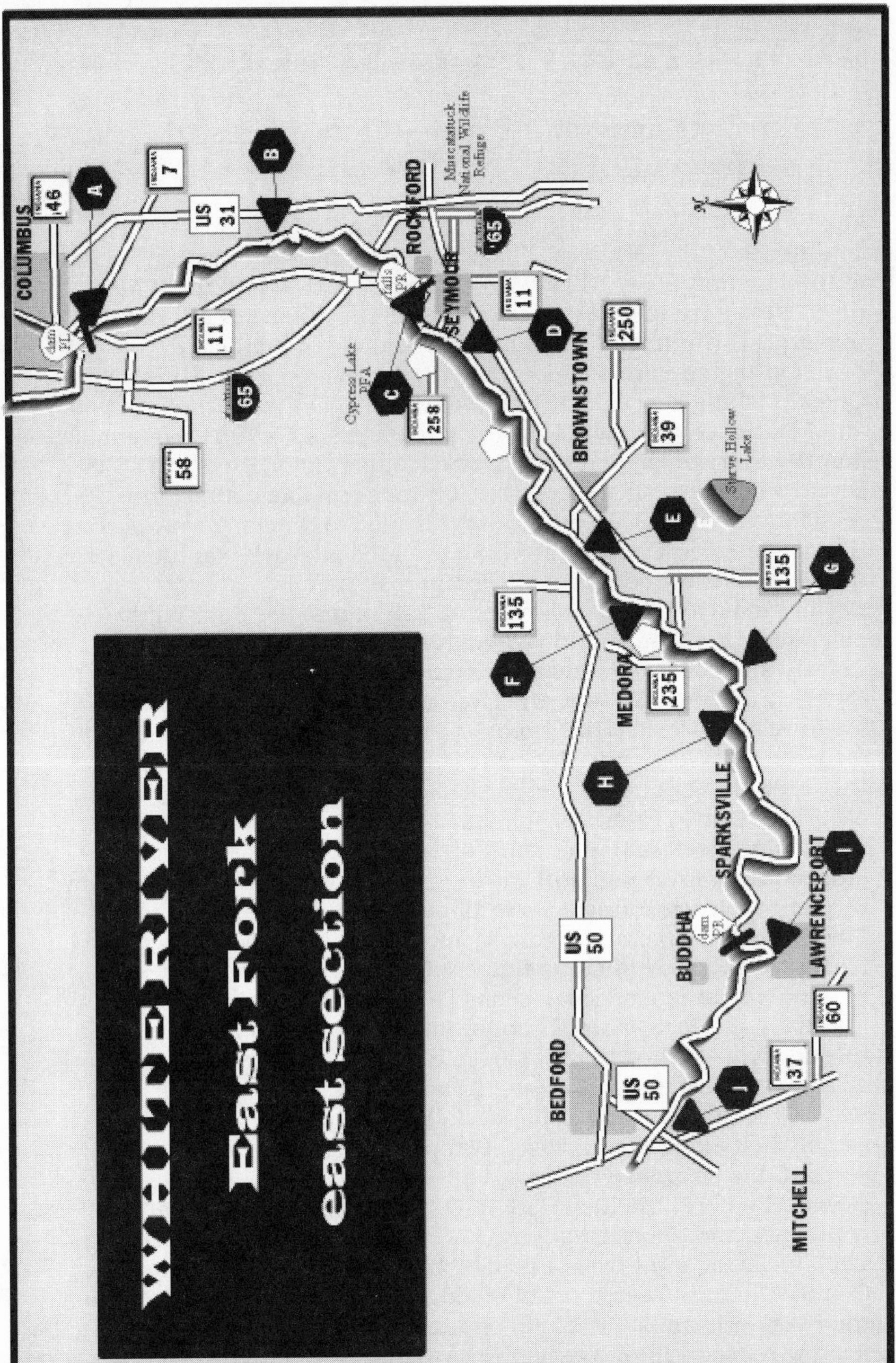
WHITE RIVER
East Fork
east section
COLUMBUS
ROCKFORD
SEYMOUR
BROWNSTOWN
MEDORA
SPARKSVILLE
LAWRENCEPORT
BUDDHA
BEDFORD
MITCHELL
Muscatatuck National Wildlife Refuge
Cypress Lake PFA
Starve Hollow Lake
46
7
US 31
65
11
58
258
250
39
135
235
US 50
60
37
A
B
C
D
E
F
G
H
I
J

27. WHITE RIVER EAST FORK

- Run along agricultural plain through forested escarpment

The White River East Fork or the Driftwood Fork, begins at the confluence of the Driftwood River and the Flat Rock River in Columbus and flows 239 miles south and west to join the White River West Fork just east of Petersburg. The Muscatatuck River is the largest tributary of the East Fork and other significant contributing streams include Clifty Creek, Sand Creek, Guthries Creek, Fishing Creek, Leatherwood Creek, Salt Creek, Indian Creek and Lost River. The slow sluggish stream drains 5,700 square miles and the average fall is less than one foot per mile. There are at least seventeen access sites along the 200-mile runable course. The best sections are from Bell Ford Covered Bridge to Shieldstown Covered Bridge, Jackson County, and from the Muscatatuck confluence to the west Martin County line near Hindostan Falls.

Beginning as a full blown stream at Columbus, the East White meanders broad and sandy through south central Bartholomew County and the wide alluvial Scottsburg Lowland floodplain. Entering Jackson County, the river goes under I-65 and veers southwest a safe distance from Seymour, Brownstown, Vallonia and Medora. There are three Jackson County historic covered bridges that arch the fork. Also, the Battle of Tipton Island, April 1, 1813, occurred near Rockford. A substantial amount of swamp forest floodplain exists west and south of Seymour. The East Fork and Muscatatuck River join and gather strength while carving their way through the rugged unglaciated Knobstone Hills near Sparksville. The East Fork becomes highly scenic in sections of Lawrence and Martin counties. Numerous timbered bluffs appear on state and national forest lands. Small seasonal fast flowing tributaries drain into the East Fork. Once through, the East Fork curves northwest through the Mitchell Karst Plain to Bedford. Although surface streams are few in karst areas, Indian Creek, Fishing Creek and Buck Creek flow into the East Fork. Delaware villages were established along their beloved Wappi-hanne, "white river" in present day Lawrence County.

Beyond Bedford, the East Fork enters the Shawnee Hills natural region and the Hoosier National Forest. Downstream from the Williams Dam and Covered Bridge, the East Fork enters Martin County the most scenic county along its course. Springs flow into the river and sandstone bluffs and rockhouses soar above the narrow rugged valley. Norman Rock Bend, Devils Elbow, Old Mans Nose, McBrides Bluff, House Rock, The Pinnacle, Bluffs of Beaver Bend and Hindostan Falls are some of the rock features and formations in Martin County.

Beyond Hindostan Falls, the East Fork returns to a flat agricultural plain of the Southwestern Lowlands natural region. The river loops west skirting Glendale FWA. Four miles above Petersburg, the East Fork joins the West Fork to form the White River.

USGS MAP(S): Columbus, Jonesville, Azalia, Seymour, Brownstown, Vallonia, Medora, Tunnelton, Campbellsburg, Bedford East, Bedford West, Williams, Huron, Logootee, Rusk, Jasper, Alfordsville, Glendale, Sandy Hook, Monroe City 1:24,000

VICINITY: Columbus, Azalia, Bartholomew County
Seymour, Brownstown, Vallonia, Medora, Sparksville, Jackson County
Ft. Ritner, Tunnelton, Bedford, Williams, Lawrence County
Shoals, Martin County
Haysville, Portersville, Dubois County

STREAM DISTANCE/TRIPS: 203 miles canoeable
16 trips or more

LEVEL OF DIFFICULTY: Class 1

HAZARDS/PORTAGES: snags, low water, submerged objects, seasonal hunting, wind, low dams: Rockford (P.R.), Lawrenceport (P.R.), Williams, Spice Valley access above dam. Do not portage. Hindostan Falls (P.L.)

INFO SOURCES: Driftwood Fish Hatchery
4931 S CR 250 W
Vallonia, IN 47281
(812) 358-4110
Avoca Fish Hatchery
POB 16
Avoca, IN 47420
(812) 279-1215
Sugar Ridge Fish & Wildlife Area
2310 E SR 364
Winslow, IN 47598
(812) 789-2724

AREA OUTFITTERS: none

GAMEFISH SPECIES: bluegill, bass, crappie, carp, sauger, drum, buffalo

CAMPING: Brown County State Park
POB 608
Nashville, IN 47448
(812) 988-6406
Class A & B
Cypress Lake PFA
I-65 &SR 11 N of Seymour
Class C
Starved Hollow SRA
4345 S. CR 275 W
Vallonia, IN 47281
(812) 358-3464
Class A & B
Jackson-Washington State Forest
1278 E. SR 250

Brownstown, IN 47220
(812) 358-2160
Class C
Spring Mill State Park
Box 376
Mitchell, IN 47446
(812) 849-4129
Class A & C
Hardin Ridge HNF
Hardin Ridge Road
Monroe Lake
c/o Hoosier National Forest
811 Constitution Ave.
Bedford, IN 47421
(812) 275-5987
Class A & C
Williams Dam PFA
below dam at Williams
S of SR 450
Class C
Martin State Forest
POB 599
Shoals, IN 47581
(812) 247-3491
Class C
Hindostan Falls PFA
SR 550 south to Hindostan
Class C
Glendale Fish and Wildlife Area
RR #2, Box 300
Montgomery, IN 47558 (812) 644-7711
Class A & C
Pike State Forest
2310 E. SR 364
Winslow, IN 47598
(812) 789-2724
Class C
Sugar Ridge Fish & Wildlife Area
2310 E. SR 364
Winslow, IN 47958 (812) 789-2724
Class C

MEDICAL ASSISTANCE: Columbus Regional Hospital
2400 E. 17th St.
Columbus, IN 47201
(812) 379-4441
Memorial Hospital
411 W. Tipton St.
Seymour, IN 47274
(812) 522-2349
Dunn Memorial Hospital
1600 23rd St.
Bedford, IN 47421

(812) 275-3331
Jasper Memorial Hospital
800 W. 9th
Jasper, IN 47546
(812) 482-2345
Daviess County Hospital
1314 Grand Ave.
Washington, IN 47501
(812) 254-2760
(800) 356-2077
Vincennes Good Samaritan Hospital
520 S. 7th
Vincennes, IN 47591
(812) 882-0582

ACCESS SITES	SECTION	RIVER MILES
A. Columbus, south of SR 46/ SR 11 bridge, 2nd St. to Lafayette Ave., S to Water St., W of sewage treatment plant	A-B	11 miles
B. Azalia public access, Bartholomew CR 800 S bridge, SE corner, SW of Azalia, 1.1 mi. east of SR 11	B-C	11 miles
C. Rockford public access, CR 725 N, west of SR 11, Falls (P.R.) below access, 0.3 mi. west of Rockford village north of Seymour	C-D	3.2 miles
D. Bell Ford Covered Bridge, NE corner public access, 3 mi. W of Seymour on SR 258	D-E	18 miles
E. Brownstown PFA public access, 0.4 mi. west of Brownstown on US 50 bridge, SE corner	E-F	9 miles
F. Medora Covered Bridge access, 1 mi. east of Medora on US 235, NW corner	F-G	6.5 miles
G. White River-Muscatatuck confluence access, 5 mi. west of SR 135 at Milport (Jackson-Washington Co. line) on Wheeler Hollow Rd., Washington County, south bank	G-H	6 miles

ACCESS SITE	SECTION	RIVER MILES
H. Sparksville, public access, 0.5 miles east on Sparksville Medora Pike, 0.3 mi W of Ferry Bridge, SW Jackson County	H-I	17 miles
I. Lawrenceport, public access, 0.1 mi. east of Spring Mill Park on SR 60, then 3.7 miles north on Lawrence CR 500 E (upstream dam P.R.)	I-J	12 miles
J. Bedford public access, 2.5 miles south of Bedford on SR 37 bridge at SW corner	J-K	14.5 miles
K. Spice Valley public access, Williams, above dam on SR 450	TAKE OUT ONLY, DANGEROUS HIGH DAM 0.5 MILES DOWNSTREAM	
L. Williams Dam PFA, Williams south of SR 450, below dam, SW bank	L-M	23.5 miles
M. Shoals public access, N of US 50 in Shoals, 8th St & Main, east bank	M-N	12 miles
N. Hindostan Falls PFA, 5 mi. E of Loogootee on SR 550, access sites above & below falls (P.L. at falls)	TAKE OUT, NORTH BANK ABOVE DANGEROUS FALLS N-O	20 miles
O. Portersville Bridge, NE corner, 0.4 mi. NE of Portersville on Daviess CR 1100 E	O-P	4.5 miles
P. Flat Rock access, Glendale Fish & Wildlife Area, S of Waco, Daviess CR 675 E (2 ½ hours downstream is the SR 257 alt. site)	P-Q	21.5 miles
Q. White River, N of Petersburg, SR 61 N bridge, NW corner		

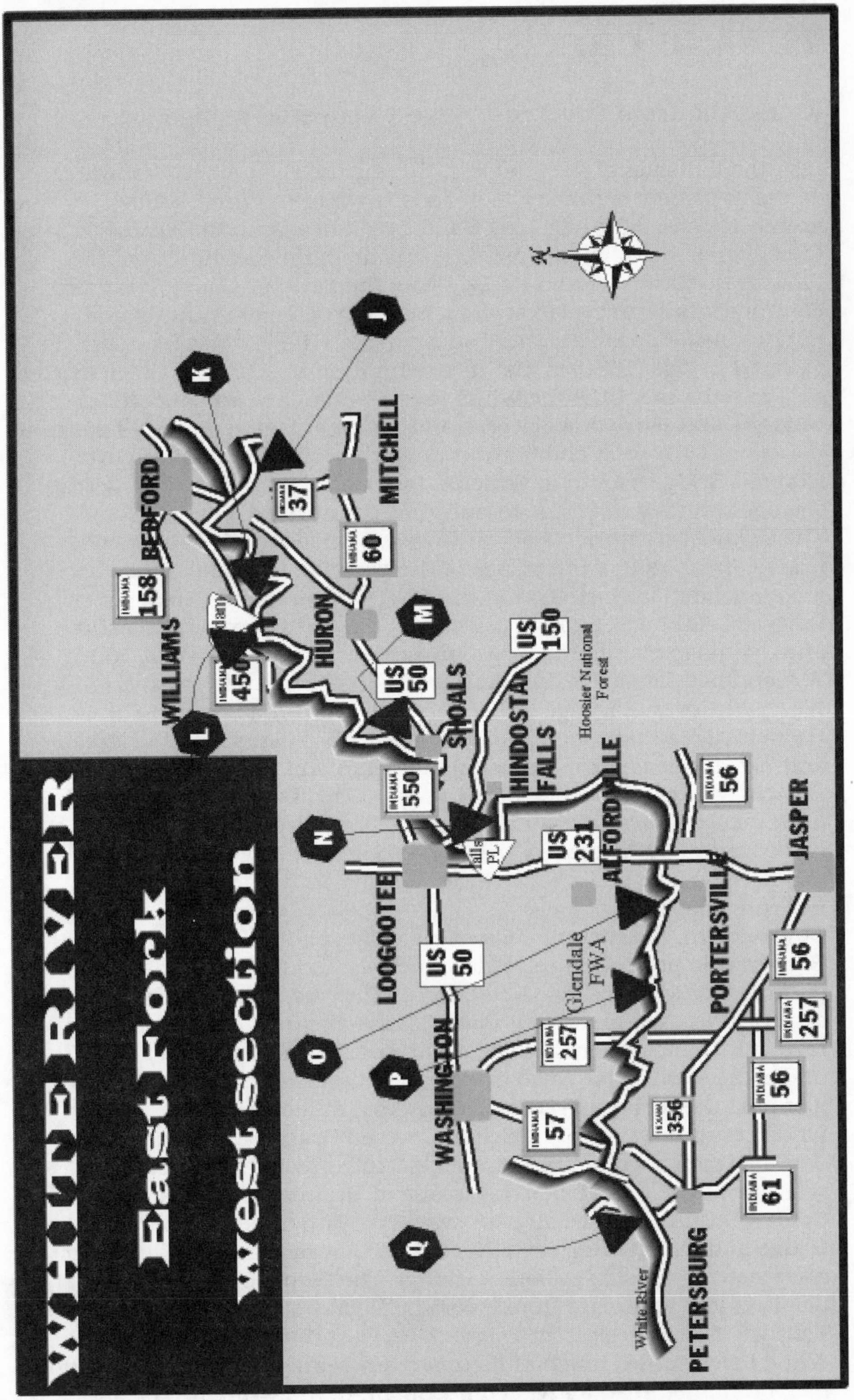
WHITE RIVER
East Fork
west section
WILLIAMS
BEDFORD
MITCHELL
HURON
SHOALS
HINDOSTAN FALLS
LOOGOOTEE
WASHINGTON
PORTERSVILLE
JASPER
PETERSBURG
Glendale FWA
Hoosier National Forest
White River
158
37
60
450
US 50
US 150
550
US 231
56
257
57
356
61
K
J
M
L
N
O
P
Q

28. SAND CREEK

- Paddle from covered bridge to covered bridge

Like the flatboats of the pioneers, finding the right amount of water at the right time is the key to a smooth voyage on this shallow scenic stream. Fifty-mile long Sand Creek heads up in Decatur County, northeast of Greensburg near the hamlet of Kingston. Flowing southwest, Sand Creek skirts the Decatur County seat and continues its countryside sojourn merging with small creeks and ditches, sometimes following county roads. The historic Westport Covered Bridge (1880) is just upstream from the Panther Creek (33 mi. from the mouth of the White River) confluence and dam (P.R.) with the first carry down access and parking. Paddlers should park roadside at the west end (Layton Road dead end) of the Westport Covered Bridge (closed to vehicles, foot traffic only) and carry across the open windowed bridge to put-in at the northeast corner.

The segment from the Westport Covered Bridge to the Brewersville bridge, just south of the village of Brewersville (12.6 miles) has been recommended for inclusion in the DNR's Natural and Scenic River Program. Although Sand Creek comes close at times with Decatur and Jennings county roads, it only crosses two (Decatur CR 500 W/Jennings CR 200 E & Jennings CR 800 N) enroute from Westport Covered Bridge to Brewersville. On the Westport to Brewersville section the meandering stream crosses morainic areas and has cut down deep exposing Devonian and Silurian bedrock especially along the bends of the karst valley. Downstream one mile from the Jennings CR 800 N bridge, a former mill race has been carved through the narrow neck of a backbone ridge at an oxbow bend. The sandy south side of the race makes a fine rest stop. Do not enter the race.

Downstream, the historic Keller Grist Mill site (est. 1823) at Brewersville provides a carry down access and limited roadside parking along North Base Road. Down the east slope face from the historical marker and North Base Road is the inlet of a second mill race cut. Do not enter the race. Continue downstream and float under the North Base Road bridge and curve back north to take out just past the west mill race outlet and old mill foundation.

When continuing on to the Scipio Covered Bridge, watch for the dam-like rough water downstream 0.3 miles from the historic mill & race site at the former railroad trestle at Brewersville (P.R.). Sand Creek continues its countryside way, crossing under the SR 3 bridge and meandering on to the Scipio Covered Bridge, (NE corner carry down, roadside pullout parking). The Scipio Covered Bridge at Scipio is just upstream from incoming Wyaloosing Creek and the SR 7 bridge. Sand Creek from Scipio flows west to the East Fork of the White River, looses much of its upstream beauty, crosses US 31 and melts into the broad alluviated floodplain of the White River East

Fork confluence.

USGS MAP(S): Westport, Butlerville, North Vernon 1:24,000
VICINITY: Westport, Decatur County
Brewersville, Scipio, North Vernon, Jennings County
STREAM DISTANCE/TRIPS: 23 miles
2 or more trips
LEVEL OF DIFFICULTY: Class 1
HAZARDS/PORTAGES: low water, rocks, logs, submerged objects,
one low dam, old RR bridge rubble
INFO SOURCES: DNR Streams & Trails
Outdoor Recreation Division
402 W. Washington St. Rm. 271
Indianapolis, IN 46204
(317) 232-4070
Driftwood State Fish Hatchery
4931 S CR 250 W
Vallonia, IN 47281
(812) 358-4110
AREA OUTFITTERS: none
GAMEFISH SPECIES: bluegilll, smallmouth bass, sunfish
CAMPING: Muscatatuck County park
325 N. SR 7
North Vernon, IN 47265
(812) 346-2953
MEDICAL ASSISTANCE: Jennings Community Hospital
301 Henry Street
North Vernon, IN 47265
(812) 346-6200

ACCESS SITES	SECTION	RIVER MILES
A. Westport Covered Bridge, east of Westport, Decatur CR 1100 S, NE corner. Parking both ends of bridge (closed to vehicles)	A-B	12.8 miles
B. Brewersville historic mill site, North Base Road, (down-stream 0.25 mi . old RR bridge rubble (P.R.)	B-C	10 miles
C. Scipio Covered Bridge, NE corner, Scipio, east of SR 7		

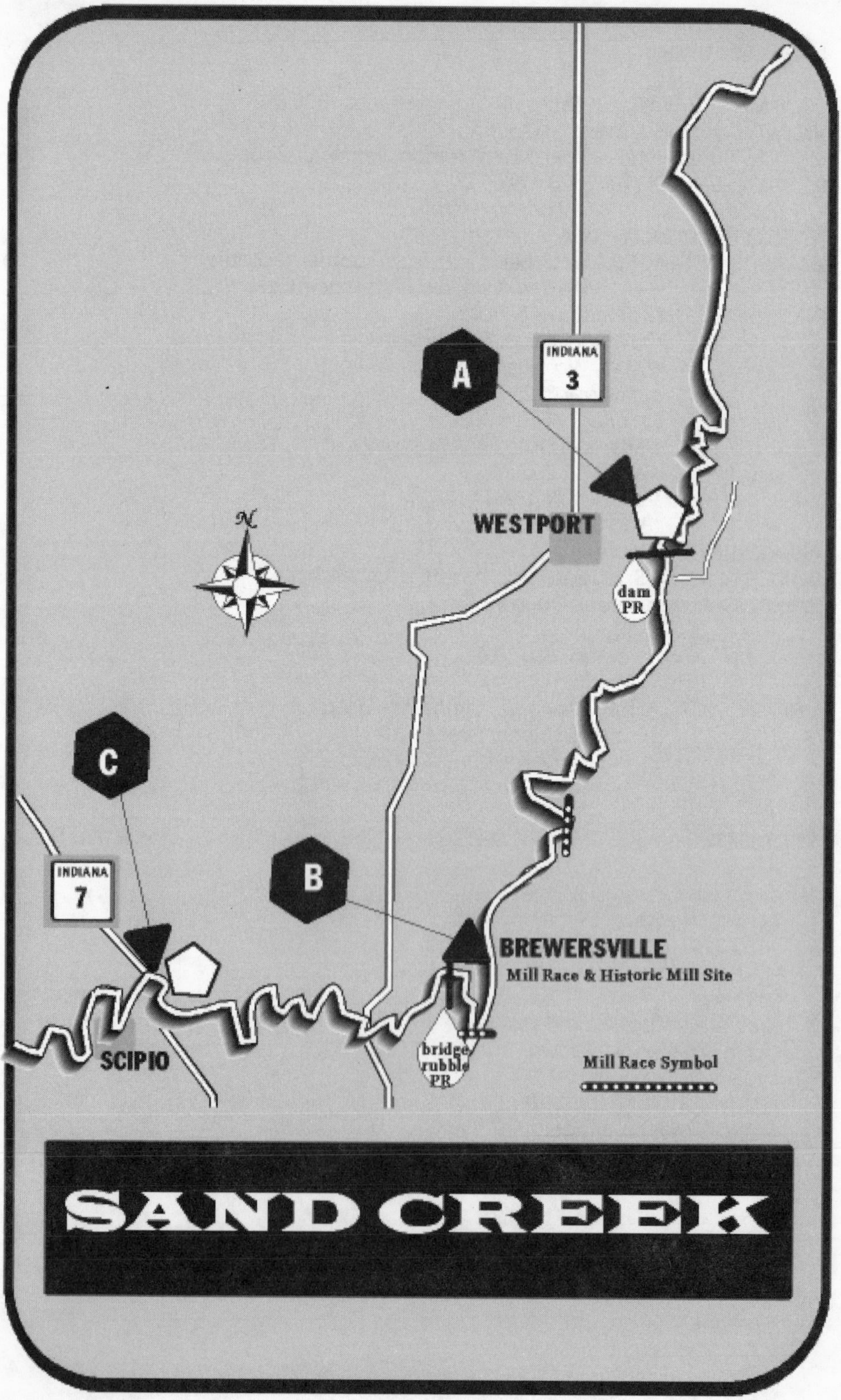

A
INDIANA
3
N
WESTPORT
dam
PR
C
INDIANA
7
B
BREWERSVILLE
Mill Race & Historic Mill Site
bridge
rubble
PR
SCIPIO
Mill Race Symbol
SAND CREEK

MUSCATATUCK VERNON FORK

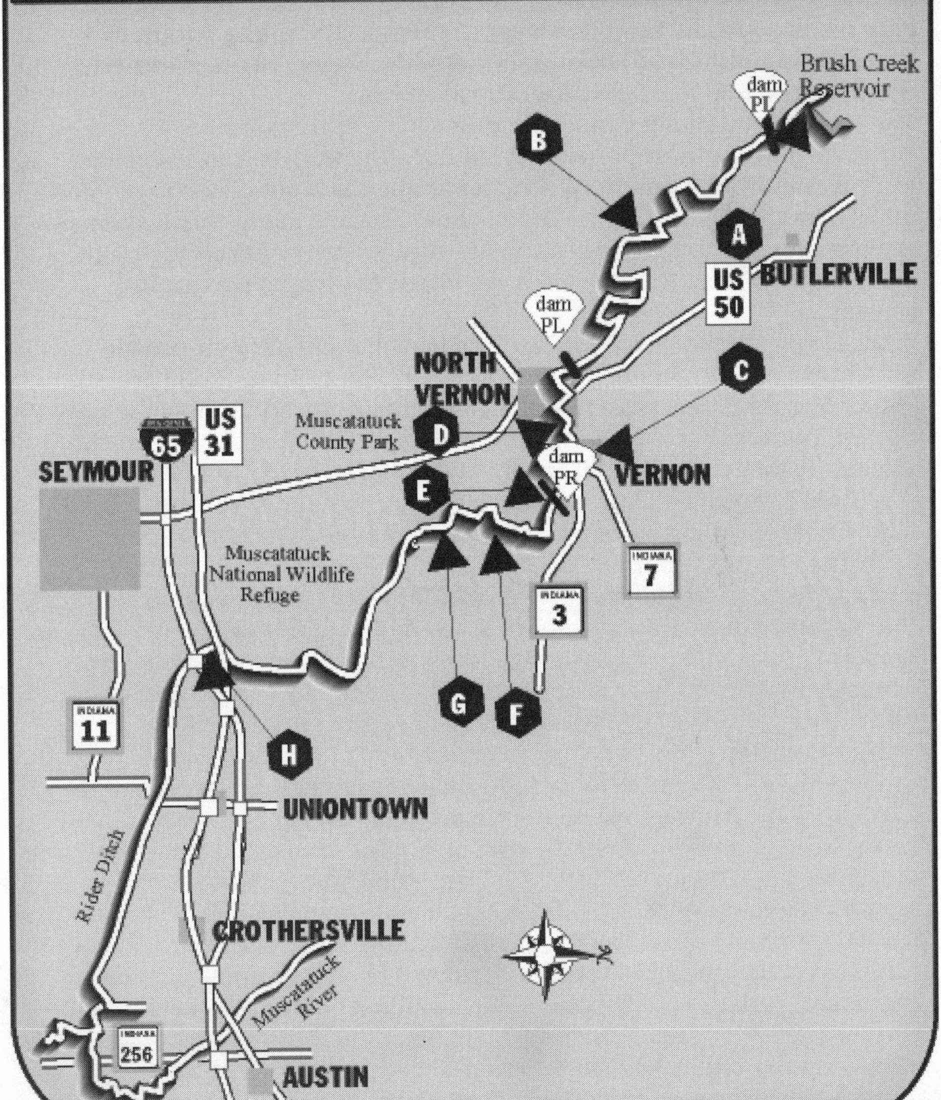
Brush Creek Reservoir
dam PL
B
A
US 50
BUTLERVILLE
dam PL
C
NORTH VERNON
Muscatatuck County Park
D
65
US 31
SEYMOUR
dam PR
VERNON
E
Muscatatuck National Wildlife Refuge
INDIANA 7
INDIANA 3
G
F
INDIANA 11
H
UNIONTOWN
Rider Ditch
CROTHERSVILLE
Muscatatuck River
INDIANA 256
AUSTIN

29. MUSCATATUCK RIVER VERNON FORK

- Wind away on the "stream of many turns"

To most paddlers, the Vernon Fork, also called North Fork, is the main stem of the Muscatatuck River. The 77 mile long Vernon Fork headwaters in southeast Decatur County, six miles east of Greensburg. The young fork flows southwestward through the extreme northwest Ripley, central Jennings and southeast Jackson counties to its confluence with the South Fork of the Muscatatuck, four miles south of Tampico, west of Austin. The many tributaries of the Vernon Fork include Square, Flatrock, Sugar, Brush, Vernon South Fork, Tea, Six Mile and Mutton creeks.

The stream is usually canoeable during the spring or after a summer downpour at above normal flow, but expect shallow riffles, logjams, and "rock gardens". The watershed is a small 1,000 square miles of southeast Indiana. The unique features along this seasonal stream are deep gorges, limestone bluffs, rock formations and outcroppings near the Vernon area where five parks border the stream.

From Brush Creek, north of Butlerville, the rocky stream travels southwest (dangerous high dam downstream, 0.5 mi.(P.L.) through Selmier State Forest, where the fork begins to meander down deeply carved, boulder-strewn, limestone canyons. Near North Vernon the stream begins to back up from the waterworks high dam (P.L.) if continuing on or (P.R.) for possible take out at North Vernon). The fork drops 55' along a six mile stretch in the vicinity of the town (county seat) of Vernon (town park access) which sits on a thin, narrow peninsular ridge nearly surrounded by the canyon stream. The Vernon Fork continues its rocky way through sharp bends of Muscatatuck County Park (carry down, Vinegar Mills site) and on down to and through Crosley Fish and Wildlife Area (bridge access, NW corner) old dam upstream breached in the middle (P.R.). Beyond Crosley FWA, the stream continues its journey along timbered and residential banks. Access is available at Jennings CR 275 W bridge and further on a mile or so at CR 400 W bridge. The valley widens as it flows southwest through farmland to the Muscatatuck National Wildlife Refuge, where the fork forms the southern boundary of the refuge between Jennings CR 900 W and US 31 (no river access in refuge). The US 31 bridge, SW corner is considered the paddling terminus. From I-65 to the confluence with the main branch, about four miles southeast of Tampico in the flat agricultural Scottsburg Lowlands, the fork has been dredged and is known as the silt-laden Rider Ditch. The Vernon Fork of the Muscatatuck lives up to its Delaware name, Mosch-ach-hit-tuck, "the stream of many turns".

USGS MAP(S): Butlerville,Vernon, Hayden, Chestnut Ridge, Crothersville,
Tampico, 1:24,000
VICINITY: Butlerville, North Vernon, Vernon, Jennings County
Seymour, Crothersville, Jackson County
STREAM DISTANCE/TRIPS: approx. 38 miles
four or more trips possible
LEVEL OF DIFFICULTY: Class 1
INFO SOURCES: Driftwood Fish Hatchery
4931 S. CR 250 W.
Vallonia, IN 47281
(812) 358-4110
Muscatatuck County Park
325 N SR 7&3
North Vernon, IN 47265
(812) 346-2953
Crosley Fish & Wildlife Area
2010 South SR 3
North Vernon, IN 47265
(812) 346-5596
Muscatatuck National Wildlife Refuge
12985 East US 50
Seymour, IN 47274 (812) 522-4352
AREA OUTFITTERS: none
GAMEFISH SPECIES: largemouth bass, smallmouth bass, rock bass, bluegill,
channel catfish, sunfish
CAMPING: Muscatatuck County Park
325 N SR 7&3,
North Vernon, IN 47265
(812) 346-2953
MEDICAL ASSISTANCE: Jennings Community Hospital
301 Henry Street
North Vernon, IN 47265
(812) 346-6200
Jackson County Hospital
200 N. Walnut
Seymour, IN 47274
(812) 522-2349
emergency 522-1400

ACCESS SITES	SECTION	RIVER MILES
A. Brush Creek DNR access, Butlerville, US 50, N to CR 460 E, N of the Muscatatuck State Development Center, downstream 0.5 mi. (high dam, (P.L.) through woods)	A-B	5 miles
B. Selmeir State Forest, SR 3 E on Jennings CR 350 N, N of North Vernon, carry down from forest road pullout at Summerfield Cemetery, if continuing on (P.L.) dam at N Vernon (P.R.) for alt. take out)	B-C	6.5 miles
C. Vernon Town Park, end of Factory St., NE of SR 7 & SR 3 bridge	C-D	2.2 miles
D. Muscatatuck County Park, staircase carry down, Vinegar Mills site, first pull out on park road	D-E	4 miles
E. Crosley FWA, bridge, NW corner, E of CR 75 W (P.R. at old breached dam upstream in low water	E-F	3.4 miles
F. Jennings CR 275 W bridge, SW corner, roadside park, follow lane to river path	F-G	3 miles
G. Jennings CR 400 W, SW corner, roadside pullout, steep bank carry down	G-H	13.5 miles
H. US 31 bridge, SW corner, utility pullout, carry down, take out only recommended		

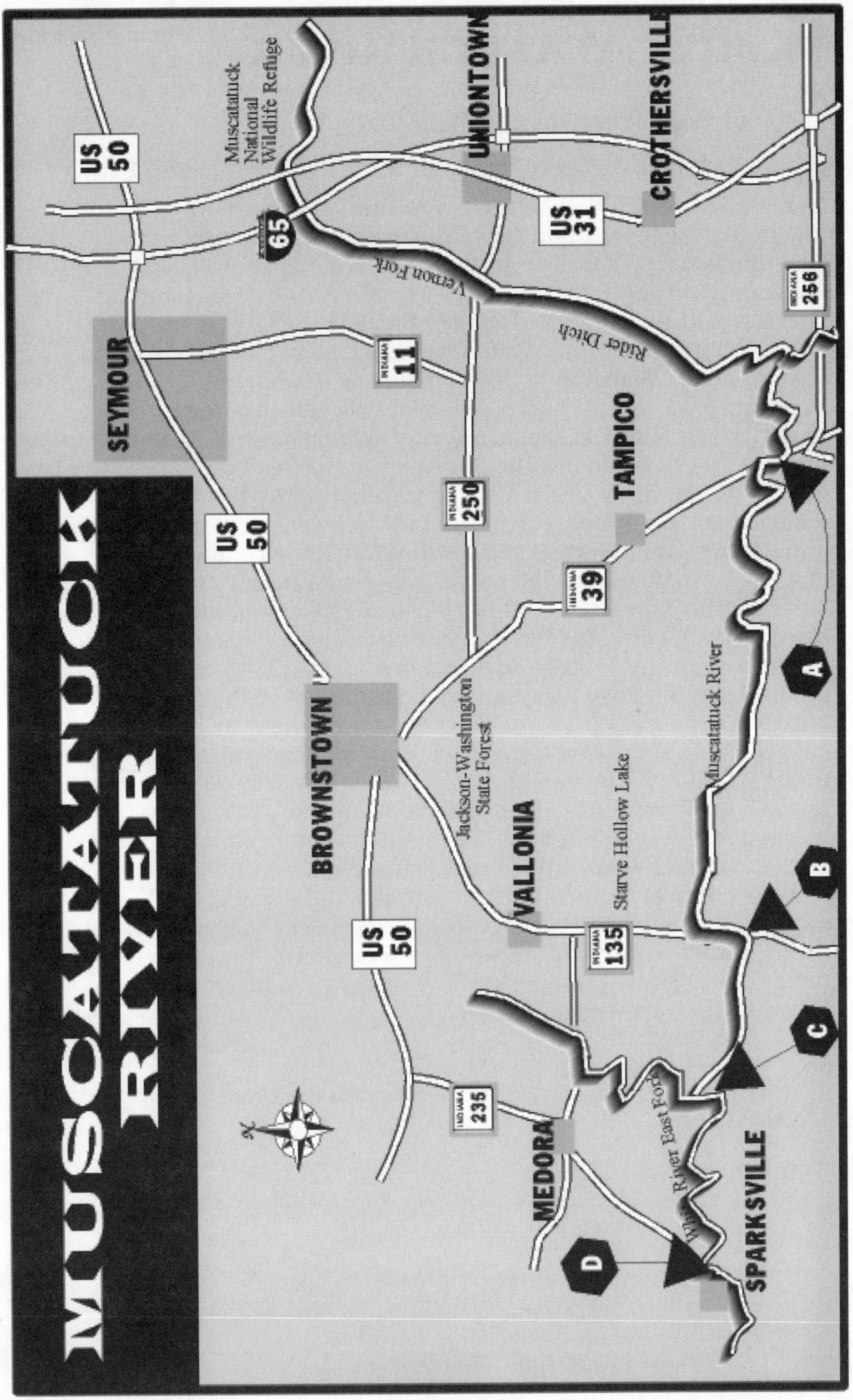
MUSCATATUCK RIVER
US 50
SEYMOUR
BROWNSTOWN
VALLONIA
TAMPICO
UNIONTOWN
CROTHERSVILLE
MEDORA
SPARKSVILLE
Muscatatuck National Wildlife Refuge
65
US 31
11
250
39
135
235
256
Vernon Fork
Rider Ditch
Jackson-Washington State Forest
Starve Hollow Lake
Muscatatuck River
White River East Fork
A
B
C
D

30. MUSCATATUCK RIVER

- Cool float fever on the "Big Cat"

The 53 mile long Muscatatuck River (the mother stream, or main fork, sometimes called the East or South Fork) heads up at the junction of Big Creek and Graham Creek, a mile or so north of Deputy, Jefferson County, and flows westward. The "Big Cat" forms the county line between Jennings and Scott as well as some of Jackson and Washington. Delaney Creek is the largest tributary. The confluence is at the White River East Fork, 3.6 miles south of Medora at the dead end of Wheeler Hollow Road.

In physiogeographical terms, the river descends from the Muscatatuck Regional Slope, a gently sloping plain of southeastern Indiana and flows across the flat valley of the Scottsburg Lowland to join the White River's East Fork at the edge of the Norman Upland. Paddle-wise, the lower reaches provide well spaced developed access and usually enough water (SR 39 to White River confluence) to make a casual trip. The deep river has a slow nearly deadwater current. The depressed stream has steep sloping, muddy banks that discourage landing. Wildlife is plentiful. Swamp forest borders the river from the SR 39 bridge to Smart Ditch. The best section is from the SR 39/Sage Ferry access downstream to the SR 135/Milport access (the two concrete county highway bridges between may serve as alternative accesses). From the Milport access to the White River confluence access, there are several permanent and seasonal dwellings along the south upland bank.

In the distance, the Knobs of Washington County shoot above the floodplain and as natural features inspire the horizons to the south. Flat agricultural lands border the stream and along several segments, only a fringe of vegetation serves as a border. For a longer trip continue on the White River East Fork from the confluence to the next access east of Sparksville, Jackson County or on to Lawrenceport, Lawrence County.

USGS MAP(S): Tampico, Vallonia, Medora 1:24,000
VICINITY: Milport, Sparksville, Brownstown, Seymour, Jackson County
STREAM DISTANCE/TRIPS: approx. 22 total miles
two or more trips
LEVEL OF DIFFICULTY: Class 1
HAZARDS/PORTAGES: low water, boulders, logs, motorboat wake
INFO SOURCE: Driftwood Fish Hatchery
4931 S. CR 250 W
Vallonia, IN 47281
(812) 358-4110
AREA OUTFITTERS: none
GAMEFISH SPECIES: catfish, carp, bass, bluegill
CAMPING: Delaney Park c/o

Washington County Parks
Salem, IN 47167
(10 miles northeast of Salem, east of SR 135 N)
(812) 883-4000
Starve Hollow SRA
4354 S. CR 275 W
Vallonia, IN 47218-9741
(812) 358-3464
Class A & B

MEDICAL ASSISTANCE: Jackson County Hospital
200 N. Walnut
Seymour, IN 47274
(812) 522-2349
emergency 522-1400

ACCESS SITES	SECTION	RIVER MILES
A. Sage's Ferry access, SR 39 bridge, SW corner	A-B	13 miles
B. SR 135 bridge, SE corner, Milport DNR access	B-C	3.5 miles
C. Confluence access site, S bank Muscatatuck & White River East Fork, 5 miles west of Milport & SR 135 on Wheeler Hollow Rd, dead end	C-D	5.8 miles
D. White River East Fork, Sparksville, Jackson County, 0.5 mi. east of Sparksville, 150 yards downstream from the Sparksville Pike Ferry bridge		

Southern Leopard Frog

31. LOST RIVER

• Survey the mystery river of southern Indiana

In the upper course of the 78-mile long stream, it flows underground and becomes a mysterious "lost river". The unique karst stream heads up in western Washington County near Smedley Station and flows through northern Orange County to join the White River East Fork in southern Martin County. In the first five miles, the stream cuts down 75 feet. The Lost River is "swallowed up" southwest of Orleans during low water near SR 337, through cracks and holes in the soft "swiss cheese-like" limestone bed. The subterranean stream has carved its way through an eight mile long straight channel. Enroute, at Wesley Chapel Gulf, the underground stream has collapsed, exposing the swallow hole. The Rise or Rises of the Lost River occur at and south of Orangeville. The water emerges quietly from a bluff at Orangeville, never reaching a boil, however the "true rise" is on a private farm one mile south of Orangeville. The stream meanders across an agricultural valley (several strainers) flowing southwest to flow under US 150, to join Lick Creek at West Baden. Crossing under SR 145 bridge at West Baden, the stream turns west and north recrossing US 150 and continuing through more agricultural valley where fields and country road come up to the wooded stream strip.

The first access is at the Orange CR 1025 bridge at the confluence of Sulfur Creek and Hoosier National Forest land at a horseshoe bend (31.3 mi. from the White River mouth). (The four access sites are evenly distributed). Lost River turns southwest again following the base of a 250' high ridge and recrossing US 150 for a third and final time. The log-choked stream runs alongside the south side of US 150 to Roland (portage low bridge) and enters Martin County. As the river curves south at Roland, a second access opportunity appears at Sam's Creek bridge, the county gravel road forks, 0.1 miles south of US 150. Beyond the Cave Creek confluence, a low dam needs portaged. Further west a few meanders is the national forest area of Paw Paw Marsh; a wildlife viewing area and where the Lost River nearly curves back on itself at an area known as The Narrows. Butler Bridge on CR 7 provides access at the southwest corner from a roadside pullout. Downstream the Lost River brushes Windom, crossing under the Windom Road bridge (no access) and meanders north for a final time. Curving south, the Lost River takes in Blue Creek and Simmons Creek, west of Yenne and flows beside CR 37 and under the last bridge (last access) before the White River East Fork.

Pioneers once utilized the stream for commerce, floating good-laden flatboats from the Orangeville Rise downstream to the White River East Fork. Thousand of hoop poles and staves, hams and bacon, and lumber were flatboated south. The limestone river bluffs produced lime and ruins of pioneers lime kilns still mar the banks. The Lost River Conservation Taskforce (1974) recommended the Lost River National Monument, a US National Park.

USGS MAP(S): French Lick, Hillham, Rusk 1:24,000
VICINITY: Orangeville, West Baden Springs, Roland, Orange County
Rusk, Yenne Windom, Martin County
STREAM DISTANCE/TRIPS: approx. 28-30 miles
three or more trips
LEVEL OF DIFFICULTY: Class 1
HAZARDS/PORTAGES: logjams, strainers, deadfalls, low water,
steep muddy banks, seasonal hunting,
low dam, low bridge
INFO SOURCES: Hoosier National Forest
811 Constitution Ave.
Bedford, IN 47421
(812) 358-2675
Sugar Ridge FWA
2310 E SR 364
Winslow, IN 47598
(812) 789-2724
Driftwood Fish Hatchery
4931 S CR 250 W
Vallonia, IN 47281
(812) 358-4110
AREA OUTFITTERS: none
GAMEFISH SPECIES: longear sunfish, channel catfish, bluegill, green sunfish,
freshwater drum, largemouth bass, flathead catfish,
warmouth, spotted bass, rock bass, carp, several
suckers
CAMPING: primitive camping permitted on HNF property
Martin State Forest
POB 599
US 50
Shoals, IN 47581
(812) 247-3491
Class C
MEDICAL ASSISTANCE: Orange County Hospital
Hospital Road
Paoli, IN 47454
(812) 723-2811
Jasper Memorial Hospital
800 W 9th
Jasper, IN 47546
(812) 482-9111 or 482-2345

ACCESS SITES	SECTION	RIVER MILES
A. Orange CR 1025 W bridge, SW corner, go 1.7 mi. on US 150 from West Baden W to Orange CR 960 W and turn N, continue 1.7 mi. to CR 1025 N & then turn N & proceed 0.5 mi. to the bridge at the Sulfur Creek confluence (easy low bank), parking for 2 cars	A-B	7 miles
B. Roland, 0.1 mi. south of US 150 on Martin CR 38/Powell Valley Rd., parking & access at the SE corner of bridge at the gravel road fork (high bank at Sam's Creek low bridge upstream & dam downstream)	B-C	9.5 miles
C. Martin CR 37, Butler bridge, SE corner carry down, two mi. S US 150 on Rush Rd	C-D	12.4 miles
D. Martin CR 37(last) bridge before White River East Fork, NE corner & alongside road shoulder, upstream near Blue Creek confluence, W of Yenne. 9 mi. S of US 150 & Lacy & on Windom Rd/CR 5 to CR 37, 4.2 mi. S of Windom bridge		

Log Jams on Lost River

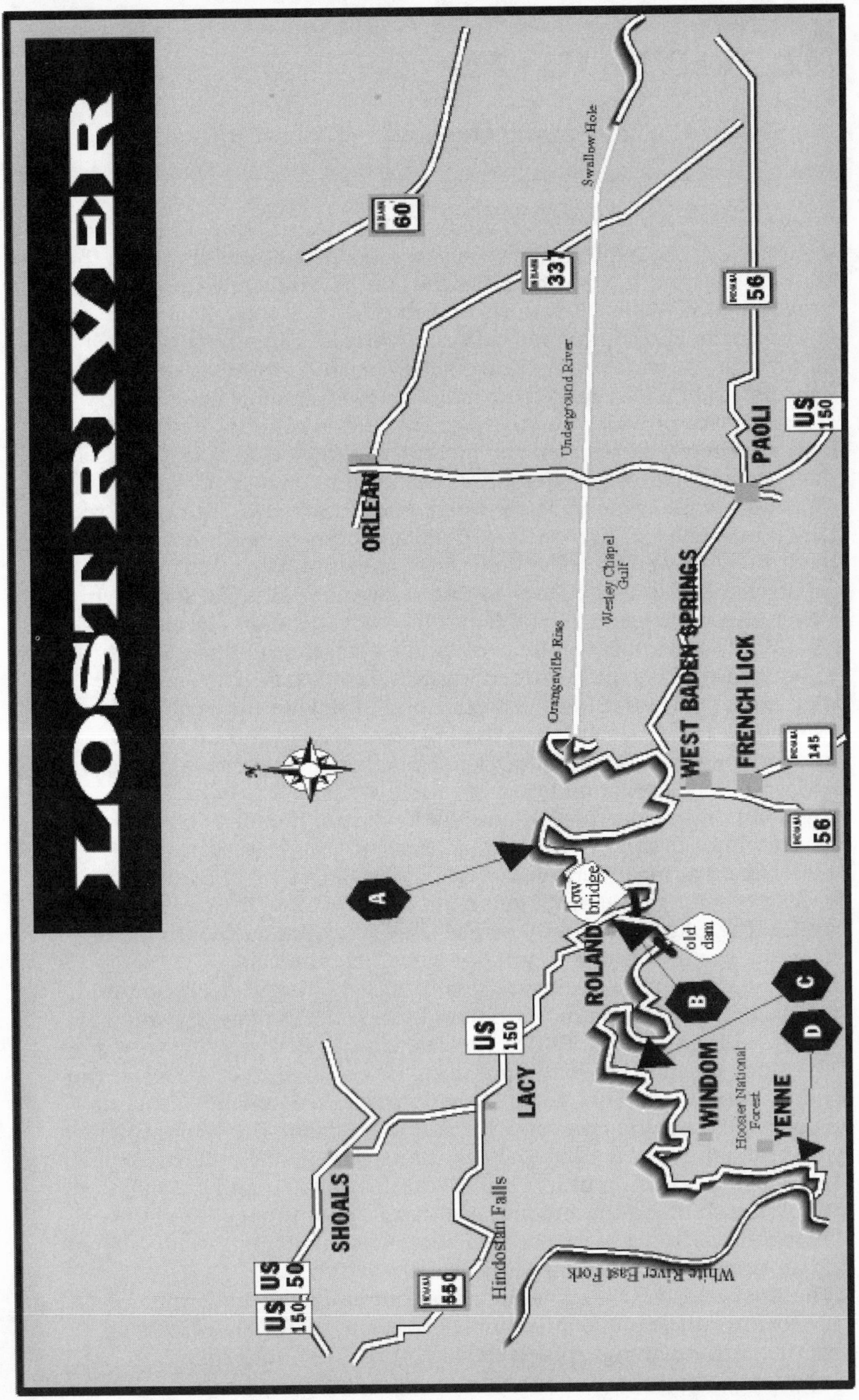
LOST RIVER
Swallow Hole
60
337
56
Underground River
US 150
PAOLI
ORLEAN
Wesley Chapel Gulf
Orangeville Rise
WEST BADEN SPRINGS
FRENCH LICK
145
56
A
low bridge
ROLAND
old dam
B
C
D
US 150
LACY
WINDOM
Hoosier National Forest
YENNE
SHOALS
Hindostan Falls
US 50
US 150
550
White River East Fork

32. WHITE RIVER

- Go for the flow along the southern bottomlands

From the riverhead downstream 50 miles to the Wabash River confluence, the White River goes at a moderate rate of flow with the gathered strength from the forks that drain nearly one third of Indiana. The White River flows at a rate of 12,300 cubic feet per second near the confluence with the Wabash. Sizeable tributaries are few in the wide valley train. The somewhat swift current closes the distance/time gap in river miles between the few access sites. The big river provides an environment that is conducive for types of fish (sturgeon, gar, goldeneye, mooneye, blue suckers) and mussels (fat pocketbook, white cats paw) not found in smaller streams. Southern cane, swamp cottonwood, sugarberry and Shumard's red oak trees thrive in the bottoms. Wildlife common to the south and west has followed the river valleys (Mississippi, Ohio, Wabash) upstream to the White River to find a lasting niche. The lower White River valley has several bayou cutoffs from the main stream.

The White River follows the county lines separating Knox County (north bank) Pike and Gibson counties (south bank). From the Petersburg access (SR 61 bridge), the White flows north along W. River Road and Beech Hills. The big river drops south and meanders around Seven Mill Bend. Further on cypress ponds and oxbow lagoons or small lakes occupy the vast floodplain. An old river cut off lies north of Buena Vista, west of the Pike-Gibson county line. Gradually turning southwest, the White forms yet another large meandering horseshoe bend at which the town of Decker occupies the northeast bend and Hazleton the southwest bend. The Old US 41 and the new US 41 bridges come into view (access, the first highway bridges since Petersburg).

Flow on the moderate current past the Dicksburg Hills, meandering south and west through bottomland forest north of Long Pond and Claypool Pond. Kelly's Riffle provides some faster water northwest of the Gordon Hills. Downstream, near the confluence (1.4 mi.) on the north bank is the once huge Little Cypress Pond swamp remnant separated from the river by a Knox County road. The White enters the Wabash just north of East Mt. Carmel, Indiana and Mt. Carmel, Illinois (access ramp at mouth). Continue downstream 1.5 miles on the Wabash along the Indiana east bank, past the mouth of the Patoka River to the east channel access at the Patoka Island site on River Road, south of East Mt. Carmel.

The East and West Fork of the river combine near the former Delaware village site of Missimimeech-hani, "Old Delaware Town " at the Lechauivitank, "place between the forks", four miles upstream from present-day Petersburg.

USGS MAP(S): Monroe City, Iona, Union, Patoka, Decker, East Mt. Carmel, Mt. Carmel, Wabash County, Ill.–Ind.1:24,000
VICINITY: Petersburg, Pike County
Hazleton, East Mt. Carmel, Gibson County
Decker, Knox County
Mt. Carmel, IL., Wabash County, IL
LEVEL OF DIFFICULTY: Class 1
HAZARDS/PORTAGES: wind, submerged objects, motorized boats, snags, limited access sites, distance
INFO SOURCES: Glendale FWA
RR#2 Box 300
Montgomery, IN 47558
(812) 644-7711
Avoca Fish Hatchery
POB 16
Avoca, IN 47420
(812) 279-1215
Sugar Ridge Fish & Wildlife Area
2310 E. SR 364
Winslow, IN 47598
(812) 789-2723
Pike State Forest
2310 E. SR 364
Winslow, IN 47598
(812) 789-2724
AREA OUTFITTERS: none
GAMEFISH SPECIES: sauger, catfish, carp
CAMPING: Sugar Ridge Fish & Wildlife Area
2310 E. SR 364
Winslow, IN 47598
(812) 789-2723
Class C
Pike State Forest
2310 E. SR 364
Winslow, IN 47598
(812) 789-2724
Class C
Pride's Creek Lake Park
1045 E. CR 400 N
Petersburg, IN 47567
(812) 354-6798
MEDICAL ASSISTANCE: Good Samaritan Hospital
520 S. 7th St.
Vincennes, IN 47591
(812) 882-5220
Gibson General Hospital
1808 Sherman Drive
Princeton, IN 47670
(812) 385-3401
Wabash General Hospital

1418 College Dr.
Mt. Carmel, IL 62863
(618) 262-8621

ACCESS SITES	SECTION	RIVER MILES
A. Petersburg north, SR 61 bridge, NW corner	A-B	27 miles
B. Hazleton, 1st St. & SR 56, upstream from US 41 bridge	B-C	20 miles
C. Wabash River, Patoka Island access, River Road, south of East Mt. Carmel, IN. also, Mt. Carmel access site at mouth		

Great Blue Heron on White River

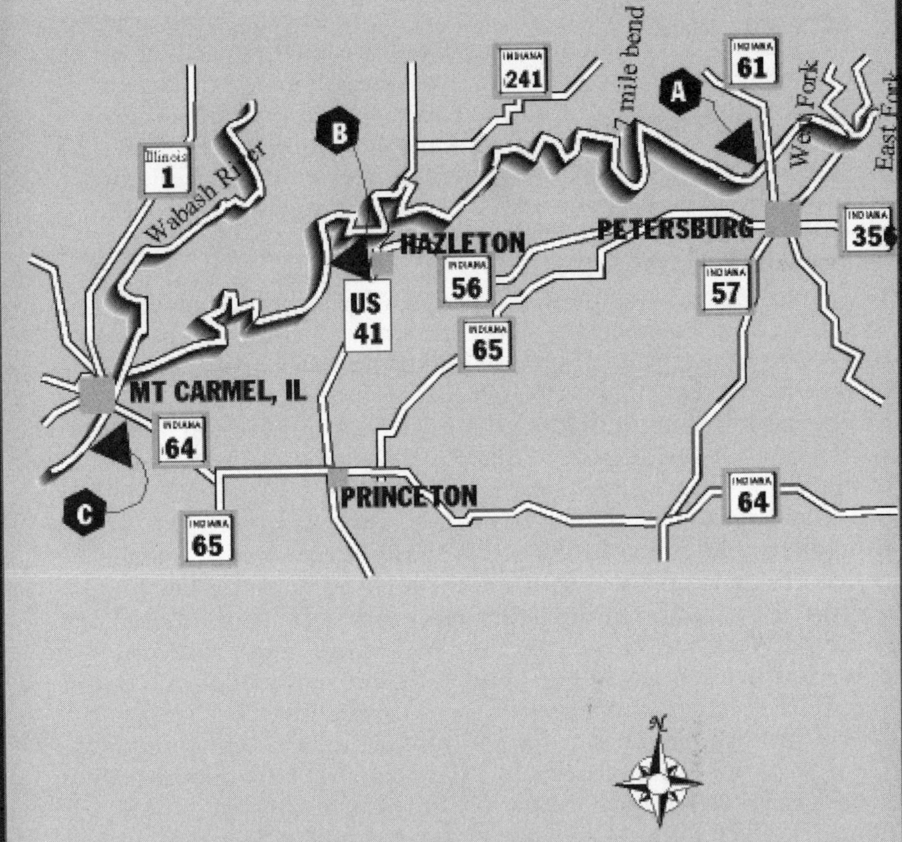
Illinois
1
Wabash River
B
INDIANA
241
mile bend
A
INDIANA
61
West Fork
East Fork
HAZLETON
PETERSBURG
INDIANA
356
INDIANA
56
INDIANA
57
US
41
INDIANA
65
MT CARMEL, IL
INDIANA
64
C
PRINCETON
INDIANA
64
INDIANA
65
N

WHITE RIVER

33. WHITEWATER RIVER

- Savor Indiana's fastest river

Only after heavy rain or as a result of hefty dam release from Brookville Lake would the Whitewater River live up to its enticing name. During normal flow or slightly above, there is no actual frothy white water however there are numerous swift riffles and rapids due to the gradient fall of nearly six feet per mile. The Delaware called the stream Wa-pa-ni-pay, "white clear water". The Whitewater valley was occupied by prehistoric mound building cultures thousands of years ago. The scenic valley is one of the most distinct in Indiana, with its majestic conical uplands and exposed ancient bedrock.

The Whitewater heads up in east central Indiana high plateau country and flows generally south as two forks that join at Brookville. The parallel forks are about ten miles apart and both have carved deep valleys through till moraine and drift. There is rarely enough water to paddle the East Fork however on foot it is spectacular at Richmond's White River Gorge Park. The "Queen City of the Whitewater Valley" allows a close up experience of some of the oldest rocks in Indiana. The valley of the East Fork is filled with Brookville Lake from Liberty south to Brookville (see Brookville Lake). The long north-to-south lake dam and tailwater lies just north of Brookville. On the south side of Brookville, the East Fork joins the West Fork. From the Franklin County seat, the Whitewater flows southeast crossing the Ohio state line and joining the Great Miami River, not far upstream from the Ohio River.

The West Fork fares better for paddling with its larger watershed. The city park at Cambridge City offers the first best opportunity to access the stream, however paddle only during normal and above flow. The West Fork picks up current, although shallow at first, south of Milton where Greens Fork joins. About four hours, between Milton and Waterloo downstream is a feeder dam (P.R.). East of Waterloo is one of the few bridges between Cambridge City Crietzs Park access and the private south Connersville Whitewater Camping access (fee site), an eighteen river mile distance.

South of Connersville, the West Fork reenters the countryside paralleling SR 121 and the Whitewater Valley railroad (seasonal excursions) to Metamora. The stream meanderings become more scenic as it crosses into Franklin County. An access site is located at the feeder dam (P.L.) d.s. of Laurel. A 28.3 mile segment of the West Fork and main stem, from Laurel to New Trenton bridge, (17.1 miles from the confluence) qualifies as a State Natural & Scenic River. A 14 mile canal section between Laurel and Brookville has been restored with a plan for an eight mile pedestrian path. The Whitewater Canal historic site includes a restored grain mill, tow

path, covered bridge aqueduct, locks and a canal boat ride at Metamora, the next village downstream. The West Fork tumbles under and runs alongside US 52 through the narrow valley floor to Brookville and the confluence with the East Fork and the start of the Whitewater River. There is local canoe livery near the river confluence and alongside US 52 (access). River and road (US 52/SR 1) continue down the swift rocky bed of Ordovician age shales, where gentle pastoral beauty meets wildness in the compact valley setting. Public access is scarce between Brookville and Harrison, Ohio (the most popular section of the river).
The experience and the river continue across the state line into Ohio. From the West Harrison (access) bridge the river continues southeast towards the Great Miami River, nine to ten miles away. Riverside homes abound near the mouth in the lower reaches. There are no opportunities for access despite roadside pullouts. The widening river goes under I-275 and enters the Great Miami near Elizabethtown downstream from Cleves, (one of the most degraded but improving streams in Ohio). Continue downstream about five miles on the Great Miami (6.2 miles to Ohio River from mouth) to the access site on the left/east shore where a cove shelters the ramp and parking area of Shawnee Lookout, a Hamilton County Park (no camping).

USGS MAP(S): Cambridge City, Jacksonburg, Brownsville, Connersville, Alpine, Metamora, Brookville, Whitcomb, Cedar Grove, Harrison 1:24,000
VICINITY: Cambridge City, Milton, Wayne County
Connersville, Fayette County
Laurel, Metamora, Brookville, Cedar Grove, New Trenton, Franklin County
West Harrison, Dearborn County
Harrison, Elizabethtown, Hamilton County, Ohio
LEVEL OF DIFFICULTY: Class 1
HAZARDS/PORTAGES: low water, submerged rocks, ltd. access
INFO SOURCES: Indiana DNR Div. of Outdoor Recreation
Streams & Trails
402 W. Washington St.
Rm. 271
Indianapolis, IN 46204
(317) 232-4070
Cikana Fish Hatchery
2650 SR 44
Martinsville, IN 46151
(765) 342-5527
Ohio DNR
Div. of Watercraft
District VII
10556 McKelvey Road

Cincinnati, OH 45240
(513) 851-1755

AREA OUTFITTERS: Morgan's Brookville Canoe Center
7040 Whitewater River Lane
Brookville, IN 47012
(800) WE-CANOE or (765) 647-4904
Metamora Canoe Rental
Rt #1
Metamora, IN 47030
(317) 647-5434
Whitewater River Canoe Rental
US Hwy 52 W, POB 2
Brookville, IN 47012
(765) 647-2330 or 647-5434

CAMPING: Brookville Lake DNR
Quakertown SRA, Mounds SRA
P.O. Box 100, Brookville, IN
47012 (765) 647-2657 & 2658
Class AA & A
Whitewater Memorial State Park
1418 S. SR 101
Liberty, IN 47353
(812) 458-5565
Class A & B
Franklin County Park
c/o Franklin County Parks & Recreation
7178 Blue Creek Rd.
Brookville, IN 47012
(765) 647-4422

MEDICAL ASSISTANCE: Fayette Memorial Hospital
1941 Virginia Ave.
Connersville, IN 47331
(765) 825-5131
Margaret Mary Community Hospital
321 Mitchell Ave.
Batesville, IN 47006
(812) 934-6624
Franciscan Medicenter at Harrison
10450 New Haven Road
Harrison, Ohio 45030
(513) 367-2222
Dearborn County Hospital
600 Wilson Creek Rd
Lawrenceburg, IN 47025
(812) 537-1010

ACCESS SITES	SECTION	RIVER MILES
A. Crietzs Park, Cambridge City, three blocks N of Main St./US 40 on Foote or Center St. (P.R.) at feeder dam, 4 hours downstream	A-B	10.6 miles
B. Waterloo bridge, Fayette CR 440, SW corner	B-C	8 miles
C. New Connersville public access, located north of Whitewater Camping, Connersville, SR 121, 1.5 mi. S of junction of SR 44 (fee)	C-D	12 miles
D. Laurel Feeder Dam, (P.L.) 1.6 mi. SE of Laurel & SR 121 on Dam Rd., 100 yd. carry (alt. downstream site, Whitewater Canal Historic site, Metamora, Goose Creek Rd., canal to river)	D-E	17 miles
E. Morgan's Canoe & Outdoor Center, Brookville, W of US 52, 7040 Whitewater River Lane	E-F	16 miles
F. West Harrison, Ohio state line Jameson Rd. bridge, S State St. & Campbell Rd., NE corner. From I-74, exit & go west on New Haven Rd. to Harrison Ave. Turn right & proceed to Main &/S State St. Turn south & continue to Jameson bridge. Access wooded lane between RR & bridge (alt. access upstream under I-74 bridge, SW corner, along River Rd. at Logan creek confluence; also Lawrenceburg Rd. & Suspension Bridge Rd., SE of Harrison, d.s. E bank, with permission)	F-G	13.6 miles
G. Great Miami River, Shawnee Lookout, Hamilton County Park, River Rd., SW of Cleves & Elizabethtown, OH, E bank		

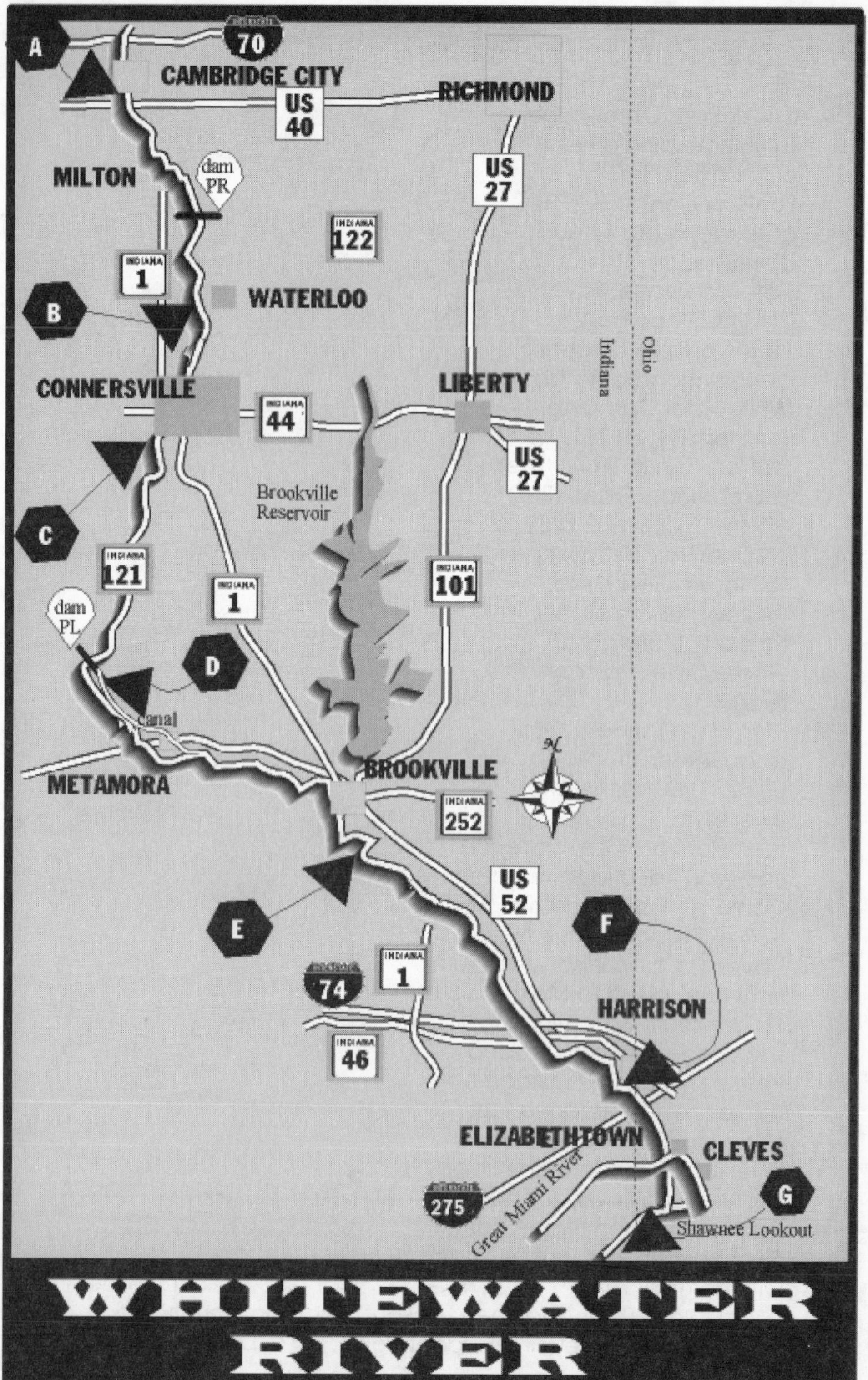
70
A
CAMBRIDGE CITY
RICHMOND
US 40
MILTON
dam PR
US 27
INDIANA 122
INDIANA 1
WATERLOO
B
CONNERSVILLE
LIBERTY
INDIANA 44
Indiana
Ohio
US 27
Brookville Reservoir
C
INDIANA 121
INDIANA 1
INDIANA 101
dam PL
D
canal
METAMORA
BROOKVILLE
INDIANA 252
E
US 52
F
74
INDIANA 1
HARRISON
INDIANA 46
ELIZABETHTOWN
CLEVES
Great Miami River
275
G
Shawnee Lookout
WHITEWATER RIVER

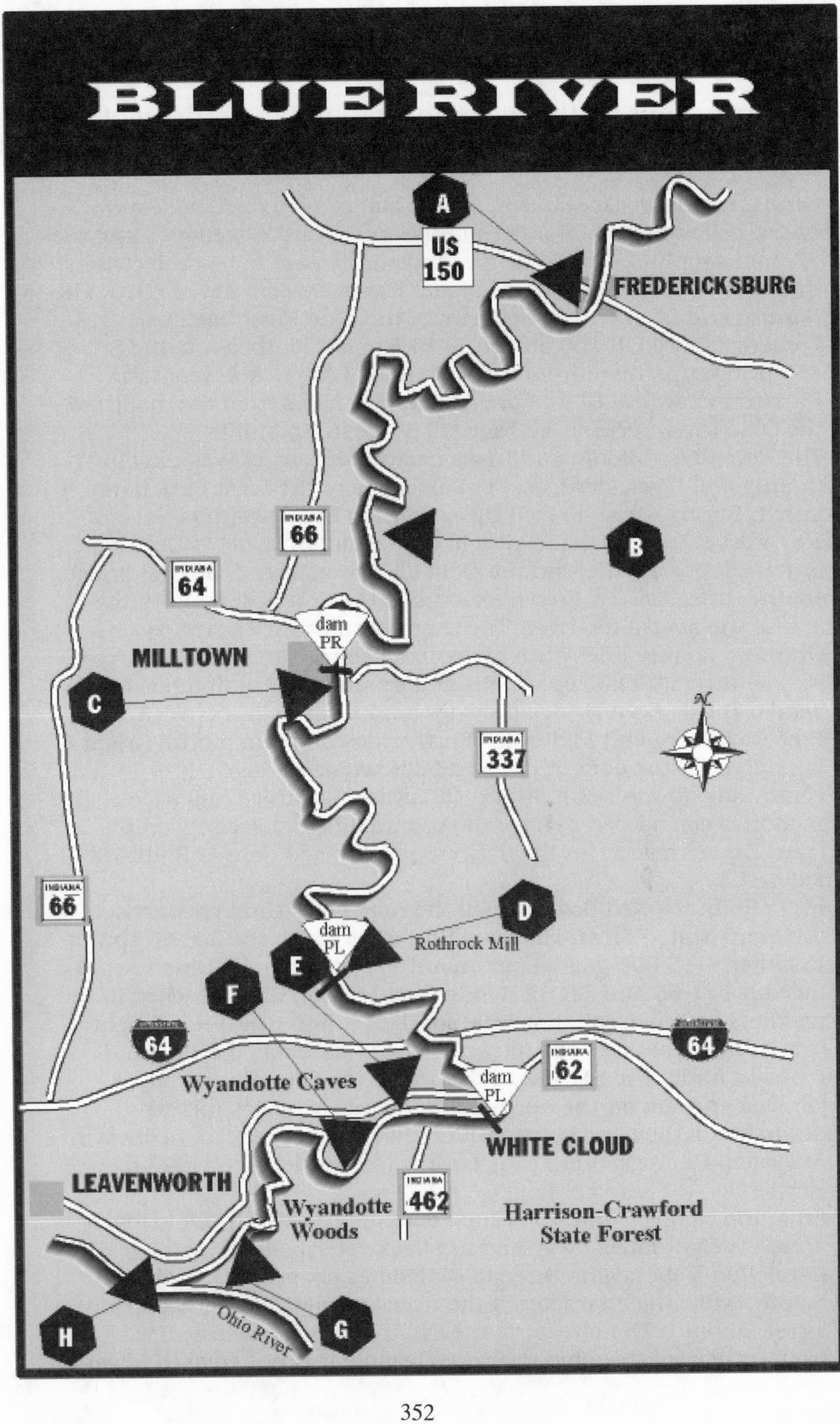
BLUE RIVER
A
US 150
FREDERICKSBURG
INDIANA 66
B
INDIANA 64
dam PR
MILLTOWN
C
INDIANA 337
N
INDIANA 66
D
dam PL
Rothrock Mill
E
F
64
64
INDIANA 62
Wyandotte Caves
dam PL
WHITE CLOUD
LEAVENWORTH
Wyandotte Woods
INDIANA 462
Harrison-Crawford State Forest
Ohio River
G
H

34. BLUE RIVER

- Ease along on the most natural Indiana stream of its size

Bends, rapids, rocks, chutes, bluffs, half canyons, islands, springs, caves, hollows and bottoms comprise much of the scenery along the 77-mile long Blue River, the first Indiana stream to be protected by the Natural Scenic and Recreational Rivers System Act of 1973. The Natural and Scenic River segment of the Blue River begins at Fredericksburg US 150 and runs 45.5 miles southeast to the SR 462 bridge upstream from the Blue River Chapel access, in the Harrison-Crawford State Forest (about 11 miles from the mouth of the Ohio River access). Average fall is 3.7 feet per mile.

The Blue River Middle Fork rises near the Knobs of Washington County and flows southwest of Salem where the West Fork flows into it. Springs arise to feed the struggling Blue, south of Salem. The most scenic spring to view (from a county bridge) is Beck's Mill (private property). Behind the Old Mill Canoe Livery, US 150 bridge, southwest corner, at Fredericksburg is the first best opportunity to access the spring-fed river. The river becomes the Harrison-Crawford county line south of Fredericksburg where it has carved its way through hills and knobs and around long bluff topped bends. Totten Ford Bridge provides a take out point between Fredericksburg and Milltown. Further downstream, portage right if taking out at the dam or livery at Milltown or portage left if continuing downstream. From Milltown to Rothrock Mill access, this section is considered to have the best rapids and scenery on the river. Do not try to run the dangerous breached dam at Rothrock Mill (P.L.).

From Rothrock Mill downstream the river flows through Harrison-Crawford State Forest. Harrison Spring (private), the largest spring in Indiana (18,000 gallons per minute), flows into the Blue River 0.3 mile above I-65 and SR 62. White Cloud dam (P.L.), breached in the middle, is downstream one mile south of (I-64), past the wrought iron bridge. The river abruptly turns west paralleling SR 62 and crossing under the SR 462 bridge where the Blue River Chapel (access) appears on the north bank. About two miles further downstream the river curves south, away from the state highway to Stagestop Campground at the base of Greenbrier Knob (822 ft. elev.).

From the campground, the Blue's confluence with the Ohio River access is eight miles away and flat backwater ponded by the Cannelton Dam begins three to sometimes six miles from the mouth, while the character of the river changes to level floodplain forest. About 0.75 mile above the Old Iron Bridge access, the backwater from the Ohio river dam begins. It is not advised to canoe the Ohio River due to the commercial river traffic. The many springs that flow through the middle of Indiana cave country account for the aqua blue color of the river referred to by the place name "Blue".

USGS MAP(S): Fredericksburg, Hardinsburg, Milltown, Depauw, Corydon West, Leavenworth 1:24,000
VICINITY: Fredericksburg, Milltown, White Cloud, Leavenworth, Corydon, Washington, Crawford & Harrison counties
STREAM DISTANCE/TRIPS: over 50 miles
seven or more trips
LEVEL OF DIFFICULTY: Class 1
HAZARDS/PORTAGES: submerged boulders & logs, low dams at Milltown (P.R.), Rothrock Mill (P.L.), White Cloud (P.L.), low water, fallen trees, seasonal hunting, deadwater in lower reaches
INFO SOURCES: Harrison-Crawford State Forest
7240 Old Forest Rd. SW
Corydon, IN 47112
(812) 738-8232
The Blue River Commission
POB 51
New Salisbury, IN 47161
Indiana DNR Div. of Outdoor Recreation
Streams & Trails
402 W. Washington St., Rm. 271
Indianapolis, IN 46204
(317) 232-4070
AREA OUTFITTERS: Old Mill Canoe Rental
SR 150 Box 60
Fredericksburg, IN 47120
(812) 472-3140
Cave Country Canoe & Kayak
POB 2171 (Milltown headquarters)
Marengo, IN 47140
(812) 365-2705
GAMEFISH SPECIES: smallmouth bass, bluegill, carp, channel catfish, sauger, black & white crappie, freshwater drum, northern bass, rock bass
CAMPING: Harrison-Crawford State Forest
7240 Old Forest Rd. SW
Corydon, IN 47112
(812) 738-8232
Class C, youth rally
Wyandotte Woods SRA
RR1 Box 85
Leavenworth, IN 47137
(812) 738-2782
Class A
MEDICAL ASSISTANCE: Harrison County Hospital
245 Atwood St. #2
Corydon, IN 47112
(812) 738-4251

ACCESS SITES	SECTION	RIVER MILES
A. Fredericksburg, US 150 bridge, SW corner, Old Mill Canoe livery (private site)	A-B	17 miles
B. Totten Ford Rd. bridge, SE corner, also Twelve Mile Camp, Cave County Canoes, (private access sites at bridge)	B-C	7 miles
C. Milltown, public access site, Cave County Canoes, (P.R.) to take out at dam & canoe livery (P.L.) to continue trip	C-D	13 miles
D. Rothrock Mill & Dam (collapsed breach) (P.L.), Harrison-Crawford SF , (P.L.) at White Cloud Dam d.s.)	D-E	9.5 miles
E. Blue River Chapel access, Wyandotte Woods SRA, Harrison-Crawford SF, downstream of SR 462 bridge, SW bank, access from SR 62	E-F	1.5 miles
F. Stagestop Campground access, Harrison-Crawford SF, access from SR 62 (seasonal)	F-G	5.7 miles
G. Old Iron Bridge access, Wyandotte Woods SRA, NE corner	G-H	2.8 miles
H. Ohio River, W bank at mouth, Lock & Dam #44, Harrison-Crawford SF		

Great Blue Heron Fishing Below White Cloud Dam

Rothrock Mill Ruins & Breached Dam

35. LITTLE BLUE RIVER

- Passage downstream to the Ohio River

The Little Blue River is entirely a Crawford County stream. It rises at the confluence of Dog Creek, Bird Hollow Creek, Brownstown Creek and Camp Fork Creek, near the town park (carry down access) in Old English (35.85 miles from the Ohio River mouth). (Flooding in recent years has resulted in relocating a New English on higher ground, northeast). Approximately two miles downstream is a low water bridge (CR 132) to portage left. The Little Blue cuts its meandering way north to south of Grantsburg, picking up Otter Creek, flowing east under new SR 37 and on to the old SR 37 bridge. The Old SR 37 bridge is now closed and may serve as an access site, carry down, southeast side of bridge (the first best access). Downstream from the Old SR 37 bridge and the Bogard Creek junction begins the Hoosier National Forest. The stream curves by the base of 810' Seton Knob. Carnes historic mill site and nature preserve is located at a hairpin bend. Watch for low dam (P.L.). There are several logjams between English and Carnes Mill. The Hoosier National Forest is on both sides of the river in some places.

The stream continues its meandering way, skirting SR 37 just north of the I-64 exit 86 ramps. A carry down is possible from the SR 37 roadside pullouts however the best access is the first pullout north of the I-64 interstate at the wildlife viewing site sign, east side of the highway. Passing under the interstate, Little Blue curves east of Sulfur and crosses under SR 62/66 between Sulfur and Beechwood. There is a second dam (P.R.) approximately one mile after passing under I-64. Parking and access is possible at the dead end barrier of Old SR 62/66, SW corner. Carry down is steep and the river is cut down (muddy banks). The Stinking Fork joins the Little Blue southeast of Sulfur Springs a mile or so, as the crow flies. The stream flows under the old Deuchars bridge (closed) and on through the national forest to the Crawford CR 4 bridge (access) south of Beechwood and SR 62/66, north of Alton and the Ohio River. Welch Dam, a third dam (P.R.), is located one mile down river of the CR 4 bridge. Little Blue picks up Turkey Fork in the final segment of national forest along the stream. There is no access at the CR 38 (iron) bridge and surrounding settlement and the water may be dead, backed up from the high water of the Ohio River. Mill Creek enters north of Alton. The last bridge and take-out before the Ohio River is on the northwest bank of High Street bridge at Alton. A short segment of the Ohio River may be sampled from the confluence to the Alton village park.

The scenic stream is eligible for for inclusion in the National Wild, Scenic and Recreational River program. There are several steep mountain laurel, blueberry, bush honeysuckle, scarlet oak and black maple are some of the forest species found along the twisting bends. The stream turns sluggish early in summer. It is legally navigable for 10.6 miles upstream from the Ohio and motor boats can be encountered up as far as four miles.

USGS MAP(S): English, Beechwood, Alton 1:24,000
VICINITY: English, Grantsburg, Sulphur, Beechwood, Alton, Crawford County
STREAM DISTANCE/TRIPS: approx. 26.5 miles
three or more trips
LEVEL OF DIFFICULTY: Class 1
HAZARDS/PORTAGES: low water, high water, low bridge portage, log jams, deadwater, strainers, submerged, boulders & logs, low dams at Carnes Mill (P.L.), Sulphur (P.R.), Welch Dam (P.R.), motor boats will venture four miles up river
INFO SOURCES: Hoosier National Forest
811 Constitution Ave
Bedford, IN 47421
(812) 275-5987
Tell City HNF Ranger District
248 15th St.
Tell City, IN 47586
(812) 547-7051
AREA OUTFITTERS: none
GAMEFISH SPECIES: bluegill, largemouth, smallmouth, rock & Kentucky bass, Ohio River muskellunge, warmouth, green sunfish, channel catfish, white bass, spotted bass, redear, white crappie, longear sunfish
CAMPING: primitive canoe camping permitted on Hoosier National Forest
developed HNF camping at Celina-Indian Lakes, Buzzard Roost HNF on Ohio River, downstream of Alton, Tipsaw Lake & Saddle Lake, Perry Co. SR 37
Contacts: Tell City HNF Ranger District
(812) 547-7051
Hoosier National Forest
(812) 275-5987
MEDICAL ASSISTANCE: Harrison County Hospital
245 Atwood St. #2
Corydon, IN 47112
(812) 738-4251
Perry County Memorial Hospital
1 Hospital Rd.
Tell City, IN 47586
(812) 547-7011

ACCESS SITE	SECTION	RIVER MILES
A. English town park, carry down headwater access, confluence of Dog Creek & Camp Fork Creek (P.L.) Crawford CR 132 low bridge, d.s. 2 mi.)	A-B	6 miles
B. Grantsburg Old SR 37 bridge, SE corner, one mi. E of new SR 37, steep carry down (P.L.) at Carnes Mill Dam	B-C	6 miles
C. SR 37, roadside pullout & carry down (steep). N of I-64, exit 86, 0.6 mi., HNF wildlife viewing site, overflow parking at I-64 ramp entry pullouts (P.R.) at Sulphur Dam	C-D	8 miles
D. Old SR 62 bridge dead end, E of Sulfur, 100 yd. downstream of new SR 62 bridge, SW corner (100 mm), carry down steep bank)	D-E	6 miles
E. Crawford CR 4 bridge (green metal), NW corner & carry down, S of SR 62 & Beechwood, N of Alton & Ohio River (P.R.) d.s. at Welch Dam	E-F	6.5 miles
F. Alton access, E High St. bridge, NW corner, last take out before Ohio River	F-G	1 mile
G. Ohio River, Alton village access, village park		

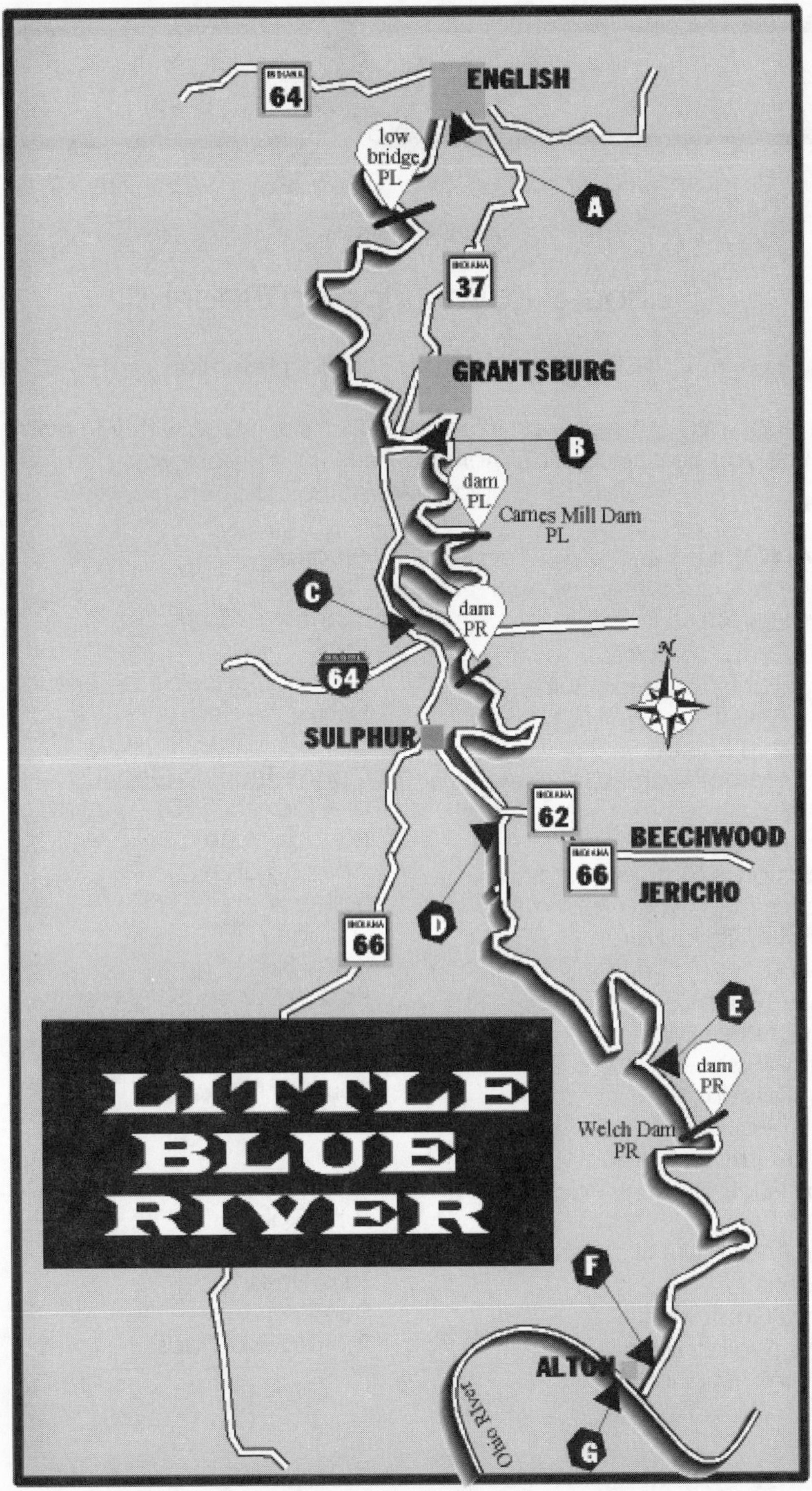

ENGLISH
64
low bridge PL
A
37
GRANTSBURG
B
dam PL
Carnes Mill Dam PL
C
dam PR
64
SULPHUR
62
BEECHWOOD
66
JERICHO
D
66
E
dam PR
Welch Dam PR
F
ALTON
G
Ohio River
N
LITTLE BLUE RIVER

Appendix A

Canoe & Kayak Tripping Gear List

Be Prepared: The Ten Paddling Essentials

The ten paddling essentials are items that should go with you every time you go afield. Using them properly will increase your comfort, safety, and enjoyment of the outdoors.

<u>CANOE LIST</u>

TEN ESSENTIALS
Map and Compass
Flashlights/Batteries, Bulbs
First Aid Kit
Knife
Waterproof Matches/Case
Fire Starter
Extra Food
Additional Clothing
Water/Filter/Aqua Tablets
Whistle/Signal Mirror

NICE TO HAVE
Insect Repellant
Sun Glasses
Sun Screen
Toilet Paper
Field Guides, Notebook, etc
Day Pack or Fanny Pack

TEN PADDLING NONESSENTIALS
Infants
Glass Containers
Keys, Wallet, Money
Guns & Weapons
Alcohol
Fireworks
Expensive Cameras
Pets
Lack of Canoeing Experience
Heavy Coolers

<u>Canoe Tripping Gear List</u>
Life Jackets (PFD)
Portage Yoke
Tracking Lines
Bailer
Sponge
Spray Skirt
Paddles (2 each)
Whistle
Waterproof Thwart Bags
Portage Packs
Duct Tape

BEDROOM
Tent/Stakes
Ground Cloth
Tarp/Lines
Sleeping Bags
Therma Rest Pads

KITCHEN
Cooking Pots
Skillet
Coffee/Tea Pot
Plates
Bowls
Mugs
Spatula
Spoons
Knife
Cooking Glove
Spices
Cooking Oil
Stove/Repair Parts
Fuel
Fire Grate/Sack
Fire Starter
Waterproof Matches
Butane Lighter
Soap/Pot Scratcher
Towel
Table Cloth-Small
Food (from menu planner)
Water
Water Bottles
Water Filter or Purifier
Aqua Tablets
Water Carrier
Trash Bags
Kitchen Pack
Snacks
Wild Foods

FURNITURE & APPLIANCES
Maps
Map Case
GPS
Compass
Permits
Lantern/Fuel
Candle Lantern/Candles
Flashlights/Batteries, Bulbs
Head Lamp/Batteries/Bulbs

FIRST AID KIT
Toilet Paper/Bag
Toilet Trowel
Journal/Pens/Pencil
Dental Floss/Needles
Saw
Dirty Clothes Bag

PERSONAL ITEMS
Knife
Insect Repellant
Sunscreen
Sunglasses/Restraint Strap
Hat
Toothbrush/Paste
Pack Towels
Camera Gear
Fishing Gear
Books/Field Guides

CLOTHES CLOSET
WARM WEATHER
Shorts (2)
Lightweight Pants (1)
Underwear (3)
Long Underwear
T-Shirts (2)
Heavyweight Shirt
Sweater or Fleece
Socks (3)
Hat
Gloves
Raingear
Camp Shoes
Boots
Old Tennis Shoes

COLD WEATHER
Wet Suit
Fleece or Wool Pants (2)
Non-Cotton Underwear (3)

Sweater or Fleece
Socks (4)
Winter Hat
Winter Gloves
Glove Liners
Poggies
Raingear
Camp Shoes
Warm, Waterproof Boots

KAYAK LIST

Life Jacket (PFD)
Paddle
Whistle
Spray Skirt
Pump
Paddle Float
Sponge
Spare Paddle
Tow System
Deck Compass
Flashlight for Night Paddling
Signal Kit;
- Flares
- Mirrors
- Smoke
- Distress Ribbon
- ERIRB

Repair Kit/Rudder Parts, etc.
Deck Bag
Gear Bags
Waterproofing

NAVIGATION GEAR
Charts/Maps
Map Case
GPS
Hand Bearing Compass
VHF Radio
Tide & Current Tables
Coast Pilots
Weather Radio
Binoculars

KITCHEN
Cooking Pots

Skillet
Coffee/Tea Pot
Plates
Bowls
Mugs
Spatula
Spoons
Knife
Cooking Glove
Spices
Cooking Oil
Stove/Repair Parts
Fuel
Fire Grate/Sack
Fire Starter
Waterproof Matches
Butane Lighter
Soap/Pot Scratcher
Towel
Table Cloth-Small
Food (from menu planner)
Water
Water Bottles
Water Filter or Purifier
Aqua Tablets
Water Carrier
Trash Bags
Kitchen Pack
Snacks
Wild Foods

FURNITURE & APPLIANCES
Lantern/Fuel
Candle Lantern/Candles
Flashlights/Batteries, Bulbs
Head Lamp/Batteries/Bulbs

FIRST AID KIT
Toilet Paper/Bag
Toilet Trowel
Journal/Pens/Pencil
Dental Floss/Needles
Saw
Dirty Clothes Bag

BEDROOM
Tent/Stakes

Ground Cloth
Tarp/Lines
Sleeping Bags
Therma Rest Pads

PERSONAL ITEMS
Knife
Insect Repellant
Sunscreen
Sunglasses/Restraint Strap
Hat
Toothbrush/Paste
Pack Towels
Camera Gear
Fishing Gear
Books/Field Guides

CLOTHES CLOSET
Paddling Jacket/Dry Top
Wetsuit/Dry Suit
Shortie Top
Paddling Sweater
Paddling Footwear
Paddling Gloves/Poggies
Shorts (2)
Lightweight Pants (1)
Underwear (1)
Long Underwear
T-Shirts (2)
Vest
Sweater or Fleece
Foul Weather Hat
Camp Shoes
Old Tennis Shoes

OTHER GEAR
Sea Anchor
Folding Crab Trap
Helmet for Surf Zones
Para Kite/Sail Rig

Source: JL Waters

Appendix B

AREA OUTFITTERS

AREA OUTFITTERS	LAKES	STREAMS
Blue's Canoe Livery 6700 W. Lowell Rd. (entrance to Heflin Memorial Park) Columbus, IN 47201 (812) 526-9851 (812) 376-6293		Driftwood River
Bristol Canoe & Kayak Bristol, IN 46507 (219) 848-4465		St. Joseph River of Lake Michigan
Canoe Country 7109 S. River Road Daleville, IN 47334 (888) 378-7358		White RIver East Fork
Cave Country Canoe & Kayak POB 2171 (Milltown Headquatrs) Marengo, IN 47140 (812) 365-2705		Blue River
Clements Canoes 613 Lafayette Ave. Crawfordsville, IN 47933 (765) 362-2781 or 362-9864		Sugar Creek
Daily Canoe Trips 313 E. 2nd Aroma Park, IL 60910 (815) 939-2486		Kankakee & Iroquois Rivers
Deam Lake seasonal boat rental	Deam Lake	
Dogwood Lake, seasonal rentals (adjacent to office)	Dogwood Lake Glendale FWA	
Eagle Creek Reservoir Seasonal rentals at marina Dandy Trail Marina	Eagle Creek Reservoir	

AREA OUTFITTERS	LAKES	STREAMS
Indianapolis, IN 46254 (317) 327-7130		
Elkhart Parks & Recreation 131 Tyler St. Elkhart, IN 46516 (219) 295-7275 or 7529		Elkhart River
Ferdinand Lake summer boat rental	Ferdinand Lake	
Ferrettie-Baugo County Park (N of US 33) Osceola, IN 46561 (219) 277-4828		St. Joseph River of Lake Michigar
Griffy Boathouse seasonal boat rentals April week ends 9 am to 6 pm, Daily (May to Sept) 7am-7pm	Griffy Lake	
Goshen Parks & Recreation 607 W. Plymouth Goshen, IN 46526 (219) 534-2901		Elkhart River
Hodges Canoe Trip 2671 N 1275 W Delphi, IN 46923 (765) 564-6806		Tippecanoe River
Hovey Lake johnboat rental at office and access site	Hovey Lake	
Jordan's Wilderness Shop & Outfitters 7940 Hawthorne Place Dyer, IN 46311 (800) 644-9955		Little Calumet Deep River
Kankakee River State Park Canoe Trips RR #1 Bourbonnais, IL 60914 (815) 932-6555		Kankakee River
Lincoln Lake seasonal boat rental near beach	Lincoln Lake	
LaPorte Memorial Park beach summer boat rental (219) 326-9600	Clear Lake Stone Lake	

AREA OUTFITTERS	LAKES	STREAMS
Mendon County Inn 440 W Main Mendon, MI 49072		St. Joseph River of Lake Michigan
Metamora Canoe Rental Rt #1 Metamora, IN 47030 (317) 647-5434		Whitewater River
Monitor Canoe Trips 7736 SR 26 E Lafayette, IN 47905 (765) 589-3506		Wildcat Creek North Fork & South Fork
Morgan's Brookville Canoe Center 7040 Whitewater River Lane Brookville, IN 47012 (800) WE-CANOE or (765) 647-4904		Whitewater River
Niles Canoe Rental 1430 N Business US 31 Niles, MI 49120 (616) 683-5110		St. Joseph River of Lake Michigan
Old Mill Canoe Rental SR 150 Box 60 Fredericksburg, IN 47120 (812) 472-3140		Blue River
Pigeon River Canoe-n-Camp 3490 S 325 Pleasant Lake, IN 46779 (219) 351-3537 (219) 475-5512	Fish, Marsh, Little Gentian, Loon, Pigeon, Little Turkey & Pigeon River FWA Lakes	Pigeon River
Pike Lake & Winona Lake summer park rentals	Pike Lake	
Ramona Canoe Rental Box 459 Ramona Rd. Spencer, IN 47460 (812) 829-0120		White River West Fork
Reed's Canoe Trips 907 N. Indiana Ave. Rt. 50 Kankakee, IL 60901 (815) WE CANOE, 939-3117		Kankakee River
River Junction Canoe Rental 6614 SR 25 W		Tippecanoe & Wabash River

AREA OUTFITTERS	LAKES	STREAMS
Lafayette, IN 47904 (765) 589-3875 (serves Lafayette area)		
River Bend Campground 21695 SR 37 N Noblesville, IN 46060 (317) 773-3333		White River West Fork
Riverside Restaurant & Marina 3001 N. White River Pkwy. West Dr. Indianapolis, IN 46222 (317) 327-2628		Fall Creek & White River West Fork
Root's 6844 N. Clinton St. (219) 484-2604		Cedar Creek & St. Joseph River Maumee
Sand Lake seasonal canoe rentals	Chain O Lakes State Park	
Lake Kickapoo seasonal boat rental , NW shore	Shakamak State Park	
Starve Hollow seasonal boat rental at beach	Starve Hollow Lake	
St. Joseph County, MI Parks & Recreation POB 427 Centreville, MI 49032 (616) 467-5519 or 6361		St. Joseph River of Lake Michigan
St. Patricks Park St. Joseph County Parks 50651 Laurel Rd. (west of US 33 at state line) South Bend, IN 46637 (219) 277-4828		St. Joseph River of Lake Michigan
St. Joseph Parks and Recreation Centreville, MI 49032 (616) 467-6361		Fawn River St. Joseph River of Lake Michigan
Sugar Valley Canoe Trips SR 47 Rt. 1, Box 166a Marshall, IN (765) 597-2364 597-2336 or (800) 422-6638		Sugar Creek

AREA OUTFITTERS	LAKES	STREAMS
Swartz's Bait & Tackle 118 Cicero Rd./SR 19 Noblesville, IN 46060 (317) 776-0129		White River West Fork
Three Rivers Canoe Rental 1509 S. Main Conservation Park Three Rivers, MI 49093 (888) 314-7444 (219) 273-9000		Fawn River St. Joseph River of Lake Michigan
Tippecanoe Rental RR# 3, Box 115 Monticello, IN 47960 (219) 278-7841		Tippecanoe River
Tippe-Canoe Float Trips 4903 N. 750 W Leiters Ford, IN 46945 (219) 542-2777		Tippecanoe River
Trading Post Canoe Rental Box 132, CR 300 N Mongo, IN 46771 (219) 367-2493 (April 1-Oct 31)		Pigeon River
Turkey Run Canoe Trips 311 W. Ohio Rockville, IN 47872 (765) 597-2456(765) 569-6705		Sugar Creek
Versailles State Park Lake boat rentals west of camp store Versailles, IN 47042	Versailles Lake	
Whitewater River Canoe Rental US Hwy 52 W, POB 2 Brookville, IN 47012 (765) 647-2330 or 647-5434		Whitewater River
Willow Slough concessionaire johnboats	JC Murphey Lake	
Worster Lake seasonal rentals	Potato Creek State Park	
Zellers Canoe Rental 412 E. Old SR 14 Winamac, IN 46996 (219) 946-3781		Tippecanoe River

Sand Bar Time Out, White River East Fork

Griffy Lake, Preparing to Cast Off

Appendix C

Canoe & Kayak Organizations

American Canoe Association
7432 Alban Station Blvd.
Suite B-232
(703) 451-0141
Springfield, VA 22150
Membership, benefit,
Paddler Magazine

American Rivers Organization
1025 Vermont Ave., NW
Suite 720
Washington, D.C. 20005-3516
(202) 347-7550

Banks of the Wabash
POB 1253
Layfayette, IN 47902
(765) 494-1330
email, wabash@hort.purdue.edu

Canoe Indiana
POB 1
Buck Creek, IN 47924

Fort Wayne Canoe & Kayak Club
email, weepee@aol.com

Friends off the St. Joseph River,
Association
POB 354
Athens, MI
(616) 729-5174
email, algs@net.link.net

Friends of Sugar Creek
POB 171
Darlington, IN 47940
Friends of South Fork Patoka Lake
Friends of the Wabash

Friends of the White River
POB 90171
Indianapolis, IN 46290

Grand Calumet Task Force
2400 New York Ave.
Whiting, IN 46394
(219) 473-4246
email, gct@lgc.org

Hoosier Canoe Club, ACA
9021 Yellowwood Ct.
Indianapolis, IN 46260
garymbledsoe@mindspring.com
(317) 773-6216

Hoosier Environmental Council
1002 E Washington
Suite 300
Indianapolis, IN 46202
email, hecindy@indy.net

Hoosier Riverwatch
IDNR, Div. of Soil Conservation
402 W Washington
W 265
Indianapolis, IN 46204
Bi-monthly periodical, Adopt-a-

River, *River Keepers*

IDNR Div. of Fish & Wildlife
402 W Washington St.
W 278
Indianapolis, IN 46204
(317) 232-4160

IDNR, Div. of Outdoor Recreation
Operation Clean Stream/Adopt-a Stream
(317) 232-4070

IDNR, Div. of Outdoor Recreation
Streams & Trails
402 W Washington St. RM 271
Indianapolis, IN 46204
(317) 232-4070

IDNR, Div. of Soil Conservation
Lake & River Enhancement Program
402 W Washington St. Rm 265
Indianapolis, IN 46204
(317) 233-3870

Illinois Paddling Council
1911 Main St.
Spring Grove, IL 60081

Indiana Canoe Racing Council
4919 N Meridian St.
Indianapolis, IN 46208

Indiana Lakes Management Society
207 Hoosier Dr., Sta. 2A
Angola, IN 46703

Indiana Recreational Waterways Association
4454 W. Washington Blvd.
Indianapolis, IN 46205

Indiana Waterways Assoc.
301 Ft. Harrison Ave.
Terre Haute, IN 47804
(812) 460-1567

Isaac Walton League
Indiana Division
2173 Pennsylvania Ave
Portage, IN 46368
(800) IKE-LINE (219) 762-4876 or 453-5463

Little River Wetlands Project
6530 W Wallen Rd.
Ft. Wayne, IN 46818

Nature Watercraft Society
515 First St. #1
Milwaukee, WI 53204

N Central IN Canoe Club
c/o Dee Gould
57749 8th Ave.
Elkhart, IN 46517-1706

OH Valley Canoe Council
Rt. 1, Box 252
Tennyson, IN 47637

Prof. Paddle Sports Assoc.
POB 248
Butler, KY 41006
(606) 472-2205

PU Canoe & Kayak Club
Purdue University
West Lafayette, IN 47907

Save the (Ohio) Valley
POB 813
Madison, IN 47250
(812) 265-4577

Sierra Club Wetlands Project
212 W 10th
Indianapolis, IN 46202

US Canoe Association
Indiana Association
POB 5743
Lafayette, IN 47903

Viking Canoe Club
1615 Corydon Place
New Albany, IN 47150

Wildcat Canoe Club
POB 6232
Kokomo, IN 46906

Wildcat Creek Foundation
Box 193
Lafayette, IN 47902

Wildcat Guardians
POB 6421
Kokomo, IN 46904-6421

INDIANA CANOE RACING

Sugar Creek Canoe Race, Crawfordsville. April
Tippecanoe Marathon, Lafayette, June

Wabash River & Wildcat Doubleheader, Lafayette, June
Hoosier Regatta, White River West Fork & Fall Creek, Indianapolis, June
Ft. Wayne Canoe & Kayak Race, St. Mary's, St. Joseph, & Maumee Rivers, June
Round Barn Festival, Tippecanoe River, Rochester, July
Three Rivers Festival, Canoe & Kayak Races, St. Marys, St. Joseph, & Maumee, Ft. Wayne, July
USCA Marathon, Canoe & Kayak Nationals, St. Joseph River, Niles, MI, August

Tiger Swallowtails on Buttonbush Flower

Yellow Spatterdock

Appendix D

Indiana Department of Natural Resources (DNR)

Fisheries Biologists
Wildlife Biologists
Law Enforcement

INDIANA'S FISHERIES BIOLOGISTS

District 1
Bass Lake Fisheries Station
6718 E Winona Ave.
Knox, IN 46534
(219) 772-2353

District 2
Fawn River State Fish Hatchery
6889 N SR 327
Orland, IN 46776
(219) 829-6241

District 3
Tri-Lakes Fisheries Station
5570 N Fish Hatchery Road
Columbia City, IN 46725
(219) 691-3181

District 4
Tri-Lakes Fisheries Station
5570 N Fish Hatchery Road
Columbia City, IN 46725
(219) 691-3181

District 5
Cikana State Fish Hatchery
2650 SR 44
Martinsville, IN 46151
(765) 342-5527

District 6
Avoca State Fish Hatcheries
POB 16
Avoca, IN 47420
(812) 279-1215

District 7
Sugar Ridge Fish & Wildlife Area
2310 E SR 364
Winslow, IN 47598
(812) 789-2724

District 8
Driftwood State Fish Hatchery
4931 S CR 250 W
Vallonia, IN 47281
(812) 358-4110

Lake Michigan Office
Lake Michigan Investigation
100 W Water St.
Michigan City, IN 46360
(219) 874-6824

Big Rivers Fisheries Program
Sugar Ridge Fish & Wildlife Area
2310 E SR 364
Winslow, IN 47598
(812) 789-2724

DISTRICT WILDLIFE BIOLOGISTS

District 1
Kankakee Fish & Wildlife Area
4320 W Toto Rd
POB 77
North Judson, IN 46366
(219) 896-3572

District 2
305 N Meadow Lane
Kendallville, IN 46755
(219) 347-2945

District 3
5047 W 600 S
Morocco, IN 47963
(219) 285-2704

District 4
Region 2 Headquarters
RR 6 Box 344
Peru, IN 46970
(765) 473-9324

District 5
Region 2 Headquarters
RR 6 Box 344
Peru, IN 46970
(765) 473-9324

District 6
3900 Soldiers Home Rd
West Lafayette, IN 47906
(765) 463-0032

District 7
Atterbury Fish & Wildlife Area
7970 S Rowe St
Edinburgh, IN 46124
(317) 232-7535 (812) 526-4891

District 8
Wilbur Wright FWA
2239 N SR 54
New Castle, IN 47362
(765) 529-6319

District 9
Minnehaha Fish & Wildlife Area
2411 E SR 54
Sullivan, IN 47882
(812) 268-0300

District 10
Glendale Fish & Wildlife Area
RR 2 Box 300
Montgomery, IN 47558
(812) 334-1137

District 11
553 E Miller Dr.
Bloomington, IN 47401
(812) 334-1137

District 12
Crosley Fish & Wildlife Area
2010 S SR 3
North Vernon, IN 47265
(812) 346-6888

District 13
Sugar Ridge Fish & Wildlife Area
2310 E SR 364
Winslow, IN 47598 (812) 789-2724

LAW ENFORCEMENT

District 1 Headquarters
9822 N Turkey Creek Rd.
Syracuse, IN 46567
(219) 457-8092

District 2 Headquarters
1903 St. Mary's Ave
Ft. Wayne, IN 46808
(219) 426-0807

District 3 Headquarters
5921 SR 43 N
West Lafayette, IN 47906
(765) 567-2080

District 4 Headquarters
3734 Mounds Rd.
Anderson, IN 46017
(765) 778-2145

District 5 Headquarters
1317 W Lieber Rd Suite 2
Cloverdale, IN 46120
(765) 795-3534

District 6 Headquarters
POB 266
Nashville, IN 47448
(812) 988-9761

District 7 Headquarters
5994 E SR 364
Pike State Forest
Winslow, IN 47598
(812) 789-9538

District 8 Headquarters
Patoka Reservoir, RR 1 Box 290
Birdseye, IN 47513
(812) 685-2498

District 9 Headquarters
POB 100
Brookville, IN 47012
(765) 647-5835

District 10 Headquarters
100 W Water St.
Michigan City, IN 46360
(219) 879-5710

North Region Headquarters
Rt 6 Box 344
Peru, IN 46970
(765) 473-9722

South Region Headquarters
4850 S SR 446
Bloomington, IN 47401
(812) 837-9536

Law Enforcement Div.Hdqtrs
402 W Washington St.
Room W 255 D
Indianapolis, IN 46204
(317) 232-4010

Ft. Harrison Office
5753 Glenn Rd.
Indianapolis, IN 46216
(317) 541-0617

Appendix E

FISH CONSUMPTION ADVISORY LIST

Due to past and present widespread use of chemicals for agriculture and industry, much of our fisheries are polluted with contaminants. Pesticides, polychlorinated biphenyls (PCBs), heavy metals and mercury are the major contaminants found in fish count in Indiana waterways. These chemical contaminants have the physical ability to accumulate and persist in the environment, exceeding safe levels. Mercury, a naturally occurring metal is also released from coal burning power plants, burning household trash and industrial wastes. PCBs are synthetic oils once widely used in industry. These contaminants build up in fish especially those that feed on other fish. Eating contaminated fish may cause build up of contaminants in the human body. Mercury damages the nervous system and PCBs cause birth defects and may cause cancer. Pregnant women and young children are particularly affected. Fish absorb PCBs which concentrate in the fat which can be cleaned and cooked before a meal to remove the toxins.

There are no cooking or cleaning methods, which will reduce the amount of mercury. Large older fish accumulate more toxins than small young ones. Contaminants are not usually detected in panfish such as bluegill or crappie. There is hardly a water body in Indiana that can escape from the chemical wrath to which modern civilization is seemingly addicted in order to function. Even Indiana's most scenic streams such as Wildcat Creek and Sugar Creek have fish that are contaminated with mercury and PCBs. (Perhaps the cleanest source for food in Indiana may be a farm pond).

An Indiana Fish Consumption Advisory is updated annually and is available from the Indiana State Department of Health, 2 N Meridian, Section 3-D, Indianapolis, IN 46204. A copy of the annual Indiana Fishing Guide is available free from the IDNR Division of Fish & Wildlife, Fisheries Section, IGC-273 W, 402 W Washington St., Indiana Government Center, Indianapolis, IN 46204 (317) 232-4080.

Source: INDIANA BOARD OF HEALTH

Note: A healthy clean stream has 10 to15 fish species and in polluted water the average is 5 species. Nutrient pollution from animal waste and farm chemical runoff and other pollution sources contributes to the growing 7,000 square mile "dead zone" in the Gulf of Mexico.

Appendix F

GLOSSARY

Abeam: To the right of center

Aboard: On or in a canoe or kayak

Access site or point: The place on the shore of a lake or river to launch (put in) or land (take out)

Afloat: Floating on water

Aground: On or onto the shore or the bottom of a body of water

Air Lock: An intermediate chamber present on the inside of an overturned canoe

Airtank: Buoyancy chamber in ends of some types of canoes which lend stability

Amidships: Middle of the canoe, in reference to its length

Astern: Toward the rear or back of the canoe

Back Ferry: Paddling backwards, to back paddle, with canoe at angle to water

Backpaddle: Paddling a canoe backward, to slow or reverse

Bail: To empty water from the bottom of a craft by sponge or container

Bang Plate: Metal strip or leading edge of bow and stern, to protect the hull, also called stem band

Balance point: The limit of lean for a kayak or canoe, before capsizing

Beam: The widest point of the canoe body

Bear off: To push off or free oneself from an obstruction

Bilge: The part of the hull of a canoe located below the water line

Blade: The flat, wide end of a paddle that is placed in water

Bladder: An air bag inside a kayak or canoe used to aide in floatation in event of a capsize

Boil: Water swelling upward, usually deflected from an obstruction; also called a pillow

Bow: The front of a canoe or kayak

Bow Draw: A paddle stroke which moves the canoe sideways

Bow Seat: The seat located at the front of the canoe

Brace: A stroke to stabilize

Bracket: A device for attaching a motor to a canoe

Breach: A gap in a dam wall

Broadside: Perpendicular to the current of a river

Broach: Turning broadside to oncoming obstacles to avoid capsizing, or to turn suddenly out of control into the wind

Canoe: A slender open watercraft propelled with a single blade paddle

Canoe Pole: A long slender pole used to propell upstream

Capsize: To tip over in water

Carry: A portage between two waterways or around obstructions

Channel: A connecting waterway between two lakes; A navigable unobstructed route of a river; passable water

Chine: The curving section of a canoe hull or point where it gradually merges with the bottom

Chute: Compressed or narrow stream channel with an accelerated waterflow

Classification: A rating applied to a steam or section of current to describe its navigability or difficulty rating

Coaming: A rim around a kayak or canoe cockpit to which a spray skirt be attached

Cockpit: The hole in the top of a kayak where the paddler sits or kneels

Cross-Bow: A paddle stroke style in which the wet blade is lifted over the bow to the water on the opposite side

Dead Falls: Fallen objects obstructing the stream

Deadwater: Motionless water usually refers to backed water on a river or flatwater on a lake

Deck: Triangular panels at the bow and stern of a canoe attached to the gunnels

Double-Blade Paddle: A paddle with a blade at each end

Draft: The depth of water needed to float; the depth of the boat below the water

Drainage Area: Watershed in a given area usually expressed in square miles

Draw or Draw Stroke: A sideways stroke placed horizontally and pulled directly toward the side of the canoe

Drip Rings: Leather or metal rings on the shaft of a double paddle which prevents water from running down the shaft

Dry Blade: Paddle that is not being used; out of water or at rest

Dry Pack: Waterproof gear bag

Double Canoe: Two paddlers (c2)

Double Kayak: Two paddlers (k2)

Eddy: Water flowing in a circular course, downstream of a major obstruction, caused by bends and obstructions

Eddy Line: A fine line between swift downstream current and a circulatory or upstream current within an eddy

Eskimo Roll: The technique of uprighting an upturned kayak with a the paddle without exiting

Face: The flat side of a paddle blade

Fathom: The nautical measurement of 6 feet

Feathering: Fast water; rapids; applied to swift, high water

Ferry: Gliding, moving laterally across the current, upstream or downstream while controlling the rate of travel

Flare: The point of a canoe paddle where it widens to become the blade

Flatwater: see deadwater

Floatation Bags: see bladder

Foot Rest: Brace; fitting inside most kayaks and some canoes which allows paddlers to paddle more efficiently

Fore: The front or bow

Forward Sweep: Paddle stroke that turns the canoe bow away from the paddle blade

Freeboard: The distance from the waterline to the top of the gunnels at their lowest point

Gator Log: Logs lurking below the surface that capsize paddlers

Gauging Station: Streamside device for measuring the flow of water

Gear: Moveable equipment, goods, paraphernalia taken along on trip

Goon Stroke: Most basic of the forward paddle strokes

Gradient: The average elevation decline per mile in a riverbed

Grab Loop: A loop of rope on the bow or stern of a kayak, handy for carrying, especially in rescue

Grip: The top of the canoe paddle shaft, usually pear shaped for general canoeing

Gunwale: The upper rails of the outer edge of a boat hull; strips along the top of the canoe side, bow to stern

Headwaters: The origin or source waters of streams and lakes

Hippo Rock: Boulders lurking beneath the surface that capsize

Hull: The main body of a canoe or kayak

Hung Up: Caught on a rock or other obstruction

Hydraulic: Souse holes and back rollers; strong reversed current at the base of a dam

Hunting Stroke: A particular type of canoe stroke forward paddle stroke, silently moving the blade through the water

Hypothermia: The dangerous lowering of body temperature while wet, that can lead to brain damage or death

Inboard: The area within the inside line of a canoe within the gunwales

Inwale: The inside portion of the gunnels

J-Stroke: A forward directional paddle stroke

Jet: A narrow channel of fast water with eddies

Kayak: A small boat resembling an Inuit vessel, paddled from a sitting position with both feet extended

Keeper: A description of a type of hydraulic wave

Keel: Strip along the entire length of the canoe bottom to provide strength

Knee Flick: An action used to right a craft during support strokes

Knob: The grip on a canoe handle

Launch: To slide a canoe onto water

Leeward: Direction into the wind; opposite of windward

Life jacket/vest: Personal floatation device

Line: A rope used to tie a canoe or pull it through obstacles in the water

Left Bank: The left side of a river as seen while looking downstream

Ledge: A projecting rock shelf which may affect stream flow

Logjam: Total or partial obstruction of a stream by trees or other debris

Low Brace: Brace stroke with entire paddle almost flat on the surface of the water

Low-Head Dam: 6" to 10' dam, usually concrete

Livery: Business where canoes or kayaks may be rented, usually from April to November 1

Maneuver: The effort of a paddle stroke on a canoe

Mouth: The place where a stream empties into another water body

Motorboat: Any boat propelled by mechanical power, including canoes

Paddle: The implement used to steer or propel a canoe or kayak through water

Painters: Lines attached to the bow and stern of a canoe, 15' to 25' long

Portage: The physical act of carrying the canoe overland between two bodies of water

Pillow: A bulge on the surface of the water, created by an underwater obstruction

Pivot: Turn sharply around a point

Pool: A stretch of water with little or no current

Port: The left side of the canoe, which faces the bow

Pry Stroke: A paddle stroke used to move the craft sideways away from the paddle

Put-In: The launching site where a canoe or kayak is placed in the water

Personal Floatation Device: Collective term for all buoyancy aids

Pinned: Trapped in boat while being pushed by the force of the water against a tree or rock; see strainer

Pry: Paddle used as a lever against the side of the boat to push the boat sideways

Rapids: Swiftly flowing water, fast and turbulent stretch of river

Riffles: Swift shallow water or light, gentle rapids

Right Bank: The right side of the river as seen while facing downstream

Rocker: The upward curvature of the keel line toward both ends of a canoe or kayak

Running: To sail with the wind by hoisting a jury sail on a canoe or kayak

Shaft: The handle of the canoe or kayak paddle between blade and grip

Shake-Out: To empty a swamped canoe while remaining in the water

Sheer: The fore and aft curving side of the hull; the gunnel lines of a canoe with gunwales

Shoe Keel: Shallow, wide, flat, keel

Skid Plate: A metal plate that prevents abrasion to the bottom skin of a canoe or kayak; see Bang Plate

Skulling Draw: A complex sideways stroke

Slack Water: Calm stream flow between riffles; see Deadwater

Shoal: Shallows caused by a sand bar especially during low water

Shuttle: Motorized transportation of canoes and kayaks between put-in points and take-out

Slicing: Moving a paddle blade through water on the flat side while keeping the paddle immersed

Starboard: The right side of the boat while facing forward

Stem: The extreme bow

Stern: Rear part of boat

Strainer: Brush or trees that become lethal hazards after falling into a river, could be deadly when pinning or swamping a craft

Strokes: Various movements of the paddle to control the direction and speed of watercraft

Solo: A single occupant

Support Strokes: Strokes used to regain or maintain stability

Swamp: Accidentally filling a canoe with water while canoeing

Sweeper: See Strainer

Sweep Stroke: A basic stroke consisting of sweeping the paddle in a wide arc from front to back

Tail: The stern on the back of a kayak or canoe

Take-out: The point at which the craft is removed from the water; the finish

Thwart: Cross braces or cross pieces between gunwales that give shape to the hull

Throwing line: A rescue emergency rope, 20 yards long, for a boat or paddler in trouble

Top Sides: The part of the hull that is above water

Trim: The angle of a canoe or kayak while in the water; level with the water; balance

Tongue: The smooth safe water running between two objects above the water line

Tumblehome: The inward curve of the sides of a canoe above the water line

Underway: Boat in motion

Upstream: Opposite direction of the flow of the stream

War Canoe: A large canoe made for many paddlers at once

Water Line: The normal water level of a loaded canoe

Watershed: Entire region drained by a lake or river

Wake: A trail of turbulent water left by watercraft that can result in capsizing a canoe

Wash: Wake

Windward: Moving into the direction of the wind; opposite of leeward

Wetsuit: Protective suit insulated to protect against hypothermia caused by cold water

Whitewater: A long stretch of foamy waves and rapids; wild water

Weir: Low dam used to direct water

Miami Dugout, Trail of Courage Festival

Red-Tailed Hawk

White Egret

Appendix G

HELPFUL BOOKS

ACRES Land Trust, *The Nature Preserves of ACRES*. Ft. Wayne, IN: Updated annually.

Addison, Corran and Power, Scott. *Kayaker's Little Book of Wisdom: A Couple Hundred Suggestions, Observations, and Reminders for Kayakers to Read, Remember and Share*, Merrillville, IN: ITS Books, 1997.

Adney, Tappan Edwin and Chappelle, Howard L. *The Bark Canoe and Skin Boats of North America*, Washington, D.C.: Smithsonian Institute Press, 1983.

American Red Cross. *Canoeing and Kayaking*. Washington, D.C.: American Red Cross, 1981.

Anderson, Luther A. *A Guide to Canoe Camping*. Chicago: Reilly & Lee, 1969.

Bailie, Marcus. *Crowood Sports Guides: Canoeing & Kayaking: Techniques, Tactics, Training*. Ramsbury, Marlborough, Wiltshire, UK: Crowood Press, 1991.

Borror, D.J. and White, R.E. *A Field Guide to the Insects of America: North of Mexico*. Boston, MA.: Houghton Mifflin, Peterson Field Guide Series, 1970.

Brailsford, John. *Canoeing*. Oxford: Oxford Illustrated Press, 1977.

Bridge, Raymond. *The Complete Canoeist's Guide*. New York: Scribner & Sons, 1978.

Bright Spot Maps, Indiana Lake Maps vol 1-14, l. Lagrange, Steuben 2. Kosciusko, Marshall, Elkhart, St. Joseph, 3. Dekalb, Noble, Whitley, 4. Lakes & Reservoirs of Indiana. 1996, 1996, 1990, 1995. POB 1342, LaPorte, IN, 46352-1342, (219) 324-3324.

Brosius, Jack and Leroy, Dave. *Building & Repairing Canoes & Kayaks*. Chicago: Contemporary Books, 1998.

Congress of Lakes Associations. *The Lake Book. Actions You Can Take to Protect Your Lake*. Hampden, ME: COLA, 1993.

Deam, Charles. *Flora of Indiana*. Indianapolis, IN: Department of Conservation, Division of Forestry, 1940.

Delorme. *Indiana Atlas & Gazetteer*. Yarmouth, ME: Delorme, 1998, First Edition.

Elvedt, Ruth. *Canoeing A-2*. Minneapolis, MN: Burgess Publishing Company, 1964.

Evans, Erie and Evans, Jay. *The Kayaking Book*. Lexington, MA: Stephen Greene Press, 1988.

Farmer, Charles J. *The Digest Book of Canoeing*. Northfield, IL: DBI Books, 1979.

Ferguson, Stuart. *Canoeing for Beginners*. Tern Hills, N.S. Wales, Australia: Reed, 1976.

Fichter, George S. and Francis, Phil. *A Guide to Fresh and Saltwater Fishes.* New York: Golden Press, 1987.

Foshee, John H. *You, Too, Can, Canoe: The Complete Book of River Canoeing*. Huntsville, AL: Strode Publishing, 1977.

Frey, Robert W. and Lane, Micheal A., eds. *A Survey of Indiana Geology*. Bloomington, IN: Indiana University, Department of Geology, 1966.

Gordon, I. Herbert. *Canoeing. Made Easy, A Manuel for Beginners with Tips for the Experienced*. Old Saybrook, CT: Globe Pequot Press, 1992.

Grant, Gordon. *Canoeing: A Trailside Guide*. New York, W.W. Norton, 1997.

Gullion, Laurie. *Canoeing*. Champaign, IL: Human Kinetics, 1994.

Gulllion, Laurie. *Canoeing & Kayaking: American Canoe Association Instructor Manual*. Birmingham, AL: Menasha Ridge Press, 1987.

Harrison, David & Harrison, Judy. *Canoe Tripping with Children*. Merrillville, IN: ICS Books, 1990.

Harrison, Dave. *Sports Illustrated Canoeing*. New York: Harper & Row, 1981.

Homoya, Michael A. *Orchids of Indiana*. Bloomington, IN: IU Press, 1992.

Indiana DNR, Division of Fish & Wildlife. *A Pocket Guide to Indiana Sportfish Identifier*. Seattle, WA: Outdoor Empire Publishing, 1997.

Indiana DNR, Division of Fish & Wildlife. *Access Sites: A Guide to Boat Ramps & Fishing Areas*. Indianapolis, IN: Indiana Government Publications, 1996.

Indiana DNR, Division of Law Enforcement. *Indiana Boating Guide*. Indianapolis, IN: Indiana Department of Natural Resources, 1998.

Indiana DNR, Division of Nature Preserves. *Directory of Indiana's Dedicated Nature Preserves*. Indianapolis, IN: Indiana DNR, government printers, 1991.

Indiana DNR, Division of Outdoor Recreation, Streams & Trail Section. *Indiana Canoeing Guide.* Indianapolis, IN: 1987, out of print, available at this web address <http://www.ai.org/dnr/outdoor/canoetra/index.htm>

Indiana DNR, Division of Waters. *Indiana Lakes Guide*, Indianapolis, IN.: government printing, 1993.

Jackson, Marion T., ed. *The Natural Heritage of Indiana*. Bloomington, IN: Indiana University Press, 1998.

Jacobson, Cliff. *Canoeing and Camping: Beyond the Basics*. Merrillville, IN: ICS Books, 1992,

Johnson, Donald Bruce. *Guide to Canoe Camping*. Martinsville, IN: American Camping Association, 1981.

Kellar, James H. *An Introduction to the Prehistory of Indiana*, Indianapolis, IN: Indiana Historical Society, 1983.

Klots, Elsie B. *Field Book of Freshwater Life*. New York: G.P. Putnam's Sons, 1966.

Mason, Bill. *Path of the Paddle. An Illustrated Guide to the Art of Canoeing*. Minoqua, WI: Northword Press, 1995.

McKown, Doug. *Canoeing Safety and Rescue*. Calgary: Rocky Mountain Books, 1992.

McNair, Robert E. *Back River Canoeing*. Martinsville, IN: American Camping Association, 1992.

McNally, Tom. *Fisherman's Bible*. Chicago: Follett Publishing Company, 1970.

McPhee, John A. *The Survival of the Bark Canoe*. New York: Noonday Press, 1992.

McPherson, Alan J. *Indian Names in Indiana*. Monticello, IN: self published, 1993.

Mead, Robert Douglas. *The Canoer's Bible*. New York: Doubleday, 1989.

Minton, Sherman A. Jr. *Amphibians and Reptiles of Indiana.* Indianapolis, IN: Indiana Academy of Science, monograph no. 3, 1972.

Mumford, Russell E. and Keller, Charles E. *The Birds of Indiana*. Bloomington, IN: Indiana University Press, 1984.

Mumford, Russell E. and Whitaker, John O. *Mammals of Indiana*.

Bloomington, IN: Indiana University Press, 1982.

Norman, Dean, ed. *The All Purpose Guide to Paddling*. Matteson, IL: Great Lakes Living Press, 1976.

Pulling, Pierre. *Canoeing the Indian Way: Straight Talk for Modern Paddlers,* New York: McKay Publishing, 1979.

Quirke, Terrence Thomas. *Canoes the World Over*. Urbana, IL: University of Illinois Press, 1952.

Slim, Ray. *The Canoe Handbook: Techniques for Mastering the Sport of Canoeing*. Harrisburg, PA: Stackpole Books, 1992.

Reid, George K. *Pond Life: A Guide to Common Plants and Animals of North America's Ponds and Lakes*. New York: Golden Press, 1987.

Riviere, Bill. *Pole, Paddle, & Portage: A Complete Guide to Canoeing*. Boston: Little, Brown & Company, 1969.

Ruck, Wolf. *Canoeing and Kayaking*. Toronto: McGraw-Hill, Ryerson, 1974.

Sanderlin, Larry W. and Brown, Wendel S. *Uncle Larry's Lake Maps*, Ft. Wayne: self-published, third edition, 1989.

Schmidt, Ernest F. *Canoeing*. Irving, Texas: Boy Scouts of America, Merit Badge Series 3308, 1981.

Shull Ernest E. *The Butterflies of Indiana*. Bloomington, IN: Indiana Academy of Science and Indiana University Press, 1987.

Simons, Richard S. *The Rivers of Indiana*. Bloomington, IN: IU Press, 1985.

Skinner, R. Dean. *Basic Canoeing Techniques*. Provo, UT: Brigham Young University, 1975.

Stuhaug, Dennis O. *Kayaking Made Easy: A Manual for Beginners with Tips for the Experienced*. Old Saybrook, CT: Globe Pequot Press, 1998.

Thompson, Peter. *Thompson's Guide to Freshwater Fishes*. Boston: Houghton Mifflin Company, 1985.

Wampler, Maryrose & Wampler, Fred. *Wiidflowers of Indiana*. Bloomington, IN: Indiana University Press, 1992.

Webre, Ann Wortham and Zeller, Janet. *Canoeing & Kayaking for Persons with Physical Disabilities*. Newington, VA: America Canoe Association,1996

Whit, Deschner. *Travels with a Kayak*. Baker, Oregon; Eddie Tern Press, 1997.

PERIODICALS

CANOE & KAYAK. Editor, POB 3146, 10526 NE 68th St., Kirkland, WA 98083, (800) 678-5432 or 829-3340.

INDIANA GAME & FISH. 2250 Newmarket Pathway, Suite 110, Marietta, GA 30061.

KANAWA. Canadian Recreational Canoeing Association., POB 398, 446 Main, W., Merrickville, ON K0 J1 N0, Canada.

NONPOINT NOTES, Indiana Association of Soil & Water Conservation Districts, 225, SE St., Suite 740, Indianapolis, IN. 46202.

OUTDOOR INDIANA. Indiana Department of Natural Resources, 402 W Washington, Room W 160, Indianapolis, IN. 46204.

PADDLER. Eagle Outdoor Publishing, POB 1341, Eagle, ID 83616, (800) 752-7951, or, Editor, POB 775450, Steamboat Springs, CO 80477.

PADDLER'S PRINT. Professional Paddle Sports Association, POB 248, Butler, KY 41006, (606) 472-2205.

RIVER. POB 1068, Bozeman, MT 59771. (406) 582-5440.

WOODEN BOAT. POB 708, Naskeag Road, Brooklin, MA 04616, (207) 359-4651.

Sunrise, Lower Tippecanoe River

Sugar Creek, Turkey Run State Park

Sunset, J.C. Murphey Lake

Index of Maps

Lake Maps

Stream Maps